FINDING THE PERFECT MATCH FOR YOUR PROJECT

Yarn labels (discussed in Book 1, Chapter 2) *suggest* appropriate needle sizes, but the best needle size for your project is dictated by your yarn, your gauge, and/or the *hand* (the way the knitted fabric feels in your hand) you want your final project to have. In general, medium- or worsted-weight yarn is knit on needles anywhere from size US 6 (4 mm) to size US 9 (5½ mm), depending on how tightly you knit and your desired look and feel for the final fabric.

After knitting a sample with the suggested needle size, you may feel that the fabric is more open than you want (needle too large) or too stiff (needle too small). In that case, try another needle size. Keep in mind that if you're making a garment or project and you want to achieve the finished measurements given in the pattern, you need to meet the gauge and live with the hand of the sample. If you're making a scarf or project where getting the exact number of stitches per inch isn't important, you can experiment to your heart's content with different needle sizes until you produce a fabric you like.

Accounting for needle makeup and tip type

Knitting needles, which were first mass-produced in steel, have been made in ivory, tortoiseshell, silver, whale bone, and more. Today you can find them made in ebony and rosewood, sherbet-colored pearly plastic, Teflon-coated aluminum, and even 14-carat gold-plated (yes, really). And that's only the beginning. Whatever your needles are made of, the material does contribute more or less to your knitting comfort, speed, and the quality of your stitches. Here are some recommendations:

>> **If you're new to knitting, working on double-pointed needles, or following color patterns, good choices include wood (bamboo, walnut, and so on) and plastic.** Wood and some plastics have a very slight grip, giving you more control over your work and discouraging dropped stitches.

>> **If you're knitting in stockinette or a straightforward stitch pattern, a slippery needle makes sense.** The fastest ones are nickel-plated brass and call themselves Turbo. Use these needles and watch your stitches fly by before your eyes. (Also watch for more-easily dropped stitches.)

Although all needles look pretty much alike, you do notice a difference in the feel of various kinds of needles and in their interaction with your knitting style and the yarn you're using. If you find that some feature of their construction or material is annoying you or interfering with the flow of your project, try a different kind of needle. Switching may make the difference between a knitting experience on cruise control and one that stops and starts and sputters along.

TIP

Needle tips can be long and tapered or rounder and blunter (see Figure 1-4). If you're working a project with a lot of stitch manipulation (as in lace or cables), or if you're a snug knitter (that is, your stitches are tight rather than loose), you'll have an easier time if you use a needle with a long, tapered tip. If you're knitting with a loosely spun yarn and/or you're a relaxed knitter with looser stitches, you may prefer a blunter point.

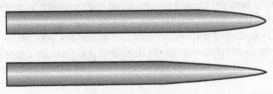

FIGURE 1-4:
Two kinds of needle tips.

Illustration by Wiley, Composition Services Graphics

TIP

Although they don't fall directly into the category of different needle composition or tip type, square needles can be a great choice if you're new to knitting. They're made of metal or wood, and the shape makes them easier for the hands to hold. Stitches don't fall off these square needles as easily as the standard round ones.

Choosing a Crochet Hook

A crochet hook is the single most important tool you use when crocheting. (It can also help you fix dropped stitches when you're knitting.) The next sections tell you everything you need to know about one, including why it's shaped the way it is, the function of each part, and the purpose of different hook materials.

Surveying the anatomy of a crochet hook

Even though you may think a crochet hook is nothing more than a straight stick with a hook on one end, it actually has five distinct and necessary parts, shown in Figure 1-5.

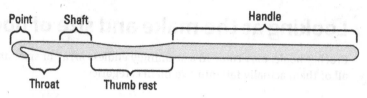

FIGURE 1-5:
The five parts of a crochet hook.

Point Shaft Handle

Throat Thumb rest

© John Wiley & Sons, Inc.

Each part of a crochet hook performs a specific function.

» **Point:** You insert the point of the hook into previously made stitches. It must be sharp enough to slide easily through the stitches yet blunt enough so that it doesn't split the yarn or stab your finger.

» **Throat:** The throat does the actual hooking of the yarn and pulls it through a stitch. It must be large enough to grab the yarn size that you're working with but small enough to prevent the previous loop from sliding off.

» **Shaft:** The shaft holds the loops that you're working with, and its diameter, for the most part, determines the size of your stitches.

» **Thumb rest:** The thumb rest helps keep the hook positioned in the right direction. Without it, the hook can twist in the wrong direction, causing you to grip the hook too tightly — and leaving you with hooker's cramp! (You'll know what this is as soon as you feel the pain in the palm of your hand and your fingers.) The thumb rest should be sandwiched between your thumb and middle finger when you hold the hook, letting you easily rotate the hook as you work each stitch.

» **Handle:** The handle is used for balance or leverage. In the under-the-hook method of holding the hook (see Book 3, Chapter 1), the handle helps keep the hook steady and well balanced. In the over-the-hook method of holding it, the handle is held against the heel or palm of your hand and provides the leverage needed to maneuver the hook properly.

TIP

Different brands of crochet hooks have slightly different shapes. Some have sharp points, whereas others have more rounded points. Some have distinct, flat, cut-out throats, whereas others have smoother, rounded throats. Nowadays, most of the standard-size and steel hooks have thumb rests, although the largest of the standard hooks don't. (See the next section for the lowdown on the different types of hooks.) Take some time to experiment with a couple of different brands of crochet hooks to find the one that you're most comfortable handling. You'll be glad you did.

Looking at the make and size of hooks

Crochet hooks may come in a seemingly endless array of sizes and materials, but all of them actually fall into two main categories:

TIP

>> **Standard hooks** are typically made of aluminum or plastic (and sometimes wood); you normally use them when working with the larger sizes of yarn, such as sport weight, worsted weight, and those that are even thicker. (We describe different yarn weights later in this chapter.) Standard hooks measure about 6 inches in length and vary in thickness from 2.5 millimeters to 19 millimeters and more. Hooks as large as 25 millimeters are now readily available for working with recycled materials or the giant-sized yarn that has become popular of late.

Plastic crochet hooks can bend or break with heavy use, so we recommend using aluminum hooks for the standard sizes simply because they literally last forever — provided they don't disappear.

>> **Steel hooks**, which are the smallest of all crochet hooks, are used for crocheting with thread and fine yarns. They're made of — wait for it — steel, and they measure about 5 inches in length and run from 0.75 millimeters to 3.5 millimeters wide.

In crochet, you work each stitch until only one loop remains on the hook, so you don't need a lot of space to hold loops (for the exception to the rule, check out the Tunisian stitch in Book 4, Chapter 4). Therefore, the hooks are a convenient length, unlike knitting needles.

The size of a crochet hook refers to the thickness of the hook, which in turn determines the size of the stitches it creates. Figure 1-6 gives you an idea of the size variation in hooks. You can expect to run across three different systems for marking hook sizes:

>> U.S. (American), which uses a letter/number combo

>> Continental (metric), which uses millimeters

>> U.K. (English), which uses numbers

REMEMBER

For standard hooks using the U.S. or metric system, the higher the number or further the letter is in the alphabet, the larger the hook. For example, a D-3 U.S. hook is smaller than a K-10½ U.S. hook. For steel hooks, which use only a number designation, the opposite holds true. The higher the number, the smaller the hook. Fortunately, you don't need to worry about keeping the different systems straight because hooks are usually labeled with both the U.S. letter/number designation as well as the numeric metric designation.

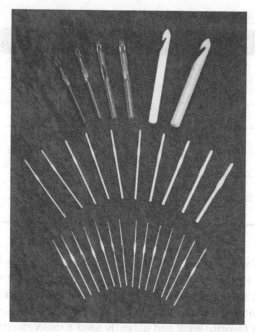

FIGURE 1-6:
Standard and
steel hooks and
the range of
available sizes.

Table 1-1 is a conversion chart showing the most commonly used sizes of standard hooks. Table 1-2 shows the most commonly used sizes of steel hooks. (*Note:* This book refers to U.S. hook sizes as well as metric sizes.)

TABLE 1-1   **Common Standard Crochet Hook Sizes**

U.S. (American)	Continental (Metric)	U.K. (English)
B-1	2.25 mm	13
C-2	2.75 mm	11
D-3	3.25 mm	10
E-4	3.5 mm	9
F-5	3.75 mm	-
G-6	4 or 4.25 mm	8
7	4.5 mm	7
H-8	5 mm	6
I-9	5.5 mm	5
J-10	6 mm	4
K-10½	6.5 mm	3

TABLE 1-2

Common Steel Crochet Hook Sizes

U.S. (American)	Continental (Metric)	U.K. (English)
2	2.25 mm	1½
4	2 mm	2½
6	1.8 mm	3½
7	1.65 mm	4
8	1.5 mm	4½
9	1.4 mm	5
10	1.3 mm	5½

REMEMBER

When shopping for crochet hooks, don't be afraid to try out lots of different brands and sizes. Hooks are inexpensive, and having extras of the most common sizes doesn't hurt. Even after you've found the style that you're comfortable with, hang on to other hooks you've collected as backups. You never know when you're going to lose your favorite hook and urgently need a replacement!

Collecting Gizmos and Gadgets

Lots of knitting and crocheting gadgets are available on the market. Some make life a little easier, and others are out-and-out lifesavers. Some you have to buy, but you can improvise others from what you already have on hand.

Stocking up on the essentials

For the most part, knitting and crocheting gadgets are small and portable. Keep these essentials in a little zippered bag, and you can carry them anywhere.

Scissors or thread cutters

Small, portable scissors are a must. In a pinch, you can break certain yarns with your hands, but others have to be cut with scissors. Collapsible scissors that fold up and don't leave any sharp points exposed are great. You can find them in most knitting stores. Other small scissors come with a little sheath that covers the tips so that you can carry them in your project bag without them poking through.

A *thread cutter* is a small, portable scissor substitute meant only for cutting yarn. It resembles a disc with notched edges and can even be worn as a necklace while you work so that it's always at hand.

TIP

If you're traveling by plane and want to carry on your knitting or crocheting, be sure to check with the Transportation Security Administration (TSA) for restrictions (www.tsa.gov/traveler-information/prohibited-items). As of this writing, knitting and crochet needles are generally permitted in carry-on luggage, but scissor size is restricted for carry-ons, and thread cutters with blades have to go in your checked baggage. When traveling, consider bringing fingernail clippers or an empty dental floss case to easily snip your yarn while in flight.

WARNING

Don't try to break your yarn with your hands — doing so is almost impossible and can stretch your yarn and hurt your hands if you actually manage it.

Tape measure

A small retractable tape measure marked for inches and centimeters can go anywhere. Use it to measure your gauge swatch and to check your knitted or crocheted pieces as you go along.

Yarn or tapestry needles

Tapestry needles, also called *yarn needles*, are simply large-eye needles with a blunt point that you use to sew knitted or crocheted pieces together. When joining pieces of fabric, you're working in the spaces around the stitches, not through the yarn strand. A blunt point ensures that you don't split the yarn.

TIP

Yarn needles come in steel or plastic styles. The steel variety are preferable because the plastic ones tend to bend and break over time.

Safety pins

Safety pins are handy for a variety of tasks. Pinned to your piece at strategic points, they can help you keep track of when you've worked a knitting increase or decrease or signal the right side of reversible fabric. They work well as miniature stitch holders for small groups of stitches and for securing dropped stitches (although you can get stich holders designed specifically for that purpose, as discussed later in this chapter).

In yarn shops and specialty catalogs, you can find several sizes of pins without coils, which are less likely to catch on your yarn than regular safety pins.

Knitting needle gauge and tension gauge

Needle gauges and tension gauges are indispensable. A *needle gauge* is a small ruler-like gadget with graduated holes in it for measuring the size of your knitting needles and crochet hooks. If you knit a lot on circular needles, which frequently aren't labeled for size, or if you're prone to finding a lost double-pointed needle under the sofa cushions, a needle gauge is essential for size identification. Buy one that shows both metric and US sizes.

A *tension gauge* (also called a *stitch gauge*) often comes as part of a needle gauge. It's a flat piece of metal or plastic with a 2-inch L-shaped window for measuring stitches and rows. You lay the tension gauge over your knitting, lining up the window along a row of stitches horizontally and vertically, and count the rows and stitches exposed. The drawback to using this tool is that 2 inches isn't always a large enough measure for an accurate gauge count. You can see a typical combination needle and tension gauge in Figure 1-7. (To find out more about tension gauge, see Book 1, Chapter 4.)

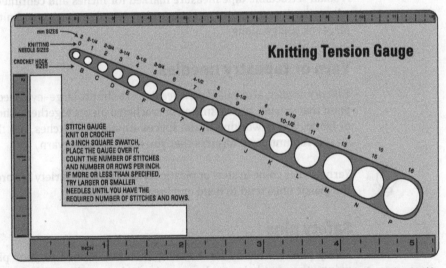

FIGURE 1-7:
A common needle and tension gauge.

Illustration by Wiley, Composition Services Graphics

TIP

You can make a great tension gauge by cutting a very accurate 4-inch window in a piece of sturdy but thin cardboard. Lay this tool over your knitting and clearly count 4 inches worth of stitches and rows.

Cable knitting needles

A *cable needle* is a short knitting needle that's pointed at both ends, has a divot or curve toward the middle, and is used to hold stitches temporarily while you work

on their neighbors. There are several versions of the two main types: U-shaped and straight (see Figure 1-8). Try out a couple of styles to see which you like better.

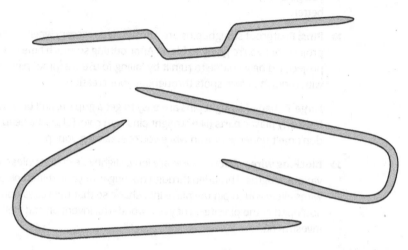

FIGURE 1-8:
Cable needles.

Illustration by Wiley, Composition Services Graphics

TIP

In a pinch, you can use a double-pointed needle or even a long nail or toothpick as a cable needle, but a tool especially designed for this task is best and a small price to pay for its convenience. Obviously, if you don't plan to knit cables, leave this item off your list.

Yarn bobbins

Yarn bobbins are usually plastic, and you use them to wrap different colors of yarn on when you're working a multicolored piece. Book 3, Chapter 5 introduces multi-color crochet. Book 4, Chapter 1 introduces multicolor knitting with stripes.

Blocking tools

When you're done with knitting or crocheting project, you need to *block* it, which means to shape it. For successful blocking, covered in detail in Book 7, Chapter 1, here's what you need:

» **Steam iron:** You probably already have a steam iron. The more steam, the better.

» **Blocking board:** A *blocking board* is not your ironing board. It's a flat surface made from a material that you can stick a pin into. It should be large enough to hold at least one pinned-out sweater piece. Ideally, it should be marked with a 1-inch grid so that you can pin out your piece to its proper dimensions

without using your tape measure. If you have enough space, you can leave the blocking board up all the time for checking your project's measurements as you go along. In a pinch, you can use your bed, but a real blocking board is better.

>> **Pins:** Rustproof straight pins are absolutely necessary when pinning down a project that you're going to block. After putting so much time into your project, it'd be a shame to ruin it by failing to use rustproof pins and ending up with reddish-brown spots throughout your creation.

Large T-shaped straight pins are easy to get a grip on, and because they don't have any plastic parts (like straight pins with colorful plastic heads do), they don't melt under your iron while you're steaming your piece.

>> **Blocking wires:** *Blocking wires* are long, slightly flexible stainless steel wires in various lengths. Threaded through the edges of your knitted piece, blocking wires allow you to pin the piece into shape so that the edges don't become scalloped at the pin sites. They're a wonderful invention and well worth the investment.

Examining nice-to-have extras

You can get by without buying the gadgets in this section, but you may find some of them worth the small investment. For example, instead of using strands of yarn tied in a circle for yarn markers, you might find using stitch markers much easier. Figure 1-9 shows some popular gadgets.

Stitch markers

In knitting, a *stitch marker* is a small ring that you slip onto your needle between stitches to alert you to places in your knitting that you need to pay attention to: the beginning of a round, the beginning and end of a repeat, the spot to work an increase or a decrease. When you reach a marker, you slip it from the LH (left hand) needle to the RH (right hand) needle and carry on. (See Book 1, Chapter 4 for an explanation of other acronyms you'll come across while knitting and crocheting.)

You can find several styles of markers on the market. Some are wafer thin, and others are small plastic coils that open and can be placed on the needle in the middle of a row. Some are made from rubber and won't come whizzing off the end of your needle when you get to them. (Of course, if you don't have any bona fide knitting markers, you can always use a contrasting yarn color tied in a loop or a safety pin.)

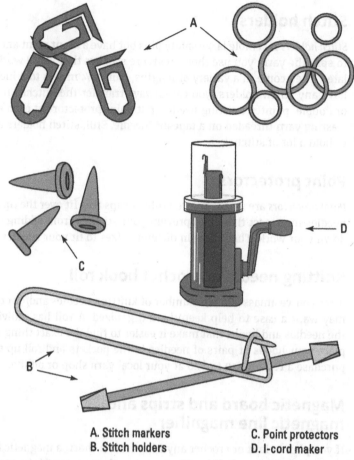

FIGURE 1-9:
Nonessential
but handy
accessories.

A. Stitch markers   C. Point protectors
B. Stitch holders   D. I-cord maker

Illustration by Wiley, Composition Services Graphics

WARNING

Choose a stitch marker that has approximately the same circumference as the needle you're using. Failing to do so may result in an unintentional column of stretched stitches where the stitch marker is placed.

Stitch markers for crocheting are a little different than those for knitting. Knitting stitch markers are closed rings, but crochet stitch markers are removable. Be sure to look for markers that have a split; they're often referred to as *split stitch markers*.

TIP

Although removable stitch markers aren't absolutely essential, having some type of marker comes in handy when you have to mark the end of a specific row or a certain stitch within the row where you're going to work an increase or decrease. However, as in knitting, a piece of contrasting colored yarn, a safety pin, or a bobby pin works just as well when you need to mark something while you crochet.

Stitch holders

Stitch holders resemble large safety pins but have a blunt point and no coil so as not to split the yarn; you use them to secure stitches that you'll work up or finish off later. They come in a variety of lengths, from 1¾ inches to 8 inches. If you don't have any stitch holders, you can always transfer the stitches to a spare circular or double-pointed knitting needle (put point protectors at each end) or to a contrasting yarn threaded on a tapestry needle. Still, stitch holders are the best tools to hold a lot of stitches.

Point protectors

Point protectors are small, pointed rubber caps that fit over the tips of your knitting needles to protect them and prevent your stitches from sliding off when you put down your work. They come in different sizes to fit your needles.

Knitting needle or crochet hook roll

After you've amassed a fair number of knitting needles and/or crochet hooks, you may want a case to help keep them organized. A roll has individual pockets for the needles and hooks that make it easier to find the exact thing you need. Simply place your hoods or pairs of needles in the pockets and roll up the case. You can purchase a roll for $10 to $20 at your local yarn shop or online.

Magnetic board and strips and magnetic line magnifier

If you plan to knit or crochet anything from a chart, a magnetic board with strips is a wonderful item to have. You put your chart on top of the magnetic board and lay the magnetized strip on the row of squares *above* the row you're working on. After you work the row shown on the chart, you move the strip up, exposing the next row to knit.

A magnetic line magnifier is a see-through ruler that works like the magnetic board and strips but also magnifies the line you're working on. You put the magnifier on top of the row you're working on.

Of course, you can use sticky notes for marking your row on a chart. The downside is that the notes often are shorter than the width of your chart and more vulnerable to cats skittering across the table or someone looking for paper to use for something (seemingly) more important than keeping your place on the knitting or crocheting chart. Another alternative is painter's tape, which has very low tack and doesn't stick to the pattern.

Yarn ball winder

A yarn ball winder can set you back about $40, but it makes winding yarn into balls much faster. Just secure one tail end of a hank or skein to the ball winder and turn the handle until all the yarn has been wound into a neat little cake. This process takes just a couple of minutes, and you end up with a string that's ready to go from the center.

Swift

Instead of relying on a friend or chair back to hold your yarn while you wind it into a ball, why not turn to a swift? Most swifts look a little like a rotating wooden umbrella. Simply unfold the hank, place it on the swift, and start winding. You can use a swift on its own or with a yarn ball winder. Either way, the cost of a swift ranges from $50 to $70.

Pompom maker

If you feel like you're creating wimpy, lopsided pompoms, try a pompom maker. What a difference they make! They help you make solid and rainbow pompoms in three sizes. This small and inexpensive gadget is one of those simple but brilliant ideas that turn a tedious job with questionable results into something quick with spectacular results. (It's so much fun to use that you may be tempted to add pompoms to everything.)

Tassel and fringe maker

Everything that's true about the pompom maker also applies to the *tassel and fringe maker*. It's a small adjustable plastic frame that allows you to wrap any number of threads around it before cutting the wraps for fringe or tassels. No more hunting around for the book or piece of cardboard just the right size for wrapping.

Graph paper

Graph paper is very useful for diagramming patterns and charting designs and motifs. Figuring on 5 or 8 squares to the inch works fine for plotting knitted sweaters and texture patterns. If you plan to design your own color patterns or motifs, look in your local yarn shop for knitter's graph paper, which has flattened-out squares (5 squares across and 7 squares up to the inch) to reflect the grid of knitted fabric — more rows per inch than stitches. You also can find knitter's graph paper online.

I-cord maker

If you find yourself making lots of I-cords for bag handles or just for decoration, a hand-cranked I-cord maker will more than pay for itself in time saved. Available at many craft and yarn stores, these small machines make quick work of I-cord. You find a few bag projects in Book 5, Chapter 4.

Notebook or folder

You'll find many good reasons to keep a notebook or folder among your knitting and crocheting supplies. It's a good place to record your projects and save labels from the yarn you're using. Never throw away the label that comes with your yarn. You may need it to match the color and/or dye lot numbers if you run out of yarn on a project. Labels are also handy records of the yardage used to make a project (especially a sweater) just in case you love it so much that you want to make another just like it. You can also write down the needle size you ended up using and the gauge you got on a specific project. In addition, you can jot down ideas, technical questions to ask a knitting or crocheting mentor, patterns you want to swatch, and so on.

Chapter 2

Yearning for Yarn

Truth be told, you can spend quite a few hours happily knitting or crocheting away with nothing more than some spare yarn and an old pair of knitting needles or a hook. If you take to knitting and crocheting, however, your satisfaction with these basic supplies will soon morph into a desire to experiment with the array of beautiful yarns.

With so many choices in stores and online, choosing the yarns that are right for you — or the project you have in mind — can be a bit daunting. This chapter's here to help. It introduces the different kinds of yarns and how to pick the right yarn for your projects.

Understanding Yarn Fundamentals

A nice yarn shop is a knitter's paradise. Heck, even the yarn section of a discount or craft store can be a little slice of heaven. Why? Because of all the traditional and specialty yarns that are available. With such an abundance of choices, how do you decide what yarn to buy? Knowing a little bit about the different types of yarn and their general characteristics helps. So first things first.

Yarn is made from short fibers that come from animals or plants or are synthetic. The fibers are combed, or *carded*, to align them into a soft untwisted rope (called *roving*). Then they're spun (twisted) into a strand or *ply* of yarn. This single ply is usually combined with other plies to form the final yarn.

The following sections explain the two main factors — fiber and weight — that account for the wide variety of yarns available. Whether you prefer your yarn plain or fancy, some knowledge of yarn basics can ensure that what looks great on the shelf will look great in your finished project, too.

Fixating on fiber

All yarn is made from natural or synthetic fibers. Different fibers have different qualities — some good, some not so good. Often, to offset an undesirable characteristic, yarn manufacturers combine different fibers. (A *blend* is a yarn made from fibers of different origins — for example, wool/cotton, wool/silk, or alpaca/cotton.) More than anything else, the combination of fibers in your yarn determines its ultimate look, feel, and wearable comfort.

Yarn consists of one or more plies. *Plied yarns* are made from two, three, or four plies of yarn twisted together. Multi-plied and firmly twisted yarns are usually strong, smooth, and even. Lightly twisted plied and single-ply yarns are closer to their roving (unspun) state and, though sturdy enough when knitted up, can pull apart into strands if they're over-handled. They also can be slightly uneven, have more loft and softness, and be warmer than their twisted sisters.

REMEMBER

A fabric's *hand* is how it feels to the touch. Just as pieces of woven fabric from silk or wool differ in *drape* (how they fall) and softness, so do knits from different fibers. But fiber isn't all that accounts for drape and softness. The size of the needle or hook you use with a given yarn affects the feel of your finished piece. The larger the needle or hook and looser the stitch, the softer and drapier the fabric. The smaller the needle or hook and tighter the stitch, the stiffer the fabric.

Wool and other fleece yarns

Wool (made from the fleece of sheep) is the queen of yarns, and it endures and remains a popular choice for a number of excellent reasons.

Wool is a good insulator — warm in winter, cool in summer. It can absorb lots of moisture without feeling wet, and it absorbs dye beautifully. It's resilient — the fibers can stretch and bend repeatedly but always return to their original shape. It's soft, relatively lightweight, and beautiful to look at. And, key to beginning knitters and crocheters, wool is easy to work with because it has just enough give. It also can be pulled out and reworked easily, a bonus when you're just learning the basic stitches.

Although all wool yarns are wonderful to work with, they vary tremendously depending on the breed of sheep or combination of breeds they come from, how they're spun, whether they're plied or single stranded, and whether they're treated for washability or not. Following are some of your wool yarn options:

» **Lamb's wool:** This wool comes from a young lamb's first shearing. It's softer and finer than wool from an older sheep's fleece.

» **Merino wool:** Merino wool is considered the finest of the fine breeds. Long, lustrous fibers make a soft and exceptionally lovely knitted fabric.

» **Pure new wool/virgin wool:** *Pure new* and *virgin* refer to wool that's made directly from animal fleece and not recycled from existing wool garments.

» **Shetland wool:** Real Shetland wool is a traditional 2-ply heathery yarn that's made from the small and hardy native sheep of Scotland's Shetland Islands and used in traditional Fair Isle sweaters. It's usually available in sport or fingering weight. (Yarn weight is discussed a little later in this chapter.) This wool originally came in sheep's colors, including all shades of charcoal and deep brown to white. Shetland wool is now also available in an extraordinary range of beautiful dyed colors.

» **Icelandic wool:** This rustic, soft, single-ply, medium-weight to heavy-weight yarn was traditionally available only in natural sheep's colors (black, charcoal, light gray, and white). Today, it's also available dyed in bright jewel and heathered colors as well as in a lighter weight appropriate for thinner "indoor" sweaters.

» **Washable or "superwash" wool:** This wool is treated chemically or electronically to destroy the outer fuzzy layer of fibers that would otherwise *felt* or bond with each other and shrink in the washing machine.

Sheep aren't the only animals to provide fibers for yarns. Fuzzy mohair and luxurious cashmere come from Angora and Kashmir goats, respectively. Warm, soft alpaca comes from members of the llama family; *alpacas* are small, South American cousins of the camel. Yarn made from yak down is one of the most luxurious fibers found. Warmer than wool and as soft as cashmere, it's an extremely durable and lightweight fiber that preserves heat in the winter yet breathes for comfort in warmer weather. The delicate underwool of the Arctic muskox is one of the most sought-after fibers in the world because of its rarity, softness, and warmth. Qiviut is softer than cashmere and is light as a feather. It's an insulating fiber and is comfortable to wear in any climate. Lighter than air and fuzziest of all, *angora* comes from the hair of Angora rabbits.

Silk, cotton, linen, and rayon

Silk, cotton, linen, and rayon yarns are the slippery yarns. Unlike rough yarns from the hairy fibers of animals, their smooth and often shiny surfaces cause them to unravel quickly if you drop a stitch. These yarns are inelastic and may stretch lengthwise over time. Often, they're blended with other fibers (natural and synthetic) to counteract their disadvantages. But silk and cotton, even in their pure state, are lovely to look at and comfortable to wear.

Silk is spun from the cocoon of the silkworm, and silk yarn has a smooth, often shiny finish. It's lightweight and absorbent, making it a perfect choice for warm-weather garments. Silk is often combined with cotton or wool to increase its elasticity and durability.

In the past, cotton was used mainly to make doilies, bedspreads, and tablecloths, but today's cotton yarn has become more versatile. It comes in a wide range of sizes, from very fine threads to worsted-weight yarn. Garments made from cotton yarn are washable, durable, and have that great cotton comfort. Cotton yarn is also a good choice for home decor items such as place mats, potholders, and curtains.

Synthetic yarns

Originally, synthetics (nylon, acrylic, and polyester) were made to mimic the look and feel of natural materials. Just as wool yarn is spun from short lengths of carded fibers from a sheep's fleece, synthetic yarns begin as a long filament made from artificial, usually petroleum-based ingredients cut into short lengths and processed to look like wool yarn.

Knitters and crocheters give mixed reviews to 100-percent synthetic yarns:

>> **On the plus side:** All-synthetic yarns are inexpensive and hold up well in the washing machine. For people who are allergic to wool, synthetics can be a look-alike substitute. Synthetic yarns are readily available in a wide range of sizes, colors, and textures and are generally less expensive than their natural counterparts. These yarns, especially those made from acrylic, are good for afghans and baby blankets because they require little care. (However, you should still be sure to check the label for washing instructions.)

>> **On the downside:** All-synthetic yarns don't have the wonderful insulating and moisture-absorbing qualities of natural yarns and therefore can be uncomfortable to wear. For the same reason, they can make your hands clammy when you're knitting. They *pill* (form small fuzz balls) more readily than wool or other fibers, and after they're exposed to heat (a hot iron is deadly), they lose resilience and become flat.

These complaints and synthetic yarns' dubious reputation have encouraged manufacturers to come up with new and better applications for synthetics. Perhaps the best use for synthetic yarns is in combination with other fibers. Manufacturers now engineer blended yarns for certain qualities. For example, nylon is extremely strong and light. Nylon adds durability when blended in small amounts with more-fragile fibers such as mohair. A little nylon blended with wool makes a superb sock yarn. A little acrylic in cotton makes the yarn lighter and promotes *memory* so that the knitted fabric doesn't stretch out of shape.

Straddling the border between natural and synthetic are soy, bamboo, corn, and other unusual yarns made using plant-based materials. Spun into microfilaments that are extruded via a process similar to that employed for acrylic and other synthetic yarns, these fibers have become increasingly popular, particularly in yarn blends such as soy/wool, bamboo/silk, and even tree-, corn-, and seaweed-derived fibers.

Novelty yarns

Novelty, or specialty, yarns are easy to recognize because their appearance is so different from traditional yarns. Their bright colors and whimsical textures can be hard to resist. Eyelash yarns, for example, feature tiny spikes of fiber that stick up, resembling eyelashes. Following are some of the more common novelty yarns you may come across:

>> **Ribbon:** This option is usually a knitted ribbon in rayon or a rayon blend with wonderful drape.

>> **Boucle:** This highly bumpy, textured yarn is comprised of loops.

>> **Chenille:** Although chenille is tricky to work with, the attractive appearance and velvety texture of this yarn make your perseverance worthwhile. It's usually available in rayon (for sheen) or cotton.

>> **Thick-thin:** Often handspun, these yarns alternate between very thick and thin sections, which lends a charmingly bumpy look to the final fabric.

>> **Railroad ribbon:** This ribbon-style yarn has tiny "tracks" of fiber strung between two parallel strands of thread.

>> **Faux fur:** Fluffy fiber strands on a strong base thread of nylon resemble faux fur when knitted. It's available in many different colors.

>> **"Traditional" novelty yarns:** Long before shiny synthetic eyelash and faux fur yarns became popular, other types of yarn were used to create special looks. Tweed, heathered, marled, and variegated yarns all create subtler effects than modern novelty yarns do and can add lovely variety to your yarn basket.

- *Tweed:* Usually wool, this yarn has a background color flecked with bits of fiber in different colors.

- *Heather:* This yarn has been blended from a number of different-colored or dyed fleeces and then spun. Heather yarns are muted in color; think of them as the yarn equivalent of watercolors.

- *Marled (ragg) yarn:* This option is a plied yarn in which the plies are different colors.

- *Variegated yarn:* This yarn is dyed in several different colors or shades of a single color. Hand-dyed yarn (often called *handpainted*) is very popular and creates a series of random color repeats that would be difficult to imitate using even a large number of different-colored yarns.

TIP

Some novelty yarns can be tricky to work with. Others — like those with complex textures, no give, or threadlike strands that are easy to lose as you create your stitches — can be downright difficult. If you're eager to work with a novelty yarn, start with a variegated dyed or painted single-ply yarn. These choices give lots of color variation and interest, but the strand of yarn is itself easy to see. Identifying individual stitches in highly textured yarns is difficult, if not impossible, making it hard to fix mistakes or rip out stitches.

Organic yarns, fair trade fibers, and sustainably sourced fibers

Ecologically friendly yarns are a growing trend in the yarn world as crafters work to lessen their hobbies' impact on the environment. Among the yarns found in this category are organic, fair trade, and sustainably sourced yarns:

>> *Organic yarns* come from companies that make their products without the use of man-made chemicals, so plants and animals are raised without synthetic pesticides or fertilizer.

>> *Fair trade fibers* come from companies who work to improve labor conditions for their farmers and workers.

>> *Sustainably sourced yarns* have been produced with minimal impact on the earth, meaning the fiber is cultivated without excess waste of or damage to the earth's resources.

MATERIALS THAT AREN'T YARN

If you're feeling adventurous, you can knit or crochet with any material that resembles a string. Throw caution to the wind and use fine, colored wire and hemp to crochet cool jewelry. Nylon cord can knit up waterproof bags and outdoor seat cushions. Or try making something with cut-up strips of fabric or plastic grocery bags to give a whole new meaning to "reduce, reuse, recycle."

Some major yarn brands and local yarn shops have added eco-friendly yarns to their line, but these still tend to be more expensive than other yarns. However, as more crafters support those brands that make a conscious effort to produce earth-friendly fibers, the more abundant and cheaper those fibers will become.

Considering yarn weight

Yarns come in different *weights*, or thicknesses. The weight of your yarn (among other things) has a huge impact on the look of your final product and certainly the amount of time it takes to knit or crochet it.

The weight of a yarn determines the *gauge*, or how many stitches it takes to knit or crochet 1 inch. For example, a medium-weight yarn that knits up 5 stitches and 7 rows to the inch takes 35 stitches to make a square inch of knitted fabric. A bulky yarn at 3 stitches and 5 rows to the inch needs 15 stitches to make a square inch. You can see how weight affects gauge in Figure 2-1. (Book 1, Chapter 3 explains gauge in more detail.)

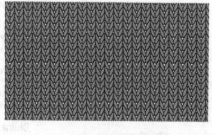 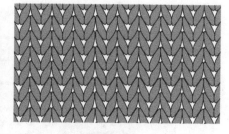

FIGURE 2-1: Different weights create different effects.

Medium-weight yarn   Bulky yarn

Illustration by Wiley, Composition Services Graphics

REMEMBER

The thickness of a given yarn is determined by the individual thickness of the plies, *not* by the number of plies. If the plies are thin, a 4-ply yarn can be finer than a heavy single-ply yarn.

Although no official categories govern yarn weights, many knitting and books and yarn manufacturers use common terms to indicate a yarn's thickness. The following list, although not all-inclusive, outlines the most common sizes of yarn in order from the thinnest to the thickest strands (check out Figure 2-2 to see how the different weights compare visually):

>> **Lace weight:** Lace weight yarns include *crochet thread* and tend to be very thin yarns commonly used for doilies, filet crochet, and shawls.

>> **Fingering weight:** Also known as *sock* or *baby weight,* this thin yarn is generally used to make lightweight garments, baby items, and designs with an open and lacy pattern.

>> **Sport weight:** This medium-weight yarn is great for many different types of patterns, including sweaters, baby blankets, scarves, and shawls.

>> **Double Knitting (DK) weight:** Sometimes referred to as *light worsted,* this yarn is slightly thicker than sport weight and can be used in the same patterns, but the resulting fabric is somewhat heavier.

>> **Worsted weight:** Worsted weight is probably the most commonly used size of yarn and also the most readily available. It's great for afghans, sweaters, scarves, hats, slippers, and toys.

>> **Chunky weight:** This yarn is sometimes referred to as *heavy worsted* or *bulky* weight. It's thicker than worsted weight and is used for afghans, jackets, and rugs.

>> **Super bulky weight:** This yarn is a very thick, warm yarn and is generally used to make jackets, afghans, rugs, and heavy outdoor sweaters.

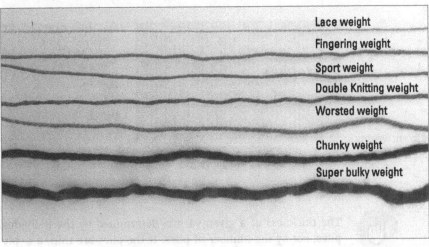

Lace weight
Fingering weight
Sport weight
Double Knitting weight
Worsted weight
Chunky weight
Super bulky weight

FIGURE 2-2:
A comparison of yarn weights.

© John Wiley & Sons, Inc.

Introduction

Knitting and crocheting are no longer considered something your grandmother did while sitting on the porch in her rocking chair. Knitted and crocheted designs are everywhere, from the racks in your favorite clothing store to fashion catalogs — even to the runways in Paris and Milan. These crafts even show up in movies and television shows. The reasons for this comeback are many, and by reading this book, you can discover some of those reasons and begin to enjoy a lifelong affair with the fiber arts.

Although knitting and crochet are time-honored crafts, that doesn't mean they are behind the times. Advances in technology have made yarns softer and more colorful, with wonderful new textures appearing every time you turn around. No longer are knitters and crocheters limited to solid or variegated colors; yarn is now hand painted and space dyed. Although worsted-weight yarn is still a staple in every yarn cache, so many varieties of weights and textures are available today that it's a challenge to categorize them all.

You're never too old or too young to discover crochet. The skills that you master, the benefits that you receive, and the beautiful heirlooms that you create can last a lifetime and, ideally, be passed on to future generations.

About This Book

Knitting & Crocheting All-in-One For Dummies gives first-time knitters and crocheters hands-on experience with new skills and serves as a reference tool for those who already have some basic know-how. The book takes you step by step through the process of gathering your materials, creating your first stitches, and finishing off a piece of knitted or crocheted fabric. If that sounds somewhat overwhelming, relax. You find detailed written instructions and easy-to-follow illustrations throughout this book.

Each minibook in *Knitting & Crocheting All-in-One For Dummies* contains chapters full of information relevant to each other, with successive parts adding more building blocks to your knowledge. If you already have some experience and are looking to refine and expand your techniques, then the later chapters are for you.

There, you can find advanced stitches and techniques, along with many tips to guide you. Finally, the projects throughout this book help you practice your new-found skills on fun and useful designs while feeling a sense of accomplishment for a job well done.

This book uses the following conventions to make the world of knitting & crocheting even easier for you to dive into:

>> When a new stitch or technique is introduced, you see its abbreviation in parentheses to help you become familiar with the shorthand used in knitting and crochet patterns. The abbreviation also appears the first time a stitch is mentioned in a set of numbered steps.

>> The specific part of an illustration that relates to the step you're working on is shaded dark gray. For example, if you're inserting your hook into a certain stitch, that stitch is shaded so you can see exactly where to go.

Foolish Assumptions

How does that saying about assuming something go? Well, never mind about that. Each step is explained as clearly and concisely as possible, so you don't need any prior experience to understand the concepts introduced in this book.

The only assumption in this book is that you have a desire to learn the art of knitting and crochet. Beyond that, you only need to give it your best shot and don't give up.

Icons Used in This Book

REMEMBER

This icon highlights important points. You should remember them and apply them when dealing with the skills shown.

TIP

This icon clues you in to some tips of the trade that more experienced knitters and crocheters have discovered over time.

WARNING

When you see this icon, read carefully. It marks potential pitfalls and helps you steer clear of frustrating and time-consuming mistakes.

Beyond the Book

In addition to all the great information and step-by-step instructions included in this book, you can find even more online! Head to dummies.com/go/ knitcrochetAIO for tutorial videos and full color images of some of the projects in this book.

You can also find a handy online Cheat Sheet with a list of international knitting and crochet symbols and stitch abbreviations and abbreviations for common terms. Go to dummies.com and search for "Knitting & Crocheting All in One For Dummies."

Where to Go from Here

Now that the introductions are over, it's time to begin. The fun part is that where you start is entirely up to you! *Knitting & Crocheting All-in-One For Dummies* is written so you can start reading whatever section best fits your skill level.

>> If you're an absolute beginner, start with Books 1, 2, and 3. They have all the essential information that you need to get started.

>> If you already have some experience with the basics and want to expand your knowledge, then look ahead to Books 4, 5, and 6, where you find advanced stitches and techniques and related projects. Whenever you need to know something that was covered in a previous chapter, you see a reference to that chapter.

>> If you used to knit or crochet and are coming back to it (sometimes life just gets too busy for fun stuff like this), skim through the chapters to reacquaint yourself with the techniques. The stitches themselves haven't changed, but the materials have, and you may come across some useful info.

Beyond the Book

In addition to all the great information and step-by-step instructions included in this book, you can find even more online. Head to dummies.com/go/knitcrochetAIO for tutorial videos and full color images of some of the projects in this book.

You can also find a handy online Cheat Sheet with a list of international knitting and crochet symbols and stitch abbreviations and abbreviations for common terms. Go to dummies.com and search for "Knitting & Crocheting All-in-One For Dummies."

Where to Go from Here

Now that the introductions are over, it's time to begin. The fun part is that where you start is entirely up to you! Knitting & Crocheting All-in-One For Dummies is written so you can start reading whatever section best fits your skill level.

- If you're an absolute beginner, start with Books 1, 2, and 3. They have all the essential information that you need to get started.

- If you already have some experience with the basics and want to expand your knowledge, then look ahead to Books 4, 5, and 6 where you'll find advanced stitches and techniques and related projects. Whenever you need to know something that was covered in a previous chapter, you see a reference to that chapter.

- If you used to knit or crochet and are returning back to it (sometimes life just gets too busy for fun stuff like that) skim through the chapters to reacquaint yourself with the terminology, the stitches themselves haven't changed, but the material has, and you may come across some useful info.

1

Getting Started

Contents at a Glance

Chapter **1**

Needles, Hooks, and Other Tools

As with any new project that you decide to undertake, you first have to figure out what tools and materials you need to get the job done. For knitting or crocheting, your needs are pretty simple. Grab a set of needles or a crochet hook and some yarn, find a comfortable seat, and you're ready to go.

In this chapter, you discover the different types of knitting needles and crochet hooks and when to use them. You also find out about other tools that aren't necessary all the time but can be useful when you're knitting or crocheting different types of designs.

Selecting Knitting Needles

Knitting needles come in a stunning assortment of materials, styles, and sizes to mesh with your knitting style, the particular project you're working on, your aesthetics, and your budget.

Exploring needles

You can choose from three kinds of knitting needles: straight, circular, and double-pointed (see Figure 1-1 and the following sections).

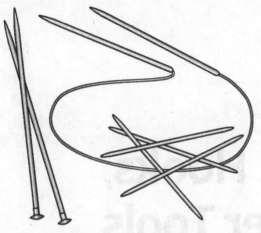

Illustration by Wiley, Composition Services Graphics

FIGURE 1-1:
Three kinds of knitting needles.

Telling it straight

Straight needles are generally used for *flat knitting* — knitting on the right side and then turning and knitting on the wrong side. Straight needles come in many standard lengths, ranging from 7-inch "scarf needles" to those that are 10, 13, and 14 inches. The larger your project, the longer the needle you need. (You also can knit flat with a circular needle for wide projects; see the next section for details about circular needles.) Figure 1-2 shows the various parts of straight needles.

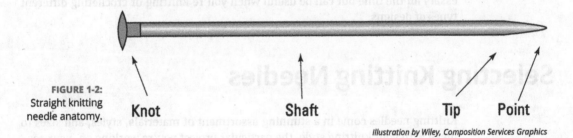

FIGURE 1-2:
Straight knitting needle anatomy.

Knot   **Shaft**   **Tip**   **Point**

Illustration by Wiley, Composition Services Graphics

Going in circles

A *circular needle* is simply a pair of straight knitting needle tips joined by a flexible cable. You can use a circular needle to *knit in the round* — knitting in a continuous, spiral-like fashion without turning your work. This technique creates a seamless tube large enough for a sweater body or small enough for a neckband. You also can use a circular needle as you would straight needles to work back and forth. This approach can be particularly handy for lengthwise-knit scarves, blankets, and other very wide pieces.

Circular needles are available in many different lengths, most frequently 16, 24, 29, and 36 inches, although they're also available as long as 60 inches! For smaller circumferences, some knitters find that double-pointed needles, described in the next section, are more comfortable to work with.

TIP

When you buy a circular needle, check to make sure the spot where the needle tip meets the cable (called the *join*) is smooth to prevent stitches from snagging. Several manufacturers now make circular needles with interchangeable needle tips and various cable lengths. These interchangeable needles are useful for a wide variety of projects and make it very easy to swap needles when you're attempting to find the right gauge for your chosen yarn.

REMEMBER

The needle size appears on the package (which you can use as a storage case), but it doesn't always appear on the needle itself, which can be a bit of a pain. To keep track of needle sizes, invest in a small metal or plastic needle gauge (discussed in "Collecting Gizmos and Gadgets" later in this chapter). A needle gauge has graduated holes to help you determine the size of your needle.

Doing rounds with double-pointed needles

Double-pointed needles (abbreviated *dpns*) have a point at each end and are sold in sets of four or five needles. They work the same way as a circular needle — in rounds. You use them to make small tubes when your knitting has too few stitches to stretch around the circumference of a circular needle — for such things as sleeve cuffs, tops of hats, socks, mittens, and so on. They come in 7- and 10-inch lengths and have even shown up in 5-inch lengths — a great boon to those who enjoy making socks and mittens.

Sizing them up

A needle's size is determined by its diameter. The smaller the size, the narrower the needle and the smaller the stitch it makes. Figure 1-3 shows needle sizes and their US and metric equivalents.

Popular Knitting Needle Sizes

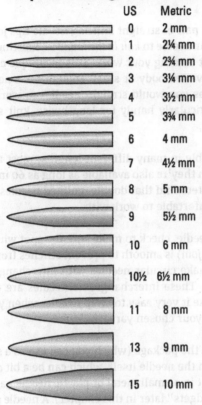

US	Metric
0	2 mm
1	2¼ mm
2	2¾ mm
3	3¼ mm
4	3½ mm
5	3¾ mm
6	4 mm
7	4½ mm
8	5 mm
9	5½ mm
10	6 mm
10½	6½ mm
11	8 mm
13	9 mm
15	10 mm

FIGURE 1-3: Chart of needle sizes.

Illustration by Wiley, Composition Services Graphics

TIP

If you aren't sure what needle sizes you'll need in the future, try a circular knitting needle set with interchangeable tips. Even though the needle is designed for circular knitting, you can also use it to knit back and forth. Some sets feature plastic needle tips, some metal. These sets allow you to combine different-sized needle tips with different connector cords to make a very large range of needle sizes on the fly. An interchangeable circular needle is especially handy when you're unsure which needle size to use for a given yarn. If the current size isn't giving you the right gauge, simply switch the tip up or down one size instead of starting over on another needle.

Table of Contents

Contents at a Glance

Knitting &
Crocheting

ALL-IN-ONE

Pam Allen
Tracy L. Barr
Marlaina "Marly" Bird
Susan Brittain
Karen Manthey
Shannon Okey
Kristi Porter

for
dummies®
A Wiley Brand

In an attempt to provide a universally accepted classification of sizes, the Craft Yarn Council of America has developed the Standard Yarn Weight System, offering yarn weight symbols that represent the categories of yarn. Many yarn manufacturers include the yarn weight symbols on the label to help you find suitable yarn substitutions. Figure 2-3 shows the symbols for lace, super fine, fine, light, medium, bulky, and super bulky weights (from 0 to 6).

FIGURE 2-3:
The Standard
Yarn Weight
System.

Yarn Weight, Symbol & Category Names	**0** LACE	**1** SUPER FINE	**2** FINE	**3** LIGHT	**4** MEDIUM	**5** BULKY	**6** SUPER BULKY
Type of Yarns in Category	Fingering 10-count crochet thread	Sock, Fingering, Baby	Sport, Baby	Double Knitting, Light Worsted	Worsted, Afghan, Aran	Chunky, Craft, Rug	Bulky, Roving

Source: Craft Yarn Council of America; www.YarnStandards.com

Even though the different thicknesses of yarns are named by weight, as in worsted weight or sport weight, the size (diameter) of the yarn is actually what that name is referring to. The terms *size* and *weight* are interchangeable when referring to the thickness of a yarn.

REMEMBER

Reading Yarn Labels

Yarn is packaged (sometimes called *put up*) in different ways — balls, skeins (rhymes with "canes"), and hanks. Each comes wrapped with a label that you should read carefully. It contains useful information and lets you know whether the yarn is a good candidate for the project you have in mind. If the yarn begs to be purchased before you know what you want to make with it, the information on the label lets you know what kind of project best suits it.

Label talk

Yarn labels contain a lot of valuable information that you need to take note of to make sure your project turns out right. Check out the label in Figure 2-4 and the following list for the lowdown on label info.

FIGURE 2-4:
Identifying key
information
on a yarn label.

© John Wiley & Sons, Inc.

Yarn labels include most, if not all, of the following information:

>> **Article number (1):** Some manufacturers assign a number to each different type of yarn they produce for identification purposes. This number comes in handy when you're ordering yarn directly from the manufacturer or another mail-order source.

>> **Brand name (2):** A yarn company may manufacture several different types or *brands* of yarn.

>> **Care instructions (3):** As with any item that needs to be cleaned, yarn has specific care instructions. Some yarns require little care; you simply throw them in the washer and dryer. Other yarns need some TLC and should be handwashed and laid flat to dry. Still others should be sent to the dry cleaner. Be sure that the care instructions will work for your finished work, or else your creation may end up on the top shelf of the closet! Many manufacturers use the International Fabric Care Symbols shown here.

REMEMBER

If you mix more than one type of yarn in a project, the care requirements should be similar. Otherwise you may end up with a stretched (or shrunken) section after you launder your piece the first time.

>> **Color name and number (4):** Yarn colors are identified in two different ways: by name and/or number.

>> **Company name and logo (5):** This is the name of the company that manufactures the yarn. Sometimes contact information, such as address, telephone number, and website, is included as well.

>> **Dye lot number (6):** The *dye lot* number identifies yarns that are dyed in the same batch. Although companies strive to match the colors as closely as possible, slight variations exist from lot to lot. Even if skeins of different dye lots look the same when you hold them together, you may end up with a distinct color difference in your finished project.

To ensure an even color throughout your work, buy enough yarn from the same dye lot to complete your entire project. If you have to go back and buy more at a later date, chances are you won't be able to find yarn from the same dye lot.

If you do end up with skeins of the same color but different dye lots, here's a trick to make the color variation less noticeable. If you have equal numbers of skeins in each dye lot, knit or crochet two rows with a skein of one dye lot, and then make the next two rows with a skein from the second dye lot. Continue to switch skeins of each dye lot after every two rows to end up with a subtle striped pattern. If you have only one skein that has a different dye lot than the remaining skeins, you can still do the same thing, but you'll want to work in the odd dye lot less frequently depending on how many skeins you have to work with.

» **Gauge (7):** Gauge is a measurement that helps you keep your knit or crochet stitches consistent. It's the number of stitches and rows in a given measurement that you should get with a particular yarn by using the recommended hook size for that yarn. If the label only gives a knitting gauge, you can use this gauge as a guide for crochet because crochet hook sizes correspond to knitting needle sizes. Flip to Book 1, Chapter 3 for more on gauge.

» **Manufacturer's address (8):** Sometimes the manufacturer's address is listed separately from the name, and it can come in handy if you have questions about the yarn or are having trouble locating a retail store that sells the product.

» **Ply (9):** *Ply* refers to the number of smaller strands twisted together to form the larger single strand of yarn. This number can be deceptive, though, because a fine yarn can be a 3- or 4-ply yarn, whereas a bulky yarn can be just 2 ply. Worsted-weight yarns are generally 4 ply, but some cotton yarns can be made up of 8 or more strands. The ply may be included on the label along with the size or weight of the yarn; for example, 4-ply worsted-weight yarn or 2-ply bulky-weight yarn.

» **Recommended needle or hook size (10):** Sometimes the label suggests a certain needle or hook size so you can work to the proper gauge for a specific yarn size. The recommended size is a good place to start, although you may find that you need to use a smaller- or larger-size hook or pair of needles, depending on how you work your stitches and how loose you want them to be. You can achieve a lacy texture by using a much larger needle or hook size than recommended. On the other hand, if you want a tight, stiff fabric (like for a tapestry bag), you should use a smaller needle or hook size than the one the label calls for.

» **Weight (11):** This number reflects the actual weight of the whole skein, ball, or hank of yarn, as opposed to the weight (size) of the yarn strand. The weight is usually quoted in ounces and/or grams.

» **Yardage (12):** The yardage is the length of the yarn (in yards or meters) that's in the ball or skein. This information is important because you don't want to get partway through your project and then realize that you don't have enough yarn.

» **Yarn content (13):** Yarn content is the stuff your yarn is made of — wool or acrylic, cotton or silk, a blend of two or more fibers, or one of the many other fibers available.

Ball, skein, or hank?

Yarn comes in balls, skeins, and hanks (shown in Figure 2-5). Balls and skeins come ready to knit. After you find the end, you can create the first row of stiches and go. Hanks need to be wound into a ball before you can use them. If you try to knit with the yarn in hank form, you'll quickly end up with a tangled mess.

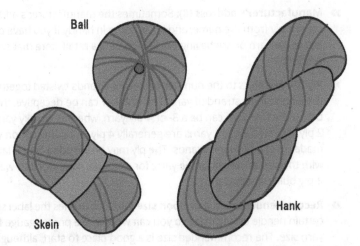

FIGURE 2-5:
Yarn comes in balls, skeins, and hanks.

Ball

Skein

Hank

Illustration by Wiley, Composition Services Graphics

To wind a hank, follow these steps:

1. Carefully unfold the hank (it's formed into a large circle) and drape it over a chair back, a friend's outstretched arms, or your bent knees if you're sitting.

2. Locate the ends of the yarn and, if they're tied, cut or unknot them.

3. **With one end, begin by making a butterfly (see Figure 2-6).**

   Wrap the yarn in a figure eight around the thumb and little finger of your hand. Make about 20 passes if you're winding a medium-weight yarn; make more passes for a finer yarn or fewer for a thick yarn.

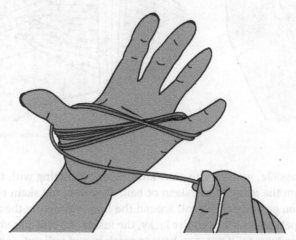

FIGURE 2-6: Making a butterfly.

Illustration by Wiley, Composition Services Graphics

4. **Take the "wings" off your finger and thumb and fold the butterfly in half, holding it between thumb and fingers.**

5. **Continue wrapping yarn *loosely* around the folded butterfly (and your fingers), as shown in Figure 2-7.**

6. **When the package gets bulky, slip it off your fingers, turn it, and continue to wrap the yarn into a ball.**

   Neatness isn't important. *Looseness* is. Always wrap the yarn around as many fingers as you can, slipping them out when you change position. The space they take up ensures that the yarn isn't stretched as it waits to be knitted or crocheted. If you work with stretched yarn, guess what happens to your final piece when the yarn springs back to size?

TIP

Your local yarn store may offer a winding service to convert hanks of yarn to center-pull balls by using a *yarn* (or *ball*) *winder* and a *swift* — two pieces of equipment that allow you to make an easy-to-use "cake" of yarn that sits flat as you knit it. If you find yourself with many hanks to wind, you can even buy your own winder and swift!

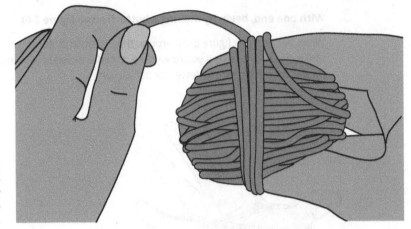

FIGURE 2-7:
Wrapping the yarn loosely around thumb and fingers.

Illustration by Wiley, Composition Services Graphics

REMEMBER

If at all possible, you want to start knitting or crocheting with the yarn end that comes from the *inside* of the skein or ball. This way, the skein or ball remains in place as you go and doesn't roll around the floor, attracting the attention of a cat (or other pet) on attack. If you're lucky, the inside end will already be pulled to the outside, ready to go. If not, you have to reach in and pull out a small hunk of yarn in order to find this end and then rewrap the extra — not ideal, but better than trying to retrieve the ball after it has rolled under the couch (for the third time).

Choosing Yarn for a Project

Yarns, garment shapes, and stitch patterns must work together for your project to be successful. With so many yarns available, how do you choose? The following questions are a good starting point:

>> **Does the yarn suit the way you'll use the piece?** If you're making a baby blanket, choose a yarn that can stand up to repeated washings. If you're making a table runner or bedspread that'll someday be an heirloom piece, invest in good-quality cotton that can withstand the test of time without falling apart. For a warm sweater, you can't beat wool for durability and warmth.

>> **Does the yarn have qualities you need to watch out for?** For example, you might want to know if the yarn will pill or stretch and whether it's colorfast.

>> **Does the yarn work well with the pattern you've chosen?** The more complicated the pattern, the plainer you probably want your yarn to be. (More on that in the next section.) When you're beginning to learn knitting or crocheting, you probably want the yarn to match the pattern's recommended yarn weight and needle or hook size. (As you gain experience, experimenting becomes easier. See "Substituting yarns" later in this chapter for pointers.)

REMEMBER

If you shop in a specialty yarn store, the people who work there likely have experience with their yarns and with knitting or crocheting in general. Feel free to ask questions about the yarn you're considering for your project. The store might also display its yarns as knitted or crocheted projects, so you can see what the yarn looks like as fabric. (The result often looks different than the yarn ball, especially if you use novelty yarn.) Many stores also offer drop-in help sessions, if you're struggling with a particular stitch or pattern and need expert help.

Working with color and texture

A wide array of wonderfully colored yarns is available today, from bright, jewel-toned solids to hand-painted, variegated yarns. If your pattern is simple, try a multicolored yarn. Using colorful yarns allows you to create a beautiful work of art without having to work a more complex stitch pattern.

If you've chosen a design with fancier stitches, stick to a more basic yarn. A smooth, solid-color yarn adds definition to your stitches and allows them to stand out. You want your cables, Fair Isle design, or other fancy stitch work to be seen! Today's vibrant, solid yarn colors are available in both matte and shiny finishes. Both finishes work equally well, so choose the one you like best.

Working with novelty yarns (think eyelash yarn or fun fur) can be tricky because seeing the stitches as you're crocheting is sometimes difficult. Don't let this downside put you off; instead, plan to take more time and effort to work up your creation. When first working with novelty yarns, try using them as an accent to your piece in borders, edgings, and collars until you get used to them. This way, if you make a mistake, at least you won't have to take your whole design apart. Besides, these novelty yarns can be overwhelming when used in excess.

REMEMBER

The more intricate your stitch design is, the simpler your yarn should be. The more interesting the yarn is, the simpler the pattern should be.

Choosing natural or man-made fibers

When picking out your yarn, think about what your design will be used for. Soft wools and shimmery silks work beautifully for winter sweaters and dressy tops. High-quality cotton produces a wonderful summer cardigan or an heirloom doily, bedspread, or tablecloth. Natural fibers cost a little more and require more TLC than man-made fibers, but they hold up well over a long period of time.

If you're making baby items or large designs, such as afghans, opt for a good-quality synthetic yarn, such as acrylic. Made to mimic the natural fibers, synthetic yarns come in a wide range of sizes and colors and can be smooth and soft to the touch. They're also easy to care for. In most cases, they can be thrown in the washer and dryer and still stand up well to the wear and tear of everyday use. Synthetic yarns are usually cheaper than their natural counterparts, which is a good thing when you're creating a design that uses a lot of yarn.

Substituting yarns

If you have your heart set on making the design exactly as you see it in the pattern picture, use the yarn listed in the pattern materials list. But if that gorgeous afghan is made in shades of pink and your decor is blue, don't be afraid to change the color scheme. Or if your budget doesn't accommodate the high-priced wool called for in that sweater design, look for a comparable synthetic or a less-expensive wool blend.

WARNING

If you're substituting for more than just color, however, make sure that the yarn you choose is the same size or weight and can accommodate the same gauge. (See Book 1, Chapter 3 for details on gauge.) For example, if the pattern calls for a worsted-weight yarn, make sure you get another worsted-weight yarn. If you choose a bulky yarn instead, you'll end up with a design that's considerably larger than planned. If you're making something wearable, substitutions can cause disastrous results.

Another important consideration when substituting yarns is total yardage. If the pattern calls for five skeins of a sport-weight yarn that has 400 yards to each skein for a total of 2,000 yards, make sure you purchase enough of whatever sport-weight yarn you choose so that you have a total of 2,000 yards.

Last but not least, consider how the fiber will affect the final piece. Yarns of different fibers, even if they have the same gauge, have different characteristics. For example, silky yarn is smoother and drapes differently than wool. Be sure you know the characteristics of the yarn and are comfortable with the way these differences will affect the finished piece. (The earlier section "Fixating on fiber" covers different kinds of yarn fibers and their characteristics.)

TIP

The manufacturer's gauge on the yarn label can help when you want to substitute one yarn for another. Just compare the gauge listed on the yarn label with the pattern gauge to determine the correct-size yarn to swap. Find out how to decipher a yarn label earlier in this chapter.

Creating your own yarn combinations

For even more variety, you can crochet with two or three different strands of yarn held together as one to create a unique blend of colors or textures. You can use two or more strands of the same weight of yarn to produce an extremely thick fabric (this is what those really big hooks are made for).

REMEMBER

If you want to use several strands in a pattern that calls for only one, make sure the yarns you put together equal the same weight yarn that the pattern calls for. For example, if a design calls for a worsted-weight yarn, you can use two or three strands of a fingering-weight yarn because that would approximately equal a worsted weight. If you're unable to come up with the correct weight, be sure to make a gauge swatch and adjust your hook size to achieve the proper gauge.

Note: Working with more than one strand of yarn at a time can be tricky. Watch out for all those extra loops of yarn that you'll encounter.

Chapter **3**

Right-Sizing with Gauge

E very knitted or crocheted fabric is made up of stitches and rows. *Gauge* is the number of stitches and rows it takes to make 1 square inch of fabric. When the size of your finished piece is important, gauge is what helps you ensure the final piece is the right size.

In this chapter, you discover more about why gauge is important. You also learn how a gauge swatch can help you achieve the correct gauge and how to measure gauge as you go.

Why (and When) Gauge Matters

Understanding how to measure and work with gauge is what allows you to go from a knitted or crocheted swatch to a finished project that has the correct measurements.

Figure 3-1 shows the stitches and rows that make up 1 square inch of a knitted stockinette *swatch* (a sample made specifically to test gauge). Stockinette and most other knitted fabrics have more vertical rows than stitches per inch.

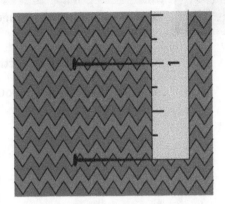

FIGURE 3-1:
One square inch
of stockinette
measured.

Illustration by Wiley, Composition Services Graphics

If you've spent some time around knitters or crocheters, you may already know that mention of the word *gauge* often elicits a groan. Gauge has a bad reputation for three reasons. First, it represents an unpleasant "should." Second, it's a tedious task that has to be accomplished before the fun part of the project can begin. Finally, it involves math. However, getting comfortable with gauge gives you a leg up in knitting and crocheting. Without knowing your gauge, you couldn't do the following:

>> Work away, comfortable in the knowledge that after you work the thousands of stitches required to complete your project, it will fit.

>> Ensure your final project is neat and attractive.

>> Substitute another yarn for the one given in the pattern.

>> Use the needle or hook size that makes the best fabric for your chosen yarn, even if it means you don't match the pattern's gauge.

>> Ensure that the amount of yarn the pattern specifies is sufficient to complete the project.

>> Design your own projects and sweaters.

The first step in any project is to determine the gauge of the fabric you're making. Gauge (sometimes called *tension*) is listed at the beginning of a pattern before the instructions begin. It's given as a number of stitches and rows over 4 inches or 10 centimeters, and it tells you which needle or hook size and which stitch pattern were used to determine the gauge. Check your pattern to see how many stitches and rows should make up 4 inches of knitted fabric. You need to measure *your* gauge against that given in the directions.

TIP

The yarn manufacturer may also recommend a particular gauge on the yarn label. This gauge may be quite different from the one in your pattern, but that's okay. Sometimes, the pattern designer wants to create a looser or tighter stitch pattern than the standard that the yarn manufacturer set. Follow the pattern gauge to get the same results as the pictured project.

REMEMBER

Gauge isn't always important, such as when you're making a scarf, an afghan, a bag, or anything else for which a precise size isn't essential. But when size *does* matter, the right or wrong gauge can make or break the finished piece.

Knowing What Affects Gauge

Gauge varies depending on the yarn, the needle or hook size, and the stitch pattern you use:

» **Yarn:** Yarns of different weights produce different gauges. A bulkier yarn produces a larger stitch, and a finer yarn produces a smaller stitch. Book 1, Chapter 2 explains how yarn weight can affect the final fabric.

» **Needle or hook size:** The same yarn knitted on different-sized needles or crocheted on a different size hook will have different gauges. Because you make a stitch by wrapping yarn around a needle or hook, the size (circumference) of the needle or hook determines the size of the stitch.

Figure 3-2 shows how needle size can affect the way the finished fabric looks. The smaller the needle is, the tighter the stitches and the denser the knitted fabric. The larger the needle is, the looser the stitches and the drapier (and stretchier) the fabric.

» **Stitch patterns and stitch size:** The same yarn knitted on the same needles or crocheted on the same hook but in different stitch patterns will have different gauges. For example, some stitches pull in, requiring more stitches to make a square inch. Other stitches spread the fabric out, so they require fewer stitches to make an inch. Figure 3-3 compares the gauges of two different stitch patterns that use the same number of stitches.

REMEMBER

Gauge also can vary with the time of day you're working, how long you've been working, and what you're thinking about. The tension you put on the yarn traveling around the needle or hook contributes to stitch size, so being tired or tense can affect the flow of your yarn and stitch size.

FIGURE 3-2: Smaller needles result in tighter stitches; bigger needles, in looser stitches.

Photograph by Wiley, Composition Services Graphics

FIGURE 3-3: Gauge on different stitch patterns.

Photograph by Wiley, Composition Services Graphics

Making a Gauge Swatch

To find out whether your gauge matches the pattern, you begin by making a gauge swatch. A gauge swatch is a small sample that you work using the same pattern, yarn, and needles or hook you intend to use for your project.

TIP

Although the gauge swatch's primary purpose is to help you create a piece that's the correct size, creating a swatch also lets you practice any new stitches found in the pattern and become familiar with the yarn you're using.

WARNING

It's important that you use the *same* yarn for your gauge swatch as for your project, not the same brand in a different color. Different dyes can affect how a specific yarn knits up, and believe it or not, a yarn in one color can give you a different gauge from the same yarn in a different color.

After you create your gauge swatch, you might need to block it. *Blocking* is a process that evens out the stitches and gets the final piece into the right shape. It usually involves getting the piece wet, whether you submerge it in a tub of water or just steam it, and then shaping the piece by hand into the correct measurements and allowing it to dry. After blocking your gauge swatch, you can measure your true gauge, therefore accurately predicting whether your finished design will be true to form. You can find details about blocking in Book 7, Chapter 1.

REMEMBER

Blocking your gauge swatch is especially important if you're working with natural fibers, such as wool and cotton.

Although the basic gauge concepts for knitting and crochet are the same, the steps for knitting or crocheting a swatch are different. The following sections explain the process for each type of stitching.

Knitting a gauge swatch

To make your swatch, follow these steps:

1. **Cast on the appropriate number of stitches.**

In general, cast on the number of stitches given in the pattern for 4 inches, plus 6 more stitches. For example, if the gauge is given as 18 stitches and 22 rows over 4 inches, cast on 24 stitches.

If the stitch pattern needs to be worked in a specific multiple, cast on any multiple that will yield a swatch larger than 4 inches in order to get an accurate gauge measurement. For example, if the pattern is worked on a multiple of 6 stitches plus 1 more, and the gauge given is 4 stitches to an inch, cast on *at least* 25 stitches (a multiple of 6 + 1). At 4 stitches to the inch, your swatch will be more than 4 inches wide, giving you a good area for measuring.

TIP

Many patterns give dimensions in centimeters rather than inches or include metric measurements alongside US ones. You can calculate inches from centimeters by dividing the centimeter number by 2.5. For example, 10 centimeters divided by 2.5 equals 4 inches. Or just use a ruler with centimeters.

2. **Work in the stitch pattern specified for the number of rows required to make 4 inches, plus 6 more rows.**

   For the same gauge specifications as in Step 1 (18 stitches and 22 rows over 4 inches), you work in the given pattern for 28 rows.

   These extra stitches and rows will give you a border around the area you're measuring. Edge stitches are frequently distorted and shouldn't be included in what you measure for gauge unless your swatch is a good 6 inches square.

3. **Bind off loosely and cut the strand of yarn, leaving an 8-inch tail, and draw it through the loops of the last row.**

4. **Block the swatch in the same manner you plan to use for your finished project.**

   Your stitches may shrink a bit when they're steamed. *Now* you're ready to measure it. For blocking instructions, head to Book 7, Chapter 1.

Crocheting a gauge swatch

In crochet, different types of patterns call for different types of gauges. A simple pattern that uses just one stitch, like a single crochet stitch, states the gauge as a certain number of stitches and rows per a given number of inches. However, some patterns have a set of several different stitches that repeats across the row. In this case, the pattern states the gauge as one entire stitch repeat per a given number of inches.

Work the stitches for your gauge swatch according to the instructions in the pattern. However, you probably want to make it bigger than what the instructions specify to get an accurate measurement.

TIP

Crocheters tend to crochet tighter at the beginning and end of rows than in the body of their work. So multiply the inches indicated in the stitch gauge by the inches indicated in the row gauge to figure out how big to make your swatch. For example, if the gauge calls for 7 stitches = 2 inches and 8 rows = 2 inches, make your swatch at least 4 inches square. That way you can measure in the center of the swatch and get an accurate measurement of your normal pace. If you're working a gauge that has a repeated set of stitches, you may need to make it bigger than 4 inches square.

Note: The crochet swatches pictured in this chapter are made up of two colors so you can better identify the center stitches, but you can just use a single color when working your own gauge swatches.

To get an accurate measurement of your stitches, you have to treat your swatch just as you plan to treat your finished project. Check whether your pattern requires you to block your final design. (Book 7, Chapter 1 explains how to block your work.)

Measuring Your Gauge

To measure your swatch, smooth it out on a flat surface; a blocking or ironing board is good for this task. Pin the edges down if they're curling in — be careful not to stretch your swatch — and follow these steps:

1. **Lay a ruler along a row of stitches and mark the beginning and end of 4 inches with pins.**

   If your second pin lands at half a stitch, don't be tempted to stretch or slightly squish your knitting to make the 4 inches end on a whole stitch.

2. **Note the number of stitches in 4 inches, fractions and all.**

3. **Lay your ruler along a vertical line of stitches, aligning the bottom of the ruler with the bottom of a stitch (the bottom of a V), and put a pin in to show where the first stitch begins. Place another pin 4 inches up.**

4. **Count the stitches between the pins and note the number of rows.**

These steps give you a gauge over a 4-inch (10-centimeter) square. Check whether your 4-inch gauge matches the one in the pattern. If it does, thank your lucky stars. If it doesn't, see "Matching Your Pattern's Gauge" later in this chapter for help.

The swatches shown in Figure 3-4 show you how to correctly measure gauge in a fabric made up of single crochet stitches. (Book 3, Chapter 1 has instructions on single crochet.) Figure 3-4a shows that you have 7 stitches in 2 inches. Figure 3-4b shows that 8 rows of single crochet = 2 inches.

TIP

If you don't work on a project for several days or weeks or months, be sure to recheck your gauge before continuing with the project. Time away can affect your gauge, which varies depending on your stress level and other outside factors. You may need to adjust your needle or hook size to maintain the original gauge.

WARNING

The cumulative effect of knitting or crocheting at a gauge as small as half a stitch less than the pattern calls for can be disastrous. For example, if your project piece is supposed to measure 20 inches and calls for a gauge of 5 stitches per inch, your finished piece will measure 22 inches if you're making 4 stitches per inch. And if you're off by 2 inches on both the front and back of a sweater, the total difference between the pattern and your sweater will be 4 inches overall. That's why gauge gets so much attention and why taking the time to measure it is so important.

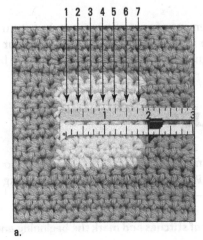

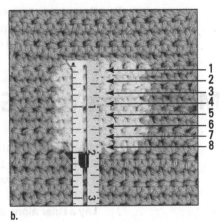

FIGURE 3-4: Measuring gauge for a single-stitch pattern.

a.

b.

© John Wiley & Sons, Inc.

The following sections explain how to measure gauge with specific types of crochet, including repeating patterns and rounds.

Measuring a swatch made with a repeating pattern

Figure 3-5 shows you how to measure crocheted fabric that uses different stitches, worked in rows.

REMEMBER

>> When measuring a stitch gauge in a swatch that has a repeating pattern of combination stitches, be sure to include the total repeat in your measurement. Figure 3-5a points out each shell for the repeating shell pattern; the width of 2 shells is 3¼ inches.

>> When measuring a row gauge, always measure the rows from the base of one row to the base of another row above it. If you measure to the top of a row, your gauge will be off because the base of the row lies in the valley of the previous row. Figure 3-5b points out each shell for the repeating pattern and shows that 4 rows in the shell pattern is equal to 2¼ inches high.

When working with a pattern such as the one in Figure 3-5, the gauge usually includes one or more repeats of the pattern, so you need to make a swatch that's at least 2 inches wider and taller than the number of inches indicated in the stitch gauge. For example, if the stitch gauge = 3¼ inches, you need to work a swatch at least 5¼ inches wide to get an accurate gauge. The row gauge for a pattern that has a 2-row repeat, such as this one, should be a multiple of 2 rows (2, 4, or 6 rows) to reflect how the pattern will work up in length. For example, the gauge for this pattern is 4 rows = 2¼ inches. For an accurate row gauge, work a swatch at least 6 rows deep, or approximately 3½ inches.

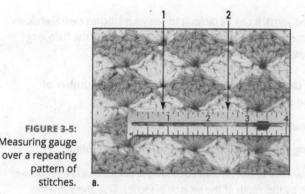 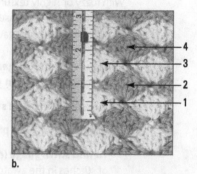

FIGURE 3-5: Measuring gauge over a repeating pattern of stitches.

a.   b.

© John Wiley & Sons, Inc.

Measuring stitches and rounds

If you're working a *round* (stitches crocheted in a circle rather than rows; see Book 3, Chapter 4 for details), such as with a doily, you figure out the gauge by measuring the diameter of the swatch after you've made a certain number of rounds. The pattern usually states how many rounds to make for the swatch; look for verbiage along the lines of "First X rounds = X inches." Figure 3-6a shows 3 rounds of double crochet stitches that equal 3½ inches in diameter. Figure 3-6b shows the first 2 rounds of a hexagon motif that equal 3 inches in diameter across the widest point.

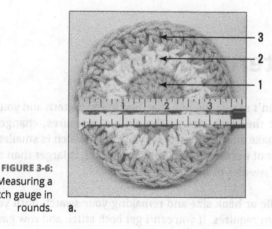 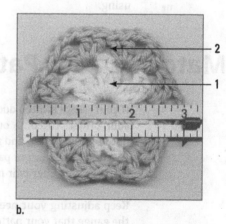

FIGURE 3-6: Measuring a stitch gauge in rounds.

a.   b.

© John Wiley & Sons, Inc.

MEASURING GAUGE ON HIGHLY TEXTURED YARNS

With fuzzy or highly textured yarns, it can be difficult to see your stitches clearly enough to take an accurate measurement by counting stitches. In this case, use the following steps to measure your gauge:

1. **Make a swatch larger than 4 inches and write down the total number of stitches and rows in your swatch.**

2. **Measure the entire swatch side to side and top to bottom.**

3. **Use a calculator to plug your numbers into the formulas that follow:**

   To find *stitch gauge* (number of horizontal stitches per inch): Divide the number of stitches in the swatch by the width of the swatch in inches. This gives you the number of stitches per inch.

   To find *row gauge* (number of vertical stitches per inch): Divide the number of rows by the overall length of the swatch in inches. This gives you the number of rows per inch.

To find your gauge over 4 inches, multiply stitches per inch or rows per inch by 4. For information on measuring gauge over cable patterns, turn to Book 4, Chapter 2.

TIP

If you're crocheting with cotton thread in rounds (or rows, for that matter), you can usually use a smaller gauge swatch than when you crochet with yarn, but you take the measurements the same way no matter what material or hook size you're using.

Matching Your Pattern's Gauge

If your gauge swatch doesn't match the one specified in the pattern and you want your project to come out the same size as the pattern measures, change your needle or hook size and make another swatch. If your first swatch is smaller than specified, use a larger pair of needles or hook. If your swatch is larger than specified, use a smaller pair of needles or hook.

Keep adjusting your needle or hook size and remaking your swatch until you get the gauge that your pattern requires. If you can't get both stitch and row gauge to match the pattern's gauge, work with the needle or hook that gives you the right *stitch* gauge.

REMEMBER

Everyone knits or crochets a little differently. After you get to know your own style (whether you tend to stitch tightly or loosely), you may be able to choose the proper needle or hook size even before making the first swatch for a pattern. Changing the size is the best way to compensate for your individual style of crochet. If you consciously try to tighten or loosen up your stitches to achieve the proper gauge, you invariably return to your natural style as you go along and then wind up with the wrong gauge.

Designing with Gauge in Mind

As you begin to knit or crochet projects, you may find yourself imagining sweaters and hats you'd like to make but can't find a pattern for. Making your own pattern for a project isn't all that difficult. No matter how fancy the pattern stitch or shaping, how large or small the project, it all comes down to stitches and inches. Figure out your gauge on the yarn and needles you want to use, and then determine the dimensions of the finished project.

To determine the number of stitches to cast on for a project you're imagining, work the formula for determining gauge in reverse: Decide how wide you want your piece to be, and then multiply that number by your gauge. For example, if you're imagining a scarf in one of the patterns found elsewhere in this book, make a gauge swatch. If your gauge is 5 stitches to the inch and you want your scarf to be 7 inches wide, cast on 35 stitches and start knitting, or crochet 35 stitches for each row.

Chapter 4

Reading Patterns

S ometimes you may work thousands of stitches for one knitting or crochet project. If these instructions were all written out, stitch by stitch by stitch without any abbreviations or shortcuts, one pattern would fill an entire book. Fortunately, both knitting and crochet instructions have their own special abbreviations and a form of shorthand that simplify the written directions, saving space and a lot of tedious reading time.

After you get a handle on the abbreviations and symbols of knitting and crochet design, reading a pattern is a cinch. In this chapter, you learn how to decipher the unique language of these instructions.

Note: If you're reading this book in order, note that the stitches are explained in order of complexity. If you want to know right away what a stockinette or double crochet stitch is, head to the table of contents or the index to find the related chapter.

Understanding Knitting Patterns

Directions for stitch patterns can be in written form or chart form. Written instructions tell you what to do with the stitches in each row as you come to them, whereas a chart shows a picture of each stitch and how it's worked. Some people prefer written instructions, and others like to follow a graphed picture of the pattern. Nowadays, the trickier the pattern, the more likely it is to be charted out. Not true for vintage patterns, however. Being familiar with both ways of describing a pattern enables you to convert a chart into written instructions if you find it easier to work with words and, conversely, to convert a convoluted set of written instructions into graph form by drawing a chart.

REMEMBER

Stitch patterns are based on *repeats* — both stitch repeats and row repeats. A given stitch sequence repeats horizontally across a row. A series of rows of given stitch sequences repeats vertically. Together, they make up a stitch pattern that determines what your knitted fabric will look like: smooth, bumpy, cabled, or striped.

Deciphering Knitterese: Common abbreviations and shorthand

To save space, patterns are written with many abbreviations and a lot of shorthand. As you work with patterns, you'll become familiar with the most common abbreviations — for example, RS (right side), WS (wrong side), beg (beginning), and rep (repeat). Pattern instructions explain any unusual abbreviations or ones that may vary from pattern to pattern. Table 4-1 presents some of the most common pattern abbreviations.

TABLE 4-1 **Common Knitting Abbreviations**

Abbreviation	What It Means	Abbreviation	What It Means
beg	beginning	pwise	purlwise (as if to purl)
CC	contrasting color	rem	remain(s) or remaining
ch	chain	rep	repeat
cn	cable needle	RH	right-hand
dec	decrease(s), decreased, or decreasing	RS	right side(s)
dpns	double-pointed needles	rnd(s)	round(s)
foll	follows or following	sc	single crochet
inc	increase(s), increased, or increasing	sl	slip, slipped, or slipping
k	knit	sl st	slip stitch
k2tog	knit 2 stitches together	ssk	slip, slip, knit the slipped stitches together
k-b	knit in stitch below	St st	stockinette stitch

Abbreviation	What It Means	Abbreviation	What It Means
kwise	knitwise (as if to knit)	st(s)	stitch(es)
LH	left-hand	tbl	through the back of the loop
lp(s)	loop(s)	tog	together
MC	main color	WS	wrong side(s)
m1 (or m)	make 1 stitch (increase 1 stitch)	wyib	with yarn in back
p	purl	wyif	with yarn in front
pat(s)	pattern(s)	yb	yarn back
p-b	purl in stitch below	yf	yarn forward
pm	place marker	yo	yarn over
psso	pass slipped stitch over (used for decreasing)		

In addition, knitting patterns use certain phrases that can be confusing until you have some experience with them. Here are some common phrases that you'll come across in knitting patterns and garments:

>> **As established:** When your instructions set up a series of steps or patterns to work instead of repeating them row by row, they tell you to continue working *as established*.

Example: If you're knitting a cardigan with the center front band knitted in, the stitches for the center front band may be worked in a pattern different from the rest of the sweater body. After the pattern tells you how many border stitches to work in the border pattern and how many stitches to work in the sweater body pattern, it tells you to continue to work the patterns in the front piece *as established*.

>> **At same time:** This phrase indicates that two things need to happen at the same time. Be on the lookout for this phrase; it's easy to get going on one task and forget to pay attention to the other.

Example: "dec 1 st every other row 4 times, *at same time,* when piece measures same length as back to shoulder, work shoulder shaping as for back." Translation: The neckline shaping (dec 1 st) continues as the shoulder shaping begins.

>> **Back of your work:** The back of your work is the side of your work that faces away from you as you hold your needles. Don't confuse this with the right side (RS) and wrong side (WS) of your work, which refer to how the piece is worn or which side should be presented as the front.

>> **Bind off from each neck edge:** When you shape the neckline on a pullover, you work both edges of the neckline at the same time, but you shape the right side (as you wear it) on right-side rows and shape the left side on wrong-side rows. Although this instruction may sound tricky, it's quite obvious and simple when you're doing it. You may see this phrase in a form like this: "Bind off from each neck edge 3 sts once, 2 sts twice. . . ."

>> **End with a WS row:** Finish the section you're working on by working a wrong-side row last. The next row you work should be a right-side row.

>> **Front of your work:** The front of your work is the side of your work that faces you as you hold your needles. It can be the wrong side or the right side.

>> **Inc (or dec) every 4 (6, 8, or whatever) rows:** This is how the increases (or decreases) along a sleeve seam are written. Increase or decrease on a (usually) right-side row, and then work 3 (5, 7, or whatever) rows without shaping.

>> **Inc (or dec) every other row:** Increase or decrease on the (usually) right-side row, and then work the following row without increasing or decreasing.

>> **Pat rep (pattern repeat):** When instructions tell you to repeat a certain stitch pattern, it's written this way. Pattern repeat refers to what's given between an asterisk and a semicolon (* . . . ;) in written patterns and between heavy black lines in a chart.

>> **Pick up and knit:** Use a separate strand of yarn to create a row of stitches on a needle by pulling loops through along a knitted edge, usually the front of a cardigan or a neckline. See more on picking up stitches in Book 6, Chapter 2.

>> **Pm (place marker):** A *marker* is a plastic ring or tied loop of yarn that sits between stitches on your needle to indicate the beginning of a round in circular knitting or to mark pattern repeats. When you see the instruction to place a marker, as in "join, pm, and begin round," you simply place a marker at that location. (As you knit, you slip the marker from one needle to the other. But usually your pattern doesn't tell you to do that — your common sense does.)

>> **Preparation row:** Some stitch patterns require a set-up row that's worked only at the beginning of the pattern and isn't part of the repeat.

>> **Reverse shaping:** When you knit a cardigan, you work two pieces that mirror each other. Most patterns have you work the side that carries the buttons before you work the side that carries the buttonholes. Instead of writing a separate set of instructions for each side, the pattern asks you to work the shaping in the opposite direction on the second piece, as in "work to correspond to front, reversing all shaping." This means that you work bind-offs and neck shaping on the reverse side of the fabric as well. If you work the shaping on the wrong side in one piece, you work it on the right side when you reverse the shaping.

- » **Right:** When a pattern specifies a right front, it means the front that would be on your right side *as you would wear the finished piece.* When in doubt, hold your knitting up to you (wrong side to your body) to determine whether you're looking at the right or left front.

- » **When armhole measures . . . :** This phrase signals that your instructions are about to change. Measure the armhole not from the beginning of the piece but from the marker you've (we hope) put near the middle of the row on which the armhole began. The pattern should have told you to place this marker.

- » **Work as for . . . :** This phrase usually refers to working the front piece the same as the back. It saves writing the same instructions twice. You may see it in a form like this: "Work as for back until piece measures 21½ inches from beg."

- » **Work even:** Continue in whatever stitch pattern you're using without doing any shaping.

- » **Work to end:** Work in whatever stitch pattern you're using to the end of the row.

You may run into other phrases that aren't as clear as they could be, but experience will make you familiar with them. Eventually, you'll be surprised at how well you understand this language, and you'll wonder why it ever seemed confusing.

Following written stitch patterns

Written instructions give you row-by-row directions for a single repeat. They follow certain conventions and use lots of abbreviations (see the preceding section). The key to understanding written instructions is paying attention to commas, asterisks, and brackets or parentheses; they mean more than you may think. Here's a punctuation translation:

- » **Single steps are separated by commas.** The instruction "Sl 1 wyif, k5" tells you to slip a stitch with the yarn on the front side of the work and *then* to knit 5 stitches as normal (meaning you have to move the yarn to the back before knitting, even though the instructions don't tell you to).

- » **An asterisk (*) indicates that whatever follows gets repeated (rep).** For example, the instruction "K1, * sl 1, k3; rep from * to last st, k1" means that you knit 1 stitch, and then you work the stitches between the asterisks (slip 1 stitch and knit 3 stitches) over and over until you reach the last stitch of the row, which you knit.

>> **Brackets (or parentheses) function much like asterisks, except you repeat the series of stitches a specified number of times.** For example, the instruction "* K5, (p1, k1) twice, p1; repeat from * to end of row" means that, after you knit 5, you purl 1/knit 1 *two times*, followed by another purl 1, and then you repeat this entire sequence across the entire row.

The following example shows a stitch pattern in written form:

Row 1 (RS): * K2, p2; rep from * to end of row.

Row 2 (WS): * P2, k2; rep from * to end of row.

Translation: On the first row (the right side is facing you on the first row in this pattern), you knit 2 stitches, purl 2 stitches, knit 2 stitches, purl 2 stitches, and so on to the end of the row. (Your row would have to be a multiple of 4 stitches for these instructions to come out evenly.) On the next row (wrong side facing now), you begin by purling 2 stitches, then knitting 2 stitches, purling 2 stitches, knitting 2 stitches, and so on to the end of the row.

As you read patterns, pay attention to row designations. To save space, many written instructions combine rows that repeat the same stitches. For example, this ribbon eyelet pattern combines a couple of rows:

Cast on multiple of 2 sts, plus 2 sts.

Row 1: Knit.

Row 2: Purl.

Rows 3 and 4: Knit.

Row 5: P1, * yo, p2tog; repeat from * to last st, p1.

Row 6: K2, * k1 tbl, k1; repeat from * to end of row.

Row 7: Knit.

Row 8: Purl.

Rep Rows 1–8.

As you can imagine, the more intricate the pattern, the more complicated the instructions. The following can help you follow the instructions without problems:

>> Read your instructions carefully.

>> Work each step between commas as a complete step.

>> Look at your work and think about what you're doing.

Reading charted stitch patterns

Charts use a square to represent each stitch and a symbol inside the square to indicate how to work the stitch. Although there's no universal set of symbols, each pattern that uses a chart also provides a key to reading it. Always begin by finding the key to the chart.

The trick to reading chart patterns without getting confused is to remember that you don't read them from top to bottom and left to right as you would a book. Instead, you read a chart from the bottom up because it shows the knitted piece as it's knitted, and in nearly all knitting, you knit from the bottom up. Whether you read from right to left or left to right depends on the row you're working:

>> **Right-side rows:** You read from right to left.

>> **Wrong-side rows:** You read from left to right.

REMEMBER

Charts represent the pattern of the knitted fabric as you're looking at it — the *right* side of the fabric. This means that on wrong-side rows (from left to right) you must purl any stitch that has a knit symbol and knit any stitch that has a purl symbol. This switch isn't difficult once you get the hang of it, and the pattern key will remind you. Of course, if you're knitting in the round, you can follow the chart without worrying about whether you have the wrong side or right side of the fabric facing. See Book 2, Chapter 4 for more about knitting in the round.

Figure 4-1 shows a very simple chart. In fact, it's the same pattern as the K2, p2 pattern from the preceding section.

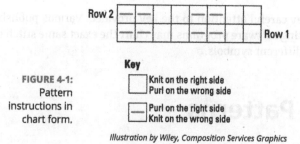

FIGURE 4-1:
Pattern instructions in chart form.

Key

Knit on the right side
Purl on the wrong side

Purl on the right side
Knit on the wrong side

Illustration by Wiley, Composition Services Graphics

Because of the way charts can condense complicated stitches and techniques into simple symbols, charts often are used for lacework, cables, and other patterns that incorporate special effects, such as bobbles and scallops, to save space. And they're indispensable for intarsia, Fair Isle, and other multicolor techniques. Figure 4-2 shows what a chart for a repeating color pattern may look like for a sweater pattern.

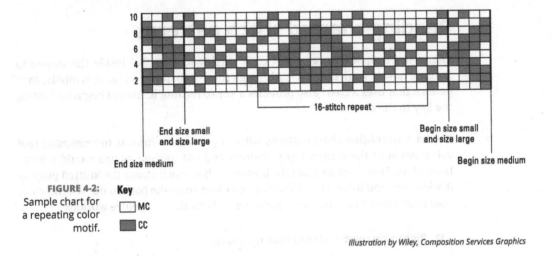

16-stitch repeat

End size small
and size large

End size medium

Begin size small
and size large

Begin size medium

FIGURE 4-2:
Sample chart for
a repeating color
motif.

Key

☐ MC

☑ CC

If the design uses a repeating pattern, as the one in Figure 4-2 does, the chart generally shows a single or double repeat and not the whole garment piece. Unless the number of stitches in the piece you're making is an exact multiple of the repeat, you'll have to begin and end on a part of the repeat. The chart tells you where to begin knitting the repeat.

TIP

If you don't have a magnetic board with strips (see Book 1, Chapter 1 for an explanation of this handy tool), buy the longest self-stick notepads you can find and keep them with your knitting project. Use them to keep track of your place on the chart by sticking them along the row *above* the row you're currently working on. Seeing only the rows on the chart that you've already worked helps you orient yourself.

REMEMBER

When reading charts, pay careful attention to the key provided. Various publishers, designers, and charting software programs may chart the exact same stitch or series of stitches using different symbols.

Following Crochet Patterns

Like knitting patterns, crochet patterns can be written in abbreviations or presented visually as a stitch diagram. In crochet, some patterns also use the International Crochet Symbols (see Figure 4-3 later in this chapter) to create pictorial diagrams of a crocheted design. You may find these diagrams easier to follow than the text when dealing with intricate patterns.

Knowing the sections of a crochet pattern

REMEMBER

Most crochet patterns found in magazines or books have several different sections that you must be familiar with if you want to concentrate on crocheting your masterpiece rather than deciphering the instructions for it. The following list introduces the most common pattern sections (some patterns will have more; others will have fewer):

>> **Level of experience:** Most patterns give you a general idea of the complexity of the pattern and whether it's suitable for a beginner, advanced beginner, intermediate crocheter, or advanced crocheter. Don't automatically shy away from a supposedly advanced pattern, though. Take a look at it before deciding that it's too complex for your ability.

>> **Materials:** The materials section lists everything you need to complete the project, specifically

- *Yarn:* The yarn section of the materials list tells you all you need to know to get the right yarn for the project: the brand name, the specific yarn name, the fiber composition of the yarn, the size of the yarn (such as sport weight or worsted weight), the weight and yardage of each skein, and how many skeins (or hanks or balls) you need as well as the color(s) used in the sample. (See Book 1, Chapter 2 for the full scoop on yarn and how to read those pesky labels.)

- *Hook:* The next item in the list is the size crochet hook (or hooks) you need.

- *Additional materials:* The materials list also includes any additional materials you need, such as a yarn needle, sewing thread, stitch markers, buttons, or beads.

>> **Size information:** This part tells you the finished dimensions of the project. If you're making a garment, this part gives you the size ranges (check out Book 6, Chapter 4 for details on sweater sizing). It may also include a *schematic,* which is a diagram showing the dimensions of each piece used to make up the finished design.

>> **Gauge:** The pattern gives the gauge for a design, each and every time. Always work to the specified gauge so you wind up with the right size design. (Book 1, Chapter 3 has information on gauge.)

>> **Stitches:** Most patterns list the stitches used and give directions for any advanced stitches or techniques. Book 3 explains how to create basic crochet stitches, and Book 4 explores more advanced techniques.

Reading Patterns

>> **Crocheting directions:** The bulk of the pattern is the step-by-step instructions for crocheting the design. They may be written row by row (or round by round), or they may include a pictorial diagram as well. If you're supposed to crochet the project in several pieces, the pattern gives instructions for each piece. If keeping track of the right and wrong sides of a project is important for a certain pattern, the instructions designate which row is which. For example, if the first row of the work is the right side, the instructions for the first row appear like this: Row 1 (RS). All subsequent odd-numbered rows are then considered right side, and even-numbered rows are considered wrong side. (See the later sections "Figuring out written instructions" and "Not just a pretty picture: Stitch symbols and diagrams" for the nitty-gritty details of reading directions.)

>> **Assembly:** If a design is made in several pieces, this section shows you how to put it all together.

>> **Finishing:** Here's where you add the final details, which can be as simple as sewing on buttons or as complex as adding borders and collars. If an item needs to be blocked, you find the specifics on that task here. (Book 7, Chapter 1 has more on blocking.)

Figuring out written instructions

Written instructions are, by far, the most common way to present a crochet pattern. The various abbreviations and symbols — and combinations of the two — may seem like a foreign language to you in the beginning. That's okay. Consider the following sections your Crochet Dictionary. They explain each of the parts used in written instructions and how they all fit together.

Keeping it short with abbreviations

Most crochet stitches have shortened names or abbreviations. For example, instead of saying *double crochet stitch* throughout a pattern, the instructions abbreviate this stitch as *dc*. As this book introduces terms and stitches, you find their abbreviations to help you become familiar with the shorthand. Table 4-2 lists the most common abbreviations (they include stitches and other pertinent information).

REMEMBER Crochet abbreviations don't have periods after them to keep the instructions as clutter free as possible. If you do come across a period that isn't at the end of the sentence or action, it's probably attached to an abbreviation that's easily confused with another word. For instance, you may see *inches* abbreviated as *in.* to avoid confusion with the word *in*.

TABLE 4-2

Common Crochet Abbreviations

Abbreviation	Spelled-Out Term
approx	approximately
beg	begin(ning)
bet	between
blp	back loop only
BP	back post
CC	contrast color
ch	chain
dc	double crochet
dec (xx2tog)	decrease(s)(d)(ing)
dtr	double triple crochet
flp	front loop only
foll	follow(ing)
FP	front post
hdc	half double crochet
inc	increase(s)(d)(ing)
MC	main color
patt	pattern
rem	remaining
rep	repeat
rib	ribbing
rnd(s)	round(s)
RS	right side
sc	single crochet
sl st	slip stitch
st(s)	stitch(es)
tog	together
tr	triple crochet
WS	wrong side
yo	yarn over the hook

Reading Patterns

DISTINGUISHING BETWEEN AMERICAN AND BRITISH CROCHET TERMINOLOGY

Just as hook sizes differ depending on where you live (as explained in Book 1, Chapter 1), the crochet terminology used in the United States is different from that used in the United Kingdom and Australia. For example, what's called a single crochet in the United States is called a double crochet in the United Kingdom.

No one is entirely sure how this different crochet terminology came about, but one theory is that the U.K. terms refer to the number of loops you have on the hook after you draw a loop through the next stitch and that the U.S. terms refer to the number of times you move the hook to complete the stitch. For example, after you've drawn the yarn through the stitch in the previous row, you have two loops on your hook, or a *double* loop, hence the U.K.'s *double crochet.* To complete the stitch, you have to draw the yarn through both loops on the hook only once, which is a *single* movement, hence the U.S.'s *single crochet.*

Following is a breakdown of what certain stitches are called in the United States and what they go by in the United Kingdom:

U.S. Stitch Name	U.K. Stitch Name
Single crochet (sc)	Double crochet (dc)
Double crochet (dc)	Treble (tr)
Half double crochet (hdc)	Half treble (htr)
Triple crochet (trc)	Double treble (dtr)
Slip stitch (sl st)	Single crochet (sc)

The bottom line: Unless a pattern comes from the United Kingdom or Australia, or it specifically states that it's using U.K. terminology, go ahead and assume it's written using the U.S. crochet terms.

One other notation that you see quite frequently in pattern instructions is the hyphen. Instructions commonly use the hyphen when referring to a chain loop; the hyphen denotes the number of chains you work to create a particular loop. For example, a *ch-5 loop* is a loop made up of five chain stitches. Don't confuse this instruction, however, with *ch 5*, which instructs you to make a chain of five chain stitches in a row.

Some patterns combine several basic stitches into a more complex stitch. For example, five double crochet stitches worked in the same stitch are collectively known as a *shell* because the result resembles the shape of a clamshell. Besides having their own names, these special stitches may also have their own abbreviations. (Book 4, Chapter 3 defines many of these combination stitches and gives you their abbreviations.)

REMEMBER

Special stitches aren't standardized and may have different definitions in each pattern that you encounter. For example, one pattern may define a shell as five double crochet stitches, but another pattern may define it as only three double crochet stitches. Before you start a new project, check the beginning of the pattern's instructions for the definition of each special stitch.

Working terms and phrases

Crochet patterns often contain jargon that isn't abbreviated, such as the following terms that explain where and how to work stitches:

» **Loop:** A *loop* is three or more chain stitches worked in a row. To work in a loop, insert your hook into the hole underneath the loop, not in any one stitch, and then complete the stitch indicated.

» **Space:** Usually, a *space* refers to the space created by working one or more chain stitches in between other stitches. To work in the space, insert your hook into the hole underneath the chain stitches and complete the stitch indicated.

» **Work across:** Crochet the designated stitch or stitches across the whole length of the row.

» **Work around:** When working in rounds, crochet the same stitch or stitch pattern repeatedly until you come back to the starting point.

» **Work across (or around) to within last 2 sts:** Crochet the designated stitches until you have two stitches left to work in at the end of the row or round; the instructions tell you what to do in the last two stitches.

Pondering parentheses

Instead of detailing each and every stitch or action involved in a row or round, instruction writers use parentheses to designate a repeated set of actions and stitches or to sum up a row. Here's a list of the different reasons instruction writers use parentheses:

» **To isolate a set of two or more stitches that you work all in one stitch:** For example, you may find something like

• (2 dc, ch 2, 2 dc) in next sc

This notation means that in the next single crochet stitch, you want to crochet two double crochet stitches, chain two, and then work two more double crochet stitches.

Reading Patterns

>> **To enclose a set of stitches that you repeat a number of times in succession:** For example:

- (dc in next 3 sts, ch 2, skip next 2 sts) twice

In plain English, this notation means that you work a double crochet stitch in each of the next three stitches, chain two, skip the next two stitches, and then repeat that by working a double crochet stitch in each of the next three stitches, chaining two, and skipping the next two stitches again.

>> **To sum up a completed row or round:** If you see (16 dc) at the end of the instructions for a row, you should have 16 double crochet stitches in that row. Likewise, (8 loops) means you've completed eight loops, and (4 ch-3 loops made) means you've made four loops that are each three chain stitches long.

>> **To distinguish different sizes in a garment pattern:** If a garment pattern is written for three sizes, it includes separate instructions for the two larger sizes in parentheses. For example:

- dc in each of next 10 (12, 14) sts

So you work 10 double crochet stitches if you're going for the small size, 12 double crochet stitches for medium, and 14 double crochet stitches for large.

TIP

To make a pattern with multiple sizes listed easier to follow, you may want to highlight, underline, or circle the numbers that pertain to your desired size throughout the pattern.

Bracing yourself for brackets

Crochet instructions use brackets in the following ways:

>> **Some patterns use brackets interchangeably with parentheses to isolate repeated phrases of stitches.** They may also appear as a set or phrase within another set of brackets or parentheses. For example:

- (2 dc, ch 5, sl st in fifth ch from hook forming a ring, [4 sc, ch 3, 4 sc] in ring just made, 2 dc) in next ch-2 space

In other words, start by working two double crochet stitches in the chain-2 space. Next, chain five stitches and slip stitch in the fifth chain from the hook to form a ring. Then work four single crochet stitches, chain three, and work four single crochet stitches again in the ring you just formed. Finally, complete the operation by working two more double crochet stitches in the same chain-2 space you started out in. See Figure 4-3 for a pictorial illustration and the section "Not just a pretty picture: Stitch symbols and diagrams," later in this chapter.

>> **Patterns use brackets within parentheses to sum up the number of stitches for different sizes.** So to sum up the number of stitches in each size, a numeric phrase at the end of a row in a sweater pattern might say

- (72 [76, 80] sts)

This notation means that when you reach the end of the row, you've worked a total of 72 stitches for a small-size sweater, 76 for a medium, and 80 for a large.

FIGURE 4-3:
Stitch diagram to illustrate stitches repeated within a bracket.

© John Wiley & Sons, Inc.

Interpreting special symbols in written patterns

Patterns use symbols such as asterisks, plus signs, and crosses in instructions to show the repetition of a series of crochet stitches. Asterisks are the most common symbol, but the symbol you see in a particular pattern really depends on the preference of the publication. This book uses only asterisks.

The following sections describe the use of symbols in written patterns. You most often see just one symbol or two symbols used.

USING ONE SYMBOL

Some patterns use only one symbol at the beginning of a phrase and then direct you to repeat from that symbol a designated number of times. Here's an example:

    * Dc in each of the next 3 sts, ch 2, skip next 2 sts; rep from * 5 times.

In this example, you work all the information after the asterisk once and then repeat the same series of steps five more times for a total of six times in all.

You may also see asterisks marking both the beginning and end of a repeated phrase. The instructions may reference this repeat again if the phrase within the asterisks is used at a different section of the row or round. Check out this example:

    Ch 3, * dc in each of next 3 dc, ch 2, skip next 2 sts *; rep from * to * once, dc in each of next 6 sts, ch 2, skip next 2 sts; rep from * to * twice, dc in each of last 4 dc.

Just to make sure you're interpreting Crochetese properly, check out the following plain-English translation of the preceding example and see whether it jives with your understanding of the abbreviated instructions:

1. Chain 3.

2. Double crochet stitch in each of the next 3 double crochet stitches, chain 2, and skip the next 2 stitches.

3. Repeat Step 2.

4. Double crochet stitch in each of the next 6 stitches, chain 2, and skip the next 2 stitches.

5. Repeat Step 2 twice.

6. Double crochet stitch in each of the last 4 double crochet stitches.

USING TWO SETS OF SYMBOLS

In more complicated patterns, you may see two sets of symbols, such as single asterisks (*) and double asterisks (**), to designate two different repeats in the same row or round.

> * Dc in dc, ch 2, skip next 2 sts *; rep from * to * 3 times, ** dc in next dc, 2 dc in next space **; rep from ** to ** 3 times.

In plain English, this notation means you need to

1. Double crochet stitch in the double crochet stitch, chain 2, and then skip the next 2 stitches.

2. Repeat Step 1 three times.

3. Double crochet stitch in the next double crochet stitch and then work 2 double crochet stitches in the following space.

4. Repeat Step 3 three times.

On the other hand, you may find the single asterisk phrase within the double asterisk phrase, denoting a repeated phrase within the larger set of repeated instructions. See for yourself in this example:

> ** 5 dc in loop, ch 2, skip next 2 dc, * dc in next dc, ch 2, skip next 2 dc *; rep from * to * 5 times **; rep from ** to ** 3 times.

In this case, you work the ** to ** phrase a total of 4 times to go around the entire piece, but within that phrase is another * to * phrase that you work a total of 6 times within each ** to ** repeat.

Confused? Here's the rundown in plain English:

1. **Work 5 double crochet stitches in the loop, chain 2, and then skip the next 2 double crochet stitches.**

2. **Work 1 double crochet stitch into the next double crochet stitch, chain 2, and then skip the next 2 double crochet stitches.**

3. **Repeat Step 2 five times, which brings you to the next loop.**

4. **Repeat Steps 1 through 3 three times.**

Repeating rows and rounds

Sometimes a pattern includes several identical rows or rounds. To save space, the instructions may group these rows together and write the directions only once, as follows:

Rows 2–7: Ch 1, sc in each sc across, *turn.*

This notation means you chain one, single crochet stitch into each single crochet stitch across the row, and then turn to complete one row. However, you work this row of single crochet consecutively for Rows 2 through 7 (for a total of six rows).

If you're to repeat two (or more) different rows in the same order, you'll see the first two rows written and then the subsequent rows written as a repeat, as follows:

Row 2: Ch 1, sc in each st across, *turn.*

Row 3: Ch 3 (turning ch for dc), dc in each sc across, *turn.*

Rows 4–9: Rep Rows 2–3 (3 times).

So for Row 2, you chain one, single crochet in each stitch across the row, and then turn your work. For Row 3, you chain three, double crochet into each single crochet stitch across the row, and turn. Then you go back and work Row 2 again and then Row 3, repeating Row 2 and Row 3 consecutively until you've worked them a total of four times each.

Not just a pretty picture: Stitch symbols and diagrams

Some pattern books and crochet magazines give you a pictorial description of the pattern design — a picture that may or may not have written directions alongside it. These *stitch diagrams* are like a road map of the pattern, laying out each individual stitch in relation to the others so you get the forest and the trees at once.

REMEMBER

The advantages of stitch diagrams are numerous:

>> You can see the number and placement of the stitches at a glance.

>> You can observe what the design should look like so that if your creation doesn't resemble the diagram, you can easily identify your mistake.

>> You can highlight or outline the repeated pattern in each row or round to make it easy to follow.

>> You can mark where you leave off when you put your work down so you know where to begin the next time you crochet.

The beauty of stitch diagrams is that anyone can read them, regardless of what language he or she speaks. That's why the individual stitch symbols that make up the diagrams are called *International Crochet Symbols*. So if you come across a terrific pattern in a Japanese book, you can make it from the diagram. Although these symbols and diagrams may look inscrutable to you now, you'll be reading them as naturally as you read this sentence after reviewing the following sections.

Cracking the International Crochet Symbols code

Although they're called International Crochet Symbols, the symbols for crochet stitches aren't universally accepted yet, which means you may find slight variations in different publications. Nonetheless, Figure 4-4 shows a list of standard symbols that appear consistently throughout this book; these are the symbols for the most common crochet stitches. The symbols for more advanced stitches appear in their respective chapters.

REMEMBER

Each symbol roughly resembles the shape and proportions of the stitch that it represents. The number of tick marks drawn diagonally across the middle of the symbols indicates the number of times that you yarn over at the beginning of the stitch. For example, the double crochet has one tick mark (yarn over once), the triple crochet has two tick marks (yarn over twice), and so on.

Following a stitch diagram

The preceding section introduces you to the individual stitch symbols and what they look like. This section helps you understand all the symbols when they appear in a stitch diagram like you'd see in a pattern.

INTERNATIONAL CROCHET SYMBOLS

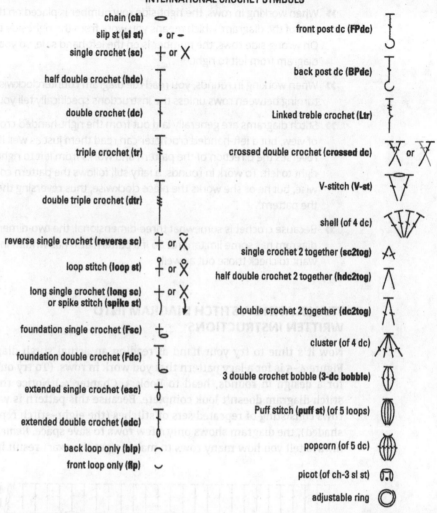

chain (**ch**)	⌒
slip st (**sl st**)	• or –
single crochet (**sc**)	+ or ✕
half double crochet (**hdc**)	T
double crochet (**dc**)	╪
triple crochet (**tr**)	╪
double triple crochet (**dtr**)	╪
reverse single crochet (**reverse sc**)	+ or X̃
loop stitch (**loop st**)	⊹ or ⸮
long single crochet (**long sc**) or spike stitch (**spike st**)	⊹ or ⸮
foundation single crochet (**Fsc**)	┼
foundation double crochet (**Fdc**)	╪
extended single crochet (**esc**)	⊦
extended double crochet (**edc**)	╪
back loop only (**blp**)	⌒
front loop only (**flp**)	⌣

front post dc (**FPdc**)	⌐
back post dc (**BPdc**)	⌐
Linked treble crochet (**Ltr**)	╪
crossed double crochet (**crossed dc**)	⋈ or ⋈
V-stitch (**V-st**)	⋎
shell (of 4 dc)	⋔
single crochet 2 together (**sc2tog**)	⋏
half double crochet 2 together (**hdc2tog**)	⋏
double crochet 2 together (**dc2tog**)	⋏
cluster (of 4 dc)	⋔
3 double crochet bobble (**3-dc bobble**)	⬭
Puff stitch (**puff st**) (of 5 loops)	⬭
popcorn (of 5 dc)	⬭
picot (of ch-3 sl st)	⌒
adjustable ring	◯

FIGURE 4-4:
The International
Crochet Symbols
for a variety
of stitches.

© John Wiley & Sons, Inc.

STITCH DIAGRAM FUNDAMENTALS

REMEMBER

Here's a quick rundown of the basics you should know before you read a stitch diagram:

>> Each row or round in a diagram is numbered so that you know where to begin — Row 1.

>> Because most crochet instructions are repetitive and most publications have limited space, a diagram may show a repeated set of stitches just a few times. But those few repeats are all you need to crochet the entire piece.

>> When working in rows, the right-side row number is placed on the right-hand side of the diagram, which means you work from the right side to the left side. On wrong-side rows, the number is on the left-hand side, so you follow the diagram from left to right.

>> When working in rounds, you read the diagram counterclockwise, without turning between rows unless the instructions specifically tell you to do so.

>> Stitch diagrams are generally laid out from the right-handed crocheter's point of view, but a left-handed crocheter can read them just as well if he or she reverses the direction of the pattern and works from left to right rather than right to left. To work in rounds, a lefty still follows the pattern counterclockwise, but he or she works the piece clockwise, thus reversing the direction of the pattern.

>> Because crochet is somewhat three-dimensional, the two-dimensional stitch diagram has some limitations. So if a pattern also has written instructions, you want to check those out as well.

TRANSLATING A STITCH DIAGRAM INTO WRITTEN INSTRUCTIONS

Now it's time to try your hand at reading an actual stitch diagram. The one in Figure 4-5 is for a lacy pattern that you work in rows. (To try out a stitch diagram for a design in rounds, head to Book 3, Chapter 4.) Notice that this particular stitch diagram doesn't look complete. Because this pattern is worked in identical rows consisting of repeated sets of stitches (the eight–stitch repeat in each row is shaded), the diagram shows only a few rows to save space. *Remember:* The pattern always tell you how many rows to make to get the exact result it shows.

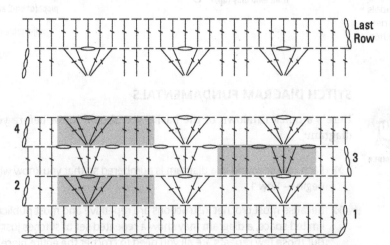

FIGURE 4-5: Stitch diagram of a repeated lacy-row pattern.

TIP

If you want to go your own way and make a piece wider, narrower, longer, or shorter than the pattern specifies — for example, a runner that's 12 inches wide or a tablecloth that's 52 inches wide — just add more sets of repeats to each row and add more rows.

To begin this design, you make a foundation chain (represented by the row of oval chain stitch symbols at the bottom of Figure 4-4) that's about the width you want, making sure it's a multiple of eight stitches (to allow for the repeat). Then you chain two more for the end of the row plus three more for the turning chain for the first double crochet of Row 1. For example, you could start with 21 chain stitches ($2 \times 8 + 2 + 3 = 21$) or 85 chain stitches ($10 \times 8 + 2 + 3 = 85$). Figure 4-5 starts with 29 chain stitches ($3 \times 8 + 2 + 3 = 29$).

The following steps take you from Row 1 to the last row. The Crochetese appears first, but it's followed by the plain-English translation so you can see how the written instructions correspond to the visual diagram. Figure 4-6 shows you what the piece should look like when you're done.

1. **Row 1: Dc in fourth ch from hook, dc in each ch across, *turn*.**

   Double crochet stitch in the fourth chain from the hook, double crochet in each chain going across, and then turn.

2. **Row 2: Ch 3 (turning ch for first dc), dc in each of next 2 dc, * skip next 2 dc (2 dc, ch 1, 2 dc) in next dc, skip next 2 dc, dc in each of next 3 dc *; rep from * to * across, ending with last dc of last rep in top of turning ch, *turn*.**

   For Row 2, chain 3 to make the turning chain for the first double crochet stitch and double crochet in each of the next 2 double crochet stitches. For the repeated part of this row (the instructions that are shown between the asterisks), skip the next 2 double crochet stitches, work 2 double crochet stitches into the next double crochet, chain 1, work 2 more double crochet stitches in the same double crochet, skip the next 2 double crochet stitches, and then work 1 double crochet in each of the next 3 double crochet stitches. Repeat this section until you reach the end of the row, ending with a double crochet in the top of the previous row's turning chain. Turn your work.

3. **Row 3: Ch 3 (turning ch for first dc), dc in each of next 2 dc, * ch 1, skip next 2 dc, 3 dc in next ch-1 sp, ch 1, skip next 2 dc, dc in each of next 3 dc *; rep from * to * across, ending with last dc of last rep in top of turning ch, *turn*.**

   To complete Row 3, chain 3 for your turning chain and then work 1 double crochet stitch in each of the next 2 double crochet stitches. For the repeated part of this row (the instructions that are shown between the asterisks), chain 1, skip the next 2 double crochet stitches, work 3 double crochet stitches in the next chain-1 space, chain 1, skip the next 2 double crochet stitches, and then

Reading Patterns

work 1 double crochet stitch in each of the next 3 double crochet stitches. Repeat this section until you reach the end of the row, ending with a double crochet in the top of the previous row's turning chain. Turn your work.

4. **Row 4: Ch 3 (turning ch for first dc), dc in each of next 2 dc, * skip next 2 sts, (2 dc, ch 1, 2 dc) in next dc, skip next 2 sts, dc in each of next 3 dc *; rep from * to * across, ending with last dc of last rep in top of turning ch, turn.**

To complete Row 4, chain 3 for your turning chain (counts as first double crochet) and then work 1 double crochet stitch into each of the next 2 double crochet stitches. For the repeated part of this row (the instructions shown between the asterisks), skip the next chain-1 space and the next double crochet stitch, work 2 double crochet stitches, chain 1, work 2 more double crochet stitches into the next double crochet stitch, skip the next double crochet stitch and the next chain-1 space, and then work 1 double crochet stitch into each of the next 3 double crochet stitches. Repeat this section until you reach the end of the row, ending with a double crochet in the top of the previous row's turning chain. Turn your work.

5. **Rep Rows 3 and 4 for desired length.**

Repeat Row 3 and then repeat Row 4, alternating these 2 rows until your piece is as long as you want it to be.

6. **Last Row: Ch 3 (turning ch for first dc), dc in each st and space across, ending with dc in top of turning ch. Fasten off.**

Begin the last row from the right side, chain 3 for your turning chain, and then work 1 double crochet stitch in each double crochet stitch and each chain-1 space across the entire row. You should have the same number of double crochet stitches in this row as you have in Row 1. Fasten off your work.

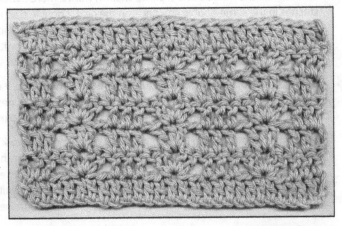

FIGURE 4-6:
A swatch of
lacy-row pattern.

© John Wiley & Sons, Inc.

2
Knitting Basics

Contents at a Glance

Chapter **1**

Knitting Fundamentals

Here you are, a ball of yarn in one hand and two knitting needles in the other. To be a successful knitter, you first need to figure out how to get the yarn onto the needles. Then you can learn how to make the thing grow. The answers? Casting on and knitting and purling. Knit and purl stitches are the two stitches upon which all other knitting techniques are based. When you're comfortable with these stitches, you can create any number of amazing things.

REMEMBER

Knitting is hugely relaxing — after you know the basics. As you pick up the techniques and practice them, keep these things in mind:

» Learning to knit can be a little stressful. Your fingers have to work in ways they're not accustomed to, and the illustrations that are decluttered for clarity make actual yarn-on-needles resemble a tangled mess — even if nothing's wrong. When you feel yourself getting tense or frustrated, set your knitting aside and do something else for a while.

» Throughout this chapter and the rest of the book, the abbreviation *LH* refers to the left hand, and *RH* refers to the right hand. These abbreviations appear whenever you're reading about the needles. You can find a list of other common abbreviations in Book 1, Chapter 4.

Casting On

Creating the first row of stitches is called *casting on.* You can cast on in various ways, and different knitters have their favorites. The following sections outline three common cast on methods. Whichever you use, be sure to cast on your stitches evenly. They make up the bottom edge of your knitting, and neatness counts.

TIP

Here are a couple of tips about casting on:

>> **Don't cast on too tightly.** Doing so makes the first row hard to work because you have to force your needle tip through each loop. If you find yourself doing this, you may want to start over and cast on with a needle one size larger to counteract the tension. Then switch to the requested size for the actual knitting.

>> **When you're casting on a lot of stitches, place a stitch marker at particular intervals — like every 50 stitches.** That way, if you get interrupted or distracted as you're counting (and you will, sometimes multiple times), you don't have to begin counting again at the first stitch. As you work the first row, just drop the markers off the needle.

TIP

No matter which method you use, before you cast on for a project, use some scrap yarn and needles to practice casting on. Cast on some stitches, and then take them off your needles and do it again. Casting on is the first thing you learn as a knitter and often the first thing you forget.

Two-strand (or long-tail) cast on

The two-strand method (sometimes called the *long-tail* method) is a great all-around cast on for your starting repertoire. It's elastic, attractive, and easy to knit from. For this cast on method, you need only one needle: the RH needle.

Visit dummies.com/go/knitcrochetAIO to watch a video demonstration of the two-strand cast on method. Then try it yourself by following these steps:

1. **Measure off enough yarn for the bottom part of your piece and make a slip knot on your needle.**

   To figure how long the tail should be, you need approximately 1 inch for every stitch you cast on plus a little extra. Alternatively, you can measure the bottom of the knitted piece and multiply this total by 4.

To make the slip knot, make a pretzel-shaped loop and place your needle into the loop, as in Figure 1-1a. Then gently pull on both ends of yarn until the stitch is firmly on the needle but still slides easily back and forth, as in Figure 1-1b.

FIGURE 1-1:
Get the slip knot (the first stitch) on your needle.

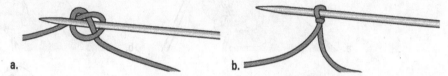

Illustration by Wiley, Composition Services Graphics

2. **Hold the needle in your right hand with the tip pointing away from your hand. Insert your left hand's thumb and forefinger into the "tent" formed by the two yarn ends falling from the slip knot on your needle.**

3. **With your left hand's ring and pinkie fingers, catch the yarn ends and hold them to your palm so they don't flap around underneath (see Figure 1-2a).**

4. **With your right hand, pull the needle between your left thumb and forefinger so that the "tent" sides aren't droopy.**

   This setup resembles a sling shot.

5. **With the RH needle tip, go around the yarn on your thumb from the left (see Figure 1-2b) and then around the yarn on your forefinger from the right (see Figure 1-2c) and pull the new loop through (see Figure 1-2d).**

   Figure 1-2e shows the finished stitch.

6. **Tighten this new loop (your first cast on stitch) onto the needle — but not too tight!**

   You'll quickly find that if you don't let go of the yarn after creating the stitch, you can use your thumb to tighten the stitch onto your needle. Finishing and tightening each stitch gets easier with practice.

   Although this is the first cast on stitch, it's the second stitch on the RH needle because you also have the initial slip knot.

REMEMBER

7. **Repeat Steps 5 and 6 until you have the number of stitches you need (see Figure 1-3).**

   If you need to put down your work or if you lose your place, you may have to pull the stitches off the needle and start from Step 2 instead.

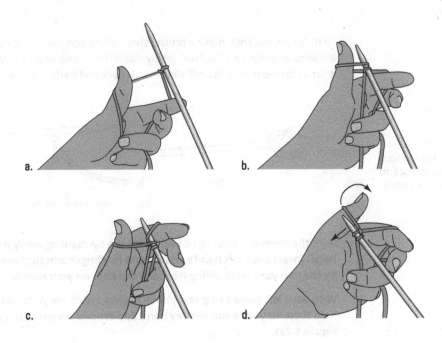

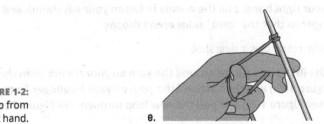

FIGURE 1-2:
Catch a loop from
your left hand.

Illustration by Wiley, Composition Services Graphics

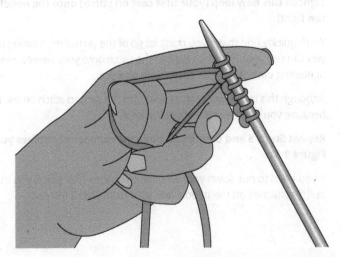

FIGURE 1-3:
Finished cast on
stitches.

Illustration by Wiley, Composition Services Graphics

Casting on may feel awkward at first, and you have to pay attention to each movement. But with time and practice, you'll no longer have to think about what your hands are doing. You'll be surprised at how quickly you'll learn the movements and make them smoothly and effortlessly while you think about something entirely unknitterish.

Cable cast on (cable co)

The cable cast on, or *knitting on*, is less elastic than the two-strand cast on. Use it when you need a sturdy, not-too-stretchy edge or when you need to cast on over buttonholes. If you're making a brand-new cast on row, start with Step 1. If you're adding on at the beginning of an existing row or making new stitches over a buttonhole, start from Step 2.

1. **Make a slip knot on your needle, leaving a 6-inch tail.**

   Refer to the preceding section for help making a slip knot.

2. **Knit into the first stitch (see Figure 1-4a), but instead of slipping the old loop off the LH needle, bring the new loop to the right (see Figure 1-4b) and slip it onto the LH needle (see Figure 1-4c).**

   If you don't know how to make this first stitch, see the later section "Knitting know-how" for instructions.

3. **Insert the RH needle *between* the 2 stitches on the LH needle (see Figure 1-4d and 1-4e).**

4. **Wrap the yarn around the RH needle, as you do when you knit, and then bring a new loop through to the front (see Figure 1-4f).**

5. **Bring this loop around to the right and place it on the LH needle (see Figure 1-4g).**

6. **Repeat Steps 3 through 5 until you have the number of cast on stitches you need.**

Thumb (or e-loop) cast on

The thumb cast on is quick and easy, but it doesn't look as nice as the cable cast on, and it isn't easy to knit into. Two-strand and cable cast ons should be your first choice for beginning a project. Still, the thumb cast on (sometimes called *e-loop*) has its uses (such as for replacing cast-off stitches in a buttonhole or for a quick and easy increase stitch in the middle of a row), so knowing how to do it is worthwhile. If you're using this cast on method at the beginning or in the middle of an existing row, skip Step 1.

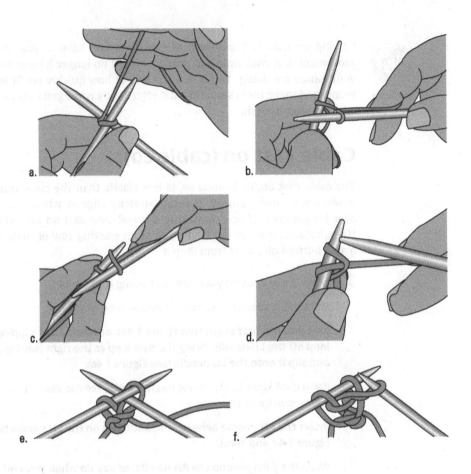

FIGURE 1-4:
Work a cable
cast on.

Illustration by Wiley, Composition Services Graphics

1. **Make a slip knot on your needle, leaving a short tail.**

    Refer to the earlier section "Two-strand (or long-tail) cast on" for help making a slip knot.

2. **Wrap the yarn around your left thumb, as in Figure 1-5a, and hold the needle in the right hand.**

3. Insert the needle through the loop around your thumb (see Figure 1-5b), slide your thumb out, and pull gently on the yarn strand to tighten the stitch (see Figure 1-5c).

The thumb cast on is very similar to the long-tail cast on. The difference between the two is that the thumb cast on uses only the yarn on the thumb, whereas the long-tail uses the yarn on the thumb and the forefinger. So if you can do this cast on, you're only one step away from the preferred long-tail method.

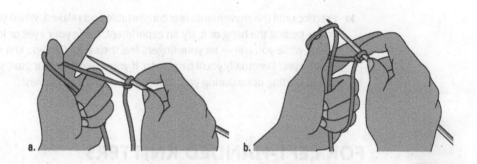

FIGURE 1-5:
Working a
thumb cast on.

Illustration by Wiley, Composition Services Graphics

Now You're Knitting and Purling

Knitted and purled stitches are made by using a continuous strand of yarn and two needles to pull new loops through old loops. That's it. The following sections explain how to create both stitches.

TIP

Here are a couple of pointers to keep in mind as you pick up knitting:

>> Finish working an entire row before putting down your knitting. It's too easy to stop midway and pick up your knitting later to find you can't tell the LH from the RH needle. Here's an easy way to tell: The yarn is always hanging down from the last stitch you made, which is generally on the RH needle, no matter what kind of stitch it is. So if you've finished the entire row as is recommended, when you pick up your needles again, the needle with stitches will be in your left hand.

>> Practice until the movements feel comfortable and relaxed. When you feel like you're getting the hang of it, try an experiment. Close your eyes or look at the ceiling while you knit — let your fingers feel their way. Can you knit without looking yet? Eventually you'll be able to. If you make this your goal, you can get lots of knitting done during your favorite TV shows and movies!

FOR LEFT-HANDED KNITTERS

Knitting is a two-handed endeavor. Whether you use your right hand or your left hand to write or stir your coffee, you use them both to knit.

For better or worse, knitting patterns are written for right-handed knitters (those who work from the LH needle to the RH needle). If you can master either of the knitting methods presented in this chapter (that is, English or Continental), you won't have to reinterpret patterns to work them in reverse. Chances are, like most right-handed knitters, sooner or later you'll work out a series of movements that feel natural and easy, and your stitches will be smooth and even.

If you find that the initial awkward feeling isn't going away, try to work in reverse — moving the stitches from the RH needle to the LH one. Follow the instructions for either the English or Continental style, substituting the word "right" for "left" and vice versa. To make the illustrations work for you, hold a mirror up to the side of the relevant illustration and mimic the hand and yarn positions visible in the mirror image.

If you find that working in reverse is the most comfortable method, be aware that some directions in knitting patterns, such as decreases, look different when worked in the opposite direction. This quirk will be most problematic for lace patterns, but it's a small price to pay for comfortable knitting.

Knitting know-how

To knit, hold the needle with the cast on stitches in your left hand, pointing to the right, and hold the yarn in your right hand. Make sure that the first stitch is no more than 1 inch from the tip of the needle.

Visit dummies.com/go/knitcrochetAIO to watch a video demonstration of the knit stitch, and then try it yourself by following these steps:

1. **Insert the tip of the empty (RH) needle into the first stitch on the LH needle from left to right and front to back, forming a T with the tips of the needles.**

    The RH needle will be behind the LH needle (see Figure 1-6).

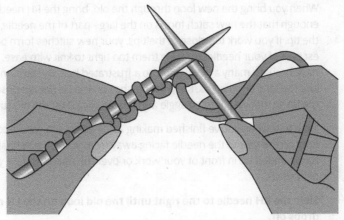

FIGURE 1-6: Insert the RH needle into the first stitch on the LH needle.

Illustration by Wiley, Composition Services Graphics

2. **With your right hand, bring the yarn to the front from the *left side* of the RH needle, and then bring it over the RH needle to the right and down between the needles.**

    You can try to maneuver the yarn with your right forefinger, as Figure 1-7a shows, or just hold it between your thumb and forefinger for now.

3. **Keeping a slight tension on the wrapped yarn, bring the tip of the RH needle with its wrap of yarn through the loop on the LH needle to the front.**

    The RH needle is now in front of the LH needle (see Figure 1-7b). Keep the tip of the left forefinger on the point of the RH needle to help guide the needle through the old stitch and prevent losing the wrap of yarn.

FIGURE 1-7:
Complete
a knit stitch.

a.

b.

WARNING

Don't hold the needles near the knob like a sword; keep your fingers in the action. Control the stitches on your needles by keeping your fingers close to the tip of the needle and use them to secure the stitches and keep them from falling off too early.

TIP

When you bring the new loop through the old, bring the RH needle up far enough that the new stitch forms on the large part of the needle, not just on the tip. If you work too close to the tips, your new stitches form on the narrowest part of your needles, making them too tight to knit with ease. Tight stitches have brought many a new knitter to a frustrated halt. By the same token, don't knit too far from the tips. Keep the stitches on the LH needle close enough to the tip so that you don't struggle and stretch to pull off the old stitch.

Note that when you've finished making a knit stitch, the yarn is coming out the *back* on the side of the needle facing away from you. Be sure that the yarn hasn't ended up in front of your work or over the needle before you start your next stitch.

4. **Slide the RH needle to the right until the old loop on the LH needle drops off.**

   You now have a new stitch/loop on the RH needle — the old stitch hangs below it (see Figure 1-8). Congratulations! You've just made your first knitted stitch!

5. **Repeat Steps 1 through 4 until you've knitted all the stitches from your LH needle.**

   Your LH needle is now empty, and your RH needle is full of beautiful new stitches.

WARNING

Some beginners worry about the tension of their knitting and make the mistake of trying to tighten up the stitches by pulling the two needles apart. Don't do this because it creates a lot of slack between the stitches and doesn't make a pretty fabric. You want the needles to be close to one another as you knit (or purl). Notice in Figure 1-8 how far apart the needles are; that's about the same amount of distance you want between your own needles.

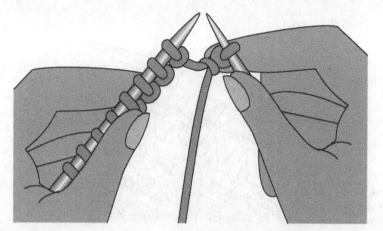

FIGURE 1-8:
Your first knitted
stitch is on your
RH needle.

Illustration by Wiley, Composition Services Graphics

In the meantime, don't worry about the tension of your knitting. As you practice more and more, you'll figure out how to control the tension of your stitches by managing the working yarn as you knit. The more snug you keep the working yarn, the more snug your stitches will be.

6. **Turn your work (that is, switch hands so that the needle with stitches is in your left hand) and knit the new row.**

   When you turn your work, the yarn strand coming out of the first stitch to knit is hanging down in the front (see Figure 1-9). Also notice that the stitch just below the first stitch (labeled "Big loop" in Figure 1-9) on your LH needle is larger than the rest and can obscure your view of where your needle should go.

   WARNING

   You may be tempted to pull the yarn strand over the needle to the back to tighten up the stitch. If you do so, it will look like you have 2 stitches on your needle rather than 1. Keep the strand in front and gently pull down on it, and the big loop if necessary, to better see the opening of the first stitch. Be sure to insert the point of the RH needle in the loop on the LH needle and not into the stitch below.

7. **Repeat these steps for several more rows (or all afternoon) until you're comfortable with the movements.**

   Aim to make these steps one continuous movement, to make even stitches, and to stay relaxed! After you've knitted a few rows, take a look at what you've created: It's the *garter stitch,* and it's one of the most common — and easiest — stitch patterns. You can find it and other common stitch patterns in Book 2, Chapter 2.

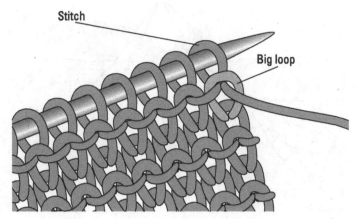

Stitch

Big loop

FIGURE 1-9:
The first stitch of
the next row.

Illustration by Wiley, Composition Services Graphics

TIP

If you're having trouble getting into the flow, change the way you carry the yarn in your hand. Or prop the knob of your RH needle under your armpit or on your hipbone to keep it stationary while you use the left hand to initiate the movements. Study how other knitters do things and be willing to try different ways until you find your knitting home. When you understand how the yarn travels around your needle to make new loops, you'll sort out the best way to hold your yarn and needles for comfort, speed, and even stitches.

Perfect purling

Purling is working a knit stitch backwards: Instead of going into the stitch from front to back, you enter it from back to front. Combining knit stitches with purl stitches enables you to make a wide variety of textured stitch patterns; many common ones are included in Book 2, Chapter 2.

If you're a visual learner, head to dummies.com/go/knitcrochetAIO to watch a video demonstration of the purl stitch. To purl, follow these steps, holding the needle with the cast on or existing stitches in your left hand and pointing to the right:

1. **Insert the tip of the RH needle into the first loop on the LH needle from right to left and back to front, forming a T with the needle tips.**

    The RH needle is in front of the LH needle, and the working yarn is in front of your needles (see Figure 1-10a). This setup is the reverse of what you do when you form a knit stitch.

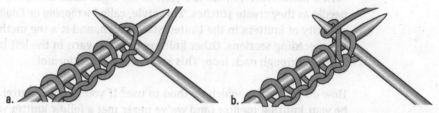

2. With your right hand, wrap the yarn around the back of the RH needle from right to left and down (see Figure 1-10b).

FIGURE 1-10:
Insert the RH needle and wrap the yarn to purl.

a.   b.

Illustration by Wiley, Composition Services Graphics

3. Keeping a slight tension on the wrap of yarn, bring the tip of the RH needle with its wrap of yarn down and through the loop on the LH needle to the *back* side of the LH needle (see Figure 1-11a).

4. Slide the old loop off the tip of the LH needle.

A new stitch is made on the RH needle. You can see how it should look in Figure 1-11b.

5. Repeat Steps 1 through 4 until you're comfortable with the movements.

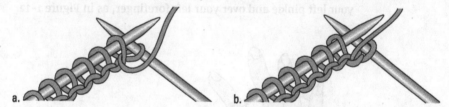

FIGURE 1-11:
Finish your purl stitch.

a.   b.

Illustration by Wiley, Composition Services Graphics

REMEMBER

When you purl, the yarn strand comes out of the new stitches on the side of the knitting facing you. When you knit, the yarn comes out of the new stitches on the side facing away from you.

A purled swatch looks just like a knitted swatch. Why? Because purling is simply the reverse of knitting. Whether you knit all the rows or purl all the rows, you're working a garter stitch. (See Book 2, Chapter 2 for more on the garter stitch.)

Knitting and purling, Continental-style

How a knitter goes about holding the yarn and needles while working stitches varies. Some knitters hold the yarn in the right hand and wrap it around the RH needle as they create stitches. This style, called *wrapping* or *English*, is the one the majority of knitters in the United States learn, and it's the method we explain in the preceding sections. Other knitters hold the yarn in the left hand and pick the stitches through each loop. This style is called *Continental.*

How do you decide which method to use? If you know a knitter who's willing to be your knitting mentor (and we've never met a fellow knitter who didn't love to show off his or her techniques), do what that person does. If you plan to knit color patterns, know that being able to knit with one color in the right hand and the other color in the left hand makes things quicker and easier.

REMEMBER

Both methods, Continental and English, give you the same result — loops pulled through loops to make knitted fabric. The most important things are that knitting feels comfortable to you and your stitches look even.

Holding the yarn and needles

When you knit Continental, you hold both the yarn *and* the needle with the stitches in your left hand. The trick is keeping the yarn slightly taut by winding it around your left pinkie and over your left forefinger, as in Figure 1-12.

Illustration by Wiley, Composition Services Graphics

FIGURE 1-12:
Carry the yarn in your left hand for Continental style.

Your left forefinger should be close to the tip of the LH needle, and the yarn between the needle and your forefinger should be a bit taut. The yarn strand is *behind* your LH needle, as in Figure 1-13.

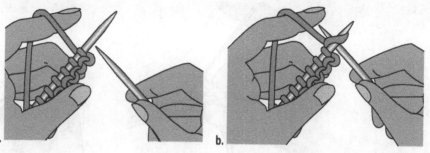

FIGURE 1-13:
Start a Continental knit stitch.

a.

b.

Illustration by Wiley, Composition Services Graphics

Swiveling to catch the yarn

When you knit or purl Continental, you don't wrap the yarn as you do in English knitting (refer to the earlier section "Knitting know-how"). Instead, you have to pick up the yarn and pull it through the old stitch. To do that, you execute a little swivel movement with your RH needle. Envision the needle as a chopstick with a cup on the end that you scoop into the stitch in order to pull up the yarn. (If you crochet, this motion should be familiar to you from working with your hook.)

Knitting the Continental way

To knit in Continental style, follow these steps:

1. **Insert the RH needle through the stitch on the LH needle from left to right and front to back (see Figure 1-14a).**

2. **Swivel the tip of the RH needle to the right and under the yarn strand, scooping up the yarn from your left forefinger (see Figure 1-14b).**

3. **Pull the yarn through the loop (see Figure 1-14c), slide the old loop off the LH needle, and let it drop (see Figure 1-14d) to complete the stitch. (Figure 1-14e shows a completed stitch.)**

TIP

To make Continental knitting a little easier, try the following:

>> Put the tip of your right forefinger on each new stitch made on the RH needle to secure it while you insert the RH needle into the next stitch on the LH needle.

>> After you've inserted the RH needle into the next stitch to be knitted, slightly stretch the loop on the LH needle to the right, opening it up somewhat, before you scoop the strand of yarn.

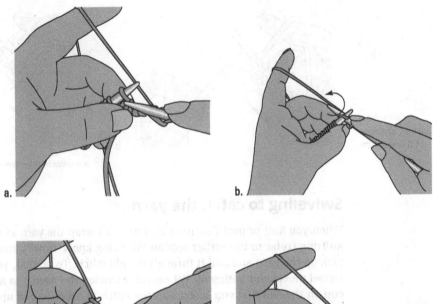

a.

b.

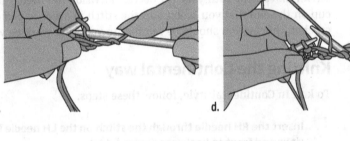

c.

d.

FIGURE 1-14:
Complete a
Continental
knit stitch.

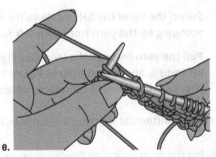

e.

Illustration by Wiley, Composition Services Graphics

Purling the Continental way

To purl in Continental style, follow these steps:

1. **Make sure the yarn between your LH needle and forefinger is in front of the needle.**

2. **Insert the tip of the RH needle into the first loop on the LH needle from right to left and back to front (see Figure 1-15a).**

FIGURE 1-15:
Set up for a
Continental
purl stitch.

a.    b.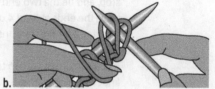

Illustration by Wiley, Composition Services Graphics

3. **Slightly swivel the RH needle tip to the right while the pad of your left forefinger brings the yarn between the needles from right to left and down between the needles (see Figure 1-15b).**

4. **Bring the tip of the RH needle with its wrap of yarn through the stitch on the LH needle to the back, away from you (Figure 1-16a).**

5. **Slip the old stitch off the LH needle, tightening it on the RH needle with the left forefinger (see Figure 1-16b).**

FIGURE 1-16:
Complete a
Continental
purl stitch.

a.    b.

Illustration by Wiley, Composition Services Graphics

Binding (or Casting) Off

To finish your knitted piece, you have to *bind off*, which is securing the stitches in the last row worked so that they don't unravel. Like casting on, you can bind off in a variety of ways, each resulting in a different look. Knowing a couple of the available methods can help you choose the right one for your project.

Standard bind-off

The standard bind-off is the most traditional option. It's easy to do if you follow these basic steps:

1. **Knit the first 2 stitches from the LH needle.**

   These become the first 2 stitches on your RH needle (see Figure 1-17a).

2. **With your LH needle in front of your RH needle, insert the LH needle into the first stitch worked on the RH needle (the one on the right, as shown in Figure 1-17b).**

3. **Bring this loop over the second stitch and off the tip of the RH needle, as shown in Figure 1-17c — sort of like leapfrogging over the stitch.**

   At this point, you have 1 stitch bound off and 1 stitch remaining on your RH needle.

4. **Knit the next stitch on the LH needle so that you again have 2 stitches on your RH needle.**

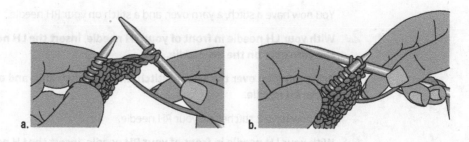

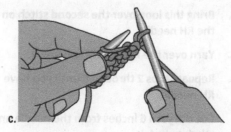

FIGURE 1-17:
Bind off a stitch.

5. **Repeat Steps 2 through 4 until you have 1 stitch remaining on your RH needle.**

6. **Cut the yarn 6 inches from the needle and pull the tail through the last stitch to lock it.**

TIP

If the piece you've just bound off will be sewn to another piece, leave a tail that's 12 inches or longer for a built-in strand to sew up a seam.

You can watch a video demonstration of the standard bind-off at dummies.com/go/knitcrochetAIO.

Yarn-over bind-off

The yarn-over bind-off is more elastic than the standard bind-off (see the preceding section) and is a bit more decorative. Use the yarn-over version when you need some stretch to the edge of your project, such as for the cuff of a toe-up sock. It's also useful for the edge of a lace shawl or for ruffles. For details on how to do a yarn over, refer to Book 2, Chapter 3.

Here's how the yarn-over bind-off works:

1. **Knit 1 stitch, yarn over the RH needle, and then knit 1 more stitch.**

   You now have a stitch, a yarn over, and a stitch on your RH needle.

2. **With your LH needle in front of your RH needle, insert the LH needle into the yarn over on the RH needle.**

3. **Bring this loop over the second stitch (the last stitch knit) and off the tip of the RH needle.**

   You now have 2 stitches on your RH needle.

4. **With your LH needle in front of your RH needle, insert the LH needle into the first stitch on the RH needle.**

5. **Bring this loop over the second stitch on the needle, leaving 1 stitch on the RH needle.**

6. **Yarn over the RH needle and knit 1.**

7. **Repeat Steps 2 through 6 until you have 1 stitch remaining on your RH needle.**

8. **Cut the yarn 6 inches from the needle and pull the tail through the last stitch to lock it.**

Helpful hints for binding off

TIP

Just as casting on evenly gives the bottom edge of your piece a neat appearance, binding off evenly ensures a neat top edge. Here are some suggestions for getting an attractive edge regardless of which bind-off method you use:

» The loop below the last bind-off stitch is often (for some mysterious reason) big and baggy. To tighten it up, when you come to the last stitch (1 stitch on the RH needle and 1 stitch on the LH needle), slip the last stitch on the RH needle back to the LH needle. Insert the tip of the RH needle into the left stitch on the LH needle and bring it over the right stitch and off the needle — binding off in the reverse direction. Cut the yarn and draw the tail through the remaining loop.

» Unless told otherwise, always bind off according to the stitch pattern given. If you'd normally be working a purl row, purl the stitches as you bind off instead of knitting them. This approach is often referred to as *binding off in pattern*.

» Don't bind off too tightly (which, unfortunately, is easy to do). Knitting should be elastic, especially around neck edges if you want to be able to get a sweater on and off comfortably (and who doesn't want that?). To avoid a tight and inelastic bound edge, try working the bind-off row on a needle one or more sizes larger than what you've been using.

Chapter **2**

Basic Stitches

When you know how to knit and purl (refer to Book 2, Chapter 1), you can combine these stitches in a seemingly endless variety of textured stitch patterns. The stitch patterns in this chapter make a good starting point.

TIP

The best way to understand how knit-and-purl patterns work is to knit them up yourself. Using a medium-weight, solid-color yarn in a light shade, cast on a multiple of the stitches required for the pattern (but no less than 24) and knit up about 4 inches in the pattern. You can save your swatches in a knitting notebook for later reference.

Go-To Stitches: Garter, Stockinette, and Seed Stitches

Knitting and purling (explained in Book 2, Chapter 1) open the door to all sorts of patterns that involve alternating between knit and purl stitches. But as a beginning knitter, you really only need to know two patterns: *garter stitch*, which you create by knitting (or purling) every row, and *stockinette stitch*, which you create by alternating a knit row with a purl row. Another stitch all knitters should have in their repertoire is *seed stitch*. Although a little more complicated than garter and stockinette stitches, seed stitches create an interesting texture and appear in many patterns.

TECHNICAL STUFF

Knits and purls have a quirky but predictable relationship to each other. When lined up horizontally, the purled rows stand out from the knitted rows. Arranged in vertical patterns, like ribbing, the purl stitches recede and the knit stitches come forward, creating an elastic fabric. When worked in a balanced manner (meaning the same number of knits and purls appear on each side of the fabric), as in seed stitch and its variations, the fabric is stable — it lies flat and doesn't have the tendency to roll in on the edges. These qualities make seed and moss stitches, as well as garter stitches, good choices for borders that need to lie flat and not pull in as ribbed borders do.

Garter stitch

Garter stitch is the most basic of all knitted fabrics. It's made by knitting every row. (You can create garter stitch by purling every row, too. Neat, huh?) You can recognize garter stitch by the horizontal ridges formed by the tops of the knitted loops on every other row (see Figure 2-1).

For a demonstration of garter stitch, check out the video at dummies.com/go/ knitcrochetAIO.

FIGURE 2-1:
Garter stitch.

Photograph by Wiley, Composition Services Graphics

Garter stitch has a lot going for it in addition to being easy to create. It's reversible, lies flat, and has a pleasant rustic look. Unlike most knitted fabrics, garter stitch has a square gauge, meaning that there are usually twice as many rows as stitches in 1 inch. To count rows in garter stitch, count the ridges and multiply by 2, or count the ridges by 2s.

WARNING

Garter stitch has a hanging gauge that stretches more *vertically*. Therefore, gravity and the weight of the garter stitch piece pull on the fabric and actually make it longer. This is important to keep in mind when you're making a garment that you want to fit properly and not grow two times larger after an hour of wearing it. Refer to Book 1, Chapter 3 for info on checking gauge.

Stockinette stitch

When you alternate a knit row with a purl row (knit the first row, purl the second, knit the third, purl the fourth, and so on), you create *stockinette stitch*; see Figure 2-2. You see stockinette stitch everywhere: in scarves, socks, sweaters, blankets, hats — you name it. In fact, most beginning and intermediate designs incorporate stockinette stitch.

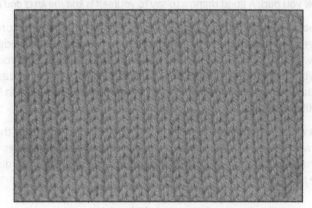

FIGURE 2-2:
Stockinette stitch showing the knit side.

Photograph by Wiley, Composition Services Graphics

In written knitting instructions, stockinette stitch (abbreviated St st) appears like this (if you're unfamiliar with the abbreviations, refer to Book 1, Chapter 4):

Row 1 (RS): Knit.

Row 2 (WS): Purl.

Rep Rows 1 and 2 for desired length.

Visit dummies.com/go/knitcrochetAIO for a video demonstration of stockinette stitch.

Stockinette fabric looks and behaves in a particular way. To successfully incorporate this stitch into your knitting repertoire, pay attention to the following:

» **Stockinette stitch has a right side and a wrong side (though, of course, either side may be the "right" side, depending on the intended design).** The right side is typically the smooth side, called *stockinette* or *knit.* On this side, the stitches look like small Vs (see Figure 2-3). The bumpy side of stockinette stitch fabric, shown in Figure 2-4, is called *reverse stockinette* or *purl.* The highlighted stitches in Figure 2-4 are the back of the highlighted knit stitches in Figure 2-3.

TIP

If you're working in stockinette stitch and you lose track of whether you knit the last row or purled it, not to worry. You can tell what to do next by looking at your knitting. Hold your needles in the ready-to-knit position (with the LH needle holding the stitches to be worked) and look at what's facing you. If you're looking at the knit (smooth) side, you knit. If you're looking at the purl (bumpy) side, you purl. A good mantra to say to yourself is *knit the knits and purl the purls.*

» **Stockinette fabric curls on the edges.** The top and bottom (horizontal) edges curl toward the front or smooth side. The side (vertical) edges roll toward the bumpy side. Sweater designers frequently use this rolling feature deliberately to create rolled hems or cuffs, and you can create easy cords or straps simply by knitting a very narrow band in stockinette stitch (say, 4 or 6 stitches across).

But when you want the piece to lie flat, you need to counteract this tendency by working the 3 or 4 stitches on the edge in some stitch that lies flat (like garter stitch, discussed in the preceding section, or seed stitch, discussed in the next section).

TIP

To figure out the gauge of a swatch knitted in stockinette stitch, count the Vs on the smooth side or right side. They're easier to see and distinguish than the bumps on the wrong side. Of course, if you find the bumps easier to count, it's okay to do so.

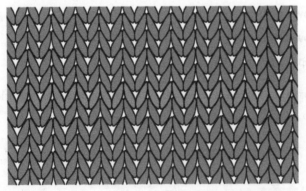

FIGURE 2-3:
Stockinette stitch showing the knit (or smooth) side.

Illustration by Wiley, Composition Services Graphics

FIGURE 2-4: Reverse stockinette showing the purl (or bumpy) side.

Illustration by Wiley, Composition Services Graphics

TECHNICAL STUFF

The names *garter stitch* and *stockinette stitch* date from the 1500s, when hand-knit stockings were a major industry in England. Garter stitch was used at the top of the stocking, where it needed to expand for the thigh, and stockinette (or *stocking stitch*) was used for the fitted leg portion.

Seed stitch

Seed stitch, shown in Figure 2-5, consists of single knits and purls alternating horizontally and vertically. Its name refers to the way the knitted fabric looks: The little purl bumps look like scattered seeds. Like garter stitch, seed stitch lies flat, making it a good edging for a sweater border and cuffs. It also looks the same from both sides, making it a nice choice for scarves and other pieces of which both sides are visible.

TIP

Seed stitch *stitch gauge* tends to be wider than a stockinette stitch stitch gauge. This is important to note if you plan to mix stitch patterns but want to maintain the same measurements in both patterns.

REMEMBER

When knitting a stitch, the loose tail of yarn is in *back* of your work. When purling a stitch, the yarn is in *front* of your work. As you switch back and forth within a row, as in seed stitch, you need to move your yarn to the front or to the back as appropriate between the needles. If you forget to do so, you create an unintentional yarn over (see Book 2, Chapter 3), resulting in an extra stitch on the next row and a hole in the work. Unfortunately for novice knitters, who often forget to move the yarn accordingly, instructions don't explicitly tell you to bring your yarn to the front or back of your work. They assume that you know where the yarn should be when you're about to knit or purl a stitch. As you practice the patterns that combine both knit and purl stitches, make sure your yarn is in the proper position for each stitch before you start it, and refer to Book 2, Chapter 1 for a quick review if necessary.

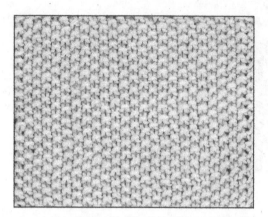

FIGURE 2-5:
Seed stitch.

Photograph by Wiley, Composition Services Graphics

To create seed stitch:

Cast on an even number of sts.

Row 1: * K1, p1; rep from * to end of row.

Row 2: * P1, k1; rep from * to end of row.

Rep Rows 1 and 2 for pattern.

When working seed stitch, you alternate between knit and purl stitches in each row. The trick to creating the little "seeds" is to knit in the purl stitches of the previous row and purl in the knit stitches of the previous row.

For a video demonstration of seed stitch, check out dummies.com/go/ knitcrochetAIO.

TIP

If you're working in seed stitch and you lose track of whether you knit the last stitch or purled it, don't worry. You can tell what to do next by looking at your knitting. Hold your needles in the ready-to-knit position (with the LH needle holding the stitches to be worked or the ones you're working on) and look at what's facing you. On the LH needle, if you're looking at a knit stitch, you purl. If you're looking at a purl (bumpy) stitch, you knit. A good mantra to say to yourself is *knit the purls and purl the knits*.

Adding Stretch with Ribbed Stitches

Knit ribs are textured vertical stripes. Ribbing is made by alternating columns of knit stitches with columns of purl stitches. Instead of alternating knit rows with purl rows, as you do in stockinette stitch, when you make a ribbed pattern, you change from knit stitches to purl stitches *within* a row, similar to seed stitch. However, unlike seed stitch, a ribbed pattern has a knit made into a knit of the previous row and a purl made into a purl of the previous row, thus making the columns of stitches.

Ribbing is the edging par excellence on most sweaters because of its elasticity; it stretches to let you in and out of cuffs and neckbands and then springs back into place to hug you. It's also used for the body of many pieces, like sweaters, scarves, and hats.

Measuring gauge of a ribbed fabric is a bit subjective in that knowing how much to stretch a ribbed fabric before measuring for stitch and row gauge is entirely up to the knitter. Some patterns state whether the ribbed fabric should not be stretched, be slightly stretched, or be stretched to fit comfortably when taking gauge; you have to decide what each one of those means for you. A good way to start is to see how stretched the finished ribbing is in the pattern picture and to measure the gauge swatch with about the same stretch. In the end, it doesn't hurt to know all of these measurements, so take the time to measure each on your gauge swatch.

TIP

A pattern may have only a stockinette stitch gauge listed, even though it's a ribbed pattern stitch. In those cases, a ribbed gauge swatch isn't necessary for measuring purposes, but you should still make a ribbed pattern swatch to see whether the needle and yarn choices create a finished fabric that's desirable.

The most common ribbing combinations are those that are even (that is, the rib uses the same number of knitted versus purl columns). Examples include 1 x 1 ribbing, in which single knit stitches alternate with single purl stitches, creating very narrow columns; and 2 x 2 ribbing, which alternates 2 knit stitches with 2 purl stitches. Although even columns are among the most common ribbed patterns, the columns don't have to be even. Many attractive and functional ribs have wider knit columns than purl columns.

REMEMBER

The elasticity of the final ribbed fabric is affected by the following:

>> **Column width:** The narrower the column of stitches, the more elastic the ribbing.

>> **Needle size:** Bigger needles result in less elasticity. Also, because ribbed edgings are intended to hug the body, you generally work them on needles one or two sizes smaller than the ones used for the body of the project.

The following sections explain how to create the most common ribbing patterns.

REMEMBER

As you switch back and forth within a row, you need to move your yarn to the front or to the back as appropriate between the needles.

Basic Stitches

1 x 1 ribbing

The 1 x 1 rib pattern alternates single knit stitches with single purl stitches to create narrow ribs. Figure 2-6 shows this ribbing stretched out a bit so you can see the purl rows (the horizontal lines in the background). When the knitting isn't stretched out, the knit columns contract, hiding the purl columns.

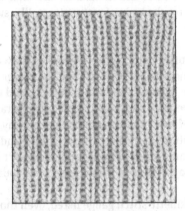

FIGURE 2-6:
1 x 1 ribbing.

Photograph by Wiley, Composition Services Graphics

To create 1 x 1 ribbing:

Cast on an even number of sts.

Work every row: * K1, p1; rep from * to end of row.

Rep this row for the length of your piece.

You can go to dummies.com/go/knitcrochetAIO for a video demonstration of ribbing stitches.

TIP

After the first row, you can look at your knitting to tell whether you should be making a knit stitch or a purl stitch. If the next stitch on your LH needle is a purl (bump) stitch, purl it. If it's a knit stitch, knit it.

2 x 2 ribbing

As you can see in Figure 2-7, 2 x 2 ribbing alternates 2 knit stitches with 2 purl stitches. It pulls in slightly less than 1 x 1 ribbing.

FIGURE 2-7:
2 x 2 ribbing.

Photograph by Wiley, Composition Services Graphics

To create 2 x 2 ribbing:

Cast on a multiple of 4 sts.

Work every row: * K2, p2; rep from * to end of row.

Rep this row for the length of your piece.

Note: If you want your piece to begin and end on 2 knit stitches, add 2 to the multiple that you cast on at the beginning.

4 x 2 and 2 x 4 ribbing

Knit ribs and purl ribs don't have to be the same number of stitches. You can work ribs in uneven combinations, such as 4 x 2, 2 x 4, and so on. Figure 2-8 shows a 4 x 2 ribbing.

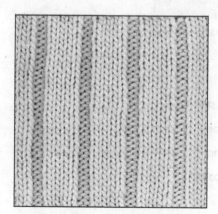

FIGURE 2-8:
4 x 2 ribbing.

Photograph by Wiley, Composition Services Graphics

To create 4 x 2 ribbing:

Cast on a multiple of 6 sts, plus 4 sts. (You can work this pattern over a multiple of 6 stitches, but it won't be symmetrical.)

Row 1: * K4, p2; rep from * to last 4 sts, k4.

Row 2: * P4, k2; rep from * to last 4 sts, p4.

Rep Rows 1 and 2 for pattern.

If you turn this swatch over, you'll have a very different looking pattern — thin vertical stripes instead of thick ones.

4 x 4 ribbing

The 4 x 4 rib shown in Figure 2-9 gives you a vertical stripe pattern that pulls in very little. It's symmetrical in that it's a simple alternation of 4 knit stitches with 4 purl stitches.

FIGURE 2-9:
4 x 4 ribbing.

Photograph by Wiley, Composition Services Graphics

To create 4 x 4 ribbing:

Cast on a multiple of 4 sts, plus 4 sts.

Row 1: * K4, p4; rep from * to last 4 sts, k4.

Row 2: * P4, k4; rep from * to last 4 sts, end p4.

Rep Rows 1 and 2 for pattern.

Chapter 3

Techniques Every Knitter Should Know

Playing around with knit and purl patterns introduced in Book 2, Chapter 2 can keep you busy for a long time, but you can do a lot more with knitted stitches. Cables, lace, and color work all lie ahead — literally (they're covered in Book 4) and figuratively. As you begin to explore stitch patterns and follow patterns for projects and garments, you'll want to familiarize yourself with the different stitch maneuvers that crop up in instructions for more demanding knitted fabrics.

Slipping Stitches

If your directions tell you to *slip a stitch* (abbreviated sl st), they mean for you to move a stitch from the left-hand (LH) needle to the right-hand (RH) needle without knitting or purling it *and* without changing its orientation (that is, without twisting it).

To slip a stitch, insert the RH needle *purlwise* (as if you were going to purl) into the first stitch on the LH needle and slip it off the LH needle onto the RH needle. Unless your instructions specifically tell you to slip a stitch *knitwise*, always slip a stitch as if you were going to purl it. Figure 3-1 shows stitches being slipped both purlwise and knitwise.

Visit dummies.com/go/knitcrochetAIO for a video demonstration of slipping stitches purlwise.

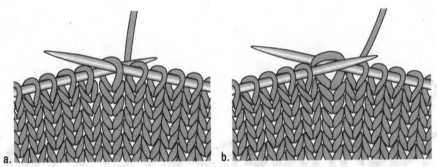

FIGURE 3-1:
Slipping stitches purlwise (a) and knitwise (b).

Illustration by Wiley, Composition Services Graphics

Slipped stitches are used in different ways. You frequently run across them in methods for decreasing stitches — when you want to reduce the number of stitches you have on your needle. They also form the basis of a family of stitch patterns. Like garter stitch, slip-stitch patterns are stable and lie flat — and they're a breeze to knit.

Making a Yarn Over

A *yarn over* (abbreviated yo) is a way of making an extra stitch on your needle and creating a deliberate little hole in your fabric. Yarn overs are an indispensable part of lace knitting. (See Book 4, Chapter 6 for more about using yarn overs in lace.) They have a multitude of other applications as well, such as decorative increases, buttonholes, and novelty stitch patterns.

To make a yarn over, you simply bring the knitting yarn (the "over" strand) over the needle between 2 existing stitches on one row and then work that strand as a stitch when you work your way back to it in the next row. You can watch an online video demonstration of a yarn over at dummies.com/go/knitcrochetAIO.

REMEMBER

At some point in your knitting experience, you may have accidentally created a yarn over when you forgot to bring the yarn between the needles from the back to the front when purling or from the front to the back when knitting. If you can do it accidentally, surely you can make a yarn over on purpose. However, until you get used to them, yarn overs can be a little confusing. Here are the things to remember in all cases:

>> **The working yarn starts in front of the needle.** Sometimes it's already there (if you've been purling); sometimes you have to put it there deliberately (if you've been knitting).

>> **You wrap the yarn around the needle from front to back and work the next stitch as normal.** Sometimes the pattern instructions ask you to wrap the yarn twice — or more times — around the needle to make a bigger hole. A double yarn over is usually written *yo twice*.

>> **As you work the row following the yarn over row, you'll recognize the yarn over by the big hole that suddenly appears on your needle where a stitch should be.** Above the hole is the strand of yarn that you've crossed over the needle. Think of the strand as a stitch and knit or purl it as you normally would.

>> **You will have 1 extra stitch for every yarn over you do.** For example, if you start with 4 stitches and then knit 2, yarn over, knit 2, on the next row, you'll have 5 stitches rather than 4.

To help you keep yarn overs straight, the following sections break down how to make a yarn over when it goes between 2 knit stitches, between a knit stitch and a purl stitch, between 2 purl stitches, and between a purl stitch and a knit stitch.

Between 2 knit stitches

To make a yarn over between 2 knit stitches (which you'd encounter in a pattern as k1, yo, k1), follow these steps:

1. Knit the first stitch.

2. Bring the yarn forward between the needles into purl position.

3. Knit the next stitch on the needle.

When you knit the next stitch, the yarn automatically crosses the RH needle, forming a yarn over (see Figure 3-2).

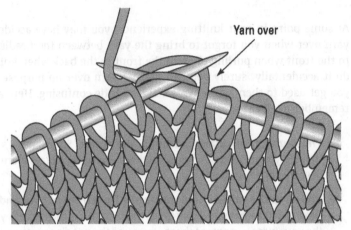

Yarn over

FIGURE 3-2:
Making a yarn over between 2 knit stitches.

Between a knit and a purl stitch

Here's how to make a yarn over that follows a knit stitch and precedes a purl stitch (which you'd encounter in a pattern as k1, yo, p1):

1. Knit the first stitch.

2. Bring the yarn to the front into the purl position, wrap it back over the top of the RH needle, and return it to the front into purl position again.

Basically you're just wrapping the yarn once around the RH needle from the front.

3. Purl the next stitch (see Figure 3-3).

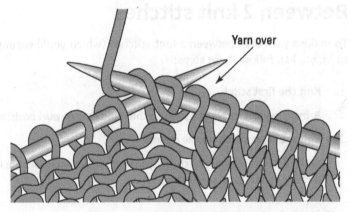

Yarn over

FIGURE 3-3:
Making a yarn over between a knit stitch and a purl stitch.

Between 2 purl stitches

To make a yarn over between 2 purl stitches (which you'd encounter in a pattern as p1, yo, p1), just do the following:

1. Purl the first stitch.

2. Wrap the yarn around the RH needle front to back to front so that it ends up in purl position again.

3. Purl the next stitch (see Figure 3-4.)

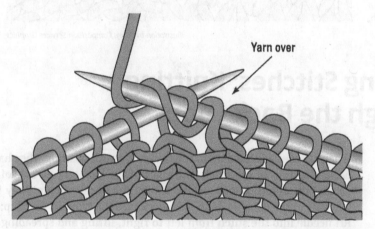

Yarn over

FIGURE 3-4:
Making a yarn over between 2 purl stitches.

Illustration by Wiley, Composition Services Graphics

Between a purl stitch and a knit stitch

To make a yarn over that follows a purl stitch and precedes a knit stitch (which you'd encounter in a pattern as p1, yo, k1), follow these steps:

1. Purl the first stitch and leave the yarn in the front of your work.

2. Knit the next stitch.

    The yarn automatically crosses the RH needle when you knit this next stitch (see Figure 3-5).

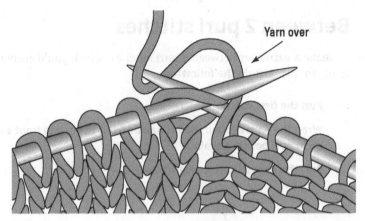

FIGURE 3-5:
Making a yarn over between a purl stitch and a knit stitch.

Twisting Stitches: Knitting through the Back Loop

When stitches are lined up in the ready-to-work position, they have a front and a back. The front of the stitch is the part of the loop on *your* side of the needle. The back of the stitch is, well, on the side of the needle facing away from you. When you knit in the usual fashion, you work into the front of the loop; you insert your RH needle into the stitch from left to right, lifting and spreading the front of the loop — the side of the loop on your side of the needle — when you insert your needle (see Figure 3-6a).

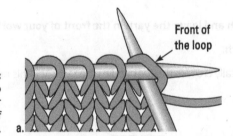
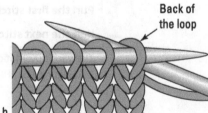

Front of the loop

Back of the loop

a.

b.

FIGURE 3-6:
You can knit into the front (a) or the back (b) of stitches.

By *knitting through back of the loop* (abbreviated ktbl), you twist the stitch and create a different effect. Stitch patterns that use twisted stitches have an etched, linear quality. On a background of reverse stockinette stitch, a vertical or wavy line of twisted stitches stands out in sharp definition. Frequently, you find twisted stitches combined with cables in traditional Aran patterns.

If your instructions tell you to knit through the back of the loop, they're asking you to change the direction from which your needle enters the stitch. When you work into the back of a stitch, you're deliberately twisting the stitch. You can purl into the front and back of a stitch as well, as shown in Figure 3-7.

» **To knit through the back of the loop:** Insert your needle from right to left, with the RH needle *behind* the LH needle, lifting and spreading the back of the loop — the side of the loop on the opposite side of the needle (see Figure 3-6b). Then wrap the yarn around the RH needle and pull a new loop through.

» **To purl through the back of the loop:** Insert your needle through the back of the loop from right to left (see Figure 3-7b) and purl as normal.

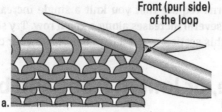
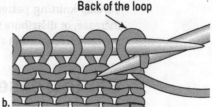

Front (purl side) of the loop

Back of the loop

FIGURE 3-7: Purling into the front (a) and the back (b) of stitches.

a.

b.

Illustration by Wiley, Composition Services Graphics

WARNING

If you find you're twisting stitches without even trying (or intending) to, check your yarn position. Wrapping the yarn around the RH needle in the opposite direction when working a stitch results in a twisted stitch on the next row. Just correct the wrapping direction, and you'll be on your way to perfect stitches.

REMEMBER

Abbreviations can vary from pattern to pattern. Some patterns use ktbl to mean "knit through back of loop"; others use k-b to mean the same thing. What can be even more confusing is that many patterns use k-b to mean "knit in the stitch below" (a technique discussed in the later section "Knitting into the stitch below"). Before you start, check your pattern to see what its abbreviations stand for.

Working Increases

Not all knitted pieces are square. Being able to increase (abbreviated inc) or decrease (abbreviated dec) stitches along the edge or within the body of a knitted piece enables you to create knitted pieces with edges that taper and expand. When you increase stitches, you add them to your needle. When you decrease stitches, you get rid of stitches on your needle.

As with everything else in knitting, you find several ways to increase and decrease stitches. Some methods are almost invisible, and others are decorative and meant to be seen. And because increases and decreases are often worked as pairs (picture adding stitches at either end of your needle when you're shaping a sleeve), if one slants to the right on the right side of your work, the other slants to the left on the wrong side.

The following sections outline the ways to work increases into your work. Keep in mind that each method has a different appearance. So how do you know which one to use? If the increase is part of a fabric stitch pattern, the pattern almost always tells you how to make the increase. Other times, you have to decide for yourself. Having a few techniques up your sleeve gives you the flexibility to decide which increase will look best in your current project.

Various knitting patterns require that you knit a single increase, work a double increase, or distribute several increases along a given row. Try some of the fundamental techniques in this section to get a firm handle on your choices.

Bar increase, or knit in front and back

So-called because it leaves a telltale horizontal bar under the increased stitch, the *bar increase* is best for increases worked at the edge of your knitting, where it will be enclosed in a seam. Knitting directions for the bar increase read, "Knit 1 into the front and back of the stitch" or "k1f&b."

Check out a video demonstration of knitting a bar increase at dummies.com/go/knitcrochetAIO.

Here's how you make a bar increase, or k1f&b, when you're working on the knit side:

1. **Knit 1 stitch as you normally would, but don't slide the old stitch off the LH needle.**

2. **Bring the tip of the RH needle behind the LH needle and enter the back of the same stitch from right to left.**

   Refer to the earlier section "Twisting Stitches: Knitting through the Back Loop" for information about the front and back of a stitch.

3. **Knit the stitch as normal and slide it off the LH needle.**

   You've worked 2 stitches from a single stitch.

To make a bar increase, or p1f&b, when you're working on the purl side, follow these steps:

1. **Purl 1 stitch as you normally would, but don't slide the old stitch off the LH needle.**

2. **Keeping the RH needle behind the LH one, insert the tip of the RH needle through the back of the loop of the same stitch, entering it from left to right.**

3. **Purl that stitch again and slide it off the LH needle.**

   You've worked 2 stitches from a single stitch.

TIP

If you're using this bar increase several stitches in from the edge as part of a paired increase, adjust the position of the stitch in which you make the increase so that the bar shows up in the same place on each side.

Working a make 1

To work the *make 1* increase (abbreviated m1), you create a new, separate stitch between 2 stitches that are already on the needle. When you get to the point where you want to make an increase, pull the LH and RH needle slightly apart. You'll notice a horizontal strand of yarn, called the *running thread*, connecting the first stitch on each needle. You use the running thread to make the new stitch. The increased stitch will be a twisted stitch that crosses to the right or to the left and leaves no little hole. (Refer to the earlier section "Twisting Stitches: Knitting through the Back Loop" for details on how twisted stitches work.)

WARNING

The make 1 increase pulls the stitches on either side of the running thread tight and therefore isn't ideal for increasing multiple times within the same row.

TIP

After you make the increase, check to make sure that it's twisted in the direction you intended. If it isn't, undo your new stitch — it will only unravel as far as the running thread — and try it again.

Twisting to the right

When you're working on the knit side and want your make 1 increase to twist to the right, work to the point between 2 stitches where you want to increase. Then follow these steps:

1. **Bring the tip of the LH needle under the running thread from back to front.**

   The running thread will be draped over the LH needle as if it were a stitch (see Figure 3-8a).

2. **Insert the RH needle through the draped strand from left to right (see Figure 3-8b) and knit as normal.**

FIGURE 3-8:
Knitting a make 1 increase that twists to the right.

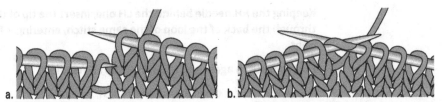

a.   b.

Illustration by Wiley, Composition Services Graphics

If you want to work a right-twisting make 1 increase on the purl side, follow the preceding steps, except change Step 2 by purling the strand by going into the front loop (the part that's closest to you) from right to left and purling as normal (see Figure 3-9).

FIGURE 3-9:
Purling a make 1 increase that twists to the right.

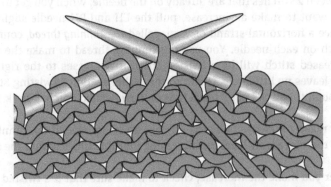

Illustration by Wiley, Composition Services Graphics

TIP

You can turn a make 1 into a decorative eyelet (a little hole) increase by knitting or purling into the running thread without twisting it.

Twisting to the left

If you're working on the knit side and want your make 1 increase to twist to the left, work to the point between 2 stitches where you want to increase. Then do the following:

1. **Insert the tip of the LH needle under the running thread from front to back (see Figure 3-10a).**

2. **With the RH needle, knit the strand through the back (see Figure 3-10b).**

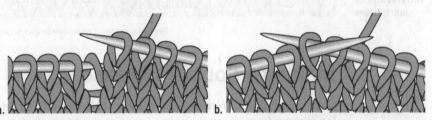

FIGURE 3-10:
Knitting a make 1 increase that twists to the left.

a.   b.

Illustration by Wiley, Composition Services Graphics

Follow the same steps when you want your make 1 increase to twist to the left from the purl side, except change Step 2 by inserting the RH needle through the back loop from left to right and purling as normal.

Knitting into the stitch below

Knitting into the stitch below is a technique often used for increasing stitches. If your instructions tell you to "knit (or purl) into the stitch below," often abbreviated k1b or k-b (or p1b or p-b for purling), follow these steps (adjust them to purl into the stitch below):

1. **Insert your needle into the stitch directly below the next stitch on the LH needle (see Figure 3-11); then wrap and knit as you normally would.**

   This step is the increase stitch.

2. **Knit the stitch on the LH needle.**

   You now have 2 stitches where 1 used to be. If you look at the purl side of your work, you'll see 2 purl bumps for the stitch you've made.

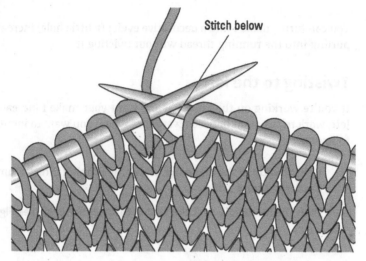

Stitch below

FIGURE 3-11:
The stitch you
knit in when
you knit into the
stitch below.

Illustration by Wiley, Composition Services Graphics

Making a double increase

Some occasions in knitting — in certain stitch patterns or when working a raglan sweater from the neck down — require you to increase 2 stitches in the same place. This task is called *working a double increase,* and it often uses an existing stitch as the increase point.

Doubling your increase with a yarn over

Doubling your increase with a yarn over results in 3 stitches being made from 1 stitch. To use this technique, work to the stitch in which you plan to make the increase and then follow these steps:

1. **Insert your RH needle as if to knit.**

2. **Wrap the yarn around the needle and bring the new loop through to the front, but don't slide the old stitch off the LH needle.**

3. **Bring the yarn between the needles to the front.**

4. **With the yarn in front and down, insert the RH needle as if to knit into the same stitch again.**

5. **Bring the yarn over the RH needle to the back.**

6. **Wrap the yarn around the tip of the RH needle as you normally would, pull the loop through, and slide the old loop off.**

   You'll see 3 stitches clustered together on your RH needle.

Doubling your increase with a make 1

Doubling your increase with a make 1 makes a new stitch on either side of an existing center stitch. Make the increase symmetrical by twisting the m1 increase before the center stitch to the right and twisting the m1 increase after the center stitch to the left. To create a double increase with a make 1, work to the stitch marked for the increase and then follow these steps:

1. **Work a m1 that twists to the right.**

As in the m1 increase presented earlier in this chapter, insert your LH needle under the running thread between the stitch just made and the stitch designated as the center stitch. Insert the RH needle from left to right through the lifted strand stitch, and knit as normal (refer to Figure 3-8).

2. **Knit the next (center) stitch as normal.**

3. **Work a m1 that twists to the left.**

With your LH needle, pick up the running thread between the knitted center stitch and the stitch that follows it; then knit the lifted strand through the back (refer to Figure 3-9).

TIP

For more ways to work a double increase, check out *Knitting from the Top* by Barbara Walker (Schoolhouse Press). She gives a whopping ten ways to make a double increase.

Increasing at several points in a single row

Patterns sometimes ask you to increase several stitches evenly across a row. It's up to you to figure out the best spacing. Here's how:

1. **Take the number of stitches to be added and add 1.**

This step gives you the number of spaces between increases.

2. **Divide the total number of stitches on your needle by the number of spaces between the increases.**

For example, if you have 40 stitches and you need to increase 4 stitches, you'll have five 8-stitch sections between the increases. If your pattern calls for you to work bar increases into existing stitches, make your increases in every 8th stitch across the row. When you're counting the stitches between increases, don't include the increased stitches.

If your numbers don't come out evenly and you have a remainder of several stitches, you can

>> Divvy up the extra stitches and knit them before the first increase and after the last increase.

>> Alternate, working an extra stitch into every other section of stitches between increases until you've used up the extras.

TIP

Graph paper is great to have on hand for charting out increases — and for all other manner of knitting math.

Doing Decreases

A *decrease* is a method for getting rid of a stitch on your needle. You use decreases for shaping at the edges and/or in the middle of a knitted piece. They're also used in conjunction with increases in various stitch patterns, most notably in lace.

A decreased stitch looks like 1 stitch overlapping another. Depending on the design you're working with, you can make your decreases slant to the left or right. When a stitch overlaps to the right, the decrease slants to the right. When a stitch overlaps to the left, the decrease slants to the left.

Knitting 2 stitches together

When you knit 2 stitches together (abbreviated k2tog), they become 1 stitch. The stitch on the left overlaps the one on the right, and the decrease slants to the right. If you're working decreases in pairs (on either side of a neckline you're shaping, for example), use the k2tog on one side and the ssk decrease (see the later section "Slip, slip, knit") on the other side.

You can find a video demonstration of knitting 2 stitches together at dummies.com/go/knitcrochetAIO.

Here's how to knit 2 stitches together on the right (knit) side of your knitted fabric:

1. **Insert the RH needle knitwise into the first 2 stitches on the LH needle at the same time.**

2. **Knit them together as if they were 1 stitch (see Figure 3-12).**

Illustration by Wiley, Composition Services Graphics

FIGURE 3-12:
Knitting 2 stitches together (k2tog).

Purling 2 stitches together

Although most knitting patterns have you decrease on right-side rows only, sometimes you may be asked to work a decrease from the purl side. When you do, you can purl 2 stitches together (abbreviated p2tog) instead of knitting them together. When you look at a p2tog decrease from the knit side, the stitches slant to the right, just as they do with a k2tog decrease.

When you need to work a single p2tog decrease on the wrong (purl) side of your knitting, follow these steps:

1. **Insert the RH needle purlwise into the next 2 stitches on the LH needle (see Figure 3-13a).**

2. **Purl the 2 stitches together as if they were 1 stitch (see Figures 3-13b and 3-13c).**

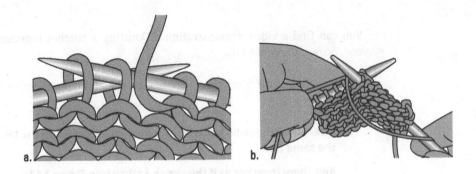

Illustration by Wiley, Composition Services Graphics

FIGURE 3-13:
Purling 2 stitches
together (p2tog).

Slip, slip, knit

Slip, slip, knit (abbreviated ssk) results in a left-slanting decrease. The ssk decrease is the mirror image of k2tog: It slants to the left. Use it when you want to work symmetrical decreases.

To work a ssk on the knit side, follow these steps:

1. **Slip the first stitch on the LH needle (as if to knit) to the RH needle without actually knitting it.**

2. **Do the same with the next stitch.**

   The 2 slipped stitches should look like the stitches in Figure 3-14a.

3. **Insert the LH needle into the front loops of these stitches (left to right), as in Figure 3-14b.**

4. **Wrap the yarn in the usual way around the RH needle and knit the 2 slipped stitches together.**

FIGURE 3-14:
Working a slip,
slip, knit (ssk)
decrease.

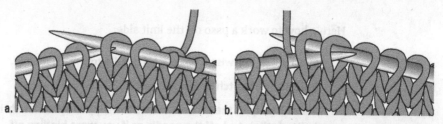

a.   b.

Illustration by Wiley, Composition Services Graphics

To complete this same decrease on the purl side — called a *slip, slip, purl* (ssp) — follow these steps:

1. **Slip the first stitch on the LH needle (as if to knit) to the RH needle.**

2. **Do the same to the next stitch.**

3. **Keeping the 2 slipped stitches facing in this direction, transfer them back to the LH needle.**

4. **Purl the 2 stitches together through the back loops (see Figure 3-15).**

FIGURE 3-15:
Purling 2 slipped
stitches through
the back of the
loops.

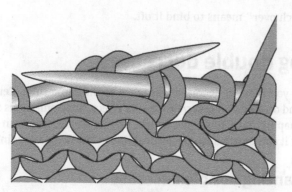

Illustration by Wiley, Composition Services Graphics

Pass slipped stitch over

Psso refers to *pass slipped stitch over*, a less attractive version of the left-slanting ssk decrease but one that's still used in certain stitch patterns and in double decreases (decreasing 2 stitches at once). Essentially, psso makes a bound-off stitch in the middle of a row. You can work it from the knit or purl side of your work.

Here's how to work a psso on the knit side:

1. **Slip 1 stitch knitwise from the LH needle to the RH needle.**

2. **Knit the next stitch on the LH needle.**

3. **Insert the tip of the LH needle into the slipped stitch and bring it over the knitted stitch and off the needle as if you were binding off.**

To work a psso on the purl side, do the following:

1. **Purl 1 stitch.**

2. **Slip the next stitch knitwise to the RH needle and return it in this changed direction to the LH needle.**

3. **Transfer the purled stitch (from Step 1) from the RH needle to the LH needle.**

4. **Insert the RH needle into the slipped stitch and bring it over the purled stitch and off the needle.**

REMEMBER

"Pass a stitch over" means to bind it off.

Making double decreases

Sometimes you need to decrease 2 stitches at the same time. Certain stitch patterns depend on this *double decrease* for its effect, and sometimes it's necessary in garment shaping. Like single decreases, the double decrease can slant to the left or right. Or it can create a single vertical line at the decrease point.

Right-slanting double decrease

To work a right-slanting double decrease on the knit side, follow these steps:

1. **Work a ssk.**

   Slip 2 stitches knitwise one at a time to the RH needle, insert the LH needle into the front of the loops, and knit them together. (Flip to the earlier section "Slip, slip, knit" for instructions on making a ssk decrease.)

2. **Slip the stitch you just worked back to the LH needle.**

3. Bring the second stitch on the LH needle over the decreased stitch and off the needle.

4. Return the decreased stitch to the RH needle.

To work a right-slanting double decrease on the purl side, do the following:

1. Slip the next stitch from the LH needle to the RH needle.

2. Purl the next 2 stitches together.

   Refer to the earlier section "Purling 2 stitches together" to find out how to do so.

3. Pass the slipped stitch over the decreased stitch.

Left-slanting double decrease

To work a left-slanting double decrease on the knit side, follow these steps:

1. Slip the next stitch on the LH needle as if to knit.

2. Knit the next 2 stitches together.

   Refer to the earlier section "Knitting 2 stitches together" to find the instructions for doing so.

3. Bring the slipped stitch over the decrease stitch as if you were binding off.

To work a left-slanting double decrease on the purl side, do the following:

1. Purl 2 stitches together.

   Flip back to the section "Purling 2 stitches together" to find out how to do so.

2. Slip this decreased stitch back to the LH needle.

3. With the RH needle, bring the second stitch on the LH needle over the decreased stitch and off the needle.

4. Return the decreased stitch to the RH needle.

Vertical double decrease

This double decrease creates a vertical line rather than a line that slants to the left or right. To make a vertical double decrease, follow these steps:

1. **Slip the first 2 stitches on the LH needle to the RH needle (as if to knit).**

2. **Knit the next stitch on the LH needle.**

3. **With the LH needle, bring both slipped stitches together over the knitted stitch and off the RH needle, as in Figure 3-16.**

FIGURE 3-16:
Bringing the 2 slipped stitches over in a vertical double decrease.

Illustration by Wiley, Composition Services Graphics

Chapter **4**

Knitting in the Round

K*nitting in the round*, in which you knit around and around on a circular needle to create a seamless tube, is deceptively simple, and many knitters of all skill levels prefer it to flat knitting. Why? The two most common reasons for beginners are that knitting proceeds faster because you don't have to turn your work and that you can create stockinette stitch — a common stitch in many beginner and intermediate patterns — without having to purl. More-advanced knitters, especially those who make garments (sweaters, socks, gloves, and so on), like knitting in the round because it cuts down on garment assembly. For these (and a variety of other) reasons, circular knitting is popular, and many books for beginning knitters include knit-in-the-round patterns.

This chapter explains everything you need to know to successfully knit in the round.

Going in Circles Can Be a Good Thing

When you knit in the round (often called *circular knitting*), you work on a circular needle or double-pointed needles (dpns) to knit a seamless tube. Years ago, circular knitting was a technique associated with more-experienced knitters.

These days, many popular patterns for beginners are written in the round. Many knitters — beginner and advanced — prefer knitting in the round because of its benefits, which include the following:

>> **The right side always faces you.** If you're averse to purling for some reason, knitting in the round allows you to skip it entirely — as long as you stick to stockinette stitch. Having the right side face you also makes working repeating color patterns easier because your pattern is always front and center; you're never looking at the back and having to flip to the front to double-check what color the next stitch should be.

>> **Although circular knitting is great for sweater bodies, sleeves, hats, socks, and mittens, you're not limited to creating tubes.** By using something called a *steek* — a means of opening the tube of knitted fabric with a line of crocheted or machine-sewn stitches — you also can create a flat piece after the fact. And that's good for such things as cardigans. (We cover steek techniques later in the chapter.)

>> **You can reduce the amount of sewing required for garments.** When you knit back and forth, you make flat pieces that have to be sewn together. Circular knitting eliminates many of these seams. In fact, some patterns let you make an entire sweater from bottom to top (or top to bottom) without having a single seam to sew up when the last stitch has been bound off.

Choosing Needles for Circular Knitting

Circular and double-pointed needles are designed for knitting in the round and (as Book 1, Chapter 1 explains) come in the same sizes as regular knitting needles. When you select circular or double-pointed needles for your projects, keep these things in mind:

>> **Circular needle:** The needle length you choose for your project must be a smaller circumference than the tube you plan to knit; otherwise, you won't be able to comfortably stretch your stitches around the needle. For example, to knit a hat that measures 21 inches around, you need a 16-inch needle because 21 inches worth of stitches won't stretch around 24 inches of needle (which is the next size up from a 16-inch needle).

We know it sounds counterintuitive to need a needle smaller in circumference than the knitted project, but the problem is that because there's no break — no first stitch or last stitch (after all, you're knitting a tube) — you can stretch the fabric only as far as you can stretch any two stitches. A 21-inch circular project won't knit comfortably on a 24-inch circular needle because you can't easily stretch 2 stitches 3 inches apart.

TIP

When you first take a circular needle from its package, it will be tightly coiled. Run the coil under hot water or immerse it in a sink of hot water for a few moments to relax the kinks. You can even hang it around the back of your neck while you get your yarn ready; your body heat will help unkink the needle.

>> **Double-pointed needles:** Lengths vary from 5 to 10 inches. The shorter ones are great for socks and mittens, and the longer ones work well for hats and sleeves. Aim for 1 inch or so of empty needle at each end. If you leave more than 1 inch, you'll spend too much time sliding stitches down to the tip so that you can knit them; if you leave less than 1 inch, you'll lose stitches off the ends.

TIP

If you've never used double-pointed needles before, choose square, wooden, or bamboo ones. Their slight grip on the stitches will keep the ones on the waiting needles from sliding off into oblivion when you're not looking. Note that with square needles especially, gauge is important because you may end up knitting bigger on square needles versus rounded ones.

Casting On for Circular Knitting

To knit on a circular needle, cast your stitches directly onto the needle as you would on a straight needle. (For a refresher on how to cast on, see Book 2, Chapter 1.) Here's the important bit: Before you start to knit, make sure that the cast on edge isn't twisted around the needle; if you have stitches that spiral around the needle, you'll feel like a cat chasing its tail when it comes time to find the bottom edge. The yarn end should be coming from the RH needle tip, as shown in Figure 4-1.

TIP

Casting on and getting started on a set of double-pointed needles can be a little trickier than using single-pointed needles. Instead of trying to cast all your stitches onto one small needle (which increases the likelihood that some will slip off the other end) or several separate needles (which leaves needles dangling and extra yarn at each needle change), cast the total number of stitches needed onto a single-pointed straight needle of the correct size. Then work the first round of the pattern onto your double-pointed needles, distributing them in equal or close-to-equal amounts and making sure that the stitches aren't twisted around any of the needles. Leave one of the needles free to start knitting.

Knitting in the Round

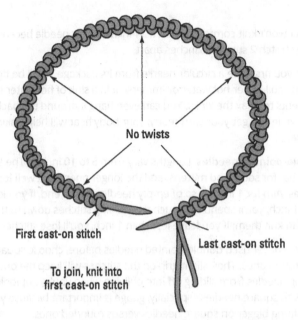

No twists

First cast-on stitch

Last cast-on stitch

FIGURE 4-1:
Ready to knit on a circular needle.

To join, knit into first cast-on stitch

Illustration by Wiley, Composition Services Graphics

If you're using a set of four double-pointed needles, use three needles for your stitches: Form them into a triangle (see Figure 4-2a) with the yarn end at the bottom point. Save the fourth (empty) needle for knitting. If you're using a set of five needles, put your stitches on four needles, as in Figure 4-2b, and knit with the fifth (empty) needle.

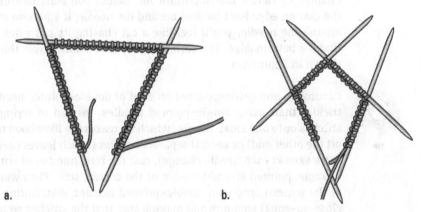

FIGURE 4-2:
Dividing stitches among three (a) and four (b) double-pointed needles.

a.

b.

Illustration by Wiley, Composition Services Graphics

TIP

Trying to focus on one of your double-pointed needles while the others are flopping around is pretty frustrating. If you lay your work on a table while transferring your cast on stitches and arranging your needles, you can keep things steady *and* pay attention to what you're doing at the same time.

Joining the Round

After you cast on your in-the-round knitting, pattern instructions tell you to join and begin knitting. *Joining* simply means that when you work the first stitch, you bring the first and last cast on stitches together, joining the circle of stitches.

The following sections walk you through joining on both circular and double-pointed needles and provide tips on creating a cleaner join. You can also visit dummies.com/go/knitcrochetAIO to watch a video demonstration of knitting in the round with common stitches.

Joining on a circular needle

To work the first stitch of the round on a circular needle, follow these steps:

1. **Place a marker on the RH needle before making the first stitch if you want to keep track of the beginning of the round.**

   Many in-the-round patterns tell you to place a marker to indicate the beginning of a round. When you're doing color work or any sort of repeating pattern, knowing where one round ends and another begins is vital. And if you have to place other markers later (common with pieces that require shaping), do something to differentiate your "beginning" marker from the others. Make it a different color from the other markers you use or attach a piece of yarn or a safety pin to it.

2. **Insert the tip of the RH needle into the first stitch on the LH needle (the first cast on stitch) and knit or purl as usual.**

   Figure 4-3 shows the first stitch being made with a marker in place.

Joining on double-pointed needles

For double-pointed needles, use the empty needle to begin working the first round. If the first stitch is a knit stitch, make sure that the yarn is in back of your work. If the first stitch is a purl stitch, bring the yarn to the front between the needles; bring the empty needle *under* the yarn and insert it to purl into the first stitch on the LH needle. After the first couple of stitches, arrange the back ends of the two working needles on top of the other needles. (Do you feel like you have a spider by one leg?) The first round or two may feel awkward, but as your piece begins to grow, the weight of your knitting will keep the needles nicely in place and you'll cruise along.

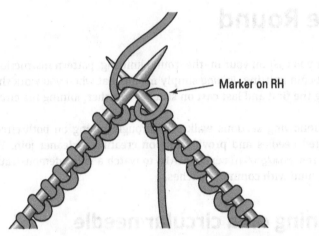

Marker on RH

FIGURE 4-3:
The first stitch in a round.

Illustration by Wiley, Composition Services Graphics

TIP

When you knit on double-pointed needles, the stitches worked where the needles meet may be looser than the rest. To keep them neat, give an extra tug on the yarn as you work the first stitch on each needle and remember to tug again after you insert the needle into the second stitch. Or when you come to the end of a needle, knit the first stitch or two from the next one before switching to the empty needle.

Tidying up the first and last stitches

Whether you're working on a circular needle or double-pointed needles, the first and last cast on stitches rarely make a neat join. To tighten up the connection, you can do one of the following:

» Cast on an extra stitch at the end, transfer it to the LH needle, and make your first stitch a k2tog, working the increased stitch with the first stitch on the LH needle ("k2tog" stands for "knit 2 stitches together," a decrease technique you can read about in Book 2, Chapter 3).

» Before working the first stitch, wrap the yarn around the first and last cast on stitches as follows:

1. Transfer the first stitch on the LH needle to the RH needle.

2. Take the ball yarn from front to back between the needles and transfer the first 2 stitches on the RH needle to the LH needle.

3. Bring the yarn forward between the needles and transfer the first stitch on the LH needle back to the RH needle.

4. Take the yarn to the back between the stitches and give a little tug on the yarn.

You're ready to knit the first stitch.

Working Common Stitches in the Round

As mentioned earlier in the chapter, when knitting in the round, the right side is always facing you — which is a good thing as long as you understand how it affects the stitches you make. For example, in flat knitting, you create a garter stitch by knitting every row, but knitting every round in circular knitting produces stockinette stitch. So here's a quick guide to getting the stitches you want:

>> **For garter stitch:** Alternate a knit round with a purl round.

>> **For stockinette stitch:** Knit all rounds.

>> **For rib stitches:** In round 1, alternate knit and purl stitches in whatever configuration you choose (1 x 1, 2 x 2, and so on). In subsequent rounds, knit over the knit stitches and purl over the purl stitches.

The trick is simply knowing how the stitch is created in flat knitting and then remembering the principle. For example, in seed stitch, you knit in the purl stitches and purl in the knit stitches. Well, you do the same in circular knitting. (Book 2, Chapter 2 has details on these flat knitting stitches.)

REMEMBER

Rounds (rnds) are what you work in circular knitting. *Rows* are what you work in flat (back-and-forth) knitting.

Using Steeks for a Clean Break

Steeks are an excellent way to open up a knitted tube. Traditionally, Nordic-style ski sweaters were knit in the round and then steeked to open the cardigan front and sleeve openings. You can use steeks for this type of project or anywhere else you want to cut open a line of knit stitches.

You can steek with a sewing machine or a crochet hook, depending on your comfort level with either and on whether you have access to a machine. Crocheted steeks are generally simpler to work with for beginners because they're easy to tear out if you make a mistake.

Sewing in a steek

To make a steek with a sewing machine, sew two vertical lines of stitches an inch or so apart (or for added security, sew four lines, as shown in Figure 4-4). Be sure to keep the line of machine stitching between the same two columns of knit stitches all the way down. Use a sturdy cotton/poly blend thread and a stitch length appropriate to the knitted stitches (shorter for finer-gauge knits, slightly longer for chunkier knits).

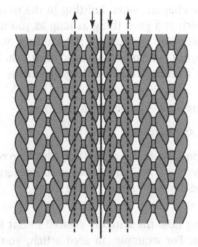

FIGURE 4-4: Sew two to four vertical lines.

Illustration by Wiley, Composition Services Graphics

Crocheting a steek

To make a steek with yarn, crochet two vertical columns of stitches an inch or more apart by using a slip stitch (see Figure 4-5). Fold the sweater at the line you plan to stitch so the vertical column of stitches looks like the top of a crochet chain; then insert your hook into the first V, yarn over the hook, pull the new loop through the V, and move to the next stitch on your left, repeating as you go. (You can read about yarn overs in Book 2, Chapter 3.) Be sure to work all your crocheted stitches on the same column of knit stitches; if you veer to the left or right, your steek will be crooked.

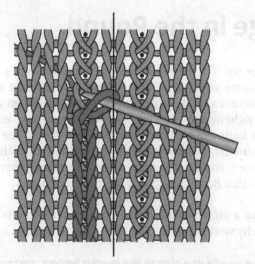

Illustration by Wiley, Composition Services Graphics

Cutting your fabric after you steek

After you've sewn or crocheted the steek in place, you can safely cut your knitted fabric between the two lines of stitching, as shown in Figure 4-6. Then you can continue with your pattern as directed.

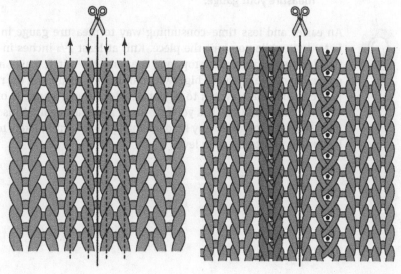

Illustration by Wiley, Composition Services Graphics

Measuring Gauge in the Round

Knitting stockinette stitch in the round can give you a different gauge than if you were knitting the same stitch flat (back and forth on straight needles). Here's why: A purl stitch is very slightly larger than a knit stitch. When you work stockinette stitch on straight needles, every other row is a purl row, and the difference in the sizes of your knits and purls averages out. However, when working stockinette stitch in the round, you always make knit stitches, which can result in a slightly smaller piece even though you're knitting the same pattern over the same number of stitches. (See Book 1, Chapter 3 for more on gauge.)

When the gauge for a project worked on a circular needle must be exact, make your gauge swatch by working all the rows from the right side as follows:

1. **Using the same needle you plan to use in your project, cast on 24 stitches or so and work 1 row.**

   Don't turn the work.

2. **Cut the yarn and slide your knitting, with the right side facing, back to the knitting end of the needle.**

3. **Knit another row and cut the yarn.**

4. **Repeat Steps 2 and 3 until you've completed your swatch and then measure your gauge.**

TIP

An easier and less time-consuming way to measure gauge in circular patterns is to do it while you knit the piece. Knit at least 1½ inches in the round on the needles you plan to use, stop, and measure the stitch gauge and 1-inch of row gauge. If your gauge is too big, switch to smaller needles on the next round; if your gauge is too small, switch to bigger needles. If your gauge is off by more than a stitch, tear out the stitches you just made and start again. This method is generally accurate enough for any kind of small project you're likely to encounter at the beginning or intermediate level.

Chapter 5

Fixing Common Mistakes

As a beginning knitter, you may not notice the mistakes in your project, and that's understandable. After all, you're trying to figure out what to do with your hands, the needles, and the yarn, which is quite enough to worry about, thank you very much! After you have the hang of knitting, however, you'll start to notice things — such as unusual bumps, unraveling stitches, and strange twists — that don't look quite right.

Take heart — all knitters at all skill levels make mistakes. The trick is to do what you can to reduce the number of mistakes you make, recognize them quickly when you do err, and fix them as soon as you recognize them. This chapter explains how to do all those things.

Stopping Mistakes or Catching Them Early

Some mistakes are minor, such as a dropped or added stitch that you can easily fix (or easily hide). Others are the whoppers of the knitting set — obvious errors that can ruin a project. Because you can't avoid mistakes entirely, your goal should be to make as few mistakes as possible and, when you do flub up, to catch 'em early. Here are suggestions for achieving this goal:

» **Read the instructions completely and make sure you understand them.**
As you read through the pattern instructions row by row, try picturing what's

happening. If you're reading a chart, talk yourself through the stitches: "I cast on 98, knit 1, purl 1 for the first 4 rows. Then in the fifth row, I work in stockinette stitch until. . .." Running through the project in your head before your hands get involved is especially important when you're working complicated patterns or garments that include shaping instructions.

>> **Practice any stitches, stitch patterns, or techniques that may trip you up.** Sometimes you can figure out what's going on simply by visualizing the steps. But when you can't picture what's going on — no matter how many times you read the instructions — take a little time to practice with real needles and yarn.

TIP

Checking gauge (covered in Book 1, Chapter 3) automatically gives you the opportunity to run through the stitch pattern. If you're one who throws caution to the wind and doesn't check gauge, practice by working up a little swatch with the stitches.

>> **Look at your work.** Although this advice seems obvious, too many knitters get so into the rhythm of actually knitting that they forget to look at their work. Looking helps you recognize how a particular combination of stitches creates the pattern growing before your eyes. When you recognize that, you're much more aware and able to keep track of the stitches as you work them. Checking your work also helps you identify mistakes early. If something is going wrong with the pattern — perhaps the rib is offset or you don't have as many stitches at the end of the row as the pattern says you should — you can address the problem before it gets worse.

>> **Beginners: Count your stitches after each row.** One stitch more or less than you cast on frequently indicates a mistake in the last row you worked. Don't panic! You don't have to count your stitches forever. Soon your fingers will alert you to a missed move, and you'll be catching mistakes before they become a nuisance to correct.

Dealing with Dropped Stitches

Dropped stitches are stitches that, for one reason or another, fall off the needle and don't get worked. Dropping stitches is pretty common for both beginning and experienced knitters. Sometimes you're lucky enough to recognize the dropped stitch right away; other times you don't notice it until much later. Either way, you need to fix the error because dropped stitches don't look good, and they unravel when the piece is pulled or stretched, leaving an unsightly ladder of yarn up your work. Think of a run in pantyhose — that's exactly what a dropped stitch resembles.

At dummies.com/go/knitcrochetAIO, you can find a video demonstration of how to spot and fix dropped stitches in your knitting.

REMEMBER Some yarns, especially *plied* (multistrand) ones, are prone to splitting. When you're fixing mistakes (or just knitting in general), take care not to let your needle separate the plies. You want to go in and out of the *holes* in the stitches, leaving the yarn strand intact.

Finding and securing a dropped stitch

When you suspect that you've dropped a stitch, the first thing to do is find it and secure it so that it doesn't unravel any more than it already has. Contrary to knitting lore, a dropped stitch doesn't immediately unravel itself into oblivion — thank goodness! — but you do need to deal with it immediately.

To find a dropped stitch, carefully spread out your stitches along the needle and slowly scan the row(s) below. The telltale sign of a dropped stitch is a horizontal strand of yarn that isn't pulled through a loop. Here's how it may look:

>> **If the dropped stitch hasn't unraveled far, or if you just recently dropped it:** It should look like the one in Figure 5-1. Note the horizontal yarn that didn't get pulled through.

>> **If the dropped stitch has worked itself down several rows, or if you didn't notice its absence immediately:** It should appear as a wayward stitch at the bottom of a ladder of unworked strands (see Figure 5-2). Each strand represents a row.

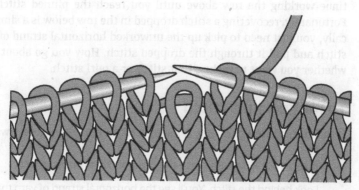

FIGURE 5-1:
A dropped stitch viewed from the knit side.

Illustration by Wiley, Composition Services Graphics

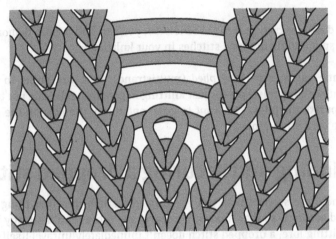

FIGURE 5-2:
A dropped knit
stitch and ladder.

Illustration by Wiley, Composition Services Graphics

When you find the dropped stitch, you need to secure it so that it doesn't unravel any more. To do so, carefully work a small needle tip, the blunt point of a tapestry needle, a toothpick, a nail, a bobby pin, or anything into it to secure it and stretch it out a bit. Then use a safety pin (you should have some with your knitting supplies) to secure the stitch.

Now take a deep breath and follow the instructions in the following sections for getting that dropped stitch back on the needle.

Rescuing a dropped stitch in the row below

After you pin the dropped stitch to secure it (refer to the preceding section), continue working the row above until you reach the pinned stitch directly below. Fortunately, recovering a stitch dropped in the row below is a simple matter. Basically, you just need to pick up the unworked horizontal strand of yarn behind the stitch and pull it through the dropped stitch. How you go about that depends on whether you want to make a knit stitch or a purl stitch.

To make a knit stitch

If the knit side of your work is facing, rescue the stitch as follows:

1. **Insert your RH needle into the *front* of the dropped stitch.**

   Look behind the stitch. You'll see the horizontal strand of yarn that didn't get pulled through. The strand is behind the stitch just like the yarn when you knit a stitch.

2. **With the RH needle, go under the lowest unworked strand from the front (see Figure 5-3). Both the strand and the stitch are on the RH needle.**

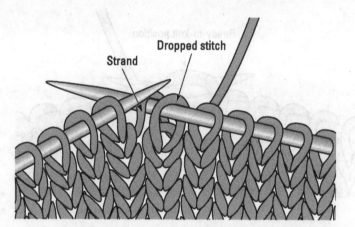

Strand **Dropped stitch**

FIGURE 5-3:
A dropped knit
stitch ready to
be worked.

Illustration by Wiley, Composition Services Graphics

3. **Insert the LH needle into the stitch from the back (see Figure 5-4) and pull
it over the strand.**

    You've just "worked" the stitch that was dropped in the last row. Now you need
    to knit the stitch in the current row, as the next step describes.

    If a stitch has dropped more than 1 row, repeat Steps 2 and 3 until all horizon-
    tal strands have been picked up and knit.

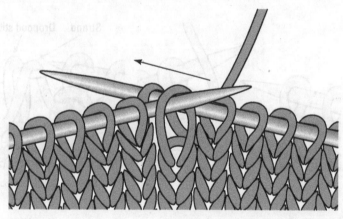

FIGURE 5-4:
Insert the LH
needle into the
dropped stitch.

Illustration by Wiley, Composition Services Graphics

4. **Put the new stitch on the LH needle in the ready-to-knit position
(see Figure 5-5) and knit as normal.**

    Check to see that you've made a smooth knitted V stitch.

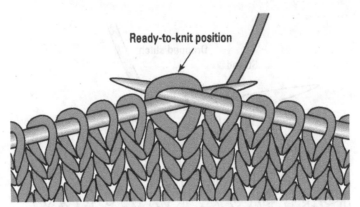

Ready-to-knit position

Illustration by Wiley, Composition Services Graphics

FIGURE 5-5:
Transfer the stitch to the ready-to-knit position.

To make a purl stitch

If the purl side is facing, or if you're working in garter stitch, rescue the dropped stitch as follows:

1. **Insert the RH needle into the dropped stitch *and* the yarn strand from the back, as in Figure 5-6.**

   If you can't readily pick up a dropped stitch from the back or front, pick it up any way you can and put it on the RH needle.

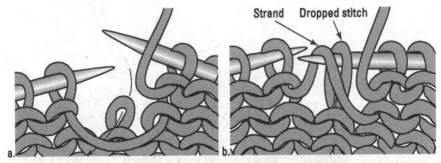

Strand   Dropped stitch

a.   b.

Illustration by Wiley, Composition Services Graphics

FIGURE 5-6:
Pick up a dropped purl stitch.

2. **Using the LH needle, pull the stitch over the strand and off the needle, forming a new stitch on the RH needle (see Figure 5-7).**

3. **Place the new stitch on the LH needle in the ready-to-work position (see Figure 5-8) and purl (or knit, for a garter stitch) as normal.**

Check to see that you have a bump below the stitch.

FIGURE 5-7:
Pull the dropped
stitch over.

Illustration by Wiley, Composition Services Graphics

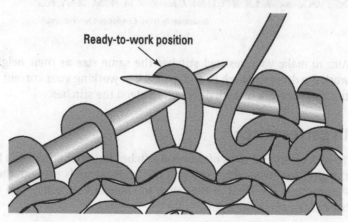

Ready-to-work position

FIGURE 5-8:
Replace the
rescued stitch in
the ready-to-work
position.

Illustration by Wiley, Composition Services Graphics

Saving a dropped stitch with a crochet hook

A crochet hook is more than just a tool for crocheters. Knitters find it handy for fixing dropped stitches as well. A crochet hook makes recovering a dropped stitch pretty easy. You just need to know whether to draw the unworked strand through the dropped stitch from the front or the back — and that depends on whether you're working with a stockinette stitch or a garter stitch.

In stockinette stitch

To rescue a dropped stitch from the knit side of stockinette stitch (if the purl side is facing, turn it around), reach through the dropped stitch with a crochet hook and pick up the bottommost strand in the ladder (see Figure 5-9). Then pull the strand through the stitch toward you to form a new stitch. Repeat this maneuver to pull each successive strand in the ladder through the loop until the last strand has been worked.

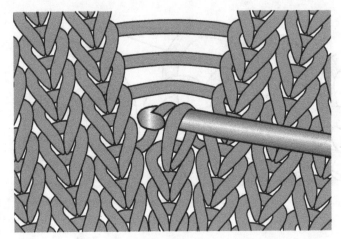

FIGURE 5-9:
Pull through the
first strand.

Illustration by Wiley, Composition Services Graphics

TIP

Aim to make your rescued stitches the same size as their neighbors. After you work the dropped stitch in and get back to working your current row, give a little tug on your work in each direction to blend the stitches.

In garter stitch

To pick up several rows of dropped stitches in garter stitch, you have to alternate the direction from which you pull the ladder strands through the dropped stitch. Pull through the front of the stitch to create a knit stitch, and pull through the back of the stitch for a purl.

To determine whether you pull through the front or back of the stitch, follow the bottom strand to the side (either way) to see what the stitch connected to it looks like. A stitch that looks like a V is a knit stitch; one that looks like a bump is a purl stitch. (Pull gently on the strand to locate the neighboring stitches if you need to.) You can see the connected stitches in Figure 5-10.

When you know whether the first stitch to be rescued is a knit or purl stitch, the fix is a cinch.

1. **Fix the first stitch.**

   If it's a knit stitch (it looks like a V), pick up the dropped stitch from the front. Refer to the preceding section and Figure 5-9 for detailed instructions. If it's a purl stitch, pick it up from the back, as shown in Figure 5-11.

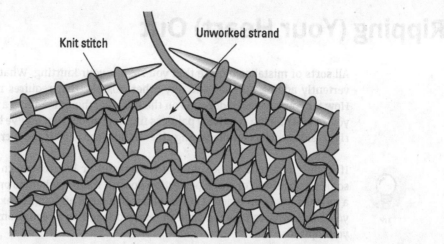

Knit stitch   Unworked strand

FIGURE 5-10: Knit stitches connected to the strand.

Illustration by Wiley, Composition Services Graphics

2. **Alternate pulling stitches from each direction until you've pulled through the last strand.**

   If you fixed the first stitch by pulling the strand through the front, fix the next stitch by pulling the strand through the back, and so on.

3. **Put the last loop onto the LH needle in the ready-to-work position and work it as normal.**

WARNING

If you pull a loop through from a strand in the wrong row, you'll have a major — and unsightly — glitch in your work. So pick up the strands of yarn in the proper order, and check to make sure that the stitch you've made matches the ones next to it.

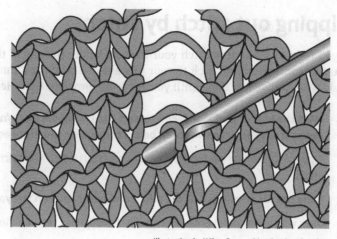

FIGURE 5-11: Pick up a dropped purl stitch from the back.

Illustration by Wiley, Composition Services Graphics

Ripping (Your Heart) Out

All sorts of mistakes require that you rip out your knitting. What are they? Inadvertently adding stitches and any other mistake that requires reknitting to fix. How far you have to go depends on the mistake, though. Adding a stitch in the row you're knitting is a relatively painless fix; finding out that you've been knitting the right-side stitches on the wrong side of the piece is a bit more cringe-inducing.

TIP

If ripping out your work sounds too stressful or like too much work, you have some alternatives for when perfection doesn't matter, when no one will know that a mistake has been made (1 added stitch in a large afghan, for example), or when you don't want to take the time to redo work you've already completed. Here are your options:

>> **Don't do anything.** If you can happily live with imperfections and the mistake doesn't bother you, let it go and keep knitting.

>> **When the mistake is a simple added stitch (or two), decrease the same number of stitches in the row you're currently working.** Use one of the decreasing techniques in Book 2, Chapter 3. This approach is a good alternative when having the extra stitch messes up the pattern and working around it in each row is a hassle.

If the thought of ripping out your knitting is making you a little sick to your stomach, take a minute to laugh at knitting shorthand that online knitters use to refer to ripping out their work: "frog" or "frogging" and "tink." *Tink* is "knit" spelled backwards, indicating you're doing the reverse. Why *frogging*? Because you need to rip it, rip it.

Ripping out stitch by stitch

If you're lucky enough to catch your mistake before the end of the row in which you made it, you can rip back to your mistake one stitch at a time. Basically, you undo what you've just done until you get to the problem spot. Here's how:

1. **With the knit or purl side facing, insert the LH needle from *front to back* (away from you) into the stitch below the one on the RH needle.**

   Figure 5-12 shows how this step looks when you undo a knit stitch or a purl stitch.

2. **Slide the RH needle out of the stitch and gently pull on the yarn to free it.**

   Your work won't unravel because your LH needle has secured the stitch below.

3. **Repeat Steps 1 and 2, stitch by stitch, to the point of your mistake.**

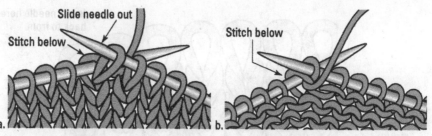

FIGURE 5-12:
Unforming a knit
stitch (a) and a
purl stitch (b).

Illustration by Wiley, Composition Services Graphics

Ripping out row by row

What's the worst-case scenario? You notice a mistake several rows down in your work — a bump or glitch that you can't easily rescue by backing up a few stitches. In such a situation, ripping back one stitch at a time may take longer than simply taking the piece off the needles, undoing your work as far back as necessary, and then starting over. It's a pain. It's no fun. And you'll mourn the time (and possibly inches of finished work) you lose, but sometimes ripping everything out is necessary. When it is, take a deep breath and follow these steps:

1. **Locate the row your mistake is on and mark it with a safety pin.**

   TIP

   You don't want to rip back any farther than absolutely necessary. If you're working with an exceptionally thin yarn, you may want to thread a so-called *safety line* of yarn through the stitches on the last good row of knitting (the last row without a mistake). Using a tapestry needle and a different, smooth yarn, thread the yarn through the center of each stitch. When you pull out the stitches above, the safety line will keep you from going too far.

2. **Slide your needle out of the stitches.**

   This point is where you probably want to take a few deep, steadying breaths.

3. **Pull gently on the working yarn, undoing the stitches; when you reach the row above the mistake (which you've marked with a safety pin), slowly rip to the end of the row.**

4. **Place your knitting so that the working yarn is on the right (flip the fabric over if you have to).**

5. **Insert the tip of the needle into the first stitch on the row below (from back to front, toward you; see Figure 5-13), and gently pull to free the yarn from the stitch.**

   You should have 1 stitch solidly planted on the RH needle.

   TIP

   Using a needle several sizes smaller to pick up the last row of your ripped-out knitting makes it easier to snag the stitches. Then, when it's time to begin knitting again, work the next row with your regular needle.

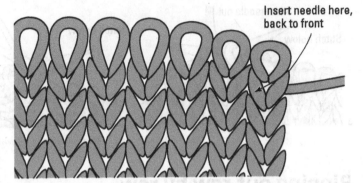

Insert needle here, back to front

FIGURE 5-13:
Insert the needle into the stitch below.

Illustration by Wiley, Composition Services Graphics

6. **Repeat Step 5 until you reach your mistake.**

   Figure 5-14 shows what it looks like as you work across the row to your mistake.

7. **Rip out your mistake, turn your work, and start knitting again!**

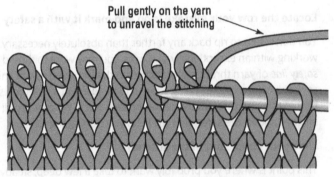

Pull gently on the yarn to unravel the stitching

FIGURE 5-14:
Put stitches on your RH needle as you work toward your mistake.

Illustration by Wiley, Composition Services Graphics

3

Crocheting Basics

Contents at a Glance

IN THIS CHAPTER

» **Getting a grip on crochet preparation**

» **Keeping you in (three) stitches and deciphering the parts of a complete stitch**

» **Creating the foundation and turning your work around**

» **Fastening off your yarn**

» **Fixing mistakes**

» **Pampering yourself with soft, luxurious washcloths**

Chapter **1**

Focusing on Fundamental Stitches

When you think about it, crochet is nothing more than a series of loops made with a hook and some yarn, worked row on row or round after round. Piece o' cake! This chapter takes you through the basics of getting your loops right: from picking up your hook and holding your yarn to completing your first rows of stitches. It also includes diagrams and instructions for both lefties and righties.

Preparing to Crochet

Before you even attempt your first stitch, you need to get some basic skills under your belt. The following sections explain which hand you should crochet with and show you how to hold the hook and yarn and how to get the yarn on the hook with slipknots and yarn overs.

Hooking with the correct hand

The correct hand for holding your crochet hook isn't necessarily the one on your right side. Your *dominant hand* — the one you write with, eat with, and do just about everything else with — is the hand you should hold your hook in. This is the hand that does most of the action; your other hand guides the yarn and holds the work you've already completed.

REMEMBER

Most of this book deals with techniques from a right-hander's point of view, but it applies to you lefties as well. Don't get discouraged. Your motions are exactly the same. If the instruction says *right*, think *left*; if it says *left*, think *right*. To make sure you get off on the right foot (or perhaps the left foot?), however, the beginning crochet techniques in this chapter include diagrams for both hands. See the nearby sidebar "For southpaws only" for additional techniques.

Getting a grip on the hook and yarn

Even though you crochet with only one hook, both hands are busy the whole time. Your dominant hand holds the hook, and your other hand holds the yarn, as explained in the next sections.

Holding the hook

Holding your crochet hook is pretty simple. You just need to get the correct grip on it. If your hand isn't comfortable, it can cramp up, resulting in uneven stitches. Crocheting should be relaxing, not a continuous fight with the hook and yarn. Experiment with the two following positions to see which one feels more comfortable for you. Both are common ways of holding the crochet hook that work just fine — for lefties *or* righties:

>> **Over-the-hook position:** Place your dominant hand over the hook with the handle resting against your palm and your thumb and middle finger grasping the thumb rest (see Figure 1-1).

>> **Under-the-hook position:** Hold the hook as you would a pencil with the thumb rest between your forefinger and thumb (see Figure 1-2).

Holding the yarn

After you decide how you want to hold the hook, you're ready for the yarn. Your *yarn hand* — the hand not holding your hook — has an important job: Not only does it feed the yarn to your crochet hook, but it also controls the tension of the yarn.

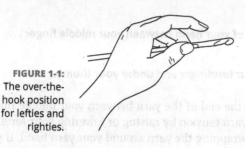

FIGURE 1-1:
The over-the-hook position for lefties and righties.

FIGURE 1-2:
The under-the-hook position for lefties and righties.

REMEMBER

Right-handed crocheters wrap the yarn over their left hand; left-handed crocheters wrap the yarn over their right hand. Figure 1-3 shows you what yarn wrapped around your hand should look like. (It may look like it, but your fingers really don't have to be contortionists to get into position.)

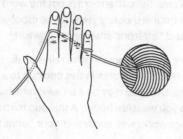
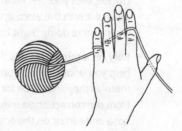

FIGURE 1-3:
Wrapping the yarn over your yarn hand.

The following steps offer one common method for wrapping the yarn around your hand:

1. **Starting from underneath your hand, bring the yarn up between your little finger and ring finger.**

2. **Wrap the yarn around your little finger to form a loop.**

3. **Draw the yarn under your ring finger and middle finger.**

4. **Bring the yarn up to the top of your hand between your middle finger and forefinger.**

5. **Finally, lay the yarn over your forefinger and under your thumb.**

To keep the yarn in place, grasp the end of the yarn between your middle finger and thumb. You can control the yarn tension by raising or lowering your forefinger, so practice wrapping and rewrapping the yarn around your yarn hand. If you ever feel that your working yarn is too loose or too tight, stop and rewrap to get the proper tension. (Don't worry. This motion soon becomes an ingrained habit.)

Note: Other methods of wrapping the yarn around your hand exist. If you prefer, you can just wrap the yarn around your forefinger twice, or you can weave the yarn through all your fingers except your little finger. Regardless of the method you choose, the goal should be to allow the yarn to flow smoothly and evenly through your fingers so you can apply just the right amount of tension.

FOR SOUTHPAWS ONLY

If thinking left rather than right just isn't concrete enough for you, use the following tips to help you work your way through a crochet pattern from the opposite perspective:

- **Replace the word *right* with *left* in pattern instructions.** If you're planning to crochet with your left hand, look over the pattern, cross out the word *right,* and replace it with the word *left.* This troubleshooting step can be especially helpful when you're doing "right front" and "left front" shaping on a sweater.

- **Rely on a mirror image.** If you're a picture person who relies on illustrations to help you understand a concept, hold the pictures in this book up to a mirror to view them as they should be for lefties. Doing so may be a bit awkward, but a quick view from the correct angle may help you visualize better. A makeup mirror that has a base and can sit on the open page works well and leaves your hands free to follow the image in the mirror.

- **Trace your way to success.** If you want a more permanent illustration, or if the mirror trick just doesn't cut it for you, trace the diagrams and illustrations on a piece of tracing paper and then flip the paper over. Doing so gives you the view from the left-hand side. (Want a more high-tech approach? If you have a scanner and a photo software application on your computer, scan the diagrams and illustrations and flip them horizontally.)

- **Try to crochet the right-handed way.** If you're brand-new to the craft and somewhat ambidextrous, you can try crocheting right-handed. You may be surprised that your hands do just what you tell them, thereby avoiding the extra work of having to translate the instructions.

TIP

When you first start working with yarn, use a light, solid-color, worsted-weight yarn (see Book 1, Chapter 2 for the basics on yarn). This type of yarn allows you to see your stitches more clearly and manipulate the yarn more easily. Textured or variegated yarn takes a little more babying.

REMEMBER

From this point on, the diagrams in this chapter aren't marked "lefty" or "righty." But here's a clue: The left diagrams in the figures are for lefties, and the right diagrams are for righties.

Working a slipknot

To get started on any crocheted piece, you first have to *join*, or attach, the yarn to the hook with a slipknot. The standard slipknot is really simple. Just follow these steps:

1. Beginning about 6 inches from the end of the yarn, make a loop that looks somewhat like a pretzel.

Refer to the pretzel-shaped loop on the hook in Figure 1-4.

2. Insert your hook through the center of the loop.

Refer to the shaded section of the pretzel-shaped loop in Figure 1-5.

3. Pull gently on both ends of the yarn to tighten the loop around the hook (see Figure 1-6).

Pulling on the tail end alone tightens the knot below the hook, and pulling on the working end adjusts the loop around the hook.

FIGURE 1-4:
Making the
pretzel-shaped
loop to begin the
slipknot.

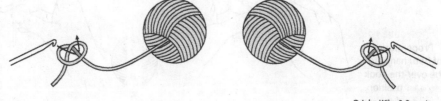

© John Wiley & Sons, Inc.

FIGURE 1-5:
Insert hook in
loop.

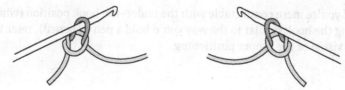

© John Wiley & Sons, Inc.

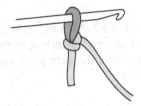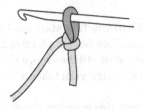

FIGURE 1-6:
Tightening the
loop around the
hook.

REMEMBER

A good slipknot should slide easily up and down the hook's shaft, but it shouldn't be so loose that it slides off over the end of the hook. If your knot is too loose, gently pull on the working end of the yarn to snug it up. Also, because you have to pull your hook back through to make your first stitch, your slipknot shouldn't be too tight either. If it is too tight, simply tug on the loop to loosen it, leaving some space below the hook where the yarn for the next stitch will pass through.

TIP

If pulling on the working end of the yarn doesn't tighten your slipknot on the hook but yanking on the tail end does, you made your slipknot backward. Simply remove the loop from the hook, tug on both ends to release the knot, and try again.

Now that you have the yarn on the hook, you're ready to begin making stitches. Make sure your hands are in the proper position, holding the slipknot with your yarn hand. If you're using the over-the-hook method for holding the hook (with your forefinger on top of the hook, your thumb underneath, and the shaft resting against your palm), see Figure 1-7 for the proper position of both hands.

FIGURE 1-7:
Proper position
of both hands for
the over-the-hook
position.

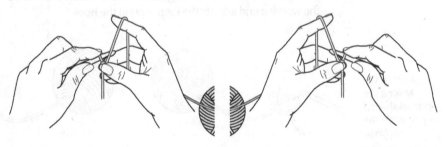

If you're more comfortable with the under-the hook position (where you're holding the hook similar to the way you'd hold a pen or pencil), refer to Figure 1-8 for a visual of the proper positioning.

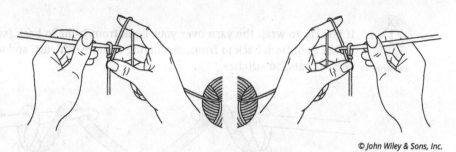

FIGURE 1-8:
Proper position of both hands for the under-the-hook position.

Wrapping the yarn over the hook

Wrapping the yarn over the hook, called a *yarn over* (abbreviated *yo*), is the most basic step to any crochet stitch. Sometimes you yarn over before you insert the hook into the next stitch, sometimes after, and sometimes you yarn over two or more times. The location and number of yarn overs really depends on the stitch.

Yarning over is very simple, but you have to do it right. Otherwise, you won't be able to draw the yarn smoothly through the stitch. Practice the yarn over motion until you're comfortable with it. To yarn over correctly, follow these steps:

1. **Make a slipknot.**

2. **Slide the slipknot onto the hook's shaft.**

3. **With your yarn hand, hold the tail of the slipknot between your thumb and middle finger.**

4. **Using the forefinger of your yarn hand, bring the yarn up behind the hook.**

5. **Lay the yarn over the hook's shaft, positioned between the slipknot and the throat of the hook, as shown in Figure 1-9.**

FIGURE 1-9:
What a finished yarn over looks like when done correctly.

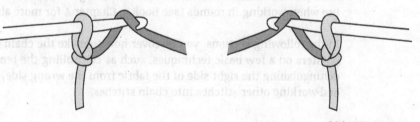

Always try to keep the loops on the hook loose enough so they slide easily on the hook.

WARNING

If you try to wrap the yarn over your hook from front to back (see Figure 1-10), rather than from back to front, crocheting is more difficult, and you end up with twisted, tangled stitches.

FIGURE 1-10:
An incorrect
yarn over.

© John Wiley & Sons, Inc.

Tied Up in Stitches: The Three Basics

Three basic stitches are used most often in crochet: the chain stitch, the slip stitch, and the single crochet. The next sections walk you through how to create these simple stitches.

REMEMBER

The first few stitches you make are often the hardest because you don't have much material to grasp onto with your yarn hand. Be patient; it gets easier.

The (almost) universal starter: Chain stitch

The *chain stitch* (abbreviated *ch*) is the basis for all crochet. Almost every pattern begins with a chain stitch. If you're working in rows, your first row is a series of chain stitches, which (not surprisingly) is called a *foundation chain*. When you're ready to start a new row, guess what? You use the chain stitch! Sometimes you work just a few chain stitches and join them together to create a ring, which you use when working in rounds (see Book 3, Chapter 4 for more about rounds).

In the following sections, you discover how to make the chain stitch and provide pointers on a few basic techniques, such as controlling the tension of your yarn, distinguishing the right side of the fabric from the wrong side, counting stitches, and working other stitches into chain stitches.

Creating your first chain stitch

Here's how to create your first chain stitch:

1. **Make a slipknot.**

   See the earlier section "Working a slipknot" for instructions.

2. Slide the slipknot onto the hook's shaft.

3. With the forefinger of your yarn hand, yarn over the hook (yo) from back to front while holding the tail of the slipknot between the thumb and middle finger of your yarn hand.

4. Slide the yarn from the yarn over onto the throat of the hook.

5. With your hook hand, rotate the hook toward you so the throat faces the slipknot.

6. With gentle pressure upward on the hook, pull the hook (which is carrying the wrapped strand of yarn) through the loop on your hook, as shown in Figure 1-11.

You now have 1 complete chain stitch (ch) and 1 loop remaining on your hook.

 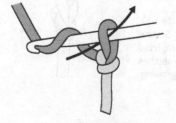

© John Wiley & Sons, Inc.

FIGURE 1-11:
Making a chain stitch.

Repeat Steps 3 through 6 until you feel comfortable with this motion.

REMEMBER

Whenever you're drawing the hook through a loop or stitch, rotate it so the throat faces slightly downward and apply gentle pressure upward on the hook so it doesn't catch on any other loops of yarn. Pulling the hook away from the knot opens up the loop on the hook slightly and helps to provide space for the new yarn to go through the loop.

Controlling your yarn tension

Each chain stitch should be the same size as the one before it, which means that you're keeping your yarn tension even for all your stitches. (See Figure 1-12.) If your stitches aren't the same size, don't get frustrated. The chain stitch takes practice, but pretty soon, you'll find yourself moving right along.

TIP

Try these tips for fixing tight and loose chain stitches:

» If you find that your stitches are very tight and it's difficult to draw the hook through the stitch, try relaxing your hands. You're probably pulling too tightly on the yarn as you're drawing it through.

>> If you find that your stitches are too loose, shorten up the distance between your yarn hand and hook hand, and lift the forefinger of your yarn hand, thereby creating more tension.

FIGURE 1-12:
Several completed chain stitches and growing.

TIP

As your chain gets longer and your hands get farther apart, you may have trouble controlling your work. Just let go of the bottom of your chain and, with the thumb and middle finger of your yarn hand, grab onto the chain closer to the hook, as Figure 1-13 shows. Holding the chain closer to the hook keeps your work stationary so you can control your stitches and maintain even tension. As your work gets longer, keep readjusting so you're always holding your completed work relatively close to the hook. (*Note:* This bit of advice applies to all your work as you're crocheting, not just chains. In fact, you'll probably find that you do it without even thinking about it after a while.)

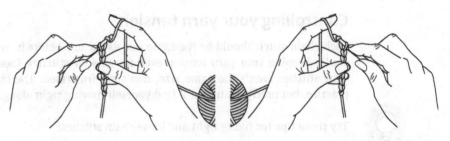

FIGURE 1-13:
Hold completed chain stitches closer to the hook to control your work.

Telling right from wrong

Each stitch has a *right side* (front) and a *wrong side* (back). The right side of the chain is smooth, and you can see each stitch clearly. The wrong side has a small bumpy loop on each stitch. Figure 1-14 shows both the right and wrong sides of a chain.

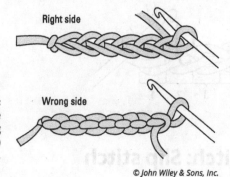

FIGURE 1-14:
Looking at the right and wrong (front and back) sides of a chain.

Right side

Wrong side

© John Wiley & Sons, Inc.

TIP

When you're talking about the right or wrong side of a piece of crocheted fabric, the first row of stitches (not counting the foundation chain) is generally considered the right side. You can always distinguish which side of the fabric you're looking at by locating the tail of the foundation chain. If it's on your left (that is, if you're right-handed), then the right side is facing you; if it's on the right, then the wrong side is toward you. (The reverse is true for lefties.)

Counting stitches

REMEMBER

Knowing what to count as a stitch is important when figuring out whether you've crocheted enough chain stitches for your foundation chain. Fortunately, it's quite easy. The loop on your hook doesn't count as a stitch. The first stitch is the one directly below your hook, and you begin counting from there, continuing down the chain until you reach the last chain stitch before the slipknot, which you don't count either. For example, Figure 1-15, in the next section, shows a chain of six chain stitches.

Working other stitches into chain stitches

To work your next row of stitches into the chain stitches, you have to know where to insert your hook. If you look at an individual stitch, you see that it consists of three separate loops or strands of yarn: two strands that create the V on the right side, which are called the *top 2 loops*, and a third that creates the bump on the wrong side. You can insert your hook anywhere in the stitch and start stitching, but you get the best results like this: With the right side of the chain facing you, insert your hook between the top loops and under the back bump loop, catching the loops on your hook (as shown in Figure 1-15). Working in the chain stitches like this gives you a neat base without any loose loops hanging down. (See the later section "The Anatomy of a Stitch" for more about top loops and the other parts of a complete crochet stitch.)

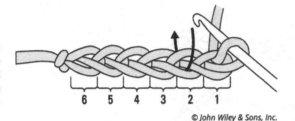

The utility stitch: Slip stitch

The *slip stitch* (abbreviated *sl st*) is the flattest (or smallest) of all the crochet stitches, and only the chain stitch is easier to make. Although you can use it to crochet a fabric, the slip stitch is really more of a utility stitch. Here are a few of its uses:

>> **Making a seam:** Slip stitching is good for joining pieces of crocheted fabric. Because the slip stitch is relatively flat, it doesn't create a bulky seam. (See Book 7, Chapter 2 for more on joining pieces of crochet.)

>> **Shaping your work:** If you have to travel from one point to another to shape a crocheted item, such as for armholes in a garment, and you don't want to fasten off your yarn and rejoin it, the slip stitch is ideal because it's so flat it's almost invisible.

>> **Joining a new ball of yarn:** When you have to join your yarn in a new place, whether for shaping purposes or to change colors (see Book 3, Chapter 5), you use the slip stitch to attach it.

>> **Creating a ring:** If you're working in rounds (like for a doily), the slip stitch joins one end of the chain to the other to create a ring. (Find out how to work in rounds in Book 3, Chapter 4.)

>> **Finishing the edges of your work:** Used as a final row or round on a design, the slip stitch creates a nice, neat border.

>> **Embellishing crocheted fabric:** You can slip stitch across the surface of a piece of crocheted fabric to create the look of embroidery.

>> **Forming combination stitches:** You can combine the slip stitch with other stitches to form fancy-schmancy stitches. For example, you can combine the chain stitch with the slip stitch to form a *picot* stitch. (For more on combination stitches, see Book 4, Chapter 3.)

The following steps show you how to make a slip stitch that forms a ring:

1. **Make a chain that's 6 chain stitches (ch 6) long.**

2. **Insert the hook into the first chain stitch you made.**

This is the stitch that's farthest from your hook, as shown in Figure 1-16.

3. **With your yarn hand, yarn over (yo) by wrapping the yarn from back to front over the hook; with your hook hand, rotate the throat of the hook toward you.**

4. **While applying gentle pressure upward, draw the hook with the wrapped yarn back through the stitch and then through the loop on the hook in one motion (see Figure 1-17).**

One slip stitch (sl st) is complete, and 1 loop remains on your hook. See Figure 1-18.

FIGURE 1-16:
Inserting the hook into the first chain stitch made.

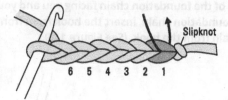

© John Wiley & Sons, Inc.

FIGURE 1-17:
Wrapping the yarn over the hook (yo) and pulling it through the loops.

© John Wiley & Sons, Inc.

REMEMBER

The slip stitch forming a ring is all you see here, but no matter where you work the stitch, you always do it the same way.

Focusing on
Fundamental Stitches

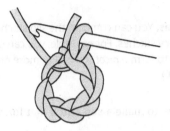

FIGURE 1-18:
Finishing up
a slip stitch.

The old standby: Single crochet

The *single crochet* (abbreviated *sc*) is the most fundamental of all stitches. A compact stitch, it creates a tight, dense fabric. You use this stitch over and over again, alone or in combination with other stitches. In the following sections, you learn how to make your first single crochet and complete a full row.

Creating your first single crochet

To begin your first row of single crochet:

1. **Make a foundation chain by doing 17 chain stitches (ch 17).**

2. **With the right side of the foundation chain facing you and your yarn hand holding the foundation chain, insert the hook from front to back into the second chain from the hook. (See Figure 1-19.)**

FIGURE 1-19:
Inserting the
hook into the
second chain
stitch from
the hook.

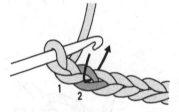 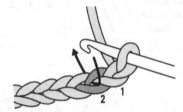

3. **With your yarn hand, yarn over (yo) by wrapping the yarn from back to front over the hook.**

4. **Rotate the throat of the hook toward you with your hook hand.**

5. **Pull the hook with the wrapped yarn through the stitch, as Figure 1-20 shows.**

    You should have 2 loops on your hook.

FIGURE 1-20:
Drawing the
yarn through
the stitch.

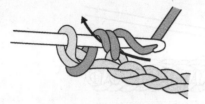
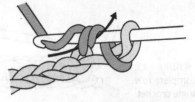

© John Wiley & Sons, Inc.

6. **With your yarn hand, yarn over again and then rotate the throat of the hook toward you with your hook hand.**

7. **Draw the hook with the wrapped yarn through both loops on the hook, as shown in Figure 1-21.**

One single crochet (sc) is complete, and 1 loop remains on your hook.

FIGURE 1-21:
Pull the yarn
gently through
both loops on
the hook.

© John Wiley & Sons, Inc.

Continuing your first row of single crochet

Here's how to work the next single crochet stitch and continue the row:

1. **Insert your hook from front to back into the next chain stitch (ch), as shown in Figure 1-22.**

2. **Repeat Steps 3 through 7 from the first single crochet stitch instructions in the preceding section to complete the second stitch.**

3. **Work 1 single crochet stitch (sc) in each chain stitch across the foundation chain.**

You should have 16 single crochet stitches, or 1 row of single crochet, as in Figure 1-23.

FIGURE 1-22:
Inserting the
hook into the
next chain stitch.

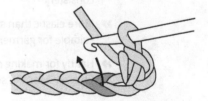

© John Wiley & Sons, Inc.

Focusing on
Fundamental Stitches

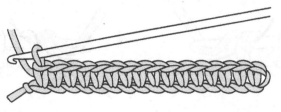

FIGURE 1-23:
A complete row
of single crochet.

© John Wiley & Sons, Inc.

If you're wondering what happened to your 17th chain stitch, remember that you worked your first single crochet into the second chain from the hook. The skipped chain stitch is considered a turning chain that brings you up to the level needed to work your first stitch of the new row (see the section "Climbing to new heights with turning chains," later in this chapter, for more on this topic).

REMEMBER

Working stitches into the foundation chain isn't easy. Even experienced crocheters can have a tough time with this technique. But after the first few rows, you have more fabric to hold on to, which makes inserting your hook much easier.

Foundation Stitches: The Chain and the First Row All in One

Sometimes a pattern may direct you to use foundation stitches rather than a foundation chain made up of chain stitches. *Foundation stitches* are a nifty way to make the foundation chain and first row of stitches all at the same time. Easily adapted to any stitch, like the single crochet described earlier in this chapter, each foundation stitch is made up of two parts: the foundation chain (which is at the base) and one standard stitch.

Foundation stitches have a few advantages over the standard foundation chain. They're generally

>> Easier to keep track of, especially when you're working a long foundation row

>> Good at keeping the tension of the foundation chain and first row even and consistent

>> More elastic than standard foundation chains, making them especially suitable for garments

>> Handy for making multiple increases at the ends of a row (see Book 3, Chapter 3 for the scoop on increases)

You can work any stitch as a foundation stitch, but to keep it simple, the following sections show you how to work several foundation single crochet (abbreviated *fsc*). *Remember:* Each *foundation single crochet* is a blend of one foundation chain stitch and one single crochet.

TIP

To make taller foundation stitches, you need to add a chain stitch to the beginning of the first row and make the required yarn overs as for the regular stitch. For example, to make a foundation double crochet (abbreviated *fdc*), begin with three chains and yarn over the hook before beginning the first stitch. Make the foundation chain as you would for the foundation single crochet and then work the loops off two at a time as you would a normal double crochet stitch. (Book 3, Chapter 2 has more on double crochet.)

Your first foundation single crochet

Follow these steps to create your first foundation single crochet:

1. **Begin with 2 chain stitches (ch 2).**

Refer to the earlier section "The (almost) universal starter: Chain stitch" for guidance on forming this stitch.

2. **Insert the hook from front to back into the chain farthest from the hook.**

3. **Yarn over (yo) by wrapping the yarn from back to front over the hook and pull the yarn through the chain stitch. See Figure 1-24.**

You should have 2 loops on the hook.

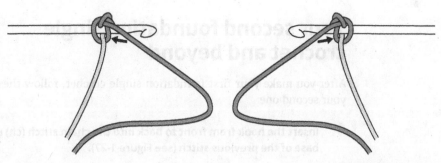

FIGURE 1-24:
Pulling your yarn through a chain stitch.

© John Wiley & Sons, Inc.

4. **Yarn over the hook and pull the yarn through the first loop (the one closest to the hook end) on the hook.**

Well done! You've just completed the foundation chain portion (shown in Figure 1-25) of your first foundation single crochet stitch (fsc).

5. **Yarn over the hook and pull the yarn through both loops on the hook.**

This completes the single crochet (sc) portion (shown in Figure 1-26) of your first foundation single crochet stitch.

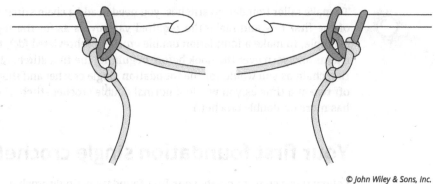

FIGURE 1-25:
Finishing the foundation chain portion.

© John Wiley & Sons, Inc.

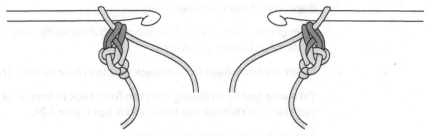

FIGURE 1-26:
Finishing the single crochet portion.

© John Wiley & Sons, Inc.

Your second foundation single crochet and beyond

After you make your first foundation single crochet, follow these steps to create your second one:

1. **Insert the hook from front to back into the chain stitch (ch) made at the base of the previous stitch (see Figure 1-27).**

2. **Yarn over (yo) by wrapping the yarn from back to front over the hook and pull the yarn through the chain stitch.**

You should have 2 loops on the hook (see Figure 1-28).

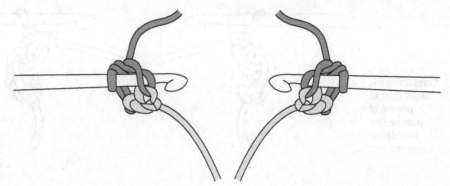

FIGURE 1-27:
Starting
your second
foundation single
crochet.

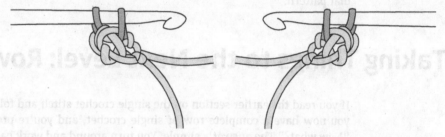

FIGURE 1-28:
Two loops are
now on the hook.

3. **Yarn over the hook and pull the yarn through the first loop on the hook (the one hanging out closer to the hook end).**

   This completes the foundation chain portion (shown in Figure 1-29) of your second foundation single crochet stitch (fsc).

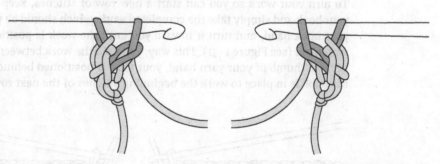

FIGURE 1-29:
Completing
the foundation
chain portion
of your second
foundation single
crochet.

4. **Yarn over the hook and pull the yarn through both loops on the hook.**

   Ta-da! You've now completed the single crochet (sc) portion (shown in Figure 1-30) of your second foundation single crochet stitch.

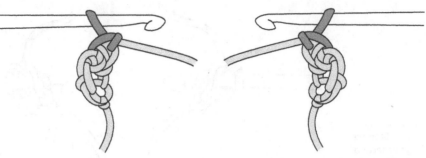

© John Wiley & Sons, Inc.

FIGURE 1-30: Completing the single crochet portion of your second foundation single crochet.

Repeat Steps 1 through 4 for each foundation single crochet you need in a particular pattern.

Taking Things to the Next Level: Row Two

If you read the earlier section on the single crochet stitch and followed the steps, you now have a complete row of single crochet, and you're probably thinking, "Now what?" The answer's simple: You turn around and work back the same way you came. The following sections show you how to turn your work around so that the tops of the stitches in the previous row are in the proper position, which way to turn, and how to begin that first stitch of the new row.

Turning your work

To turn your work so you can start a new row of stitches, keep the last loop on your hook and simply take the completed work, which should be positioned under your hook hand, and turn it toward you until the work is positioned under your yarn hand (see Figure 1-31). This way, you hold the work between the middle finger and thumb of your yarn hand, your yarn is positioned behind your work, and the hook is in place to work the beginning stitches of the next row.

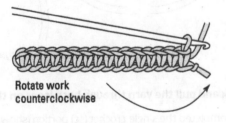

Rotate work
counterclockwise

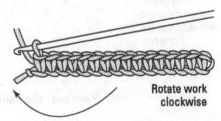

Rotate work
clockwise

FIGURE 1-31: Turning your work to crochet back across the row.

© John Wiley & Sons, Inc.

TIP

Keep in mind that each time you turn your work to crochet back across the previous row, a different side of the piece will be facing you. If the first row is designated as the right side of the piece, then when you turn to work the second row, the wrong side is facing you. The third row again has the right side facing you, and so on. (See the earlier section "Telling right from wrong" for a refresher on what the right and wrong sides of a piece look like.)

Climbing to new heights with turning chains

After you turn your piece around, you're ready to crochet the *turning chain*, the one or more chain stitches that you make after you've turned your work and are about to begin your next row. The purpose of the turning chain is to bring your yarn to the height necessary in order to work the first stitch of your next row or round.

The number of chain stitches you make in the turning chain depends on what the next stitch in the row is, because some stitches are taller than others. Figure 1-32 shows the height differences of several turning chains used for successively taller stitches. (See Book 3, Chapter 2 for more info on taller stitches.)

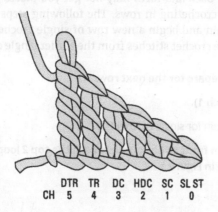

FIGURE 1-32:
A comparison
of turning chain
heights.

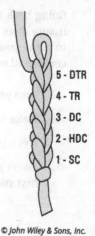

5 - DTR
4 - TR
3 - DC
2 - HDC
1 - SC

DTR TR DC HDC SC SL ST
CH   5   4   3   2   1   0

© John Wiley & Sons, Inc.

Table 1-1 lists the number of chain stitches you need for several frequently used stitches.

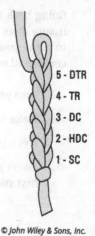

Focusing on
Fundamental Stitches

How Many Chain Stitches Make a Turning Chain?

Stitch Name	Number of Turning Chains Needed
Slip stitch (sl st)	0
Single crochet (sc)	1
Half double crochet (hdc)	2
Double crochet (dc)	3
Triple crochet (tr)	4
Double triple crochet (dtr)	5

REMEMBER

The turning chain almost always counts as the first stitch of the next row, except for the single crochet. (The single crochet turning chain isn't wide enough to substitute for the first single crochet of the row and creates a rough edge to your rows. Working a single crochet stitch in the first stitch of the row fills out each row on the end.)

Starting the next row

Going back and forth and back and forth may not get you places in real life, but it sure does when you're crocheting in rows. The following steps show you how to make your turning chain and begin a new row of single crochet, so grab your completed row of 16 single crochet stitches from the earlier single crochet section:

1. Turn your work to prepare for the next row.

2. Make 1 chain stitch (ch 1).

   This is your turning chain for single crochet (sc).

3. Insert your hook from front to back underneath the top 2 loops of the first stitch, as shown in Figure 1-33.

FIGURE 1-33:
Inserting the hook under the top 2 loops of the first stitch.

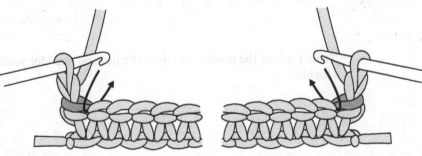

© John Wiley & Sons, Inc.

4. Yarn over (yo) by wrapping the yarn from back to front over the hook.

5. Draw your yarn through the stitch, as shown in Figure 1-34.

6. Yarn over again by wrapping the yarn from back to front over the hook.

7. Draw your yarn through the 2 loops on the hook.

Now you have 1 single crochet in the second row completed, and 1 loop remains on the hook. (See Figure 1-35.)

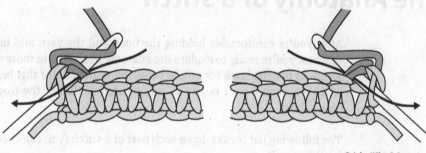

FIGURE 1-34:
Drawing the yarn through the stitch.

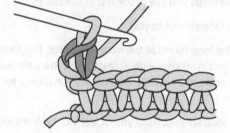
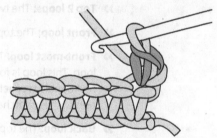

FIGURE 1-35:
A new row with one complete single crochet.

To complete the row, work one single crochet stitch in each single crochet stitch from the previous row and continue doing so all the way to the end. You work the stitches exactly the same way as when you're working them into the foundation chain; you just place your hook in the top of a stitch from a previous row instead. Make sure to count your stitches when you get to the end of the row. You should have exactly the same number of stitches in the second row as in the first (in this case, 16).

REMEMBER

Some patterns like to change things up and may tell you to insert your hook in a different place in the previous row. But if no specific instructions are given, always work the stitches in each subsequent row under the top 2 loops of the stitch in the previous row. This is the best way to create a smooth, even fabric.

TIP

Working a practice swatch helps you figure out new stitches and start making them like a pro. Use worsted-weight yarn (it's easiest to work with) and a size H-8 U.S. (5 mm) hook (see Book 1 for more on yarn weights and hook sizes) to make a foundation chain that's approximately 4 inches long and then chain 1 for your turning chain. Work as many rows of single crochet as you need to until you feel comfortable with the new stitch and your stitches have a smooth, even look.

The Anatomy of a Stitch

After you're comfortable holding the hook and the yarn and making a few basic stitches, you're ready to explore the anatomy of a stitch in more detail so you know where to put the hook for stitches covered in the rest of this book. Fortunately, a stitch's anatomy isn't nearly as complicated as that of the frog you dissected in high school.

The following list breaks down each part of a stitch (you can check out Figure 1-36 for the visual):

>> **Top 2 loops:** The two loops you see at the top of the stitch.

>> **Front loop:** The top loop closest to you.

>> **Front-most loop:** The loop found at the front of a stitch, just below the front loop. This loop is found in stitches with at least one extra yarn over, like the half double crochet or double crochet. (See Book 3, Chapter 2 for an introduction to these stitches.)

>> **Back loop:** The top loop farthest from you or behind the front loop.

>> **Back-most loop:** The loop found at the back of a stitch just below the back loop. This loop is found in stitches with at least one extra yarn over, like the half double crochet or double crochet.

>> **Base:** The two loops at the bottom of the stitch. The base of a new stitch is the top of the stitch below it.

TIP

The base is the most stable part of a stitch to work into when working a border or sewing pieces together.

>> **Post:** The body of the stitch, located between the top 2 loops and the base. It varies in height depending on the stitch and is also referred to as the *stem*. When it's located at the end of a row and you're working into it when adding a border or edging, the post is also considered the side of the stitch.

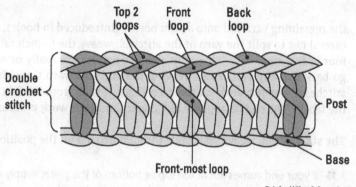

FIGURE 1-36:
The various parts
of a stitch.

Top 2 loops
Front loop
Back loop
Double crochet stitch
Post
Base
Front-most loop

© John Wiley & Sons, Inc.

All's Well That Ends Well: Fastening Off

Sooner or later, you're going to come to the end of your design and need to *fasten off* (cut) the yarn. Or maybe you're working with different colors and need to fasten off one color to join the new color. (See Book 3, Chapter 5 for more on switching colors.) The next sections show you how and where to cut the yarn and what to do with the leftover tail.

Cutting the yarn

To fasten off your yarn, cut it about 6 inches from the hook. (See the next section to find out why you leave this much yarn.) Using your hook, draw the cut end of the yarn through the last remaining loop on your hook, as shown in Figure 1-37. Pull gently on the tail of yarn to snug up the end. This action keeps your work from coming apart without you having to make large, unsightly knots.

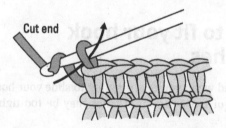

Cut end

FIGURE 1-37:
Fastening off.

© John Wiley & Sons, Inc.

Weaving in the end

Weaving in the leftover tail through a few stitches ensures that your yarn ends are secured and hidden, resulting in a neatly finished appearance. To do this, thread the remaining yarn tail onto a yarn needle (introduced in Book 1, Chapter 1). Being careful not to split the yarn of the stitches, weave the 6-inch tail of yarn through four or five stitches — kind of in a zigzag pattern. To really make the end secure, go back the way you came, weaving the end backward through those same few stitches. When finished, cut the yarn about ¼ inch from the fabric and gently pull the fabric. The end disappears like magic, and your work is secure.

REMEMBER

The stitches you weave your ends through depend on the position of the tail end.

>> If your end comes out at the top or bottom of the piece, simply weave it back and forth under the top loops of the stitches along the same row.

>> If your end emerges along the side of the fabric, weave it vertically, either up or down, through the stitches found along the same edge.

REMEMBER

Always check to make sure your woven ends aren't visible from the right side of the work. If you find that one is, simply pull it through the fabric to the wrong side.

Troubleshooting Mistakes as You Crochet

No matter how much experience you have as a crocheter, you *will* make mistakes — and that's perfectly okay! Sure, discovering that you've lost a stitch or made some other typical error can be a frustrating experience, but knowing how to identify the problem and how to fix it will get you back on track in no time. The sections that follow explain some common crocheting problems. You discover why they happen, how to fix them, and how to keep them from happening again. Well, what are you waiting for? The key to stress-free crocheting awaits!

You struggle to fit your hook into the stitches

It's easy to get frustrated when you're struggling to slide your hook into stitches. Following are a couple of reasons your stitches may be too tight (along with a couple of easy fixes):

>> **You're pulling the working yarn too tight as you work.** Try loosening up your tension by adjusting how you hold the yarn. (Head to "Holding the yarn" earlier in this chapter for pointers on how to hold yarn properly.)

>> **The loop is sitting on the skinny end of the hook.** Make sure that when you finish the stitch, the loop on the hook is on the fat portion of the hook, not near the hook part.

>> **The hook's too small for the yarn you're working with.** By switching to a larger hook, you can make bigger stitches that are easier to work with. (Flip to Book 1, Chapter 1 for the scoop on hook sizes.)

TIP

To keep from having too-tight stitches ever again, make sure you're checking your gauge against the pattern before you begin to crochet. Taking the time to make a gauge swatch early on saves you serious time in the long run. Check out Book 1, Chapter 3 for more on gauge.

The fabric edges are shrinking

You're crocheting along when suddenly you realize that your work is getting skinnier — something it's not supposed to do. This problem is a common one for those who are still getting the hang of crocheting. If your project is growing narrower as you work, then you probably lost one or more stitches somewhere along the way.

To fix this problem, count the number of stitches in the last row. If you've lost stitches, hold up the fabric and look for any spots where you may have skipped a stitch. If you can't easily see where you began losing stitches, carefully pull out the last row and count the number of stitches in the next row. (To pull out a row, simply remove the yarn loop from your hook and then gently pull on the tail end of the yarn to unravel the stitches. Be careful not to pull too fast, because you may end up pulling out more stitches than you need to.) Continue to pull rows out one by one, counting as you go, until you're back to the correct number of stitches, and then try, try again.

Alternatively, if you've lost just one or two stitches, you can simply add the same number of stitches to the next row by working two stitches in the same space until you're back to the correct stitch count. When you're done adding stitches, hold up your work to make sure the edges still look even.

TIP

Stitches are commonly lost at the beginning or end of a row because it's hard to tell where the first or last stitch of the row is due to the fact that both are typically turning chains and therefore have a different appearance than a regular stitch. To help you distinguish where different rows start and end, place a removable stitch marker in the first and last stitches of a row. When you work your way back to the marker, you'll know exactly where you need to place the stitch. (See "Climbing to new heights with turning chains" earlier in this chapter for more on turning chains.)

The fabric edges are getting wider

If your work is getting wider and you didn't intend for it to, you've unknowingly added stitches somewhere.

To trim your project back down to size, count the stitches in the last row to determine how many extra stitches you have. If you have more stitches than you're supposed to, carefully pull out the last row (as explained in the preceding section) and count the number of stitches in the next row. Continue pulling rows out one by one, counting as you go, until you're back to the correct number of stitches. Then you can start over safely.

What to do if you've added only one or two stitches? Just subtract the same number of stitches in the next row by working two stitches together until you're back to the correct stitch count. After you've decreased the stitches, hold up your work to make sure the decrease isn't noticeable. (Book 3, Chapter 3 explains how to decrease stitches.)

TIP

To keep from having to redo your work in the future, make sure to count your stitches after every row until you feel more confident in your crochet skills. And don't forget that turning chains count as the first stitch in taller stitches; make sure to work into them at the end of a row. Refer to "Climbing to new heights with turning chains" earlier in this chapter and Book 3, Chapter 2 for details on how to work into the turning chain.

The foundation edge is tighter than the rest of the fabric

If after working a few inches of your project you notice that the piece is getting wider and you didn't add any stitches, there's a chance your foundation edge may be too tight. The chain stitch is easy to make narrower than the other, more structured stitches, so accidentally making the foundation chain too tight is quite common. To avoid this issue, try to keep your chain stitches loose as you work the foundation chain. To keep your stitches loose, you can either consciously make loose stitches by keeping your tension looser than you would for regular stitches or you can use a hook that's one size larger than the one the pattern calls for. The resulting chain may look a little messy, but some of the slack will be taken up when you work the following row of stitches. (Keep in mind that your foundation chain should look like a big fat worm!)

The corners are curled

When the corners of your work are starting to curl and just won't lie flat, you may need to try adjusting your tension. Stitches that are worked too tightly together result in a stiff fabric, which often causes the corners to curl in.

To fix this problem, try stretching the fabric. That just might loosen up the stitches and allow the piece to lie flat. If the corners begin to curl again, make sure you're using the appropriately sized hook for the yarn you're working with. Switching to a larger hook size will create bigger stitches and loosen up the fabric, allowing it to lie flat. If all else fails, you may need to adjust your tension by changing the way you hold the yarn. See "Holding the yarn" earlier in this chapter for guidance.

TIP

Sometimes you won't realize that the corners of a project are curling until you're all done with it. Instead of tossing your work away in a heap of frustration, try blocking it (using one of the processes covered in Book 7, Chapter 1). With some yarns, such as wool, blocking loosens up the fibers, allowing you to stretch out any curls.

One way to prevent curled corners is by simply loosening your stitches. If you find that your hands are cramping up, chances are you're holding the hook too tightly and therefore creating stitches that are too tight as well. Relax your grip for looser stitches.

REMEMBER

Making a gauge swatch helps you identify and prevent any potential problems early on. If your swatch is curling, then your project will probably curl as well. Always make sure you're working to the gauge specified in your pattern if you want to wind up with a successful project.

Luxurious Washcloth Projects

The following projects let you practice your newfound basic skills while creating luxuriously soft and absorbent washcloths that are suitable for yourself or as gifts for friends. To see a color photo of this project, visit dummies.com/go/knitcrochetAIO.

Simple Luxurious Washcloth project

The yarn used in this project is a lofty, organic, worsted-weight cotton that grows softer with each wash and is easy to find in an array of natural or bright colors. Feel free to use the given color or choose your own to match your style. One skein contains enough yarn to make two cloths.

Materials and vital statistics

>> **Yarn:** Blue Sky Alpacas "Organic Cotton" worsted-weight yarn (100% organic cotton), (3.5 oz. [100 g], 150 yds [137 m] each skein): 1 skein of #80 Bone

Note: If you can't find the Blue Sky Alpacas cotton, a suitable substitution is Lion Brand "Nature's Choice Organic Cotton" or other worsted-weight cotton yarn of your choice.

» **Hook:** Standard crochet hook size I-9 U.S. (5.5 mm) or size needed to obtain gauge

» **Large-eyed yarn needle**

» **Measurements:** 10 in. x 10 in. square

» **Gauge:** 14 sts and 16 rows in sc = 4 in.

» **Stitches used:** Chain stitch (ch), single crochet (sc)

Directions

The following directions are written in plain English, not Crochetese, to help walk you through your first project. Refer to the chain stitch section and single crochet section earlier in this chapter for details on each stitch.

1. **Create your foundation chain by working 36 chain stitches in a row (ch 36).**

2. **To complete Row 1, work 1 single crochet stitch (sc) in the second chain from the hook and then work 1 single crochet stitch in each chain across the row.**

   You should have 35 complete single crochet stitches.

3. **Turn your work, and then chain 1 for the single crochet turning chain to prepare for the next row.**

4. **To complete the next row, work 1 single crochet stitch in each single crochet stitch across the row.**

   You should have 35 complete single crochet stitches in this row.

5. **Repeat Steps 3 and 4 until you have 40 rows on your work.**

6. **Fasten off your yarn and weave in the loose ends using the yarn needle.**

Luxurious Washcloth with Border project

This project, a simple adaptation of the previous washcloth, takes your skills to the next level with the addition of a bright and colorful border. Working on this project requires a few additional techniques, such as adding a new yarn color (see Book 3, Chapter 5) and working into the sides of the rows (refer to Book 4, Chapter 3). The recommended yarn is soft and comes in a variety of beautiful colors.

Materials and vital statistics

>> **Yarn:** Blue Sky Alpacas "Organic Cotton" worsted-weight yarn (100% organic cotton), (3.5 oz. [100 g], 150 yds [137 m] each skein): 1 skein of #80 Bone (A)

Blue Sky Alpacas "Dyed Cotton" worsted-weight yarn (100% organic cotton), (3.5 oz. [100 g], 150 yds [137 m] each skein): 1 skein each of

- #601 Poppy (B)

- #634 Periwinkle (B)

Note: The pattern calls for only one color to be used in the border. Choose whichever color you prefer for your border, or choose another one to suit your decor.

Note: If you can't find the Blue Sky Alpacas cotton, a suitable substitution is Lion Brand "Nature's Choice Organic Cotton."

>> **Hook:** Standard crochet hook size I-9 U.S. (5.5 mm) or size needed to obtain gauge

>> **Large-eyed yarn needle**

>> **Measurements:** 10 in. x 10 in. square

>> **Gauge:** 14 sts and 16 rows in sc = 4 in.

>> **Stitches used:** Chain stitch (ch), single crochet (sc), slip stitch (sl st)

Directions

As in the preceding project, the following directions are written in plain English rather than Crochetese to help walk you through each step. Refer to the chain stitch, slip stitch, and single crochet sections earlier in this chapter for details on each stitch. Figure 1-38 shows the stitch diagram for this washcloth.

To make the washcloth's body, follow these steps:

1. **With A, create your foundation chain by working 29 chain stitches in a row (ch 29).**

2. **To complete Row 1, work 1 single crochet stitch (sc) in the second chain from the hook and then work 1 single crochet stitch in each chain across the row.**

   You should have 28 complete single crochet stitches.

3. **Turn your work and then chain 1 for the single crochet turning chain to prepare for the next row.**

Washcloth border

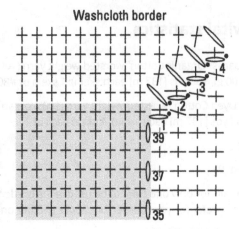

FIGURE 1-38:
The stitch diagram for the Luxurious Washcloth with Border project.

© John Wiley & Sons, Inc.

4. **To complete the next row, work 1 single crochet stitch in each single crochet stitch across the row.**

You should have 28 complete single crochet stitches in this row.

5. **Repeat Steps 3 and 4 until you have 32 rows on your work.**

6. **Fasten off your yarn and weave in the loose ends using the yarn needle.**

After you finish crocheting the washcloth's body, follow these steps to start the border:

1. **Insert your hook in the last stitch of the last row you worked and draw B through so you have 1 loop on the hook.**

See Book 3, Chapter 5 for information on how to join a new color.

2. **Make a corner by working 1 chain (ch 1) and then work 1 single crochet (sc), 1 chain, and 1 more single crochet all in the same stitch.**

3. **Working across the side edge of the washcloth, work 1 single crochet in each row-end stitch across to the last row-end stitch.**

4. **Make a corner by working 1 single crochet, 1 chain, and 1 more single crochet all in the last row-end stitch.**

You should have 33 single crochet stitches between the 2 chain spaces.

5. **Working across the foundation edge, work 1 single crochet stitch in each chain stitch across to the last chain.**

6. **Work 1 single crochet, 1 chain, and 1 more single crochet all in the last chain stitch of the foundation edge.**

7. Repeat Steps 3 and 4 once.

8. Work 1 single crochet stitch in the next stitch and in each stitch across until you reach the first single crochet of the border.

9. Work 1 slip stitch (sl st) in the first single crochet stitch to join.

To continue Round 2 of the border:

1. Continuing in the same direction, and without turning the piece, work 1 slip stitch (sl st) into the chain space.

2. Work 1 single crochet (sc), 1 chain (ch), and 1 more single crochet all in the same chain space.

3. Work 1 single crochet in the next single crochet and in each single crochet across to the chain space at the next corner.

   There should be 33 single crochets between the 2 chain spaces.

4. Work 1 single crochet, 1 chain, and 1 more single crochet all in the corner chain space.

5. Repeat Steps 3 and 4 twice.

6. Work 1 single crochet in the next single crochet and in each single crochet across to the first single crochet stitch of Round 2.

7. Work 1 slip stitch in the first single crochet stitch to join.

8. Repeat Round 2 twice more before fastening off the yarn and weaving in the loose ends.

TIP

The two washcloth patterns in this chapter make a generously portioned washcloth, but you can easily adjust the size to create a smaller washcloth or one that's perfect for a baby. All you need to do is work half the number of chains for either the basic washcloth or the washcloth with a border.

Chapter **2**

Expanding Your Stitch Choices

The beauty of crochet is that you can create so many patterns and textures by combining just three basic motions:

» Yarning over the hook

» Inserting your hook

» Drawing your yarn through

The first three stitches in this chapter — the double crochet, the triple crochet, and the double triple crochet — are each made a step taller than the one before with one extra yarn over. How simple is that? The fourth stitch, the half double crochet, is slightly different but makes sense after you master the other stitches in this chapter. You also learn about a couple of extra stitches that are simple, extended variations on some basics. Each stitch presented in this chapter produces a slightly different textured fabric. When you combine them, the variety of possible patterns is endless!

Of course, now that you're making so many stitches, you're going to run out of yarn, so this chapter also shows you how to join a new skein without any unsightly lumps, bumps, or knots.

Doing a Double Crochet

The *double crochet* (abbreviated *dc*) is one of the most common crochet stitches and is about twice as tall as a single crochet, which debuts in Book 3, Chapter 1. A fabric made of all double crochet stitches is fairly solid, but not stiff, and is great for sweaters, shawls, afghans, place mats, or any number of other home decor items. You can also combine the double crochet stitch with other stitches to produce many interesting patterns and textures. The next sections show you how to create the first two rows of the double crochet stitch.

First things first: Row 1

The following steps set you up to work your first double crochet stitch (see Book 3, Chapter 1 for a refresher on foundation chains and turning chains):

1. **Make a foundation chain by doing 15 chain stitches (ch 15).**

2. **Chain 3 more stitches for the turning chain.**

   The double crochet turning chain makes your edges even with the height of the new row and is counted as a double crochet stitch (dc).

TIP

Most pattern books combine the steps for making a foundation chain and turning chain into one by telling you to chain a total of 18.

Now you're ready for your first double crochet.

1. **Yarn over the hook (yo).**

   Always yarn over from back to front when any of the taller stitches call for it.

REMEMBER

2. **Insert your hook between the 2 front loops and under the back bump loop of the fourth chain (ch) from the hook.**

   Figure 2-1a provides the visual for this step. Refer to Book 3, Chapter 1 for details on working into chain stitches.

3. **Yarn over the hook.**

4. **Gently pull the wrapped hook through the center of the chain stitch, carrying the wrapped yarn through the stitch.**

   You should now have 3 loops on your hook, as shown in Figure 2-1b.

5. **Yarn over the hook.**

6. **Draw your yarn through the first 2 loops on your hook, like in Figure 2-2a.**

7. Yarn over the hook.

8. Draw your yarn through the last 2 loops on the hook, as in Figure 2-2b.

One double crochet stitch (dc) is now complete. You should have 1 loop remaining on your hook.

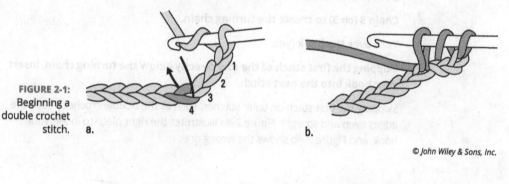

FIGURE 2-1:
Beginning a
double crochet
stitch.

a.

b.

© John Wiley & Sons, Inc.

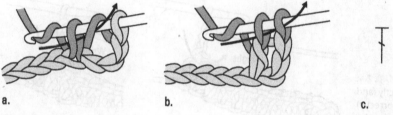

FIGURE 2-2:
Drawing your
yarn through the
loops.

a.

b.

c.

© John Wiley & Sons, Inc.

To finish your first row of double crochet, work one double crochet stitch in each successive chain stitch across the foundation chain, beginning in the next chain of the foundation chain, as shown in Figure 2-3a. You should have 16 double crochet stitches in Row 1 (counting the turning chain as the first double crochet). Take a look at Figure 2-3b to see what the end of the first row of double crochet looks like.

FIGURE 2-3:
Finishing the first
row of double
crochet.

a.

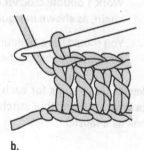

b.

© John Wiley & Sons, Inc.

Turning around and beginning again: Row 2

To work the second row of double crochet, follow these steps:

1. **Turn your work so that the back side is facing you.**

Book 3, Chapter 1 explains how to turn your work correctly.

2. **Chain 3 (ch 3) to create the turning chain.**

3. **Yarn over the hook (yo).**

4. **Skipping the first stitch of the row directly below the turning chain, insert your hook into the next stitch.**

Skipping the first stitch on taller stitches, such as the double crochet, keeps the edges even and straight. Figure 2-4a illustrates the right place to insert your hook, and Figure 2-4b shows the wrong one.

FIGURE 2-4:
Correctly (and incorrectly) inserting the hook for the first stitch of Row 2.

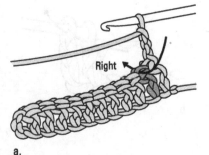 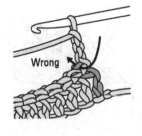

a. b.

© John Wiley & Sons, Inc.

5. **Repeat Steps 3 through 8 from the preceding section in each of the next 14 double crochet stitches (dc).**

Be sure to yarn over before inserting your hook into each stitch.

6. **Work 1 double crochet in the top chain of the previous row's turning chain, as shown in Figure 2-5.**

You should have 16 double crochet stitches in Row 2 (counting the turning chain as 1 double crochet).

Repeat these steps for each additional row of double crochet until you feel comfortable working this stitch. Figure 2-6 shows you how rows of double crochet look as a fabric.

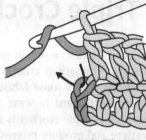

FIGURE 2-5:
Inserting the hook in the top chain of the turning chain.

© John Wiley & Sons, Inc.

FIGURE 2-6:
Several rows of double crochet.

© John Wiley & Sons, Inc.

WARNING

Don't work a stitch into the first stitch of the row after the turning chain. Doing so produces an extra stitch, and if you continue to add a stitch in each row, your design grows ever wider as it gets longer and longer. Also, don't forget to put a double crochet into the top of the turning chain when you get to the end of a row. If you do, you'll lose a stitch, and continuing to drop a stitch per row makes your design narrower and narrower as it grows longer and longer. Be sure to count your stitches frequently to make sure you haven't inadvertently gained (or lost) any along the way.

TIP

Sometimes, especially when you're working with bulky yarn or a larger-than-usual hook, the turning chain on a double crochet row leaves a gap at the beginning of the row. To get a neater edge, try chaining two rather than three stitches for the turning chain.

Expanding Your Stitch Choices

Trying Your Hand at the Triple Crochet

The *triple crochet* (abbreviated *tr*), also called a *treble crochet* in many publications, is slightly longer than the double crochet. This stitch creates longer openings between the stitches and therefore produces a very loose fabric. For example, if you make a sweater with triple crochet, you'll want to wear a blouse under it or else risk revealing too much. However, the triple crochet is usually combined with other stitches to create pattern variety and produce interesting textures and fancier stitches. The following sections break down how to crochet your first two rows of triple crochet.

Starting with Row 1

Follow these steps so you're ready to make your first row of triple crochet (and, if necessary, check out Book 3, Chapter 1 to refresh your memory on chains):

1. **Make a foundation chain by doing 15 chain stitches (ch 15).**

2. **Chain 4 more stitches for the turning chain.**

TIP

If a particular pattern tells you to start Row 1 of triple crochet by chaining 19, don't be surprised. It has merely combined the steps for making a foundation chain and turning chain into one.

To begin your first triple crochet stitch:

REMEMBER

1. **Yarn over the hook (yo) 2 times.**

   Don't forget to yarn over from back to front.

2. **Insert your hook into the fifth chain (ch) from the hook, as shown in Figure 2-7a.**

3. **Yarn over the hook.**

4. **Gently pull the wrapped hook through the center of the chain stitch, carrying the wrapped yarn through the stitch.**

   You should have 4 loops on your hook, like in Figure 2-7b.

5. **Yarn over the hook.**

6. **Draw your yarn through the first 2 loops on your hook, as in Figure 2-8a.**

7. **Yarn over the hook.**

8. **Draw your yarn through the next 2 loops on your hook.**

   See Figure 2-8b for the visual.

9. Yarn over the hook.

10. Draw your yarn through the last 2 loops on your hook.

Figure 2-9a illustrates Step 10, and Figure 2-9b depicts a finished triple crochet stitch (tr) with 1 loop remaining on the hook. Figure 2-9c shows how a stitch pattern indicates a triple crochet stitch.

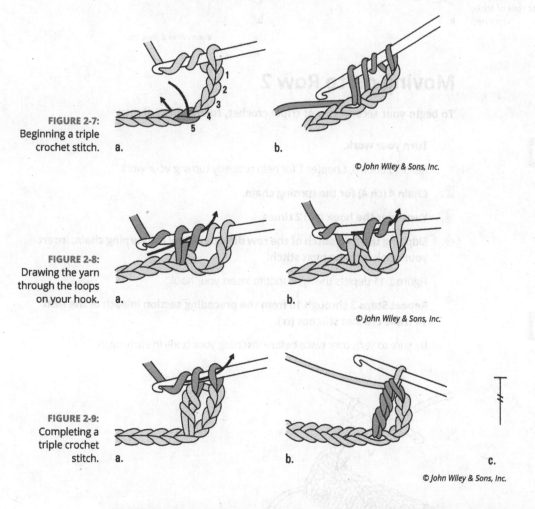

FIGURE 2-7: Beginning a triple crochet stitch.

a.   b.

© John Wiley & Sons, Inc.

FIGURE 2-8: Drawing the yarn through the loops on your hook.

a.   b.

© John Wiley & Sons, Inc.

FIGURE 2-9: Completing a triple crochet stitch.

a.   b.   c.

© John Wiley & Sons, Inc.

To finish the row, yarn over twice and insert your hook into the next chain of the foundation chain, just like in Figure 2-10a. Work one triple crochet in each successive chain across the foundation chain. You should have 16 triple crochet stitches in Row 1 (counting the turning chain as 1 triple crochet). Figure 2-10b shows the end of the first triple crochet row.

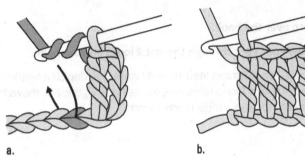

FIGURE 2-10:
Finishing your
first row of triple
crochet.

a.   b.

Moving on to Row 2

To begin your second row of triple crochet, follow these steps:

1. **Turn your work.**

   Refer to Book 3, Chapter 1 for help properly turning your work.

2. **Chain 4 (ch 4) for the turning chain.**

3. **Yarn over the hook (yo) 2 times.**

4. **Skipping the first stitch of the row directly below the turning chain, insert your hook into the next stitch.**

   Figure 2-11 depicts the right spot to insert your hook.

5. **Repeat Steps 3 through 10 from the preceding section in each of the next 14 triple crochet stitches (tr).**

   Be sure to yarn over twice before inserting your hook in each stitch.

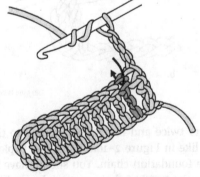

FIGURE 2-11:
Inserting your
hook in the
second stitch.

6. **Work 1 triple crochet in the top chain of the previous row's turning chain.**

When you count the turning chain as 1 triple crochet, you should have 16 triple crochet stitches in Row 2.

Repeat these six steps for each additional row of triple crochet. Continue working rows of triple crochet until you feel comfortable with this stitch. To see how rows of triple crochet look as a fabric, check out Figure 2-12.

FIGURE 2-12: Several rows of triple crochet.

© John Wiley & Sons, Inc.

Diving into Double Triple Crochet

The *double triple crochet* (abbreviated *dtr*) is even taller than a triple crochet. As a fabric, it's loose and holey and commonly used in lacy designs, particularly doilies and other fine cotton crochet patterns. The following sections will have you stitching your first two rows of double triple crochet in no time.

First things first: Row 1

Before you begin a double triple crochet stitch, follow these steps:

1. **Make a foundation chain by working 15 chain stitches (ch 15).**

2. **Chain 5 more stitches for the turning chain.**

Check out Book 3, Chapter 1 for details about chains.

Most patterns combine these two steps and have you chain 20 to start, so don't be thrown off if you see that somewhere.

To complete your first double triple crochet stitch, perform the following seven steps:

1. **Yarn over the hook (yo) 3 times.**

Always yarn over from back to front. Otherwise, you'll get frustrated when the yarn you're drawing through the stitch falls off the hook.

If you're using the over-the-hook position to hold the hook, press the yarn-over loops to the hook with your index finger to prevent the chain from coiling around the hook.

2. **Insert the hook into the sixth chain (ch) from the hook, as shown in Figure 2-13a.**

3. **Yarn over the hook.**

4. **Gently pull the wrapped hook through the center of the chain stitch, carrying the wrapped yarn through the stitch.**

You should now have 5 loops on your hook (see Figure 2-13b).

5. **Yarn over the hook.**

6. **Draw your yarn through the first 2 loops on your hook.**

You should have 4 loops remaining.

7. **Repeat Steps 5 and 6 three more times until you have only 1 loop left on the hook.**

Congratulations! Your first double triple crochet stitch (dtr) is now complete.

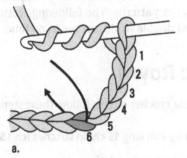

FIGURE 2-13: Inserting your hook into the sixth chain from the hook.

a.

b.

© John Wiley & Sons, Inc.

To finish the row, begin a new double triple crochet stitch in the next chain of your foundation chain, as indicated in Figure 2-14a. Work one double triple crochet in each successive chain across the foundation chain, taking care to yarn over three times before inserting the hook in each chain. When you finish the row, you should have 16 double triple crochet stitches in Row 1 (counting the turning chain as 1 double triple crochet). Figure 2-14b illustrates what the end of the first row of double triple crochet looks like. Figure 2-14c shows how a stitch diagram indicates a double triple crochet stitch.

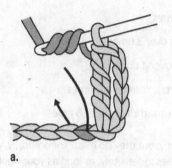 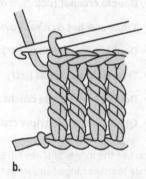 

FIGURE 2-14: Finishing the first row of double triple crochet.

a.　　　　　　　　　　b.　　　　　　　　　　c.

© John Wiley & Sons, Inc.

Turning around and beginning again: Row 2

To work the second row of double triple crochet, follow these steps:

1. **Turn your work.**

   Book 3, Chapter 1 explains how to turn your work correctly.

2. **Chain 5 (ch 5) for the turning chain.**

3. **Yarn over the hook (yo) 3 times.**

4. **Skipping the first stitch of the row directly below the turning chain, insert your hook into the next stitch.**

5. **Repeat Steps 3 through 7 in the preceding section in each of the next 14 double triple crochet stitches (dtr).**

   Be sure to yarn over 3 times before inserting your hook in each stitch.

6. **Work 1 double triple crochet stitch in the top chain of the previous row's turning chain.**

   You should have 16 double triple crochet stitches in Row 2 (counting the turning chain as 1 double triple crochet).

MAKING YOUR STITCHES EVEN LONGER

Each additional yarn over that you make at the beginning of a stitch adds length to the completed stitch. So if you continue to add yarn overs, you produce longer and longer stitches. Here's a breakdown of the yarn overs involved in several different stitches (note that the stitch names may vary in different publications):

- **Single crochet (sc):** No yarn over

- **Double crochet (dc):** Yarn over 1 time

- **Triple crochet (tr):** Yarn over 2 times

- **Double triple crochet (dtr):** Yarn over 3 times

- **Triple triple crochet (trtr):** Yarn over 4 times

- **Double triple triple crochet (dtrtr):** Yarn over 5 times

- **Quadruple triple triple crochet (quad):** Yarn over 6 times

You use the longer stitches infrequently, but they do exist. Theoretically, you can continue to make longer and longer stitches indefinitely, as long as your hook can hold all the loops.

Repeat these six steps for each additional row of double triple crochet, continuing until you feel comfortable with this stitch. Figure 2-15 shows you how rows of double triple crochet look as a fabric.

FIGURE 2-15: Several rows of double triple crochet.

© John Wiley & Sons, Inc.

Hooking a Half Double Crochet

The *half double crochet* (abbreviated *hdc*) is kind of an oddball stitch, and you make it differently from all the other stitches that appear earlier in this chapter. It falls in between a single crochet and a double crochet in height, but instead of working off two loops at a time, you draw the yarn through three loops on the hook. This action produces a fairly tight fabric similar to one made with a single crochet stitch. The following sections explain how to make the first two rows of half double crochet.

Starting with Row 1

Follow these steps to get started:

1. **Make a foundation chain with 15 chain stitches (ch 15).**

2. **Chain 2 more for the turning chain.**

   Check out Book 3, Chapter 1 for the scoop on chains.

TIP

Most pattern books combine the steps for making a foundation chain and turning chain into one by telling you to chain a total of 17.

To create your first half double crochet stitch:

REMEMBER

1. **Yarn over the hook (yo).**

   Don't forget to yarn over from back to front.

2. **Insert your hook into the third chain (ch) from the hook, as shown in Figure 2-16a.**

3. **Yarn over the hook.**

4. **Gently pull the wrapped hook through the center of the chain stitch, carrying the wrapped yarn through the stitch.**

   You should have 3 loops on your hook, just like in Figure 2-16b.

5. **Yarn over the hook.**

6. **Draw your yarn through all 3 loops on your hook.**

   Figure 2-17a depicts Step 6, and Figure 2-17b shows a completed half double crochet stitch (hdc).

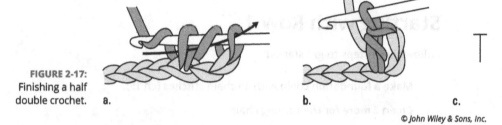

FIGURE 2-16:
Beginning a half double crochet.

a.

b.

© John Wiley & Sons, Inc.

FIGURE 2-17:
Finishing a half double crochet.

a.

b.

c.

© John Wiley & Sons, Inc.

To complete a full row of half double crochet stitches, begin in the next chain of the foundation chain, as indicated in Figure 2-18a. Work one half double crochet stitch in each successive chain across the foundation chain. When you count the turning chain as one half double crochet stitch, you should have 16 half double crochets at the end of Row 1. Figure 2-18b shows the end of the first half double crochet row.

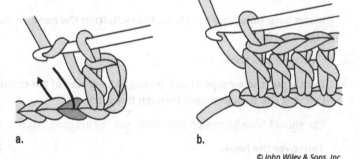

FIGURE 2-18:
Finishing your first row of half double crochet.

a.

b.

© John Wiley & Sons, Inc.

Moving on to Row 2

Here's how to begin the second row of half double crochet:

1. **Turn your work.**

Refer to Book 3, Chapter 1 for help properly turning your work.

2. **Chain 2 (ch 2) for the turning chain.**

3. **Yarn over the hook (yo).**

4. **Skipping the first stitch of the row directly below the turning chain, insert your hook into the next stitch, as in Figure 2-19.**

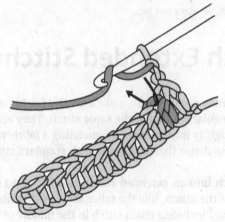

FIGURE 2-19:
Working a half double crochet into the second stitch.

© John Wiley & Sons, Inc.

5. **Repeat Steps 3 through 6 from the preceding section in each of the next 14 half double crochet stitches (hdc).**

Be sure to yarn over before inserting your hook into each stitch.

6. **Work 1 half double crochet in the top chain of the previous row's turning chain.**

You should have 16 half double crochet stitches in Row 2 if you count the turning chain as 1 half double crochet.

Repeat these steps for each additional row of half double crochet and continue working rows of half double crochet until you feel comfortable with this stitch. To see how rows of half double crochet look as a fabric, check out Figure 2-20.

FIGURE 2-20:
Several rows
of half double
crochet.

© John Wiley & Sons, Inc.

Adding Height with Extended Stitches

Occasionally a pattern may direct you to make *extended crochet stitches*, which are a little taller than the regular version of the same stitch. They also provide variation in texture with a slightly improved drape, meaning a fabric made of extended stitches is softer and less dense than one made with standard stitches.

REMEMBER

You can adapt any stitch into an extended stitch. How? Instead of adding a yarn over to the beginning of the stitch, like the taller stitches described earlier in this chapter, extended stitches include a chain stitch in the middle of the stitch to give a little extra lift.

In the following sections, you discover how to work two common extended stitches — the extended single crochet and the extended double crochet.

TIP

An extended stitch is usually abbreviated by adding an *E* before the standard abbreviation. So the abbreviation for extended double crochet, for example, is Edc.

Extended single crochet

The *extended single crochet* (abbreviated *Esc*) is a simple variation on the standard single crochet (abbreviated *sc*), which is covered in Book 3, Chapter 1. Follow these steps to start:

1. **Create a foundation chain by working 15 chain stitches (ch 15).**

2. **Chain 1 more for the turning chain.**

Now you're ready to begin your first extended single crochet stitch.

1. **Insert your hook into the second chain (ch) from the hook.**

2. **Yarn over the hook (yo).**

   Move from back to front, never front to back.

REMEMBER

3. **Gently pull the wrapped hook through the center of the chain stitch, carrying the wrapped yarn through the stitch (as shown in Figure 2-21).**

   Now you should have 2 loops on your hook.

4. **Yarn over the hook.**

5. **Work a chain stitch by drawing the hook, with the wrapped yarn, through the first loop on the hook.**

   Refer to Figure 2-22a for the visual.

6. **Yarn over the hook.**

7. **Draw the yarn through both loops on the hook, as shown in Figure 2-22b.**

   Well done! Your first extended single crochet stitch (Esc) is now complete.

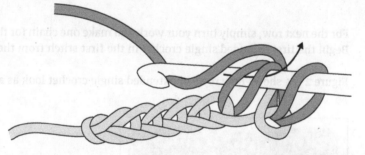

FIGURE 2-21:
Beginning an
extended single
crochet.

© John Wiley & Sons, Inc.

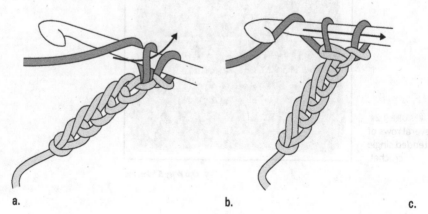

FIGURE 2-22:
Finishing an
extended single
crochet.

a.

b.

c.

© John Wiley & Sons, Inc.

To work the next extended single crochet stitch and continue the row:

1. **Insert your hook into the next chain stitch (ch), yarn over the hook (yo), and pull the yarn through the chain stitch.**

   You should have 2 loops on the hook.

2. **Repeat Steps 4 through 7 from the preceding instructions to complete the second extended single crochet stitch (Esc).**

3. **Work 1 extended single crochet stitch in each chain stitch across the foundation chain by repeating Steps 1 and 2.**

   You should have 15 extended single crochet stitches in the row. Figure 2-23 shows you what a completed row of extended single crochet looks like.

For the next row, simply turn your work and make one chain for the turning chain. Begin the first extended single crochet in the first stitch from the previous row.

Figure 2-24 shows how rows of extended single crochet look as a fabric.

Extended double crochet

The *extended double crochet* (abbreviated *Edc*) is a variation on the standard double crochet stitch (abbreviated *dc*) that's covered earlier in this chapter. To get started:

1. **Make a foundation chain by working 15 chain stitches (ch 15).**

2. **Chain 3 more stitches for the turning chain.**

To create your first extended double crochet stitch, follow these steps:

REMEMBER

1. **Yarn over the hook (yo).**

   Always yarn over from back to front.

2. **Insert your hook into the fourth chain (ch) from the hook.**

   Refer to Figure 2-1a, earlier in this chapter, for the proper positioning.

3. **Yarn over the hook.**

4. **Gently pull the wrapped hook through the center of the chain stitch, carrying the wrapped yarn through the stitch.**

   You should now have 3 loops on your hook. (Refer to Figure 2-1b, earlier in this chapter, for the visual of this step.)

5. **Yarn over the hook.**

6. **Work a chain stitch by drawing the yarn through the first loop on the hook, as in Figure 2-25.**

7. **Yarn over the hook.**

8. **Draw the yarn through the first 2 loops on your hook, like in Figure 2-26a.**

9. **Yarn over the hook.**

FIGURE 2-25:
Making a chain stitch for your extended double crochet.

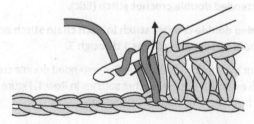

10. Draw the yarn through the last 2 loops on the hook, as shown in Figure 2-26b.

One extended double crochet stitch (Edc) is now complete, and you should have 1 loop remaining on your hook. When a stitch diagram indicates an extended double crochet stitch, you see the symbol shown in Figure 2-26c.

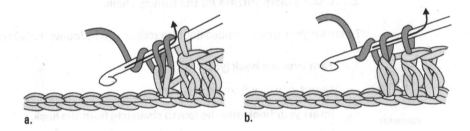

a.   b.

FIGURE 2-26:
Finishing an
extended double
crochet stitch.   c.

© John Wiley & Sons, Inc.

To work your next extended double crochet and continue the row, perform these steps:

1. Yarn over the hook (yo) and insert your hook into the next chain stitch (ch).

2. Yarn over and pull the yarn through the chain stitch.

You should have 3 loops on the hook.

3. Repeat Steps 5 through 10 from the preceding instructions to complete the second extended double crochet stitch (Edc).

4. Work 1 extended double crochet stitch in each chain stitch across the foundation chain by repeating Steps 1 through 3.

When you count the turning chain as the first extended double crochet, you should have 16 extended double crochet stitches in Row 1. Figure 2-27 shows the end of the first extended double crochet row.

To begin the next row of extended double crochet, turn your piece and make three chains for the turning chain. Skipping the first stitch, work your first extended double crochet stitch into the next stitch on the previous row and follow Steps 1 through 3 of the preceding instructions. Take a look at Figure 2-28 to see what rows of extended double crochet look like as a fabric.

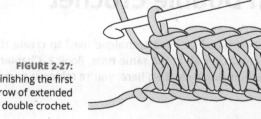

FIGURE 2-27: Finishing the first row of extended double crochet.

FIGURE 2-28: Several rows of extended double crochet.

A CROCHETING CONSTANT: STITCH WIDTH

Crochet stitches vary in either length or height, never width. That's because all stitches are the same width when worked properly with the same yarn and hook. Whether you're making a row of 16 chain stitches or fancy three-dimensional stitches, the width of your piece should be the same. After you complete the stitch and have one loop remaining on your hook, the top of the stitch is still the same width as all the other stitches because the size of hook you're using determines the size of both that last loop and the width of the stitch.

Creating a Foundation Double Crochet

The *foundation double crochet* (abbreviated *fdc*) is a technique used to create the foundation chain and first row of stitches all at the same time. Book 3, Chapter 1 shows you how to work a foundation single crochet; here, you're taking it to new heights. Follow these steps:

1. **Begin with 3 chain stitches (ch 3).**

2. **Yarn over the hook.**

3. **Insert the hook from front to back into the chain farthest from the hook.**

   See Figure 2-29 for an illustration of this step.

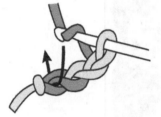

FIGURE 2-29: Beginning your first foundation double crochet.

© John Wiley & Sons, Inc.

4. **Yarn over the hook and pull the yarn through the chain stitch.**

   You should have 3 loops on the hook.

5. **Yarn over the hook and pull through the first loop (the one closest to the hook end) on the hook.**

   You have completed the foundation chain portion of the first foundation double crochet (shown in Figure 2-30).

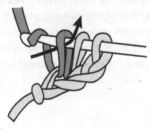

FIGURE 2-30: Finishing the foundation chain portion of the stitch.

© John Wiley & Sons, Inc.

6. Yarn over the hook and pull through the first 2 loops on the hook
(see Figure 2-31).

You should have 2 loops on the hook.

7. Yarn over the hook and pull through both loops on the hook
(see Figure 2-32a).

This completes the double crochet (dc) portion of your first foundation
double crochet (fdc), as shown in Figure 2-32b.

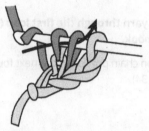

FIGURE 2-31:
Pulling the yarn
through the first
2 loops on the
hook.

© John Wiley & Sons, Inc.

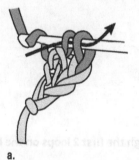 

FIGURE 2-32:
Completing the
first foundation
double crochet.   a.   b.

© John Wiley & Sons, Inc.

Now, to create the second foundation double crochet, follow these steps:

1. Yarn over the hook.

2. Insert the hook from front to back into the chain stitch (ch) made at the
base of the previous foundation double crochet (fdc; see Figure 2-33).

3. Yarn over the hook and pull the yarn through the chain stitch.

You should have 3 loops on the hook.

FIGURE 2-33:
Starting your second foundation double crochet.

© John Wiley & Sons, Inc.

4. **Yarn over the hook and pull the yarn through the first loop (the one closest to the hook end) on the hook.**

   You have completed the foundation chain portion of the next foundation double crochet (shown in Figure 2-34).

FIGURE 2-34:
Completing the foundation chain portion.

© John Wiley & Sons, Inc.

5. **Yarn over the hook and pull through the first 2 loops on the hook (see Figure 2-35).**

   You should have 2 loops on your hook.

6. **Yarn over the hook and pull through both loops on the hook (shown in Figure 2-36a).**

   Voila! You have now completed the double crochet portion of the next foundation double crochet (fdc; see Figure 2-36b).

7. **Repeat Steps 1 through 6 for each foundation double crochet you need in a particular pattern.**

FIGURE 2-35:
Pulling yarn through the first 2 loops on the hook.

© John Wiley & Sons, Inc.

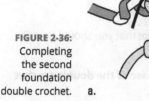

FIGURE 2-36:
Completing the second foundation double crochet.

a.

b.

© John Wiley & Sons, Inc.

Running on Empty: Joining a New Ball of Yarn

Every ball or skein has a limited amount of yarn on it. Sooner or later, you'll run out of yarn in the middle of a project. Joining a new ball or skein of yarn correctly is as important to the appearance of your work as the actual stitches. You may find the process awkward at first, but you'll be an old hand at it in no time.

TIP

You can join a new ball of yarn in any stitch of a row, but making the transition at the end of a row creates a neater appearance. The sections that follow explain how to do both methods.

WARNING

Avoid tying the beginning end of the new ball to the tail end of the first ball, because doing so produces an unsightly knot in your work.

Joining at the end of a row

The following steps use a swatch of fabric made with double crochet stitches, so if you haven't already made a swatch, refer to the "Doing a Double Crochet" section, earlier in this chapter, to get ready. After you've completed a few rows, follow these steps to join new yarn at the end of a row:

1. **Double crochet (dc) across the row, stopping before the last stitch of the row.**

2. **Work the last double crochet to the point where only 2 loops are left on the hook.**

3. **Wrap the cut end of the new yarn around the hook, from back to front.**

   The *working end* of the yarn (the end that's attached to the ball or skein) should be the end closest to you.

4. **Draw the new yarn through the 2 loops on your hook.**

   Figure 2-37 illustrates how to perform this step. Note that you should have 2 strands of yarn hanging down.

5. **Tug on the dropped end of the old yarn at the base of the double crochet to tighten the stitch.**

   The remaining tail of the old yarn is the *tail end*. It goes into hiding when you weave it into the fabric later on.

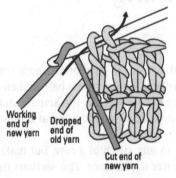

FIGURE 2-37: Drawing new yarn through both loops on your hook.

Working end of new yarn

Dropped end of old yarn

Cut end of new yarn

© *John Wiley & Sons, Inc.*

Joining in the middle of a row

Sometimes you have no choice but to join new yarn in the middle of a row, such as when you shape necklines or armholes in a garment. To join a new ball or skein in such cases, work as follows:

1. **Make a slipknot on the end of the new ball of yarn.**

   See Book 3, Chapter 1, for details on making a slipknot.

2. **Insert your hook into the stitch where you want to join in the new yarn.**

3. **Place the new yarn's slipknot on the hook.**

4. **Draw the slipknot through the stitch, as shown in Figure 2-38.**

   One loop is now on your hook, and you're ready to begin crocheting the new row.

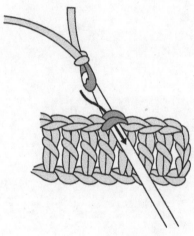

FIGURE 2-38:
Joining yarn with
a slipknot.

© John Wiley & Sons, Inc.

You can weave the ends of the yarn in later with a yarn needle, but a better approach is working over the strands while crocheting the next row because it saves time. To work over the strands, lay them down over the tops of the stitches in the current row; then when you work your stitches, you capture the strands in the bases of your stitches. Cut off any excess yarn after you've covered a few inches.

TIP

Weaving in yarn ends is a tedious, thankless job — and one you should avoid whenever you can. Some projects allow you to leave ends dangling off to the side to be incorporated into fringe. You can also leave ends dangling on the side if they can be sewn into a seam later on. Border stitches are also good for covering your ends. However you go about avoiding weaving in your yarn ends, just don't try to cover too many strands in one area, or else you'll create a messy lump along the edge of your project.

Chapter **3**

Increasing and Decreasing Stitches

Crocheting would be pretty boring if all you could make were squares and rectangles. Sure, you could make armloads of scarves or afghans, but you probably want to branch out and create some shape. In this chapter, you discover how to widen and narrow your designs by simply adding or taking away a few stitches.

Note: This chapter shows you how to increase and decrease with single crochet stitches (see Book 3, Chapter 1) or double crochet stitches (see Book 3, Chapter 2), but you work increases and decreases with other stitches exactly the same way. Most patterns explain how to work the increases and decreases necessary for that particular design, so be sure to read all the pattern instructions before beginning.

REMEMBER

When increasing or decreasing stitches, always count your stitches to make sure you have the correct number on your work.

Increasing Stitches

Increasing stitches (abbreviated *inc*) is just what it sounds like: You add stitches to a row so it has more stitches than the previous one to broaden the shape of your design. Depending on the type of design you're making, you can increase stitches anywhere in the row — at the beginning, end, or middle; in every other stitch; or any place where you want the shaping to occur. If you're working from a pattern, it'll always tell you exactly where to place your extra stitches. No guesswork necessary!

REMEMBER

Adding a stitch at the beginning or end of a row is a common way to increase stitches while working in rows. This method creates a smooth, tapered edge to your piece. Adding stitches to the middle of a row makes the shaping more subtle, allowing your piece to bend or angle out from the center, as with many shawl patterns.

Regardless of where the increase occurs, you usually make it by working two or more stitches into one stitch. Most stitches, no matter how tall they are, have the same steps for working an increase in the middle or end of a row. Working an increase at the beginning of a row of single crochet, however, is a little different from the taller stitches.

In the following sections, you find out how to increase with single crochet and double crochet at the beginning of a row. Keep in mind that increases at the beginning of a row for stitches taller than single crochet are worked in the same way as the double crochet, counting their own specific turning chain as the first stitch of the increase. (Flip to Book 3, Chapter 1 for more on turning chains.)

TIP

If you're working in rounds, increasing usually occurs in each successive round to accommodate the larger circumference of the design. See Book 3, Chapter 4 for more on working in rounds.

Increasing anywhere with single crochet

Because the turning chain in a single crochet row doesn't count as a stitch, increasing one single crochet at the beginning of a row is the same as doing it in the middle or at the end of a row. Wherever you want to increase one single crochet (the pattern will tell you where to do this), work two single crochet stitches in the designated stitch, like in Figure 3-1a. Figure 3-1b illustrates a completed single crochet increase, and Figure 3-1c shows the stitch symbol you'd see in a diagram.

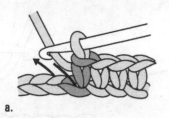

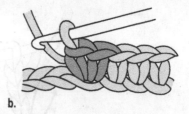

FIGURE 3-1:
Increasing with
single crochet.

© *John Wiley & Sons, Inc.*

Increasing with double crochet at the beginning of a row

If the pattern calls for an increase in stitches at the beginning of a row and you're working with stitches taller than single crochet, adding stitches to the beginning of a row is a little different from adding them in the middle or at the end. The main difference is that taller stitches require a turning chain at the beginning of a row. To figure out how to add one double crochet stitch at the beginning of a row, make a swatch of double crochet stitches and then follow these steps:

1. **Chain 3 (ch 3).**

   This is the same number of chains required for a double crochet turning chain, which counts as the first stitch.

2. **Work your next double crochet stitch (dc) into the first stitch of the row.**

   The first stitch of the row is the stitch directly below the turning chain, the one that you usually skip — see Figure 3-2a. Check out the completed stitch in Figure 3-2b and its symbol as you'd see it in pictorial crochet diagrams in Figure 3-2c. *Note:* The stitch you make in this step is the increase stitch.

3. **Finish the rest of the row as you normally would, working 1 double crochet stitch in each stitch across the row.**

   To double-check your work, count your stitches (including the turning chain). You should have 1 more stitch in this row than you have in the previous row.

TIP

Increasing and
Decreasing Stitches

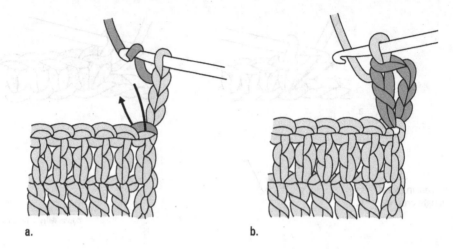

a.   b.

FIGURE 3-2:
Working a double
crochet increase
at the beginning
of a row.

c.

Increasing with double crochet in the middle or end of a row

Sometimes a pattern may call for an increase at the end of a row or while you're working your way across a row. Basically, you work an increase in the middle or at the end of a row the same way you work an increase at the beginning of a row, except you don't have to worry about the turning chain. The following instructions explain how:

1. Work across your row until you get to the designated increase stitch or the last stitch of the row.

2. Work 2 double crochet stitches (dc) into the designated stitch.

Figure 3-3a illustrates how to perform Step 2, and Figure 3-3b shows a completed increase in the middle of a row. Figure 3-3c is the symbol for a double crochet increase in the middle or end of a row as you'd see it in pictorial crochet diagrams.

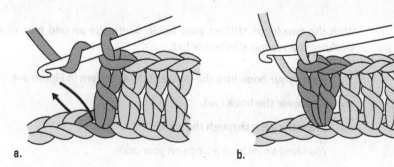

FIGURE 3-3:
Working a double crochet increase in the middle of a row.

a.

b.

c.

Decreasing Stitches

When you want to shape your design so that it gets smaller, you need to decrease your stitches. You can *decrease* a stitch (abbreviated *sc2tog, dc2tog,* and so on), which is really just subtracting a stitch, in the same places that you increase stitches — at the beginning or end of a row or somewhere in the middle. Decreasing takes a few more steps, but it's as simple as increasing. In the following sections, you find several useful methods for decreasing stitches.

Decreasing with single crochet

REMEMBER

When a single crochet decrease (*sc2tog*) is called for, the pattern will typically tell you where the decrease(s) should be made. You decrease single crochet stitches in the middle or end of a row by turning two separate stitches into one, which is a two-step process. But because of these two steps, you have to think ahead and start the first part one stitch before your pattern designates the actual decrease.

To begin the two-part process of turning two single crochet stitches into one, start the first single crochet as you normally would.

1. **Insert your hook into the first stitch of the decrease.**

2. **Yarn over the hook (yo).**

3. **Draw the yarn through the stitch.**

   You should have 2 loops remaining on your hook.

Increasing and
Decreasing Stitches

With the two loops still on your hook, begin the second part of the decrease by working the second single crochet.

1. **Insert your hook into the next stitch, as shown in Figure 3-4.**

2. **Yarn over the hook (yo).**

3. **Draw the yarn through the stitch.**

   You should now have 3 loops on your hook.

4. **Yarn over.**

5. **Draw the yarn through all 3 loops on your hook, just like in Figure 3-5a.**

   Figure 3-5b shows 1 complete single crochet decrease, and Figure 3-5c denotes the stitch symbol for this action.

FIGURE 3-4:
Beginning the second part of a single crochet decrease.

© John Wiley & Sons, Inc.

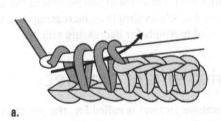

a.   b.

FIGURE 3-5:
Finishing a single crochet decrease.   c.

© John Wiley & Sons, Inc.

Decreasing with double crochet

The double crochet decrease (*dc2tog*) can be used in the middle of a row or round or at the beginning or end of a row or round (the pattern you're working with should tell you exactly where). It's almost identical to the single crochet decrease described in the preceding section except it has one more step.

Begin the first part of the decrease by starting the first double crochet as you would for a normal double crochet stitch.

1. **Yarn over the hook (yo).**

2. **Insert your hook into the next stitch.**

3. **Yarn over.**

4. **Draw the yarn through the stitch.**

   You should have 3 loops on the hook.

5. **Yarn over.**

6. **Draw the yarn through the first 2 loops on your hook.**

   As you can see from Figure 3-6, 2 loops remain on the hook.

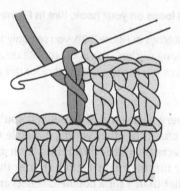

FIGURE 3-6: Completing the first part of a double crochet decrease.

© John Wiley & Sons, Inc.

In the second part of the decrease, you work the second double crochet stitch and join it with the first to complete the decrease. (*Note:* At this point, your first stitch is actually a *half-closed stitch:* in other words, one that has been partially completed.) With the two loops still on your hook, start to work the second double crochet stitch as you would a regular stitch.

1. **Yarn over the hook (yo).**

2. **Insert your hook into the next stitch, as shown in Figure 3-7.**

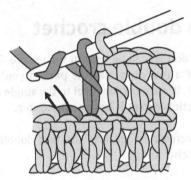

FIGURE 3-7:
Beginning the
second part of a
double crochet
decrease.

© John Wiley & Sons, Inc.

3. **Yarn over.**

4. **Draw the yarn through the stitch.**

You should now have 4 loops on your hook.

5. **Yarn over.**

6. **Draw the yarn through the first 2 loops on your hook.**

Three loops should still be on your hook.

7. **Yarn over.**

8. **Draw the yarn through all 3 loops on your hook, like in Figure 3-8a.**

If you look at the tops of the stitches in Figure 3-8b, you see only 1 stitch across the top of the 2 underlying stitches. This is 1 complete double crochet decrease. Figure 3-8c introduces you to the stitch symbol for this particular decrease.

REMEMBER

If you want to decrease at the very beginning of a row and you're working with a stitch that requires a turning chain (in other words, a double crochet stitch or anything taller), you work the decrease a little differently from one in the middle or at the end of a row. Make your turning chain a stitch shorter than you normally would (for example, chain 2 rather than 3 for a double crochet) and then continue across the row as normal. When you work the next row, don't work a stitch in the shortened turning chain. This process takes care of the decrease and leaves a smooth edge.

To avoid this kind of a decrease at the beginning of a double crochet row, a pattern may place a decrease in the second and third stitch rather than in the first two stitches. The opposite end of the row would then have the decrease placed one stitch in from the end to be symmetrical with the beginning of the row. This way you continue to work the turning chain and last stitch like usual and the decrease still falls toward the beginning and end of the row.

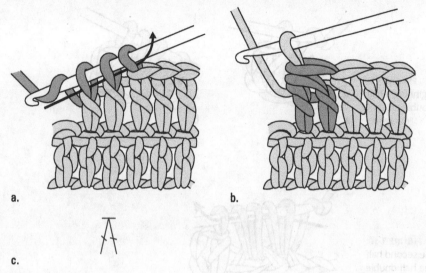

FIGURE 3-8:
Finishing a
double crochet
decrease.

a.

b.

c.

Decreasing with a half double crochet stitch

The half double crochet decrease (*hdc2tog*) is worked in a slightly different manner from either the single crochet decrease or the double crochet decrease, due to the fact that the stitch itself is somewhat of a hybrid between the two. The following steps detail how to decrease a half double crochet in the middle of a row.

The first part of the decrease begins by starting the first half double crochet as you would for a normal half double crochet stitch:

1. **Yarn over the hook (yo).**

2. **Insert your hook into the next stitch (see Figure 3-9a).**

3. **Yarn over.**

4. **Draw the yarn through the stitch.**

   You should have 3 loops on the hook (see Figure 3-9b).

5. **Yarn over.**

6. **Insert your hook into the next stitch.**

7. **Yarn over.**

8. **Draw the yarn through the stitch.**

   You should have 5 loops on the hook (see Figure 3-10).

Increasing and
Decreasing Stitches

FIGURE 3-9:
Beginning a half double crochet decrease.

a.   b.

© John Wiley & Sons, Inc.

FIGURE 3-10:
The second half of the half double crochet decrease.

© John Wiley & Sons, Inc.

9. **Yarn over the hook and pull the yarn through all 5 loops on the hook, as shown in Figure 3-11a.**

Figure 3-11b shows the symbol you see when a stitch diagram indicates a half double crochet stitch.

FIGURE 3-11:
A completed half double crochet decrease.

a.   b.

© John Wiley & Sons, Inc.

Decreasing with slip stitches at the start of a row

One handy method for decreasing at the beginning of a row is to slip stitch across the number of stitches that you want to decrease. You use this method when you need to decrease more than just one or two stitches, typically for shaping the armholes or neck edges in a garment. The resulting look is a squared-off corner.

To find out exactly how decreasing with slip stitches works, take a swatch of double crochet stitches and work the following steps to decrease three stitches at the beginning of a row:

1. **Work 1 slip stitch (sl st) in each of the first 4 stitches.**

Book 3, Chapter 1 has instructions on working a slip stitch.

2. **Chain 3 (ch 3) for the turning chain, which also counts as the first double crochet stitch (dc).**

3. **Skip the stitch under the turning chain and then work a double crochet in the next stitch.**

4. **Continue to work a double crochet in each stitch across the row.**

Figure 3-12 shows you how this decrease should look.

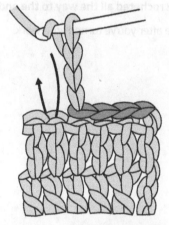

FIGURE 3-12:
Decreasing three double crochet stitches with slip stitches.

© John Wiley & Sons, Inc.

Decreasing by skipping stitches

Skipping stitches is an easy way to decrease stitches in a row. It's an especially good tactic when you're shaping armholes or necklines, but you can actually decrease by skipping stitches anywhere in the row — at the beginning, middle, or end. You can skip any number of stitches, but the more you skip, the larger the gap created by the skipped stitches will be. That's why decreasing by skipping stitches works best when you're dealing with single crochet stitches.

REMEMBER

To decrease by skipping stitches, simply work to the stitch that the pattern tells you to decrease. Then skip the designated stitch, working the stitch before and after it as usual.

Decreasing by stopping and turning before you reach the end of a row

An alternate method of decreasing stitches at the end of a row is to just stop before you get to the last stitch. This technique, which can be used with any stitch, gives you a rather squared-off look and is quite often used when shaping garments. Here's how to perform this pretty simple decreasing tactic:

1. **Work across the row until you have the number of stitches that your work requires.**

2. **Stop crocheting and turn your work, leaving the remaining stitches on the current row unworked.**

    Book 3, Chapter 1 has instructions on properly turning your work.

3. **Make your turning chain and then work back across the previous row in the same manner as if you'd crocheted all the way to the end.**

    Figure 3-13 shows this decrease after you've turned your work.

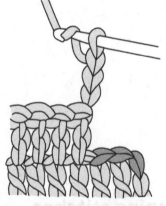

FIGURE 3-13: Decreasing double crochet by stopping and turning your work.

© John Wiley & Sons, Inc.

Simple Ripple Blanket Project

Practice your new shaping skills with this fun, colorful blanket. The larger size is perfect for a twin bed, or even as a cozy throw to brighten up your couch, but you can easily change the size by using the optional instructions. The gentle waves in the pattern are shaped by alternating an even number of increase stitches with decrease stitches so you always end each row with the same number of stitches. (To see a color photo of this blanket, visit dummies.com/go/knitcrochetAIO.)

The easy-care acrylic yarn used to make this blanket comes in a wide variety of colors, so feel free to play with the number of colors and the size of each color block. You can even change up the brand of yarn if you want to. Just make sure that the yarn you buy is the same size and weight as the yarn noted in the pattern (see Book 1, Chapter 2 for more on yarn substitution) and that you can come up with the right gauge. (Find out all about gauge in Book 1, Chapter 3.)

Materials and vital statistics

>> **Yarn:** Coats & Clark Red Heart "Super Saver" worsted-weight yarn (100% acrylic), Article #E300 (7 oz. [198 g], 364 yds [333 m] each skein): 2 skeins each of

- #624 Tea Leaf (green) (A)
- #724 Baby Pink (pink) (B)
- #360 Café (brown) (C)
- #381 Light Blue (blue) (D)
- #579 Pale Plum (purple) (E)
- #316 Soft White (white) (F)

>> **Hook:** Crochet hook size I-9 U.S. (5.5 mm) or size needed to obtain gauge

>> **Large-eyed yarn needle**

>> **Measurements:** 40 in. wide x 60 in. long

>> **Gauge:** 14 sts and 8 rows = 4 in. in wave patt

Note: For the gauge swatch, make 31 chain stitches. Work Rows 2 through 10 all in the same color. Then place your ruler straight across the width of your swatch and count the stitches across 4 inches of one row, following the wave pattern. Count each increase as 2 double crochet and each decrease as 1 double crochet.

>> **Stitches used:** Chain stitch (ch), double crochet (dc), **dc2tog:** * (Yo, insert hook in next st, yo, draw yarn through st, yo, draw yarn through first 2 loops on hook) twice, yo, draw yarn through 3 loops on hook *.

Directions

The directions for the following project appear as you'd see them in the real world of crochet, complete with abbreviations, followed by the plain-English format. (Figure 3-14 shows the blanket's stitch diagram.) Feel free to follow whichever set of instructions you're most comfortable with (and check out Book 1, Chapter 4 to brush up on the abbreviations). Your design will turn out super no matter which format you follow.

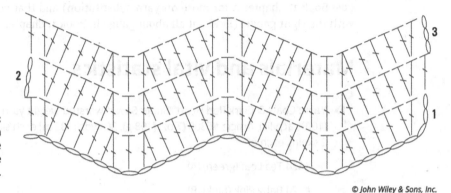

FIGURE 3-14:
The stitch diagram for the Simple Ripple Blanket.

1. **Foundation chain: With A, ch 143.**

   Create your foundation chain by working 143 chain stitches with green.

2. **Row 1: Skip first 3 ch from hook (counts as first dc), * 2 dc in next ch (inc made), dc in each of next 3 ch, dc2tog over next 2 ch, dc in next ch, dc2tog over next 2 ch, dc in each of next 3 ch, 2 dc in next ch, dc in next ch *; rep from * to * 9 more times across, *turn* — 141 dc.**

   To complete Row 1, skip the first 3 chain stitches from the hook (the 3 skipped stitches are the turning chain and count as your first double crochet stitch), * work 2 double crochet in the next chain, work 1 double crochet in each of the next 3 chain stitches, double crochet 2 together over the next 2 chain stitches, work 1 double crochet in the next chain, double crochet 2 together over the next 2 chain stitches, work 1 double crochet in each of the next 3 chain stitches, work 2 double crochet in the next chain, work 1 double crochet in the next chain *; repeat the instructions from * to * 9 more times and then turn your work. You'll have 141 double crochet stitches.

3. **Rows 2–3: Ch 3 (counts as first dc), * 2 dc in next dc, dc in each of next 3 dc, dc2tog over next 2 dc, dc in next dc, dc2tog over next 2 dc, dc in each of next 3 dc, 2 dc in next dc, dc in next dc *; rep from * to * across, *turn*.**

   To complete Row 2, chain 3 for your turning chain (which counts as the first double crochet), * work 2 double crochet in the next double crochet, work 1 double crochet in each of the next 3 double crochet stitches, double crochet 2 together over the next 2 double crochet stitches, work 1 double crochet in the next double crochet, double crochet 2 together over the next 2 double crochet stitches, work 1 double crochet in each of the next 3 double crochet stitches, work 2 double crochet in the next double crochet, work 1 double crochet in the next double crochet *; repeat the instructions from * to * across the row and then turn your work. Work Row 3 the same way as Row 2.

4. **Row 4: Rep Row 2 across until 1 st remains. In the last st, work the first part of the dc, with A, until 2 loops remain on the hook, join B and complete the dc as usual, *turn*.**

To complete Row 4, repeat Row 2 across the row to the last stitch. Work 1 double crochet in the last stitch until 2 loops remain on the hook. Drop green, yarn over with pink, draw through the last 2 loops on the hook, and then turn. (See Book 3, Chapter 5, to find out how to change colors.)

5. **Rows 5–7: With B, rep Row 2.**

To complete Rows 5 through 7, work as for Row 2 using pink rather than green.

6. **Row 8: Rep Row 2 across until 1 st remains. In the last st, work the first part of the dc, with B, until 2 loops remain on the hook, join C and complete the dc as usual, *turn*.**

To complete Row 8, repeat Row 2 across the row to the last stitch. Work 1 double crochet in the last stitch until 2 loops remain on the hook. Drop pink, yarn over with brown, and draw through the last 2 loops on the hook; then turn.

7. **Rows 9–20: Rep Rows 5–8 for D and E and then rep Rows 5–8 for F until 1 st remains on the last row. In the last st, work the first part of the dc, with F, until 2 loops remain on the hook, join A and complete the dc as usual, *turn*.**

To complete Rows 9 through 20, work Rows 5 through 8 for blue, then purple, then white until 1 stitch remains. Work 1 double crochet, with white, in the last stitch until 2 loops remain on the hook. Drop white, yarn over with green, draw through the last 2 loops on the hook, and then turn.

8. **Work in est patt working 4 rows each in the following color sequence: A, B, C, D, E, F until blanket measures 60 in. and each color has been worked a total of 5 times. Don't turn on the last row. Fasten off. Weave in loose ends.**

Continue to work Rows 5 through 8, working 4 rows each in the following color order: green, pink, brown, blue, purple, white. Work until the blanket is about 60 inches long and each color block has been worked a total of 5 times. On the last row, don't turn. Fasten off instead and weave in loose ends with your yarn needle.

Optional directions for different sizes

To lengthen or shorten the blanket, simply adjust the number of rows you work until it's the desired size. To change the width of the blanket, add or subtract 10 chains from the first step for every 3 inches of width, and then follow the pattern adjusting how many times you repeat the stitch pattern in Step 2 (10 chains = 1 repeat).

IN THIS CHAPTER

» **Creating and joining a center ring**

» **Adding additional rounds to your ring**

» **Spiraling to avoid visible seams**

» **Giving your work dimension**

» **Crocheting the perfect hat**

Chapter 4

Crocheting in Circles

Who says that going in circles doesn't get you anywhere? Obviously that person has never crocheted! To crochet hats, mittens, bags, stuffed animals, and more, you need to be able to crochet a circle by working in rounds.

Crocheting rounds is no more difficult than working rows. Instead of working back and forth, you work around in a circle, increasing the number of stitches you work in each round to accommodate the growing circumference. This chapter shows you three common methods for creating a center ring, which is the basis for all rounds, and how to work rounds of stitches off of it. You also discover how to work in a spiral and make three-dimensional shapes.

Practice your new skills on the fashionable Slouch Hat project, worked in increasing rounds of double crochet stitches.

Lord of the Center Rings

To begin a design that you work in rounds, you must first create a center ring. The *center ring* is the foundation for all crocheted designs that are worked in rounds — just like the foundation chain you use when working in rows (see Book 3,

Chapter 1). The three most frequently used methods for creating a center ring are as follows:

>> Working chain stitches into a ring

>> Working a round of stitches into one chain stitch

>> Working stitches into an adjustable loop of yarn

The following sections show you these three methods and explain when to use each. You also learn how to end a round and be in the proper position to start the next round.

Joining chain stitches into a ring

REMEMBER

The most common method for creating a center ring is to make a chain and close it into a ring with a slip stitch. (See Book 3, Chapter 1 for the how-to on making chain stitches and slip stitches.) Use this method when your first round is made up of a fairly large number of stitches and you need the room in which to fit them, or if the design calls for an obvious hole in the center of the piece.

The next sections explain how to create the center ring and work your first round off of that ring.

Making a center ring

The following steps show you how to create a simple center ring of six chain stitches:

1. **Chain 6 (ch 6).**

2. **Insert your hook from front to back into the first chain stitch you made, as shown in Figure 4-1, to form a ring.**

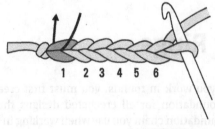

FIGURE 4-1:
Making the center ring chain.

© John Wiley & Sons, Inc.

3. **Yarn over your hook (yo).**

4. **Draw the yarn through the stitch and through the loop on your hook, like in Figure 4-2a.**

   Your center ring is now complete. It should look like the one in Figure 4-2b.

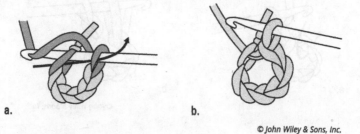

FIGURE 4-2:
Completing the center ring.

a.   b.

© John Wiley & Sons, Inc.

REMEMBER

The number of stitches in the beginning chain determines the size of the hole that the center ring creates as well as how many stitches you can work into the center ring. Make sure the ring is large enough to accommodate the number of stitches you'll be working in it. On the other hand, make sure it's not so long that you have a big loose hole in the center. *Note:* When you're working a pattern, it tells you how many chain stitches you need for the proper size center ring.

Working the first round

After you make the center ring, you're ready to crochet your first round. Just as when you're beginning a new row, you first need to determine the number of turning chain stitches necessary to bring your hook up to the proper level for the next round of stitches. (The number of turning chains you need depends on the stitch you're about to work; Book 3, Chapter 1 has a chart that shows how many turning chain stitches the basic crochet stitches require.)

Now here's the easy part about working with a center ring: Instead of inserting your hook into the actual stitches of the center ring, just go through the center hole! The following steps show you how to work single crochet stitches into the center ring:

1. **Chain 1 (ch 1) to make the turning chain for single crochet (sc).**

2. **Insert your hook into the center ring so that the hook end is behind the ring. (See Figure 4-3a.)**

3. Yarn over the hook (yo).

4. Draw the yarn through the center ring to the front of the ring. (Refer to Figure 4-3b.)

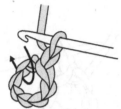 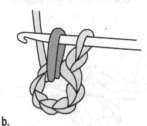

FIGURE 4-3:
Working a single crochet into the center ring.

a.   b.

5. Yarn over the hook.

6. Draw the yarn through the 2 loops on your hook.

Your first completed single crochet stitch should look like the one in Figure 4-4a, where the arrow shows how you must insert the hook for the next stitch.

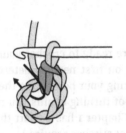 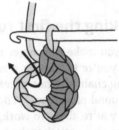

FIGURE 4-4:
Working a round of single crochet.

a.   b.

Continue to work single crochet stitches into the ring until you can't fit anymore (see Figure 4-4b for the visual). You may fit in more stitches than you expect because the center ring will stretch somewhat.

Working stitches in the chain stitch

REMEMBER

The second most common method for creating a center ring is to work all the stitches for the first round in one chain stitch. You generally use this method when the design calls for a small hole in the center of the pattern or almost no hole at all.

To start a center ring this way, chain one stitch (this is what you work the stitches in) plus the number of stitches required for the turning chain, depending on which particular stitch you work in the first round. (See Book 3, Chapter 1 for a list of the most common turning chain lengths.)

Follow these steps to work your first round of double crochet stitches into a chain stitch. *Note:* Although the double crochet is starting stitch in the following steps, the process works the same whichever stitch you choose to start with.

1. **Chain 1 (ch 1).**

2. **Chain 3 more for the double crochet stitch's (dc) turning chain.**

3. **Yarn over the hook (yo).**

4. **Insert your hook into the fourth chain from the hook, as shown in Figure 4-5.**

   This is the first chain stitch you made; it becomes your center ring chain stitch.

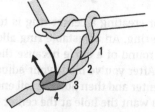

FIGURE 4-5: Inserting the hook into your first chain stitch.

© John Wiley & Sons, Inc.

5. **Work 1 complete double crochet stitch in the center ring chain stitch.**

   Do this by yarning over, drawing the yarn through the center ring chain stitch, yarning over, drawing the yarn through the first 2 loops on the hook, yarning over, and drawing the yarn through the first 2 loops on the hook. (See Book 3, Chapter 2 for more on how to make a double crochet stitch.)

6. **Continue working double crochet stitches in the same center ring chain stitch until you're comfortable with the process.**

For the next stitch, yarn over, insert your hook into the center ring chain stitch, and complete the stitch as you would a regular double crochet. Figure 4-6a shows you how to begin the third stitch, and Figure 4-6b shows a growing number of completed stitches.

REMEMBER

The turning chain for double crochet stitches worked in the round always counts as the first stitch.

FIGURE 4-6:
Making your
first round of
double crochet
in the center ring
chain stitch.

a.

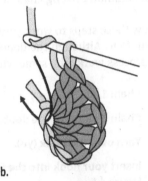

b.

© John Wiley & Sons, Inc.

Working stitches in an adjustable ring

REMEMBER

The third most common method for creating a center ring is to work your first round of stitches into an adjustable ring. An adjustable ring allows you to make any number of stitches in the first round of a circle because the beginning loop can slide open or closed as needed. After you've made your adjustable ring, work the first round of stitches into the center and then pull the tail end until the center is closed. Use this method when you want the hole at the center of a project to be completely closed.

You can work an adjustable ring with any stitch; just remember to work the required number of turning chains before working your first stitch into the ring (see Book 3, Chapter 1 for a refresher on turning chains). Follow these steps to work one round of single crochet into the center of an adjustable ring:

1. **Leaving a 2-inch tail, make a loop by crossing the working end of the yarn over the tail end and pinching the loop where the ends cross with the thumb and index finger of your nondominant hand.**

The *working end* is the one attached to the ball of yarn. Figure 4-7a shows what this step looks like.

2. **Insert your hook through the center of the ring.**

3. **Yarn over (yo) with the working end of the yarn and draw the yarn through the ring, as shown in Figure 4-7b.**

   You now have 1 loop on your hook. Figure 4-7c shows how a stitch diagram indicates what you need to begin making an adjustable ring.

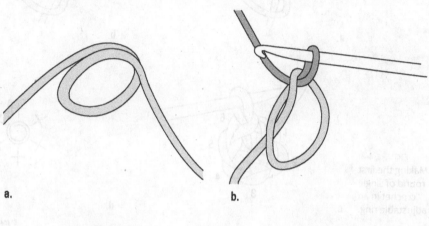

a.   b.

FIGURE 4-7:
Setting up the
adjustable ring.   c.

© John Wiley & Sons, Inc.

4. **Chain 1 (ch 1).**

   This is the turning chain for a single crochet (sc).

5. **Insert the hook through the center of the ring, yarn over, and draw up a loop (see Figure 4-8a).**

   You now have 2 loops on your hook.

6. **Yarn over and draw the yarn through both loops on your hook.**

   One single crochet in the center of the ring is now complete (see Figure 4-8b).

7. **Work 5 more single crochets in the center of the ring, and then pull the tail end of the yarn until the center of the ring is closed.**

   Figure 4-8c shows 6 single crochet stitches in an adjustable ring with the tail end pulled tight to close the hole at the center of the ring. Figure 4-8d shows how a stitch diagram provides these instructions.

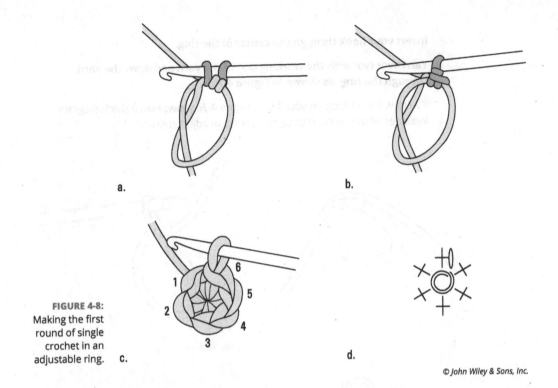

FIGURE 4-8: Making the first round of single crochet in an adjustable ring.

a.

b.

c.

d.

© John Wiley & Sons, Inc.

Uniting Your Ring

After you complete the number of stitches you need for your first round, you must join the first and last stitches of the round to complete the circle. The most popular way of doing that is by working a slip stitch in the top of the round's first stitch; doing so puts you in the proper position to begin the next round. You join each successive round in the same place, which creates a slightly visible seam. (To make a round without a seam, see the later section "Another Option: Spiraling Up and Up.")

You join single crochet rounds a little bit differently than rounds of other stitches, so the following sections include one example of each.

Single crochet

To join a round of single crochet stitches, proceed as follows:

1. **After completing the last single crochet (sc) of the round, insert your hook under the top 2 loops of the first single crochet stitch you made.**

REMEMBER

The chain-1 turning chain at the beginning of a single crochet round doesn't count as a stitch, so skip over it and work the slip stitch in the first single crochet.

2. **Yarn over the hook (yo).**

3. **Draw the yarn through the stitch and the loop on your hook to complete 1 slip stitch (sl st), as shown in Figure 4-9a.**

   Congratulations! You've just joined the first round of single crochet. Figure 4-9b shows a stitch diagram depicting the placement of the joining slip stitch, which is the dot at the top. (See Book 1, Chapter 4 for help reading stitch diagrams.)

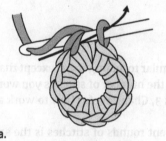

FIGURE 4-9:
Joining a single crochet round with a slip stitch.

a.   b.

© John Wiley & Sons, Inc.

Double crochet and other stitches

To join a round of double crochet (or any other stitch), you must do the following:

1. **Insert your hook in the top of the turning chain after completing the last double crochet (dc) of the round.**

   Note that the turning chain counts as the first stitch of the round.

2. **Yarn over the hook (yo).**

3. **Draw the yarn through the turning chain and the loop on your hook to complete 1 slip stitch (sl st), as shown in Figure 4-10a.**

   You've just joined the first round of double crochet. Figure 4-10b is a stitch diagram depicting the placement of the joining slip stitch, which is the dot at the top, by the turning chain. (Not sure how to read stitch diagrams? Refer to Book 1, Chapter 4.)

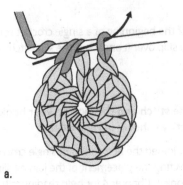

FIGURE 4-10:
Joining a double
crochet round
with a slip stitch. **a.**

b.

© John Wiley & Sons, Inc.

Adding Rounds

Adding rounds to your work is similar to adding rows, except that you usually don't turn your work and you increase the number of stitches you work in each round so that the piece lies flat. (See Book 3, Chapter 3 for how to work an increase.)

The method of working subsequent rounds of stitches is the same for all stitches except the single crochet, as you discover in the following sections. However, the number of stitches you start with changes depending on the height of the stitch you're working with. Taller stitches, such as double and triple crochet, require more stitches in each round because the circumference of the circle they create is larger than a circle created with shorter stitches. The pattern you're working with should tell you how many stitches to work for your project.

REMEMBER

The slip stitch that joins each round doesn't count as a stitch (regardless of whether you're working in single crochet or a taller stitch). When you join the last stitch to the first stitch, make sure you're working the slip stitch into the first stitch of the round and not the slip stitch from the previous round. So you don't accidentally work stitches into the slip stitch, be sure to count your stitches at the end of each round to ensure that you have the correct amount.

The second round of single crochet

Working rounds of single crochet is different from most other stitches because the turning chain doesn't count as a stitch. To work a second round of single crochet, follow these steps:

1. After joining the first round, chain 1 (ch 1) for the turning chain.

2. Without turning your piece, work 2 single crochet stitches (sc) under the top 2 loops of the first stitch.

The first stitch is the one directly below the turning chain; it's the same stitch you worked the joining slip stitch into.

3. **Work 2 single crochet stitches in each stitch around.**

4. **Join the first and last stitches of the round with a slip stitch (sl st).**

The second round of double crochet

When working rounds of taller stitches, remember that the turning chain does in fact count as the first stitch. To work the second round of double crochet stitches, follow the instructions in the preceding section, but omit the chain 1 in Step 1 and substitute a chain 3 turning chain for the first stitch. (See Book 3, Chapter 1 for a refresher on turning chains.) And, of course, use double crochet stitches in place of single crochet stitches.

REMEMBER

For your piece to lie flat, the number of stitches in each round should increase by the number of stitches worked in the first round. (If you don't increase enough stitches, your piece will begin to turn up in a cuplike shape.) For example, if your first round has a total of 6 stitches, then your second round should increase by 6 stitches for a total of 12 stitches. The third round should again increase by 6 stitches, giving you a total of 18 stitches at the end of the round.

Table 4-1 presents three different examples of round increases as well as how to work them.

TABLE 4-1   **Increasing Stitches in Rounds**

Round Number	Number of Stitches in the Round			How to Work the Increase
Round 1	6	8	12	N/A
Round 2	12	16	24	Increase 1 stitch in each stitch around
Round 3	18	24	36	Increase 1 stitch in every other stitch around
Round 4	24	32	48	Increase 1 stitch in every third stitch around
Round 5	30	40	60	Increase 1 stitch in every fourth stitch around
Round 6	36	48	72	Increase 1 stitch in every fifth stitch around

REMEMBER

These guidelines apply to one specific form of increasing in rounds. You can increase in rounds many different ways, although the principle of increasing in a regular sequence remains the same. Always follow whatever increasing instructions are provided in your pattern.

Because you don't turn your work at the end of each round, you get a definite front and back to your piece. Figure 4-11a shows the *right* (front) side of a round. Notice how the stitches lean toward you? Figure 4-11b shows the *wrong* (back) side. It's a little smoother, and the stitches angle away from you somewhat.

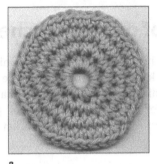

FIGURE 4-11:
Two definite sides: the right/front side (a) and the wrong/back side (b).

a.   b.

© John Wiley & Sons, Inc.

TIP

Sometimes, though, you want to avoid this front-and-back business and create a reversible fabric — especially for projects such as an afghan that you want to look good on both sides. To create a reversible fabric, just turn your piece after you've joined each round. (If you happen to forget this tip while working a pattern that requires a reversible fabric, don't worry. The directions will show you how to turn and where to work the stitches.) When you turn at the end of each joined round, be sure to skip the slip stitch and work your first stitch of the next round into the last stitch worked on the last round.

Another Option: Spiraling Up and Up

Working in a spiral is a way to crochet in rounds when you prefer not to have a visible seam. The usual reasons for working in a spiral are to make hats, mittens, bags, and toys with a three-dimensional shape. Another advantage of working in a spiral is that you don't need to join the end of each round or make a turning chain; this perk makes crocheting items faster and neater. This section introduces spiral basics and shows you how to work one from a stitch diagram, such as you may find in a pattern you want to try.

WARNING

Working tall stitches (like triple crochet) in a spiral gives your work an uneven edge, so use this technique *only* for single crochet stitches.

The first round of a spiral design begins the same way as any other round. You create a center ring by using one of the three methods described earlier in this chapter and then work the required number of stitches in the first round. The stitch diagram in Figure 4-12 shows a center ring of 6 chain stitches and a first round of 12 single crochet stitches. (Book 1, Chapter 4 has more on how to read a stitch diagram.) The twist comes in at the end of the round.

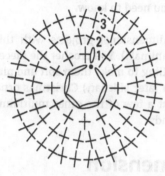

FIGURE 4-12:
Single crochet
stitch diagram
for working
in a spiral.

© John Wiley & Sons, Inc.

Instead of joining the round, you work the first stitch of the next round into the first stitch of the last round, and so on for each successive round. The only time you should slip stitch to complete the round is when you've finished the required number of rounds for the design. Reading the diagram in Figure 4-12 counter-clockwise, that means you work the 13th stitch in the first single crochet stitch of Round 1, skipping the turning chain from the first round. This now becomes the first stitch of the second round.

TIP

Before continuing on with Round 2, mark the first stitch of the second round with a stitch marker or a safety pin because losing your place or miscounting the stitches in each round is easy to do. (Stitch markers are handy gadgets introduced in Book 1, Chapter 1.) When you work your way back around, you work the first stitch of Round 3 into the marked stitch. Remove the marker from Round 2 and place it in the first stitch of Round 3. Continue spiraling until you're too dizzy to go any further or until your design is the size you want.

The last stitch in the last round of a spiral design is raised above the level of the previous round. To finish the round and make the edge smooth, you need to slip stitch in the next stitch (the first stitch of the previous round) before fastening off. (Book 3, Chapter 1 explains how to fasten off.)

Adding Another Dimension

Not all designs that you work in the round have to be flat. A perfect example is the Slouch Hat project at the end of this chapter. It's a flat round at the top, but then it takes on a tubular shape to fit over your head. If you're worried that transforming a round shape into a tubular one is a difficult technique, don't be — it's actually easier than getting the darn round to lie flat in the first place! The following sections explain what you need to know.

TIP

You can make some fun three-dimensional projects with this shaping technique (think crocheted dolls and animals). You crochet the pieces into the proper shape and then stuff them with filling to make them soft and plump. (Read about Amigurumi, a Japanese craft, in a later sidebar.) Christmas ornaments, mittens, slippers, and leg warmers are just a few of the other multidimensional designs that you shape by working in rounds.

Starting to add dimension

In the earlier section "Adding Rounds," you find out how to keep a round flat by increasing the number of stitches in each successive round. To get the round to start curving up, you simply stop adding new stitches in each round. Here's how:

1. **Make a center ring of 6 chain stitches (ch) and work a complete round of 12 single crochet (sc). Join with a slip stitch (sl st).**

   See the sections "Joining chain stitches into a ring" and "Uniting Your Ring," earlier in this chapter, to find out how to perform this step.

2. **Work 2 more rounds, increasing 12 stitches for Round 2 and 12 more stitches for Round 3, joining after each round.**

   See the earlier section "Adding Rounds" for how to make the turning chain and add new rounds.

   You don't have to stop after 3 rounds. Add more rounds to make a larger design, but keep increasing the stitches by 12 for each round.

REMEMBER

3. **To start adding depth, don't add any extra stitches to Round 4. Instead, work 1 single crochet stitch in each stitch of the previous round and join with a slip stitch.**

   Working 1 stitch in each stitch like this causes the edges of your work to turn in. Repeat Step 3 until the piece is as deep as you want.

AMIGURUMI: THE ART OF JAPANESE TOY-MAKING

Amigurumi is the popular Japanese craft of crocheting (or knitting) cute stuffed dolls. Most *amigurumi* projects tend to be animals (such as bears, cats, dogs, birds, or monkeys), but the craft is often seen giving other objects (such as cupcakes, milk cartons, eggs, and mushrooms) *anthropomorphic* features. In other words, the craft bestows human features upon animals and inanimate objects. No matter the subject, the main aesthetic goal of any *amigurumi* project is to be sweet and cute.

Amigurumi is very simple in design and only a little more challenging in construction. The dolls are usually created with tight single crochet stitches (to keep any stuffing bits from coming through) that are worked in a spiral method to avoid a seam. The pieces and parts of the toys are worked separately and then sewn together at the end. Embellishments and facial features are added before the pieces are stuffed and finished.

Amigurumi patterns usually let you know exactly what you need to make the project, but here are a few basics you can expect to find in a typical pattern:

- **Yarn:** You can use any type of yarn, but *amigurumi* projects are usually made with worsted-weight acrylic, wool, or wool-blend yarns. You may use scraps of various colors to add embroidery for the mouth or nose. ***Remember:*** The dolls are small, so you don't need a ton of yarn; check your stash first before buying anything new.

- **Hooks:** Your stitches need to be tight so the stuffing doesn't fall out, so the recommended hook may be at least two sizes smaller than the one normally recommended for the yarn.

- **Notions:** You'll probably want a stitch marker to help you keep track of your rounds as well as a yarn needle to sew up the pieces and parts.

- **Facial features:** Many craft stores sell plastic safety eyes and noses, which are great for toys that are given to children because they don't pull off very easily. You can also use beads, buttons, crocheted circles, or embroidery.

- **Stuffing:** The most commonly used stuffing is fiberfill, found at most craft stores, but you can also use fabric or yarn scraps. Plastic pellets or pony beads are sometimes added to give the toy weight. Whatever you opt for, don't use rice or beans (which can attract bugs).

If you want your piece to start curving in more gradually, don't add as many increase stitches to the rounds in Step 2. Add a few so that the circumference grows but not enough to keep it lying flat. Try adding just eight stitches to each round. Play around with the number of increases: The fewer you add, the more dramatic the curve; the more you add, the shallower the curve.

Deciding how to wrap up your work

After your work is as deep (or as long) as you want, you have three choices:

>> **Fasten off your work.** You now have something that looks like a cap or a tube sock, depending on how big you made the initial flat round and how many rounds you added for depth.

>> **Begin increasing stitches in each round.** This makes your piece begin to widen and flatten out, kind of like the brim on a hat.

>> **Begin decreasing stitches in each round.** Decreasing the number of stitches starts to close up the edges of your piece, creating a spherical design. You decrease rounds the same way you decrease rows, by combining two stitches into one. (Refer to Book 3, Chapter 3 for more on decreasing.)

Decreasing evenly in each successive round creates a smooth, even curve, but if you work a large number of decreases in one round, the work will pull in sharply. If you want your design to be symmetrical, decrease at the same rate as you increased on the first half of your piece.

Slouch Hat Project

The pattern for this warm and fashionable hat uses double crochet stitches worked in the back loops of the stitches in the row below and allows you to practice increasing in rounds. The brim is then worked in single crochet stitches also worked in the back loops by using a hook one size smaller to tighten the fit. The yarn in this design is a super soft, easy-care acrylic, available in a multitude of colors to suit your own personal style. To see a color photo of this project, visit dummies.com/go/knitcrochetAIO.

Materials and vital statistics

- **Yarn:** Lion Brand Yarns "Hometown USA" Super Bulky-weight yarn (100% acrylic), (5 oz. [142 g], 81 yds [74 m] each skein): 2 skeins of #176 Galveston Green

- **Hook:** Crochet hook sizes M-9 (9 mm) and L-8 U.S. (8 mm) or sizes needed to obtain gauge

- **Yarn Needle**

- **Measurements:** 20 in. in circumference; one size fits most adults

- **Gauge:** First 3 rnds = 4½ in. in diameter

- **Stitches used:** Chain stitch (ch), slip stitch (sl st), single crochet (sc), double crochet (dc), **Dc2tog:** * (Yo, insert hook in next st, yo, draw yarn through st, yo, draw yarn through 2 loops on hook) twice, yo, draw yarn through 3 loops on hook *

Directions

The instructions for this project are just as you'd see them in any regular crochet publication, complete with abbreviations. Figure 4-13 gives you a stitch diagram for extra guidance. If you need more info on how to read Crochetese or stitch diagrams, head to Book 1, Chapter 4 for the scoop on what each abbreviation means and how to work with asterisks. For complete instructions on how to increase and decrease stitches, refer to Book 3, Chapter 3. Book 4, Chapter 3 shows you how to work in the back loops of stitches.

Foundation chain: With M-9 hook, ch 4 (counts as ch 1 and first dc).

Rnd 1: Work 7 dc in 4th ch from hook, sl st in first dc to join (8 dc).

Rnd 2: Ch 3 (counts as first dc now and throughout), dc in same st, 2 dc in blp of each st around, sl st in first dc to join (16 dc).

Rnd 3: Ch 3, dc in same st, * dc in blp of next dc, 2 dc in blp of next dc, repeat from * around, sl st in first dc to join (24 dc).

Rnd 4: Ch 3, dc in same st, * dc in blp of next 2 dc, 2 dc in blp of next dc, repeat from * around, sl st in first dc to join (32 dc).

Rnd 5: Ch 3, dc in same st, * dc in blp of next 3 dc, 2 dc in blp of next dc, repeat from * around, sl st in first dc to join (40 dc).

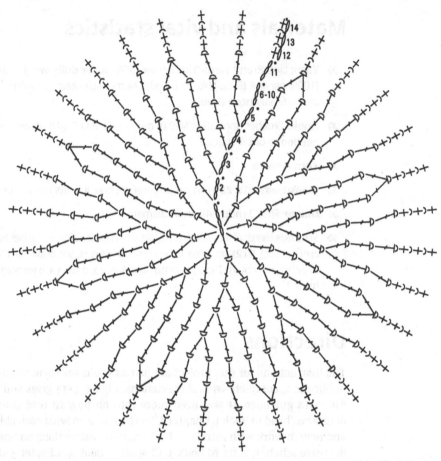

FIGURE 4-13:
The stitch diagram for the Slouch Hat project.

Rnds 6–10: Ch 3, dc in blp of each dc around, sl st in first dc to join (40 dc).

Rnd 11: Ch 3, dc in next st (counts as dc2tog), dc in blp of next 3 dc, * dc2tog in blp of next 2 dc, dc in blp of next 3 dc, rep from * around, sl st in first dc to join (32 dc).

Switch to L-8 hook.

Rnd 12: With L-8 hook, ch 1, sc in blp of each dc around, sl st in first sc to join (32 sc).

Rnds 13–14: Ch 1, sc in blp of each sc around, sl st in first sc to join (32 sc).

Fasten off and weave in loose ends with the yarn needle.

IN THIS CHAPTER

» **Changing from one color to another**

» **Avoiding the snipping and rejoining part by carrying your yarn**

» **Deciphering color codes and color charts**

» **Getting crafty with the Fibonacci sequence (not as scary as it sounds!)**

» **Decorating with a colorful pillow**

Chapter **5**

Multicolored Crochet

Have you ever stopped to imagine what the world would be like without color? Everywhere you look, from outside your windows to inside your home to the clothes on your body, color shapes your life and the way you view things. Well, the same holds true for the designs you crochet. Take, for example, an afghan. Worked in a single color, it provides warmth but not much else. Add one or more colors, though, and not only do you have a warm blanket to snuggle up with, but you also have a work of art to display.

Whether you want to create a simple stripe pattern or a complex mosaic design in many colors, this chapter explains the various techniques for working with color and reading color charts. If you work the fun Mod Pillow project at the end of this chapter, you can practice your newfound techniques.

Bringing Designs to Life: Joining Colors

Working color changes properly gives your finished project a smooth, clean appearance with no unsightly bumps and knots. You usually switch colors at one of two different places within your design:

>> **At the beginning (or end) of a row or round:** You typically change colors at the beginning of a row when working a striped pattern. Of course, you can also look at this as changing color at the end of a row or round because the end of one is the beginning of another.

>> **In the middle of a row or round:** For *charted patterns,* which have a picture in the middle of the design, you need to change colors in the middle of a row. (See the later section "Charting color change" for more details.)

The next sections show you how to create a smooth, clean transition between colors regardless of whether you need to switch in the beginning, middle, or end of a row or round.

Changing color at the beginning (or end)

TIP

If you're going for stripes, master changing colors at the beginning (or end) of a row because you'll be doing this a lot. Fortunately, you change colors at the beginning (or end) of a row or round the same way you join a new strand of yarn of the same color — by making the change while working the last stitch of the previous row or round. (Need a refresher on joining yarn? See Book 3, Chapter 2.)

Practice this technique by crocheting a swatch of double crochet several rows long with your first color; then follow these steps to join the new color:

1. **Using the first color, double crochet (dc) in each stitch across to the next-to-last stitch of the row.**

2. **Work the last double crochet to the point where only 2 loops are left on the hook.**

3. **Drop the first yarn color and pick up the second color.**

4. **Wrap the end of the second yarn color around the hook.**

5. **Draw the second yarn color through the 2 loops of the first yarn color that are on your hook, as in Figure 5-1.**

   At this point, you should have 2 strands of yarn hanging down.

6. **Tug on the end of the first color at the base of the double crochet to tighten the stitch.**

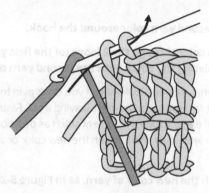

FIGURE 5-1:
Joining a new color at the beginning (or end) of a row.

REMEMBER

If you plan to pick up the first color in a later row, leave the first color of yarn hanging and continue on with the second color. (See the section "Hitching a Ride: Carrying the Yarn," later in this chapter, to find out what to do with the unused first color strand of yarn.) If you don't plan to pick up the first color in a nearby row, cut the yarn (after joining the second color as explained in Step 5 of the preceding list). Be sure to leave a 6-inch tail for weaving in later.

To hide the tail end of the first yarn color, lay it across the tops of the stitches in the previous row and work over it or weave it in with a yarn needle when you finish crocheting.

REMEMBER

When you join a new yarn color, always finish the last stitch of the first color with the second color, regardless of the type of stitch you're working. Doing so gets you ready to start the first stitch of the second color with the correct color loop on your hook, thereby preventing *color drag*, which happens when part of a stitch is one color and the rest of the stitch is another color. This holds true regardless of where the color change is made — at the beginning, end, or middle of a row or round.

Changing color midstream

If you're making a design with a picture in the middle (a *charted pattern*), you change colors in the middle of a row. As when changing colors at the beginning of a row, correctly switching to a new color is important in order to prevent color drag.

Practice this technique by crocheting a swatch of double crochet several rows long with your first color. To add a new color within a row, follow these steps:

1. **Work the last stitch prior to the stitch where you're going to make the color change up to the point where only 2 loops are left on the hook.**

2. **Drop the first yarn color to the wrong (back) side and pick up the second color.**

3. **Wrap the end of the second yarn color around the hook.**

4. **Draw the second yarn color through the 2 loops (of the first yarn color) on your hook, thus completing the stitch with the second yarn color.**

   Figure 5-2a illustrates what this step looks like. If you don't plan to use the first color of yarn in the next few rows, cut the yarn, leaving a tail. Fasten off the first color by drawing the tail end through the current stitch as described in the preceding section. Then work over this tail with the new color or weave it in later with a yarn needle.

5. **Continue working with the new color of yarn, as in Figure 5-2b.**

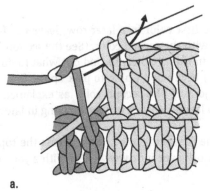 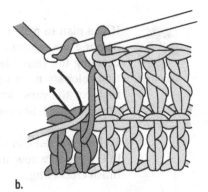

FIGURE 5-2:
Changing to a
new color of yarn
within a row,
wrong side facing.   a.   b.

© John Wiley & Sons, Inc.

REMEMBER

You can change color with either the right side or the wrong side of the work facing you. Just remember to drop the tail end of the first color of yarn to the wrong side, even if it's the side of the work that's facing you.

Hitching a Ride: Carrying the Yarn

When you're crocheting with two or more colors, you often carry the yarn that you're not presently working with to avoid having to fasten it off and rejoin a new strand each time you make a color change. As you find out in the following sections, you have several different options for carrying the yarn, each of which produces a different result.

TIP

If you're carrying several different colors, you can end up with a tangled mess in seconds. The simple act of turning your work at the end of each row becomes a nightmare if you have many different balls of yarn attached to your work at the same time. For small areas of color, cutting off a few yards of the required color and winding it around a bobbin alleviates this mess. (See Book 1, Chapter 1 for more on yarn bobbins.) For the most prominent colors, however, leave the whole skein intact.

Carrying on the wrong side

Carrying the yarn across the row on the wrong side of the fabric is probably the easiest method to use when working with different colors. When you're working a design that changes colors fairly frequently, such as vertical stripes or multicolored charted designs, fastening off each color each time you have to change is too much of a hassle. It also produces an incredibly sloppy finished product.

To carry a strand on the wrong side of the fabric, work over the strand every few stitches with the second color, as shown in Figure 5-3. (Please note that Figure 5-3 shows the wrong side of the fabric.) To do this, lay the strand horizontally across the tops of the stitches along the wrong side of the fabric. When you complete the next stitch, make sure to encase the yarn as you draw it through the first two loops.

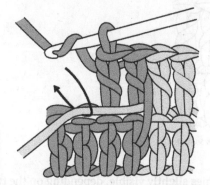

FIGURE 5-3:
Carrying a strand across the wrong side.

© John Wiley & Sons, Inc.

REMEMBER

The *wrong* (back) side of your piece is facing you as you work every other row, so make sure you're always carrying the yarn on the same side. If you're changing color on a *right* (front) side row, you carry the first color on the wrong side of your work.

If you'll be switching back to the carried color several times across the row, then carry the yarn all the way across. If the design is only in a particular section of the work, such as a picture in the middle of a sweater back, carry the yarn only in the part of the row where the design is featured and then let it drop while you finish the row. When you work back across the row, the color will be available for you to pick up in the spot dictated by the design.

Keep the carried strand tight enough so that it lies flat against the wrong side of the fabric and doesn't catch on anything, but don't pull the strand too taut, or else the fabric can pucker.

Working over a carried strand

Working over the carried strand produces a neater appearance on the wrong side of the fabric, which is especially important in a design where the backside is visible, such as an afghan or a scarf.

The technique for working over a carried strand is basically the same as working over the end of the yarn when joining a new ball in the middle of a row (refer to Book 3, Chapter 2). Just lay the unused strand of yarn across the tops of the stitches of the previous row. Then, using the new color, work the stitches in the current row and encase the strand, as in Figure 5-4.

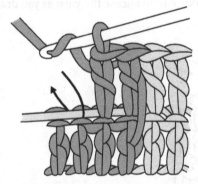

FIGURE 5-4:
Working over a
carried strand.

© John Wiley & Sons, Inc.

The carried color is sometimes slightly visible, depending on the type and color of the yarn and stitches you're using. Don't worry, though; more often than not this visibility adds depth and contrast to the design.

Carrying on the right side

The only reason you ever carry the yarn on the right side of the fabric is if the carried strand is an integral part of your design. For example, carrying a thin strand studded with sequins or mirrors across the right side can add fancy flash to a project made with otherwise simple yarn.

You carry the yarn across the right side the same way you carry it across the wrong side (as explained in the earlier "Carrying on the wrong side" section).

However, you may want to catch the strand every other stitch or even every stitch, depending on the pattern, to make sure that no long, loose loops are hanging around. If your pattern calls for this carrying method, the instructions will indicate how often to catch the yarn.

Carrying up the side

WARNING

Carrying the yarn up the side comes in handy when you're working a horizontal stripe pattern. However, this technique works only when you're crocheting stripes in even numbers of rows. If you're working a stripe pattern that changes color every row, the carried yarn won't be on the side you need it to be when you want to pick it up in the next row.

To carry a strand of yarn up the side edge of your work:

1. **Work 2 rows in the first color, switching colors of yarn in the last stitch of the second row.**

   To switch colors of yarn, follow the first set of steps in the earlier "Changing color at the beginning (or end)" section.

2. **Work 2 rows with the second color.**

3. **Draw up the first color from 2 rows below to complete the last stitch of the second row (see Figure 5-5) and drop the second color, which you'll pick up later.**

WARNING

   If you pull the strand too tightly up the side, your design will pucker.

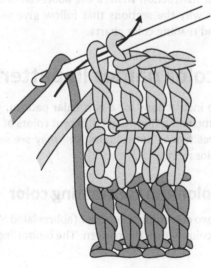

FIGURE 5-5:
Carrying the unused strand up the side of your work.

Choosing different colors for a design may turn into a more daunting process than you originally bargained for. Here are some tips to make combining colors well a tad easier:

- **Use a color wheel.** This handy little gadget is available in most craft and yarn stores. Choose colors within the same segment to get several tones that work well together, or for a more vibrant look, choose colors that are exactly opposite each other on the color wheel.

- **Pick a multicolored yarn and a solid color yarn.** Many yarn companies create variegated or multicolored yarns to coordinate with their solid colors. Choose a multicolored yarn that appeals to you and then match it up with a solid color yarn. Doing so gives the appearance of using many different yarns, when you actually use only two or three.

- **Rely on basic white or off-white to add contrast.** White and off-white work well with almost any other color. If you're looking for a stark contrast, go with a dark secondary color. A lighter color works fine if you want something subtler.

- **Use dark and light tones of the same color.** If you favor a particular color, why not use its many shades?

Demystifying Color Codes and Charts

Working with color has its own special language. To make the instructions more compact and concise, most instruction writers use abbreviations when referring to colorful designs. That's why the sections that follow give you the skinny on deciphering color codes and reading color charts.

Abbreviating color names in patterns

When you first look at the instructions for a particular pattern, you check to see what materials you need, including how many different colors of yarn the pattern uses. If the pattern involves two or more colors, you may see some funny letter designations after each color name.

Pairing up: Main color and contrasting color

If a pattern requires only two colors, the *main color* (abbreviated MC) is usually the first and most prominent color within the pattern. The *contrasting color* (CC) is the secondary color.

If the materials call for three skeins of white as the main color (MC) and two skeins of red as the contrasting color (CC) and the instruction is for a striped pattern, you may see something like this:

1. **Row 2: With MC, ch 1, sc in each sc across, complete last st with CC, *turn*. Fasten off MC.**

   Here's what that gobbledygook means: Working with the main color (white), chain 1 and then work 1 single crochet stitch in each single crochet stitch across until you reach the next-to-last stitch. Then work the last stitch, completing it with the contrasting color (red). Fasten off the main color (white). Then turn your work.

2. **Row 3: With CC, ch 1, sc in each sc across, *turn*.**

   Again, an English translation: Working now with the contrasting color (red), chain 1, work 1 single crochet in each single crochet stitch across the row, and then turn your work.

Three's a crowd: Letter abbreviations

When a design calls for three or more colors, patterns use letters of the alphabet to designate the colors. For example, a materials list that calls for six different colors may appear like this:

> 4 balls of Yellow (A); 3 balls each of White (B), Green (C), and Blue (D); 1 ball each of Pink (E) and Lilac (F)

Some patterns may use the initials of color names to abbreviate, such as G for green, W for white, and so on. Then again, sometimes a pattern has a main color (MC) along with several other colors designated A, B, C, and so on. Whichever abbreviation style they use, patterns usually list the yarns needed in order of appearance in the pattern or by the quantity required.

REMEMBER

Be sure to read through the materials list at the beginning of each project so you're familiar with the color abbreviations. You may want to write a separate list of the abbreviations and the color names to help keep things straight.

Charting color change

Many patterns use a color chart rather than written instructions to show designs that have frequent color changes or use several different colors. A *color chart* is a grid, with each square representing one stitch (see Figure 5-6a). Because most crochet publications are in black and white, symbols in each square indicate the different colors. Always refer to the chart key (which looks like Figure 5-6b) to determine which symbol stands for which color.

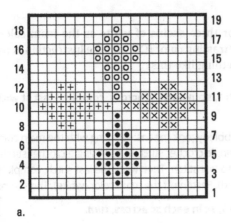

FIGURE 5-6:
A sample color chart and key.

CHART KEY

☐ = White sc
⦿ = Red sc
+ = Yellow sc
☒ = Aqua sc
Ⓞ = Green sc

a.　　　　　　　b.

© John Wiley & Sons, Inc.

REMEMBER

When reading a color chart, you generally read the odd-numbered rows from right to left and the even-numbered rows from left to right, unless otherwise specified. This is simply because you work your first row after the foundation chain from right to left and the second row from left to right. Figure 5-7 shows a swatch made from the chart in Figure 5-6a.

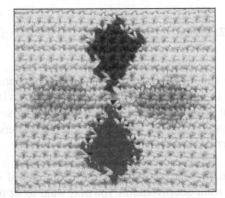

FIGURE 5-7:
Sample swatch worked from a color chart.

© John Wiley & Sons, Inc.

Crafty Math: Understanding the Fibonacci Sequence

Like it or not, math and crochet go hand in hand. From calculating gauge (explained in Book 1, Chapter 3) to determining how to work increases to make a flat or curved circle (described in Book 3, Chapters 3 and 4), you use math whenever you pick up your hook. The Fibonacci sequence is a math concept allows you to add balance and interest in crochet patterns involving multiple colors.

The *Fibonacci sequence* is a simple series of numbers that follows a predictable pattern. Here's the beginning of the basic sequence:

0, 1, 1, 2, 3, 5, 8, 13, 21, 34, 55, 89, 144, 233, 377 . . .

To break the pattern down, begin with the first two numbers and add them together to get the third number: $0 + 1 = 1$. Next, add the previous two numbers in the sequence to get the fourth number: $1 + 1 = 2$. Now the sequence reads 0, 1, 1, 2. Find the fifth number by adding the third and fourth numbers together: $1 + 2 = 3$. As you can see, the Fibonacci sequence can go on indefinitely as you continue to add the previous two numbers to find the next number in the series.

Many eye-pleasing objects in nature follow the Fibonacci sequence. Picture the number of petals on your favorite flower. Now count them. You probably count three, five, or eight petals. Sequences can also occur in the arrangement of petals on a pinecone or the spiraling rings of seeds at the center of a sunflower. If these sequences produce such an orderly appearance in nature, why not apply the same concepts to crochet?

TIP

To create an interesting color pattern in your piece, simply apply the basic Fibonacci sequence using two or more colors, as shown in the Mod Pillow project in the next section. You can apply part of the sequence to the number of rows or stitches in a pattern. For example, you can use a 1-1-2 pattern or a 2-3-5-8-13 pattern. (*Note:* You can also create texture patterns using the same concept and a variety of basic stitches.)

All patterns involving multiple colors will instruct you on how to create the color patterns for the piece, but you can make a project your own by choosing the colors that reflect your style or by substituting your own Fibonacci sequence.

Mod Pillow Project

One side of this contemporary pillow allows you to practice the technique of changing color; the other side uses a Fibonacci sequence to determine the number of rows for each stripe in the following order: 1, 1, 2, 3, 5, 8. You can see a color photo of the stripes by visiting dummies.com/go/knitcrochetAIO.

The recommended worsted-weight yarn is easy to work with and comes in a bountiful array of colors. Use the colors listed here. Or choose colors that suit your decor and let the Fibonacci sequence do all the work of coordinating them for you.

Materials and vital statistics

>> **Yarn:** Brown Sheep Company, Inc. "Lamb's Pride" worsted-weight yarn (85% wool/15% mohair), (4 oz. [113 g], 190 yds [173 m] each skein):

- 2 skeins of #M28 Chianti (MC)

- 1 skein of #M83 Raspberry (A)

- 1 skein of #M89 Roasted Coffee (B)

- 1 skein of #M105 RPM Pink (C)

- 1 skein of #M191 Kiwi (D)

>> **Hook:** Crochet hook size I-9 U.S. (5.5 mm) or size needed to obtain gauge

>> **Large-eyed yarn needle**

>> **Pillow form:** 14 in. x 14 in. square

>> **Measurements:** 14 in. wide x 14 in. long

>> **Gauge:** 13 sts and 12 rows sc = 4 in. in Esc

>> **Stitches used:** Chain stitch (ch), extended single crochet (Esc), single crochet (sc), slip stitch (sl st)

Directions

Work the pillow front using the Fibonacci striping sequence. Work the pillow back following the color chart in Figure 5-8a; the chart key is in Figure 5-8b. Read all the odd-numbered rows from right to left and all the even-numbered rows from left to right. To change colors, complete the last single crochet of the first color with the next color. Drop the first color to the wrong side to be picked up later. Attach separate balls of color as needed and fasten off colors when they're not needed in the following row.

TIP

To help you keep track of which side is the right side and which side is the wrong side, use a safety pin, stitch marker, or scrap of yarn to mark the right side for both the front and the back of the pillow.

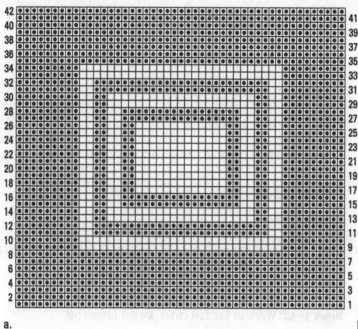

FIGURE 5-8:
The color chart
and key for the
back of the
Mod Pillow.

a.

b.

CHART KEY
⊙ = Esc in MC
☐ = Esc in C

© *John Wiley & Sons, Inc.*

Pillow front

With MC, ch 48.

Row 1 (RS): Esc in second ch from hook, Esc in each ch across changing to A with last Esc (47 Esc), *turn.*

Row 2: Ch 1, Esc in each sc across changing to B with last Esc (47 Esc), *turn.*

Rows 3–4: Rep Row 2 with B.

Rows 5–7: Rep Row 2 with C.

Rows 8–12: Rep Row 2 with D.

Rows 13–20: Rep Row 2 with MC.

Row 21: Rep Row 2 with A.

Row 22: Rep Row 2 with B.

Rows 23–24: Rep Row 2 with C.

Rows 25–27: Rep Row 2 with D.

Rows 28–32: Rep Row 2 with MC.

Rows 33–40: Rep Row 2 with A.

Row 41: Rep Row 2 with B.

Row 42: Rep Row 2 with C. Fasten off and weave in the loose ends.

Pillow back

With MC, ch 48.

Row 1 (RS): Esc in second ch from hook, Esc in each ch across (47 Esc), *turn.*

Row 2: Ch 1, Esc in each Esc across (47 Esc), *turn.*

Rows 3–42: Work in Esc foll chart. *Do not* fasten off.

Finishing

With the WS of the front and back facing each other, align the top edges so the sts are lined up together. Working through the sts of the front panel and the back panel at the same time, ch 1, * sc in each set of front and back sc across to the next corner, work 3 sc in the next corner *; rep from * to * around, working sts into each row end on the side edges of the panels. Insert the pillow form into the cover before joining the last side and sl st in first sc to join. Fasten off.

4

Expanding Your Skills

Contents at a Glance

Chapter **1**
Knitting Stripes

I f you can knit and purl (see Book 2, Chapter 1 for how-to info), you already have the skills to knit stripes. If your mind goes straight to prison uniforms or kiddie rompers, take heart: Stripes can be as subtle and elegant or as loud and crazy as you want them to be. The key is knowing how to create the desired effect, and that's exactly the kind of information you find in this chapter. Here you discover how to create textured stripes and stripes of many (or a few) different colors. And because knowing a couple of easy tricks can make stripe patterns easier, you find those here, too.

TIP

Now is the time to get out that collection of odd balls of yarn culled from the sale bin of your favorite yarn shop and the bits and pieces of leftovers you've saved. Color patterns in general and stripe patterns in particular are great ways to incorporate your precious collection into an original project.

This chapter explains how to knit horizontal stripes. If you want vertical stripes, a ribbed stitch pattern is just the thing. See Book 2, Chapter 2 for common ribbed patterns.

Seeking the Story on Stripes

Never think that stripes are boring. Far from being a single thing, stripes are many-splendored. They offer great variety in scale, balance, sequence, color, and texture. Here are a few ideas of the ways you can arrange stripes:

>> **Balanced stripes:** One of the most common types of stripe is alternating stripes of equal width.

>> **Wide stripes:** If you want a stripe pattern that's easy to read (that is, to recognize), use a wide stripe. There'll be no mistaking your intentions, and then you can make the look bolder or more subtle with the colors you choose.

>> **Narrow stripes:** Narrow stripes can be bold or subtle, depending on the colors you choose; combining colors in the same shade, for example, creates a blurred effect, and contrasting colors make the stripes more crisp.

TIP

The eye tends to blend very narrow bands of colors together, so before you settle on a particular combination, knit a swatch and view it from a distance to make sure you like the effect.

>> **Alternating stripes:** For added visual effect (and to avoid the prison uniform effect that stripes of equal width tend to create), deliberately vary the width of your stripes.

>> **One stripe:** A single stripe draws the eye and creates an effect all its own. A wide stripe across the bust or chest creates a sporty look, and a narrow stripe beneath the bust creates the impression of a flattering empire waist.

>> **Wild stripes:** These stripes break the rules. Make yours zigzag or start and stop them randomly. Incorporate outlandish colors or textures by using novelty yarn or multicolored yarns. Vary the width of every stripe in the piece.

TIP

If you find a striped pattern you like, you can simply follow the instructions to get the look you want. For those times when you're happy with the pattern but not so happy with the colors it uses, substitute colors you like better. Occasionally, you may want to design your own stripe pattern. To discover the myriad options you have, start a collection of stripe ideas by tearing pages from catalogs and magazines when you see interesting striped patterns or color combinations. You also can use a mathematical sequence, such as the Fibonacci sequence, to determine how many rows of each stripe color to knit. (The *Fibonacci sequence* is 1, 1, 2, 3, 5, 8, 13, 21, and so on, with each number the sum of the two before it; Fibonacci-inspired scarves are particularly charming.) Or ask a mathematician for other ideas!

Textured Stripes, or How to Stand Out in a Crowd

When you think of stripes, you may automatically think of alternating bands of different colors. That's fine, but you also can create stripes simply through texture. Here are some options:

>> **Vary your stitches.** As Book 2, Chapter 2 explains, you create stockinette stitch — a stitch with a smooth face — by alternating a row of knit stitches with a row of purl stitches. By varying the sequence of knit rows and purl rows, you can create horizontal stripes (sometimes called by their ancient name, *welts*). The two patterns in this section illustrate how you can create stripes through texture. In the section "Reverse stockinette stitch stripes," you create the stripes with rows of reverse stockinette stitch on a plain stockinette stitch background. In "Garter stitch stripes," you make the stripes with garter stitch ridges.

>> **Vary the weight and texture of the yarns you use.** You can mix and match smooth and fuzzy yarns, shiny and pebbly yarns, and others to create stripes. If your stripes are narrow, you can even work with yarns of different weights as long as the difference isn't too extreme.

TIP

To balance the different weights, knit the heavier yarns on a smaller needle and the lighter ones on a larger needle; head to Book 1, Chapter 2 to read more about yarn weights and Book 1, Chapter 3 to find out about gauge. This situation is one time when a circular needle set with interchangeable tips comes in handy because you can swap the tips as you switch between yarn weights.

TIP

Using same-color yarns to create textured stripes has a subtle effect. For a bolder stripe, make your textured stripes different colors, too.

Reverse stockinette stitch stripes

Reverse stockinette stitch (rev St st) is just one way to make textured stripes (see Figure 1-1). This stitch pattern uses rows of reverse stockinette on a plain stockinette background.

Try the following pattern for a basic reverse stockinette stitch stripe:

Cast on any number of stitches.

Rows 1, 3, and 6: Knit.

Rows 2, 4, and 5: Purl.

Rep Rows 1–6.

FIGURE 1-1:
Reverse
stockinette
stripes.

Photograph by Wiley, Composition Services Graphics

Here's what's happening: As you work Rows 1, 2, 3, and 4, you create your stockinette stitch (the smooth background). Then at Row 5, because you purl again rather than alternate back to a knit row, you begin the reverse stockinette stitch, which creates the bumped-out stripe, and you continue it with Row 6, which alternates with Row 5. When you return to Row 1, you return to the stockinette stitch and the whole pattern starts over again.

TIP

To vary the width of your stripes or the space between them, simply increase the number of alternating rows in either the stockinette portion or the reverse stockinette portion.

Garter stitch stripes

Garter stitch stripes have a different texture from the stripes made in reverse stockinette stitch. Whereas reverse stockinette stitch stripes create a rolled bump, garter stitch stripes create a flat ridge (see Figure 1-2).

Follow this pattern to create the garter stitch stripes shown in Figure 1-2:

Cast on any number of stitches.

Rows 1, 3, 5–11, 13, 15, and 16 (RS): Knit.

Rows 2, 4, 12, and 14: Purl.

Rep Rows 1–16.

FIGURE 1-2:
Garter stitch
stripes.

Photograph by Wiley, Composition Services Graphics

By alternating knit and purl rows, you create stockinette stitch. When you work knit rows in succession, you create the garter stitch stripe. To change the width of the background, simply work more or fewer rows in the stockinette pattern; to vary the width of the stripes, simply knit more or fewer rows in succession.

Knitting Colorful Stripes

Gorgeous yarn colors are the primary appeal for many knitters. When scanning the jewel-colored skeins in a yarn shop, who can resist gathering together a palette to take home and knit up? Who can walk by the odd topaz- or hyacinth-colored ball in the sale bin? Who can give away the remaining bit of rose and the tail end of periwinkle from the last project? Not us. But what do you do with a basket of single skeins? You knit in color, that's what!

Knitting colored stripes is a quick and easy way to get started in color work. Unlike color techniques that require you to go back and forth between colors in a single row (such as Fair Isle and intarsia techniques, which are beyond the scope of this book), colored stripes allow you to use as many colors as you please while working with only one color at a time.

TIP

Maybe you're a little timid about changing colors on a project but still want to have that look. No problem; just pick up some self-striping yarn from your local yarn store. With self-striping yarn, you get an impressive, deceptively complex look while the yarn does all the work. No need to tell anybody that you didn't change yarn colors to create the beautiful pattern; let folks praise your skill and talent with needles and yarn.

Although knitting different colored stripes can be a lot of fun and an opportunity to let your creative juices flow, you need to be able to do a few things before you jump in. The following sections get you ready.

Picking colors for your project

You can knit stripes in two colors, three colors, or as many colors as you like. Use color at random, or plan for a particular mood in your color combination. Stripes in clean, bright colors with a balance of light and dark are pert and lively; stripes in a few close shades of a single color or colors close to each other on the color wheel (such as blue, purple, magenta, and red) are subtle and sophisticated.

You can look for a striped project pattern and follow the sequence, colors, and spacing given in the design; or you can use the stripe pattern as a template and plug in your own colors and yarns. If you're in a spontaneous mood, gather your yarns together and start knitting, changing yarns as you feel like it.

REMEMBER

Patterns with multiple colors use a standard set of abbreviations:

MC: Main color (for patterns that use two colors)

CC: Contrasting color (for patterns that use two colors)

A, B, C, and so on: For patterns that use more than two colors

TIP

If, before diving in, you want to get an idea of what a stripe pattern may look like knitted in a specific group of yarns, try wrapping samples of the yarns in the proposed pattern around a stiff piece of cardboard or a cardboard toilet paper roll for a sneak preview.

Counting rows

When you knit stripes, you count rows (or if you're knitting in the round, you count rounds). Why? Because it's an easy way to keep track of the stripe's width. For example, knowing that a stripe spans 7 rows and counting as you go is easier and more accurate than getting out the tape measure. Here's the thing you need to know about counting rows, especially if you're using only two colors: Odd and even rows affect where the yarn ends up — whether it's right there where you want it or at the opposite end of your knitting. Fortunately, a few easy fixes get you out of this dilemma:

» **Work on a circular needle.** It doesn't matter where the yarn ends up. If it's not on the end where you need it, simply slide your knitting to the other needle and — voila! — problem solved. Just pick up the yarn and carry on.

» **Cut the yarn, leaving the ends to weave in later, and begin anew at the next row.** Weaving in ends isn't hard, but it's a bit tedious, especially if you have many loose ends. Head to the later section "Dealing with old colors and loose ends" for instructions.

» **Use three or more colors.** If you use three or more colors, you can organize odd- and even-row stripes so that the yarn for the next stripe will be in the right place. If you use this strategy, you have to start some colors on wrong-side rows and carry the yarn colors up both the left and right edges of your work. ("Carrying the yarn up the side as you go" later in this chapter shows you how to do just that.) Changing colors on both sides rather than just one is a good idea anyway if you're using lots of colors because it keeps the side edges from being too bulky.

Joining colors

When you're ready to change colors in a stripe pattern, you need to join the new color. Unless you're creating random stripes that start and stop anywhere, you usually join colors at the edge. For garments and other pieces that get sewn along the seam, you use one technique. For pieces whose edges remain open, you need to use a technique that lets you hide the join. You find both techniques in the following sections.

When the edge is hidden in a seam

When you're ready to add a new color in a stripe pattern, secure the new yarn by working the first stitch in the row with the old and new colors held together. To do so, follow these steps:

1. Insert the RH needle into the first stitch.

2. Drape the end of the new yarn behind your work.

3. Grab the old and new yarn strands together and work the first stitch.

4. Drop the old color and continue on in the new color until it's time to change again.

When you work back to the edge stitch made with two strands, remember to knit the strands *together*. Otherwise, you inadvertently increase a stitch on the edge. After you work a few more rows, pull on the strand of the old yarn to tighten up the edge stitch.

You don't need to cut the end of the old color if you'll be using it again in the next few inches. When it's time to change back, simply drop the new (now old) color, pick up the old (now new) color, and carry on. Be careful not to pull the color from below too tight, or the side seam will pucker.

When the edge isn't hidden

When you're adding a new color somewhere in the middle of a row or another location where you can't hide your ends at the edge, you need to weave in ends. Follow these steps to make the color switch:

1. Insert the RH needle into the next stitch on your needle.

2. Drape the end of the new yarn over your needle, as if to knit, leaving a 4- to 5-inch tail.

3. Work the next stitch with your new yarn.

4. Cut the old color, leaving a 4- to 5-inch tail, tie the new and old tails together in a bow, and continue in the new color until it's time to change again.

5. When you finish knitting your piece, weave in the ends (see the next section).

   Make sure you weave the yarns over the small hole created by adding in the new yarn in opposite directions (with the WS-facing old yarn to the right, new yarn to the left).

Dealing with old colors and loose ends

When you're joining all these colors to make stripes, what do you do with all the ends you create every time you start and stop a color? You can either carry them up or cut and weave them in. Which option is better? It depends. If you don't use a color for several inches, it's better to cut the yarn and weave in the end. If you use it again soon, you can carry the yarn along the edge as you go.

Weaving in ends

When you're obliged to cut the yarn, you can weave the end in vertically along the edge of your knitting or horizontally along the edge of a stripe.

When you look at your work from the wrong side, you should see the usual purl bumps. Look below them to see the running threads that connect the stitches. To weave ends horizontally along a stripe, grab a tapestry needle and weave your loose end through four or five of these running threads. Turn to Book 7, Chapter 1 for more on tying up loose ends. (In stripe work, don't weave ends vertically, because you'll invariably end up in a stripe of the wrong color.)

Carrying the yarn up the side as you go

To avoid cutting and weaving, you can carry the yarn not in use up the side, tucking it around the working yarn and keeping it close to the edge as you go until you need it again.

1. **When you finish working with Color A, work a few rows with Color B, following the instructions for joining in the earlier section "When the edge is hidden in a seam."**

2. **When you're back at the edge where Color A is waiting and about to start the next row with Color B, insert the RH needle into the first stitch.**

3. **With the working strand (A) on the left, bring Color B up the side.**

4. **Pick up Color A from under Color B and make the first stitch.**

   The working strand catches the carried strand (see Figure 1-3). This technique works the same on the purl side as it does on the knit side.

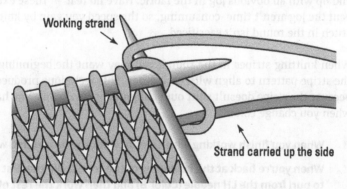

Working strand

Strand carried up the side

FIGURE 1-3:
Carry yarn up the side and tuck it in as you go.

Illustration by Wiley, Composition Services Graphics

You can carry yarn up the side of your piece every time you're at the beginning of the row if you're making a scarf and want a tidy edge. If the edge will be enclosed in a seam, you need to catch it only every 4 to 6 rows to maintain even tension on the edge stitches and keep the strand along the side from getting out of hand.

WARNING

Be conscious of the tension on the strand you carry up the side of your work: If it's too loose, you get sloppy edge stitches, and if it's too taut, your sides pull in and have no give. Take a stitch or two in the new stripe color, and then check the strand carried up the side to make sure that it isn't gaping or pulling.

TIP

For a scarf or shawlette that changes colors every 2 rows, try a simple detail to carry the yarn up the side of a piece and keep a clean edge. On the row where you're changing colors, bring the old color to the front, slip the first stitch as if to purl, and bring the yarn to the back. Then continue in the established pattern with the new color. This strategy will keep the slipped first stitch in the color opposite to the rest of the row but will otherwise keep the edge nice and tidy.

REMEMBER

Untwist your yarns periodically for sanity's sake when you're working them around each other up the side edges. And give a gentle tug on the carried strand now and then to make it neat — but don't pull hard enough to draw up the edge.

Knitting Stripes in the Round

Knitting in the round is a wonderful way to make any object, but it's important to remember that the nature of circular knitting causes stripes to *jog*, or not line up (see Figure 1-4). When you knit in the round, you're actually knitting a large spiral. If you don't take extra steps to make sure the color changes line up, you end up with an obvious jog in the fabric. Have no fear — these extra steps to prevent the jog aren't time-consuming, so the speed you gain by knitting stockinette stitch in the round isn't sacrificed.

When knitting stripes in the round, you may want the beginning and the end of the stripe pattern to align with each other. This technique produces a *jogless stripe* because the stripe doesn't shift out of alignment. To do this, you have to add a step when you change colors:

1. When you finish working with Color A, work the next round with Color B.

2. When you're back at the beginning of the round, slip the first stitch as if to purl from the LH needle (Color B) and then work the rest of the stitches in the established pattern.

3. Continue in the pattern for the number of rounds necessary.

4. When making more stripes, repeat Steps 1 and 2.

   To see this technique in action, take a look at the jogless stripe in Figure 1-4.

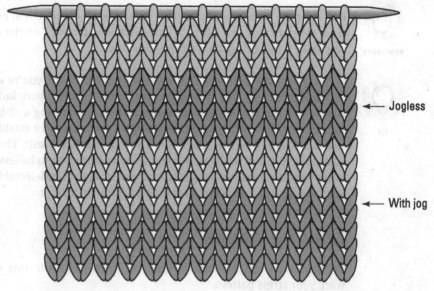

← Jogless

← With jog

FIGURE 1-4:
Compare a jogless stripe to one with a jog at the color change.

Illustration by Wiley, Composition Services Graphics

Stirring Up Stripes: Combining Texture and Color

You can work stripes in flat stockinette stitch, or you can make them more interesting by adding texture. Knit an entire project in a stitch pattern with colored stripes running through it or add different textures to different stripes.

If the simplicity and creative pleasure of knitting stripes appeal to you but standard stripes don't inspire you (or you'd rather not wear horizontal stripes), don't give up quite yet. The sections that follow introduce some unconventional ways to work stripes into your knitting.

Varying your stitch pattern

Stitch patterns can affect the way your stripe pattern (or color change) looks. In stockinette stitch, if you knit a row in one color and the next row in another color, from the right side the line where the rows meet is sharp and clean. From the wrong side, the line is broken into dots of color by the purl bumps — different effects, different design possibilities. In ribbing or other stitch patterns where purl bumps show on the right side of the fabric, striped patterns show the dots of color unless both the row of the old and the row of the new show the knit side of the stockinette on the right side.

REMEMBER

Knit refers to both how you make a certain kind of stitch *and* how a stitch looks from the right side of a fabric. A knit stitch is a smooth V on the right side, even if you make it by purling on a wrong-side row.

TIP

If you want a sharp no-dot line between your colors and you're working a pattern on which the right side shows the purl bumps, simply work knit stitches for the first row of the new color. For example, if you're knitting a ribbed pattern, work the last row of the old color in the knit/purl pattern you've established. If the next row is a wrong-side row, purl; if it's a right-side row, knit. Then continue on in your pattern stitch in the new color. Hard as it may be to believe, as long as your stripes are several rows deep, the knit row is almost undetectable in your pattern stitch, and you have a distinct transition between stripes.

Making waves

To make wavy stripes, knit the chevron stitch pattern in this section while you work your stripe pattern.

When you stack increases on top of increases and decreases on top of decreases, the stitches slant away from the column of increases and toward the column of decreases, creating chevron patterns (see Figure 1-5). The bottom edge of this pattern forms points or scalloped borders, depending on whether the decreases and increases are worked in a single stitch or spread over several stitches. Although this pattern looks tricky to execute, it's relatively simple.

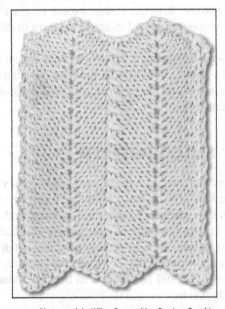

FIGURE 1-5:
Chevron pattern.

Photograph by Wiley, Composition Services Graphics

The chevron pattern uses the following abbreviations:

dbl dec = Double decrease: sl next 2 sts as if to knit, k1, pass 2 sl sts over.

dbl inc = Double increase: (k1, yo, k1) into next st.

Cast on a multiple of 12 sts, plus 3 sts (includes 1 extra st on each side for a selvedge stitch).

Row 1 (RS): K1, k2tog, * k4, dbl inc, k4, dbl dec; rep from * to last 3 sts, ssk, k1.

Row 2: Purl.

Rep Rows 1 and 2 for pattern.

TIP

If you've found a good basic sweater pattern and want to add a wavy striped border to the bottom and sleeves, sample the chevron stitch on different needles until you match the gauge given in your sweater pattern. Then work the border on the body and sleeves as deep as you like before switching to stockinette stitch for the sweater body.

Striping any which way

You can also break up the strong horizontal feel of stripes by knitting randomly striped strips and sewing them together. (Or you can work mismatched stripes in vertical panels by using the intarsia method of color knitting, which is beyond the scope of this book.) Breaking up stripes prevents them from traveling across the width of the entire piece. Finally, you can make patches of stripes (lots of gauge swatches!) and sew them together at 90-degree angles for a patchwork effect.

Practice Striped Projects

If you have doubts about your creative abilities, or if you feel like you wouldn't know where to begin to invent a color pattern, try knitting the projects in this section. Earlier in this chapter, you find out how to tackle the striped elements in these projects: how to change colors and how to carry yarn up the side edge of your knitting. Now, all you need is to relax and indulge in a little color spontaneity. You'll be amazed at the great-looking pieces you can turn out from such simple techniques. (For a refresher on any of the basic techniques used in these projects, check out the chapters in Book 2.)

Bold and Bright Scarf

A striped scarf is the classic knitted item par excellence. And the scarf is the classic garment on which to practice stripes! This scarf pattern varies in texture as well as colors. You can follow the pattern given here by using the suggested yarns or substituting yarns from your own collection.

Materials and vital statistics

» **Measurements:** 7 inches x 54 inches

» **Yarn:** Red Heart "With Wool" (80% acrylic/20% wool; CYC #4, 146 yards, 3.5 ounces [100 grams]):

- **Color A:** Tangerine; 1 skein

- **Color B:** Dahlia; 1 skein

- **Color C:** Pixie; 1 skein

- **Color D:** Gumball; 1 skein

- **Color E:** Tropical; 1 skein

» **Needles:** One pair of size US 10 (6 mm) needles or size needed to obtain gauge

» **Gauge:** 20 stitches and 20 to 24 rows per 4 inches in the various patterns of the scarf

Directions

Note: Most of the color changes for this scarf occur when the RS is facing. Be on the alert, however, because some of the changes begin with the WS facing.

Using Color A, cast on 30 sts and work 6 rows in garter stitch (knit every row).

Begin stripe pattern as follows:

With Color A, work 8 rows in St st (knit on RS rows, purl on WS rows).

With Color B, work 2 rows in St st.

With Color C, work 2 rows in St st.

With Color D, work 6 rows in St st.

With Color E, work 4 rows in St st.

With Color A, work 7 rows in St st and 4 rows in garter stitch.

With Color D, work 13 rows in St st.

With Color C, work 4 rows in St st and 6 rows in garter stitch.

With Color B, work 2 rows in St st.

With Color A, work 6 rows in St st.

With Color E, work 4 rows in St st.

With Color D, work 6 rows in St st.

With Color C, work 2 rows in St st.

With Color B, work 2 rows in St st.

With Color A, work 6 rows in St st.

Repeat the stripe pattern 2 more times for a total of three repeats.

End the scarf by working 6 rows in garter stitch in Color A.
Bind off.

Weave in the ends horizontally along color change lines.

Finishing: Block the scarf (see Book 7, Chapter 1 for blocking instructions).

Variations

Striped projects are easy to improvise. The following variations are just a few ideas to get you going:

» Use yarns in different fibers and textures. They needn't be labeled for the same gauge, but it helps if their gauges are within half a stitch of each other.

» Use different stitch patterns in the different stripes. Try seed stitch (see Book 2, Chapter 2) or one of its variations.

» Keep the color change sequence but work the entire scarf in a rib or another single-pattern stitch.

» Play around with scale by doubling or halving the number of rows in each stripe.

Slouchy Hat with Pompom

This trendy hat is quick to knit up and cozy when finished — and you don't have to worry about sewing any seams! Make it in a soft yarn in colors of your choice, and you'll end up with a striped hat that is as bold and bright as the scarf in the preceding section. Visit dummies.com/go/knitcrochetAIO for a video showing how to knit up this fantastic slouchy hat.

Materials and vital statistics

>> **Measurements:** 24 inches in circumference x 11 inches

>> **Yarn:** Red Heart "With Wool" (80% acrylic/20% wool; CYC #4, 146 yards, 3.5 ounces [100 grams]):

- Color A: Tropical; 1 skein

- Color B: Dahlia; 1 skein

- Color C: Pixie; 1 skein

- Color D: Lapis; 1 skein

- Color E: Tangerine; 1 skein

>> **Needles:** One 16-inch size US 8 (5 mm) circular needle; four or five size US 8 (5 mm) dpns or size needed to obtain gauge

>> **Gauge:** 20 stitches and 24 rows per 4 inches in the various patterns of the scarf

Directions

With the 16-inch circular needle and Color A, cast on 80 sts, place marker to denote beginning of round, and join round, being careful not to twist the stitches.

Work in k2, p2 ribbing pattern until brim measures 1½ inches from cast on edge.

Increase round: Change to Color B, * k1, kfb; rep from * to end of round — 120 stitches.

Work each color change as a jogless join (refer to the earlier section "Knitting Stripes in the Round") in the following stripe pattern:

With Color B, work 3 rounds in St st.

With Color C, work 4 rounds in St st.

With Color D, work 4 rounds in St st.

With Color E, work 4 rounds in St st.

With Color A, work 4 rounds in St st.

With Color D, work 4 rounds in St st.

With Color C, work 4 rounds in St st.

With Color B, work 4 rounds in St st.

With Color A, work 4 rounds in St st.

With Color E, work 4 rounds in St st.

With Color D, work 4 rounds in St st.

With Color C, work 4 rounds in St st.

With Color B, work 4 rounds in St st.

With Color A, work 4 rounds in St st.

With Color D, work 4 rounds in St st.

Begin decreases:

Round 1: * K8, k2tog; rep from * to end of round — 108 sts.

Round 2 and all even rounds: Knit without decreasing.

Round 3: * K7, k2tog; rep from * to end of round — 96 sts.

Round 5: * K6, k2tog; rep from * to end of round — 84 sts.

Round 7: * K5, k2tog; rep from * to end of round — 72 sts.

Note: At this point, you may want to switch to dpns because the circumference of the round is much smaller than the circular needle's length. Simply distribute the remaining stitches evenly over three or four dpns and knit with the remaining needle (the fourth or fifth, depending on how many you're using).

Round 9: * K4, k2tog; rep from * to end of round — 60 sts.

Round 11: * K3, k2tog; rep from * to end of round — 48 sts.

Round 13: * K2, k2tog; rep from * to end of round — 36 sts.

Rounds 15 and 17: Continue knitting (* k2, k2tog *) until 12 stitches remain.

Cut yarn, leaving at least a 12-inch tail.

Finishing: Thread tail onto yarn needle and then slip remaining stitches onto yarn needle (check out Book 2, Chapter 3 for a refresher on how to slip stitches). Pull opening closed, push yarn tail to reverse side of fabric, and weave in ends.

Using a pompom maker and all colors of yarn, create a pompom for the top of the hat. Tie a 12-inch piece of yarn to the center of the pompom. Thread the yarn tail through a tapestry needle, and pull the yarn through the center of the top of the hat so that the pompom sits in the right place. Secure the yarn tail to the inside of the hat to keep the pompom in place.

Variations

You can express your creativity — and practice new skills at the same time — by altering the basic stockinette stitch with a texture stitch instead.

Let the color changes show differently on the RS by alternating a stockinette stitch stripe with a reverse stockinette stitch stripe (covered earlier in this chapter). To get reverse stockinette when knitting in the round, you purl every round.

TIP

Get a random look by making the number of rounds for each stripe different. If random is difficult for you, try tossing a die and using the number that shows up as the number of rounds you stripe. That's guaranteed to be random.

Chapter **2**

Creating Cables

Cables, like knit and purl patterns, offer endless design possibilities. If you're familiar with the creamy cabled sweaters of the Aran Isles, which feature intertwining cable motifs in vertical panels arranged symmetrically across a sweater front, then you're already aware of the wealth of traditional cable designs.

The simple technique of *cabling* — crossing one group of stitches over another by knitting them out of order — lends itself to many interpretations. After you master the basic technique (and it's very easy to do), you can make all kinds of interesting and imaginative cable patterns. All it takes is a little patience and practice.

And that's just the beginning. This chapter presents cable basics that beginners can follow as well as some more intricate cables for when you want to stretch your cabling skills.

Cable Basics

You can make any kind of cable by suspending (or holding) a number of stitches on a cable needle (abbreviated cn) while you knit a specified number of stitches from the LH needle. Then you knit the suspended stitches either by returning them to the LH needle and knitting them or by knitting them straight from the cable needle. (See Book 1, Chapter 1 for more on cable needles.) This process of knitting stitches out of order enables you to cross stitches to create cables. Whether you're making simple or intricate cables, all you're doing is crossing stitches. Easy, right? Right!

Twisting to the right or left

A cable can twist to the right or left, depending on where you hold the suspended stitches.

>> **Left:** To make a cable that twists to the left, hold the suspended stitches in *front* of your work while you knit from the LH needle.

>> **Right:** To make a cable that twists to the right, hold the suspended stitches in *back* of your work.

Cable instructions typically tell you whether you hold the stitches in front or back. Consider these instructions, which create a 6-stitch left-twisting cable:

Sl next 3 sts to cn and hold in *front,* k3, k3 from cn.

Instructions for the same cable, but twisting to the right, read like this:

Sl next 3 sts to cn and hold in *back,* k3, k3 from cn.

You may also see abbreviations like C3F and C3B. The C before the number tells you that these stitches are cable stitches. The number tells you how many stitches are involved with this particular maneuver. The F or B indicates whether to suspend the stitches to the front or the back of your work. So C3F means that you slip 3 stitches to the cable needle and hold it in front. *Note:* Some patterns may list the same cable pattern as C6F and C6B, referring to 6 stitches rather than 3 because you suspend 3 and then knit 3 stitches from the LH needle (3 + 3 = 6). Read the pattern abbreviations for every pattern to make sure you are in fact doing the stitch that the designer intended you to do.

FINDING THE RIGHT CABLE NEEDLE

Various styles of cable needles are available. A needle shaped like a U with a short leg seems to stay out of the way better than the other kinds and the stitches on hold don't slide off. The other versions have different advantages. For example, the straight-needle type makes it easier to knit cable stitches being held directly from the cable needle, but some knitters lose stitches with this version and have trouble figuring out what to do with the LH needle while knitting stitches from the cable needle. Try the different types as you practice cables to see which best suits your knitting style. Refer to Book 1, Chapter 1 for info on the types of cable needles.

Reading cable charts

Most knitting patterns give cable instructions in chart form. These charts show the cable stitches, cable rows, and often some background stitches. Depending on how complicated the cable pattern is, the chart may show you one repeat of the cable or an entire piece.

Although chart symbols aren't standardized, every pattern has a key to the symbols used. Figure 2-1 shows a chart for a 6-stitch left-twisting cable.

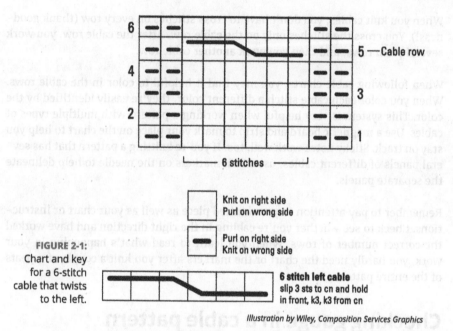

FIGURE 2-1:
Chart and key for a 6-stitch cable that twists to the left.

Illustration by Wiley, Composition Services Graphics

The chart represents the front side of your knitting. Each square in the chart represents a stitch. Here's a breakdown of this chart according to its legend:

>> **A horizontal line** in the square indicates a stitch that you purl on the right side and knit on the wrong side.

>> **The empty squares** represent the cable stitches, which you knit on the right side and purl on the wrong side. In Figure 2-1, the six empty squares tell you that the cable is 6 stitches wide.

>> **The cable symbol in the cable row** indicates (via the key) whether to hold the stitches in the front or the back. Usually, the symbols mean the following, but be sure to check your pattern's chart key before you begin knitting:

- When the cable symbol begins at the bottom of the square and jogs to the top (as it does in Figure 2-1, reading Row 5 from right to left), you hold the yarn in front.

- When the cable symbol begins at the top of the square and jogs to the bottom, you hold the yarn in back.

REMEMBER

When you knit cables, you don't have to cross stitches on every row (thank goodness!). You cross the stitches only on the cable row. After the cable row, you work several plain rows, and then you work another cable row.

TIP

When following cable charts, you may find it helpful to color in the cable rows. When you color each cable stitch a different color, they're easily identified by the color. This system is very helpful when working a pattern with multiple types of cables. Use a magnetic board and strip to mark your place on the chart to help you stay on track. Sticky notes work well, too. If you're knitting a pattern that has several panels of different cables, use stitch markers on the needle to help delineate the separate panels.

REMEMBER

Remember to pay attention to your knitted piece as well as your chart or instructions. Check to see whether you're cabling in the right direction and have worked the correct number of rows. When you learn to read what's happening in your work, you hardly need the chart or the markers after you knit a couple of repeats of the entire pattern.

Checking gauge in a cable pattern

If you're making a project in a repeating cable pattern, be sure to work a large enough swatch to be able to measure gauge accurately. (See Book 1, Chapter 3 if you don't understand measuring gauge.) The swatch should include at least two repeats of the cable pattern horizontally and vertically. If you're working several different cables, you have to check your gauge over each one.

TIP

Feel like you're wasting time making swatches to check gauge? Make two gauge swatches and sew them together for a cabled pillow or bag.

ADDING CABLES TO A BASIC PATTERN

The combination of knit panels with purl panels (think ribs) and crossing stitches over stitches causes cable patterns to pull in widthwise. A sweater worked in a cable pattern is significantly narrower than one worked using the same number of stitches in stockinette stitch. You need more yarn and more stitches for a cable sweater than for one of the same dimensions in a knit/purl pattern.

If you decide to add a cable (or several) to a plain sweater, be sure to increase enough stitches after you knit your border to maintain the overall width. Your gauge swatch is very important here. Use it to play around with the number of stitches you need to add a cable stitch to a plain sweater. Although there are no hard and fast rules, you'll be safe if you add 1 to 2 extra stitches for every 4 stitches in your cable. If you have a ribbed border, you can add the stitches evenly on the last ribbed row. Book 2, Chapter 3, has instructions on making increases.

A Cornucopia of Cables

The patterns in this section are designed to give you an idea of the many ways you can use a simple crossing technique to create a rich variety of cables. Although standard or rope cables are the most basic cables, you aren't limited to those. You can also create

>> A double cable that looks like a horseshoe

>> *Open* cables, where the cable strands separate

>> A braid cable that uses three rather than two cable strands

>> Allover cable patterns, like honeycomb cable

Practice the cable patterns in the following sections to improve your cabling technique. Each cable panel includes 3 set-up stitches on both sides of the cable. These set-up stitches make a crisp transition between the background fabric and the cable itself.

Standard (rope) cable

Standard, or rope, cables have the same number of plain rows between cable rows as there are stitches in the cable. If the cable is 6 stitches wide, for example, you work the cable row every 6 rows. These cable patterns generally cross stitches predictably up a single column of stitches. You can make a rope cable over almost any even number of stitches.

Creating Cables

Here's the pattern for a 6-stitch left-twisting cable, where the first and last 4 stitches make up the background and the 6 central stitches form your cable (you can see the cable row in Figure 2-2):

Cast on 14 sts.

Rows 1 and 3 (RS): P4, k6, p4.

Rows 2, 4, and 6: K4, p6, k4.

Row 5, the cable row: P4, sl next 3 sts to cn and hold in front, k3 from LH needle, k3 from cn, p4.

Rep Rows 1–6 and watch your stockinette stitches become a cabled rope.

TIP

When you suspend stitches on the cable needle, let the cable needle dangle down in front of your work, giving the yarn a slight tug to keep it taut (you don't need to close the gap).

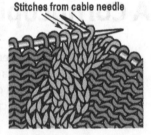

Stitches from cable needle

FIGURE 2-2:
Work the
cable row.

a. Slip the cable stitches to the cable needle and hold in front.

b. Knit 3 from the LH needle.

c. Knit the stitches from the cable needle.

Illustration by Wiley, Composition Services Graphics

Instead of knitting stitches directly from the cable needle, you may prefer to return the suspended stitches to the LH needle before you knit them. Try both ways and use the technique that's more comfortable for you.

REMEMBER

When you work cables, you go back and forth from purl stitches to knit stitches. To switch from a knit to a purl stitch, bring your yarn to the front before you make the next stitch. From a purl to a knit stitch, bring your yarn to the back before you make the next stitch.

COUNTING CABLE ROWS

Get used to counting the rows between cable crossings, and you won't have to rely on your memory. (It's always good to have an alternative to memory.) Look carefully at the cable row: If the cable crosses to the right, you should see a small hole created by the pull of the stitches just to the left of the cable crossing. (You may have to stretch the knitting vertically a bit to see it.) If the cable crosses to the left, the hole is on the right. Just below the hole is a horizontal running thread stretching between the last crossed stitch and the background. The following figure shows you what to look for.

Starting with the running thread *above* the hole, count up running threads to determine the number of rows worked since the last cable row. Alternatively, you can follow the thread to the stitch it connects to — the knit stitch in the cable or the purled stitch in the background. Starting with the stitch *above* the connected stitch, count up to and include the stitch on the needle for the number of rows worked. If you're working a 6-stitch cable and you count 6 running threads or stitches, you're ready for a cable row.

Small hole

Illustration by Wiley, Composition Services Graphics

Open cable

Not all cables are worked on the same stitches over and over. Using basic cabling techniques, you can cross stitches over the background as well to make open cables (sometimes called *traveling cables*). Picture the strands of a basic rope cable separating and moving away from each other and then returning and twisting around each other again, as in Figure 2-3.

FIGURE 2-3:
Open cable.

Photograph by Wiley, Composition Services Graphics

To work an open cable, you simply cross stitches as in a basic cable, but instead of crossing stockinette stitches over stockinette stitches, you cross stockinette stitches over one or more background (usually purl) stitches. You can open a cable and have the strands move away from each other by using the same crossing technique used for the 6-stitch rope cable in the preceding section.

The open cable pattern in Figure 2-3 consists of a panel of 11 stitches. The point at which they cross is simply a 4-stitch cable row. To knit this open cable, you need two new techniques:

>> **Back cross:** Sl next p stitch to cn and hold in back, k2, p the stitch from the cn.

>> **Front cross:** Sl next 2 sts to cn and hold in front, p1, k2 from cn.

Knit the open cable pattern as follows:

Cast on 11 sts.

Rows 1 and 3 (WS): K3, p2, k1, p2, k3.

Row 2: P3, sl next 3 sts to cn (2 k sts and 1 p st) and hold in back, k2, sl next p st back to LH needle and p it, k2 from cn, p3.

Row 4: P2, back cross, p1, front cross, p2.

Row 5: K2, p2, k3, p2, k2.

Row 6: P1, back cross, p3, front cross, p1.

Rows 7 and 9: K1, p2, k5, p2, k1.

Row 8: P1, k2, p5, k2, p1.

Row 10: P1, front cross, p3, back cross, p1.

Row 11: K2, p2, k3, p2, k2.

Row 12: P2, front cross, p1, back cross, p2.

Rep Rows 1–12.

Double cable

Also known as a *horseshoe cable*, a *double cable* (see Figure 2-4) consists of a panel of 18 stitches (the cable is 12 stitches wide with 3 set-up stitches on either side of it). Visit `dummies.com/go/knitcrochetAIO` for a video demonstration of how this double cable comes together.

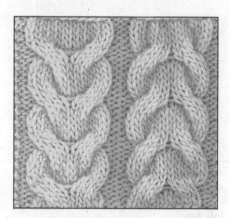

FIGURE 2-4:
Double cable.

Photograph by Wiley, Composition Services Graphics

Follow these instructions to work this double cable pattern:

Cast on 18 sts.

Rows 1 and 3 (RS): P3, k12, p3.

Rows 2, 4, and 6: K3, p12, k3.

Row 5: P3, sl next 3 sts to cn and hold in back, k3, k3 from cn, sl next 3 sts to cn and hold in front, k3, k3 from cn, p3.

Rep Rows 1–6.

Did you notice that this is nothing more than a right cable next to a left cable? You can turn the cable upside down by working a left cable first and then a right one.

Wave cable

A *wave cable* (see Figure 2-5) consists of a panel of 12 stitches (the cable itself is 6 stitches wide). This cable gets its appearance from crossing inconsistently — to the right on one cable row and to the left on the next cable row.

FIGURE 2-5:
Wave cables.

Photograph by Wiley, Composition Services Graphics

Work the wave cable as follows:

> Cast on 12 sts.
>
> **Rows 1, 3, 7, and 9 (RS):** P3, k6, p3.
>
> **Rows 2, 4, 6, 8, 10, and 12:** K3, p6, k3.
>
> **Row 5:** P3, sl next 3 sts to cn and hold in back, k3, k3 from cn, p3.
>
> **Row 11:** P3, sl next 3 to cn and hold in front, k3, k3 from cn, p3.
>
> Rep Rows 1–12.

Chain cable

A chain panel (shown in Figure 2-6) consists of 14 stitches; the cable itself is 8 stitches wide.

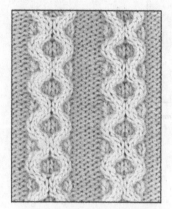

Photograph by Wiley, Composition Services Graphics

FIGURE 2-6:
Chain cable.

Work this cable as follows:

Cast on 14 sts.

Rows 1 and 5 (RS): P3, k8, p3.

Rows 2, 4, 6, and 8: K3, p8, k3.

Row 3: P3, sl next 2 sts to cn and hold in back, k2, k2 from cn, sl next 2 sts to cn and hold in front, k2, k2 from cn, p3.

Row 7: P3, sl next 2 sts to cn and hold in front, k2, k2 from cn, sl next 2 sts to cn and hold in back, k2, k2 from cn, p3.

Rep Rows 1–8.

Did you notice that a chain cable is just two wave cables waving in opposite directions and lined up side by side?

Honeycomb cable

A *honeycomb cable* (see Figure 2-7) is made of a multiple of 8 stitches. Because this cable pattern is an allover pattern (that is, it makes up the whole knitted fabric), it's set up as a multiple of stitches rather than as a panel.

FIGURE 2-7: Honeycomb cable.

Knit this pattern as follows:

Cast on a multiple of 8 sts.

Rows 1 and 5 (RS): Knit.

Row 2, 4, 6, and 8: Purl.

Row 3: * Sl next 2 sts to cn and hold in back, k2, k2 from cn, sl next 2 sts to cn and hold in front, k2, k2 from cn; rep from * to end of row.

Row 7: * Sl next 2 sts to cn and hold in front, k2, k2 from cn, sl next 2 sts to cn and hold in back, k2, k2 from cn; rep from * to end of row.

Rep Rows 1–8.

Braid cable

A *braid cable* (shown in Figure 2-8) consists of a panel of 15 stitches; the cable itself is 9 stitches wide.

Knit this pattern as follows:

Cast on 15 sts.

Rows 1 and 5 (RS): P3, k9, p3.

Rows 2, 4, 6, and 8: K3, p9, k3.

Row 3: P3, sl next 3 sts to cn and hold in front, k3, k3 from cn, k3, p3.

Row 7: P3, k3, sl next 3 sts to cn and hold in back, k3, k3 from cn, p3.

Rep Rows 1–8.

FIGURE 2-8:
Braid cable.

Photograph by Wiley, Composition Services Graphics

TIP

You can make a petite version of the braid cable simply by reducing the number of cable stitches (the stitches between the set-up stitches on the edge) to 6. Cross 2 stitches over 2 for this variation.

Varying a cable

Even the simplest cable lends itself to variation. Here are some ideas to try when you're in an experimental mood (keep some graph paper nearby):

>> Change the width of the cable strands.

>> Play around with the number of rows between cable rows.

>> Change the background stitch. Instead of stockinette stitch, work the cable on garter stitch, seed stitch, moss stitch, or something else.

>> Work one cable strand in a different color (which uses intarsia knitting, a topic beyond the scope of this book).

>> Work one cable strand in a different pattern stitch.

>> Work a twist (essentially a mini cable) in one of the strands; see the next section for a how-to.

THE STUBBORN STITCH ON THE LEFT EDGE

Often, the left-end knit stitch on a rib or in a cable is noticeably larger than the other knit stitches. When you move from a knit to a purl stitch, the yarn travels a tiny bit farther than it does between 2 knit or 2 purl stitches, resulting in this looser stitch. You can remedy this problem by working the first 2 purl stitches after the cable tighter than normal. After you knit the last stitch, insert your needle into the neighboring purl stitch and give a good tug on the yarn before wrapping and making the stitch. Do so again for the next stitch. This technique helps tighten the last cable stitch, but *don't* let it tighten the rest of your stitches.

If you find that you still have a sloppy knit stitch on the left edge of your cable, try this trick: On the right side, work the last knit stitch of the cable. Bring the yarn to the front, slip the next (purl) stitch, and continue on. When you come to the slipped stitch on the next wrong-side row, go into it as if to knit and, at the same time, go under the unworked strand on the right side. With the tip of the LH needle, bring the slipped stitch over the strand, transfer the newly formed stitch to the LH needle in the ready-to-work position, and knit it.

Making Twists

Twists are diminutive cousins of the cable. A twist consists of 2 stitches — 1 stitch crossing over its neighbor. You can twist in either direction: left over right or right over left. To make a 2-stitch twist, you can use a cable needle to take 1 stitch to the front or back while you knit the other stitch. But another method lets you accomplish the crossing, doesn't require a cable needle, saves time, and is easier to do. The following sections show you how to do it.

Twisting to the right

To work a twist to the right, follow these steps:

1. **Slip the 2 designated twist stitches one at a time from the LH needle to the RH needle.**

Always slip a stitch as if to purl unless your instructions tell you to do otherwise.

2. **Move the tip of the LH needle behind the RH needle, pass up the first slipped stitch, and enter the second slipped stitch from left to right, as shown in Figure 2-9.**

Leave the tip of the LH needle in the slipped stitch.

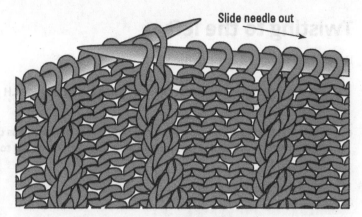

FIGURE 2-9: Insert the LH needle through the second slipped stitch from left to right.

3. **Gently slide the RH needle out of both stitches, leaving the second stitch on the LH needle hanging.**

4. **Bring the tip of the RH needle around to the *front* and insert it into the hanging stitch (see Figure 2-10).**

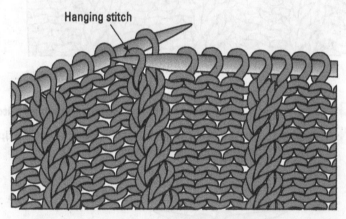

FIGURE 2-10: Insert the RH needle tip into the hanging stitch.

5. **Transfer this stitch to the LH needle.**

   Both stitches are back on the LH needle, with the second one overlapping the first to the right.

6. **Knit both stitches in the usual way.**

Creating Cables

Twisting to the left

Here's how to work a twist to the left:

1. **Slip the 2 designated twist stitches one at a time from the LH needle to the RH needle.**

2. **Move the tip of the LH needle in front of the RH needle, pass up the first slipped stitch, and enter the second slipped stitch from left to right (see Figure 2-11).**

   Leave the tip of the LH needle in the slipped stitch.

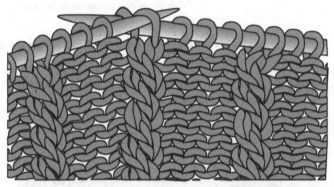

FIGURE 2-11:
Insert the LH needle from left to right.

Illustration by Wiley, Composition Services Graphics

3. **Gently slide the RH needle out of both stitches, leaving 1 stitch hanging.**

4. **Keeping the RH needle in *back* of the LH needle, insert the tip of your RH needle into the hanging stitch (see Figure 2-12).**

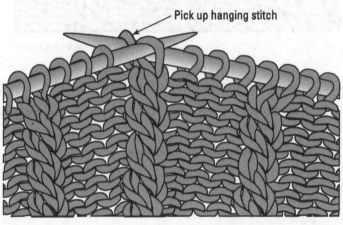

Pick up hanging stitch

FIGURE 2-12:
Pick up the hanging stitch.

Illustration by Wiley, Composition Services Graphics

5. **Transfer this stitch to the LH needle.**

Both stitches are back on the LH needle, with the first one overlapping the second to the left.

6. **Knit both stitches in the usual way.**

Practice Cable Projects

Cables lend themselves to almost anything you can knit: hats, pillows, scarves, and sweaters. Even the most basic cables look intriguing, whether alone or in multiples. Follow the patterns for the projects in this section as they are, or use them as guidelines and plug in different types of cables.

Cable Hat with Pompoms

This Cable Hat with Pompoms is a straightforward hat pattern that uses only one kind of cable: a 6-stitch cable twisting to the right. You make the front and back as separate pieces and seam them along the top and sides.

Materials and vital statistics

➤➤ **Measurements:** 21 inches in circumference (each piece measures 10½ inches wide) x 8 inches

➤➤ **Yarn:** Classic Elite Yarns "Montera" (50% llama/50% wool; CYC #4, 127 yards, 3.5 ounces [100 grams]): Color #3827, 2 hanks

➤➤ **Needles:** One pair each of size US 7 (4½ mm) and US 9 (5½ mm) needles or sizes needed to obtain gauge, cable needle

➤➤ **Other materials:** Pompom maker

➤➤ **Gauge:** 22 stitches and 22 to 24 rows per 4 inches over cable pattern

Directions

With size US 7 needles, cast on 50 sts.

Rows 1–4: * K1, p1; rep from * to end of row.

Change to size US 9 needles.

Row 5 (RS): P2, inc 1, * k2, inc 1, k3, p3; rep from * to end of row (57 sts).

Row 6: * K3, p6; rep from * to last 3 sts, k3.

Work the cable chart (see Figure 2-13), being sure to begin and end each RS row with k3 and to begin and end each WS row with p3:

Row 7 (WS): * P3, work Row 1 of 6-st cable chart; rep from * to last 3 sts, p3.

Row 8 (RS): * K3, work Row 2 of cable chart; rep from * to last 3 sts, k3.

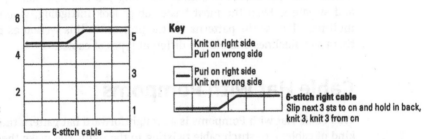

FIGURE 2-13: 6-stitch cable chart with key.

Illustration by Wiley, Composition Services Graphics

Continue working the chart as established.

Rep the cable chart pattern until the piece measures approximately 8 inches in length, ending with Row 4 (WS) of the pattern.

Note: When working with cables, try to begin and end on a flat part of the cable, between cable rows.

Next row (RS): * P3, k2, k2tog, k2; rep from * to last 3 sts, p3 (51 sts).

Decreasing 1 st in each cable on the final row brings the fabric back to normal width.

Bind off, or if you want to seam your pieces together using the three-needle bind-off (see Book 7, Chapter 1), run a piece of scrap yarn through the stitches to secure them.

Make a second piece to match the first.

Finishing: After knitting the pieces of your hat, follow these steps to finish it like a pro:

Gently block the squares. Cables are best blocked by using the wet-blocking method (refer to Book 7, Chapter 1), which allows you to shape and mold the cable pattern.

Seam the top of the hat. Use backstitch or the three-needle bind-off covered in Book 7, Chapter 1 and then steam the seam.

Sew up the side seams by using mattress stitch and steam the seam.

Add the pompoms. Follow the instructions for using your pompom maker to make pompoms. You can make as many or as few as you like, in the same or different sizes. Leave enough of a tail on the pompoms to braid or twist into a cord. Using a tapestry needle, thread the cords to the inside of the hat and secure them in a seam.

Variations

>> Use a different kind of 6-stitch cable — for example, the wave cable presented earlier in this chapter.

>> Make the hat longer.

>> Use any combination of cable patterns that appeals to you.

Horseshoe Cable Hand Warmers

These stylish Horseshoe Cable Hand Warmers are super-simple to knit. Earlier in the chapter, you find out how to make a 6-stitch horseshoe cable. This pattern uses a 4-stitch horseshoe cable because the pattern uses a heavier weight yarn.

Materials and vital statistics

>> **Measurements:** Approximately 8 inches in circumference x 6 inches; can be shortened or lengthened as desired

>> **Yarn:** Schachenmayr SMC "Big Bravo" (100% acrylic; CYC #6, 131 yards, 7 ounces [200 grams]): Tan, 1 skein

>> **Needles:** One pair of US size 13 (9 mm) needles or size needed to obtain gauge, cable needle

>> **Gauge:** The horseshoe cable is 3 inches wide, and the seed stitch gauge is approximately 8 stitches and 10 rows per 4 inches with the yarn listed here

Directions

It's necessary to have two sets of instructions — one for the left hand and one for the right — for the cable to end on the top of the hand as intended.

LEFT HAND

Cast on 18 sts.

Setup row (RS): P1, k1, place marker, k8, place marker, (k1, p1) four times.

Row 1, 3 (WS): (P1, k1) four times, slip marker, p8, slip marker, k1, p1.

You've now begun the seed stitch outside the markers and stockinette stitch inside the markers. This division remains the same throughout the pattern on every row except the cable row.

Row 2 cable row (RS): Maintain the seed stitch pattern to marker, slip marker, sl next 2 sts to cn and hold in back, k2 from LH needle, k2 from cn, sl next 2 sts to cn and hold in front, k2 from LH needle, k2 from cn, slip marker, work established seed stitch pattern to end.

Row 4: Maintain the seed stitch pattern to marker, slip marker, k8, slip marker, work established seed stitch pattern to end.

Rep Rows 1–4 until hand warmers are long enough to cover the space between the base of your thumb and 1 to 2 inches past your wrist bone. You can make them even longer if you want. Bind off.

Finishing: Seam the right and left sides of the piece together and try it on.

RIGHT HAND

Cast on 18 sts.

Setup row (RS): (P1, k1) four times, place marker, k8, place marker, k1, p1.

Row 1, 3 (WS): P1, k1, slip marker, p8, slip marker, (k1, p1) four times.

You have now begun the seed stitch outside the markers and stockinette stitch inside the markers. This division remains the same throughout the pattern on every row except the cable row.

Row 2 cable row (RS): Maintain the seed stitch pattern to marker, slip marker, sl next 2 sts to cn and hold in back, k2 from LH needle, k2 from cn, sl next 2 sts to cn and hold in front, k2 from LH needle, k2 from cn, slip marker, work established seed stitch pattern to end.

Row 4: Maintain the seed stitch pattern to marker, slip marker, k8, slip marker, work established seed stitch pattern to end.

Rep Rows 1–4 until hand warmers are long enough to cover the space between the base of your thumb and 1 to 2 inches past your wrist bone. You can make them even longer if you want. Bind off.

Finishing: Seam the right and left sides of the piece together and try it on.

Chapter **3**

Crochet Stitches That Create Pattern and Texture

One of the qualities of crochet that makes it so unique is its flexibility — you can fashion an almost endless array of patterns and textures based on a few simple stitches. (Book 3, Chapters 1 and 2 show you how to create these basic stitches.) You can combine stitches to make pattern stitches, such as shells and clusters, and textured stitches, such as bobbles, popcorns, and loops. You can also create interesting textures and designs by working a stitch in the top loops, and inserting your hook in the bottom loops, around the middle loops, or even in loops on the fronts or backs of stitches!

Along with illustrations of the completed stitches, you find the International Crochet Symbol for each stitch so you're prepared to read stitch diagrams whenever you encounter them. (See Book 1, Chapter 4 for the basics of stitch diagrams.) The Elegant All-Season Wrap, cowl, and blanket projects at the end of this chapter incorporate many of the fancy stitches and techniques introduced in the following pages so you can practice them while creating beautiful accessories.

A stitch is a stitch is a stitch. Regardless of where you insert your hook, you always work a particular stitch in the same way.

Spicing Things Up with Pattern Stitches

The versatile V-stitch, crossed double crochet, shell, cluster, picot, and reverse single crochet stitches can create stitch designs that are open and lacy or tight and compact. As you become familiar with these stitches, you'll recognize them in numerous patterns that span the range from home decor to fashion.

As you branch out in the crocheting world, you'll probably come across variations of the pattern stitches in this section. So don't assume that you always work a cluster stitch exactly as it's defined here. Trust your pattern instructions; they usually tell you exactly how to work a pattern stitch, so be sure to carefully read the notes at the beginning.

Showing the V: The V-stitch

The *V-stitch* (abbreviated *V-st*) combination got its name because it resembles a *V*. To create a V-stitch, work one double crochet stitch, chain one, and then work another double crochet stitch all in the same stitch (check out Figure 3-1a to see a completed V-stitch). In Crochetese, that's dc, ch 1, dc in the same stitch. Figure 3-1b shows the International Crochet Symbol for the V-stitch.

FIGURE 3-1: The common V-stitch with its symbol.

a. b.

© *John Wiley & Sons, Inc.*

Seeing Xs: The crossed double crochet stitch

For the *crossed double crochet stitch* (abbreviated *crossed dc*), you work two double crochet stitches on an angle, producing a pattern that looks like an *X*. To make a crossed double crochet stitch, follow these steps:

1. **Skip the next stitch in the row.**

2. **Work 1 double crochet (dc) in the next stitch.**

3. **Working behind the double crochet you just made, work 1 double crochet in the stitch that you skipped, as shown in Figure 3-2a.**

Keeping the double crochet stitch you just made in front of your hook, insert your hook from front to back in the specified skipped stitch. Figure 3-2b illustrates the completed stitch, and Figure 3-2c denotes the symbol for the crossed double crochet stitch.

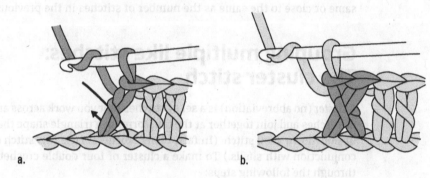

FIGURE 3-2:
Working a
crossed double
crochet stitch.

© John Wiley & Sons, Inc.

To continue working crossed double crochet stitches across the row, repeat Steps 1 through 3.

REMEMBER

Some patterns using the crossed double crochet stitch may specify that you work the second double crochet in front of the first, or even wrapped around the first (having the second double crochet enclose the first). That's all the more reason to read your pattern's instructions so you can crochet the way it wants you to from the start.

Spreading out: The shell stitch

The *shell stitch* (abbreviated *shell*) is very versatile, and you can find it just about anywhere. The variation shown here is a common version of this adaptable stitch. To make a shell stitch, work four double crochet stitches in the same stitch. (See Figure 3-3a for the completed stitch and Figure 3-3b for the stitch symbol.)

FIGURE 3-3:
A completed
shell stitch and
its symbol.

a.

b.

© John Wiley & Sons, Inc.

Usually the base of a shell stitch is surrounded by unworked stitches. However, most shell stitch patterns make sure that the total number of stitches is either the same or close to the same as the number of stitches in the previous row.

Grouping multiple like stitches: The cluster stitch

A *cluster* (no abbreviation) is a set of stitches that you work across an equal number of stitches and join together at the top, forming a triangle shape that resembles an upside-down shell stitch. (In fact, many crocheters use this stitch combination in conjunction with shells.) To make a cluster of four double crochet stitches, work through the following steps:

1. **Yarn over (yo), insert the hook into the next stitch, yarn over, draw the yarn through the stitch, yarn over, and draw the yarn through 2 loops on the hook. (2 loops should remain on the hook, as shown in Figure 3-4a.)**

   One half-closed double crochet is now complete. A *half-closed stitch* is one that's only worked partway and then finished at the end of the combination.

2. **Repeat Step 1 three times (see Figure 3-4a).**

   You should end up with 5 loops on your hook, like in Figure 3-4b.

3. **Yarn over and draw the yarn through all 5 loops on the hook (refer to Figure 3-4b).**

   Well done. You've just completed one 4-double-crochet (4-dc) cluster. See Figure 3-5a for a visual of what the completed cluster should look like and Figure 3-5b for its symbol.

Getting decorative: The picot stitch

Picots (no abbreviation) are pretty little round-shaped stitches that add a decorative touch to an edging or fill an empty space in a mesh design. You see them quite often in thread crochet, but you can also make them with yarn. To make a picot, follow these steps:

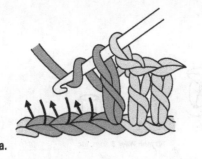 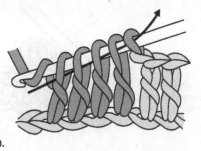

FIGURE 3-4:
Working a
4-double-crochet
cluster.   **a.**

b.

© John Wiley & Sons, Inc.

FIGURE 3-5:
A completed
4-double-crochet
cluster stitch
with symbol.   **a.**

b.

© John Wiley & Sons, Inc.

1. Chain 3 (ch 3).

2. Insert your hook into the third chain from the hook, as shown in Figure 3-6a.

3. Yarn over (yo).

4. Draw the yarn through the stitch and through the loop on the hook, like in Figure 3-6b.

Figure 3-7a depicts a completed picot. Check out this stitch's symbol in Figure 3-7b.

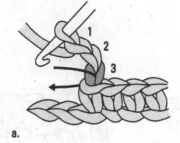 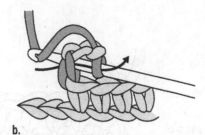

FIGURE 3-6:
Making a
picot stitch.   **a.**

b.

© John Wiley & Sons, Inc.

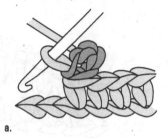

FIGURE 3-7:
A finished picot
stitch and its
symbol.

a.

b.

© John Wiley & Sons, Inc.

Working backward: The reverse single crochet stitch

The *reverse single crochet stitch* (abbreviated *reverse sc*) is sometimes called the *crab stitch*. The mechanics are the same as for a regular single crochet — except in reverse. Instead of working from right to left, you work from left to right. This stitch creates a somewhat twisted, rounded edge that's good for making a simple finished edge for your work. *Note:* You usually don't work stitches into the tops of the reverse single crochet, so you won't find this stitch in the middle of a project.

To work reverse single crochet, follow these steps:

1. **With the right side of your work facing you, insert the hook from front to back in the next stitch to the right, as shown in Figure 3-8a.**

2. **Yarn over (yo) and draw the yarn through the stitch, as in Figure 3-8b.**

3. **Yarn over and draw the yarn through the 2 loops on your hook (see Figure 3-9a).**

   One reverse single crochet is now complete.

4. **Repeat Steps 1 through 3 in each stitch across the row.**

   Figure 3-9b shows several completed reverse single crochet stitches, and Figure 3-9c denotes the stitch symbol.

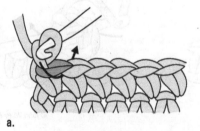
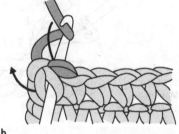

FIGURE 3-8:
Working a reverse
single crochet.

a.

b.

© John Wiley & Sons, Inc.

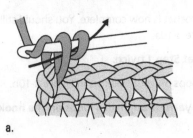 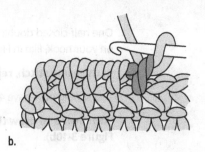

a.   b.

FIGURE 3-9:
Finishing the
reverse single
crochet.
c. $\tilde{\mathsf{T}}$ or $\tilde{\mathsf{X}}$

Moving into the Third Dimension with Texture Stitches

If you want to add even more pizzazz to your crocheting, the three-dimensional stitch combinations in the following sections create great textures in your crocheted fabric. You can interchange the first three stitches because they all look like different versions of a bumpy oval. The last one, the loop stitch, creates long, fun loops that come in handy when making toys, sweaters, slippers, and wall hangings.

REMEMBER

Because stitches aren't standardized in any way, you may come across many different names for them. For example, *puff stitches* are sometimes referred to as *bobbles*, even though they're created in completely different ways. So always read the specifics for each stitch before beginning your work.

Gently bumping along: The bobble stitch

The *bobble stitch* (no abbreviation) creates a smooth, oval bump and works well with a heavier-weight yarn. Making a bobble stitch is similar to making a cluster (described earlier in this chapter) in that you half-close several stitches worked in the same stitch and then join them together to finish the stitch. To make a 3-double-crochet bobble stitch, follow these simple steps:

1. **Yarn over (yo), insert your hook into the stitch, yarn over, draw the yarn through the stitch, yarn over, and draw the yarn through the 2 loops on your hook.**

One half-closed double crochet is now complete. You should still have 2 loops on your hook, like in Figure 3-10a.

2. **In the same stitch, repeat Step 1 twice.**

You should now have 4 loops on your hook, as in Figure 3-10b.

3. **Yarn over and draw the yarn through all 4 loops on the hook (refer to Figure 3-10b).**

One 3-double-crochet bobble stitch is now complete. Take a look at Figure 3-11a for the completed stitch and Figure 3-11b for the stitch symbol.

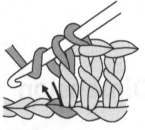 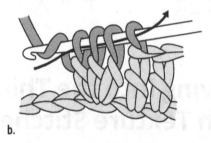

FIGURE 3-10:
Creating a bobble stitch.

a.   b.

© John Wiley & Sons, Inc.

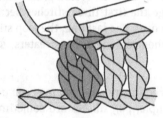

FIGURE 3-11:
A completed bobble stitch and its symbol.

a.   b.

© John Wiley & Sons, Inc.

In some instances, you can make the bobble stitch with more than three double crochet stitches, as in the Elegant All-Season Wrap project (featured later in this chapter), which uses four double crochet stitches to form the bobble stitch. To increase a 3-double-crochet bobble stitch to a 4-double-crochet bobble stitch, simply work one more partial double crochet into the stitch and finish as you normally would. (Don't worry that you'll have to figure this type of thing out on your own. A good pattern always instructs you on exactly how to make specialized stitches such as the bobble stitch.)

Not a magic dragon: The puff stitch

A *puff stitch* (abbreviated *puff st*) is aptly named because it gently puffs up into an oval shape. The puff stitch differs slightly from other raised stitches because you make it with a series of loops rather than stitches. Follow these few steps to create a puff stitch:

1. **Yarn over (yo) and insert your hook into the stitch (refer to Figure 3-12a).**

2. **Yarn over and draw the yarn through the stitch, bringing the loop up to the height of the previous stitch.**

   You should have 3 loops on your hook, as shown in Figure 3-12b.

3. **Working in the same stitch, repeat Steps 1 through 2 four times.**

   At the end of this step, you should have 11 loops on your hook.

4. **Yarn over and draw the yarn through all 11 loops on your hook, as in Figure 3-13a.**

   Ta-da! You've just completed your first puff stitch. Check out Figure 3-13b to see the completed stitch and Figure 3-13c for its symbol.

FIGURE 3-12:
Fashioning
a puff stitch.   a.

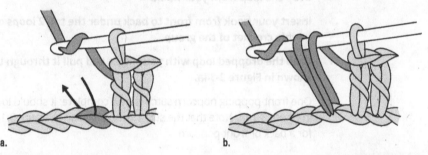

b.

© *John Wiley & Sons, Inc.*

TIP

Puff stitches, clusters, bobbles, and popcorn stitches (see the next section) sometimes need an extra chain stitch at the top of the stitch to close them securely. If this is the case, your pattern should tell you so.

Forget the butter: The popcorn stitch

This stitch really pops! The *popcorn stitch* (abbreviated *pop* or *pc*) is a nicely rounded, compact oval that stands out from the fabric. It takes a bit more time to make than other raised stitches, but it's well worth the effort. For even more fun, you can work popcorn stitches so that they "pop" to the front or the back of a fabric, depending on where you want them to stand out. The following steps show you how to work a 5-double-crochet popcorn stitch both ways.

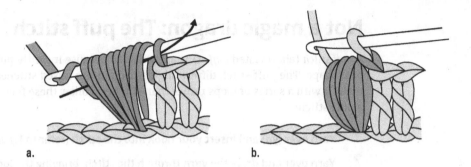

a.   b.

FIGURE 3-13:
Finishing the
puff stitch.   **c.**

To pop to the front of your design:

1. **Work 5 double crochet stitches (dc) in the same stitch.**

2. **Drop the loop from your hook.**

3. **Insert your hook from front to back under the top 2 loops of the first double crochet of the group.**

4. **Grab the dropped loop with your hook and pull it through the stitch, as shown in Figure 3-14a.**

   One front-popping popcorn stitch is now complete; it should look like the stitch in Figure 3-14b. Note that the stitch symbol shown in Figure 3-14c is the same for a back or front popcorn.

To pop to the back of your piece:

1. **Work 5 double crochet stitches (dc) in the same stitch.**

2. **Drop the loop from your hook.**

3. **Insert your hook from back to front under the top 2 loops of the first double crochet of the group.**

4. **Grab the dropped loop with your hook and pull it through the stitch, like in Figure 3-15a.**

   Figure 3-15b illustrates how a completed back-popping popcorn should look.

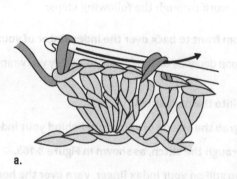
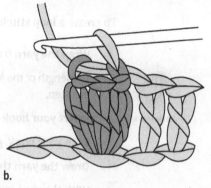

a.

b.

FIGURE 3-14:
Completing a
front popcorn
stitch.

c.

© John Wiley & Sons, Inc.

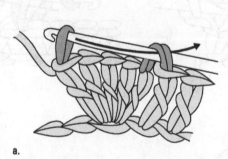

FIGURE 3-15:
Completing a
back popcorn
stitch.

a.

b.

© John Wiley & Sons, Inc.

Feeling loopy: The loop stitch

The *loop stitch* (no abbreviation) gets its name from the long, loose loops it leaves behind. Getting the loops to be all the same length takes some practice, but when you get the hang of it, the loop stitch adds a lot of interest to garments. It also works great to make a beard for Santa when worked in several consecutive rows.

To create a loop stitch, work through the following steps:

1. **Wrap the yarn from front to back over the index finger of your yarn hand.**

   The length of the loop depends on how loosely or tightly you wrap the yarn in this step.

2. **Insert your hook into the next stitch.**

3. **With your hook, grab the strand of yarn from behind your index finger.**

4. **Draw the yarn through the stitch, as shown in Figure 3-16a.**

5. **With the yarn loop still on your index finger, yarn over the hook (yo) and draw the yarn through the 2 loops on your hook (refer to Figure 3-16b).**

   One loop stitch is now complete. Figure 3-17a shows the completed stitch, and Figure 3-17b shows its symbol.

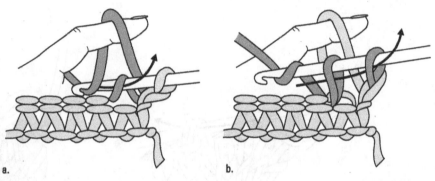

FIGURE 3-16:
Making a
loop stitch. a.

b.

© John Wiley & Sons, Inc.

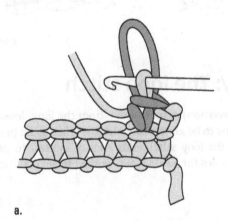

FIGURE 3-17:
A completed loop
stitch and its
symbol. a.

b.

© John Wiley & Sons, Inc.

REMEMBER

Make sure that all the loops you create are the same length to achieve a finished look.

After working an area of loop stitch, you can cut all the loops to create a shaggy dog look.

Switching Up Your Stitch Placement

Depending on the type of look you're trying to achieve, you can work a stitch pretty much anywhere you can fit your hook — nothing is off-limits. Normally you work a new stitch into both top loops of a stitch you've already made, but to switch things up, you can also work a new stitch into a single top loop, into the base, or into other loops on the front or back of your piece. In Book 3, Chapter 1 you learn about all the parts of a stitch; the next sections show you what you can do with them.

Working into the top and other loops

You can work one stitch into another in a few different ways, regardless of whether you're working in rows or rounds, and each method creates a unique effect in your finished fabric. The resulting look can be either smooth or textured, depending on which loop you choose to use (as shown in Figure 3-18a; Figure 3-18b notes the symbols):

>> **Crocheting under both top loops:** Working under both top loops is the typical way to crochet a stitch; it creates a smooth, flat fabric. This method is presented in earlier chapters.

>> **Crocheting in the front loop only:** Working under the front loop only creates a ridge on the opposite side of the fabric. This approach is great for making a rib at the bottom edge and cuffs of a sweater. Another reason to leave the back loop free is so you can work a stitch from a later row into it.

>> **Crocheting in the back loop only:** Like front-loop-only stitching, working new stitches in the back loop creates a rib, except it's on the opposite side of the fabric. You may also work in just the back loops when joining two pieces of crocheted fabric together. (See Book 7, Chapter 2 for the scoop on this technique.) Leaving the front loops free when joining pieces together creates a decorative raised seam on the front of your work.

>> **Crocheting in a loop found on the front or back side of the stitch:** Usually, you look at the stitch from the top to see the front and back loops; however, look at a stitch from the front (right) or back (wrong) side of the fabric, and you'll find additional loops available for your use.

- Working stitches into a loop on the front side of the stitch pushes the top two loops outward to the back of the fabric and is referred to as the *front-most loop* (see Book 3, Chapter 1).

- Working stitches into a loop on the back side of the stitch pushes the top two loops outward to the front of the fabric, creating a faux knit-like rib, and is called the *back-most loop* (see Book 3, Chapter 1).

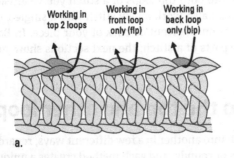

FIGURE 3-18: Working in the different loops at the top of a stitch, plus the relevant stitch symbols.

⌒ = worked in back loop only

⌄ = worked in front loop only

⌣ = worked in front-most loop

⌒ = worked in back-most loop

a.   b.

© *John Wiley & Sons, Inc.*

TIP

Working in just one loop at the top of a stitch adds a bit of stretch to your piece that working in both top loops just doesn't offer. This flexibility comes in handy when you're working with a yarn that doesn't offer much elasticity, such as cotton, or when you're making a rib around the bottom or cuff edges of a sweater where you want the fabric to have some stretch.

REMEMBER

Working in the front or back loop of a stitch doesn't necessarily designate the design's front or back side. After you turn your work at the end of a row (see Book 3, Chapter 1), the front loop on the previous row becomes the back loop on the current row.

Stitching up the sides

You often work around the side of a stitch when you're adding a border to a crocheted item, smoothing out an edge, or joining two pieces of fabric. Only the stitches that are at the end of a row come into play, which is why most pattern instructions refer to working in the side of a stitch as working in *row-end stitches*.

Figure 3-19 shows the proper placement for your hook in a row-end stitch. To avoid gaping holes across the edges, insert your hook where two stitches join together, whether at the base or the top of the stitches or both. You work the new stitch in the same way whether you're working into a complete row-end stitch or a turning chain.

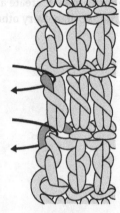

FIGURE 3-19: Proper hook placement for crocheting into the side of a stitch.

© John Wiley & Sons, Inc.

Working Stitches in Spaces and Other Interesting Places

Who says you have to work in a stitch at all? You can create some nice stitch effects by working outside the box — or shall we say stitch? The following sections introduce you to working stitches into the spaces *between* stitches or those created by chain loops and working a stitch in and around the middle of another one.

Squeezing into spaces

Unlike the tight weave of knitted fabric, crocheted fabric has spaces between the stitches because they're not linked on the sides, which unlocks a whole new world of opportunity in which to create new stitches. Even though the spaces between stitches aren't always obvious, they're there. In the sections that follow, you find out how to work in spaces between stitches and in chain spaces and loops.

Working in the spaces between stitches

Because crocheted stitches aren't linked at the sides, you can work your stitches in between other stitches by inserting your hook into the space between two stitches rather than the loop(s) at the top of a stitch (see Figure 3-20). When you work in between stitches, you lower the base of the new stitch, altering the alignment of the row. You can use this technique to create a zigzag effect: Just work one stitch in between stitches and the next one in the top of the row. Or create a brick pattern by alternating every four stitches, for example, rather than every other one.

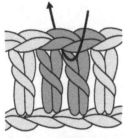

FIGURE 3-20:
Crocheting in the space between stitches.

TIP

Working in between stitches is a great help when you're using novelty yarns. (See Book 1, Chapter 2 for a description of these.) Because highly textured yarns can make individual stitches hard to see, working between them keeps your design untangled and you out of the loony bin. You can make a whole design this way without ever working into the top of another stitch.

Working in chain spaces and loops

Many lacy patterns, such as filet crochet (see Book 4, Chapter 6), use chain loops and spaces in their designs to achieve a loose, airy look. Although these loops and spaces may appear fancy and complicated, working a stitch into them is a piece of cake because you don't have to be too particular about where you stick your hook. As long as it lands somewhere within the loop or space, you're good to go. Figure 3-21 shows where to put your hook.

REMEMBER

Patterns identify the space or loop you're supposed to work into by how many chain stitches were used to create it. For example, if you need to work into a space created by one chain, the pattern tells you to work into the *chain-1 space*, which may be abbreviated as *ch-1 sp*. If you need to work into a loop created by five chain stitches, the pattern directs you to the *chain-5 loop* (or *ch-5 lp* for short).

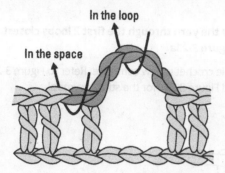

FIGURE 3-21:
Working stitches
into a chain
space or loop.

© John Wiley & Sons, Inc.

Going around the middle with post stitches

You can insert your hook around the *post* (body) of a stitch that's one or more rows below the current row to make — you guessed it — a *post stitch*. Post stitches create raised patterns, such as ribbing and cables. The way you insert your hook around the post determines whether you're creating a front post or a back post. The following sections show you how to make both.

Front post stitches

Front post stitches are raised on the surface of the fabric facing you and have a ridge on the opposite side of the fabric. To create a front post double crochet (abbreviated *FPdc*), follow these steps:

1. **Work a row of normal double crochet (dc) for the first row and turn.**

2. **Chain 2 (ch 2) for your first double crochet.**

   REMEMBER

   Because a post stitch is shorter than a normal stitch, you make the turning chain with 1 chain stitch less than the normal turning chain requires. (Book 3, Chapter 1 covers the basics of turning chains.) In addition, the last stitch in the row may be a shorter stitch to keep the whole row level. For example, if you're working a row of double crochet stitches in the front post of the stitches from the previous row, you make a turning chain with 2 chains rather than 3, and your final stitch is a half double crochet (hdc).

3. **Yarn over (yo) and insert your hook from front to back between the posts of the first and second double crochet of the row below and then from back to front again between the posts of the second and third stitches (see Figure 3-22a).**

   The hook should now be positioned horizontally behind the double crochet that you're working around, as shown in Figure 3-22b.

4. **Yarn over and draw the yarn around the post of the stitch.**

   You should now have 3 loops on your hook.

5. **Yarn over and draw the yarn through the first 2 loops closest to the hook end twice, like in Figure 3-23a.**

One front post double crochet is now complete. Refer to Figure 3-23b for the completed stitch and Figure 3-23c for the stitch's symbol.

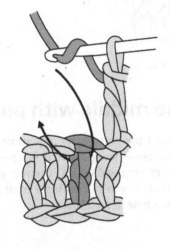

FIGURE 3-22: Inserting the hook for the front post double crochet. **a.**

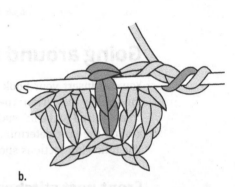

b.

© John Wiley & Sons, Inc.

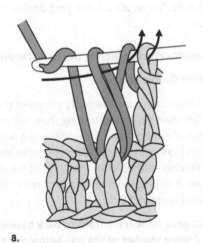

a.

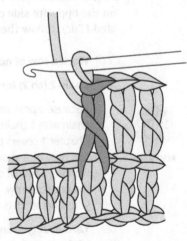

b.

FIGURE 3-23: Finishing a front post double crochet and noting its symbol. **c.**

© John Wiley & Sons, Inc.

Back post stitches

Back post stitches appear to recede on the side of the fabric facing you, creating a ridge. To form a back post double crochet (abbreviated *BPdc*), follow these steps:

1. **Work a row of normal double crochet (dc) for the first row and turn.**

2. **Chain 2 (ch 2) for the first double crochet.**

   REMEMBER

   Because a post stitch is shorter than a normal stitch, you make the turning chain with 1 chain stitch less than the turning chain normally requires. (Flip to Book 3, Chapter 1 for the basics of turning chains.)

3. **Yarn over (yo) and insert your hook from back to front between the posts of the first and second double crochets in the row below and then from front to back again between the posts of the second and third stitches (see Figure 3-24a).**

   Your hook should now be positioned horizontally in front of the double crochet that you're working around, as in Figure 3-24b.

4. **Yarn over and draw the yarn around the post of the stitch.**

   You now have 3 loops on your hook.

5. **Yarn over and draw the yarn through the first 2 loops closest to the hook end twice, as shown in Figure 3-25a.**

   Figure 3-25b shows 1 complete back post double crochet, and Figure 3-25c denotes the stitch symbol.

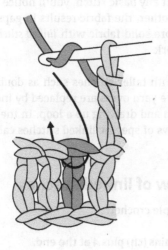
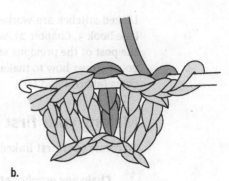

FIGURE 3-24:
Inserting your hook for the back post double crochet.

a.

b.

© John Wiley & Sons, Inc.

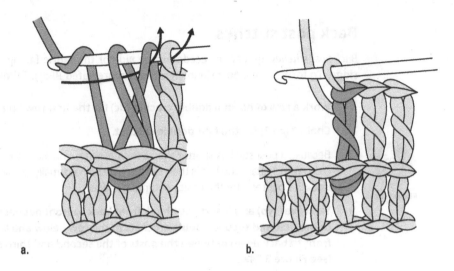

a.

b.

© John Wiley & Sons, Inc.

FIGURE 3-25: Completing a back post double crochet and noting its stitch symbol.

c.

Solidifying fabric with linked stitches

If you work a swatch of almost any basic stitch, you'll notice that by working each stitch independently of each other, the fabric results in gaps, or spaces, between stitches. You can create a more solid fabric with *linked stitches*, stitches that you link to one another as you work.

Linked stitches are worked with taller stitches such as double and triple crochet (see Book 3, Chapter 2), where yarn overs are replaced by inserting the hook into the post of the previous stitch and drawing up a loop. In the sections that follow, you discover how to make rows of specific linked stitches called linked triple crochets (abbreviated *Ltr*).

Making your first row of linked stitches

To create your first linked triple crochet:

1. **Chain any number of chains (ch) plus 4 at the end.**

   The 4 stitches at the end create the triple crochet turning chain.

2. **Insert your hook into the second chain away from the hook, yarn over (yo), and draw up a loop.**

   There are 2 loops on the hook (see Figure 3-26a).

3. **Insert your hook into the third chain away from the hook, yarn over, and draw up a loop.**

   Now you have 3 loops on the hook (refer to Figure 3-26b).

4. **Insert your hook into the fifth chain away from the hook, yarn over, and draw up a loop.**

   The reason you skip the fourth chain is so that the first linked triple stitch looks just like the other stitches in the row. There are 4 loops on the hook (see Figure 3-26c).

5. **Yarn over and draw through the first 2 loops on your hook.**

   Now you have 3 loops on the hook (see Figure 3-27a).

6. **Yarn over and draw through the first 2 loops on your hook.**

   You're left with 2 loops on the hook (see Figure 3-27b).

7. **Yarn over and draw through the last 2 loops on your hook.**

   Nice work! You've just finished 1 linked triple crochet (see how yours matches up with Figure 3-27c). Want to know the symbol for this particular stitch? Check out Figure 3-27d.

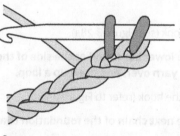 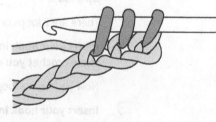

a.   b.

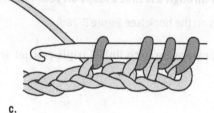

FIGURE 3-26:
Creating a linked
triple crochet.   c.

© John Wiley & Sons, Inc.

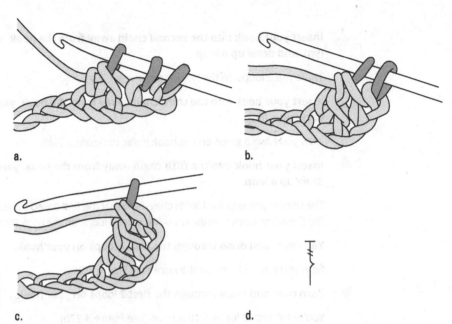

FIGURE 3-27:
A complete linked
triple crochet and
its stitch symbol.

a.

b.

c.

d.

© John Wiley & Sons, Inc.

To create the second linked triple crochet in the first row:

1. **Insert your hook into the upper horizontal bar found at the side of the last linked triple crochet (Ltr) you made, yarn over (yo), and draw up a loop.**

   There are 2 loops on the hook (see Figure 3-28a).

2. **Insert your hook into the lower bar found at the side of the last linked triple crochet you made, yarn over, and draw up a loop.**

   Now you have 3 loops on the hook (refer to Figure 3-28b).

3. **Insert your hook into the next chain of the foundation chain, yarn over, and draw up a loop.**

   There are 4 loops on the hook (see Figure 3-28c).

4. **Yarn over and draw through the first 2 loops on your hook, 3 times.**

   You're left with 1 loop on the hook (see Figure 3-28d).

Repeat the preceding four steps for each linked triple crochet across to the end of the row.

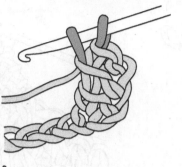
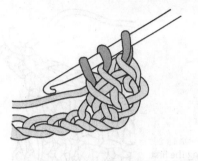

a.

b.

FIGURE 3-28:
Working
subsequent
linked triple
crochets.

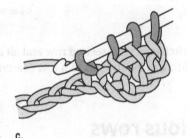
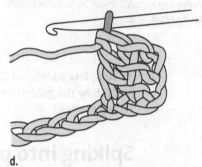

c.

d.

© John Wiley & Sons, Inc.

Creating your second row of linked stitches

After you've made your first row of linked stitches, follow these steps to transition to the first linked stitch of the second row (and all subsequent rows):

1. **Chain 4 (ch 4) for the turning chain.**

2. **Insert your hook into the second chain away from the hook, yarn over (yo), and draw up a loop.**

You now have 2 loops on your hook.

3. **Insert your hook into the third chain away from the hook, yarn over, and draw up a loop.**

A total of 3 loops are now on your hook.

4. **Insert your hook into the top 2 loops of the next stitch, yarn over, and draw up a loop (refer to Figure 3-29a).**

You now have 4 loops on your hook.

5. **Yarn over and draw through the first 2 loops on your hook, 3 times.**

Figure 3-29b shows the first linked triple crochet (Ltr) in the second row.

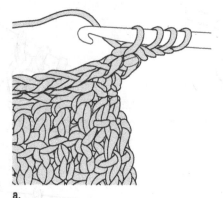 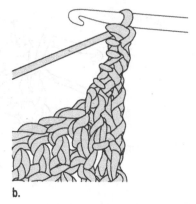

FIGURE 3-29: Working the first linked triple crochet in the second row.

a.   b.

© John Wiley & Sons, Inc.

To complete additional linked stitches in your second row and all additional rows, just follow the guidelines for adding more stitches to a row (described in the preceding section).

Spiking into previous rows

Long stitches (also known as *spikes*) are usually single crochet stitches that you work into either the tops of stitches or the spaces between stitches one or more rows below the current row to create a vertical spike of yarn that extends over several rows of stitches.

TIP

Long stitches produce a spike on both sides of the fabric, so they're well suited for a design that's reversible, such as an afghan. They're also particularly striking in a contrasting color.

To create a long single crochet stitch:

1. **Insert your hook from front to back under the top 2 loops of the designated stitch 1 or more rows below the row you're currently working in, as shown in Figure 3-30.**

2. **Draw the yarn through the stitch and up to the current level of work.**

   You should now have 2 loops on your hook.

3. **Yarn over (yo) and draw the yarn through the 2 loops on your hook.**

   Figure 3-31a shows a complete long single crochet stitch (although the length varies depending on where you stick your hook, of course). Figure 3-31b shows a few long-single-crochet stitch symbols, while Figure 3-31c depicts the couple of different ways you may see it shown.

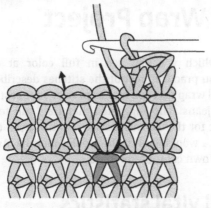

FIGURE 3-30:
Working a long
single crochet
stitch 3 rows
below the
current row.

© John Wiley & Sons, Inc.

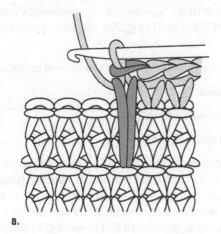

XXX = Long stitches
      or spikes

a.

b.

FIGURE 3-31:
A completed long
stitch in single
crochet.

c.   ┼ or ✕

© John Wiley & Sons, Inc.

REMEMBER

To make other types of long stitches, such as a long double crochet, you follow
the same steps as for the long single crochet. Just remember to yarn over first as
necessary and then make the stitch the same way you always do. The only variation is that you're sticking the hook in a different spot.

Elegant All-Season Wrap Project

This stylish project (which you can see in full color at dummies.com/go/knitcrochetAIO) lets you practice most of the stitches described in this chapter while creating a beautiful wrap that you can drape over your best dress or pair with your most comfortable jeans. The suggested materials call for an acrylic yarn with a strand of metallic for the warmer seasons, but you can easily substitute a worsted-weight wool or a wool blend for the cooler months. As always, feel free to experiment with your own color preferences.

Materials and vital statistics

- **Yarn:** Coats & Clark Red Heart "Sparkle Soft" worsted-weight yarn (99% acrylic; 1% metallic), Article #E728 (4 oz. [113 g], 208 yds [190 m] each ball): 3 balls of #9001 White

- **Hook:** Crochet hook size H-8 U.S. (5 mm) or size needed to obtain gauge

- **Large-eyed yarn needle**

- **Measurements:** 11 in. wide x 62 in. long

- **Gauge:** 14 sts and 8 rows in dc = 4 in.

- **Stitches used:** Foundation double crochet (fdc), chain stitch (ch), single crochet (sc), double crochet (dc), triple crochet (tr). **Popcorn (pop):** * Work 4 dc in same st, drop loop from hook, insert hook from back to front in top of first dc of group, pull dropped loop through st *. **V-st:** * (Dc, ch 1, dc) in same st or space *. **Bobble:** * 4 dc (half closed and joined tog) worked in same st *. **Shell:** * 5 dc in same st or space *. **Picot:** * Ch 3, sl st in third ch from hook *.

Directions

Work this project in three parts so that the stitches run outward from the center in opposite directions. Begin with the center strip, which consists of only two rows, and then work the first half of the pattern off of the center. Next, simply turn the crocheted piece so the foundation row is facing up. Then complete the second half (which is nearly identical to the first half) by working off of the foundation row. Crocheters use this method quite frequently to create a symmetrical design.

Figure 3-32 presents you with the stitch diagram for the Elegant All-Season Wrap. The steps for this project follow, and they look just as you'd see them in a regular crochet publication. If you need to refresh your memory a bit of what all the abbreviations mean, flip to Book 1, Chapter 4.

FIGURE 3-32:
Stitch diagram
for the Elegant
All-Season Wrap.

Center strip

Ch 3 (counts as first fdc), fdc in 3rd ch from hook, work 210 fdc, *turn.*

Row 1 (WS): Ch 4 (counts as the first dc and 1 ch), skip the first 2 dc, * pop in next dc, ch 1, skip 2 dc, V-st in next dc, ch 1, skip next 2 dc *; rep from * to * across until 6 dc remain, pop in next dc, ch 1, skip 2 dc, V-st in next dc, skip next dc, dc in top of tch (35 pop sts and 35 V-sts), *turn.*

Row 2: Ch 3 (first dc), dc in each dc, chain space (ch sp) and pop across to tch, dc in top of tch (212 dc), *turn.*

First half

Row 1: Ch 3 (first dc), * skip next dc, dc in next dc, working behind dc just made, dc in skipped dc (crossed dc made) *; rep from * to * across to tch, dc in top of tch (105 crossed dc), *turn.*

Row 2: Ch 3 (first dc), dc in each dc across to tch, dc in top of tch (212 dc), *turn.*

Row 3: Ch 3 (first dc), ch 1, skip next dc, * bobble in next dc, ch 1, skip next 2 dc, V-st in next dc, ch 1, skip next 2 dc *; rep from * to * across until 6 dc remain, bobble in next dc, ch 1, skip next 2 dc, V-st in next dc, skip next dc, dc in top of tch (35 bobble sts and 35 V-sts), *turn.*

Row 4: Ch 3 (first dc), work 1 dc in each dc, ch sp and bobble st across to tch, dc in top of tch (212 dc), *turn.*

Row 5: Ch 3 (first dc), skip next 2 dc, * shell in next dc, skip next 4 dc *; rep from * to * across until 4 dc remain, shell in next dc, skip next 2 dc, dc in top of tch (42 shell sts), *turn.*

Fasten off.

Second half

Row 1: With the WS facing and working across the opposite side of the fdc row, join yarn in first fdc, ch 3 (first dc), * skip next fdc, dc in next fdc, working behind dc just made, dc in skipped fdc (crossed dc made) *; rep from * to * across to last fdc, dc in last fdc (105 crossed dc), *turn.*

Rows 2–5: Rep Rows 2–5 of "First half," *turn.* Don't fasten off.

Border

Row 1: Ch 6 (counts as tr and ch 2), * (tr, ch 1, tr) in center dc of next shell in the previous row, ch 2 *; rep from * to * across to last shell, (tr, ch 1, tr) in center dc of last shell, ch 2, (tr, ch 3, tr) in top of tch in previous row, rotate piece to continue work across row ends of short edge, ch 2, skip 1 row end (the shell row), ** (tr, ch 1, tr) in space at end of next row (the dc row), ch 2, skip next row end **; rep from ** to ** 5 times across short end, (tr, ch 3, tr) in first dc of last row of first half; rep from * to * across to last shell, (tr, ch 1, tr) in center dc of last shell, ch 2, (tr, ch 3, tr) in top of last dc, rotate piece to continue work across row ends of second short edge, ch 2, skip 1 row end (the shell row); rep from ** to ** 6 times across short end, (tr, ch 3) in top of dc from previous row (at the base of the tch from the beg of the rnd), sl st in fourth ch of beg ch-6 to join.

Row 2: Ch 1, sc in first ch-2 sp, * ch 1, work ([2 tr, picot] twice, tr) all in ch-1 sp of V-st from previous row, ch 1, sc in next ch-2 sp (between V-sts) *; rep from * to * across to corner ch-3 sp, ch 1, ([2 tr, picot] 3 times, tr) all in corner ch-3 sp **; rep from * to ** for each side of the wrap, ch 1, sl st in first sc to join.

Fasten off. Weave in loose ends with the yarn needle.

Finishing

Block your wrap by washing it in cool water with a mild soap and then rolling it in a towel to remove any excess water. Pull and shape the wrap to the finished measurements and leave it to dry. (See Book 7, Chapter 1 for the full details on blocking.)

Comfy Cowl Project

The textured fabric in this cowl comes from alternating between working stitches in the back top loop and the front top loop. Worked in single crochet with an extra large hook and super bulky yarn, the back loop/front loop pattern creates a pleasing design, and the buttons (no button holes needed!) secure it perfectly. The cowl (which you can see in full color at dummies.com/go/knitcrochetAIO) is a perfect accessory for a cold winter day, and you can find the recommended yarn (which by the way is pretty reasonably priced) in a wide variety of colors to match your wardrobe. If you do change your yarn, be sure to check your gauge. (Book 1, Chapter 3 explains how gauge affects your projects.)

TIP

When working with the heavier weight yarns and larger sized hooks that are so popular these days, you'll probably find that you need to adjust your hold on both the hook and yarn. This is fine; just be sure to keep your yarn tension consistent, and check your gauge so that the measurements of your finished project are as those specified in the directions.

Materials and vital statistics

>> **Yarn:** Coats & Clark Red Heart "Grande" super bulky-weight yarn (78% acrylic/22% wool), Article #E826 (5.29 oz. [150 g], 46 yds [42 m] each skein): 3 skeins of #0110 Aran

>> **Hook:** Crochet hook size Q-19 U.S. (15.75 mm) or size needed to obtain gauge

>> **Buttons:** (3) 1⅜-in. size buttons

>> **Sewing needle and thread to match buttons**

>> **Scissors**

>> **Measurements:** 8½ in. wide x 40 in. long before closing into a circle with buttons

>> **Gauge:** 6 sts and 6 rows sc = 4 in.

>> **Stitches used:** Chain stitch (ch), single crochet (sc)

Directions

If the directions in this project look a little foreign to you, flip to Book 1, Chapter 4 for a little Reading Crochetese 101. The stitch diagram for this project is shown in Figure 3-33. Refer to the schematics in Figure 3-34 for measurements and button placements.

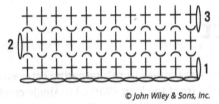

FIGURE 3-33: Stitch diagram for the Comfy Cowl project.

© John Wiley & Sons, Inc.

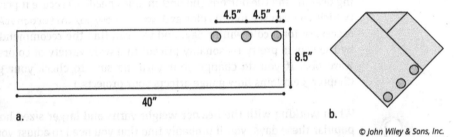

FIGURE 3-34: Schematic for the Comfy Cowl project.

© John Wiley & Sons, Inc.

Ch 13 for the foundation chain.

Row 1: Sc in second ch from hook, sc in each ch across (12 sc), *turn.*

Row 2: Ch 1, sc in blp of first sc, sc in flp of next sc, * sc in blp of next sc, sc in flp of next sc *; rep from * to * across (12 sc), *turn.*

Row 3: Ch 1, sc in flp of first sc, sc in blp of next sc, * sc in flp of next sc, sc in blp of next sc *; rep from * to * across (12 sc), *turn.*

Rep Rows 2–3 for patt until fabric measures 40 in. long.

Last Row: Ch 1, sc in both loops of each sc across (20 sc). Fasten off.

Finishing

With right side facing, using sewing needle and thread, place buttons across one long edge and sew first button 1 in. from corner, sew the second button 9 in. from the first, and sew the third button centered equally between the two. See the full color image of this project online (dummies.com/go/knitcrochetAIO) for placement.

Fold opposite side of cowl across, pull buttons through fabric to secure.

Gingham Baby Blanket Project

The gingham-like pattern in this blanket is created by working one row each of the three colors throughout. The blanket (which you can see in full color at dummies.com/go/knitcrochetAIO) is worked by alternating double crochet stitches and spike double crochet stitches, which are worked by crocheting a regular double crochet stitch over a chain space and into the stitches one row below. Don't be intimidated, though; it's quite simple once you get started, and you'll have another stitch to add to your repertoire. If you're making a blanket for a baby girl, simply switch the colors to shades of pink! Book 3, Chapter 5 walks you through color changes.

Materials and vital statistics

» **Yarn:** Caron Yarns "Simply Soft" 4-ply worsted-weight yarn (100% acrylic), (6 oz. [170 g], 315 yds [288 m] each skein): 1 skein each of Country Blue (A), White (B), and Sage (C).

» **Hook:** Crochet hook size H-8 U.S. (5 mm) or size needed to obtain gauge

» **Measurements:** 28 in. x 28 in. square.

» **Gauge:** 16 sts and 12 rows in pattern = 4 in.

» **Stitches used:** Chain stitch (ch), double crochet (dc), single crochet (sc), spike double crochet (sdc): Work dc over ch space by inserting hook into corresponding st one row below, reverse single crochet (reverse sc).

Directions

If the directions in this project look a little foreign to you, flip to Book 1, Chapter 4 for the lowdown on reading Crochetese. The stitch diagram for this project is shown in Figure 3-35.

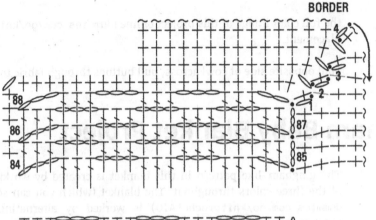

BORDER

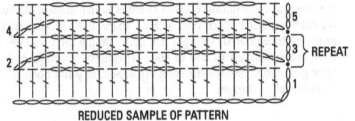

> REPEAT

REDUCED SAMPLE OF PATTERN

FIGURE 3-35: Stitch diagram for the Gingham Baby Blanket project.

© John Wiley & Sons, Inc.

With Color A, ch 116 for the foundation chain.

Row 1: Dc in 4th ch from hook (counts as first 2 dc), dc in next ch, * ch 3, skip next 3 ch, dc in each of next 3 ch, rep from * across (114 sts; 37 ch-3 spaces), *turn.* Fasten off color A, join B.

Row 2: With B, * ch 3, skip next 3 dc, Sdc over each of next 3 sts, rep from * across to last 3 sts, ch 2, skip next 2 dc, sl st in top of turning ch (114 sts; 38 ch-spaces), *turn.* Fasten off color B, join C.

Row 3: With C, ch 3 (counts as first Sdc), Sdc over next 2 ch, * ch 3, skip next 3 sts, Sdc over each of next 3 sts, rep from * across (114 sts; 37 ch-3 spaces), *turn.* Fasten off C, join A.

Rows 4–88: Rep Rows 2–3, ending with Row 2 and working in the following color sequence: * 1 row A, 1 row B, 1 row C, rep from * throughout, ending with A. Do not fasten off.

Finishing

Follow these directions to finish the blanket with a border.

Rnd 1: With A, ch 1, *(sc, ch 1, sc) in same st to create the first corner, working across the side edge of blanket, sc evenly across to next corner, rep from * around, sl st in first sc to join. Fasten off A, join B in next corner ch–1 space.

Rnd 2: With B, ch 1, *(sc, ch1, sc) in corner ch–1 space, sc in each sc across to next corner, rep from * around, sl st in first sc to join. Fasten off B, join A in next corner ch–1 space.

Rnd 3: With A, ch 1, **(sc, ch 1, sc) in corner ch–1 space, * sc in next sc, ch 1, skip next sc*, rep from * to * across to next corner, rep from ** around, sl st in first sc to join. Fasten off A, join C in next corner ch–1 space.

Rnd 4: With C, ch 1, working from left to right, reverse sc in each st and space around sl st in first sc to join. Fasten off.

IN THIS CHAPTER

» **Gathering tools for Tunisian crochet**

» **Making the Tunisian simple stitch**

» **Adding variety with the Tunisian knit and purl stitches**

» **Working with color and design**

» **Making an absorbent hand towel**

Chapter **4**

Tunisian Crochet

Tunisian crochet is a special kind of stitch that you can use to make anything from home decor items, such as afghans, place mats, and rugs, to sweaters, coats, and accessories. This type of crochet is different from standard crochet stitches in that each row is worked in two separate halves: The first half adds the loops to your hook, and the second half takes them off. Tunisian crochet produces a rather solid fabric that closely resembles knitted fabric, although it uses much more yarn and therefore produces a heavier fabric than knitting does. (When making clothing using Tunisian crochet, use a lighter-weight yarn, such as a sport weight. Worsted-weight yarn is more suitable for afghans, and rugs work up beautifully using bulky-weight yarn.) The stitches themselves are squarish, which makes the fabric perfect for working multicolored designs or as a base for cross-stitch designs.

Tunisian crochet stitches have many variations that look quite different from each other, but in this chapter you find out how to work three of the most common ones: the basic Tunisian stitch and the knit and purl variations. You also learn what special hooks you need, how to increase and decrease stitches, and how to work from a chart for designs with color changes as well as for cross-stitch designs. After you master the Tunisian crochet technique, try out the Absorbent Hand Towel project at the end of this chapter.

Note: Tunisian crochet has many names attached to it. So if you come across any of the following names, know that they're referring to Tunisian crochet: *afghan stitch, tricot crochet, shepherd's knitting, hook knitting,* and *railroad knitting.*

Taking a Look at Tunisian Crochet Tools

Tunisian crochet is a unique form of crochet that calls for a unique hook. Unlike standard crochet, where you work each stitch off to one loop before going on to the next stitch, Tunisian crochet requires you to pick up a whole row of stitches on the hook before you work off the loops on a second pass. To accommodate all these stitches, you need a hook with a cap or a stopper on the end to hold the stitches. Standard Tunisian hooks are long and straight with a cap, but you can also find hooks with longer cable attachments and even double-ended hooks that give you more flexibility when working wider projects.

Tunisian hooks are longer than standard hooks, too, coming in a variety of lengths and sizes; the most popular Tunisian hooks are 10 to 14 inches long and range in size from size G to size K. The longest hooks, like those with cable-cord attachments, are ideal for making large afghans. You can see a sampling of Tunisian crochet hooks in Figure 4-1.

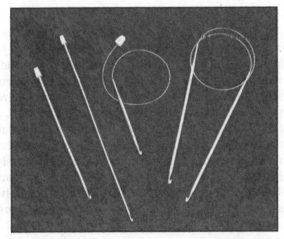

FIGURE 4-1:
A sampling of Tunisian crochet hooks.

© John Wiley & Sons, Inc.

REMEMBER

Longer hooks can be cumbersome if you don't need the extra length. The best way to determine what hook length suits your purpose is to refer to the beginning of your pattern's instructions. If the materials list doesn't mention a specific length, take a look at the measurements of the pieces you'll be working and use a hook that fits the size of each piece. For example, if each piece is 13 inches wide, use a 14-inch hook. If you work an afghan in one piece that measures 40 inches wide, then the 22-inch flexible hook or the 40-inch double-ended hook is appropriate.

TIP

When you want to crochet small pieces in Tunisian crochet (or when you just want to try out the technique), you can actually use a standard crochet hook rather than a Tunisian crochet hook. Simply wrap a rubber band several times around the base of the standard hook to keep the stitches from falling off the end. If you want to try Tunisian crochet with finer yarn or cotton thread, use a smaller crochet hook.

Creating the Tunisian Simple Stitch

If a pattern calls for Tunisian crochet, it's usually referring to the *Tunisian simple stitch*, abbreviated *Tss*. Tunisian simple stitches are shaped like little squares with two horizontal strands of yarn and a vertical bar on top of them. (You can see a sample in Figure 4-2.)

FIGURE 4-2:
A swatch of
Tunisian simple
stitch.

© John Wiley & Sons, Inc.

REMEMBER

Each row of Tunisian simple stitch is worked in two halves:

» **Forward (first) half:** Picking up the loops. (The forward half is sometimes called the *forward pass* or *forward row*.)

» **Return (second) half:** Working off the loops, without turning your work between rows. (The return half is sometimes called the *return pass* or *return row*.)

As you discover in the next sections, you start out with a foundation row that you work the same way for all variations of Tunisian crochet. The forward half of the second row, and beyond, establishes the pattern — in this case, the Tunisian simple stitch. (Check out the section "Varying Your Tunisian Crochet" for instructions on the knit stitch and purl stitch variations.) You usually work the return half of each row (from the second row on) in the same way for all variations of Tunisian crochet.

To practice working the Tunisian simple stitch, use a worsted-weight yarn and a 10-inch size H-8 U.S. (5 mm) Tunisian crochet hook.

Starting with a foundation row

Because Tunisian stitches require you to pull loops up through existing stitches, you need to start with a foundation row, which is actually the first row of the design. Chain 16 stitches for your foundation chain, and you're ready to begin the forward half of your foundation row of Tunisian crochet.

Working the forward half of your foundation row

Follow these steps to work the forward half of the foundation row, drawing up the loops of each stitch onto your hook:

1. **Insert your hook into the second chain stitch (ch) from the hook.**

    See Book 3, Chapter 1 for more on counting chain stitches.

2. **Yarn over the hook (yo).**

3. **Draw your yarn through the chain stitch, as shown in Figure 4-3a.**

    You should have 2 loops on your hook.

4. **Insert your hook into the next chain stitch and repeat Steps 2 and 3 in each chain stitch across the foundation chain until your hook is loaded with loops (like in Figure 4-3b).**

    This technique is known as *drawing up the loops*. If you have 16 loops on your hook — 1 for each chain stitch in your foundation chain — then the forward half of your foundation row of Tunisian crochet is complete.

FIGURE 4-3:
Working the forward half of the foundation row.

a. b.

© John Wiley & Sons, Inc.

Working the return half of your foundation row

To work the return half of the foundation row, work the loops off the hook by doing the following:

1. **Yarn over the hook (yo).**

2. **Draw your yarn through the first loop on the hook, as shown in Figure 4-4a.**

3. **Yarn over the hook.**

4. **Draw your yarn through the next 2 loops on the hook (see Figure 4-4b).**

5. **Repeat Steps 3 and 4 across the row until 1 loop remains on the hook.**

You've just successfully worked Tunisian crochet across your foundation row. Well done! One loop remains on your hook (see Figure 4-5), and it counts as the first stitch of the next row.

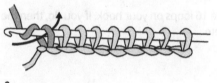 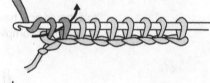

FIGURE 4-4:
Working off the loops on the return half.

a.   b.

© John Wiley & Sons, Inc.

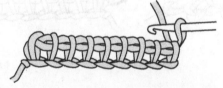

FIGURE 4-5:
A completed foundation row of Tunisian crochet.

© John Wiley & Sons, Inc.

Continuing to the second row and beyond

You place your hook differently for the stitches in the second row of Tunisian crochet, but otherwise, you work them across the row in the same manner as for the foundation row. You then work each successive row the same way as the second row.

Working the forward half of the second row

To begin the forward half of your next row of Tunisian simple stitch:

WARNING

1. **Insert your hook behind the next vertical bar in the row below.**

   Don't work into the vertical bar directly below the loop on your hook; if you do, you'll end up adding a stitch to the row.

2. **Yarn over the hook (yo).**

3. **Draw the yarn through the stitch, as shown in Figure 4-6a.**

4. **Repeat Steps 1 through 3 in each vertical bar across the row until you reach the next-to-last stitch.**

5. **Insert your hook under the last 2 vertical bars at the end of the row (refer to Figure 4-6b).**

6. **Yarn over the hook.**

7. **Draw your yarn through both vertical bars.**

   You should now have 16 loops on your hook. If you do, then the forward half of this row is complete.

FIGURE 4-6:
Working the
forward half of
your second row.

a.

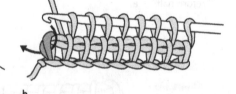
b.

© John Wiley & Sons, Inc.

Working the return half of the second row

To work the return half of the second row, repeat Steps 1 through 5 from the earlier section "Working the return half of your foundation row." Continue working rows of Tunisian simple stitch until you feel comfortable with this technique (a good length for a practice swatch is 4 inches).

Binding off

When you finish your last row of Tunisian simple stitch, you can't just fasten off your yarn like you do with other standard crochet stitches. Instead, you need to *bind off* the top edge of your last row of Tunisian crochet with a row of slip stitches. If you don't bind off the last row, the stitches will have gaps in them and won't look like the rest of the piece. So, using the same hook, work a slip stitch under each vertical bar across the last row. (See Book 3, Chapter 1 for instructions on making slip stitches.)

REMEMBER

The different variations of Tunisian crochet may call for a different binding-off stitch (like a row of single crochet, for example). The specific pattern you're following indicates what stitch to use when binding off, so make sure you check for this info before you automatically start binding off with slip stitches.

Shaping the Tunisian Simple Stitch

When working in Tunisian crochet, you may occasionally need to shape your work, particularly when you're making sweaters. The great thing about Tunisian crochet stitches is that you increase and decrease in the same way whether you do it at the beginning, middle, or end of a row. And the same general technique applies to all variations of Tunisian crochet — you do all your increasing and decreasing on the forward half of a row. In the following sections, you discover how to increase and decrease in Tunisian simple stitch.

Increasing in Tunisian simple stitch

REMEMBER

You always make increases in the forward half of a row of Tunisian simple stitch, creating the extra loops on your hook; then you work off all the loops in the return half, as usual.

To practice making increases, grab the swatch you made in the earlier section "Creating the Tunisian Simple Stitch" or head there to make one. To increase by one stitch, work the forward half of the row as follows:

1. **With 1 loop on your hook from the previous row, insert your hook into the space between the first and second stitch (not under the vertical bar). (Refer to Figure 4-7a.)**

2. **Yarn over (yo).**

3. **Draw the yarn through the stitch.**

   One increase at the beginning of the row is now complete.

4. **Work in Tunisian simple stitch (Tss) across the rest of the row, starting in the next vertical bar.**

   You should have 17 loops on your hook because you added 1. (The extra loop is highlighted in Figure 4-7b.)

FIGURE 4-7:
Increasing at the
beginning of the
forward half of
a row.

a.   b.

© John Wiley & Sons, Inc.

Working the return half of a row is pretty standard, whether you're working the foundation row or Row 12 of Tunisian crochet. To work the return half of the increase row, repeat Steps 1 through 5 from the earlier section "Working the return half of your foundation row."

Decreasing in Tunisian simple stitch

REMEMBER Making a decrease in the Tunisian simple stitch is pretty similar to making an increase: You decrease in the forward half of a row of Tunisian simple stitch, subtracting loops from your hook; then you work off all the loops in the return half, just like you always do.

To practice making decreases, use the swatch you just made the increase on (if you're following this chapter in order), or head to the earlier section "Creating the Tunisian Simple Stitch" to make a swatch. To decrease one stitch, work the forward half of the row as follows:

1. **With 1 loop on your hook from the previous row, insert your hook behind the second and third vertical bars in the row below. (See Figure 4-8a.)**

2. **Yarn over (yo).**

3. **Draw the yarn through both stitches.**

   One decrease at the beginning of the row is now complete.

4. **Work in Tunisian simple stitch (Tss) across the rest of the row.**

   You should have 15 loops on your hook because you decreased by 1 stitch. (Refer to Figure 4-8b.)

To work the return half of the decrease row, repeat Steps 1 through 5 of the section "Working the return half of your foundation row," found earlier in this chapter.

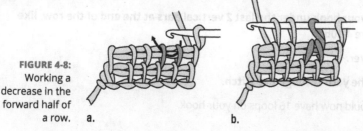

FIGURE 4-8:
Working a
decrease in the
forward half of
a row.

a.   b.

© John Wiley & Sons, Inc.

Varying Your Tunisian Crochet

Two of the most common variations of the Tunisian simple stitch are the *Tunisian knit stitch* and the *Tunisian purl stitch*, which, not surprisingly, resemble the knitting stitches they're named after — *knit* and *purl*. The crocheted fabric is thicker than the knitted, however, and you can see a noticeable ridge on the back of it.

REMEMBER

When working any variation of Tunisian crochet, begin the pattern on the second row of your piece, after the foundation row of Tunisian simple stitch (which you always work the same way).

Tunisian knit stitch

Tunisian knit stitch, abbreviated *Tks*, is also known as *stockinette stitch*. It looks like rows of Vs nesting in the row below (see for yourself in Figure 4-9). You can use the Tunisian knit stitch for afghans as well as for home decor and fashion items. Like working with any kind of Tunisian crochet, you begin with a foundation row made up of Tunisian simple stitch. For the purposes of this exercise, work a foundation row of 16 stitches. (Refer to the section "Starting with a foundation row," earlier in this chapter, to find out how.)

To begin the forward half of the first row of Tunisian knit stitch:

1. **Insert your hook, from front to back, between the front and back strands of the next vertical stitch.**

2. **Yarn over (yo).**

3. **Draw the yarn through the stitch, as in Figure 4-10a.**

4. **Repeat Steps 1 through 3 across the row until you reach the next-to-last stitch.**

5. **Insert your hook under the last 2 vertical bars at the end of the row, like in Figure 4-10b.**

6. **Yarn over.**

7. **Draw the yarn through the stitch.**

   You should now have 16 loops on your hook.

FIGURE 4-9:
A swatch of
Tunisian knit
stitch.

© John Wiley & Sons, Inc.

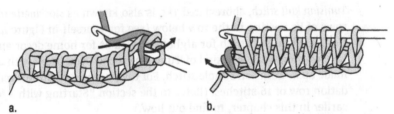

FIGURE 4-10:
Working the
forward half of
the Tunisian knit
stitch row.   **a.**   **b.**

© John Wiley & Sons, Inc.

To work the return half of the first row, repeat Steps 1 through 5 of the earlier section "Working the return half of your foundation row" across the row. The first row of Tunisian knit stitch is now complete; yours should look like the example in Figure 4-11.

For each additional row of Tunisian knit stitch, repeat the preceding steps. Work this stitch until you feel comfortable with it.

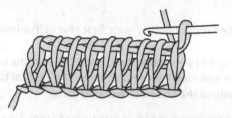

FIGURE 4-11:
A completed first row of Tunisian knit stitch.

Tunisian purl stitch

Tunisian purl stitch, abbreviated *Tps*, is also known as *purl stitch* and looks like rows of rounded bumps (see Figure 4-12). Tunisian purl stitch is useful by itself or in combination with other Tunisian stitches to produce textured patterns. Like working any other type of Tunisian crochet, you need to build from a foundation row. To get started, work a 16-stitch foundation row (follow the instructions in the earlier section "Starting with a foundation row").

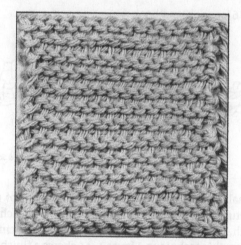

FIGURE 4-12:
A swatch of Tunisian purl stitch.

WARNING

People tend to tighten their stitches when working in Tunisian purl stitch. Be very conscious of tension and be sure to double-check your gauge when working this stitch. If you feel that you can't loosen up with the hook that a pattern suggests, change to a larger hook to get the desired gauge. (For more on gauge, refer to Book 1, Chapter 3.)

Here's how to begin the forward half of your first row of Tunisian purl stitch:

1. **With the index finger of your yarn hand, bring the working yarn to the front of your work and insert your hook under the vertical bar of the next stitch (but behind the strand of working yarn).**

   Figure 4-13a shows this action as well as how to work Steps 2 and 3 that follow.

2. **Yarn over (yo).**

3. **Draw the yarn through the stitch.**

4. **Repeat Steps 1 through 3 across the row until you reach the next-to-last stitch.**

5. **Insert your hook under the last 2 vertical bars at the end of the row, as shown in Figure 4-13b.**

6. **Yarn over.**

7. **Draw the yarn through the stitch.**

   You should have 16 loops on your hook.

FIGURE 4-13: Working the forward half of the Tunisian purl stitch.

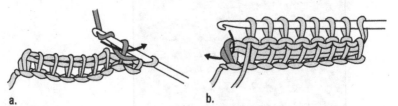

a.   b.

© John Wiley & Sons, Inc.

To work the return half of the row, repeat Steps 1 through 5 of the earlier section "Working the return half of your foundation row." For each additional row of Tunisian purl stitch, repeat the preceding steps; keep practicing until you feel comfortable performing this technique. Figure 4-14 shows a finished row of Tunisian purl stitch for your reference.

FIGURE 4-14: A completed row of Tunisian purl stitch.

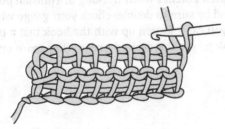

© John Wiley & Sons, Inc.

ADDRESSING THE CURLING PROBLEM

Fabric made of Tunisian crochet tends to curl up along the bottom edge. This is normal and happens because more yarn is on the back of the work than on the front. If you're having problems with curling, try working your Tunisian crochet in one of the following ways:

- Work the foundation row in just the *top loop* (the one at the top when the right side is facing you) of the foundation chain. (Refer to Book 3, Chapter 1 for more on foundation chains.)

- Work the foundation row in the top 2 loops (the part of each chain stitch that forms a *V*) of the foundation chain.

- Work the foundation row in the back loop of the foundation chain. To do so, turn your foundation chain over. Notice one little raised-up loop on the backside of each stitch? Work your foundation row in these loops.

- After working the foundation row, purl the first row or two. Because Tunisian purl stitch tends to have just as much yarn on the front of the work as it does on the back, it doesn't curl much. Working a few rows of Tunisian purl stitch before beginning the pattern may solve your curling problem. (See the section "Tunisian purl stitch," earlier in this chapter, for more on this particular stitch.)

If your work still curls after trying these methods, don't despair. You can remedy the curling problem by

- Blocking your design while working on it or after you finish it. (See Book 7, Chapter 1 for blocking directions.)

- Placing a heavy object (such as a large book) on the edge of your work for a few days to flatten it out.

- Working a border around the design, especially a heavy border with lots of stitches.

Coloring Your Tunisian Crochet

Because Tunisian crochet produces a gridlike stitch pattern, it's an excellent medium for creating colored designs. You can work color into the design while you're crocheting, or you can cross-stitch a colored design onto the surface after you've finished crocheting. Either of these techniques works great for afghans, wall hangings, rugs, place mats, potholders, and even sweaters. The sections that follow delve into the ins and outs of adding color to your Tunisian crochet pieces.

Crocheting with more than one color

Most patterns that call for color changes in Tunisian crochet provide a chart to show where you switch colors. If you're going to use a color again in the same row with no more than three stitches in between, you can carry the color loosely on the wrong side of the work and pick it up later, as Book 3, Chapter 5 shows you how to do. However, be aware that the carried strand is visible on the back of your work. If you have more than three stitches in between, fasten off and rejoin the yarn when you need it.

TIP

When working with several different colors and different balls of yarn, alleviate the inevitable tangle on the back of your work by joining small balls of yarn rather than whole skeins of each color. If you're going to work just a few stitches of a certain color, estimate the amount of yarn that you need for a patch of color by counting the number of stitches in the patch and allowing 2 inches for each stitch plus 4 more inches at each end. Wind the allotted amount of yarn into a small ball or wrap it around a yarn bobbin (Book 1, Chapter 1 fills you in on this cool crocheting tool).

Figure 4-15 shows you an example of a color chart, a chart key, and the end product. To use the color chart, read all the rows from right to left when working the forward half of the rows. After you work the return half of the row, you're back at the right side to begin the next row. Each square counts as one complete stitch.

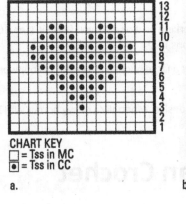

CHART KEY
□ = Tss in MC
⊡ = Tss in CC

FIGURE 4-15: Charted design and chart key (a) and a swatch (b) created from the chart.

a.

b.

© John Wiley & Sons, Inc.

Note that the following steps for using a color chart for Tunisian simple stitch changes are general and don't correspond with the chart in Figure 4-15:

REMEMBER

1. **Draw up the designated number of loops of the first color according to the squares on the chart.**

   The first loop on the hook counts as the first stitch of the row.

2. **When you need to switch to a new color, drop the first color to the wrong side so you can pick it up in the return half of the row.**

3. **With the new color behind your work, insert your hook into the next stitch, yarn over (yo) with the new color, and draw that yarn through the stitch.**

4. **Continue by drawing up the designated number of loops of the new color.**

   Figure 4-16 shows 4 loops of the old color and 1 loop of the new color being drawn up.

5. **Repeat Steps 2 through 4 for each section of a new color across the row of the chart.**

6. **For the return half of the row, work off the loops with the matching color until 1 loop of the current color remains on the hook.**

7. **Pick up the next color in sequence from the wrong side of the work, drawing it under the working end of the first color (thereby twisting the yarn to prevent holes in the work), and yarn over.**

8. **Draw the new color through 1 loop of the previous color and 1 loop of the matching color, as shown in Figure 4-17.**

9. **Repeat Steps 6 through 8 as needed across the row until 1 loop remains on the hook.**

   One row of the chart is now complete. Each time you finish changing colors, continue working off the loops as you normally would. Then repeat Steps 6 through 8 as necessary to change colors.

10. **Repeat Steps 1 through 9 for each row of the chart.**

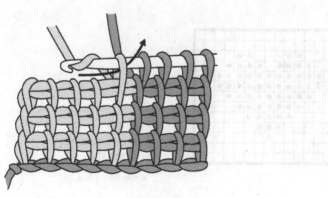

FIGURE 4-16:
Drawing up the designated number of loops of the next color.

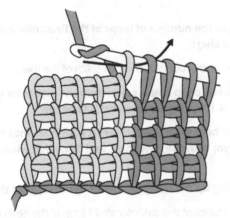

FIGURE 4-17:
Working off the
next color.

© John Wiley & Sons, Inc.

Cross-stitching on top of Tunisian crochet

Tunisian crochet, especially Tunisian simple stitch, makes an ideal base for working cross-stitch designs and is often used for just that. You can produce a more delicate color pattern, as well as a more elaborate one, when cross-stitching on Tunisian crochet fabric rather than working color changes within the crochet. Plus you don't have to deal with changing colors in the middle of a row while crocheting. In the sections that follow, you find a few pointers on cross-stitching on top of Tunisian crochet and details about making a complete cross-stitch row.

A few handy tips before you begin

You work cross-stitch designs by following a chart (see Figure 4-18) so you can see where to place the stitches. Each square on the chart represents one stitch in Tunisian crochet and one cross-stitch. If you're working a small design on a large piece of crocheted fabric, the instructions tell you where to position the design on your piece. A chart key accompanies the chart, indicating what color the symbols on the chart stand for.

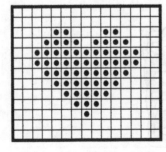

FIGURE 4-18:
Cross-stitch chart
and key.

CHART KEY
☐ = Background Tss
⊡ = Cross st

© John Wiley & Sons, Inc.

Cross-stitch in one color at a time, following the chart from left to right in rows. If you're going to work several stitches in a row with the same color, work the first half of each stitch across the row and then come back from right to left to work the second half of each stitch.

REMEMBER

Standard cross-stitch technique, where the needle goes through the fabric to the back and then up through the fabric to the front, produces a rather sloppy back on your item. To avoid the yarn showing on the back, be careful to slide your needle under the two horizontal strands of the Tunisian stitch near the surface of your work. Check the back of your work frequently to make sure nothing is showing.

WARNING

If you make your cross-stitches too tight, you can ruin your design. The cross-stitches should lay over the Tunisian crochet without causing the background to pucker.

The first part of a cross-stitch row

To work cross-stitch on Tunisian simple stitch, follow these steps (which reference Figure 4-19) to make the first half of a row:

1. **Thread a length of the designated color yarn onto a yarn needle.**

   Use a length of yarn that's comfortable to work with. An 18-inch length is about average.

2. **Insert the needle from back to front at Position A (the bottom left-hand corner of the designated stitch) and draw the needle up, leaving a 4-inch length of yarn on the back (which you'll later weave in).**

3. **Insert the needle at Position B (the top right-hand corner of the same stitch), angled vertically down, behind the 2 horizontal threads.**

4. **Bring the needle out at Position C (the bottom right-hand corner of the same stitch) and draw the yarn through until it stretches neatly across the stitch.**

5. **Position C now becomes Position A of the next stitch.**

6. **Repeat Steps 3 through 5 across the row in the stitches where the chart calls for cross-stitching.**

The second part of a cross-stitch row

To make the second half of a cross-stitch row, follow these steps (which refer to Figure 4-20):

1. **Insert your needle at Position D (the top left-hand corner of the same stitch you ended the first half with), angled vertically down, behind the 2 horizontal threads.**

   The thread should form an *X* with the already-completed first half of the stitch.

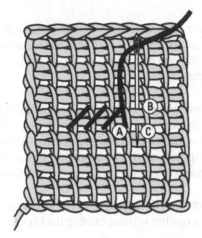

FIGURE 4-19:
Working the first half of a row of cross-stitch on Tunisian simple stitch.

© John Wiley & Sons, Inc.

2. **Bring the needle out at Position E (the bottom left-hand corner of the same stitch) and draw the yarn through until it stretches neatly across the stitch.**

3. **Repeat Steps 1 and 2 across the row, completing each cross-stitch.**

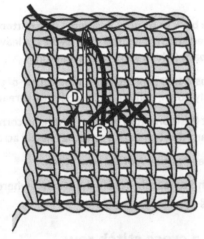

FIGURE 4-20:
Working the second half of a row of cross-stitch on Tunisian simple stitch.

© John Wiley & Sons, Inc.

When you're finished working cross-stitches with a particular color, weave the ends through the Tunisian background for several inches to hide the strands. Then clip off the excess yarn (see Book 3, Chapter 1 for more information on weaving in ends). Figure 4-21 shows a finished cross-stitch design.

FIGURE 4-21:
A swatch of cross-stitch on Tunisian simple stitch.

REMEMBER

Always work cross-stitches with the thread crossing on top in the same direction. And don't tie knots in the yarn at the beginning or the end of your work. Simply weave in the ends to secure them and snip off the excess.

Absorbent Hand Towel Project

This project uses Tunisian simple stitch and Tunisian purl stitch to make a thick and thirsty hand towel. The yarn is made of absorbent cotton and comes in a nice selection of colors so you can put together colors that complement your bathroom or kitchen. The project is finished with simple cross-stitches on bands of Tunisian simple stitch to add classic contrast and design, as shown in the color image of this towel, which you can see at dummies.com/go/knitcrochetAIO.

Materials and vital statistics

>> **Yarn:** Elmore-Pisgah "Peaches & Crème" 4-ply worsted-weight yarn (100% cotton), Article #930 (2.5 oz. [70.8 g], 122 yds [112 m] each ball): 2 balls of #1 White (MC) and 1 ball of #10 Yellow (CC)

Note: Lily Sugar 'n Cream yarn is a great substitute.

>> **Hooks:**

- 10-in. Tunisian crochet hook size J-9 U.S. (6 mm) or size needed to obtain gauge

- Standard crochet hook size J-9 U.S. (6 mm) or size needed to obtain gauge

- » **Large-eyed yarn needle**

- » **Measurements:** 27 in. long x 17 in. wide

- » **Gauge:** 14 sts and 12 rows = 4 in. in alternating Tunisian simple stitch (Tss) and Tunisian purl stitch (Tps) pattern

- » **Stitches used:** Chain stitch (ch), Tunisian simple stitch (Tss), Tunisian purl stitch (Tps), single crochet (sc), slip stitch (sl st)

Directions

The Absorbent Hand Towel is worked lengthwise in five sections using two different stitch patterns. The first, third, and fifth sections are created by alternating one stitch of Tunisian simple stitch with one stitch of Tunisian purl stitch to create a honeycomb pattern. The second and fourth sections are worked in plain Tunisian simple stitch, which creates the background for cross-stitching embellishment at the end. Follow the chart in Figure 4-22.

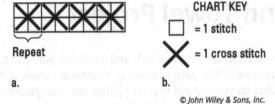

FIGURE 4-22:
Absorbent Hand Towel chart and chart key.

CHART KEY

☐ = 1 stitch

✕ = 1 cross stitch

Repeat

a.

b.

© John Wiley & Sons, Inc.

Making the foundation row

With the Tunisian crochet hook and MC, ch 95.

The following steps explain in detail how to work your foundation row for this project: Insert hook in second ch from hook, yo, draw yarn through ch, * insert hook in next ch, yo, draw yarn through ch *; rep from * to * across, keeping all loops on the hook (95 loops — forward half of foundation row complete), beg return half of row, yo, draw yarn through 1 loop on hook, ** yo, draw yarn through 2 loops on hook **; rep from ** to ** across (1 loop remains and counts as first st of next row).

Working the rest of the pattern

Row 1: Skip first st, * Tps in next st, Tss in next st; rep from * across; work return half.

Row 2: Skip first st, * Tss in next st, Tps in next st; rep from * across; work return half.

Rows 3–4: Rep Rows 1–2.

Row 5: Rep Row 1.

Row 6: Skip first st, Tps in next st and each st across; work return half, change to CC with last st.

Rows 7–12: Skip first st, Tss in next st and each st across; work return half, changing to MC with last st.

Row 13: Skip first st, Tps in next st and each st across; work return half.

Rows 14–35: Rep Rows 1–2 eleven times.

Row 36: Rep Row 1.

Rows 37–44: Rep Rows 6–13 once.

Rows 45–49: Rep Rows 1–2 twice, then rep Row 1.

Row 50: Skip first st, Tss in next st and each st across; work return half.

Bind off: Skip first st, sl st under each vertical bar across the last row.

Finishing

With a standard crochet hook, ch 1, working across side edge * sc in each row-end st across side edge to next corner, work 3 sc in next corner st, sc in each st across bottom edge to next corner, work 3 sc in next corner st *; rep from * to * around, sl st in first sc to join. Fasten off. Weave in loose ends with yarn needle.

With MC and yarn needle, cross-stitch across center 2 rows of each Tss stitch section (Rows 10 and 11 and Rows 41 and 42), making each cross-stitch 2 stitches (Tss "boxes") wide by 2 rows tall (as shown in Figure 4-22).

Chapter **5**

Crocheting Motifs

A fter you know a few basic stitches and techniques, you're ready to crochet motifs. Considered the building blocks of crochet, motifs are small pieces that can be used on their own as doilies, jewelry, or appliqués. You can also join them together to create larger projects such as scarves, bags, or afghans. Because they're small and quick to stitch, motifs are great for using up bits and pieces of leftover yarn. If you like to take your projects with you, motifs are the perfect project for the crocheter on the go, fitting easily into your purse or bag.

Often using a foundation of simple geometric or nature-inspired patterns, motifs can be a variety of shapes, sizes, and colors. The possibilities are endless. This chapter shows you how to morph rounds (introduced in Book 3, Chapter 4) into granny squares, which are the foundation of many square motifs. You also find examples of a few playful motifs that you can use as decorative accents for your home or wardrobe, or as inspiration for your own designs. Motifs are a great way to get used to looking at stitch diagrams, so each motif includes text instructions and a stitch diagram.

At the end of this chapter, you can try out the Flower Power project, which leaves you with a three-dimensional appliqué flower you can use to garnish gifts and accessories.

Granny's a Square: Cornering Your Rounds

Just because you can work in rounds doesn't mean you can only make circles. Turning a circle into a square is very simple to do; just add four corners to your round. The *granny square* is an extremely common circle-turned-square that has been the foundation of crochet fashion for decades. In the following sections, you find out how to work a few rounds of the granny square motif; see Book 3, Chapter 4 for an introduction to crocheting in the round.

The first round

Figure 5-1 is the stitch diagram for the granny square; it shows you how the rounds square off with the addition of four short chain loops for the corners. To start a typical granny square, follow these steps:

1. **Chain 4 (ch 4).**

2. **Close into a ring with 1 slip stitch (sl st) in the first chain.**

   This is your center ring.

FIGURE 5-1:
The stitch diagram of a basic granny square motif.

© John Wiley & Sons, Inc.

Next, follow these instructions to complete the first round of your granny square:

1. **Chain 3 (ch 3) for your first double crochet (dc) and then work 2 more double crochet stitches into the ring. Chain 2.**

   Here's your first corner.

2. **Work 3 more double crochet stitches into the ring and chain 2.**

3. **Repeat Step 2 twice.**

   Ta-da! You now have your 4 corners, and each one is made of a chain-2 space between the sets of 3 double crochets.

4. **Join the round by working 1 slip stitch in the top of the turning chain (without turning your work).**

The second round

To go on to the second round of the granny square, proceed as follows:

1. **Slip stitch (sl st) across to the first chain-2 space (ch-2 sp) and then chain 3 (ch 3) for the first double crochet (dc).**

   Refer to Book 3, Chapter 1 for info on traveling across stitches with the slip stitch.

2. **Work 2 double crochet stitches in the first chain-2 space, chain 2, and then work 3 more double crochet stitches in the same chain-2 space. Chain 1.**

3. **Work 3 double crochet stitches, chain 2, and then work 3 more double crochet stitches all in the next chain-2 space. Chain 1.**

4. **Repeat Step 3 twice to get to the last side of the motif; work 1 slip stitch in the top of the turning chain to join.**

The third round and beyond

1. **Slip stitch (sl st) across to the first chain-2 space (ch-2 sp) and then chain 3 (ch 3) for the first double crochet (dc).**

2. **Work 2 double crochet stitches in the first chain-2 space, chain 2, and then work 3 more double crochet stitches in the same chain-2 space. Chain 1.**

3. **Work 3 double crochet stitches in the next chain-1 space. Chain 1.**

4. Work 3 double crochet stitches, chain 2, and then work 3 more double crochet stitches all in the next chain-2 space. Chain 1.

5. Repeat Steps 3 and 4 twice to get to the last side of the motif; repeat Step 3 once more; work 1 slip stitch in the top of the turning chain to join.

REMEMBER

You can add as many rounds as you want to the granny square. Heck, you can make it as big as an entire afghan if you want to. Just remember that each successive round has additional chain-1 spaces across the sides. Simply work three double crochet stitches, followed by a chain 1, in each space across the sides and work your corners the same way. (To see a completed granny square with four rounds, check out Figure 5-2.)

FIGURE 5-2:
A granny
square swatch.

© John Wiley & Sons, Inc.

Don't Be Square: Motifs of Different Shapes

Squares and circles aren't the only ways to create motifs. They can have other geometric angles, such as stars and hexagons, or they can be fun shapes such as hearts, raindrops, or flowers. Start with the motifs in the next sections, and then use your newfound skills to try motifs on your own.

The lacy hexagon motif

Commonly worked in the round, polygons such as triangles (which have three sides) and hexagons (which have six sides) follow the same concept as the granny square described earlier in this chapter; to shape them, you just need a different number of corners. Figure 5-3 shows the stitch diagram for a lacy hexagon motif with four rounds. Follow these simple instructions to start the motif:

1. **Chain 4 (ch 4).**

2. **Close into a ring with 1 slip stitch (sl st) in the first chain.**

   This is the center ring.

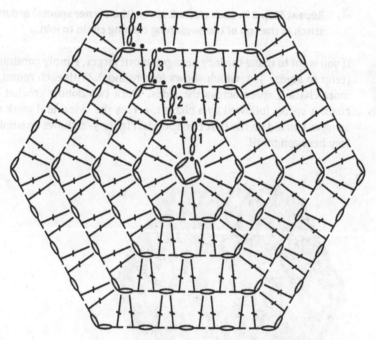

FIGURE 5-3:
The stitch diagram for the lacy hexagon motif.

Work the first round as follows:

1. **Chain 3 (ch 3) to create the first double crochet (dc); then work 1 double crochet into the ring and chain 2.**

2. **Work 2 double crochet stitches and 2 chains into the ring 5 times; slip stitch (sl st) into the top of the turning chain to join.**

   You should have 6 chain-2 spaces (ch-2 sp) and 6 pairs of double crochet stitches.

To make the second round:

1. **Slip stitch (sl st) across to the next chain-2 space (ch-2 sp); then chain 3 (ch 3) for the first double crochet (dc).**

2. **Work 1 double crochet, 2 chains, and 2 double crochet in the same chain-2 space. Chain 1.**

3. **Work 2 double crochet, 2 chains, and 2 double crochet in the next chain-2 space. Chain 1.**

4. **Repeat Step 3 in each chain-2 space (the corner spaces) around; then slip stitch in the top of the beginning turning chain to join.**

REMEMBER

If you want to make the lacy hexagon motif larger, simply continue adding rounds (refer to Figure 5-3, which shows four rounds). With each round, you'll have one more chain-1 space across the sides. Work two double crochet stitches in each chain-1 space, followed by a chain 1, across the sides, and work your corners the same as you did on the first two rounds. Figure 5-4 shows a sample of a completed lacy hexagon motif.

FIGURE 5-4:
A finished
sample of the lacy
hexagon motif.

© John Wiley & Sons, Inc.

TIP

You can also form many geometric shapes (such as hexagons and triangles) by working in rows and using the increasing and decreasing techniques found in Book 3, Chapter 3.

The flat flower motif

Motif shapes don't have to be found in the geometry classroom; you may be inspired to make them from objects you find in nature or around your home.

For example, attach a chain of green yarn to a circle crocheted in red yarn, and you have a delicious cherry. This section features instructions for creating a wonderful flat flower motif. Treat it as a topper for gifts and hats, or use it to add a little beauty to everyday items such as barrettes, bags, and even jeans.

Figure 5-5 shows the stitch diagram for three rounds of the flat flower motif. To start creating the motif, follow these steps:

1. **Chain 6 (ch 6).**

2. **Close into a ring with 1 slip stitch (sl st) in the first ch.**

   This is the center ring.

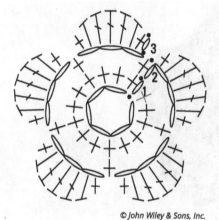

FIGURE 5-5:
The stitch diagram for the flat flower motif.

© John Wiley & Sons, Inc.

Now, follow these instructions to complete the first three rounds:

1. **Chain 1 (ch 1) and work 15 single crochet stitches (sc) into the ring; slip stitch (sl st) in the first single crochet to join.**

   The first round is complete.

2. **Chain 1 and single crochet in the first single crochet.**

3. **Chain 3, skip the next 2 single crochet, and then single crochet in the next single crochet.**

4. **Repeat Step 3 three more times.**

5. **Chain 3, skip the next 2 single crochet, and slip stitch in the first single crochet to join.**

   You've just made 5 chain-3 loops for the second round. (See Book 4, Chapter 3 for more about spaces and loops.)

6. Slip stitch into the first chain-3 loop (ch-3 lp) and then chain 1.

7. Work the following in each chain-3 loop: 1 single crochet, 1 half double crochet (hdc), 3 double crochet, 1 half double crochet, and 1 single crochet. Slip stitch in the first single crochet to join.

Your final round should leave you with 5 petals.

8. Fasten off.

REMEMBER

Figure 5-6 depicts a completed flower motif that you can use on its own or as the foundation for multiple layers, as shown in the next section.

FIGURE 5-6:
A completed
sample of the flat
flower motif.

© John Wiley & Sons, Inc.

The layered flower motif

Some motifs have multiple layers for a pleasing three-dimensional appearance. These types of motifs are good decorative accents for your wardrobe all on their own, but if you want, you can join them together to make a larger piece. In the preceding section, you learn how to make a flat flower motif (a flower with only one layer). In this section, you find out how to add layers to create a blossoming flower.

Figure 5-7 shows the stitch diagram for the layered flower motif. Begin with the flat flower motif described in the preceding section, but don't fasten off. To work the second layer of petals (which consists of two rounds), follow these steps:

1. Chain 4 (ch 4), working behind petals in previous round, skip the next 6 stitches, and then slip stitch (sl st) in the next single crochet (sc).

2. Repeat Step 1 around the motif 4 times to make a total of 5 chain-4 loops (ch-4 lps).

3. Slip stitch in the first chain-4 loop. Chain 1.

4. Work 1 single crochet (sc), 1 half double crochet (hdc), 2 double crochet (dc), 1 triple crochet (tr), 2 double crochet, 1 half double crochet, and 1 single crochet in each chain-4 loop around.

5. Slip stitch in the first single crochet to join.

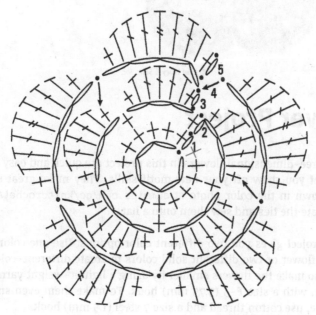

FIGURE 5-7:
The stitch diagram for the layered flower motif with two layers of petals.

© John Wiley & Sons, Inc.

You've worked two rounds of a multilayered flower with these instructions, so now you're ready to compare your work to the sample in Figure 5-8. Continue adding layers with the Flower Power project at the end of this chapter to make a bigger blossoming flower.

TIP

Joining flower motifs is pretty easy if you sew petals at the tips or join them on the last round as you go (refer to Book 7, Chapter 2 for joining methods). To join the flower petals on the last round, begin the last round of the flower as usual until you've made the first triple crochet stitch. Work one slip stitch in the triple crochet stitch on an already completed flower motif; then continue working the petals as before. Repeat the slip stitch method of joining stitches on the next petal so the flowers are connected at two petals. Make several flower motifs, using a variety of colors, and then join them together in a single row for a colorful scarf. Or try joining multiple rows together to make a garden-inspired shawl, bag, or blanket.

FIGURE 5-8:
A finished sample
of the layered
flower motif.

Flower Power Project

The three-dimensional flowers in this project are quick and easy to make — plus they let you show off your new motif skills. They make great package toppers (as shown in the color photo at dummies.com/go/knitcrochetAIO) or you can eliminate the ties and sew them onto a hat.

TIP

This project gives you two different color options: Use one color of yarn for the whole flower or two different solid colors to create different-colored petals. You can also make the flowers smaller by using a lighter-weight yarn, such as sport-weight, with a size F-5 (3.75 mm) hook. To make them even smaller and more delicate, use cotton thread and a size 7 steel (1.5 mm) hook.

Materials and vital statistics

» **For solid and two-color flowers:** Coats & Clark Red Heart "Classic" worsted-weight yarn (100% acrylic), Article #E267 (3.5 oz. [100 g], 190 yds [174 m] each skein): 1 skein each of

- #1 White

- #230 Yellow

- #912 Cherry Red

» **Hook:** Crochet hook size F-5 U.S. (3.75 mm) or size needed to obtain gauge

» **Yarn needle**

» **Measurements:** Approximately 3 in. in diameter

» **Gauge:** First 3 rnds = 1¾ in. in diameter

» **Stitches used:** Chain stitch (ch), slip stitch (sl st), single crochet (sc), half double crochet (hdc), double crochet (dc), triple crochet (tr)

Directions

The following instructions use Crochetese to explain how to make a flower motif with three layers. If you need to refresh your memory of crochet abbreviations, head to Book 1, Chapter 4. Refer to the stitch diagram in Figure 5-9 as another way to see where to make your stitches.

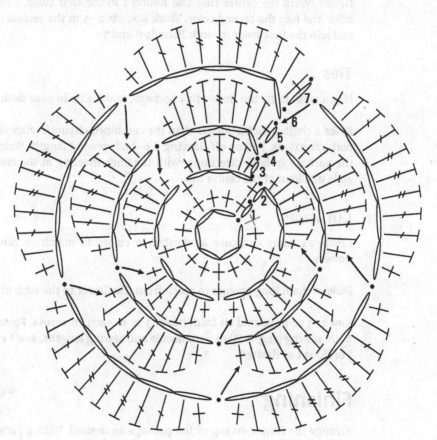

FIGURE 5-9:
The stitch diagram for the Flower Power project.

© John Wiley & Sons, Inc.

One-color flower

Work the layered flower motif described earlier in this chapter. Then work an additional layer of petals as follows:

Rnd 1: * Ch 5, **working behind petal in previous round,** skip next 8 sts, sl st in next sc *; rep from * to * around (5 chain-5 loops [ch-5 lps] made).

Rnd 2: Sl st in first ch-5 lp, ch 1, (sc, hdc, 2 dc, 3 tr, 2 dc, hdc, sc) in each ch-5 lp around (5 petals made), sl st in first sc to join. Fasten off.

Two-toned flower

For a two-toned flower, you work the stitches the same way as in the one-color flower. Work the center ring and Round 1 in the first color. Fasten off the first color and join the second color. Work Rounds 2–5 in the second color. Fasten off and join the first color to work Rounds 6 and 7.

Ties

If you want to tie the flower to a package, make a tie in your desired color.

Make a chain 2 inches longer than the combined circumference of the package in both directions. Fasten off, leaving a 6-inch sewing length. Wrap the tie around the package in both directions, with the ends meeting at the center top. Tie the ends in a knot at the center top.

Curlicues

Create as many curlicues as desired in colors to match or contrast with your flowers.

Make a chain long enough to reach from the flower to the edge of the package.

Row 1: 3 sc in second ch from hook, 3 sc in each ch across. Fasten off, leaving a 6-in. sewing length. With yarn needle and sewing lengths, sew 1 end to WS of Rnd 1 of flower as desired.

Finishing

Arrange the flower on top of the package as desired. With a yarn needle and the extra sewing lengths, sew the flower to the ties.

IN THIS CHAPTER

» **Decoding lace charts**

» **Exploring knitted lace patterns and how they enhance your projects**

» **Fixing mistakes while knitting lace**

» **Making lacy designs with filet crochet**

» **Practicing your skills with a scarf, shawl, and butterfly runner**

Chapter **6**

Making Lace

Knitted lace is versatile. It can be the fabric of an entire garment, the edging on a sleeve, a panel down the front of a sweater, or a single motif in a yoke, to name a few ideas. In a fine yarn on a small needle, it can be intricate and delicate. Worked randomly in a heavy, rustic yarn, it can be minimalist and modern. It can be a small eyelet motif sparsely arranged over an otherwise solid fabric, or it can be light, airy, and full of holes.

And believe it or not, even beginning knitters can make lace. If you can knit and purl, knit 2 stitches together, and work a yarn over (explained in Book 2, Chapter 3), you can make lace. The hardest thing is to keep track of where you are in the pattern. When you can identify a yarn over on your needle and see the difference between an ssk and a k2tog decrease in your knitting (both are explained in detail in Book 2, Chapter 3), you're on your way to becoming a lace expert.

Filet crochet is similar to lace and simpler than it looks, which makes it another great technique for beginners. You can use it to create distinct mesh-like designs, usually worked in white cotton thread. You've probably seen filet crochet without knowing it many times because it's often used for tablecloths, table runners, curtains, and wall hangings. Filet crochet looks especially elegant against a dark wood surface or brightly colored cloth background.

To familiarize yourself with knitted lace and filet crochet, sample the patterns at the end of this chapter.

Reading Lace Charts

Knitted lace makes use of two simple knitting moves — a *yarn over* (an increase that makes a small hole) and a decrease — to create myriad stitch patterns. Every opening in a lace fabric is made from a yarn-over increase, and every yarn over is paired with a decrease to compensate for the increase. When you understand the basis of lace's increase/decrease structure, even the most complicated lace patterns become intelligible. Of course, you can follow the instructions for a lace stitch without understanding the underlying structure, but being able to recognize how the pattern manipulates the basic yarn over/decrease unit is a great confidence builder.

TIP

Knitted lace is a fabric made with yarn overs and decreases, but you can use other ways to get lace-type fabrics. Using a very large needle with a fine yarn makes an open and airy piece of knitting. You can make a beautiful shawl with a simple garter stitch triangle (with increases worked at either end of every row) made in a fingering- or sport-weight yarn and worked on size US 13 (8 mm) needles. For extra visual interest, use a self-patterning sock yarn. Try it!

Yarn-over increase and decrease symbols

Like other charts for knitted stitch patterns, charts for knitted lace "picture" the patterns they represent. As you may expect, the two symbols you find most often in lace charts are the one for a yarn-over increase (usually presented as an *0*) and some kind of slanted line to mimic the direction of a decrease. Take a look at Figure 6-1 for an example.

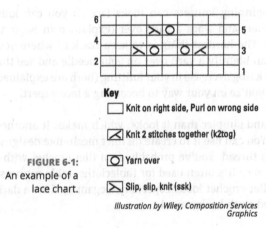

FIGURE 6-1:
An example of a lace chart.

Illustration by Wiley, Composition Services Graphics

Notice that each decrease symbol (k2tog or ssk) appears in only one square, even though a decrease involves 2 stitches. Charting the decrease this way allows the yarn-over symbol to occupy the square for the decreased stitch. Sometimes the yarn over shows up adjacent to the decrease, as it does in this pattern. Other times, the yarn over isn't placed directly before or after the decrease but rather somewhere else entirely in the pattern row. In either case, in most patterns the number of decrease symbols is the same as the number of yarn-over symbols because every increase has a corresponding decrease.

REMEMBER

A k2tog (knit 2 stitches together) decrease slants to the right. A ssk (slip, slip, knit) decrease slants to the left. For instructions on these techniques, refer to Book 2, Chapter 3.

No-stitch symbol

A lace chart sometimes has to show a changing number of stitches from one row to the next. To keep the stitches lined up on the chart the way they are in the fabric, the chart indicates that a stitch has been eliminated temporarily from the pattern by using the no-stitch symbol in the square that represents the decreased stitch. This symbol repeats in a vertical row until an increase is made and the stitch is back in play, as shown in Figure 6-2.

The chart in Figure 6-2 shows a pattern in which one stitch is decreased and left out for 10 rows and then created again and left in for the next 10 rows. The take-out/put-back-in pattern repeats every 20 rows. The black squares in the chart hold the place of the disappearing and reappearing stitch. Using the no-stitch symbol allows the grid to remain uniformly square. Otherwise, the edges of the grid would have to go in and out to match the number of stitches in each row.

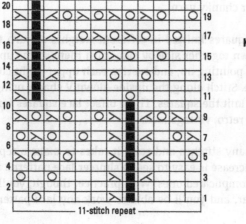

FIGURE 6-2: Chart that includes the no-stitch symbol.

Key

☐ Knit on right side, Purl on wrong side

⊡ Yarn over

■ NO stitch

◢ Knit 2 stitches together (k2tog)

◣ Slip, slip, knit (ssk)

Illustration by Wiley, Composition Services Graphics

Making Lace

When you're working from a chart that uses the no-stitch symbol, skip the symbol when you get to it and work the next stitch on your needle from the chart square just after the no-stitch symbol.

TIP

When you suspect that your stitch count is changing, it probably is! If the stitch pattern doesn't say anything about the stitch count changing on different rows and you suspect that it does, you can sort it out by checking the instructions. Add up the number of yarn overs and decreases in each row of a written or charted pattern to see if they're the same (don't forget that double decreases take out 2 stitches).

Knitting Different Kinds of Lace

Knitted lace is varied enough that different categories have been created to describe (loosely) the different types, such as *eyelet lace, open lace,* and *faggot lace.*

The divisions between one kind of lace and another are porous. Better to think of lace patterns as belonging on a continuum — the more solid fabrics with scattered openings (eyelet) at one end, the lacy and open fabrics (allover and faggot patterns) at the other. The lace patterns in this section provide a good introduction to lacework for both beginning and intermediate knitters.

If you're really interested in lacework, here's a project that gives you a lot of practice and lets you create something useful: Make a series of swatches with all the patterns in this section and then sew them together — or simply work one pattern after the other — to create a great scarf. Use the same yarn throughout unless you want to observe the effect of different yarns on the same pattern. Lace worked on light-weight yarns intended for lace looks very different from lace worked with a worsted-weight or chunky yarn.

TIP

If you have lace squares knitted in different weights of yarn that don't line up perfectly to be sewn together side by side, turn them so the upper-right corners of the squares are pointing up, and overlap each upper-right corner to the center of the next square. Stitch along the upside-down V shape, using one of the same yarns you used to knit the squares. These offset lace squares form an appealingly uneven edge for a retro, vintage look.

REMEMBER

No matter how many stitches and rows it takes to make a repeat, the marriage of increase and decrease is easy to see in simpler lace patterns and a little harder to track in more complicated ones. With practice, though, you'll quickly see how they work together, and you'll be able to work any lace pattern you fancy with confidence.

For your first forays into lace knitting, choose easier patterns. Specifically look for

>> **Patterns that tell you right at the beginning to purl all the wrong-side rows:** In general, the simplest lace patterns call for yarn-over/decrease maneuvers on right-side rows only. More-advanced patterns have you make openings on every row.

>> **Patterns made from vertical panels:** You can fairly easily tell if a pattern is organized as a series of vertical repeats because you'll see "lines" running up and down the fabric. You can place a marker after each repeat and keep track of one repeat at a time.

>> **Patterns that maintain the same number of stitches on every row:** To maintain the number, every yarn-over increase has an equivalent decrease on the same row. Other patterns call for a yarn-over increase on one row and the corresponding decrease on another. In these latter patterns, the stitch count changes from row to row. Often, the pattern alerts you to these changes and tells you which rows you have to look out for, but even at that, this type of lace is still a bit more challenging.

TIP

When you knit lace, always work the edge stitch (or two) in plain stockinette stitch to stabilize the sides of your pieces and make it easier to sew them together. The same is true for cast on and bound-off edges. If you use stockinette stitch at the edges, be sure to include these selvedge stitches in the number of stitches you cast on. (*Selvedge stitches* are extra stitches at the edge of your knitted fabric that serve to create an even, stable border.) For example, if the lace pattern calls for a multiple of 6 stitches plus 1 more and you want to include 2 stockinette stitches on either end, you add 4 selvedge stitches to the total cast on count.

DESIGNING YOUR OWN LACE

If you can work eyelet patterns, don't hesitate to try designing your own lace. On a sheet of graph paper, plot yarn overs with adjacent decreases in any arrangement you think is attractive. Keep the following in mind:

- Horizontal eyelets should be spaced 1 stitch apart.

- Vertical rows should be spaced 4 rows apart.

- Diagonal eyelets can be spaced every other row.

Eyelet patterns

Eyelet patterns generally have fewer openings than out-and-out lace patterns and are characterized by small openwork motifs distributed over a solid stockinette (or other closed-stitch pattern) fabric. The increase/decrease structure is usually easy to see in eyelet patterns, making them a good place to begin your lace exploration.

Ridged ribbon eyelet

You can thread a ribbon through these eyelets or use them in a colored stripe pattern. Figure 6-3 shows both a chart and a sample of this pattern.

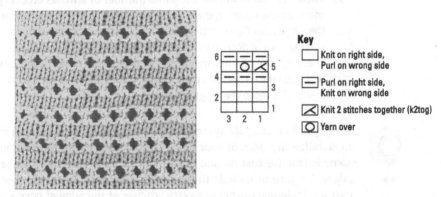

Key

	Knit on right side, Purl on wrong side
—	Purl on right side, Knit on wrong side
⧄	Knit 2 stitches together (k2tog)
⃝	Yarn over

FIGURE 6-3:
Ridged ribbon eyelet and chart.

Photograph and Illustration by Wiley, Composition Services Graphics

You work this pattern as follows:

Cast on an odd number of sts.

Rows 1 and 3 (RS): Knit.

Row 2: Purl.

Rows 4 and 6: Knit.

Row 5: * K2tog, yo; rep from * to last st, k1.

Cloverleaf eyelet

Figure 6-4 shows a three-eyelet cloverleaf arranged over a stockinette background.

This cloverleaf pattern requires a multiple of 8 stitches, plus 7 more. You work a double decrease between the two bottom eyelets. To knit this pattern, follow these steps:

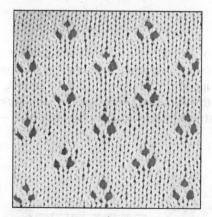

FIGURE 6-4:
Cloverleaf eyelet
pattern.

Photograph by Wiley, Composition Services Graphics

Cast on a multiple of 8 sts, plus 7 sts.

Row 1 (RS): Knit.

Row 2 and all WS rows: Purl.

Row 3: K2, yo, sl 1, k2tog, psso, yo, * k5, yo, sl 1, k2tog, psso, yo; rep from * to last 2 sts, k2.

Row 5: K3, yo, ssk, * k6, yo, ssk; rep from * to last 2 sts, k2.

Row 7: K1, * k5, yo, sl 1, k2tog, psso, yo; rep from * to last 6 sts, k6.

Row 9: K7, * yo, ssk, k6; rep from * to end of row.

Row 10: Purl.

Rep Rows 3–10.

Open lace patterns

Out-and-out lace patterns have more openings than solid spaces in their composition. They're frequently used in shawls or any project that cries out for a more traditional lace look.

The patterns in this section are more *open* — meaning that they have more holes — than the eyelet patterns earlier. Try them in fine yarns on fine needles (think elegant cashmere scarves) or in chunky yarn on big needles for a nontraditional look.

Arrowhead lace

Arrowhead lace (see Figure 6-5) requires a multiple of 6 stitches, plus 1. Row 4 of this pattern uses the double decrease psso, meaning "pass slipped stitch over." "P2sso" means "pass 2 slipped stitches over." (Flip to Book 2, Chapter 3 for a refresher on how to make this decrease.) Visit dummies.com/go/knitcrochetAIO to see a video that demonstrates just how easy arrowhead lace — and other lace patterns — are to knit.

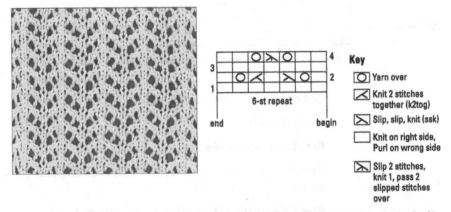

FIGURE 6-5:
Arrowhead lace and chart.

Key

[O] Yarn over

Knit 2 stitches together (k2tog)

Slip, slip, knit (ssk)

Knit on right side, Purl on wrong side

Slip 2 stitches, knit 1, pass 2 slipped stitches over

Photograph and Illustration by Wiley, Composition Services Graphics

Knit this pattern as follows:

Cast on a multiple of 6 sts, plus 1 st.

Rows 1 and 3 (WS): Purl.

Row 2: K1, * yo, ssk, k1, k2tog, yo, k1; rep from * to end of row.

Row 4: K2, * yo, sl 2 kwise, k1, p2sso, yo, k3; rep from * to last 5 sts, yo, sl 2 kwise, k1, p2sso, yo, k2.

Rep Rows 1–4.

Miniature leaf pattern

Figure 6-6 shows a simple miniature leaf pattern in which each little "leaf" is surrounded by lace openings.

Knit this pattern as follows (if you prefer charts over written instructions, see the chart in Figure 6-7):

Cast on a multiple of 6 sts, plus 1 st.

Row 1 and all WS rows: Purl.

Row 2: K1, * k2tog, yo, k1, yo, ssk, k1; rep from * to end of row.

Row 4: K2tog, * yo, k3, yo, sl 2 kwise, k1, p2sso; rep from * to last 5 sts, yo, k3, yo, ssk.

Row 6: K1, * yo, ssk, k1, k2tog, yo, k1; rep from * to end of row.

Row 8: K2, * yo, sl 2 kwise, k1, p2sso, yo, k3; rep from * to last 5 sts, yo, sl 2 kwise, k1, p2sso, yo, k2.

Rep Rows 1–8.

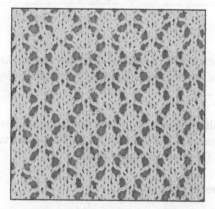

FIGURE 6-6: Miniature leaf open lace pattern.

Photograph by Wiley, Composition Services Graphics

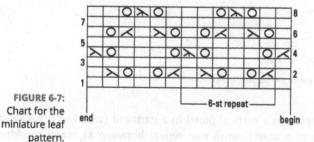

FIGURE 6-7: Chart for the miniature leaf pattern.

Key

◻ Yarn over

◻ Knit 2 stitches together (k2tog)

◻ Slip, slip, knit (ssk)

◻ Slip 2 stitches, knit 1, pass 2 slipped stitches over

◻ Knit on right side, Purl on wrong side

Illustration by Wiley, Composition Services Graphics

Faggot lace

Faggot patterns (basic lace) are really a category unto themselves. They're composed of nothing but the simplest lace-making unit: a yarn over followed (or preceded) by a decrease. You can work a faggot unit over and over for a very open mesh-like fabric, as shown in Figure 6-8a. Or try working a faggot grouping as a vertical panel in an otherwise solid fabric or as a vertical panel alternating with other lace or cable panels, as shown in Figure 6-8b.

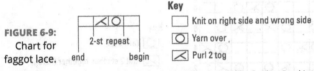

FIGURE 6-8:
Faggot lace by itself (a) and combined with another lace pattern (b).

a. b.

Photographs by Wiley, Composition Services Graphics

You can work faggot patterns with a knitted decrease (ssk or k2tog) or a purled decrease. The appearance of the lace changes very subtly depending on the decrease you use.

Basic faggot is made by alternating a yarn over and a p2tog decrease. You might find this variation (called *purse stitch*) faster and easier to work than others. Follow these instructions (or see the chart in Figure 6-9):

Cast on an even number of sts.

Every row: K1; * yo, p2tog; rep from * to last st, k1.

FIGURE 6-9:
Chart for faggot lace.

2-st repeat

end   begin

Key

☐ Knit on right side and wrong side

☐ Yarn over

☑ Purl 2 tog

Illustration by Wiley, Composition Services Graphics

TIP

To use the faggot repeat as a vertical panel in a garment (whether it's a sweater front or the middle of a scarf), work one repeat between as many stockinette stitches as you like.

Incorporating Lace into Other Pieces

If you want to incorporate knitted lace into a sweater and can't find a pattern that appeals to you, you can work in a lace pattern without a specific set of pattern instructions.

TIP

Numerous stitch dictionaries offer a variety of lace patterns to draw from. To start, check out Barbara Walker's *Treasury of Knitting Patterns* books.

Lace insertions

The simplest way to incorporate lace into a knitted project is to work a vertical lace panel or eyelet motif (otherwise known as a lace *insertion*) into a plain stockinette or simple stitch sweater. Place the panel or motif anywhere in your sweater body, far enough away from a shaped edge so that the panel won't be involved in any increases or decreases. This way, you can concentrate on the lace stitches and avoid having to work any garment shaping around the yarn overs and decreases of your lace stitch.

TIP

If you insert an open lace stitch as a vertical panel, you may want to cast on a few stitches less than the pattern calls for because lace spreads out more than stockinette. Of course, if you want to be exact, you can work out the gauge of your lace insertion and the gauge of the stitch pattern in the sweater body and adjust the numbers accordingly.

You also can add lace as a horizontal insertion. Figure 6-10 shows arrowhead lace, but this time several row repeats have been inserted across a piece of stockinette stitch fabric.

TIP

Some stitch pattern books separate lace insertions from allover lace patterns, but if you find a pattern with a vertical orientation (arrowhead, for example), you can isolate a repeat and work it by itself as an insertion.

FIGURE 6-10:
Arrowhead lace used as a horizontal insertion.

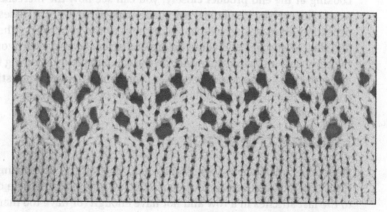

Photograph by Wiley, Composition Services Graphics

Lace edgings

Dress up any sweater by adding a lace edge at the bottom of the sweater body or sleeve. Knitted lace edgings are borders designed with a scalloped or pointed edge. Frequently, they're made in garter stitch to give body to the edging and to ensure that it lies flat. Some edgings, such as hems and cuffs, are worked horizontally; you cast on the number of stitches required for the width of your piece, work the edging, and then continue in stockinette or whatever stitch your garment pattern calls for.

Other edgings are worked vertically and then sewn on later. In this case, you simply cast on the number of stitches required for the depth of the lace edging (from 7 to 20 sts, depending on the pattern) and work the edging until its length matches the width of the piece to which you plan to attach it. Then you bind off, turn the edging on its side, and sew it onto the edge of your project. Or, better yet, you can pick up stitches along the border of the edging itself and knit the rest of the piece from there. (See Book 6, Chapter 3 for details on how to pick up stitches.)

Handling Mistakes While Making Lace

The best way to avoid mistakes in lace-making is to envision how the yarn overs and decreases combine to create the pattern. Take, for example, the cloverleaf eyelet pattern (refer to Figure 6-1 earlier in the chapter to see its chart). This pattern creates the lace shown in Figure 6-11.

Looking at the end product closely, you can see how the increases and decreases work. The eyelets (the holes) are made with yarn-over increases, and the compensating decreases are worked right next to the yarn overs. The decreases look like slanted stitches and come before and after the two eyelets on the bottom of the cloverleaf and after the eyelet on the top. Simply by knowing what's happening with the increases and decreases, you can anticipate what stitch comes next and, in so doing, better avoid missing a yarn over or decrease.

Finding the error

Sometimes mistakes happen despite your best efforts. In knitting lace, you may "feel" the mistake before you see it. That is, your count will be off, or you'll get to the last stitches in a row and not have enough (or have too many) to knit them according to the pattern, or you'll realize that the hole you're creating is in the wrong place. When this happens, the first thing you need to do is find the error.

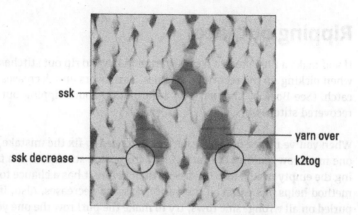

ssk

yarn over

ssk decrease

k2tog

FIGURE 6-11:
Detail of the cloverleaf eyelet pattern.

The way to do that is to look at the stitches on your needle and check each repeat for the right number of stitches. This point is where it really helps to be able to recognize yarn overs and decreases. Figure 6-12 illustrates a yarn over, an ssk decrease, and a k2tog decrease.

TIP

If you're working a pattern in which the stitch count is consistent on every row, tracking an extra or lost stitch is easy. If you're short a stitch, you've probably neglected to make a yarn over. If you find yourself with an extra stitch, you've probably forgotten to make a decrease.

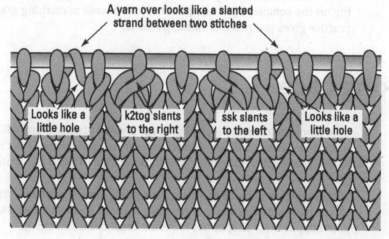

A yarn over looks like a slanted strand between two stitches

Looks like a little hole

k2tog slants to the right

ssk slants to the left

Looks like a little hole

FIGURE 6-12:
Recognizing yarn overs and decreases on your needle.

Ripping out lace

If you make a mistake in a lace pattern and have to rip out stitches, take your time when picking up the recovered stitches. Yarn overs and decreases can be tricky to catch. (See Book 2, Chapter 5 for information about ripping out and picking up recovered stitches.)

REMEMBER

When you've ripped out as far back as you need to fix the mistake, slowly take out one more row, pulling the yarn gently from each stitch one at a time and inserting the empty needle into the freed stitch before it has a chance to disappear. This method helps you catch all the yarn overs and decreases. Also, if your pattern is purled on all wrong-side rows, try to make the purl row the one you pick up from.

As you go, check that stitches end up in the ready-to-work position. Before starting work on your pattern again, read the last pattern row and compare it with the stitches on your needle to make sure that they're all there and that all yarn overs and decreases are in the right place.

TIP

Lifelines are truly a lifesaver when ripping out lace, especially if you've caught a mistake that's more than a few rows down. Using a slick, smooth strand that won't rub colored fibers onto your knitting (such as embroidery floss or cotton yarn), use a needle to thread the lifeline through the last row of stitches below your mistake. If you accidentally tear out more than you intended, you can put stitches back onto your needle from the lifeline. Some extra-cautious lace knitters make a habit of threading a lifeline into their knitting every 5 to 10 rows (depending on the complexity of the pattern) just in case something goes wrong! If this practice gives you peace of mind, go for it.

Blocking Lace

Lace fabrics need to be blocked for their patterns to show up well. The best way to block a lace piece is to wet-block it: Get it wet and spread it out in its final shape to dry. (See Book 7, Chapter 1 for additional tips to block like a pro.)

Whether you wet-block or steam your piece, spread out the fabric in both directions, using blocking wires if you have them. If the bottom edges are scalloped or pointed, pin these shapes out to define them before blocking.

Filet Crochet for Newbies

Not to be confused with filet mignon or filet of sole, filet crochet (also known as net stitch) is a technique that imitates a 17th-century form of lace worked on mesh netting stretched across a frame. Over the years, the technique evolved into what it is today — a series of blocks and spaces that form a design. Because of the uniformity of the designs, the directions are shown in a chart, with each square of the chart representing specific stitches.

Filet crochet is usually worked in white cotton thread and is often used for tablecloths, table runners, curtains, and wall hangings; they're especially elegant against a dark wood surface or brightly colored cloth background. In the sections that follow, you find an introduction to the basics of making filet crochet; one project at the end of this chapter, the Butterfly Runner (shown in full color at dummies.com/go/knitcrochetAIO) is a typical example of the filet crochet technique.

Breaking down filet crochet stitches

Perhaps you've seen a drawing or painting made of small dots or squares. Looking at the drawing from a distance, you see only the design or picture, but as you come closer, you can see the tiny dots/squares that make up the larger picture. Similar to the tiny dots/squares in the drawing, filet crochet is a grid of blocks and spaces that make up a design. The spaces form the background, and the blocks create the design. Patterns for these designs are given as charts (see the next section). Because of its detail, filet crochet is commonly used for lettering. (Here's an interesting tidbit for you: The earliest-known text depicted with filet crochet is *The Lord's Prayer*.)

REMEMBER

Each space and block is made up of three stitches:

>> **Spaces** begin with two chain stitches, followed by a double crochet stitch.

>> **Blocks** are made up of three double crochet stitches, which you can work in the stitches or spaces of the previous row.

TIP

To make sure your design is clear, work filet crochet patterns with cotton thread. Start with size 10 thread and a size 7 steel (1.50 mm) hook. After you have some experience with this technique, move on to a smaller size 20 or size 30 thread and a size 12 (0.75 mm) or 14 (0.60 mm) steel hook to create a much more delicate and elegant design. (Flip to Book 1, Chapters 1 and 2 for the basics on different types of threads and hooks.)

Following a chart

Because of the repetitive nature of filet crochet, the instructions are usually depicted in chart form. (Not only would written instructions be really lengthy, but you'd probably lose your place and become cross-eyed in no time at all.) After you understand how to read a chart, you'll find it's much easier to follow than written instructions.

Filet crochet charts look somewhat like graph paper. They're made up of tons of squares, some of which are empty (spaces), and some of which are filled in (blocks). Each pattern also provides you with a chart key that explains what each square means and whether you work each space or block with three stitches or with another number of stitches that the designer may have chosen. Long empty spaces are bars, and the small, curved lines — the ones that look kind of like Vs — are the lacets. (See the later section "Spacing Filet Crochet with Lacets and Bars" for the scoop on these two stitches.) Figure 6-13a shows a sample filet crochet chart, and Figure 6-13b shows a sample chart key. *Note:* The first double crochet in each of the groups of stitches in the chart key represents the last stitch of the previous space or block.

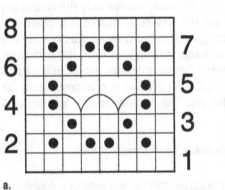 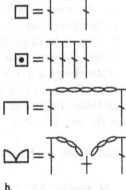

FIGURE 6-13: A sample filet crochet chart and key.

a.　　　　　　　　　　b.

© John Wiley & Sons, Inc.

TIP Each row of the chart has a number, beginning with Row 1 at the bottom and ending with the last row at the top. The instructions normally tell you the number of chains you need to make for the foundation chain, and they may or may not write the first row's instructions. Read all the odd-numbered rows from right to left and all the even-numbered rows from left to right (because you actually work the second row from the left-hand side of the piece to the right-hand side).

Sometimes large patterns that repeat a series of rows over and over again show you the repeated rows only once in the chart. The instructions tell you to work the chart from Row 1 to the last row and then repeat the chart, beginning at Row 1 again, a designated number of times to complete the project. This is often the case when you're making a table runner, tablecloth, or curtains.

If the filet crochet chart is for a large piece, the squares may be small and hard to read. Make a copy of the chart and enlarge it for easier reading instead of working directly from the original instructions. With a copy, you can also mark up the chart without destroying the original. You can highlight the row you're working on or place a mark next to the last row that you worked when you have to put your project down for a while.

Chaining the foundation

You need to do some simple math to make your foundation chain of filet crochet. Each block or space in a filet crochet chart is actually three stitches. This means that each row of filet crochet has a multiple of three stitches plus one double crochet at the end to complete the last space or block.

Here's how to create a foundation chain for a sample design that calls for five spaces across the first row:

1. **Multiply the number of spaces (or blocks) in the row by 3.**

- 5 × 3 = 15 chain stitches (ch)

2. **Add 3 more chain stitches for the turning chain (refer to Book 3, Chapter 2) of the next row's first double crochet stitch (dc).**

- 15 + 3 (first double crochet) = 18 chain stitches

WARNING

Getting the tension just right for your foundation chain is important. If your foundation chain is too tight, your design can pucker or be misshapen. If it's too loose, you'll have a lot of droopy loops hanging off the edge. The stitches in your foundation chain should be the same size and just big enough to fit your hook into comfortably. Most people have a tendency to chain too tightly. If you fall into this category, go to the next-largest hook size to work the foundation chain. If you chain too loosely, try the next size down.

TIP

Nothing is more frustrating than getting to the end of your first row in a large design and finding out that you don't have enough stitches. If you're working on a large filet crochet design, chances are your foundation chain is several hundred stitches long. To avoid miscounting, crochet your foundation chain with a separate ball of thread. When you think you have the right number of chain stitches, attach a new ball of thread in the first chain stitch that you created, working your first row from there. If you miscounted, you can easily add (or subtract) chain stitches at the end of the foundation row with the first ball of thread that you used. Fasten off the first ball of thread when you complete the first row and weave in the end to keep it from unraveling.

Creating spaces

If you're armed with the foundation chain you created in the preceding section, you're ready to start working your first row of filet crochet. To work a first row of spaces, proceed as follows:

1. **Chain 2 (ch 2) to create the top of the first space.**

   You already chained the turning chain for the first stitch when you crocheted your foundation chain.

2. **Double crochet (dc) in the eighth chain from your hook to make the first space.**

   Not sure how to make a double crochet stitch? See Book 3, Chapter 2.

3. **Chain 2.**

4. **Skip the next 2 chain stitches.**

5. **Double crochet in the next chain to make the second space.**

6. **Repeat Steps 3 through 5 across the row.**

   You work your last double crochet in the last chain of the foundation chain, and you should have 5 spaces at the end of the row, as in Figure 6-14.

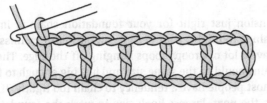

FIGURE 6-14:
The first row of filet crochet spaces.

© John Wiley & Sons, Inc.

To work a second row of spaces:

1. **Turn your work.**

   Refer to Book 3, Chapter 1 for the how-to on turning your work.

2. **Chain 3 (ch 3) for the turning chain for your first double crochet (dc).**

3. **Chain 2 to make the first space.**

4. **Skip the next 2 chain stitches.**

5. **Double crochet in the next double crochet stitch to make the first space of the second row.**

6. **Repeat Steps 3 through 5 across the row.**

   You should wind up with 5 spaces at the end of the second row.

Work each successive row the same way as the second row until you're comfortable with the technique.

REMEMBER Take care to notice the way that the spaces form squares and that they line up one on top of another. Filet crochet is a symmetrical design technique, and if the squares are skewed, then your whole piece will look out of kilter. If you find that you've made a mistake, tear out your work to that spot and rework your design from there. You can't hide mistakes in filet crochet.

Building blocks

Blocks are what create the actual substance of a filet crochet design. Some designs also start with a row of blocks for the first row to create a border. Using the foundation chain of 15 chain stitches plus 3 for the turning chain (see the earlier section "Chaining the foundation"), work a first row of blocks.

1. **Double crochet (dc) in the fourth chain (ch) from the hook.**

   Flip to Book 3, Chapter 2 to see how to make a double crochet stitch.

2. **Double crochet in each of the next 2 chain stitches to complete the first block.**

3. **Double crochet in each of the next 3 chain stitches to complete the second block.**

4. **Repeat Step 3 across the row.**

   You should have 5 blocks at the end of the row (or 15 double crochet stitches plus the turning chain), as shown in Figure 6-15. *Remember:* You always have 1 more stitch than the multiple of 3.

FIGURE 6-15: The first row of filet crochet blocks.

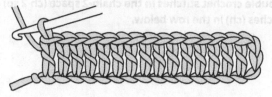

© John Wiley & Sons, Inc.

To work the second row of blocks, follow these steps:

1. **Turn your work.**

   See Book 3, Chapter 1 for pointers on turning your work.

2. **Chain 3 (ch 3) for the turning chain for your first double crochet (dc).**

3. **Double crochet in each of the next 3 double crochet stitches to make the first block.**

4. **Double crochet in each of the next 3 double crochet stitches to complete the second block.**

5. **Repeat Step 4 across the row.**

   You should have 5 blocks at the end of the second row.

Combining spaces and blocks

To create the design you're going for, you must combine spaces and blocks, which is easy to do because both techniques are based on three stitches.

REMEMBER

As you're crocheting, make sure your blocks and spaces line up with all the vertical and horizontal lines lying at right angles. The double crochet stitches that form the beginning and end of each block or space must line up one on top of the other to create the grid-like appearance.

To work a space in the next row over a block:

1. **Work the first double crochet (dc).**

2. **Chain 2 (ch 2).**

3. **Skip the next 2 double crochet stitches.**

   The double crochet that closes the space is actually considered the first stitch of the next space or block in the row.

To work a block over a space:

1. **Double crochet (dc) in the first double crochet stitch of the space below.**

2. **Work 2 double crochet stitches in the chain-2 space (ch-2 sp) or in the 2 chain stitches (ch) in the row below.**

You can either work your stitches in the chain space or work them directly into the chain stitches — try it both ways to see which one you prefer. Most crocheters find working in the space easier and neater. (Flip to Book 4, Chapter 3 for the lowdown on working in the spaces between stitches.)

TIP

Don't worry if the stitches look a bit skewed as you're crocheting. After you finish the design, you can pin it out and starch it (see Book 7, Chapter 1 for more on this process, which is commonly referred to as blocking) to straighten out the stitches.

Figure 6-16 shows a swatch of filet crochet that combines spaces and blocks. In this figure, the stitches are worked in the chain space.

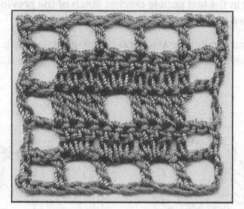

FIGURE 6-16:
A swatch of filet crochet that combines spaces and blocks.

© John Wiley & Sons, Inc.

Shaping Your Filet Crochet Design

You're not limited to straight-edged, rectangular pieces in filet crochet. Instead, you can add interest to corners and edges by increasing or decreasing the number of spaces and blocks in a row to make inset corners and step-like edges, as explained in the following sections.

Increasing spaces and blocks

Increasing the number of spaces and blocks at the end of a row shapes the edges of the design. Because most filet crochet designs are symmetrical, if you increase at the beginning of a row, you need to increase at the end of the row, too. However, the process is a little different for each end.

Increasing one space at the beginning of a row

To increase one space at the beginning of a row, you must chain enough stitches to make up a space. Here's how to work a one-space increase at the beginning of a row:

1. **At the end of the row that precedes the row you're going to increase, turn your work and then chain 2 (ch 2) to create the base of the first increase space.**

2. **Chain 3 more for the turning chain of the space's first double crochet (dc).**

3. **Chain 2 more to complete the top of the first space.**

4. **Double crochet in the last double crochet stitch of the previous row, as shown in Figure 6-17a.**

   One increase is now complete, which you can see in Figure 6-17b. Continue across the row with blocks or spaces, as detailed earlier in this chapter.

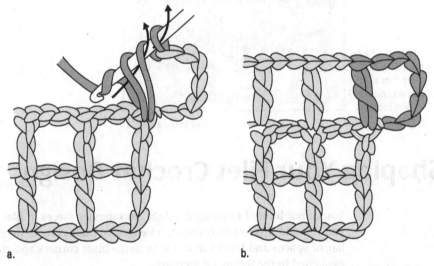

FIGURE 6-17:
Increasing one filet crochet space at the beginning of a row.

a.

b.

© John Wiley & Sons, Inc.

Increasing more than one space at the beginning of a row

Increasing more than one space at the beginning of a row works the same way as increasing one space; you just have to know how many additional chain stitches to make for each additional space.

REMEMBER

When increasing spaces, chain 2 for the first space increase and then chain 3 more for each additional space required. The first double crochet of a row is always a chain 3.

Follow these steps to increase more than one space:

1. **When you reach the end of the row that precedes the row you're going to increase, turn your work and then chain 2 (ch 2) for the base of the first increase space.**

2. **Chain 3 more for each additional space required.**

    The example in these steps adds 1 more space for a total of 2 increases. Therefore, you're chaining a total of 5 stitches for the 2 increases.

3. **Chain 3 more for the turning chain of the row's first double crochet stitch (dc).**

4. **Chain 2 more for the top of the first space.**

5. **Double crochet in the eighth chain from the hook, as shown in Figure 6-18a.**

6. **Chain 2 for the top of the second increase space.**

7. **Skip the next 2 chain stitches.**

8. **Double crochet in the next chain stitch.**

    You've now increased the row by 2 spaces.

9. **Chain 2 to make the top of the next space.**

10. **Skip the next 2 stitches.**

11. **Double crochet in the next double crochet stitch to make the next space of the row.**

12. **Repeat Steps 9 through 11 across the row to complete a row of spaces.**

    Your completed row should look similar to Figure 6-18b.

Increasing one or more blocks at the beginning of a row

Increasing one block at the beginning of a row is similar to increasing one space. The big difference is that you replace the two chain stitches you make for the top of the space with two double crochet stitches. To increase one block at the beginning of a row, proceed as follows:

1. **At the end of the row that precedes the row you're going to increase, turn your work and then chain 2 (ch 2) to make the base of the first increase block.**

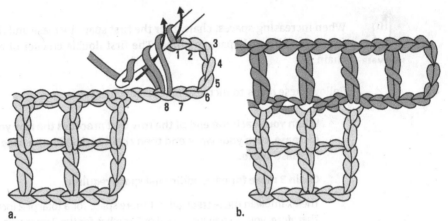

FIGURE 6-18:
Increasing two spaces at the start of a row.

a.   b.

© John Wiley & Sons, Inc.

2. **Chain 3 more to complete the turning chain of the block's first double crochet stitch (dc).**

3. **Double crochet in the fourth chain from the hook to complete the second double crochet stitch of the block. (See Figure 6-19a.)**

4. **Double crochet in each of the next 2 chain stitches to complete the block.**

   The first block increase is now complete; yours should look like the one in Figure 6-19b. From here, continue making blocks or spaces across the row.

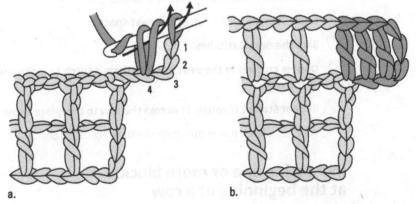

FIGURE 6-19:
Increasing one block at the start of a row.

a.   b.

© John Wiley & Sons, Inc.

REMEMBER

To increase additional blocks, follow the same steps for increasing one block, but remember the additional chain stitches you need to make for the additional blocks. Here's the simple math: Chain 2 for your first increase block, chain 3 more for each additional block, and then chain 3 for the turning chain of the row's first double crochet. So if you want to increase 2 blocks at the beginning of a row, you chain 2 for the first block, 3 for the second block, and 3 more for the turning chain, which is 11 chain stitches total.

After you chain the required number of stitches, follow Steps 3 and 4 in the previous list to make the first block; then work another set of three double crochet stitches for the other increase block (see Figure 6-20).

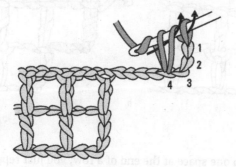

FIGURE 6-20:
The beginning of a two-block increase at the start of a row.

© John Wiley & Sons, Inc.

Increasing one or more spaces at the end of a row

When you need to increase a space at the end of a row, you start at the *top* of the last double crochet in the row just prior to the increase. To create the extra space(s), you work a chain-2 space followed by a stitch called a *triple triple crochet* (abbreviated *trtr*), which is one step taller than a double triple crochet stitch (presented in Book 3, Chapter 2). By working a triple triple crochet stitch, you create a length equivalent to five chain stitches, which is what you need to make one filet space — two chain stitches for the width of the space plus three chain stitches for the height of one double crochet.

To increase one space at the end of a row, follow these instructions:

1. **Chain 2 (ch 2) to create the top of the first space.**

2. **Yarn over the hook (yo) 4 times.**

3. **Insert your hook into the same stitch as the last double crochet stitch (dc) that you worked, like in Figure 6-21a.**

4. **Yarn over and draw the yarn through the stitch.**

5. **Yarn over and draw the yarn through the first 2 loops on the hook.**

Making Lace

6. **Repeat Step 5 three times until you have 1 loop on the hook, completing 1 triple triple crochet (trtr).**

Figure 6-21b shows 1 completed space increase at the end of a row.

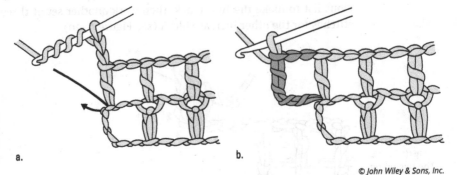

FIGURE 6-21: Working an increase space at the end of a row.

a.   b.

REMEMBER

To increase more than one space at the end of a row, you just repeat the steps for increasing one space. The only difference is that in Step 3, you insert the hook in the middle of the post of the triple triple crochet that you made for the first space increase, as shown in Figure 6-22. Flip to Book 3, Chapter 1 if you need a refresher on stitch parts.

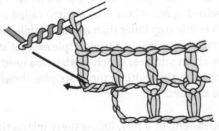

FIGURE 6-22: Working additional spaces at the end of a row.

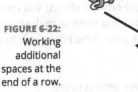

Increasing one or more blocks at the end of a row

Increasing a block at the end of a row is a bit tricky but still relatively simple. The key is to make sure you don't tighten up too much on your stitches.

REMEMBER

When increasing blocks, you use a triple crochet stitch rather than a double crochet. The extra length compensates for not having a row of chain stitches to serve as the base.

Here's how to increase one block at the end of a row:

1. **Yarn over (yo) twice.**

2. **Insert your hook into the top of the last stitch of the previous row, which is where you just worked the last double crochet (dc) of the current row. (Refer to Figure 6-23a.)**

3. **Yarn over and draw the yarn through the stitch.**

4. **Yarn over and draw the yarn through the first 2 loops on the hook.**

5. **Repeat Step 4 twice.**

   You now have 1 loop remaining on your hook and have completed 1 triple crochet (tr) as well as the second stitch of the block.

6. **Yarn over twice.**

7. **Insert your hook near the bottom of the post of the last triple crochet that you made, as shown in Figure 6-23b.**

8. **Yarn over and draw the yarn through the first 2 loops on the hook.**

9. **Repeat Step 8 twice until you have just 1 loop on the hook (completing 1 triple crochet).**

10. **Repeat Steps 7 through 9 (completing the third stitch of the block).**

    See Figure 6-24 for the visual.

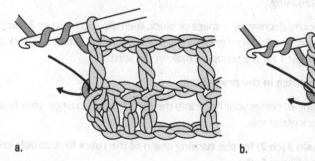

FIGURE 6-23:
Working an extra block at the end of a row.

a.   b.

© John Wiley & Sons, Inc.

After you master increasing one block, increasing more than one is easy. You just repeat Steps 7 through 9 three times for each additional block that you want.

TIP

Making Lace

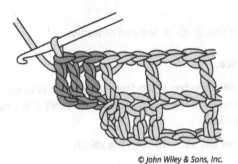

FIGURE 6-24:
A complete block
increase at the
end of a row.

© John Wiley & Sons, Inc.

Decreasing spaces and blocks

The method for decreasing both spaces and blocks is the same. It's simply a matter of counting.

Decreasing spaces or blocks at the beginning of a row

To decrease one space or block at the beginning of a row, simply slip stitch across to where you want to begin the first space or block.

1. **At the end of the row immediately before the row you're decreasing, turn your work.**

2. **Slip stitch (sl st) across 3 stitches for each space or block that you're decreasing.**

   If you're decreasing 1 space or block, then slip stitch across 3 stitches; if you're decreasing 2 spaces or blocks, slip stitch across 6 stitches. (Check out Book 3, Chapter 1 for the scoop on making slip stitches.)

3. **Slip stitch in the next stitch.**

   Doing so brings your hook into the correct stitch to begin your first space or block of the row.

4. **Chain 3 (ch 3) for the turning chain of the row's first double crochet (dc). (See Figure 6-25.)**

5. **Work across the row with either blocks or spaces.**

Decreasing spaces or blocks at the end of a row

The method for decreasing spaces or blocks at the end of a row is the same regardless of how many you need to decrease. You work across the row following the chart, stop crocheting at the point where you want to make the decrease, and then turn your work to begin the next row. Keep in mind that the decrease must end with a double crochet stitch or a complete space or block. Figure 6-26 shows the decrease at the end of a row after you've turned and are ready to begin the next row.

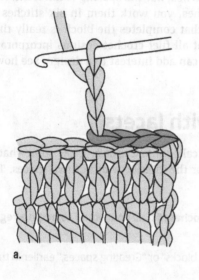

FIGURE 6-25:
Decreasing at
the beginning of
a row: (a) blocks
and (b) spaces.

a.　　　　　　　　b.

© John Wiley & Sons, Inc.

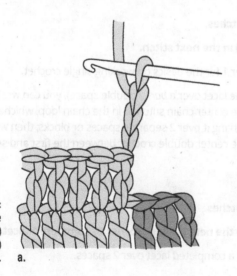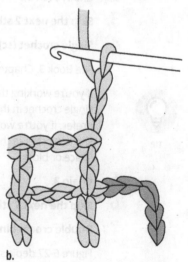

FIGURE 6-26:
Decreasing at the
end of a row: (a)
blocks and (b)
spaces.

a.　　　　　　　　b.

© John Wiley & Sons, Inc.

Spacing Filet Crochet with Lacets and Bars

Lacets and bars are two more filet crochet stitches that create an elegant, lacy look. Despite their fancy names, you work them with just double crochet, chain, and single crochet stitches, but the spacing is different. Instead of working them across three stitches, you work them in six stitches or two spaces. (*Remember:* The last stitch that completes the block is really the first stitch of the next space or block.) Not all filet crochet designs incorporate these fancy-schmancy stitches, but they can add interest to a design. See how to make them in the next sections.

Getting fancy with lacets

A *lacet*, which is sometimes called a *fancy stitch*, looks somewhat like a *V* and is worked across five stitches or the interior width of two spaces. To make a lacet, proceed as follows:

1. **Work the first double crochet (dc) as you would to begin a regular block or space.**

   See the sections "Building blocks" or "Creating spaces," earlier in this chapter, for guidance.

2. **Chain 3 (ch 3).**

3. **Skip the next 2 stitches.**

4. **Single crochet (sc) in the next stitch.**

   See Book 3, Chapter 1 for the basics on working single crochet.

TIP

   If you're working the lacet over a *bar* (a double space), you can work the single crochet in the center chain stitch or in the chain loop, whichever you prefer. If you're working it over 2 separate spaces or blocks, then work the single crochet in the center double crochet between the first and second space or block.

5. **Chain 3.**

6. **Skip the next 2 stitches.**

7. **Double crochet in the next double crochet to complete 1 lacet.**

   Figure 6-27 depicts a completed lacet over 2 spaces.

FIGURE 6-27:
A finished lacet over two spaces.

Bridging the gap with bars

Bars, sometimes referred to as *double spaces*, are long spaces that cross over the two blocks or spaces or the one lacet below them. They're generally worked over a lacet. To make a bar:

1. **Work the first double crochet (dc) as you would to begin a regular block or space.**

   Refer to the sections "Building blocks" or "Creating spaces," earlier in this chapter, for help with this step.

2. **Chain 5 (ch 5).**

3. **Skip the next 5 stitches or 2 spaces.**

4. **Double crochet in the next double crochet stitch to complete 1 bar.**

   To see what a completed bar looks like, check out Figure 6-28.

FIGURE 6-28:
A bar worked over a lacet.

Figure 6-29 shows a swatch of filet crochet worked with all four stitches: blocks, spaces, lacets, and bars. Pretty cool, huh?

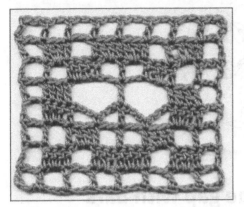

FIGURE 6-29:
A finished swatch of filet crochet featuring all four stitches.

Practice Lace Projects

Accessories are natural projects for practicing lace patterns: You don't have any shaping to consider, and the flat panels really showcase the lace patterns. Try making the scarf and shawl in this section; not only will you improve your lace-making techniques, but you'll also have terrific accessories!

Scarf with Faggot Lace

This scarf is simple to make. Work it up in a soft, cozy yarn, and you'll never want to be without it — except perhaps in the heat of summer.

Materials and vital statistics

- » **Measurements:** 9 inches x 60 inches; can be shortened or lengthened as desired

- » **Yarn:** Kollage Yarns "Creamy Flame" (80% milk/20% cotton; CYC #2, 200 yards, 1.8 ounces [50 grams]): Spearmint, 3 skeins

- » **Needles:** One pair of size US 5 (3¾ mm) needles or size needed to obtain gauge

- » **Other materials:** 2 stitch markers

- » **Gauge:** 24 stitches per 4 inches in faggot lace scarf pattern

Directions

Cast on 52 sts.

Row 1 (RS): K5, place marker, * yo, p2tog, k4; rep from * to last 5 sts, place marker, k5.

Row 2: K2, p3, slip marker, * yo, p2tog, p4; rep from * to marker, slip marker, p3, k2.

Row 3 (RS): K5, slip marker, *yo, p2tog, k4; rep from * to marker, slip marker, k5.

Rep Rows 2 and 3 until the scarf reaches the desired length.

MOSS STITCH

Moss stitch, shown in the following figure, is an elongated version of seed stitch (see Book 2, Chapter 2). Instead of alternating the pattern every other row, however, you work 2 rows of the same sequence of knits and purls before you alternate them.

Photograph by Wiley, Composition Services Graphics

Cast on an uneven number of sts. (An uneven number makes this pattern symmetrical — either side can be the right side.)

Rows 1 and 4: K1, * p1, k1; rep from * to end of row.

Rows 2 and 3: P1,* k1, p1; rep from * to end of row.

Rep Rows 1–4 for pattern.

Making Lace

Variations

To make a different scarf on the same theme, try one of the following variations:

>> Make the scarf in a different yarn. Use a heavier yarn for an entirely different fabric and feel. Remember to do a gauge swatch to determine whether you may also need to change the number of cast on stitches to get the correct size scarf. This pattern has a stitch repeat of 6 stitches plus 10 stitches, so as long as you cast on a multiple of 6 plus 10, the scarf will be perfect.

>> Add tassels or fringe to the ends of the scarf.

>> Instead of using stockinette stitch between the faggot panels, work garter or moss stitch. (See Book 2, Chapter 2 for garter stitch and the nearby sidebar for moss stitch.)

>> Instead of including the k4 panel in the pattern, work a cable panel between the faggot patterns. For an entire selection of cable patterns, head to Book 4, Chapter 2.

Lace Leaf Shawl

You make this shawl as a basic rectangle with a built-in garter stitch border so that it's very easy to knit. When knitting lace, thinking about how the lace stitches will look in the fiber and the color you choose is important. A smooth wool or wool blend in a solid or semi-solid color will make the stitches visible and crisp on your shawl.

TIP

The last thing you want to do is put all that work into a project that doesn't show off the beautiful stitches. Here's where your gauge swatch is vital in choosing the right yarn. Make sure you wash and block your gauge swatch to see whether you like the finished fabric. If you do, then you're good to go! This project uses a 100-percent yak yarn that blocks out lace stitches brilliantly.

Materials and vital statistics

>> **Measurements:** Approximately 25 inches x 72 inches

>> **Yarn:** Bijou Basin Ranch "Sport Weight" (100% yak; CYC #3, 328 yards, 3.5 ounces [100 grams]): Gray, 2 skeins

>> **Needles:** One pair of size US 6 (4 mm) needles or size needed to obtain gauge

>> **Gauge:** 24 stitches and 32 rows per 4 inches in miniature leaf pattern in a blocked gauge. Because this shawl isn't a fitted piece, checking gauge isn't vital, but if your gauge varies, you may not get the desired look.

Directions

Cast on 151 sts.

Preparation rows: Purl 6 rows for a garter stitch border.

Row 1 and all WS rows: Purl.

Row 2: Purl 6, place marker, k1, * k2tog, yo, k1, yo, ssk, k1; rep from * to last 6 sts, place marker, purl to end of row.

Row 4: Purl to marker, slip marker, k2tog, * yo, k3, yo, sl 2 kwise, k1, p2sso; rep from * to last 5 sts before marker, yo, k3, yo, ssk, slip marker, purl to end of row.

Row 6: Purl to marker, slip marker, k1, * yo, ssk, k1, k2tog, yo, k1; rep from * to marker, slip marker, purl to end of row.

Row 8: Purl to marker, slip marker, k2, * yo, sl 2 kwise, k1, p2sso, yo, k3; rep from * to last 5 sts before marker, yo, sl 2 kwise, k1, p2sso, yo, k2, slip marker, purl to end of row.

Rep Rows 1–8 until piece measures approximately 68 inches from the beginning. End with 6 rows of garter stitch. Bind off loosely.

Finishing: Weave in any loose ends; then wash and block your shawl to the finished measurements. See Book 7, Chapter 1 on how to block.

Butterfly Runner Project

This beautiful filet crochet runner is a simple rectangle that uses spaces, blocks, bars, and lacets. The sample (shown in the online photos at dummies.com/go/knitcrochetAIO) uses size 20 thread with a size 12 (0.75 mm) steel hook, but if you'd feel more comfortable using the larger size 10 thread with a size 7 (1.50 mm) steel hook, go right ahead. Your finished design will be larger but just as pretty.

TIP

If you're feeling pretty confident and want to spice up the runner a tad, you can shape the corners of it by using the increasing and decreasing technique. The runner shown online at dummies.com/go/knitcrochetAIO features this corner variation. (Don't worry. Another chart and directions help you with this change.)

Materials and vital statistics

>> **Cotton thread:** DMC "Cebelia" size 20 crochet cotton (100% mercerized cotton), Article #167 (1.76 oz. [50 g], 405 yds [370 m] each ball): 1 ball of White

» **Hook:** Steel crochet hook size 12 U.S. (0.75 mm) or size needed to obtain gauge

» **Measurements:** 10 in. wide x 12½ in. long

» **Gauge:** 7 spaces = 2 in.; 9 rows dc = 2 in.

» **Stitches used:** Chain stitch (ch), slip stitch (sl st), single crochet (sc), double crochet (dc). **Filet st:** * Dc in dc, ch 2, skip next 2 sts *, 1 space made. * Dc in dc, dc in each of next 2 sts *, 1 block made. * Dc in dc, ch 3, skip next 2 sts, sc in next st, ch 3, skip next 2 sts *, 1 lacet made. * Dc in dc, ch 5, skip next 5 sts, or 2 spaces *, 1 bar made.

» **Additional stitches for corner option: To dec 1 space at beg of row:** Sl st to designated dc, ch 3 (first dc) to beg row. **To dec 1 space at end of row:** Work to designated dc, *turn* to beg next row.

Directions

For complete information on reading crochet instructions, refer to Book 1, Chapter 4. With that said, have fun creating your first filet crochet masterpiece!

Ch 180 + 3 (first dc) + 2 (first space).

Row 1: Dc in eighth ch from hook, (ch 2, skip next 2 ch, dc in next ch) 4 times, * dc in each of next 6 ch, (ch 2, skip next 2 ch, dc in next ch) 4 times, * rep from * to * across until 3 ch remains, ch 2, skip next 2 ch, dc in last ch (first row of chart complete — 60 spaces and blocks), *turn*.

Rows 2–48: Work in blocks, spaces, bars, and lacets following chart (see Figure 6-30). Read all odd-numbered rows from right to left and all even-numbered rows from left to right. Fasten off at end of last row.

Optional directions for corner variation

Ch 150 + 3 (first dc).

Row 1: Dc in fourth ch from hook, dc in each of next 5 ch, * (ch 2, skip next 2 ch, dc in next ch) 4 times, dc in each of next 6 ch *; rep from * to * across (first row of chart complete — 50 spaces and blocks), *turn*.

Rows 2–48: Work in blocks, spaces, bars, and lacets following chart (see Figure 6-31). Read all odd-numbered rows from right to left and all even-numbered rows from left to right. Fasten off at end of last row.

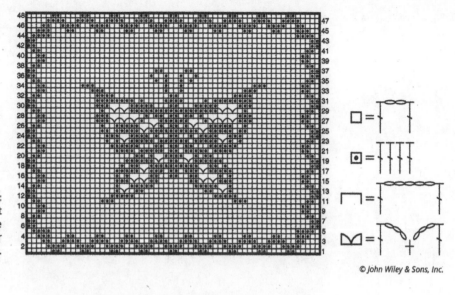

FIGURE 6-30: Chart and chart key for the Butterfly Runner project.

© John Wiley & Sons, Inc.

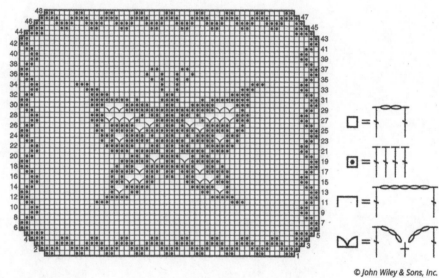

FIGURE 6-31: Butterfly Runner chart with shaped edges and chart key.

© John Wiley & Sons, Inc.

Finishing

Using liquid starch, block the finished piece. (See Book 7, Chapter 1 for instructions.)

5 Popular Projects

Contents at a Glance

Chapter **1**

Scarves, Wraps, and Hats

When you're learning to knit and crochet, scarves and hats are popular projects. These projects tend to be quick and easy (compared to an afghan or sweater) and result is something warm to wear. This chapter offers a variety of scarf, wrap, and hat projects for both knitting and crocheting. In many cases, the project includes details about how you can modify the pattern for a slightly different result.

Box Stitch Scarf

Box stitch (shown in Figure 1-1) is a great choice for blankets and scarves, but it can also give a great allover texture to a piece such as a jacket. Box stitch also makes a great edging. For instance, if you don't like the bottom of your sweater to pull in at the hips, box stitch makes a fine substitute for 2 x 2 rib (introduced in Book 2, Chapter 2).

To knit box stitch when knitting flat, you need a number of stitches that's equal to a multiple of 4 plus 2:

Rows 1 and 4: *K2, p2, repeat from * to last 2 sts, k2.

Rows 2 and 3: *P2, k2, repeat from * to last 2 sts, p2.

Repeat these 4 rows for the pattern.

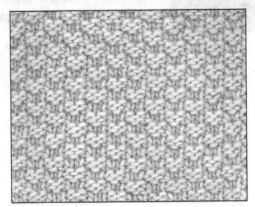

FIGURE 1-1:
Box stitch.

© John Wiley & Sons, Inc.

To knit box stitch in the round (see Book 2, Chapter 4), you need a multiple of 4 stitches:

Rounds 1 and 2: *K2, p2, repeat from * to end of round.

Rounds 3 and 4: *P2, k2, repeat from * to end of round.

Repeat these 4 rounds for the pattern.

To make a box stitch swatch for your block, cast on 18 stitches. Follow the directions for working box stitch flat. Bind off when your swatch measures 4 inches.

The basic box stitch scarf has so many variations that it's always sure to be fresh and interesting. Try the stitch by holding two yarns together or the twins scarf, a variation that features two different takes on box stitch. See a box stitch scarf in Figure 1-2 or check out a color photo at dummies.com/go/knitcrochetAIO.

Materials and vital statistics

» **Yarn:** Rowan Kid Classic (70% lambswool, 26% kid mohair, 4% nylon); 151 yards (140 meters) per 50 grams; 2 balls; color: Straw

» **Needles:** US 9 (5.5 mm) needles, or the size needed to match gauge

» **Other materials:** Yarn needle for weaving in ends

» **Size:** 6 inches wide by 60 inches long

» **Gauge:** 18 stitches and 24 rows per 4 inches in stockinette stitch

FIGURE 1-2:
A box stitch scarf
is always fresh.

Working box stitch is a lot like knitting ribs — you're regularly alternating between knits and purls.

Directions

Cast on 28 sts.

Rows 1, 3, and 5: *K4, p4, repeat from * to last 4 sts, k4.

Rows 2 and 4: *P4, k4, repeat from * to last 4 sts, p4.

You now switch so that the boxes that were purled are now knit and vice versa.

Rows 6, 8, and 10: *K4, p4, repeat from * to last 4 sts, k4.

Rows 7 and 9: *P4, k4, repeat from * to last 4 sts, p4.

Repeat these 10 rows until scarf measures 60 inches, or your desired length, ending with Row 5 or Row 10.

Bind off and weave in ends.

Variation: Twins scarf

Work the first half of the scarf exactly the same as the basic pattern. When your scarf measures 30 inches, or half the desired length, end with Row 10 of the box stitch pattern, and switch to the leaning box stitch as follows:

Row 1: *K4, p4, repeat from * to last 4 sts, k4.

Row 2: K1, *p4, k4, repeat from * to last 3 sts, p3.

Row 3: K2, *p4, k4, repeat from * to last 2 sts, p2.

Row 4: K3, *p4, k4, repeat from * to last st, p1.

Row 5: *P4, k4, repeat from * to last 4 sts, p4.

Now the boxes switch from knit to purl and switch to lean the opposite direction.

Row 6: P4, *k4, p4, repeat from * to end.

Row 7: P1, *k4, p4, repeat from * to last 3 sts, k3.

Row 8: P2, *k4, p4, repeat from * to last 2 sts, k2.

Row 9: P3, *k4, p4, repeat from * to last st, k1.

Row 10: *K4, p4, repeat from * to last 4 sts, k4.

Repeat Rows 1–10 of leaning box stitch until scarf measures 60 inches, or your desired length, ending with Row 5 or Row 10.

Bind off and weave in ends.

Variation: Two-yarns scarf

This variation uses two yarns — a mohair yarn and a ribbon yarn — held together. Why not give it a try? It's a great way to make something totally unique because you're making your own multistrand yarn. Not only are you doing something interesting with the texture of the scarf, but you're also playing with color. For example, a yarn that's too bright can be toned down when paired with a subdued mohair. Or a novelty yarn can gain both structure and substance when you use it with a more conventional yarn.

When trying this variation, hold both strands of yarn together and treat them as a single strand of yarn (see Figure 1-3). Be sure to pick up both strands of yarn for each stitch. If you're worried that the strands will tangle, put each yarn in its own zippered sandwich bag. And don't limit yourself to two yarns: You can use three, five, or even a dozen yarns held together!

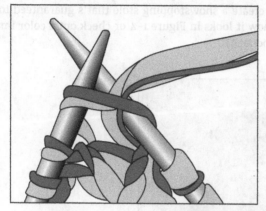

FIGURE 1-3:
Knitting with two yarns held together.

© John Wiley & Sons, Inc.

TIP

To get an idea of what needles to use, add the needle sizes (in millimeters) that are recommended for each yarn. (This information is found on the yarn's label.) The resulting number of millimeters tells you what size needles to use. For example, if you want to use a yarn that suggests a US 6 (4 mm) needle paired with a yarn that suggests a US 8 (5 mm) needle, you should knit them on a 9 mm needle (4 mm + 5 mm = 9 mm). A 9 mm needle is a US 13 needle. It's handy to have a needle gauge close by when you're making this sort of calculation. (Book 1, Chapter 1 introduces this tool and Book 1, Chapter 3 explains how to determine gauge.)

Remember, though, this calculation gives you only a suggestion for needle size. Cast on a few stitches, knit a few rows, and see if you like the fabric you're creating. Switch to smaller or larger needles to get the look and feel that you're after.

Ready to knit? Use one strand of Crystal Palace Deco Ribbon and one strand of Crystal Palace Kid Merino held together. (Or try any ribbon combined with a mohair blend, depending on the look you want.) Use a US 13 (9 mm) needle, or the needle that makes a fabric you like.

Cast on 20 stitches and follow the earlier basic pattern. You can also try 28 or 36 stitches if you want something even larger and more dramatic.

Longways Multiyarn Stole

This multiyarn stole lets a collection of beautiful yarns do the work for you — the knitting could hardly be simpler, yet the result is stunning. The suggested yarns are a mohair yarn, a thick and thin wool, and a shiny ribbon with glints of silver. But choose any combination of yarns with a variety of textures and colors you love, and you'll create a showstopping stole that's guaranteed to bring drama to any outfit. See how it looks in Figure 1-4 or check out a color image at dummies. com/go/knitcrochetAIO.

FIGURE 1-4:
A longways multiyarn stole is breathtaking.

© John Wiley & Sons, Inc.

TIP

In this pattern, you have to change yarns, which many new knitters find intimidating. However, a little practice is all you need to get the hang of it. Just remember that when making this wrap, you carry the mohair (yarn A) loosely up the side of the work because you're using it every other stripe. The other two yarns are cut and rejoined as indicated in the pattern. For more help joining a new color an existing one, see Book 4, Chapter 1.

Materials and vital statistics

>> **Yarn:** You need the following three types of yarn:

- Yarn A: Divé Mohair Kiss Ombre (73% mohair, 22% wool, 5% polyamide); 98 yards (90 meters) per 50 grams; 3 skeins; color: 40377

- Yarn B: Divé Fiamma (100% wool); 55 yards (50 meters) per 50 grams; 2 skeins; color: 40377

- Yarn C: Divé Luxus (91% nylon, 9% polyester); 51 yards (47 meters) per 50 grams; 2 skeins; color: 40377

>> **Needles:** US 15 (10 mm) circular needle, 24-inch length or longer, or the size needed to match gauge (if you tend to cast on tightly, use an even bigger needle to cast on and bind off)

>> **Other materials:** Large crochet hook; yarn needle to weave in ends

>> **Size:** 65 inches long by 16 inches wide, without fringe

>> **Gauge:** 8 stitches and 12 rows per 4 inches in garter stitch

Directions

With yarn B (the thick and thin wool), cast on 130 sts loosely.

Knit 1 row. Cut yarn B.

Rows 1 and 2: Join yarn A (the mohair) and knit 2 rows. Don't cut yarn A.

Rows 3 and 4: Join yarn C (the ribbon) and knit 2 rows. Cut yarn C.

Rows 5 and 6: Knit 2 rows with yarn A. Don't cut yarn A.

Rows 7 and 8: Join yarn B and knit 2 rows. Cut yarn B.

Repeat these 8 rows until your stole measures approximately 16 inches, ending with Row 7. Bind off loosely with yarn B.

Weave in any loose ends.

Finishing: From the remaining yarn, cut 20-inch lengths for the fringe. Cut 18 pieces each from yarn B and yarn C. Cut 36 pieces from yarn A. Divide the pieces of fringe into 18 groups with 2 strands of A, 1 strand of B, and 1 strand of C in each group. Attach fringe every 2 inches along each short side of the stole. See "Making Fringe" later in this chapter for details about making and attaching fringe.

TIP

If you like, use scissors to give the ends of your fringe a trim.

Variation: Changing yarns

TIP

The sky's the limit in selecting yarns for your multiyarn stole. Choose any three yarns you like — or choose more than three. Just be sure to stick to the basic formula of going back to yarn A between the other yarns you've chosen. This formula gives your project the continuity it needs. The suggested yards create a monochromatic palette, but you can vary the look by going for greater contrast in color as well as texture. Even yarns that don't "go" together at first glance can create a pleasing result. Don't be afraid to experiment!

Making Fringe

Adding fringe to a piece of clothing can totally change its personality. Fringe can be long or short, widely or narrowly spaced, knotted, beaded, or plain. Fringe showcases particularly well yarns that vary in color, texture, or size, but any yarn adds movement and visual interest to a finished piece. Fringe also adds length to knitting projects that come up a little short. If you've run out of yarn, consider adding fringe in a contrasting color or texture.

You may typically think of fringe as being on the two short ends of a scarf, but you can also consider fringing two short sides and one long side of a stole for something more out of the ordinary. Or you might consider fringing the edges of a shawl or poncho, the cuff of a mitten, or the hem of a sweater.

To make fringe, begin by calculating how many pieces of fringe you want and how long you want the fringe to be. The lengths of yarn used to make fringe are doubled over, so use two strands of yarn to make four lengths of fringe in one spot. You can use just a couple of strands for each group and space them closer together or hold several strands together for tassel-like fringe and space them farther apart. You don't have to follow any rules — just experiment to your heart's content.

TIP

The fringe lengths need to be twice as long as you want your fringe to be, plus about an inch for the knot at the top. As you can imagine, fringe can use a lot of yarn. So, plan for it in the yarn-buying phase. A quick way to make uniform lengths of fringe is to wrap your yarn around an appropriately sized book, and then make a single cut along the spine of the book.

To attach your fringe:

1. **Stick your crochet hook through the edge of the work from the wrong side to the right side.**

2. Grab the center of the length of fringe with the hook, and then pull through a loop of yarn about 1 inch long.

3. Using your fingers or the crochet hook, pull the tails of the fringe through the loop and give them a gentle tug to secure them.

A Scarf of a Different Color

Crocheting this scarf is really fun, and it'll certainly brighten up your wardrobe. Not only are you changing colors with each row, but textures as well (see Figure 1-5). You work the scarf completely with single crochet stitches, but you'd never know to look at it. Sometimes it's okay to mix and match yarns, and this design is a great example.

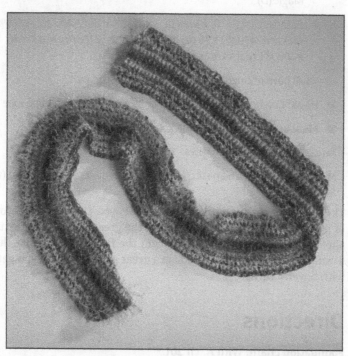

FIGURE 1-5:
By using the single crochet stitch in this scarf, you can focus on changing colors.

© John Wiley & Sons, Inc.

Materials and vital statistics

>> **Yarn:**

- Bernat "Matrix" railroad yarn (62% nylon/38% polyester), Article #166102 (1.75 oz. [50 g], 140 yds [128 m] each ball): 1 ball of #02430 Web Wines (A)

- Patons "Silverlash" eyelash yarn (98% polyester/2% lurex), Article #244081 (1.75 oz. [50 g], 164 yds [150 m] each skein): 1 skein of #81415 Rose Quartz (B)

- Patons "Lacette" fine-weight yarn (39% nylon/36% acrylic/25% mohair), Article #243030 (1.75 oz. [50 g], 235 yds [215 m] each skein): 1 skein of #30040 Touch of Black (C)

- Patons "Silverlash" eyelash yarn (98% polyester/2% lurex), Article #244081 (1.75 oz. [50 g], 164 yds [150 m] each skein): 1 skein of #81405 Maroon Magic (D).

- Patons "Lacette" fine-weight yarn (39% nylon/36% acrylic/25% mohair), Article #243030 (1.75 oz. [50 g], 235 yds [215 m] each skein): 1 skein of #30008 Cream Caress (E)

You'll have enough yarn to make several scarves.

>> **Hook:** Crochet hook size H-8 US or size needed to obtain gauge

>> **Measurements:** 3¼ in. wide x 45 in. long

>> **Gauge:** 8 sts = 2 in.; 6 rows = 1 in.

>> **Stitches used:** Chain stitch (ch), slip stitch (sl st), single crochet (sc)

The beauty of this design reveals itself as you complete each row. You'll get lots of practice changing yarn colors, and the great thing is the textures will hide any slip-ups if you don't get it quite right the first time. Because the scarf is worked in single crochet stitches, it's also a great project to help you get used to working with novelty yarns.

Directions

Foundation chain: With A, ch 201.

Row 1 (right side): Sc in 2nd ch from hook, sc in each ch across (200 sc), turn. Fasten off A, join B.

Row 2: With B, ch 1, sc in each sc across (200 sc), turn. Fasten off B, join C.

Row 3: With C, ch 1, sc in each sc across (200 sc), turn. Fasten off C, join B.

Row 4: With B, ch 1, sc in each sc across (200 sc), turn. Fasten off B, join A.

Row 5: With A, ch 1, sc in each sc across (200 sc), turn. Fasten off A, join D.

Row 6: With D, ch 1, sc in each sc across (200 sc), turn. Fasten off D, join E.

Row 7: With E, ch 1, sc in each sc across (200 sc), turn. Fasten off E, join D.

Row 8: With D, ch 1, sc in each sc across (200 sc), turn. Fasten off D, join A.

Row 9: With A, ch 1, sc in each sc across (200 sc), turn. Fasten off A, join C.

Row 10: With C, ch 1, sc in each sc across (200 sc), turn. Fasten off C, join A.

Row 11: With A, ch 1, sc in each sc across (200 sc), turn. Fasten off A, join D.

Row 12: With D, ch 1, sc in each sc across (200 sc), turn. Fasten off D, join E.

Row 13: With E, ch 1, sc in each sc across (200 sc), turn. Fasten off E, join D.

Row 14: With D, ch 1, sc in each sc across (200 sc), turn. Fasten off D, join A.

Row 15: With A, ch 1, sc in each sc across (200 sc), turn. Fasten off A, join B.

Row 16: With B, ch 1, sc in each sc across (200 sc), turn. Fasten off B, join C.

Row 17: With C, ch 1, sc in each sc across (200 sc), turn. Fasten off C, join B.

Row 18: With B, ch 1, sc in each sc across (200 sc), turn. Fasten off B, join A.

Row 19: With A, ch 1, sc in each sc across (200 sc), turn.

Row 20: Ch 1, sc in each sc across (200 sc). Fasten off.

The Most Basic Shawl Ever

Although this shawl is simple to knit, it's not ho-hum. With a dramatic ribbon yarn and large-gauged needles, this quick shawl has plenty of pizzazz, as shown in Figure 1-6. You can see a color photo of the shawl at dummies.com/go/knitcrochetAIO.

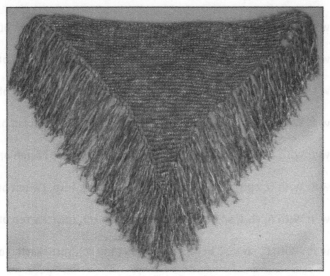

FIGURE 1-6:
A stunning
(and stunningly
simple) shawl.

© John Wiley & Sons, Inc.

Materials and vital statistics

» **Yarn:** Colinette Giotto (50% cotton, 40% rayon, 10% nylon); 151 yards
(140 meters) per 100 grams; 4 hanks; color: Lichen

» **Needles:** US 15 (10 mm) circular needle, 36-inch length or longer, or the size
needed to match gauge

» **Other materials:** Crochet hook to attach fringe; yarn needle to weave in ends

» **Size:** 60 inches wide by 40 inches long from tip to center of widest edge
(without fringe)

» **Gauge:** 10 stitches and 20 rows per 4 inches in garter stitch

To make this eye-catching wrap, you start with just 2 stitches. From there you
increase at the beginning of every row until your shawl is as large as you want it
to be. Long, dramatic fringe completes the wrap.

Directions

Cast on 2 sts.

Row 1 (RS): K1, yo, k1.

Row 2: K1, yo, k2.

Row 3: K1, yo, knit to end.

Repeat Row 3 until there are 150 sts (or more). Every 10 sts you add will increase the width by 4 inches.

Bind off loosely.

Finishing: Weave in any ends. Cut 2 20-inch lengths of yarn for each eyelet, and then use these pieces to make fringe. (See "Making Fringe" earlier in this chapter for details about fringe.)

Variation: Changing up your yarn

TIP

This basic shawl lends itself well to some variations and substitutions in yarns. For example:

>> Choose any ribbon or tape yarn and a very large needle size to achieve a lacy look. If you're substituting a thicker yarn, use US 17 or larger needles.

>> Consider knitting with one yarn and fringing with a second color or texture to vary the look of your shawl. Or you can leave the fringe off all together for a sleeker look.

Variation: Making a poncho

If you're more of a poncho person, make two shawls, each with a hypotenuse of about 45 inches (or about 115 stitches, if you're knitting at the same gauge given in the basic pattern). Lay the shawls out so they make a square, as shown in Figure 1-7. Now seam the two hypotenuses together from the points toward the center, leaving a 10-inch wide slit in the center for the neck opening. (To find out how to sew a seam, head to Book 7, Chapter 2.)

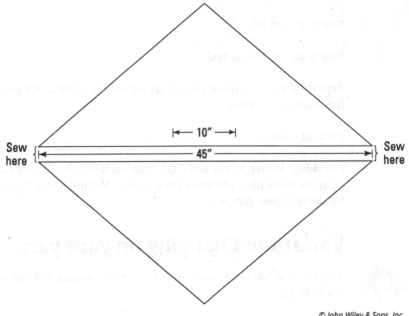

FIGURE 1-7:
Two smaller
triangular shawls
make a great
poncho.

Lacy Shawl

Even though this knitting project is called "lacy," don't be scared away. You simply work stockinette stitch and yarn overs on a needle large enough to let plenty of light shine through. Worked with two strands of a classic mohair blend held together, this lightweight shawl adds warmth and drama to any outfit. (See Figure 1-8 or the color photo at dummies.com/go/knitcrochetAIO.)

Loads of yarns now on the market shift from one color to the next on their own. But you also can create gradual color changes yourself — and control how they change. Changing colors highlights the chevron shape that you create when you knit this shawl.

TIP

With this project you use three different colors. So, using two strands of yarn at a time with three colors to choose from means that you can create five different colors — AA, AB, BB, BC, and CC. Choose wild, surprising combinations or colors within the same family. Whatever colors you choose, do think about value as well as hue. In other words, if you want a strong gradient, consider using a very light or very dark color to contrast with two medium-valued colors. (Check out Book 4, Chapter 1 for the basics of changing colors in a knitting pattern.)

FIGURE 1-8:
A lacy shawl is dramatic and flattering.

Materials and vital statistics

>> **Yarn:** Crystal Palace Yarns Kid Merino (28% kid mohair, 28% merino wool, 44% micro nylon); 240 yards (221 meters) per 25 grams

  - Color A: Charcoal; 2 balls

  - Color B: Misty Blue; 2 balls

  - Color C: Pacific Blue; 2 balls

>> **Needles:** US 13 (9 mm) circular needle, 24-inch length or longer, or the size needed to match gauge

>> **Other materials:** Yarn needle to weave in ends

>> **Size:** 34 inches from tip to center of widest edge by 68 inches wide (see the schematic in Figure 1-9)

>> **Gauge:** 10 stitches and 14 rows per 4 inches in stockinette stitch

The lacy shawl starts with just a few stitches at the nape of the neck and grows out in a triangle due to the placement of your increases. You bind off at the two short sides of the triangle. This construction technique means that it's easy to vary the size of your shawl by knitting more or fewer rows.

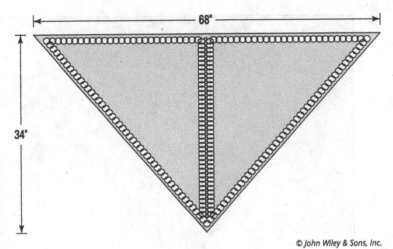

FIGURE 1-9:
Two triangles
worked together
to create an
easy-to-wear
shawl.

68"

34"

© John Wiley & Sons, Inc.

Directions

With 2 strands of color A held together as if they were 1, cast on 3 sts.

Row 1 (RS): K1, yo, k1, yo, k1. There are 5 sts.

Row 2 and all following WS rows: Purl.

Row 3 (RS): K1, yo, k1, yo, k1, yo, k1, yo, k1. There are 9 sts.

Row 5 (RS): K1, yo, k3, yo, k1, yo, k3, yo, k1. There are 13 sts.

Row 7 (RS): K1, yo, k5, yo, k1, yo, k5, yo, k1. There are 17 sts.

Row 9 (RS): K1, yo, k7, yo, k1, yo, k7, yo, k1. There are 21 sts.

Continue pattern as set, increasing 4 sts every RS row by making yarn overs at each edge and working 2 more sts between each edge and the central pair of yarn overs.

Continue until you've worked 28 rows with 2 strands of color A. There are 57 sts.

Switch to 1 strand of color A and 1 strand of color B held together as 1 yarn and work 24 rows of the pattern. There are 105 sts.

Switch to 2 strands of color B held together and work 20 rows of the pattern. There are 145 sts.

Switch to 1 strand of color B and 1 strand of color C held together and work 16 rows of the pattern. There are 177 sts.

Switch to 2 strands of color C held together and work 8 rows of the pattern, and then work the border as follows:

Next RS row: K1, yo, *k2tog, yo, repeat from * to center 3 sts, k1, yo, k1, yo, k1, **yo, k2tog, repeat from ** to last st, yo, k1. There are 197 sts.

Next row: Purl.

Bind off all sts loosely.

Finishing: Weave in ends. Block shawl by wetting it and laying it flat to dry. (Book 7, Chapter 1 explains how to block.)

Variation: Knitting through thick and thin

TIP

Because this shawl is a triangle right from the start and grows along its outer edges, it's a great shawl pattern to use with just about any yarn. You can use the suggested yarn in the original pattern held singly and use smaller needles for a very delicate shawl. Or, you can use a yarn that borders on ridiculously thick and get something interesting — just be sure that the needles you use are large enough to create a shawl that drapes beautifully and lets the light shine through. If you need help choosing the right needles for the job, head to Book 1, Chapter 1.

Geometric Wrap

If you look around at almost any clothing store, you're bound to see a design such as the one in this wrap (see Figure 1-10). Worked in the shape of a triangle, the V-stitch, which is comprised of two double crochet stitches joined by a chain stitch, creates an open and lacy pattern that makes this wrap ideal for when there's a touch of chill in the air. The yarn adds a slight shimmer and is available in several colors. If you don't want to wear it as a wrap, go for the modern look and wrap it around your waist (sideways, of course) as a great accent to a pair of jeans.

Materials and vital statistics

» **Size:** One size fits most adults

» **Yarn:** Aunt Lydia's "Shimmer Fashion" fine sport-weight yarn (64% cotton/36% rayon), Article #188 (2 oz. [57 g], 124 yds [113 m] each ball): 5 balls of #2242 Light Linen

» **Hook:** Crochet hook size I-9 US or size needed to obtain gauge

FIGURE 1-10:
You can wear the geometric wrap traditionally or wrapped around your waist.

© John Wiley & Sons, Inc.

» **Measurements:** 31½ in. from bottom point to top edge; 45 in. across top edge

» **Gauge:** 7 V-sts = 5 in.; 10 rows in pat = 5 in.

» **Stitches used:** Chain stitch (ch), double crochet (dc). V-stitch: (Dc, ch 1, dc) in same st or space. (For a quick reminder on how to create a V-stitch, refer to Book 4, Chapter 3.)

Because the V-stitch creates an open fabric, watch where you put your hook. Make sure to work your next row of stitches in the space created by the chain-one stitch of the V-stitch directly below it, and not between the V-stitches themselves (see Figure 1-11). The triangle shape of this pattern is created by starting with a single V-stitch, then increasing them as you go along. The increases take place across two rows, in this case Rows 4 and 5, until you reach the desired width.

Directions

Foundation chain: Ch 2 + 3 (first dc).

(See Figure 1-11 for a reduced sample of the stitch pattern.)

Row 1 (right side): Dc in 5th ch from hook (1 V-st), turn.

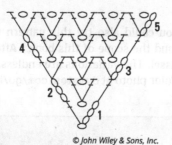

FIGURE 1-11:
Reduced sample
of stitch pattern.

© John Wiley & Sons, Inc.

Row 2: Ch 3 (first dc), V-st in next ch-1 space, dc in last dc (1 V-st and 2 dc), turn.

Row 3: Ch 3 (first dc), (ch 1, dc) in first dc, V-st in next ch-1 space, V-st in last dc (3 V-sts), turn.

Row 4: Ch 3 (first dc), V-st in each ch-1 space across, dc in last dc (3 V-sts and 2 dc), turn.

Row 5: Ch 3 (first dc), (ch 1, dc) in first dc, V-st in each ch-1 space across, V-st in last dc (5 V-sts), turn.

Rows 6–63: Rep Rows 4–5 (29 times) (63 V-sts at end of last row). Fasten off.

Fringe: Cut yarn into 130 9-in. lengths. Using 2 strands of yarn held together as one for each fringe, starting at the bottom point of wrap, single-knot one fringe in bottom point, then in every even-numbered row across sides of wrap. Trim ends even. (See "Making Fringe" earlier in this chapter for details about adding fringe.)

TIP

When cutting yarn for fringe, try to find something to wrap the yarn around that will produce the lengths you need. You might try a book, a sturdy piece of cardboard, a CD case, and so on.

Variation: Why knot add beads?

For a different twist, add some beads to the fringe. Just keep them small and light so they don't add too much weight.

Basic Beanies

A good hat is a must-have in your knitting repertoire, and this basic beanie, sized for babies through adults, fits the bill. Make it plain or cabled. Add in stripes or a color pattern. (Any of the 8-stitch mosaic patterns in Book 5, Chapter 4 can be used with this pattern, but remember to leave out the extra edge stitches because you're working in the round. You could also try this pattern with Fair Isle or intarsia knitting, which are beyond the scope of this book.) After your beanie is knit, top it with a pompom or tassel. The variations are endless. Check out some beanies in Figure 1-12 or in the color photo at dummies.com/go/knitcrochetAIO.

FIGURE 1-12: A basic beanie and its cabled cousin.

Materials and vital statistics

>> **Yarn:** Berrocco Smart Mohair (41% mohair, 54% acrylic, 5% polyester); 108 yards (100 meters) per 50 grams; 1 (1, 1, 2, 2) balls; color: Pink

>> **Needles:** US 10 (6 mm) circular needle, 16-inch length, or the size needed to match gauge; US 8 (5 mm) circular needle, 16-inch length; US 10 (6 mm) double-pointed needles

>> **Other materials:** Eight stitch markers; yarn needle to weave in ends

>> **Size:** Baby (toddler, child, small adult, large adult); circumference: 14 (16, 18, 20, 22) inches, unstretched

>> **Gauge:** 16 stitches and 20 rows per 4 inches in stockinette stitch on larger needles

This beanie is worked in the round, starting on circular needles and switching to double-pointed needles when you shape the crown of the hat. If you want to include any color patterning, add it to the body of the hat between the ribbing and the decreases. If you'd like to knit cables on your hat, see the variation at the end of the pattern.

Directions

Cast on 56 (64, 72, 80, 88) sts with the smaller circular needles. Place marker and join in the round, being careful not to twist.

Round 1: *K2, p2, repeat from * to end of round.

Repeat this round for ¾ (1, 1, 1½, 2) inches.

Switch to larger circular needles and begin knitting in stockinette stitch (knit all rounds).

When your hat measures 4½ (5, 5½, 6½, 7) inches, begin the crown shaping as follows:

Next round: *K7 (8, 9, 10, 11), place marker, repeat from * to end.

Next round (Decrease Round): *K2tog, knit to marker, slip marker, repeat from * to end. 8 sts have been decreased.

Next round: Knit.

Repeat these 2 rounds until 8 sts remain, switching to double-pointed needles when you have too few sts to fit comfortably on your circular needle.

Cut yarn, leaving a 12-inch tail.

Finishing: Thread the tail of the yarn onto the yarn needle. Slip the stitches from the knitting needle to the yarn needle, making sure that you go through each stitch. Pull the yarn firmly to tighten the top of the hat, and then run the yarn through the stitches again before weaving in the yarn end on the inside to secure. Weave in any remaining ends.

TIP

If you want, you can top your beanie with a pompom, knitted flower, or other adornment for extra flair.

Variation: Creating a cabled beanie

This cabled hat features straightforward six-stitch cables (see Book 4, Chapter 2). It is made with the same yarn and needles as the basic beanie, fits a toddler (child, small adult, large adult), and measures 16 (17½, 19, 22) inches around. You need six stitch markers to help keep your decreases lined up.

Using the smaller circular needles, cast on 66 (72, 78, 90) sts. Place a marker and join in the round, being careful not to twist.

Ribbing round: *K1, p1, repeat from * to end.

Repeat this round for 1 (1, 2, 2) inches.

Switch to the larger circular needles and begin the six-stitch right cable pattern as follows, placing markers on the first round as indicated:

Rounds 1, 2, 3, 4, and 5: *K6, p5 (6, 7, 9), place marker, repeat from * to end of round.

Round 6: *Slip 3 sts to the cable needle and hold to back, k3, k3 from cable needle, p5 (6, 7, 9), repeat from * to end of round.

Repeat these 6 rounds until the hat measures 5½ (6, 6½, 7) inches, and then begin decreasing as follows:

Continue the cable pattern as set on the columns of 6 knit sts. In other words, you should cable every 6th round (even though the decreasing is occurring too).

Next round: *K6, p2tog, purl to marker, repeat from * to end of round.

TIP

If you're unfamiliar with purling 2 stitches together (p2tog), here's how to do it: Insert the right needle into the next 2 stitches purlwise, wrap the yarn around the right-hand needle, and then purl them to decrease 1 stitch.

Next round: Work even, knitting and purling the sts as they appear.

Repeat the previous 2 rounds 3 (4, 5, 7) more times. There are 42 sts on the needles.

Stop the cable pattern and finish the hat in stockinette stitch (knit all rounds).

Next round: *K5, k2tog, repeat from * to end of round. 36 sts remain.

Next round: Knit.

Next round: *K4, k2tog, repeat from * to end of round. 30 sts remain.

Next round: Knit.

Next round: *K3, k2tog, repeat from * to end of round. 24 sts remain.

Next round: Knit.

Next round: *K2, k2tog, repeat from * to end of round. 18 sts remain.

Next round: *K1, k2tog, repeat from * to end of round. 12 sts remain.

Next round: *K2tog, repeat from * to end of round. 6 sts remain.

Cut the yarn leaving a 12-inch tail.

Finishing: Use the same technique described in the basic pattern to finish your cabled beanie.

Red Velvet Crusher Hat

This crocheted hat will make you stand out in a crowd! The resulting fabric resembles crushed red velvet and is just as soft to the touch. You can see the classic result in Figure 1-13 or in the color photo at dummies.com/go/knitcrochetAIO.

FIGURE 1-13:
You can toss this crusher hat in a bag when you're not wearing it, and it will retain its shape when you put it back on.

© John Wiley & Sons, Inc.

With hats featured so prominently these days, this pattern is a must. You use basic stitches and techniques and get ample opportunity to practice working in the round, but the results will make you look like an expert. If red isn't your color, go ahead and choose another color, but by all means, grab your hook and yarn and work up a fabulous fashion accessory.

Materials and vital statistics

- ≫ **Size:** One size fits most adults
- ≫ **Yarn:** Caron "Jewel Box" medium-weight yarn (64% acrylic/20% rayon/16% polyester), Article #JB1000 (2.5 oz. [70g], 100 yds [91 m] each skein): 2 skeins of #0020 Ruby
- ≫ **Hook:** Crochet hook size H-8 US or size needed to obtain gauge
- ≫ **Stitch markers**
- ≫ **Measurement:** 22 in. in circumference
- ≫ **Gauge:** First 4 rnds = 2 in. in diameter
- ≫ **Stitches used:** Chain stitch (ch), slip stitch (sl st), single crochet (sc)

When making the transition from the crown of the hat to the sides, then again from the sides to the brim, you work your stitches into the back loops and front loops of the stitches, respectively. Remember, the back loops are the ones farthest from you, and the front loops are the ones closest to you.

Directions

Foundation chain: Ch 4 and close into ring with sl st in first ch.

Rnd 1: Ch 1, work 6 sc in ring, do not join. Continue to work in a spiral, marking beginning of each rnd and moving marker up as work progresses.

Rnd 2: Work 2 sc in each sc around (12 sc).

Rnd 3: · Sc in next sc, 2 sc in next sc ·, rep from · to · around (18 sc).

Rnd 4: · Sc in each of next 2 sc, 2 sc in next sc ·, rep from · to · around (24 sc).

Rnd 5: · Sc in each of next 3 sc, 2 sc in next sc ·, rep from · to · around (30 sc).

Rnd 6: · Sc in each of next 4 sc, 2 sc in next sc ·, rep from · to · around (36 sc).

Rnd 7: · Sc in each of next 5 sc, 2 sc in next sc ·, rep from · to · around (42 sc).

Rnd 8: · Sc in each of next 6 sc, 2 sc in next sc ·, rep from · to · around (48 sc).

Rnd 9: · Sc in each of next 7 sc, 2 sc in next sc ·, rep from · to · around (54 sc).

Rnd 10: · Sc in each of next 8 sc, 2 sc in next sc ·, rep from · to · around (60 sc).

Rnd 11: · Sc in each of next 9 sc, 2 sc in next sc ·, rep from · to · around (66 sc).

Rnd 12: Sc in each sc around (66 sc), sl st in first sc to join.

Rnd 13: Ch 1, working in back loops of sts, sc in each sc around (66 sc), do not join. Continue to work in a spiral as before.

Rnds 14–25: Sc in each sc around (66 sc).

Rnd 26: Working in front loops of sts, · sc in each of next 10 sc, 2 sc in next sc ·, rep from · to · around (72 sc).

Rnd 27: Working in both loops of sts, · sc in each of next 11 sc, 2 sc in next sc ·, rep from · to · around (78 sc).

Rnd 28: · Sc in each of next 12 sc, 2 sc in next sc ·, rep from · to · around (84 sc).

Rnd 29: · Sc in each of next 13 sc, 2 sc in next sc ·, rep from · to · around (90 sc).

Rnd 30: · Sc in each of next 14 sc, 2 sc in next sc ·, rep from · to · around (96 sc).

Rnd 31: · Sc in each of next 15 sc, 2 sc in next sc ·, rep from · to · around (102 sc).

Rnd 32: · Sc in each of next 16 sc, 2 sc in next sc ·, rep from · to · around (108 sc).

Rnd 33: · Sc in each of next 17 sc, 2 sc in next sc ·, rep from · to · around (114 sc).

Rnd 34: · Sc in each of next 18 sc, 2 sc in next sc ·, rep from · to · around (120 sc), sl st in first sc to join. Fasten off.

Chapter **2**

Home Decor

K nitting and crocheted items help your home feel cozy and give it a personal touch. When you make blankets, pillows, and baskets yourself, you can also ensure the yarn or other material you use works well with the decor you already have. In this chapter, you find projects for warm afghans, pillows and pillow accents, and a basket you can use to hold whatever you need.

Wooly Warmer Afghan

You can use this crocheted afghan on those really cold nights when you want to curl up with a soft, warm blanket and forget about the outside temperature. See the final result in Figure 2-1 or in the color photo at dummies.com/go/knitcrochetAIO.

The pattern uses most of the basic stitches and is worked vertically, or lengthwise, rather than in the traditional side-to-side manner. The yarn is a super-bulky-weight wool blend, which allows you to work it up faster than you could using a worsted-weight yarn. (See Book 1, Chapter 2 for more on yarns.) Throw this afghan over the back of the sofa, or fold it at the foot of your bed, ready to provide an extra layer of warmth.

FIGURE 2-1:
The wooly
warmer afghan
will protect
you from
winter's chill.

Materials and vital statistics

>> **Yarn:** Lion Brand Yarn "Wool-Ease Thick & Quick" super-bulky-weight yarn (80% acrylic/20% wool), Article #640 (6 oz. [170 g], 106 yds [97 m] each skein): 13 skeins of #143 Claret

>> **Hook:** Crochet hook size M-13 US or size needed to obtain gauge (refer to Book 1, Chapter 3 for more information on gauge)

>> **Measurements:** 50½ in. wide x 76 in. long

>> **Gauge:** 6 sts = 4 in.; 5 rows in pat = 4 in.

>> **Stitches used:** Chain stitch (ch), single crochet (sc), half double crochet (hdc), double crochet (dc), triple crochet (tr)

Because this afghan is worked in long rows, it's a great project to work on when you can sit down in a comfortable chair or on the sofa. After you get a few rows finished, you'll find that the afghan gets somewhat awkward to shift around, and the arms of the chair or seat cushions of the sofa make a great support tool. You'll also need to add new skeins of yarn regularly, so refer to Book 3, Chapter 2 for detailed instructions.

Directions

TIP

The bulky nature of this yarn requires the use of a larger hook, so you may find that you have to adjust your hold on the hook. Keep your hands and stitches loose, and the afghan will be finished in no time.

Foundation chain: Ch 124 + 2 (first hdc).

Row 1: Hdc in 3rd ch from hook, hdc in each ch across (125 hdc), turn.

Row 2: Ch 1, sc in first hdc, · tr in next hdc, sc in next hdc ·, rep from · to · across to within last 2 hdc, tr in next hdc, sc in turning ch (125 sts), turn.

Row 3: Ch 2 (first hdc), hdc in each st across (125 hdc), turn.

Row 4: Ch 3 (first dc), dc in each hdc across, dc in turning ch (125 dc), turn.

Row 5: Ch 2 (first hdc), hdc in each dc across, hdc in turning ch (125 hdc), turn.

Rows 6–57: Rep Rows 2–5 (13 times).

Rows 58–59: Rep Rows 2–3. Fasten off.

Variation: Supersize it!

To make the afghan bigger, add stitches to your foundation chain until you reach the desired length. Just make sure you end with an odd number of stitches so the pattern in Row 2 works. Adjust the width by repeating Rows 2–5 as many times as you want and be sure to buy extra skeins of yarn.

Variation: Trying a different yarn

This company also makes a super-bulky-weight chenille yarn that would work well with this pattern. You can use the same size hook suggested in the original pattern.

Wavy Chevron Throw

Sometimes, there's nothing like having a soft, warm blanket to throw over your legs or wrap around your shoulders to keep the chill out (see Figure 2-2 or the color photo at dummies.com/go/knitcrochetAIO). The crocheted chevron pattern (a fancy way to describe the repeated V shape) features shells at the peaks and clusters at the valleys.

This crochet pattern probably falls into the intermediate skill-level category because of the stitch combination involved in creating the pattern. The pattern is commonly used, and it's a great way for you to become familiar with a design that you'll see repeatedly throughout your crochet experience.

The yarn used here is a wonderfully soft acrylic, which stands up to daily use and repeated washings. You should be able to find the yarn in most craft stores, and it comes in a multitude of colors if you decide on a different color palette.

FIGURE 2-2:
Complementary colors draw attention to the chevron design of this afghan.

© *John Wiley & Sons, Inc.*

Materials and vital statistics

>> **Yarn:** Lion Brand Yarn "Homespun" bulky-weight yarn, (98% acrylic/2% polyester), Article #790 (6 oz. [170 g], 185 yds [169 m] each skein):

- 5 skeins of #347 Mediterranean (A)

- 3 skeins of #318 Sierra (B)

- 3 skeins of #326 Ranch (C)

>> **Hook:** Crochet hook size K-10½ US or size needed to obtain gauge

>> **Measurements:** 36 in. wide x 58 in. long, excluding tassels

>> **Gauge:** 11 sts in pat = 4 in.; 6 rows in pat = 4 in.

>> **Stitches used:** Chain stitch (ch), double crochet (dc). Shell: • 3 dc in same stitch •. Cluster: • 3 dc (half closed and joined tog) worked across 3 consecutive stitches •. (See Book 4, Chapter 3, for detailed instructions on shells and clusters.)

The stitch pattern used to make this throw is a simple chevron pattern, comprised of shell stitches and clusters. The shells are made with three double crochet stitches worked into one stitch, and the clusters are three double crochet stitches, half-closed and joined together, worked across three separate stitches (see Figure 2-3). The shells form the peaks, while the clusters draw the fabric together to form the valleys of the pattern.

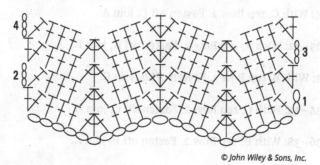

FIGURE 2-3: Reduced sample of stitch pattern.

© John Wiley & Sons, Inc.

Directions

Foundation chain: With A, chain 101 + 2 (first dc).

TIP

Normally, the first dc in a row is made by working 3 chain stitches, not 2. However, for the foundation row in this pattern, a chain of only 2 stitches is used. The rest of the pattern uses a turning ch of 3 for the first dc in a row.

Row 1 (right side): Dc in 3rd ch from hook, • dc in each of next 3 ch, work one cluster of 3 dc across next 3 ch, dc in each of next 3 ch, shell in next ch •, rep from • to • across to within last ch, 2 dc in last ch (102 sts), turn.

Row 2: Ch 3 (first dc), dc in first dc, • dc in each of next 3 dc, work one cluster of 3 dc across next 3 sts (the center dc of the cluster will be worked in the top of the cluster in the row below), dc in each of next 3 dc, shell in next dc (the shell will be worked in the center dc of the shell from the row below) ·, rep from · to · across to within last dc, 2 dc in last dc (102 sts), turn.

Rows 3–7: Rep Row 2. Fasten off A, join B.

Rows 8–10: With B, rep Row 2. Fasten off B, join C.

Rows 11–12: With C, rep Row 2. Fasten off C, join B.

Row 13: With B, rep Row 2. Fasten off B, join A.

Rows 14–21: With A, rep Row 2. Fasten off A, join C.

Row 22: With C, rep Row 2. Fasten off C, join B.

Row 23: With B, rep Row 2. Fasten off B, join C.

Row 24: With C, rep Row 2. Fasten off C, join A.

Rows 25–32: With A, rep Row 2. Fasten off A, join B.

Row 33: With B, rep Row 2. Fasten off B, join C.

Rows 34–35: With C, rep Row 2. Fasten off C, join B.

Rows 36–38: With B, rep Row 2. Fasten off B, join A.

Rows 39–46: With A, rep Row 2. Fasten off A, join B.

Rows 47–78: Rep Rows 8–38. Fasten off B, join A.

Rows 79–85: With A, rep Row 2. Fasten off.

Adding tassels: To make a tassel, cut two 8-inch lengths of colors A, B, and C. Holding all lengths together as one, fold in half. Cut two more 6-inch lengths of color A. Using one 6-inch length of yarn, tie the bundle securely together through the center fold, leaving equal lengths on each side. With the bundle folded in half, wrap the second length of yarn several times around the folded bundle approximately ¾ in. below folded end. Tie tightly to secure. Make 20 tassels.

To attach the tassels, use the ends of yarn from the first tie at the center top of the tassel to tie one tassel to each point across each short edge of throw.

Variation: Highlight the stitches, not the colors

This stitch pattern also looks great worked in a solid color. The yarn used comes in a multitude of shades, so choose your own solid or color combination.

Throw Pillows

Use this knitting pattern to create some great throw pillows for your sofa or bed (check some out in Figure 2-4 or in the color photo at dummies.com/go/knitcrochetAIO). A couple of new pillows can really liven up your decor, and the knitting will give you a chance to hone some new skills. The basic pattern creates a simply textured pillow in a single color; the later variations give you two different options for slip-stitch color patterns.

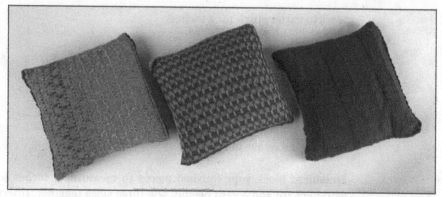

FIGURE 2-4:
Spruce up your living space with throw pillows.

© John Wiley & Sons, Inc.

Materials and vital statistics

>> **Yarn:** Berrocco Ultra Alpaca (50% alpaca, 50% wool); 215 yards (198 meters) per 100 grams; 2 skeins; color: 6282 Cranberry

>> **Needles:** US 7 (4.5 mm) needles, or the size needed to match gauge

>> **Other materials:** Yarn needle; 14-inch pillow form

>> **Size:** 14 inches square

>> **Gauge:** 20 stitches and 26 rows per 4 inches in stockinette stitch

This throw pillow is worked in two pieces and then stitched up. If you want more pillows with less knitting, use cloth for the backs of your pillows. Cut the fabric into a 15½-inch square, and then hem the edges so that the backing measures 14 inches square. Then you can attach the fabric to your knitted piece with a needle and thread.

Directions

Make 2 pieces the same. To make the simplest pillow, make the back piece exactly the same way as you made the front. But, if you want to vary the sides, follow one of the later variations.

Cast on 70 sts and work 1 inch in stockinette stitch (knit RS rows, purl WS rows).

Work in garter stitch (knit all rows) for 2 inches.

Work in stockinette stitch for 3 inches.

Work in garter stitch for 2 inches.

Work in stockinette stitch for 3 inches.

Work in garter stitch for 2 inches.

Work in stockinette stitch for 1 inch.

Bind off and weave in ends.

Finishing: Block your finished pieces to measure 14 inches square. Using the working yarn and a yarn needle, sew three sides together. Insert the pillow form and sew the last side closed. You can find details on blocking and sewing seams in Book 7.

Variation: Retro check pillow

Lots of knitting abbreviations look funny, and wyif and wyib (featured in this variation and the next) are right near the top of the list! Here's what they mean:

>> *Wyif* stands for "with yarn in front." What this phrase means is that you need to bring the yarn to the front (or into the purl position) before you perform the next step. If your yarn is already in front, don't do anything; just carry on with the next instruction.

>> *Wyib* stands for "with yarn in back." This phrase means that you need to bring the yarn to the back of the work (or into the knit position) before you perform the next step. If your yarn is already in back, you don't have to move it.

REMEMBER

When you change your yarn's position to the front or back, remember to bring it between and under the needles and not up over the needle. (Book 2, Chapter 1 introduces how to turn your knitting.)

Usually wyif and wyib accompany slipped stitches (find the basics of slipping knitting stitches in Book 2, Chapter 3). The position of the yarn, at the front or the back of the work, dictates where the horizontal float will be. You create floats when dragging the yarn over an unworked stitch. If the float is in the front on the right side, or in the back on the wrong side, it shows and becomes part of the decoration. Check out wyif and wyib stitches in Figure 2-5.

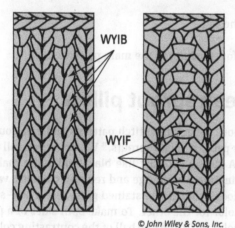

FIGURE 2-5:
Stitches made with yarn in back and with yarn in front.

© John Wiley & Sons, Inc.

TIP

For the retro check pillow, you need two colors of yarn. Choose two colors with high contrast such as orange and avocado green for a retro look. Or choose two shades of the same color if you're looking for a more subtle pattern. For each side of the pillow, you need one skein of each color.

Because you're alternating colors every 4 rows, you don't need to cut the yarn each time you switch colors. Just carry the unused color loosely up the side.

Cast on 71 sts with the first color.

Purl 1 row.

Row 1 (RS): With the second color, k3, *slip 1 st wyib, k3, repeat from * to end.

Row 2 (WS): With the second color, p3, *slip 1 st wyif, p3, repeat from * to end.

Row 3 (RS): With the second color, repeat Row 1.

Row 4 (WS): With the second color, purl.

Row 5 (RS): With the first color, k3, *slip 1 st wyib, k3, repeat from * to end.

Row 6 (WS): With the first color, p3, *slip 1 stitch wyif, p3, repeat from * to end.

Row 7 (RS): With the first color, repeat Row 5.

Row 8 (WS): With the first color, purl.

Repeat these 8 rows 11 more times or until piece measures 14 inches.

Bind off and weave in ends.

Make a second piece the same.

Follow the directions for finishing in the main pattern.

Variation: Bean sprout pillow

Barbara Walker, a famous collector of stitch patterns and a profoundly influential knitter, calls this color pattern "bean sprouts." Whatever you call it, it's a fun slip stitch pattern to try. A strong contrast like black and white makes this pattern stand out, but a combination like orange and red also creates a wonderful result. Or, for an effect that looks almost like stained glass, use a self-striping yarn for one yarn and a plain color for the other. To make both sides of a pillow, you need two balls of the main color (MC) and one ball of the contrasting color (CC). You can see a color photo of the pillow at dummies.com/go/knitcrochetAIO.

TIP

In this pattern, you work 6 rows in the main color between the rows you work in the contrasting color. You can carry the contrasting yarn up the side, twisting it with the main color at the beginning of each odd-numbered row. But take care not to pull it too tight, because if you do, that side of the pillow will pucker. If you prefer, cut the contrasting color each time and weave in the ends when you're finished. You don't need to cut the main color yarn because the contrasting color is only worked for 2 rows. (You can find more information about changing colors while knitting in Book 4, Chapter 1.)

Cast on 71 sts with MC.

Row 1 (RS): With MC, knit.

Row 2 (WS): With MC, purl.

Row 3 (RS): With CC, k2, *slip 1 st wyib, k1, repeat from * to last st, k1.

Row 4 (WS): With CC, k1, *k1, slip 1 st wyif, repeat from * to last 2 sts, k2.

Note that this WS row (Row 4) is knit rather than purled.

WARNING

Rows 5 and 7 (RS): Using MC, k5, *slip 1 st wyib, k5, repeat from * to end.

Rows 6 and 8 (WS): Using MC, p5, *slip 1 st wyif, p5, repeat from * to end.

Rows 9 and 10: Repeat Rows 1 and 2.

Row 11 (RS): With CC, k1, *slip 1 st wyib, k1, repeat from * to end.

Row 12 (WS): With CC, k1, *slip 1 st wyif, k1, repeat from * to end.

Again, this WS row (Row 12) is knit rather than purled.

WARNING

Rows 13 and 15 (RS): With MC, k2, *slip 1 st wyib, k5, repeat from * to last 3 sts, slip 1 st wyib, k2.

Rows 14 and 16 (WS): With MC, p2, *slip 1 st wyib, k5, repeat from * to last 3 sts, slip 1 st wyib, k2.

Repeat these 16 rows until the pillow measures approximately 14 inches. End with Row 2 or Row 10 of the pattern repeat. Bind off and weave in ends. Make a second piece the same, and then follow the directions for finishing in the earlier pattern.

Shells and Lace Pillowcase Edging

The design of this crocheted pillowcase edging (see Figure 2-6 or the color photo at dummies.com/go/knitcrochetAIO) was popular years ago, especially when women were still putting together hope chests for their daughters. A beautifully made bed is something that has never gone out of style, though, and the pillowcase edging here allows you to create a look that you won't see in any store.

When you decide to add edging to something, you can choose from literally hundreds of different edging designs. This one incorporates a variation of the shell stitch and works up into a narrow band that you sew across the front of the pillow. Make it in the beige color suggested here or go for a brighter look to add some pizzazz. This project is good for an intermediate-level crocheter, mainly because you use crochet thread, which is much finer and can be harder to work with. Don't let that put you off, though. Thread crochet makes some really beautiful designs.

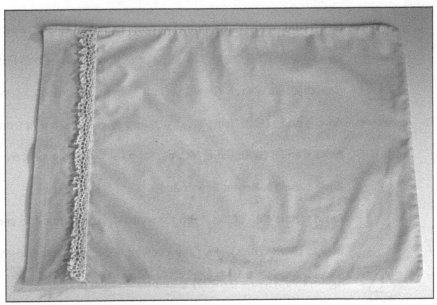

FIGURE 2-6:
Dress up your
pillows with this
elegant edging.

Materials and vital statistics

» **Yarn:** DMC "Cebelia" size 10 crochet thread (100% double mercerized cotton), Article #167G (1.75 oz. [50 g], 284 yds [260 m] each ball): 1 ball of #712 ecru makes several edgings

» **Hook:** Steel crochet hook size 4 US or size needed to obtain gauge

» **Sewing needle and matching sewing thread**

» **Measurements:** 1½ in. wide x 19½ in. long

» **Gauge:** 3 pat repeats = 4 in.

» **Stitches used:** Chain stitch (ch), slip stitch (sl st), single crochet (sc), double crochet (dc). Shell: • 5 dc in same st •. Cluster: • 2 dc (half closed and joined together) worked across 2 designated sts •. Picot: • Ch 6, sl st in 3rd ch from hook •. (For refreshers on the shell, cluster, and picot stitches, turn to Book 4, Chapter 3.)

This is a great pattern to crochet for someone who's relatively new to thread crochet. It's not too complicated, yet the results look like you've been crocheting for years. The design is actually an expanded shell pattern (see Figure 2-7), one that you'll likely see if you do any amount of thread crochet. You may find that the edges curl a bit as you work, but once you're finished, wet the edging, shape it, lay it flat to dry, and it'll be just fine.

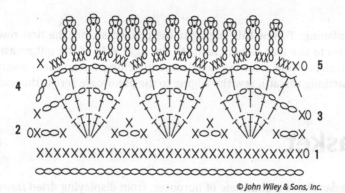

FIGURE 2-7:
Reduced sample
of edging stitch
diagram.

© John Wiley & Sons, Inc.

Directions

TIP

The length of this edging is long enough to cover the edge of one side of a standard pillowcase. If you'd like to make your edging go all the way around the pillow, or if you want to make a matching edging for your sheets, make a foundation chain that is long enough for your needs and is a multiple of 9 sts + 5 to accommodate the pattern.

Foundation chain: Ch 122.

Row 1: Sc in 2nd ch from hook, sc in each ch across (121 sc), turn.

Row 2: Ch 1, sc in first sc, ch 2, skip next 2 sc, sc in next sc, · skip next 2 sc, shell in next sc, skip next 2 sc, sc in next sc, ch 2, skip next 2 sc, sc in next sc ·, rep from · to · across (13 shells made), turn.

Row 3: Ch 1, sc in first sc, ch 2, · dc in first dc of next shell, (ch 1, dc in next dc) 4 times, sc in next ch-2 space ·, rep from · to · across to within last shell, dc in first dc of last shell, (ch 1, dc in next dc) 4 times, ch 2, skip next ch-2 space, sc in last sc, turn.

Row 4: Ch 3 (first dc), skip next ch-2 space, (dc in next dc, ch 2) 4 times, · work one cluster of 2 dc across next 2 dc, with first dc of cluster in next dc, skip next sc, and second dc of cluster in next dc, ch 2, (dc in next dc, ch 2) 3 times ·, rep from · to · across to within last dc, work one cluster of 2 dc across next 2 sts, with first dc of cluster in next dc, skip next ch-2 space, and second dc of cluster in last sc, turn.

Row 5: Ch 1, sc in top of first cluster, 3 sc in first ch-2 space, · ch 6, sl st in 3rd ch from hook (picot made), ch 4, 3 sc in next ch-2 space ·, rep from · to · across to within last 2 dc, skip next dc, sc in last dc. Fasten off.

Finishing: To sew this edging to the pillowcase, pin the first row of the edging, close to the foundation chain, to the right side of the pillowcase in the desired location. Using a sewing needle and matching thread (or a sewing machine and matching thread), sew the edging to the pillowcase across the entire front edge.

Hemp Basket

Baskets have a multitude of purposes, from displaying dried flowers in the living room to holding pretty soaps in the bathroom. Large or small, square or round, they're one of the most useful items to have around the house. Now you can create your own baskets. This project uses hemp cord instead of yarn (see Figure 2-8 or the color photo at `dummies.com/go/knitcrochetAIO`), and one ball will make enough baskets so you can have several to place around the house or share with friends. It also proves that you don't always have to crochet with yarn. Almost any flexible material will work. Just use your imagination!

FIGURE 2-8: After you see how handy this basket is, you'll want to shout, "Hemp, hemp, hooray!"

© John Wiley & Sons, Inc.

Materials and vital statistics

- » **Yarn:** Hemp jewelry cord (worsted weight) (73 yds [67 m] each ball): 1 ball
- » **Hook:** Crochet hook size J-10 US or size needed to obtain gauge
- » **Stitch marker**
- » **Measurements:** 5½ in. in diameter across top x 2½ in. tall
- » **Gauge:** First 4 rnds of base = 2¾ in. in diameter
- » **Stitches used:** Chain stitch (ch), slip stitch (sl st), single crochet (sc)

The pattern for this basket is typical of any round item you may come across, such as hats. The difference is in the material. Hemp cord is a little stiffer than yarn, so you may have to work a little harder to create each stitch.

Building the base

Center ring: Ch 4 and close into a ring with one sl st in first ch.

Rnd 1: Ch 1, work 4 sc in ring (4 sc), sl st in first sc to join.

Rnd 2: Ch 1, 2 sc in each sc around (8 sc), sl st in first sc to join.

Rnd 3: Ch 1, 2 sc in each sc around (16 sc), sl st in first sc to join.

Rnd 4: Ch 1, sc in each of first 3 sc, 2 sc in next sc, · sc in each of next 3 sc, 2 sc in next sc ·, rep from · to · around (20 sc), sl st in first sc to join.

Working your way up the sides

Rnd 1: Ch 1, working in blps of sts only, sc in each sc around (20 sc), do not join. Continue working in a spiral, marking beg of each rnd and moving marker up as work progresses.

Rnd 2: Working in both loops of sts, · sc in each of next 4 sc, 2 sc in next sc ·, rep from · to · around (24 sc).

Rnd 3: Sc in each sc around (24 sc).

Rnd 4: · Sc in each of next 5 sc, 2 sc in next sc ·, rep from · to · around (28 sc).

Rnd 5: Sc in each sc around (28 sc), sl st in first sc to join. Fasten off.

Variation: Making the basket just the right size

You can make bigger or smaller baskets. Increase or decrease the size of your base, then the sides accordingly. If you want to make a taller basket, keep going up, up, and around until the basket is the height you want.

Variation: Using different sizes of hemp cord

Hemp cord comes in different sizes. You can use a finer-weight cord and smaller hook, or a heavier-weight cord and a larger hook.

If you use a finer-weight cord, your basket will be smaller in size. You can compensate for this by making the base larger, then the sides taller to arrive at the same dimensions as above.

If you use a heavier-weight cord, the basket will be larger. If that's what you're looking for, then that's just fine. But if you want to keep it the same size, decrease the size of your base, and work the sides until they reach the desired height.

Chapter **3**

Baby and Kid Projects

This chapter is all about projects for young people — and even the young at heart. Handmade knitted or crocheted items are a special way to welcome a new baby. And as those babies grow, they'll love lighthearted storybook hats made just for them.

Retro Slippers for Baby

This retro slipper (see Figure 3-1 or the color photo at dummies.com/go/ knitcrochetAIO) is hardly more than a swatch. Still, if you grew up around knitters, chances are they'll fill you with nostalgia. Just because these slippers are labeled as "nostalgic" and "retro," however, doesn't mean that they aren't cute! You can adorn them with old-school pompoms, bows, or buttons that match the ones you use on the one-piece baby sweater later in this chapter for an oh-so-cute matching ensemble.

Materials and vital statistics

» **Yarn:** Cascade 220 Superwash (100% superwash wool); 220 yards (203 meters) per 100 grams; 1 skein; color: 860 Gray Heather

» **Needles:** US 7 (4.5 mm), or the size needed to match gauge

FIGURE 3-1:
Try these easy slippers for baby — and the whole family!

>> **Other materials:** Yarn needle

>> **Size:** Newborn (6–12 months, 1–2 years), 4 (5, 6) inches square

>> **Gauge:** 18 stitches and 36 rows per 4 inches in garter stitch

These slippers are a cinch to make. They're quick to knit and a great way to use leftover yarn. Essentially, all you have to do is knit your rectangle and then sew it up. After making some for baby, why not try making some for yourself? See the variations that follow.

Directions

Make 2 slippers with the following pattern:

Cast on 18 (22, 26) sts.

Work in garter stitch (knit all rows) for 3 (3½, 4) inches.

Switch to rib as follows:

Row 1 (RS): K2, *p2, k2, repeat from * to end of row.

Row 2 (WS): P2, *k2, p2, repeat from * to end of row.

When slipper measures 4 (5, 6) inches, stop knitting, but don't bind off.

Finishing: Cut the yarn, leaving a 12-inch tail.

Thread the end of the tail through the yarn needle, and then pass the yarn through all the stitches on the needle. Pull snugly to gather the stitches, and then draw the yarn through the stitches again to secure. This creates the toe.

Without breaking the yarn, use mattress stitch (Book 7, Chapter 2) to sew the edge of the slipper from the end of the toe about halfway up the edge of the work to form the top of the slipper.

Cut the yarn and weave in the end.

Fold the cast on edge of the slipper in half and sew together to form the back of the slipper, as shown in Figure 3-2.

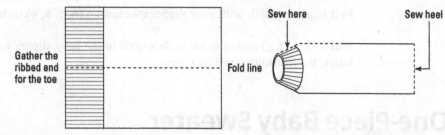

FIGURE 3-2:
Folding and sewing your slippers.

Gather the ribbed end for the toe — Sew here — Fold line — Sew heel

© John Wiley & Sons, Inc.

Variation: Using different yarns

You can knit these slippers with any sturdy yarn. But if you're knitting for someone other than a baby (whose feet will never touch the ground), look for a washable yarn. For babies learning to walk, use caution: Slippers can be slippery!

TIP

Yarn labels give an estimated gauge in stockinette stitch, but you're knitting these slippers in garter stitch. The perfectionists will swatch. But if you're making baby slippers, you're more or less making a swatch anyway. So just go for it. A typical worsted-weight yarn that knits at 20 stitches per 4 inches in stockinette stitch gives you the garter stitch gauge that you're after.

Variation: Sizing up

Sure these slippers are cute on baby feet, but you can easily scale them up to fit anyone. Use Table 3-1 to find the correct cast on number.

TIP

You're better off making the slippers a little smaller if you're in doubt of the proper size — they'll stretch, and you don't want them to slip off.

TABLE 3-1

Cast On Chart for Adult Retro Slippers

Size	Cast on	Foot Length
4–6 years	30 stitches	7 inches
6–10 years	34 stitches	8 inches
Small adult	38 stitches	9 inches
Medium adult	42 stitches	10 inches
Large adult	46 stitches	11 inches

Cast on the number of stitches specified for your size.

Knit in garter stitch until your slipper measures 5 (6, 7, 8, 9) inches.

Knit 2 (2, 3, 3, 3) inches in rib as described in the baby slipper pattern, and then follow the finishing directions there.

One-Piece Baby Sweater

Legions of baby sweater patterns claim to be quick and easy. Here's an updated take on the classic baby kimono (see Figure 3-3 or the color photo at dummies. com/go/knitcrochetAIO). It's unrealistic to expect to finish this sweater in one day, but you can still finish it pretty quickly. Pair this sweater with the retro slippers in the preceding section and one of the great hats in Book 5, Chapter 1, and baby will have a fantastic cold-weather outfit. (You can also find a full layette project later in this chapter.)

This sweater pattern includes a buttonhole. For details about making buttonholes, turn to Book 6, Chapter 3.

Materials and vital statistics

>> **Yarn:** Cascade 220 Superwash (100% superwash wool); 220 yards (201 meters) per 100 grams; 2 (2, 3) skeins; color: 860 Gray Heather

>> **Needles:** US 7 (4.5 mm), or the size needed to match gauge

>> **Other materials:** Two 1-inch buttons; sewing needle and thread to match buttons; yarn needle for sewing up seams

FIGURE 3-3:
This baby
sweater is knit
all in one piece.

» **Size:** Newborn (6–12 months, 1–2 years)

- Finished chest circumference: 18 (22, 26) inches

- Finished length: 9 (11, 13) inches

See the schematic in Figure 3-4.

» **Gauge:** 18 stitches and 36 rows per 4 inches in garter stitch

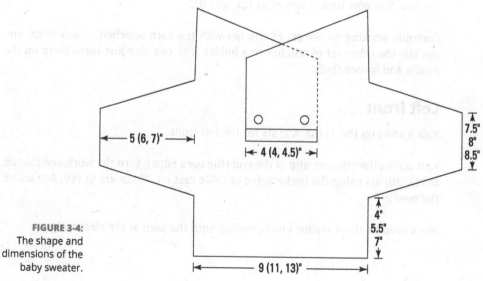

FIGURE 3-4:
The shape and
dimensions of the
baby sweater.

This sweater is worked in one piece. You start at the lower edge of the back and knit straight to the beginning of the sleeves, which are increased gradually. When you get to the shoulders, you bind off stitches for the neck opening, and then work each side of the front separately, casting on stitches for the front neckline. When you're done knitting, you have just one seam to sew on each side from the cuff to the waist. Then you attach the buttons.

Directions

Cast on 36 (44, 54) sts.

Work in garter stitch (knit all rows) until the sweater measures 4 (5½, 7) inches.

Sleeves

You'll cast on gradually for both sleeves. Using the cable cast on (see Book 2, Chapter 1) or your preferred method, cast on 4 sts at the beginning of the next 12 (14, 16) rows. There are now 84 (100, 118) sts on the needle.

Work even until the sweater measures 9 (11, 13) inches. The back is now complete.

Neck

You now bind off stitches for the neck and work the left front and right front separately.

Next row: Knit 33 (41, 49) sts; bind off the center 18 (18, 20) sts; knit to the end of the row. You now have 2 sets of 33 (41, 49) sts.

Continue working on the set of stitches with the yarn attached. If you want, you can slip the other set of stitches to a holder. You can also just leave them on the needle and ignore them.

Left front

Knit 6 rows on the 33 (41, 49) sts for the left front.

Knit across the 7th row, and at the end (the neck edge), turn the work and cast on 18 (18, 20) sts using the backward-e or cable cast on. There are 51 (59, 69) sts on the needle.

Work even on these sts for 1 inch, ending with the yarn at the sleeve edge.

Now work buttonholes over the next 2 rows as follows:

Next row: K37 (45, 53) sts, bind off 2 sts, k5 (5, 7) sts, bind off 2 sts, k3. There are 6 (6, 8) sts between the 2 buttonholes.

Next row: K4, cast on 2 sts, k6 (6, 8) sts, cast on 2 sts, knit to end.

Work even until the left side measures 10¾ (14, 17¼) inches from the cast on edge, ending with the yarn at the sleeve edge.

Next WS row (at the wrist edge): Bind off 4 sts, knit to end.

Next row: Knit.

Repeat the previous 2 rows 5 (6, 7) more times. There are 27 (31, 37) sts.

Work even until the sweater measures 2½ (3¾, 5) inches from the bottom of the sleeve, ending with the yarn at the front (tummy) edge.

Next row: Bind off 4 sts, knit across.

Next row: Knit.

Repeat the previous 2 rows 6 (7, 8) more times, and then bind off the remaining sts.

TIP

Some people care which side their sweaters button on (for example, right over left or left over right). This sweater has buttons on two sides, and the left side of the lapel goes on top. But if you want the right side of the lapel to go on top, turn the sweater inside out before you do the finishing.

Right front

Reattach the yarn at the neck edge and knit 5 rows on the 33 (41, 49) sts for the right front.

Knit across the 6th row, and at the end (the neck edge), cast on 18 (18, 20) sts using the backward-e, knitted, or cable cast on. There are 51 (59, 69) sts on the needle.

Work even until this side of the sweater measures 10¾ (14, 17¼) inches from the cast on edge, ending with the yarn at the sleeve edge.

Next RS row (at the wrist edge): Bind off 4 sts, knit to end.

Next row: Knit.

Repeat the previous 2 rows 5 (6, 7) more times. There are 27 (31, 37) sts.

Work even until the sweater measures 2½ (3¾, 5) inches from the bottom of the sleeve, ending with the yarn at the tummy edge.

Next row: Bind off 4 sts, knit to end.

Next row: Knit.

Repeat the previous 2 rows 6 (7, 8) more times, and then bind off the remaining stitches.

Finishing

Block the sweater so the edges are smooth and the side seams are the same length. Sew the seam on each side from cuff to underarm to hem. Using the buttonholes as guides, place the buttons on the opposite lapel and then sew them firmly in place using a needle and thread. (Read more on blocking and sewing seams in Book 7.)

TIP

You can make a good sweater great with the right buttons. If you wait until the sweater is done to pick them, you'll know you've chosen the right ones.

Baby's Layette: Cardigan, Booties, Hat, and Blanket

Layettes make for great starter projects because they knit up quickly and use the same pattern for multiple pieces. This knitted layette consists of a cardigan, booties, a hat, and a blanket that any new parent will love.

Cardigan

This cardigan is quite possibly the simplest construction imaginable — garter stitch with a few seams. It knits fast and looks great on any baby. (Then again, what *doesn't* look great on a baby?) Figure 3-5 shows the schematic for the layette cardigan. (See a color photo of the cardigan and hat at dummies.com/go/knitcrochetAIO.)

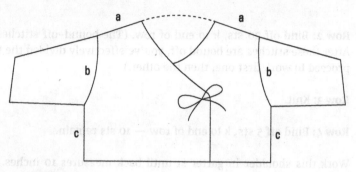

FIGURE 3-5:
The layette
cardigan
construction.

a. shoulder seam
b. sleeve seam
c. side seam

Illustration by Wiley, Composition Services Graphics

Materials and vital statistics

>> **Size:** Newborn to 3 months

- **Finished chest circumference:** 17 inches

- **Finished sleeve length:** 6 inches

- **Finished length:** 10 inches

>> **Yarn:** Berroco "Comfort DK" (50% superfine nylon/50% superfine acrylic; CYC #3, 178 yards, 1.76 ounces [50 grams]): Color 2740, 2 skeins

>> **Needles:** One pair each of size US 6 (4 mm) and US 4 (31/4 mm) needles or size needed to obtain gauge

>> **Gauge:** 22 stitches and 24 rows per 4 inches

Directions

The following sections break down the instructions for creating this cardigan piece by piece.

BACK

Using size US 6 needles, cast on 50 sts and work in garter st for 9 inches.

Neck and shoulder shaping:

To shape the neck, you bind off stitches in the middle of the row. Doing so creates the shoulders, which you then work separately:

Row 1: K35, turn.

Row 2: Bind off 20 sts, k to end of row. (The bound-off stitches form the neck. After these stitches are bound off, you've effectively divided the shoulders; you'll proceed to work first one, then the other.)

Row 3: Knit.

Row 4: Bind off 5 sts, k to end of row — 10 sts remain.

Work this shoulder in garter st until back measures 10 inches. Bind off shoulder sts.

Pick up remaining sts and repeat shaping from Row 3 for the second shoulder.

FRONT

Make 2 (both the same).

With size US 6 needles, cast on 34 sts and work in garter st for 5 inches.

Neck shaping:

To create the neck, you decrease stitches along what will become the neck edge.

Row 1: Ssk, k to end of row.

Row 2: Knit.

Rep Rows 1 and 2 until 10 sts remain, then knit until same length as back. Bind off.

SLEEVE

Make 2 (both the same).

With size US 6 needles, cast on 35 sts and work 10 rows in garter st.

Inc at each end every 4th row until you have 55 sts. Work straight until sleeve measures 6 inches. Bind off loosely.

FINISHING

Block the pieces to size.

Sew the shoulder seams and then set the sleeves into the body.

Sew the side seams and sleeves together.

Make a fastener by adding ribbon, a button and buttonhole, or three sets of I-cord ties evenly down the front. (For the I-cord, work six 5-inch ties of 5 sts each on size US 4 needles.)

Booties

Booties look complex, but these are anything but. The ribbon trim pulls together the edges to create the top and close across the foot — just right for teeny tiny baby feet! (The materials list 1 skein of yarn, but you won't use it all on one pair of booties; use the rest in the other layette pieces.)

Materials and vital statistics

>> **Size:** Newborn to 3 months

>> **Yarn:** Berroco "Comfort DK" (50% superfine nylon/50% superfine acrylic; CYC #3, 178 yards, 1.76 ounces [50 grams]): Color 2740, 1 skein

>> **Needles:** One pair of size US 6 (4 mm) needles or size needed to obtain gauge

>> **Gauge:** 5½ stitches and 6 rows per 1 inch

Directions

With size US 6 needles, cast on 38 sts.

Rows 1–6: Work in garter st.

Row 7: K2, m1 in next 2 sts, k10, m1 in next 4 sts, k2, m1 in next 4 sts, k10, m1 in next 2 sts, k2 (50 sts).

Row 8: Knit.

Row 9: K17, m1 in next 4 sts, k8, m1 in next 4 sts, k17.

Rows 10–13: Work in garter st.

Row 14: K17, (k2tog, k2) twice, k2tog, k4, (k2tog, k2) twice, k2tog, k17.

Row 15: Knit.

Row 16: K17, (k2tog, k1) twice, k1, (k2tog, k1) twice, k2tog, k17 — 46 sts.

Row 17: Knit.

Row 18: K17, k2tog 6 times, k17.

Row 19: Bind off.

Finishing: Starting at cast on seam, sew along seam and up side of work to form the bootie. Thread ribbon or I-cord through the final row for decoration if desired.

Hat

Knit flat and seamed, this adorable hat will keep sun and chill off baby's head. It also knits up super-quick. Make more than one in different colors for the ultimate accessory. (The materials list 1 skein of yarn, but you won't use it all on one hat; use the rest in the other layette pieces.)

Materials and vital statistics

» **Size:** Newborn to 3 months

» **Yarn:** Berroco "Comfort DK" (50% superfine nylon/50% superfine acrylic; CYC #3, 178 yards, 1.76 ounces [50 grams]): Color 2740, 1 skein

» **Needles:** One pair of size US 6 (4 mm) needles or size needed to obtain gauge

» **Gauge:** 5½ stitches and 6 rows per 1 inch

Directions

Using size US 6 needles, cast on 74 sts and work in garter st for 3 inches.

Begin decreases:

Row 1: K3, k2tog tbl, (k10, k2tog tbl) 5 times, k to end of row.

Row 2: Knit.

Row 3: K3, k2tog tbl, (k9, k2tog tbl) 5 times, k to end of row.

Row 4: Knit.

Continue in this manner, decreasing k9, k8, k7, and so on, until 14 sts remain.

Last row: (K2tog tbl) 7 times.

Finishing: Cut yarn about 18 inches from work. Draw yarn through remaining 7 sts and pull tightly. Use the remaining yarn to sew down the side seam.

Blanket

This blanket isn't square or rectangular . . . it's actually kite-shaped, with lengthy edges perfect for wrapping baby tight or (some time from now) dragging behind a toddler's cautious steps. In other words, it's not just a blanket, it's a capital-B Blankie, knit in the same sturdy, washable yarn used throughout the layette.

Materials and vital statistics

>> **Size:** Approximately 30 inches x 30 inches, slightly stretched

>> **Yarn:** Berroco "Comfort DK" (50% superfine nylon/50% superfine acrylic; CYC #3, 178 yards, 1.76 ounces [50 grams]): Color 2740, 6 skeins

>> **Needles:** 36-inch size US 11 (7½ mm) circular needle or size needed to obtain gauge

>> **Gauge:** 3½ stitches and 4 rows per 1 inch in garter stitch

Directions

Use double strands throughout:

Using a size US 11 circular needle, cast on 3 sts.

Row 1: M1, k to end (4 sts).

Row 2: M1, k to end (5 sts).

Rep Row 2, increasing 1 st each row until you have 16 sts total.

Begin stockinette insert:

Row 14: M1, k6, p1, k to end of row (17 sts).

Row 15: M1, k to end of row (18 sts).

Row 16: M1, k6, p3, k to end of row (19 sts).

Row 17: M1, k to end of row (20 sts).

Continue working the odd and even rows as established, increasing the number of purl sts by 2 on each even row until you have 130 sts total.

Dec Row 1: K2tog, work in pattern as established to end of row.

Work the decreases as established, decreasing the number of purl sts by 2 on each odd row, until the stockinette insert is finished; then continue in garter st until 3 sts remain.

REMEMBER

"Work in pattern as established" simply means that after you work the edge stitches (whether decreases or increases), you continue to knit or purl every row between those edge stitches.

Finishing: Bind off and weave in ends very securely.

Tunisian Crochet Baby Blanket

Baby items are among the most popular designs to crochet. Whether for you, a family member, or a friend, crocheted baby items are not only useful, but they also quite often become heirlooms to be passed down through generations.

Tunisian crochet (also called *afghan stitch*) lends itself wonderfully to baby blankets because of the tight stitch pattern. It creates a warm fabric without any loose holes for tiny fingers and toes to get caught in. The size of this blanket (see Figure 3-6 or the color photo at dummies.com/go/knitcrochetAIO) was designed with a bassinet or stroller in mind, so it's large enough to cover a baby without the risk of getting tangled up.

For an introduction to Tunisian crochet, see Book 4, Chapter 4. For another crocheted baby blanket pattern, check out the project in Book 4, Chapter 3.

TIP

As the saying goes, practice makes perfect. If you're new to Tunisian crochet, be sure to work a gauge swatch so you can get the hang of the stitch and make sure your gauge is accurate. Swatches should be about 4 inches square, so if you're using the yarn for this project, start with a foundation chain of 17 stitches, and work 16 rows to make a square. You'll know you've got it right if the vertical bars line up one on top of another.

Materials and vital statistics

>> **Yarn:** Caron "Simply Soft" 4-ply worsted-weight yarn (100% acrylic), Article #H3000 (3 oz. [85 g], 165 yds [151 m] each skein): 1 skein each of

- #2615 Soft Blue (A)

- #2613 Soft Yellow (B)

FIGURE 3-6:
This baby blanket, worked in basic afghan stitch, keeps a little one warm and snuggly.

© John Wiley & Sons, Inc.

- #2705 Soft Green (C)
- #2601 White (D)

>> **Hooks:**

- Tunisian crochet hook size J-10 U.S. or size needed to obtain gauge
- Standard crochet hook size J-10 U.S. or size needed to obtain gauge

>> **Measurements:** Panel = 5¾ in. wide x 19½ in. long; blanket = 22½ in. wide x 22½ in. long

>> **Gauge:** Working in simple Tunisian crochet stitch with Tunisian crochet hook, 17 sts and 16 rows = 4 in.

>> **Stitches used:** Chain stitch (ch), slip stitch (sl st), single crochet (sc), double crochet (dc), simple Tunisian stitch. Shell: • 5 dc in same st •.

No one will realize how easy it is to make this design when you show them the finished product. The afghan consists of three separate panels worked in the simple Tunisian stitch with no increasing or decreasing necessary. After the panels are complete, you crochet a simple edging consisting of single crochet stitches, then join those together with slip stitches. This is a perfect example of how the joining seam becomes part of the design. Add a pretty border with the shell stitch, and you're done.

Creating a couple of panels

This afghan is made up of 3 panels, one each in colors A, B, and C.

Foundation row: With Tunisian crochet hook and first color, ch 25. Insert hook in second ch from hook, yo, draw yarn through st, · insert hook in next st, yo, draw yarn through st ·, rep from · to · across, keeping all loops on hook (25 loops — first half of foundation row complete), beg 2nd half of row, yo, draw yarn through 1 loop on hook, ·· yo, draw yarn through 2 loops on hook ··, rep from ·· to ·· across (1 loop remains and counts as first st of next row).

Second and successive rows: Work in simple Tunisian stitch across all 25 stitches until panel measures 19½ in.

Last row: Sl st in each vertical stitch across. Fasten off.

Panel border

Work border around each panel.

Rnd 1: With right side facing, using standard crochet hook, join D in any corner st, ch 1, sc in each st and row-end st around panel, working 3 sc in each corner st, sl st in first sc to join. Fasten off D, join color to match panel.

Rnd 2: Ch 1, sc in each sc around, working 3 sc in each corner st. Fasten off, join D.

Rnd 3: With D, rep Rnd 2. Fasten off.

Putting the panels together and adding the final touch

With right sides facing, matching stitches across long edges of each panel, using standard crochet hook and D, sl st panels tog through back loops of sts in the foll color sequence: A, B, C to form a square.

Edging

Rnd 1: With right side facing, using standard crochet hook, join D in any corner st, ch 1, sc in corner st, · ch 1, skip next sc, sc in next sc ·, rep from · to · around, working (sc, ch 1, sc) in each corner st, to within last corner st, (sc, ch 1) in corner st, sl st in first sc to join.

Rnd 2: Ch 1, sc in first ch-1 space, skip next sc, ·· shell in next ch-1 space, skip next sc, sc in next ch-1 space, skip next sc ·, rep from · to · across to next corner, shell in corner ch-1 space ··, rep from ·· to ·· around, sl st in first sc to join. Fasten off.

Variation: Making a bigger blankie

If you want to make this afghan for a toddler, increase the size of each panel by making a longer foundation chain. For instance, to make it twice the size, double the number of stitches in the foundation chain, then keep working rows until the panel reaches the desired length. Follow the directions for the edging and border as written above. Don't forget to buy extra yarn.

Variation: Picking a new color palette

This afghan would look really great worked in different colors. Choose colors that match baby's nursery or child's bedroom. Both pastels and primary colors would look great.

Storybook Hats

Sometimes it's fun to have a silly hat, and the Dr. Seuss-meets-Waldo chapeau in Figure 3-7 certainly fits the bill. (See color photos of this pattern at dummies.com/go/knitcrochetAIO.) With a thick yarn, this hat is a quick knit and makes a great gift for your favorite snowboarder or snowman maker (or anyone who appreciates the absurd). The later variations show you to how use almost any yarn to make a similar hat. These hats are sure to chase away the winter blues.

Materials and vital statistics

» **Yarn:** Cascade Lana Grande (100% Peruvian wool); 87 yards (80 meters) per 50 grams

- **Color A:** Cream; 1 skein
- **Color B:** Pink; 1 skein

» **Needles:** US 15 (10 mm) circular needle, 16-inch length; US 15 (10 mm) double-pointed needles; US 11 (8 mm) circular needle, 16-inch length

» **Other materials:** Two stitch markers; yarn needle

FIGURE 3-7:
A storybook hat chases away the winter blues.

© John Wiley & Sons, Inc.

>> **Size:** Baby (toddler, child, small adult, large adult)

  • **Circumference:** 14 (16, 17½, 19, 21) inches unstretched

  • **Length (without tassel):** 12 (14, 16, 16, 18) inches

>> **Gauge:** 10 stitches and 12 rows per 4 inches in stockinette stitch

This hat is worked in the round and goes quickly on big needles. You can make it with a single color, but the broad stripes make it extra fun and colorful. For information on changing colors, see Book 4, Chapter 1.

Directions

With the larger circular needles and color A, cast on 36 (40, 44, 48, 52) sts. Place a marker and join in the round, being careful not to twist.

Round 1: Using the smaller needles, *k1, p1, repeat from * to end.

Continue in rib until your hat measures 2 inches. Cut color A, leaving a 6-inch tail.

REMEMBER

As you make this hat, cut and rejoin the yarns each time you switch colors.

Switch to color B and the larger circular needles. Work 6 rounds in stockinette stitch (knit all rounds).

Switch to color A.

Round 1: K9 (10, 11, 12, 13), place marker, k18 (20, 22, 24, 26), place marker, knit to end of round.

Round 2: Knit.

Round 3 (Decrease Round): Knit to 2 sts before marker, k2tog, slip marker, ssk, knit to 2 sts before marker, k2tog, slip marker, ssk, knit to end of round.

Head to Book 2, Chapter 3 to find out more about the k2tog and ssk decreases if you aren't familiar with them.

TIP

Rounds 4, 5, and 6: Knit.

Switch to color B.

Round 7 (Decrease Round): Repeat Round 3.

Rounds 8, 9, and 10: Knit.

Round 11: Repeat Round 3.

Round 12: Knit.

Switch to double-pointed needles when there are too few sts on the needles to knit comfortably.

Continue repeating these 12 rounds until only 8 sts remain. Continue working even on these 8 sts to the end of the 6-round stripe if necessary.

Cut an 8-inch tail and, using a yarn needle, thread it through the remaining sts, pulling gently to gather them in. Run the yarn through the sts once more, and then weave in the tail on the inside. Weave in ends.

To make the tassel, start by wrapping the yarn around a paperback book about 40 times.

Cut the yarn and wrap the tail tightly around all the strands a couple of times. Then tie with a firm knot, leaving the tail to use later to attach the tassel to the hat.

Slip the rounds of yarn off the book and wrap a 1-foot length of yarn around the tassel 1 inch below the knot. Pull firmly before knotting in place. Cut through the loops at the opposite end of the tassel and then trim the ends so that they're even.

To attach the tassel, thread the tail of yarn from the tassel onto a yarn needle. Insert the needle through the tip of the hat and pull the yarn through. Bring the needle through the base of the tassel. Insert the needle into the tip of the hat, bringing the yarn to the inside and then knot it firmly in place.

Variation: Changing yarns

TIP

If you want to knit this hat with a different weight yarn, use Table 3-2 to figure out your cast on number, and then follow the directions in the basic pattern. You can use more than one color of yarn (which is a great way to use up your odds and ends!) or try a self-striping yarn.

TABLE 3-2   ### Cast On Numbers for Different Yarns and Gauges

Gauge per Inch	Cast on Number
3	44 (48, 52, 56, 64)
4	56 (64, 72, 76, 84)
4½	64 (72, 80, 88, 96)
5	68 (80, 88, 96, 104)
5½	76 (88, 96, 104, 116)

TIP

Knit the ribbing with needles that are two sizes smaller than the needles you use to get the gauge needed for the body of the hat.

Begin decreasing when the hat measures 4 inches. Place your markers as follows for your gauge:

>> **3 sts per inch:** K11 (12, 13, 14, 16), place marker, k22 (24, 26, 28, 32), place marker, knit to end of round.

>> **4 sts per inch:** K14 (16, 18, 19, 21), place marker, k28, (32, 36, 38, 42), place marker, knit to end of round.

>> **4½ sts per inch:** K16 (18, 20 22, 24), place marker, k32 (36, 40, 44, 48), place marker, knit to end of round.

>> **5 sts per inch:** K17 (20, 22, 24, 26), place marker, k34 (40, 44, 48, 52), place marker, knit to end of round.

>> **5½ sts per inch:** K19 (22, 24, 26, 29), place marker, k38, (44, 48, 52, 58), place marker, knit to end of round.

Follow the 12-round color and decrease pattern outlined in the basic pattern.

Chapter **4**

Bags for All Occasions

With your knitting and crocheting skills, you can create all kinds of bags. The mosaic bag pattern in this chapter creates a purse that you can use every day or save for fancy occasions. The knitted messenger bag is suitable for work, school, or running errands. The crocheted tote is a durable bag for shopping or everyday use.

REMEMBER

All the bags in this chapter are felted, which means they're made of wool that's washed and dried to create a fabric that's denser and stronger. This process also makes your project smaller, so keep that in mind as you stitch or modify the patterns in this chapter. If you've ever shrunk a wool sweater in the dryer, you have some idea of what felting is. You can find much more detail about felting in Book 7, Chapter 1.

Mosaic Bags

Mosaics create wonderful color patterns. (The color photos at dummies.com/go/knitcrochetAIO speak for themselves.) A mosaic's repeating geometry is pleasing, and mosaic patterns are much easier to knit than other multicolor techniques. The mosaic bags shown in Figure 4-1 look complicated, but if you can knit a stripe and slip a stitch, you're ready to try them.

FIGURE 4-1:
The felted mosaic
purse and tote.

© John Wiley & Sons, Inc.

In mosaic knitting, instead of knitting with two strands of yarn, you only use one at a time. On right-side rows, any stitch that needs to be the "new" color (the color of yarn you're holding), you knit. Any stitch that's supposed to stay the old color (the color from the previous row), you slip, bringing the new color along on the wrong side of the work. And wrong-side rows are even easier: If the stitch is the same color as the yarn in your hand, purl it; if it isn't the same, slip it.

REMEMBER

Here are a few things to remember about mosaic knitting:

>> Choose yarns that have the same weight. If one yarn is thicker than the other, the design won't look its best.

>> When it comes to yarn color, contrast is vital to a pleasing final result. Choose two colors that have different values (one darker and one lighter) so that the pattern pops. To get more complex color results without the fuss of changing yarns all the time, choose a plain-colored yarn and a variegated yarn. A bright multicolored foreground with a black background, for example, looks almost like stained glass.

>> Work two rows in the first color and then two rows in the second color. Repeat. In the second row of a color, knit or purl the stitches that were worked in the previous row, and slip the slipped stitches. No stitches change color in this row.

>> Always slip stitches purlwise with the yarn held to the wrong side of the work. (See Book 2, Chapter 3 for how-to on slipping stitches.)

>> Mosaic patterns that are knit flat usually include some extra stitches for the edges so that the patterns stay evenly centered. For example, you're likely to see directions that ask you to use, say, a multiple of 16 stitches plus 3 edge stitches. When you knit a mosaic in the round, though, throw out those extra stitches and stick to the even multiple only.

>> Stitches are slipped exactly twice. If you find yourself slipping a stitch more (or fewer) times, back up and read your knitting to see what went wrong.

>> If you tend to knit tightly, remember that the yarn carried behind the slipped stitch should be as wide as the normal stitches. Keep the stitches on the right needle stretched out a bit to help you overcome the tendency to pull too tight. Use a needle long enough to do so; working back and forth on a circular needle may help.

In this mosaic bag pattern, you find both written directions and a chart for the pinbox mosaic. Both sets of instructions give the same information, but some people find one easier to follow than the other.

The pattern for this bag presents you with lots of options. The featured pattern is for the pinbox mosaic purse. Later in this section, you find several other mosaic patterns you can substitute for the pinbox mosaic. Or if you want your bag striped or plain, check out the later variations. A plain purse can be stunning if you adorn it with a brooch, knitted flowers, or needle-felted designs. Craft stores and yarn shops carry beautiful ready-made handles that can jazz up any bag. Or you can knit the handle with the bag. This pattern gives you both options.

You can use colors on this mosaic bag in many ways. The materials list calls for two shades of the main color (dark brown and lighter brown) and two shades of the contrasting color (yellow and gold) for the pinbox mosaic. You can easily choose to use a single main color and two contrasting colors if you decide on a three-color mosaic pattern. Simpler still is sticking with just two colors. The results are fantastic any way you choose to do it!

Materials and vital statistics

>> **Yarn:** Cascade 220 (100% Peruvian highland wool); 220 yards (201 meters) per 100 grams

- **Main color 1 (MC1):** 2403 Dark Brown; 1 skein

- **Main color 2 (MC2):** 2411 Brown; 1 skein

- **Contrasting color 1 (CC1):** 7825 Gold; 1 skein

- **Contrasting color 2 (CC2):** 7827 Yellow; 1 skein

>> **Needles:** US 10½ (6.5 mm) circular needles, 24- or 36-inch length

>> **Other:** One stitch marker; yarn needle to weave in ends

>> **Size:**

Approximate size before felting for a purse (tote):

- **Width:** 16 (21) inches

- **Height:** 18 (21) inches (without handles)

- **Depth:** 5 inches

Approximate size after felting for a purse (tote):

- **Width:** 9½ (12) inches

- **Height:** 8 (10½) inches (without handles)

- **Depth:** 3 inches

Felting is both art and science. The sizes given here are guidelines, and your results may vary.

>> **Gauge:** 12 stitches and 16 rows per 4 inches in stockinette stitch

This bag is worked in one piece. The bottom is worked back and forth in garter stitch, and from there, you pick up stitches around the rectangle that you've created and work in the round. When the bag is complete, you felt it in the washing machine.

Directions

With MC1, cast on 48 (64) sts.

Work 32 rows in garter stitch (knit all rows). There will be 16 garter ridges. Don't cut the yarn.

With your 48 (64) sts still on the needles, continue with MC1 and pick up and knit 16 sts down the first short side, 48 (64) sts along the cast on edge, and 16 sts along the second short side of the base. There will be 128 (160) sts on the needles. Place a marker to indicate the beginning of the round.

Switch to CC1 and knit 2 rounds.

Use the pinbox mosaic pattern presented here or any other 16-stitch mosaic pattern from the list of variations later in this chapter. Figure 4-2 shows a chart for the pinbox mosaic pattern information, or you can follow the written instructions. Use the method that's easiest for you to follow. For each row, the stitches shown in the working color are worked, and the stitches shown in the other color are slipped. Each chart row represents two consecutive pattern rows.

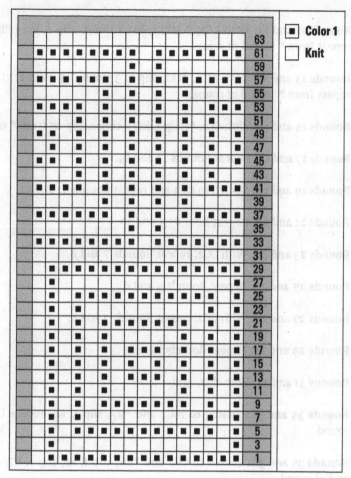

FIGURE 4-2:
The pinbox
mosaic pattern
repeat presented
in a chart.

© John Wiley & Sons, Inc.

REMEMBER

When you're working a mosaic pattern, always slip stitches purlwise.

Rounds 1 and 2: With MC1, *k15, slip 1, repeat from * to end of round.

Rounds 3 and 4: With CC1, *slip 1, k13, slip 1, k1, repeat from * to end of round.

Rounds 5 and 6: With MC1, *k1, slip 1, k11, slip 1, k1, slip 1, repeat from * to end of round.

Rounds 7 and 8: With CC1, *slip 1, k1, slip 1, k9, slip 1, k1, slip 1, k1, repeat from * to end of round.

Rounds 9 and 10: With MC1, *(k1, slip 1) 2 times, k7, (slip 1, k1) 2 times, slip 1, repeat from * to end of round.

Bags for All Occasions

Rounds 11 and 12: With CC1, *(slip 1, k1) 2 times, slip 1, k5, (slip 1, k1) 3 times, repeat from * to end of round.

Rounds 13 and 14: With MC1, *(k1, slip 1) 3 times, k3, (slip 1, k1) 3 times, slip 1, repeat from * to end of round.

Rounds 15 and 16: With CC1, *(slip 1, k1) 8 times, repeat from * to end of round.

Rounds 17 and 18: Repeat Rounds 13 and 14.

Rounds 19 and 20: Switch to CC2 and repeat Rounds 11 and 12.

Rounds 21 and 22: Repeat Rounds 9 and 10.

Rounds 23 and 24: With CC2, repeat Rounds 7 and 8.

Rounds 25 and 26: Repeat Rounds 5 and 6.

Rounds 27 and 28: With CC2, repeat Rounds 3 and 4.

Rounds 29 and 30: Repeat Rounds 1 and 2.

Rounds 31 and 32: With CC2, knit.

Rounds 33 and 34: Switch to MC2 and *k7, slip 1, k8, repeat from * to end of round.

Rounds 35 and 36: Switch to CC2 and *k6, slip 1, k1, slip 1, k7, repeat from * to end of round.

Rounds 37 and 38: Switch to MC2 and *k5, (slip 1, k1) 2 times, slip 1, k6, repeat from * to end of round.

Rounds 39 and 40: Switch to CC2 and *k4, (slip 1, k1) 3 times, slip 1, k5, repeat from * to end of round.

Rounds 41 and 42: Switch to MC2 and *k3, (slip 1, k1) 4 times, slip 1, k4, repeat from * to end of round.

Rounds 43 and 44: Switch to CC2 and *k2, (slip 1, k1) 5 times, slip 1, k3, repeat from * to end of round.

Rounds 45 and 46: Switch to MC2 and *(k1, slip 1) 7 times, k2, repeat from * to end of round.

Rounds 47 and 48: Switch to CC2 and *(slip 1, k1) 8 times, repeat from * to end of round.

Rounds 49 and 50: Repeat Rounds 45 and 46.

Rounds 51 and 52: Switch to CC1 and repeat Rounds 43 and 44.

Rounds 53 and 54: Repeat Rounds 41 and 42.

Rounds 55 and 56: With CC1, repeat Rounds 39 and 40.

Rounds 57 and 58: Repeat Rounds 37 and 38.

Rounds 59 and 60: With CC1, repeat Rounds 35 and 36.

Rounds 61 and 62: Repeat Rounds 33 and 34.

Rounds 63 and 64: With CC1, knit.

For the tote only, work Rounds 1–32 again before moving on to the next step.

For both purse and tote, work 4 more rounds with MC in stockinette stitch.

If you want to attach ready-made handles, bind off; you attach the handles after finishing and felting. If you want to knit in your handles, continue with the directions that follow. These knitted handles are made like big buttonholes. (See more on buttonholes in Book 6, Chapter 3.)

Next round: K16 (22), bind off 16 (20) sts, k47 (59), (there are 48 (60) sts on the right needle after the last set of bound-off sts), bind off 16 (20) sts, knit to end of round.

Next round: Knit, casting on 16 (20) sts over each set of bound-off sts, using the cable cast on (see Book 2, Chapter 1). Be sure to turn your work so the WS is facing you as you cast on each set of stitches.

Knit 5 (7) more rounds, and then bind off. Weave in any ends.

Felt your bag in the washing machine. (You can find step-by-step instructions on felting in Book 7, Chapter 1.) You'll know your bag is done when it's firm and you can no longer see the stitches. Your bag should be the approximate finished size that's noted in the "Materials and vital statistics" section.

If you have purchased handles, you can attach them now. Follow any instructions provided with the handles or sew them on with a needle and heavy-duty sewing thread that matches the bag.

Variation: Other mosaics

In the following sections, you find two 16-stitch mosaics and three 8-stitch mosaics. Here are some general facts about each of them:

WARNING

>> Mosaics with 16 stitches, such as the puzzle piece mosaic and woven cord mosaic, can be substituted directly into the mosaic bags pattern. The pattern for this eye-catching bag is a good one to help you get comfortable with mosaic knitting. Because you're knitting in the round, you'll find it easy to keep things lined up.

The written directions for both 16-stitch mosaics in this chapter are designed for knitting in the round (so they're easy to use in the mosaic bags pattern); if you're using this pattern to knit flat, add the 3 edge stitches shown in the following charts (1 at the beginning of the row and 2 at the end of the row) to complete the pattern. If you're using the charted pattern to work in the round, read only the outlined 16-stitch pattern repeat.

>> Smaller mosaics, such as the little mosaic, little boxes mosaic, and miniature mosaic are 8 stitches wide. You can also use these smaller mosaics in the mosaic bags pattern. Just remember to throw out the 3 edge stitches given in the directions for knitting flat; you won't need them to work in the round. Or try them on the throw pillows in Book 5, Chapter 2, using 67 or 75 stitches.

TIP

If you want to get your hands on more mosaic patterns, any of the brilliant treasuries by Barbara G. Walker offer lots of inspiring options.

Puzzle piece mosaic

The puzzle piece mosaic, as the name suggests, looks a bit like jigsaw puzzle pieces. You can see this mosaic in Figure 4-3. You'll find this mosaic to be quite predictable: After you get going with it, you can see what comes next and soon fall into its rhythm.

You can get a feel for this mosaic by making a swatch with 35 stitches. You'll use two colors, main color (MC) and contrasting color (CC), and the colors are used equally. Cast on 35 stitches with CC and knit 2 rows, and then follow the chart in Figure 4-4 or the upcoming written directions. Remember, because you're knitting flat, you need to use those 3 edge stitches!

FIGURE 4-3:
Puzzle piece mosaic.

Set-up rounds: Knit 2 rounds with CC.

Round 1: With MC, *(k1, sl 1) 8 times, repeat from * to end.

Round 2 and all even-numbered rounds:

If a stitch was knit in the previous row (it will be the same color as the yarn in your hand), knit it (or purl it if you're working back and forth).

If a stitch was slipped in the previous row (it won't be the color of the yarn in your hand), slip the stitch purlwise with the yarn held to the wrong side of the work.

Round 3: With CC, *k2, sl 1, k11, sl 1, k1, repeat from * to end.

Round 5: With MC, *k1, sl 1, k3, sl 1, k5, sl 1, k3, sl 1, repeat from * to end.

Round 7: With CC, *k4, sl 1, k1, sl 1, k3, sl 1, k1, sl 1, k3, repeat from * to end.

Round 9: With MC, *k1, sl 1, k5, sl 1, k1, sl 1, k5, sl 1, repeat from * to end.

Round 11: With CC, *k2, sl 1, k1, sl 1, k7, sl 1, k1, sl 1, k1, repeat from * to end.

Round 13: With MC, *k3, sl 1, k3, sl 1, k1, sl 1, k3, sl 1, k2, repeat from * to end.

Round 15: With CC, *k6, sl 1, k3, sl 1, k5, repeat from * to end.

Round 17: With MC, *(k1, sl 1) 8 times, repeat from * to end.

Round 19: Repeat Round 15.

Round 21: Repeat Round 13.

Round 23: Repeat Round 11.

Round 25: Repeat Round 9.

Round 27: Repeat Round 7.

Round 29: Repeat Round 5.

Round 31: Repeat Round 3.

Repeat Rounds 1–32 for pattern.

When your swatch is large enough to measure accurately and you feel comfortable knitting the mosaic pattern, bind off.

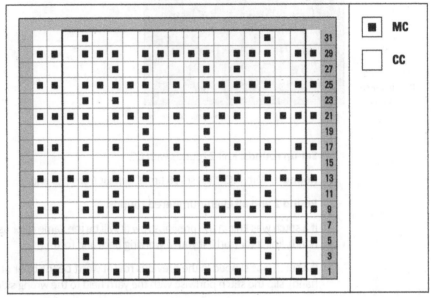

FIGURE 4-4:
Puzzle piece
mosaic chart.

Woven cord mosaic

The woven cord mosaic, shown in Figure 4-5, creates a dynamic design with strong diagonal elements.

REMEMBER

If you're knitting flat, remember that you need the 3 edge stitches shown in the chart. If you're knitting in the round, ignore the edge stitches and use only the 16-stitch pattern repeat outlined by the dark box. The written directions describe how to work the pattern in the round, so they're easy to use with the mosaic bag pattern. But remember not to include the 3 edge stitches.

You can practice this mosaic by making a swatch that's made with 35 stitches or any multiple of 16 plus 3. Choose two colors, referred to as MC and CC. MC is the foreground color, represented as black in the chart in Figure 4-6. CC is the background color, represented by white in the chart. To begin your swatch, cast on 35 stitches, knit 2 rows with CC, and then follow the chart or these written directions:

Set-up rounds: Knit 2 rounds with CC.

Round 1: With MC, *k8, sl 1, k1, sl 1, k5, repeat from * to end.

FIGURE 4-5:
The woven cord mosaic.

Round 2 and all even-numbered rounds:

If a stitch was knit in the previous row (it will be the same color as the yarn in your hand), knit it (or purl it if you're working back and forth).

If a stitch was slipped in the previous row (it won't be the color of the yarn in your hand), slip the stitch purlwise with the yarn held to the wrong side of the work.

Round 3: With CC, *k1, sl 1, k5, sl 1, k8, repeat from * to end.

Round 5: With MC, *k2, sl 1, k1, sl 1, k1, sl 1, k3, sl 1, k1, sl 1, k1, sl 1, k1, repeat from * to end.

Round 7: With CC, *k9, sl 1, k5, sl 1, repeat from * to end.

Round 9: With MC, *sl 1, k1, sl 1, k13, repeat from * to end.

Round 11: With CC, *k3, sl 1, k9, sl 1, k2, repeat from * to end.

Round 13: With MC, *sl 1, k13, sl 1, k1, repeat from * to end.

Round 15: With CC, *k1, sl 1, k5, sl 1, k8, repeat from * to end.

Round 17: With MC, *k2, sl 1, k1, sl 1, k1, sl 1, k3, sl 1, k1, sl 1, k1, sl 1, k1, repeat from * to end.

Round 19: With CC *k9, sl 1, k5, sl 1, repeat from * to end.

Round 21: With MC, *k6, sl 1, k1, sl 1, k7, repeat from * to end.

Round 23: With CC, *k5, sl 1, k5, sl 1, k4, repeat from * to end.

Repeat Rounds 1–24 for pattern. To complete your swatch, repeat the 24 rows of the chart, and then bind off.

Little mosaic

The little mosaic is shown at the bottom of Figure 4-7.

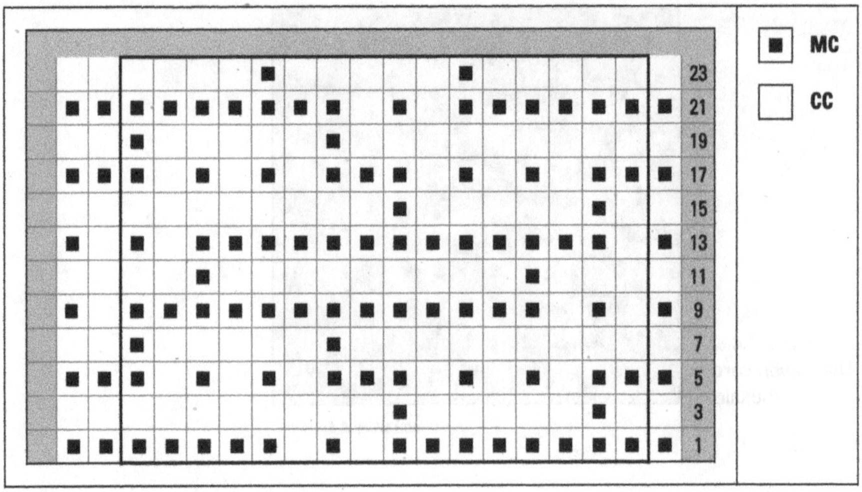

FIGURE 4-6: The woven cord mosaic, charted.

© *John Wiley & Sons, Inc.*

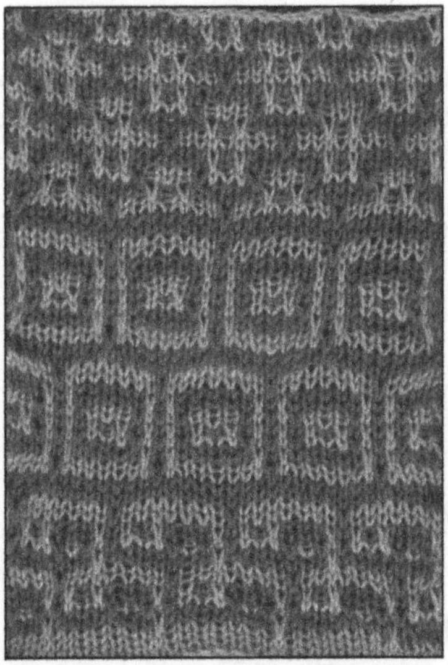

FIGURE 4-7: Three 8-stitch mosaics from top to bottom.

© *John Wiley & Sons, Inc.*

To practice the little mosaic, use two colors, referred to as MC and CC. Cast on 27 stitches with MC and follow these directions to get started (or check out Figure 4-8 for a chart):

Set-up rows: With MC, knit a row, purl a row.

Row 1: With CC, k1, *k4, sl 1, k3, repeat from * to last 2 sts, k2.

Row 2 and all wrong-side rows: Purl the sts knit in the previous row and slip the sts slipped in the previous row.

Row 3: With MC, k1, *k3, sl 1, k1, sl 1, k1, sl 1, repeat from * to last 2 sts, k2.

Row 5: With CC, k1, *sl 1, k1, sl 1, k1, sl 1, k3, repeat from *to last 2 sts, sl 1, k1.

Row 7: With MC, k1, *k3, sl 1, k4, repeat from * to last 2 sts, k2.

Row 9: With CC, k1, *sl 1, k7, repeat from * to last 2 sts, sl 1, k1.

Row 11: With MC, k1, *k1, sl 1, k1, sl 1, k3, sl 1, repeat from * to last 2 sts, k2.

Row 13: With CC, k1, *sl 1, k3, sl 1, k1, sl 1, k1, repeat from * to last 2 sts, sl 1, k1.

Row 15: With MC, k1, *k7, sl 1, repeat from * to last 2 sts, k2.

Repeat Rows 1–16 for pattern. To complete your swatch, repeat the 16 rows once more and then bind off.

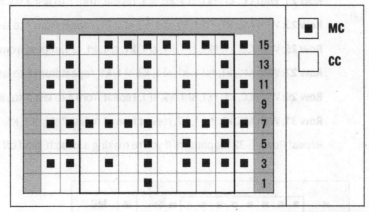

FIGURE 4-8: Little mosaic chart.

© John Wiley & Sons, Inc.

Little boxes mosaic

The little boxes mosaic is a miniaturized version of the larger pinbox mosaic that appears earlier in this chapter. This mosaic is shown in the center of Figure 4-7 and charted in Figure 4-9.

To practice the little boxes mosaic, use 27 stitches to make a swatch. Use two colors, referred to as MC and CC. For your swatch, cast on 27 stitches with MC and follow these directions (or the chart in Figure 4-9):

Set-up rows: With MC, knit a row, purl a row.

Row 1: With CC, knit.

Row 2 and all wrong-side rows: Purl the sts knit in the previous row and slip the sts slipped in the previous row.

Row 3: With MC, k1, *k4, sl 1, k3, repeat from * to last 2 sts, k2.

Row 5: With CC, k1, *k3, sl 1, k1, sl 1, k2, repeat from * to last 2 sts, k2.

Row 7: With MC, k1, *k2, sl 1, k1, sl 1, k1, sl 1, k1, repeat from * to last 2 sts, k2.

Row 9: With CC, k1, *k1, sl 1, k1, sl 1, k1, sl 1, k1, sl 1, repeat from * to last 2 sts, k2.

Row 11: With MC, k1, *k2, sl 1, k1, sl 1, k1, sl 1, k1, repeat from * to last 2 sts, k2.

Row 13: With CC, k1, *k3, sl 1, k1, sl 1, k2, repeat from * to last 2 sts, k2.

Row 15: With MC, k1, *k4, sl 1, k3, repeat from * to last 2 sts, k2.

Row 17: With CC, knit.

Row 19: With MC, k1, *sl 1, k7, repeat from * to last 2 sts, sl 1, k1.

Row 21: With CC, k1, *k1, sl 1, k6, sl 1, repeat from * to last 2 sts, k2.

Row 23: With MC, k1, *sl 1, k1, sl 1, k3, sl 1, k1, repeat from * to last 2 sts, sl 1, k1.

Row 25: With CC, k1, *k1, sl 1, k1, sl 1, k1, sl 1, k1, sl 1, repeat from * to last 2 sts, k2.

Row 27: With MC, k1, *sl 1, k1, sl 1, k3, sl 1, k1, repeat from * to last 2 sts, sl 1, k1.

Row 29: With CC, k1, *k1, sl 1, k6, sl 1, repeat from * to last 2 sts, k2.

Row 31: With MC, k1, *sl 1, k7, repeat from * to last 2 sts, sl 1, k1.

Repeat Rows 1–32 for pattern. If you're making a swatch, bind off after Row 32.

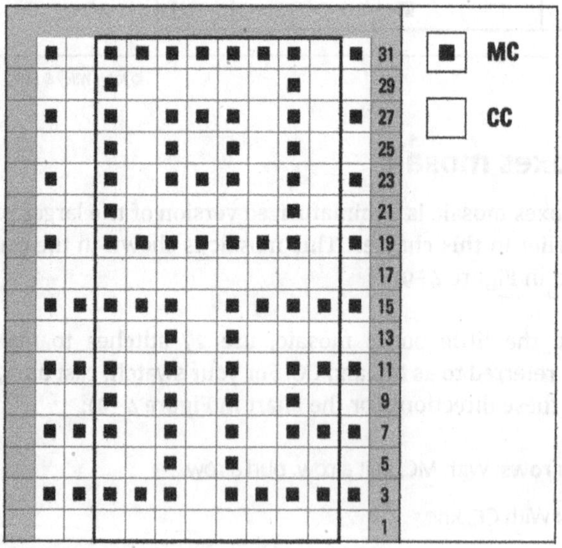

FIGURE 4-9:
The chart for the little boxes mosaic.

Miniature mosaic

The miniature mosaic, another 8-stitch mosaic pattern, can be used in the same places as the other small mosaic patterns. It's also a great allover pattern. Or you can knit it as a scarf using garter stitch instead of stockinette stitch — just remember to keep the yarn to the wrong-side when you slip your stitches! This mosaic is shown at the top of Figure 4-7 and is charted in Figure 4-10.

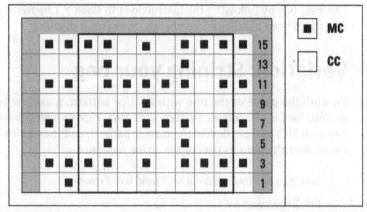

FIGURE 4-10:
Miniature mosaic
chart.

© John Wiley & Sons, Inc.

To practice this mosaic pattern with a swatch, cast on 27 stitches with MC and follow these directions (or the chart in Figure 4-10):

Set-up rows: With MC, knit a row, purl a row.

Row 1: With CC, k1, *sl 1, k7, repeat from * to last 2 sts, sl 1, k1.

Row 2 and all wrong-side rows: Purl the sts knit in the previous row and slip the sts slipped in the previous row.

Row 3: With MC, k1, *k3, sl 1, k1, sl 1, k2, repeat from * to last 2 sts, k2.

Row 5: With CC, k1, *k2, sl 1, k3, sl 1, k1, repeat from * to last 2 sts, k2.

Row 7: With MC, k1, *k1, sl 1, k5, sl 1, repeat from * to last 2 sts, k2.

Row 9: With CC, k1, *k4, sl 1, k3, repeat from * to last 2 sts, k2.

Row 11: With MC, k1, *k1, sl 1, k5, sl 1, repeat from * to last 2 sts, k2.

Row 13: With CC, k1, *k2, sl 1, k3, sl 1, k1, repeat from * to last 2 sts, k2.

Row 15: With MC, k1, *k3, sl 1, k1, sl 1, k2, repeat from * to last 2 sts, k2.

Repeat Rows 1–16 for pattern. To complete your swatch, repeat the 16 rows once more and then bind off.

Variation: Keeping your bag plain and simple

If you'd rather make a bag in a single color, knit the base and pick up stitches as outlined in the mosaic bag pattern. Begin working in the round and knit for 70 (90) rounds. If you have ready-made handles, bind off. If you want to knit handles, follow the directions given in the main pattern.

Felt your bag by following the instructions in Book 7, Chapter 1. After felting, you can attach your handles and embellish your bag if desired.

Variation: Striping your bag

To work the purse or the tote with a stripe pattern, make the bottom of the bag as described in the mosaic pattern with MC1. Pick up stitches for the sides of the bag with MC1 as described in the mosaic pattern, and then knit 1 round. *Note:* This round doesn't count as part of the stripe sequence.

> Switch to CC1 (but don't cut MC1) and knit 2 rows.
>
> Knit 2 rows with MC1.
>
> Repeat the previous 4 rounds until you've worked 3 stripes each of MC1 and CC1.
>
> Cut MC1 and join MC2. Work 3 stripes each of CC1 and MC2.
>
> Cut CC1 and join CC2. Work 3 stripes each of CC2 and MC2.
>
> Cut MC2 and join MC1. Work 3 stripes each of CC2 and MC1.
>
> Repeat this stripe sequence until you've knit 72 (96) rounds.

If you're adding ready-made handles, bind off and felt your bag. If you're making the knit-in handle, stop striping and, using MC1 only, follow the directions in the basic pattern. Follow the directions for the mosaic bag on finishing and felting.

REMEMBER

When you alternate colors, twist the two yarns around one another at the beginning of each round to keep things tidy and to prevent any gaps. Book 4, Chapter 1 covers the basics on changing colors as you knit.

Felted Messenger Bag

This stylish knit bag can go everywhere with you — it has plenty of room and a stylish strap that you can adjust to fit your needs. The matching buckle closure adds panache and keeps your belongings safely inside. You can see this great bag in Figure 4-11 or in color at dummies.com/go/knitcrochetAIO.

FIGURE 4-11:
The felted
messenger bag
has linen stitch
straps.

This messenger bag, like the other patterns in this chapter, relies on casting on and binding off to create its shape. But because you cast on in the middle of the project instead of just at the beginning, you can't use the long-tail cast on (you won't have a long tail; indeed, you won't have any tail at all!). So what do you do? There are several ways, but the cable cast on is recommended for this project. See Book 2, Chapter 1 for details about how it's done.

Working linen stitch by slipping stitches

To create the strap for this bag, you use linen stitch, which creates a beautiful woven texture that resists stretching, lays obediently flat, and looks great on both the front and the back. The stitch is also compact; you'll get a very firm gauge even on big needles. Linen stitch acts as it does because each stitch is knit only every other row, which means that stitches are slipped as often as they are knit.

As you might guess, linen stitch has a lot in common with half linen stitch. With linen stitch, you slip stitches every row. In half linen stitch, you slip stitches only on right-side rows. So, half linen stitch is stretchier and less dense than true linen stitch.

The linen stitch pattern is composed of 2 rows: a right-side row and a wrong-side row. The pattern works over any odd number of stitches.

Starting with the right-side row, follow these steps:

1. **Knit 1 stitch.**

2. **Bring the yarn to the front as if to purl.**

   Be sure to bring the yarn between and under the needles when you do this.

3. **Slip the next stitch purlwise. That is, put the right needle into the stitch as though you were going to purl and transfer the stitch to the right needle without purling it.**

4. **Bring the yarn back between stitches to the knit position.**

   This step leaves a horizontal float across the front of the slipped stitch.

5. **Repeat these four steps until you've reached the last stitch. Knit the last stitch.**

Wrong-side rows are a bit more difficult to describe because you're slipping the first and last stitches of the row. Do it as you read it and the steps will fall into place!

1. **With the yarn in front as if to purl, slip the first stitch purlwise.**

2. **Bring the yarn around the outside of the work to the back and then between the first and second stitch, return it to the purl position.**

   You've wrapped the yarn around the edge stitch counterclockwise (see Figure 4-12).

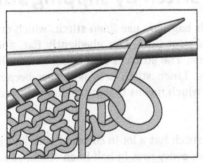

FIGURE 4-12: Wrapping the yarn around the edge stitch.

© John Wiley & Sons, Inc.

3. **Purl the next stitch.**
4. **Bring the yarn to the back of the work, as if to knit.**
5. **Slip the next stitch purlwise.**
6. **Bring the yarn back to the front of the work.**

7. **Repeat Steps 3 through 6 until you've reached the last stitch.**

8. **Bring the yarn to the back of the work.**

9. **Slip the last stitch purlwise.**

10. **Bring the yarn to the front of the work, wrapping the last stitch and putting the yarn in the correct position to knit the first stitch of the next row.**

Continue repeating these 2 rows (right-side and wrong-side) as directed in the pattern you're working.

Materials and vital statistics

>> **Yarn:** You need two kinds of yarn for this project:

- For the bag: Cascade 128 (100% wool); 128 yards (118 meters) per 100 grams; 4 skeins; color: 627 Grey Tweed

- For the straps: Schaefer Yarns Miss Priss (100% merino wool); 280 yards (256 meters) per 115 grams; 1 skein; color: Rosa Parks

>> **Needles:** You need two types of needles for this project:

- For the bag: US 13 (9 mm) needles

- For the straps: US 10½ (6.5 mm) needles

TIP

It's easiest to work with short straight needles or 2 double-pointed needles for the straps and a long circular needle for the bag, but any straight or circular needles of the appropriate size will work.

>> **Other materials:** Two D-rings, 2 inches wide; 2 buckles, 2 inches wide; yarn needle; sewing needle and matching heavy-duty thread to attach the straps to the bag

>> **Size:** See a schematic of the bag in Figure 4-13.

- Before felting: 18½ inches wide, 17 inches tall, and 3½ inches deep

- Finished size: 15 inches wide, 12 inches tall, and 3 inches deep

>> **Gauge:** You'll work at two different gauges on this project:

- For the bag: 9 stitches and 18 rows per 4 inches in garter stitch before felting; 11 stitches and 26 rows per 4 inches in garter stitch after felting

- For the straps: 26 stitches and 40 rows per 4 inches in linen stitch

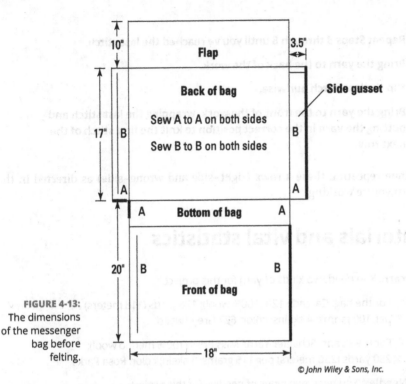

FIGURE 4-13:
The dimensions
of the messenger
bag before
felting.

© John Wiley & Sons, Inc.

This bag is knit in one piece starting with the front. From there you cast on a few stitches on each side to form the sides of the bag, which are knit at the same time as the back. After you bind off the side gusset stitches, you continue working the flap. When the knitting is complete, you sew the bag together and felt it in the washing machine. While it's drying, cast on for the eye-catching straps.

Knitting the bag

Cast on 42 sts with a US 13 (9 mm) needle and the Cascade 128 yarn.

Knit 94 rows in garter stitch (knit all rows); 47 garter ridges will be visible.

Side gussets and back

To give the bag depth, stitches are cast on each side of the work. The sides are created as you knit the back of the bag.

Using the cable cast on, cast on 8 sts at the beginning of the next 2 rows. There are 58 sts on the needles.

Knit 76 rows. There are 39 garter ridges visible from the beginning of the side gussets.

Bind off 8 sts at the beginning of the next 2 rows. There are 42 sts on the needle. (See Book 2, Chapter 1 details on binding off.)

Flap

Knit 44 rows. There will be 22 garter ridges visible after the last bind-off.

Bind off remaining 42 sts.

Creating the straps

Using US 10½ (6.5 mm) needles and the Miss Priss yarn, cast on 13 sts.

Begin working in linen stitch.

Row 1: *K1, slip 1 purlwise wyif, repeat from * to last st, k1.

Row 2: *Slip 1 purlwise wyib, purl 1, repeat from * to last st, slip 1 purlwise wyib.

TIP

The abbreviation "wyif" stands for "with yarn in front"; the abbreviation "wyib" stands for "with yarn in back." See Book 1, Chapter 4 for a table of knitting abbreviations. See the retro check pillow section in Book 5, Chapter 2 for an explanation of how these techniques work.

Repeat these 2 rows until the piece measures 45 inches.

Bind off and weave in ends.

For the buckle closure, you need 2 more straps:

For each one, cast on 13 sts and work in linen stitch. Make one piece that's 5 inches long and another piece that's 3 inches long.

Finishing your bag

Using Cascade 128 and the yarn needle, sew the bottom of the side gusset to the front (the sections marked A on Figure 4-13) using mattress stitch. Sew the long vertical edges of the gussets to the sides of the front (the sections marked B), being sure that the top edge of the bag front is aligned with the top (bound-off) edges of the gussets. (You can read up on finishing in Book 7, Chapter 2.)

Now it's time to felt your bag. Felting, which will make your bag smaller and sturdier, is accomplished by exposing the knitted bag to hot water and agitation in the washing machine. See Book 7, Chapter 1 for step-by-step felting instructions.

WARNING

Don't felt the beautiful straps you've made! Only put the bag itself in the washing machine!

When the bag is dry (which may take a couple of days depending on your climate) attach the straps by following these steps:

1. Sew the two D-rings to the top edges of the side gussets using a sewing needle and matching thread.

2. Slip one end of the longest strap through a D-ring from the outside toward the bag, making sure that the right side of the strap is out.

3. Fold an inch of the loose end of the strap over the D-ring and stitch it down.

4. Thread one buckle onto the long strap, placing it roughly in the middle of the strap.

   Because it's adjustable, it doesn't matter where you put it for now.

5. Insert the free end of the strap through the D-ring on the opposite side of the bag, putting it through from the outside toward the bag and bringing the free end up along the wrong side of the strap.

6. Bring the strap under the center bar of the buckle and fold it over the bar, and then stitch it down using a sewing needle and thread.

7. Attach the 5-inch-long strap to the center of the front flap, as shown in Figure 4-14. Attach the first 2 inches of the strap to the flap itself, with the remaining 3 inches hanging down from the edge of the flap.

8. Attach one end of the 3-inch-long strap to the center bar of the second buckle using a sewing needle and thread.

   The buckle will be at the top of the strap. Be sure that the right side of the strap faces out.

9. Thread the strap from the flap through the buckle to determine the correct placement of the strap with the buckle on the front of the bag.

10. Close the bag and sew the last strap in place.

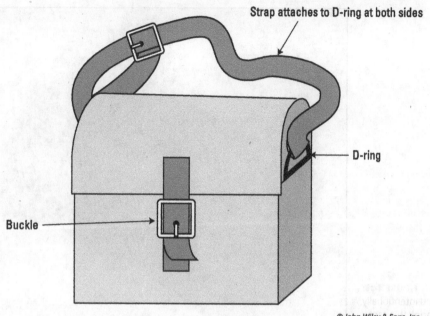

Strap attaches to D-ring at both sides

D-ring

Buckle

FIGURE 4-14: Attaching the straps to your bag.

© John Wiley & Sons, Inc.

Crocheted Tote Bag

Crocheting this felted carry-all is really fun! You start with one design and end up with another. The resulting fabric is soft, warm, and extremely durable (see Figure 4-15).

Materials and vital statistics

>> **Yarn:** Lion Brand "Lion Wool" worsted-weight yarn (100% wool), Article #820 (3 oz. [85 g], 158 yds [144 m] each skein for solids; 2¾ oz. [78 g], 143 yds [131 m] each skein for multis):

- 3 skeins of #140 Rose (MC)

- 1 skein of #201 Autumn Sunset (CC)

>> **Hook:** Crochet hook size K-10½ US or size needed to obtain gauge

>> **Measurements:** 22 in. wide x 12½ in. deep, excluding handles, and before felting

- **Note:** The finished measurements after felting will vary, but the carry-all will be considerably smaller. The bag shown here measured 17 in. wide x 9 in. deep, excluding the handles, after felting.

FIGURE 4-15:
You intentionally shrink this carry-all after you're done crocheting.

>> **Gauge:** First 2 rnds of base = 1¾ in.

>> **Stitches used:** Chain stitch (ch), slip stitch (sl st), single crochet (sc), half double crochet (hdc)

The beauty of this design is that the stitches are basic, and when you get done, you don't really see them at all. Whether you tend to crochet on the loose side or make your stitches tight, the final outcome will be unique. The felting process blends the stitches together, so the look you get is one of a solid fabric.

Crafting the tote

You create the base and sides of the bag as you crochet by working in rounds, instead of making the pieces individually and putting everything together at the end.

Base

Foundation chain: With MC, ch 62.

Rnd 1 (wrong side): Hdc in 3rd ch from hook, hdc in each of next 58 ch, 3 hdc in last ch, working across opposite side of foundation ch, hdc in each of next 58 ch, hdc in same ch as first hdc (122 hdc), sl st in turning ch to join.

Rnd 2: Ch 2 (first hdc), 2 hdc in next hdc, hdc in each of next 58 hdc, 2 hdc in each of next 3 hdc, hdc in each of next 58 hdc, 2 hdc in next hdc, hdc in same st as first hdc (128 hdc), sl st in first hdc to join, turn.

Beg sides

Rnd 1 (right side): Ch 2 (first hdc), working in flps only, hdc in each hdc around (128 hdc), sl st in first hdc to join.

Rnd 2: Ch 2 (first hdc), working in both loops of sts, hdc in each hdc around (128 hdc), sl st in first hdc to join.

Rep Row 2 in the foll color sequence: 5 rows MC; 3 rows CC; 9 rows MC; 2 rows CC; 3 rows MC; 2 rows CC; 3 rows MC; 2 rows CC; 9 rows MC; 1 row CC.

Last Row: With MC, sl st in each hdc around. Fasten off.

Getting the hang of the handles

Row 1: With right side facing, join MC in 11th st from side, ch 100, join with sl st in corresponding st on same side edge of bag being careful not to twist ch, sl st in next st on edge of bag, turn.

Row 2: Ch 1, sc in each st across handle, sl st in next st on side edge of bag, turn.

Rows 3–4: Rep Row 2. Fasten off.

Rep handle in corresponding sts on opposite side of bag.

Variation: Felting? Fuhgeddaboudit!

If you really like the way the bag looks before the felting process, go ahead and use it that way. If it gets wet or dirty, don't worry — it won't automatically felt. Just hand wash the bag in cool water and lay flat to dry.

Sweaters

Contents at a Glance

Chapter **1**

Anatomy of a Knitted Sweater Pattern

Sweater patterns tell you how to make the individual pieces of a sweater and how to put them together. Whether from a book, magazine, leaflet, or website, sweater patterns are set up in a predictable way. You find information about sizes, materials needed, gauge, and any special pattern stitches or abbreviations listed before the actual piece-by-piece instructions. This chapter runs you through the kinds of information you find in a typical sweater pattern.

You don't have to go deep into a sweater pattern before you see things like "sl 1, k1, psso," "yb," and "ssk" — common abbreviations to knitters. If they look indecipherable to you, refer to Book 1, Chapter 4, where these and other terms are conveniently listed and explained.

Picture This: Studying the Garment Photo

When you sit down with a new sweater pattern — or better yet, when you're choosing one — begin by paying close attention to the picture of the sweater you want to knit. This step may seem obvious, but studying the photograph or drawing and noting the details will clarify parts of the instructions that may otherwise be confusing. Study the picture of your sweater and answer these questions:

» Is it a pullover or a cardigan?

» How is it constructed? Can you tell from the picture whether the sweater is designed with a drop shoulder or a set-in sleeve, two common sleeve styles?

» Does the shoulder slope, or is it worked straight across? (If you can't tell from the photo, check the schematic. The shoulder design will be clear in the line drawing that often comes with the instructions.)

» Is the body of the sweater shaped in any way, or is it a simple rectangle?

» Is the sweater worked primarily in stockinette stitch? If other pattern stitches are used, can you identify them? Are they knit-and-purl patterns, cables, or something else?

» Is there a color pattern? If so, is it an allover pattern, or is it placed along the hem or across the yoke?

» Is there ribbing at the bottom edges, or does the sweater begin some other way?

» Does it have a round neckline or a V-neck? Is it finished with a ribbed neckband? A collar? A crocheted edge?

» If the sweater is pictured on a model, how's the fit? Does the collar lie properly around the neck? Does the sleeve cap pull? If the sweater doesn't fit the model well, chances are that it won't look good on you. (Then again, it just might.)

The point of all these questions? Know thy sweater.

Assessing the Pattern at a Glance

Looking at a picture of the knitted garment can tell you only so much about how the sweater is constructed. For the nitty-gritty details, you need to read the pattern — preferably before you begin.

REMEMBER Knowing as much as you can about your sweater upfront helps you anticipate the steps in the instructions and forestall many a mistake. If you find that something in the instructions is confusing in the first read-through, don't be alarmed; it may make sense by the time you get to that point in the instructions with needles and yarn in hand.

The following sections walk you through the various bits of info a typical sweater pattern contains.

TIP

It's a good idea to photocopy the pattern so you have a working copy that you can highlight, take notes on, or make changes to without messing up the original pattern.

How hard is "easy"? Level of difficulty

Many patterns tell you right away the level of difficulty the pattern writer has assigned to it. Here are the categories:

>> A *beginner* sweater uses basic stitches (knits and purls) and involves minimal shaping and simple finishing.

>> An *intermediate* project uses more-challenging stitch patterns and/or shaping and finishing.

>> An *experienced* or *expert* pattern may require all your powers of concentration. It frequently features tricky pattern or color work, and it may involve complicated shaping or construction details. Work on it only when you can give it all your attention.

TIP

Having more than one project going at a time is always a good idea. Make one of those projects something portable and rather brainless to give you a feeling of accomplishment and to keep your hands going while you watch TV or wait for a website to load. And have another more challenging project to work on when you have the time and quiet to concentrate on it.

How big is "big"? Knitted measurements

Most patterns begin by listing the sizes given in the instructions. Older patterns may list them in numbered chest sizes — for example, 38 (40, 42, 44, 46). Most current patterns give sizes in the designations small (medium, large) or in some combination of the two systems. Be sure you know your measurements before choosing the size to knit!

The size section is the first place you see parentheses in a knitting pattern, and it pays to notice where the size you want to make is located in the pattern: before or inside the parentheses. Every time a number or measurement is given in the pattern, the one for your size will be in the same place in relation to the parentheses. For example, if the pattern is written for small, medium, and large sizes — presented "small (medium, large)" — and you're making a small, the numbers for your size will always be written first outside the parentheses. If you're making a large, your numbers will always be last in the parentheses.

TIP

Before you start knitting, take the time to circle all the instructions in your size throughout the entire pattern (this is when your photocopy comes in handy). If you use a pencil, you can then erase the circles when finished so you can knit the pattern again later in a different size without confusion.

Sweater patterns generally tell you what the finished garment should measure when laid out on a flat surface. Sometimes only the chest/bust width is given. Other times, you find measurements for overall length, sleeve length, and/or upper arm circumference. Use this info to help you determine which size to knit. For more information about choosing which size to make, see Book 6, Chapter 2.

Materials

The pattern tells you what materials and equipment you need to make your sweater. In the "Materials" section of the pattern, you can find the following:

>> **The brand and specific name of the yarn used:** It gives the fiber content of the yarn, the weight and often the number of yards per skein, the color number and name of the yarn, and the number of skeins or balls required for the sweater. If the sweater hasn't been designed for a specific yarn company and isn't a vehicle for selling a particular brand, the pattern may simply call for yarn in a specific weight — for example, worsted-weight. (See Book 1, Chapter 2 for more on different yarn weights.)

>> **The size and type of needles you need:** Often, needles in two sizes are listed — the smaller for cuffs and bottom borders and the larger for the body of the sweater. If the pattern uses double-pointed needles or a circular needle (say for a neckband or collar), or if the entire sweater is worked in the round, the pattern tells you which size needle(s) to use and in what length.

Following the particular needles specified, you always see the phrase "or size to obtain gauge." This phrase often appears in full capitalization or in italics. Why? Because gauge matters. Head to Book 1, Chapter 3 for everything you need to know about gauge and why it's so important.

>> **Any special equipment or gadgets required:** Constructing some sweaters requires special tools — for example, a cable needle, stitch markers, stitch holders, and so on. These tools are listed after the needles.

>> **Buttons or other finishing materials:** If the sweater is a cardigan, the number and size of the buttons called for are listed. If pompoms, embroidery, or other embellishments are in order, the materials needed to make them are listed here.

TIP

Check the materials list and make sure that you have what you need when you're purchasing yarn and needles for a project. You don't want to find yourself unable to continue working on your project after the stores have closed because you don't have a particular tool in your supply box.

Gauge

In the "Gauge" section of the pattern, you find a formula that reads something like this:

14 sts and 21 rows to 4" (10 cm) over St st, using larger needles.

This notation is the gauge formula. It tells you how many stitches and rows are in a 4-inch square of the sweater fabric (in this case, stockinette stitch). If you want to make a sweater that corresponds to the measurements given, you must duplicate this gauge. You can't underestimate the importance of gauge! Find more information on gauge in Book 1, Chapter 3.

REMEMBER

Gauge isn't a standard, and you should make a gauge swatch for everything you plan to knit — especially if you want the finished project to fit when you're done.

Special pattern stitches

If your sweater has any special pattern stitches or instructions, they may be listed and explained separately and not given again in the body of the instructions. For example, you may see the following:

Seed Stitch

Row 1 (RS): * K1, p1; rep from * to end of row.

Row 2: K the purl sts and p the knit sts.

Rep Row 2 for pattern.

Then, in the instructions proper, when you read "work seed stitch for 8 rows," come back to this section to find out how to work seed stitch.

You also may find that a special abbreviation is explained. For example, you may see the following:

C3R (cross 3 right): Sl 1 st to cn and hold to back, k2, p1 from cn.

When you come across C3R in your instructions, you don't have to scratch your head and wonder, "What the heck?" You can look in the opening information for an explanation. (And if the instruction used in this example is making you wonder, "What the heck?" refer to the abbreviations in Book 1, Chapter 4.)

Schematics and charts

The *schematic* is a small outline drawing of each sweater piece in the pattern. The pattern usually includes one schematic showing the body front and back with the neckline sketched in and another schematic of one sleeve. Cardigans usually show a single front, a back, and a sleeve.

Listed along the edges of the drawing are the dimensions of the piece in each size — for example, the width and length of the sweater, the distance from the bottom of the sweater to the armhole, the depth of the armhole, and the depth and width of the neck. Figure 1-1 shows a schematic for a toggle jacket.

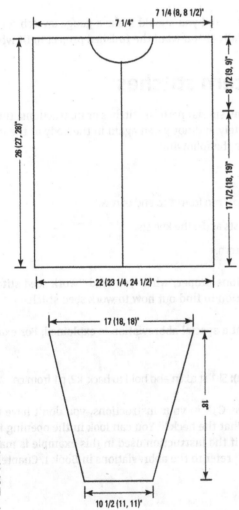

FIGURE 1-1:
A sample schematic showing shape and measurements.

Illustration by Wiley, Composition Services Graphics

Schematics are a big help because they show you the structure of the sweater at a glance: whether the armhole is straight or shaped and whether the sleeve cap is tall and narrow or short and wide. As you become more familiar with the way actual measurements fit you, you'll be able to tell quickly from the schematic whether you want to knit the pattern as-is or make changes.

Depending on the design of the sweater and the way the pattern's written, a sweater pattern may include a chart to show a stitch, cable, or color pattern. Or it may include a chart to show an unusual feature of the garment, such as a shawl collar. Figure 1-2 shows a chart for a repeating color motif and indicates how you should use it.

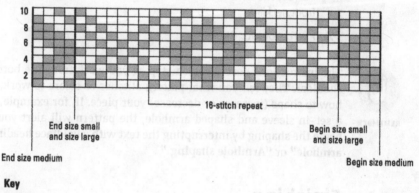

FIGURE 1-2:
Sample chart
for a repeating
color motif.

Key
☐ MC
▨ CC

Illustration by Wiley, Composition Services Graphics

REMEMBER

On right-side rows, work the chart from right to left. On wrong-side rows, work the chart from left to right. Refer to Book 1, Chapter 4 for more on how to read charts.

TIP

If you collect vintage knitting patterns, you'll seldom see a chart or schematic. Instead, all the moves are painstakingly written out. Some people who learned to knit under the row-by-written-row system regret its demise. Others welcome the picture over the written instructions. The good news is that if you understand better when things are described with words, you can write charts in word form — and vice versa. If you have a pattern with interminable and obscure directions, read them carefully with graph paper and pencil in hand and make yourself a chart to better understand the text.

Knitting instructions

After all the introductory information, the instructions for knitting your sweater begin. In general, most patterns for cardigans and pullovers begin with the back piece. Here the pattern tells you how many stitches to cast on and what to do with them.

The instructions are usually sequenced like this:

>> Instructions for the back

>> Instructions for the front (or fronts if you're knitting a cardigan); generally, the instructions for the front mirror those of the back until it's time to shape the front neckline

>> Instructions for the sleeves

REMEMBER

The instructions describe each step as you work from the bottom border to the shoulder. They tell you what pattern stitches or colors to work, and they tell you how to shape (increase or decrease) your piece. If, for example, your sweater has a set-in sleeve and shaped armhole, the pattern will alert you that it's time to begin the shaping by interrupting the text with a boldface heading such as **"Shape armhole"** or **"Armhole shaping."**

Finishing

The "Finishing" section of the pattern tells you what to do with your knitted pieces to make them into a complete sweater. It gives any special blocking instructions and tells you the order in which to sew the pieces together. You also find instructions for additional sweater details, such as how to make the neckband, cardigan bands, collar, crochet edge, and so on.

Chapter **2**

Knitting a Sweater, Step by Step

Being able to knit and purl, manipulate stitches (increasing, decreasing, and so on), and create special effects such as cables and stripes is fun in and of itself, no matter what you create. You can happily knit for years, using these techniques to make hats, scarves, afghans, bags, and other pieces that require just a little simple shaping or assembly. At some point, though, you may want to try your hand at something more challenging: knitting sweaters.

Before you cast on your first stitch, take a little time for a few simple preparatory steps: deciding on the perfect size, determining your gauge, and drawing a quick diagram of your sweater pieces. Of course, you can forget these steps and jump right in, just as you can toss your map in the backseat and drive from Maine to California by following the sun. But your trip is more likely to go smoothly if, before leaving, you check your oil and tires, study your map, and highlight the route to follow. This approach may be less spontaneous, but after you're on the road, you won't hit any dead ends that halt your progress.

This chapter runs you through the sweater-making process, from getting ready to knit to making the back, front, and sleeves. After you complete your back, front, and sleeves, you're ready to finish your sweater. Turn to Book 6, Chapter 3 and Book 7, Chapters 1 and 2 for information on those tasks.

Gathering Your Materials

To knit your first sweater, you need three things: a good pattern, good yarn, and needles. If possible, look for your materials in a knitting shop rather than a big-box or craft store. People who work in a yarn shop are generally very knowledge-able and can steer you to good pattern choices and quality yarn. If you run into any problems with the pattern or find that something confuses you, they'll be delighted to help you figure it out.

The following sections offer some tips to give you a good start in gathering your materials.

A good pattern

For your first sweater, choose a simple style with minimal shaping. A dropped-shoulder pullover is a good choice. Save a cardigan with buttonholes for your next project.

Also look for a pattern that calls for size US 7, 8, or 9 needles (that's 4½ mm, 5 mm, and 5½ mm, respectively). On needles this size, your project will knit up relatively quickly. You'll also be able to see, count, and manipulate individual stitches without straining your eyes — or patience. Plus, if a pattern calls for US 7, 8, or 9 needles, the yarn will be medium weight, one of the easier weights to work with. (Refer to Book 1, Chapter 2 for details on yarn weights.)

TIP
A child's sweater that knits up quickly is a good practice sweater. You get to work through all the steps of sweater making in miniature — and little kids look great in anything, whether the sleeves are an exact match or not. Plus, if you make it too big, the child will grow into it; if you make it too small, you have a ready-made gift or a doll's outfit. See Book 5, Chapter 3 for some baby sweater patterns.

TIP
Make a photocopy of your pattern so that you can write on it freely as you knit. Keep the copy in a protective plastic sleeve to carry around with your knitting. The same goes for any charts that come with the pattern.

Book 6, Chapter 1 guides you through the parts of a typical sweater pattern. You'll find it helpful to review before starting a sweater project.

Yarn

Choosing materials for your first sweater may be daunting if your local knitting store is a yarn and color wonderland. This section gives you some suggestions to help you narrow the choices.

Wool is the best choice for a first sweater because it knits up easily, blocks beautifully, and looks great. Choose a color on the lighter side so that it's easy to see individual stitches, and make sure that the yarn is a pretty color you'll enjoy knitting. When selecting yarn, look for a *superwash* wool. With superwash, you can launder the sweater in the washing machine and tumble dry, whereas regular wool tends to felt under those conditions.

If you're averse to wool for some reason, look into a blend of other natural fibers before turning to synthetics. Avoid all-cotton yarn for your first sweater unless you've worked up a lot of the smaller projects in this book and feel that you've had plenty of practice making stitches. Cotton yarn doesn't have much give and can be frustrating to work if your hands are new to needles and yarn.

If you must use a 100-percent synthetic yarn, choose a good-quality one (check with the salesperson at your local yarn shop for a recommendation) and resolve to be very careful in the blocking process. (You may want to take a quick look through Book 1, Chapter 2 before you head to the yarn shop to choose materials for your first sweater.)

Knitting needles

If you're using straight needles, they should be at least 12 to 14 inches long. If you have trouble with stitches slipping off your needles, choose wooden or plastic needles for your first sweater.

Depending on the size of the sweater, you may choose to use a longer circular needle instead. When you have many stitches on a short, straight needle, getting the stitches spread out comfortably can be difficult, which can affect the finished gauge. Using a 24-inch or longer circular needle as a straight needle (meaning that you don't connect the ends to knit in the round) eliminates this problem.

Other supplies to have handy

Before you leave the knitting store, double-check the materials list in the pattern to see whether you need to have any other supplies at the ready, such as stitch holders, markers, a pompom maker, or a tapestry needle for sewing seams or adding buttons.

TIP

Keep the following supplies together in a zippered bag with your knitting projects, and you won't have to get up and hunt around for them when you'd rather be knitting. See Book 1, Chapter 1 for more information on some of these tools.

>> Calculator

>> Crochet hook

>> Pencil and paper

>> Ring stitch markers

>> Safety pins

>> Scissors

>> Scrap yarn (preferably smooth, white cotton)

>> Spare double-pointed needle

>> Tape measure and a small ruler

>> Tapestry needle

TIP

Including an emery board for taming a renegade nail that keeps snagging on your yarn isn't a bad idea, either.

Before You Cast On

Before you put yarn to needles, you have a couple of small tasks to accomplish: Determine the best size sweater to make and check your gauge thoroughly.

Step 1: Pick a size

Sit down with your materials and take your pattern in hand. Go past the section that says "Sizes" and look for "Knitted Measurements." Don't be tempted to choose a size arbitrarily; one designer's medium is another designer's small. Instead, choose the size in the pattern that most closely matches the size you want your garment to measure. Choose according to the bust or chest measurement, or measure a sweater you love that fits you well and then find the closest match.

Most patterns are written for more than one size. Generally, instructions for the smallest size are listed first, followed by those for the larger sizes. So a pattern that includes instructions for small, medium, large, and extra-large sizes would present info in this form: S (M, L, XL). If the instructions say, "Cast on 100 (112, 120, 128) stitches," you cast on 100 stitches for a size small, 112 stitches for a size medium, 120 for a size large, and 128 for a size extra-large. Similarly, if the instructions say, "Repeat last 2 rows 8 (9, 11, 12) times" you know to knit these last 2 rows 8 times for a small sweater, 9 times for a medium sweater, and so on. *Note:* Many patterns give a size measurement *in addition to* an actual measurement: for example, "chest 32 (34, 36), actual size 36 (38, 40)."

FINDING THE PERFECT SIZE

If you're wondering whether 21 inches across the chest would fit better than 23 inches, there's an easy way to find out. Unfold your favorite sweater from the shelf (or dig it out of the pile on the chair), find your tape measure, and see what measurements feel good to you.

Obviously, if your most comfortable sweater is oversized and baggy and the sweater you're planning to knit is short and fitted, you shouldn't use your favorite sweater as a starting point. Look through your closet for something that fits the way you envision your future sweater will fit, measure it, and compare the measurements to those given in the pattern. Or pocket your tape measure along with your knitting notebook and a pen and head to your favorite clothing store. Fill your fitting room with sweaters, try them on, measure the ones that fit well, note the numbers in your knitting notebook, neatly refold the sweaters, and return them with a gracious smile to the salesperson. You'll know what sizes fit you best based on accurate measurements and styles.

What if you're knitting for someone else and you don't have that person's favorite sweater on hand to measure? Unless you're making a present for this person, call and ask. If it's a gift and the person is of average height and build, you're probably safe knitting a medium. Or if it's for someone who's taller than average, you can't go wrong with a large (or extra-large).

One wonderful thing about knitted fabric is that it's forgiving. It stretches. In desperation, you can even block it out or block it in — to a point. (See Book 7, Chapter 1 for information about blocking.) Width is really the only measurement you need to be concerned with when you start your sweater. Length can be adjusted fairly easily after you're underway. It's worth a little (or a lot of) investigation time upfront to ensure that, at the long-awaited moment when the sweater pieces have been knit and blocked and sewn together, you have a masterpiece that fits.

TIP

When you've determined which set of measurements to follow, get out a yellow highlighter or a pencil and carefully mark every number that refers to your size. If you've made a copy of your pattern as recommend earlier, you won't have to mark on the original.

Step 2: Find your gauge

Go to the section in your pattern that gives the required — that's *required* — gauge for the pattern. How is the gauge in your pattern measured? What size needles do you use, and which pattern stitch do you work? To brush up on the process of measuring gauge, refer to Book 1, Chapter 3.

REMEMBER

Always work your gauge swatch on the exact same needles and with the very same yarn you'll use for your project, not just needles of the same size and/or the same yarn in a different color. Needles of the same size but made out of different material, such as wood or Teflon-coated steel, can make a difference in the size of the stitch you make.

To find your gauge, follow these steps:

1. **Work a swatch to a length and width of 5 inches or more and then thread a piece of scrap yarn through the stitches on the needle.**

2. **Block your swatch, ideally in the same manner you'll block your sweater and let it rest.**

   See Book 7, Chapter 1 for blocking instructions.

3. **After the swatch has rested, measure it to determine your gauge.**

4. **Reknit the swatch as necessary to get the exact gauge you need.**

   - If you have more stitches per inch than the pattern calls for, go up one needle size.
   - If you have fewer stitches per inch than the pattern calls for, go down one needle size.

Tinker with your needle size until you come as close as you can to the *stitch gauge* required by the pattern. Stitch gauge determines how wide a sweater is, so if you're off on stitch gauge, your sweater will be off widthwise. After you cast on and start knitting the actual sweater, you can't do much to make your sweater wider or narrower.

Row gauge *will* affect your sleeve shaping and raglan shaping, and the placement of a cable or other distinctive vertical pattern may be interrupted in an awkward place if your row gauge is off. But you can work around a not-so-perfect row gauge with a little diagramming and planning, as explained in the later section "Graphing sleeves (it's worth it)."

Knitting . . . at Last!

After you've read through the instructions and established your gauge, it's time to cast on and launch your sweater. Most sweater patterns proceed in a predictable way, usually beginning with the back, followed by the front and then the sleeves.

If you're knitting in the round, you'll proceed a bit differently, depending on the type of sweater:

>> **Top-down sweaters:** When you knit a *top-down sweater,* you begin at the neck and knit your way down to just under the arms, knitting the tops of the sleeves as you go. (It may sound confusing, but these garments are some of the easiest and fastest sweaters to knit.) After you finish the body, you return to the sleeves and finish them separately.

>> **Bottom-up sweaters:** For these sweaters, you knit the bottom portion of the sweater first, all the way to the underarms. Then you join the sleeves, which have been knit separately, and decrease the sweater yoke all the way to the neck opening.

Knitting the back

Most sweater patterns instruct you to begin with the back. They tell you which needles to use to get started, how many stitches to cast on, and which stitches to begin with. This section offers helpful advice on getting off to a good start.

TIP

Get into the habit of keeping track of how many rows you've knit as you work the sweater back (and front). Why? Because if the back and front match row for row, you can sew them together using the mattress stitch (explained in Book 7, Chapter 2). Using safety pins, pin the first stitch from which you want to count. Then, as you knit, stop every once in a while, count 20 rows, and pin the next stitch. If you pin a stitch every 20 rows, it's easy to keep track of the row number, and you won't have to count from the very beginning each time.

Casting on

For the two-strand cast on method (refer to Book 2, Chapter 1), you have to know how much yarn to allow for the number of stitches you'll be casting on. Allow 1 to 1½ inches for each stitch to be cast on.

TIP

Leave enough of a tail to use later to seam up the side of the sweater. For this tail, add 12 inches to the amount you need for the cast on stitches. If this extra-long end gets in your way as you knit, try using a plastic bread clip as a bobbin for the extra-long tail.

Strengthening the cast on edge

Cast on edges take a lot of wear, and a well-worn and loved sweater can begin to fray or even break along the bottom edge. You can discourage this wear by casting on with a double strand of yarn (simply cast on with two balls of yarn) and then continuing with a single strand. After the cast on row, simply drop the second strand and cut it off, leaving an end long enough to weave in later.

Selecting the right side

After you've worked a few rows, take a look at the cast on edge. You'll see that it looks different from each side: One side shows small neat bumps, and the other shows overlapping diagonal stitches. It's up to you to decide which side you prefer for the right side of your sweater. If you use the two-strand cast on method and make the first row a right-side row, the little bumps will show on the right side. If you'd rather use the other side of the cast on row as the right side, make the first row of your knitting a wrong-side row.

REMEMBER

When you move on to the front and the sleeves, be sure to use the same side as the right side. Otherwise, the edges of your piece won't be the same.

Switching needles when it's time

Many sweaters use smaller needles for cuffs, hems, and necks and use larger needles for the body. The instructions tell you when to change to the larger or smaller needles. At the change row, simply knit the next row with one of the smaller (or larger needles). Here's an example from a pattern:

> With smaller needles and the MC, cast on 101 (107, 117) sts.
>
> Work k1, p1 rib for 3½ inches.
>
> Change to larger needles and work in St st until piece measures 12½ (13, 13) inches from beg.

To switch needles in this example, you work to the end of the change row and knit the next row by using one of the larger needles. Essentially, you're knitting from the smaller needle to the larger one. At the end of this row, the stitches are now on the larger needle, and the smaller needle is empty. Put aside the smaller needles and continue on in the stitch pattern(s) given in your pattern with the larger needles.

Measuring your piece

As accurate as your gauge swatch may be, knitting a piece so much larger than a swatch can throw off your careful measurements. For peace of mind, take a gauge reading after you work a good 4 inches or so. Work to the halfway point in your row so that you can spread out the stitches along both needles to the width of the fabric. Lay out your piece on a flat surface and measure it. If it's supposed to measure 22 inches across, check to see that it does.

When it's time to measure the length of your piece, work to the center of the row, lay the piece flat, and measure it from the very bottom — the first row — to the knitting needle. Take your measurement somewhere in the middle, not on the edge; your edges will be more stretched and wobbly and not as stable as the center knitting.

Shaping an armhole

If your sweater has a shaped armhole, the instructions tell you when to begin the armhole shaping, where and how to decrease, and how many stitches you should have left after you complete the shaping. It may say something like this:

Armhole shaping

Bind off 3 sts at beg of next 2 rows. Dec 1 st each side every other row 1 (3, 5) times — 56 (60, 62) sts. Work even until armhole measures 5 (5½, 6) inches.

TIP

Before starting any decreasing, put a safety pin into one of the stitches on the LH needle to mark the beginning of the armhole. You'll measure from that mark when you're determining the depth of the armhole. Be sure to lay the measuring tape flat; do not follow the curved edge of the armhole.

Continue to work the back until you've worked the number of inches to the shoulder given in your pattern.

Shaping the shoulder and neck

If the shoulder is shaped, you work the shoulder and neck shaping right after you work the armhole shaping. You're likely to see instructions like this:

Shoulder and neck shaping

Bind off 6 sts at beg of next 4 (2, 2) rows, 7 sts at beg of next 2 (4, 4) rows. Bind off rem 18 (20, 22) sts for back neck.

Some patterns with straight shoulders tell you to bind off all the stitches on the last row of the back piece and don't distinguish shoulder stitches from back-neck stitches. If the instructions don't give specific numbers for shoulder stitches, look at the final line in the instructions for the front. There, you should be able to find the number of stitches remaining for each shoulder after you've worked the neckline shaping.

Sometimes the shoulder and neck shaping are separated, with the shoulder shaping coming first and the neck shaping later. Simply follow the instructions as they're given, and you'll be fine.

At this point, you've completed your sweater back. You're a quarter of the way to a finished sweater, and you have a useful tool: a very accurate gauge swatch. Block the back (see Book 7, Chapter 1) and have it at the ready in case you need to measure the gauge one more time.

SLOPING THE SHOULDERS

If your pattern is designed with a straight shoulder and you want it to angle up slightly from shoulder edge to neck, changing your pattern is easy. Instead of binding off all the shoulder stitches at once, bind off several groups of stitches over several rows in stair-step fashion.

For an average gauge of 4 to 6 stitches an inch, three steps make a good slope. Divide the number of stitches for one shoulder by 3 to determine how many stitches to bind off for each shoulder step. If the number of stitches in the shoulder isn't evenly divisible by 3, make the first two steps the same number of stitches and the third step at the neckline the odd one.

On a piece of graph paper, mark off enough squares in a horizontal line to represent the right shoulder and fill in the steps. (If you have enough room on your graph paper, map enough squares to represent the back neck and both shoulders, too.) See the following figure.

When you reach the shoulder and are ready to bind off, with the right side facing, bind off the number of stitches for the first "step" at the beginning of the next 2 rows. Then bind off the number of stitches for the second step at the beginning of the next 2 rows. Then bind off the remaining shoulder stitches at the beginning of the next 2 rows. Finally, bind off the back neck stitches.

Original shoulder bind-off

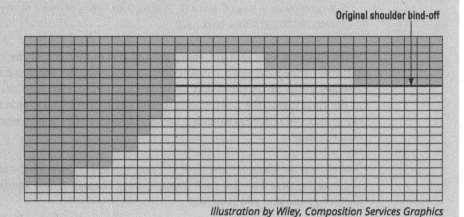

Illustration by Wiley, Composition Services Graphics

Knitting the front

The front of a sweater is generally worked in the same way as the back as far as the neckline. Your pattern tells you to work the front until it measures a certain length and to "end with a WS (wrong-side) row." You begin the neckline on the next RS (right-side) row.

Shaping the front neck

To shape a neckline, you begin by binding off a group of stitches at the center of your sweater piece. Your pattern tells you to "join a second ball of yarn" before you begin to bind the stitches off. You need two balls of yarn to work the remainder of the neckline, one for each side.

To join the second ball of yarn, simply start knitting and binding off with the strand from the second ball. When you return to shape the left side of your neckline, pick up and use the yarn from the first ball.

Shaping the shoulders

Often the shoulder shaping begins while the neckline is still being worked (your pattern says "at the same time" if this is the case). At this point, get out the graph paper. It's helpful to chart the neckline shaping stitch by stitch, especially if the shoulders are shaped as well, because the chart clearly shows what you should be doing and when.

Here's a set of example instructions for front neck and shoulder shaping:

Next row (RS): Work 27 sts, join second ball of yarn and bind off center 15 sts, work to end. Working both sides at once, bind off from each neck edge 3 sts once, 2 sts twice, then dec 1 st every other row twice. AT SAME TIME when piece measures same length as back to shoulder, shape shoulder as for back.

Because the back shoulder shaping instructions were "Bind off 9 sts at beg of next 6 rows," you do the same for the front shoulder shaping. Figure 2-1 shows this pattern charted.

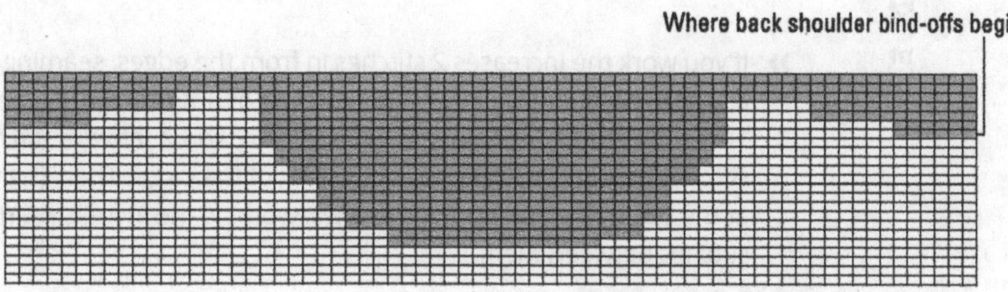

Where back shoulder bind-offs begin

FIGURE 2-1:
Charting shoulder and neck shaping for easy reference.

Illustration by Wiley, Composition Services Graphics

Note: When you begin shoulder shaping while still working the neckline, you shape the right and left sides of your piece on different rows. Your shaping is symmetrical but off by one row. You can see this difference by checking the bind-offs at either side of the center front neck edge.

Putting the front and back together

If you take the time to count rows as you knit up the back (a tip mentioned in the earlier section "Knitting the back") and you make the front the exact same number of rows, you can use the nearly invisible and fun-to-do mattress stitch to seam them together. If, on the other hand, you rely on measuring your pieces to check their sameness, you don't necessarily have the *exact* same number of rows in both front and back pieces, and you have to seam up your sweater by using the less-than-wonderful backstitch. Head to Book 7, Chapter 2 for a variety of ways to assemble sweater pieces.

Knitting sleeves

When you've worked your way to the sleeves, you're almost home free. Sleeves are smaller than body parts and therefore go quickly. And shaping makes them interesting to knit.

In general, sleeves begin at the cuff, are worked in the same stitch patterns as the back and front, and are shaped by regular increases along the sides. Your pattern tells you how many stitches to cast on, what stitch to work, when to change needles to a larger size if required, when to begin increasing, and how often to increase. In general, patterns instruct you to increase at regular row intervals, although sometimes they tell you to increase at intervals measured in inches.

Advice for making sleeves easy

Here are some tips for knitting sleeves:

>> If you work the increases 2 stitches in from the edges, seaming your sleeve is a breeze because you have a straight line of undistorted stitches to work with. To do so without throwing off your pattern, add 2 *selvedge stitches* (border stitches that add stability) on both sides of the piece. Then knit these 2 stitches at the beginning and end of the rows, working the increases and pattern stitches between them.

>> Using two balls of yarn and one (circular) needle, cast on for two sleeves and work them both at the same time. Doing so ensures that you end up with identical pieces. Just cast on the number of stitches required for one sleeve. Then use the second ball of yarn as you cast on the same number of stitches

on the same needle. Work each sleeve with its own ball of yarn. (This strategy is also helpful when working two fronts of a cardigan.)

>> If you're working a sweater with a dropped shoulder, you can pick up stitches along the armhole edge of the body and knit from the armhole down to the cuff, saving yourself from having to sew the sleeve to the body. (Find out about picking up stitches in Book 6, Chapter 3.) Check to see how many stitches your sleeve is supposed to have when you've worked all the increases; that's the number to pick up. Work 1 inch before you begin decreasing.

Graphing sleeves (it's worth it)

Once in a while, you may run into a glitch in sleeve-making if the pattern tells you to increase every so many rows and your row gauge is different from the designer's. Your sleeve may measure the correct length before you've worked all the necessary increases, but you end up with a sleeve that's the right length but the wrong width at the armhole.

If you're working an angled or shaped-sleeve cap, the top of your sleeve needs to fit *exactly* into the carved-out shape in the sweater body. To ensure that your sleeve is the correct length *and* width when you reach the armhole, graph it. (You can buy large sheets of graph paper at an artist's supply store or simply tape two pieces together lengthwise.) If you're working a cable or lace pattern that requires a certain number of stitches, graphing your sleeve offers the further advantage of helping you see when you've increased enough stitches to begin working the pattern over them.

To graph a sleeve, follow these steps:

1. **Draw a line at the bottom of your graph paper to represent the first row after the bottom rib or border of the cuff; mark the center.**

2. **Go to the sweater back you've finished and blocked and take a new and improved gauge reading.**

   Subtract the cuff measurement from the length that your sleeve should measure to the armhole. Multiply the row gauge per inch by the length that your sleeve should measure from the end of the rib or border to the underarm.

3. **Count this number of rows from your bottom line and mark the top row to represent the underarm.**

4. **At the underarm mark, count out a horizontal line of squares to represent the width your sleeve should be at this point.**

   Make sure that the centers of top and bottom rows are aligned.

5. **Mark a row about 1 inch below the underarm; check your pattern for the first increase row and mark it.**

   The rows of squares between the marked rows represent the number of rows you have in which to make your increases.

6. **Draw in the rest of the increases.**

   If you get them all in *before* reaching the top line, you're all set. If not, reconfigure the increases so that they're closer together, and you can be sure of ending up with the correct number of stitches when your sleeve measures the right length.

Figure 2-2 shows a chart of a sleeve with increases.

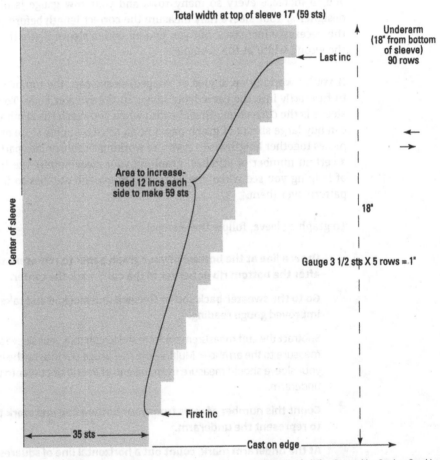

Total width at top of sleeve 17" (59 sts)

Last inc

Underarm
(18" from bottom
of sleeve)
90 rows

Area to increase-
need 12 incs each
side to make 59 sts

Center of sleeve

18"

Gauge 3 1/2 sts X 5 rows = 1"

First inc

35 sts

Cast on edge

FIGURE 2-2:
Charting a sleeve
with increases
(looking at the
right half of the
sleeve).

Illustration by Wiley, Composition Services Graphics

The Big Picture: Keeping Track of Where You Are

You don't knit a sweater in one sitting. No matter how much you love to knit, eventually you have to put it down. For this reason, it's helpful to develop a system that reminds you of where you are at the moment you put down your knitting and where you're going when you pick it up again later.

For example, to track a sweater in progress, you can make a diagram, similar to the method explained in Gertrude Taylor's *America's Knitting Book* (Simon & Schuster Trade). The following approach is an adaption of her system.

A *diagram* is a quick outline drawing you make of your sweater piece. On it, you can show all the knitting information embedded in the text of your pattern. If your sweater pattern is a map of your entire sweater, the diagram you make is a map of the piece you're working on at the moment. It gives you an instant visual picture of where you are, where you're headed, and the steps you have to take to get there. Figure 2-3 shows a diagram of a sweater back.

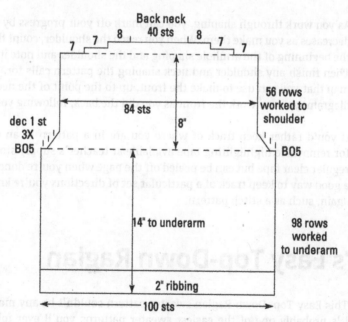

FIGURE 2-3:
A diagram of a sweater back.

Illustration by Wiley, Composition Services Graphics

You can work from a general diagram on plain white paper until you get to the shaping area. At that point, move to graph paper and chart every stitch. Because most sweater patterns have you begin with the back, draw a diagram for that piece first and enter the information that will remind you of the steps en route to the finished piece, such as the following:

>> How many stitches to cast on

>> How many inches to work in the border stitch

>> Where to begin binding off the armhole

>> How many stitches to bind off

>> How many stitches to decrease

As you work through the sweater, you can mark off your route as you go (doing so is helpful if you put your work down for a few days) and make notes on things you want to remember. For example, if you're working on a sweater with armhole shaping, you can note on the diagram the number of rows you're worked to the first shaping row. This way, when you work on the front, you know exactly how many rows to work for the piece to be the same as the back.

As you work through shaping, you can mark off your progress by checking off the decreases as you make them. When you reach the shoulder, count the rows between the beginning of the armhole shaping and the shoulder and note it on the diagram. Then finish any shoulder and neck shaping the pattern calls for. This gives you a map that you can use to make the front, up to the point of the neckline. Using the diagram, you can work the front as you did the back, following your notes.

TIP

If you'd rather keep track of where you are in a pattern in an easier way, look for removable highlighting tape available at teacher's supply stores. It looks like regular clear tape but can be peeled off the page when you're done with it. It's also a good way to keep track of a particular set of directions you're knitting again and again, such as a stitch pattern.

Women's Easy Top-Down Raglan

This Easy Top-Down Raglan sweater pattern couldn't be any more basic. In fact, it's probably one of the easiest sweater patterns you'll ever follow. Figure 2-4 shows the schematic for this top-down sweater.

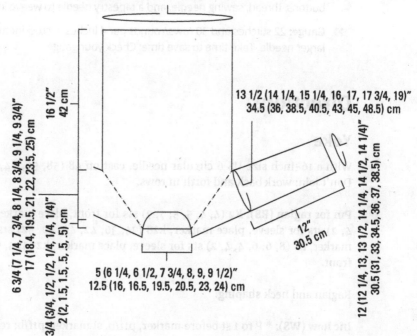

34 1/4 (37 3/4, 41 1/2, 45, 48 3/4, 52 1/4, 56)"
87 (96, 105.5, 114.5, 124, 132.5, 142) cm

13 1/2 (14 1/4, 15 1/4, 16, 17, 17 3/4, 19)"
34.5 (36, 38.5, 40.5, 43, 45, 48.5) cm

16 1/2"
42 cm

6 3/4 (7 1/4, 7 3/4, 8 1/4, 8 3/4, 9 1/4, 9 3/4)"
17 (18.4, 19.5, 21, 22, 23.5, 25) cm

3/4 (3/4, 1/2, 1/2, 1/2, .5, .5, 1/4)"
2 (2, 1.5, 1.5, .5, .5, .5) cm

5 (6 1/4, 6 1/2, 7 3/4, 8, 9, 9 1/2)"
12.5 (16, 16.5, 19.5, 20.5, 23, 24) cm

12"
30.5 cm

12 (12 1/4, 13, 13 1/4, 14 1/4, 14 1/2, 14 1/4)"
30.5 (31, 33, 34.5, 36, 37, 38.5) cm

FIGURE 2-4:
Diagram of the
Women's Easy
Top-Down Raglan
sweater.

Illustration by Wiley, Composition Services Graphics

Materials and vital statistics

» **Measurements:** 34¼ (37¾, 41½, 45, 48¾, 52¼, 56) inches. The instructions are for the smallest size, with larger numbers in parentheses. When only one number is given, it applies to all sizes. The sweater is shown in size 37¾ inches.

Measure yourself around the chest under your arms (armpit level); this number is your chest measurement. Because most sweater patterns give a finished measurement, measuring a favorite sweater that fits well is also a good idea. That way, you know exactly what finished measurement you prefer in a sweater. For more help with taking your measurements, see the sidebar in Book 6, Chapter 1.

» **Yarn:** Lion Brand "Superwash Merino" (100% superwash merino; CYC #3, 306 yards, 3.5 ounces [100 grams]): Dijon #486-170, 4 (4, 5, 5, 5, 6, 6) balls

» **Needles:** 16-inch and 32-inch sizes US 5 (3¾ mm) and US 6 (4 mm) circular needles, sizes US 5 and 6 dpns or sizes needed to obtain gauge

> » **Other materials:** Stitch markers, stitch holders or waste yarn, five small buttons, thread, sewing needle, and a tapestry needle to weave in ends

> » **Gauge:** 22 stitches and 30 rows/rounds per 4 inches in stockinette stitch with larger needle. Take time to save time: Check your gauge.

Directions

Yoke

With a 16-inch size US 6 circular needle, cast on 48 (58, 56, 64, 62, 72, 70) sts. Don't join; work back and forth in rows.

Pm for raglan (RS): K2 (4, 4, 5, 5, 7, 7) sts for front, place marker, k8 (8, 6, 6, 4, 4, 2) sts for sleeve, place marker, k28 (34, 36, 42, 44, 50, 52) sts for back, place marker, k8 (8, 6, 6, 4, 4, 2) sts for sleeve, place marker, k2 (4, 4, 5, 5, 7, 7) sts for front.

Raglan and neck shaping:

Inc Row (WS): * P to 1 st before marker, p1f/b, sl marker, p1f/b; rep from * 3 more times, p to end — 8 sts increased.

Inc Row (RS): K1, m1, * k to 1 st before marker, k1f/b, sl marker, k1f/b; rep from * 3 more times, k to last st, m1, k1 — 10 sts increased.

Rep the last 2 rows 4 (4, 5, 6, 7, 7, 8) more times — 138 (148, 164, 190, 206, 216, 232) sts total; 17 (19, 22, 26, 29, 31, 34) sts each front, 28 (28, 30, 34, 36, 36, 38) sts each sleeve, 48 (54, 60, 70, 76, 82, 88) sts for back.

Purl 1 WS row even.

Inc Row (RS): K1, m1, * k to 1 st before marker, k1f/b, sl marker, k1f/b; rep from * 3 more times, k to last st, m1, k1 — 10 sts increased.

Rep the last 2 rows once more. Do not turn after the last RS row — 158 (168, 184, 210, 226, 236, 252) sts total; 21 (23, 26, 30, 33, 35, 38) sts each front, 32 (32, 34, 38, 40, 40, 42) sts each sleeve, 52 (58, 64, 74, 80, 86, 92) sts for back.

To shape the neck, place marker for beg of round, then use the cable method to CO 10 (12, 12, 14, 14, 16, 16) sts for front neck, join to work in the round and knit to end of round — 168 (180, 196, 224, 240, 252, 268) sts total; 52 (58, 64, 74, 80, 86, 92) sts each front and back; 32 (32, 34, 38, 40, 40, 42) sts each sleeve.

Raglan shaping:

Inc Round: * K to 1 st before marker, k1f/b, sl marker, k1f/b; rep from * 3 more times, knit to end — 8 sts increased.

Knit 1 round even.

When you have too many stitches on the 16-inch circular, change to the longer circular needle by holding the new needle in your right hand and knitting the stitches from the old needle onto the new needle.

Rep the last 2 rounds 17 (19, 20, 20, 21, 23, 24) more times — 312 (340, 364, 392, 416, 444, 468) sts total; 88 (98, 106, 116, 124, 134, 142) sts each front and back, 68 (72, 76, 80, 84, 88, 92) sts each sleeve.

Dividing body and sleeves:

Remove beg of round marker and knit to the next raglan marker (left front), remove marker, place the next 68 (72, 76, 80, 84, 88, 92) sleeve sts onto stitch holder or waste yarn, remove marker, use the cable method to CO 3 (3, 4, 4, 5, 5, 6) sts, place marker for new beg of round, CO 3 (3, 4, 4, 5, 5, 6) more sts, knit across back sts to next raglan marker (right back), remove marker, place the next 68 (72, 76, 80, 84, 88, 92) sleeve sts onto stitch holder or waste yarn, remove marker, use the cable method to CO 6 (6, 8, 8, 10, 10, 12) sts, knit to end of round — 188 (208, 228, 248, 268, 288, 308) sts.

Body

Continue working in stockinette st in the round until piece measures 16 inches from underarm.

Change to smaller needle and work in garter st for 6 rounds, ending after a knit round. Bind off all sts purlwise.

Sleeve

Return 68 (72, 76, 80, 84, 88, 92) held sts from one sleeve onto larger dpns. Beg at center of underarm CO sts, pick up and knit 3 (3, 4, 4, 5, 5, 6) sts, knit across held sts, then pick up and knit another 3 (3, 4, 4, 5, 5, 6) sts along rem underarm CO sts — 74 (78, 84, 88, 94, 98, 104) sts. Place marker for beg of round.

Work in stockinette st in the round until piece measures 1 inch from underarm.

Sleeve shaping:

Dec Round: K1, k2tog, knit to last 3 sts, ssk, k1 — 2 sts decreased.

Knit 17 (13, 11, 9, 8, 7, 6) rounds even.

Rep the last 18 (14, 12, 10, 9, 8, 7) rounds 3 (4, 5, 6, 7, 8, 9) more times — 66 (68, 72, 74, 78, 80, 84) sts remain.

Continue to work in stockinette st in the round until piece measures 11½ inches from underarm.

Change to smaller dpns and work in garter st for 6 rounds, ending after a knit round. Bind off all sts purlwise.

Rep for second sleeve.

Finishing

Block piece to measurements.

Neck trim: With smaller circular needle or dpns, beg at center of back, pick up and knit 14 (17, 18, 21, 22, 25, 26) sts along first half of back, 8 (8, 6, 6, 4, 4, 2) sts along sleeve, 12 (14, 15, 17, 18, 20, 21) sts along front neck to CO sts, 10 (12, 12, 14, 14, 16, 16) sts along CO sts, 12 (14, 15, 17, 18, 20, 21) sts along front neck to sleeve, 8 (8, 6, 6, 4, 4, 2) sts along sleeve, then 14 (17, 18, 21, 22, 25, 26) sts along rem half of back — 78 (90, 90, 102, 102, 114, 114) sts. Place marker for beg of round work in garter st for 6 rounds, ending after a knit round. Bind off all sts purlwise.

Sew decorative buttons along raglan lines at one shoulder.

Chapter 3

Knitting Neckbands, Edging, Buttonholes, and More

Most knitting patterns for sweaters give you the most basic, generic plan for making a sweater. After you work the pieces, block them, and seam the shoulders, you must bring your own expertise to the finishing details — neckbands, edgings, buttonholes, and cardigan bands. This chapter takes you on a beginner's tour of techniques for picking up stitches evenly, making cardigan bands, and installing buttonholes. By no means do the procedures shown here exhaust the possibilities for finishing your sweater, but they're a great place to start.

Picking Up Stitches to Knit

The cast on edges of knitted garments are generally very presentable and need no finishing. Not true for the other edges of a knitted piece. Edges not encased in a seam, such as necklines, the center front edges of a cardigan, and the armholes on a vest, require some kind of finishing or edging. Usually, a neckline gets a neckband or collar, and cardigans feature knitted bands along the front edges for buttons and buttonholes.

Picking up stitches is a knitter's way to avoid sewing on these extra edgings. Instead of creating a collar or button band separately and sewing it onto a knitted garment, you can use needles and yarn to pull up new loops along a knitted edge and knit a border right then and there. Some knitters are so enamored of picking up stitches that they make sleeves for garments by picking up stitches around the armholes and knitting the sleeves upside down to the cuffs. (Knitters are very ingenious.) Follow the instructions in this section to pick up a row of completely new stitches and knit from there.

You can pick up stitches from three kinds of edges:

>> Horizontal, such as the bound-off stitches along a back neck

>> Vertical, such as the center front of a cardigan

>> Diagonal or curved, such as the shaped section of a front neckline

To pick up stitches, you need the yarn for your project and one needle in the size you plan to use for your band or collar. Most patterns specify the needle size required for collars, cuffs, and other bands; if yours doesn't, one or two sizes smaller than the needles used for the main part of your knitting generally works well.

WARNING

Be sure to block your sweater back and fronts before picking up stitches. (See Book 7, Chapter 1 for details on blocking.) You won't have to cope with edges that want to curl in or out; your blocked edges to be picked up will lie nice and flat — and therefore be easy to work.

Picking up stitches along a horizontal edge

The easiest, most straightforward form of picking up stitches is along a horizontal edge because you pick up 1 stitch in each bound-off stitch. When you're done, you should barely see a transition between the stitches you picked up and the new set of stitches. You use this method when picking up stitches along a back neck edge and for the center front stitches that form the base of a round neckline. Follow these simple steps:

1. **With the RS facing, starting at the right end of the work, insert the needle into the first stitch (the V) from front to back just below the bound-off edge.**

   Make sure that your needle isn't just going under the threads of the bound-off stitches but into the entire stitch below (the one you can see clearly), as shown in Figure 3-1.

2. **Wrap the yarn around the needle just as if you were knitting and then pull a loop through.**

You can secure the loose yarn end temporarily by tying it onto your knitting, or you can just keep picking up stitches and secure it later. After you pick up the first stitch, the yarn will be taut.

3. **Repeat Steps 1 and 2, pulling through one loop in each stitch across the row.**

4. **After you finish picking up all the stitches you need for your finished edge, turn your work around (so that the WS is facing you) and work the first WS row in your stitch pattern.**

That's all there is to it!

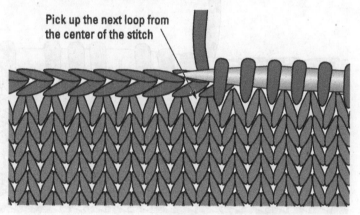

Pick up the next loop from the center of the stitch

FIGURE 3-1:
Pick up stitches along a bound-off horizontal edge.

Illustration by Wiley, Composition Services Graphics

Picking up stitches on a vertical edge

To pick up stitches along a vertical edge, such as a cardigan front, use the same pull-through-a-stitch procedure covered in the preceding section for a horizontal edge. This time, however, bring the loop up between the running threads connecting the first 2 stitches along the edge, as shown in Figure 3-2. Here's how to do it:

1. **With the RS facing and starting at the right end of the work, insert your needle between the running threads of the first 2 stitches from front to back.**

2. **Wrap the yarn as if to knit, and pull the new loop through.**

3. Repeat Steps 1 and 2, pulling stitches up through the column of running threads until you've picked up the number of stitches you need for your finished edge.

There are more vertical rows of stitches per inch than there are stitches across. When you pick up stitches along a vertical edge, you match stitches to rows. To keep the correct ratio of stitches to rows, you need to skip a running thread interval every few stitches. The rule is to pick up 3 stitches out of every 4 rows. You can see this technique in Figure 3-2 and find more information about it in the section "Bring on the Bands" later in this chapter.

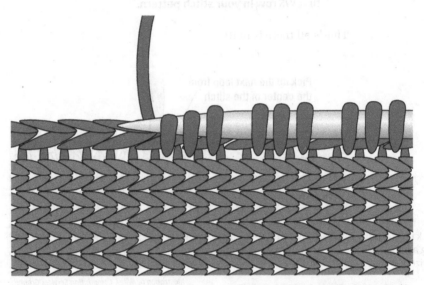

FIGURE 3-2:
Pick up stitches along a bound-off vertical edge.

Illustration by Wiley, Composition Services Graphics

Picking up stitches on a diagonal or curved edge

Most curved edges are made by a series of stepped bind-offs followed by decreases that give a far-from-smooth curved line. Not to worry. The picked-up band saves the day with an attractive continuous curve.

When you pick up stitches along a curved edge, avoid working in the very edge stitch. Instead, work into a stitch or between stitches at least 1 full stitch in from the edge. Your aim is to make a nice-looking line for your border to begin on, not to see how close you can work to the uneven edge of your knitting.

Pick up stitches on the bound-off edge of the back neck and the center front bound-off section as shown in the earlier section "Picking up stitches along a horizontal edge." Along the side neck edges, pick up between running threads and then in the center of stitches as you follow the line of stitches marking the curve of the neck. In Figure 3-3, the darkened stitches show you where to insert your needle to pick up stitches along a curve.

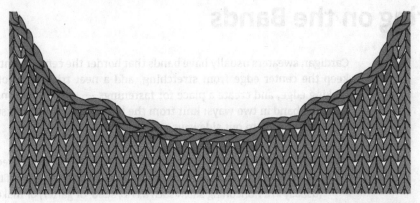

Illustration by Wiley, Composition Services Graphics

FIGURE 3-3:
Pick up stitches on a bound-off curved neckline.

TIP

When you have to pick stitches up along the neck edge for a collar that isn't rib, pick up with the WS facing. That way, when the collar is turned, the fabric faces the right way.

Picking up: A reality check

Picking up stitches is relatively simple when you get the hang of it. The rub comes when you painstakingly pick up a cardigan border or neckband according to your pattern instructions. You pick up the exact number of stitches called for, knit the correct number of rows given in the stitch pattern, and bind off the last stitch. Then, after all your effort, you find that your otherwise lovely cardigan has a stretched and droopy button band or that you can't squeeze your head through the neck of your pullover.

TIP

Your pattern tells you how many stitches to pick up around the neck, but it may or may not tell you how to distribute them: so many along the back neck and so many along the left and right front neck edges. It may be up to you to figure out how many stitches to pick up where. Also, if the gauge on your border pattern is different from the sweater designer's or if you alter the pattern in any way, your border may not fit as planned. Use your pattern as a guide, but keep a critical eye on your own work. At the first sign that your band is starting to gape or your neckband is shrinking the neck opening, be prepared to toss your sweater map in the backseat. Resolve to pick up stitches according to your knitted pieces, *not* according to your pattern. Just remember that if you're changing the number of stitches to pick up, you must come out with a number that works as a multiple of your stitch pattern.

Bring on the Bands

Cardigan sweaters usually have bands that border the center front. Cardigan bands keep the center edge from stretching, add a neat trim to an otherwise rough-looking edge, and create a place for fastenings — usually buttons. You can knit a cardigan band in two ways: knit from the bottom up, or pick up stitches along the edge and knit them out sideways.

>> **Vertically knit bands:** These bands are knitted in the same direction as the sweater body, from bottom to top. You can knit them as part of the front (usually in a noncurling stitch such as rib, seed, or garter) or make them separately and sew them on later.

>> **Horizontally knit bands:** These bands are usually made by picking up stitches along the center front edge and knitting at a right angle to the sweater body for an inch or so. Like vertical bands, you can knit them separately to be sewn on later if, unlike most knitters, you'd rather sew than knit.

It's a good idea to have some understanding of how these bands work — how to plan and make them. When you're familiar with both types, you just may decide to turn your perfectly fitting pullover pattern into a cardigan.

TIP

When you're making a vertical or horizontal band in a ribbed stitch (1 x 1 or 2 x 2), end your band on a knit rib and add an extra knit stitch at the outside edge. Edge stitches never look great and tend to curl and disappear. The extra knit stitch tucks itself in and becomes an unobtrusive facing. What you notice is a symmetrical band with a tidy edge. Try it!

Bottoms up! Vertical bands

On a vertical band, you work the stitches in the band in the same direction as the body of the sweater. A vertical band allows you to create a ribbed band that matches the bottom ribbed edge of your sweater.

Knitted-in vertical bands

Vertical cardigan bands knitted in at the same time as the sweater are convenient and easy. No need for further finishing — you just knit to the end of the row for your front panel and continue to knit the stitches for the band. Their drawback is their lack of stability. Worked on the same size needle as the sweater body, the bands don't always make a taut edge. If you find your band less than successful, try one of the following remedies:

» Work the band in a stitch pattern with a shorter row gauge, such as a garter stitch band on a stockinette stitch body.

» Work the band on separate double-pointed needles in a smaller size (slightly awkward but doable). Just work the band on the smaller short needle and then work the body on the larger needles. When you come back to the band, pick up the other double-pointed needle, work back and forth on the band, leave the smaller needle suspended in the band, and return to the larger needle.

Vertical bands knitted separately

You can work vertical bands as separate pieces and later join them to the front of the cardigan. You just cast on the number of stitches you need to achieve the width of your band and then knit it up — be prepared for a lot of turning! Generally, you make the band on a smaller needle than the sweater body to give it more stability. Sew the band to the sweater edge by using the mattress stitch, which you can find in Book 7, Chapter 2.

Horizontal picked-up bands

The key to knitting attractive horizontal picked-up bands is to find the right number of stitches to pick up along the front edge of your sweater. Too many, and you have a droopy band that stretches the sweater front; too few, and the band draws up the sweater at the center front. Sweater patterns tell you how many stitches to pick up along a cardigan edge in one of two ways: They give you a pick-up rhythm, something like, "Pick up 3 out of every 4 rows," or they give you a total number of stitches to pick up.

When you pick up stitches along a vertical edge and knit the band from there, you're working at a right angle to your knitted piece — stitches to rows. One inch of rows on the vertical edge has to match 1 inch of stitches on the band you're knitting. Most of the time, this means picking up a few stitches and then skipping 1 stitch at regular intervals — a pick-up rhythm.

The rhythm method

Be grateful when instructions give you the pick-up rhythm. You don't have to worry about getting a particular number of stitches into a band. Instead, you're concerned with a ratio of rows to stitches.

Rhythm instructions are easy to test. Along the cardigan edge (or along your gauge swatch), pick up 32 stitches and work in the rhythm your pattern gives you. Work the stitches for 1 inch (see Figure 3-4), and then check the edge you've made. Be honest. If the band is nice and flat and doesn't pucker, stretch, or distort the front edge in any way, you're on. Rip out those test stitches and pick up the stitches in the same way all along the edge.

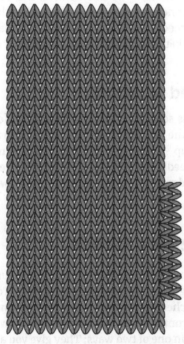

Knit a test band to see if you have the correct ratio of stitches to rows.

FIGURE 3-4:
Knit a test band.

Illustration by Wiley, Composition Services Graphics

If the test band puckers and draws in, you're skipping too many stitches. Instead of 3 out of 4 rows, try 4 out of 5 or 5 out of 6. And if the band stretches the edge of your sweater, you aren't skipping enough stitches. Try picking up 2 out of 3. Keep experimenting until you get the right ratio; then rip out the test band and proceed with your plan.

The section method

If your pattern gives you a total number of stitches to pick up, you have to ration the total out in equal sections along the front edge and pick up stitches evenly along the edge. The following steps tell you how to do this:

1. **Divide the front edge into equal sections about 2 inches long.**

   You can measure out sections with a ruler, but it's better to count rows. Use safety pins to mark them.

2. **Count the number of sections you've marked.**

3. **Divide the number of stitches the pattern says to pick up by the number of sections, and pick up that number of stitches between pins.**

   For example, if the pattern tells you to pick up 120 stitches and you've made 12 sections, pick up 10 stitches in each section.

TIP

You may want to test your band by picking up stitches in a few sections (about 6 inches or so total) and knitting a band from them to ensure that the band doesn't distort the edge.

Hole in One: Buttonholes

Unless you plan to tie it, snap it, or leave it hanging open, you need to add buttons and buttonholes to a cardigan. Knitted buttonholes are rarely gorgeous, but with a little thought and planning, you can make buttonholes that don't sacrifice good looks to workaday function.

The appearance of a buttonhole has a lot to do with how it fits into the background stitch on which it's worked. A buttonhole that looks great on stockinette fabric may look clumsy on a ribbed band, for example. Take the time to practice a buttonhole in the stitch pattern you're using. Aim to make the buttonhole and stitch pattern work together. If you plan ahead and buy your buttons before working your buttonholes, you can test your buttons in your practice buttonholes to guarantee a good fit.

REMEMBER

Horizontal and *vertical* describe how a buttonhole is worked — between rows or between stitches, respectively — and/or how it looks in a finished band. Keep in mind that a vertical buttonhole is horizontal on a picked-up cardigan band.

All-purpose horizontal buttonhole

Most knitting patterns give instructions for a generic cast-off/cast on 2-row buttonhole that read like this: "Bind off 3 stitches, cast on 3 stitches over bound-off stitches on next row." Although this method works, it makes a loose and unattractive buttonhole. The technique for a horizontal buttonhole creates a more durable buttonhole — and it looks better, too (see Figure 3-5).

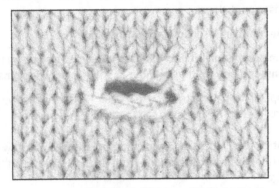

FIGURE 3-5:
All-purpose horizontal buttonhole.

Photograph by Wiley, Composition Services Graphics

These instructions are for a 4-stitch buttonhole, which takes 2 rows to complete. To make it, you need to know how to cast on by using the thumb or cable method (refer to Book 2, Chapter 1).

1. **Work Row 1 (RS).**

   1. Work to the position of the buttonhole.

   2. Bind off 4 stitches.

   3. Knit the next stitch tightly (hold the yarn taut).

   4. Continue working in the pattern to the end of the row.

      If you count your stitches, you should have 4 fewer stitches on your needle for each buttonhole you've worked on the row.

2. **Work Row 2.**

   1. Work to the bound-off stitches of the buttonhole.

   2. Using the thumb or cable cast on method, tightly cast on 4 stitches.

3. With the tip of the LH needle, pick up the outer edge of the loop from the first bound-off stitch (see Figure 3-6) and purl it together with the next stitch.

Turn your fabric around to easily see the loop you need to pick up.

4. Continue to purl or work in the pattern to the end of the row.

All done!

TIP

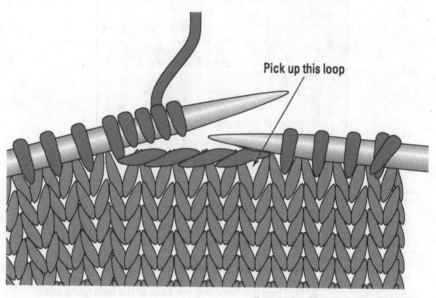

Pick up this loop

FIGURE 3-6:
Picking up the loop from the bound-off stitch.

FITTING IN

When you practice a horizontal buttonhole, keep in mind that it must work with your button choice *and* with the stitch pattern of your fabric. Whether you make your buttonhole over an odd or even number of stitches helps determine how it fits into its background. If possible, use the following pointers to ensure that your buttonholes blend neatly into their setting:

- In a 1 x 1 rib, seed stitch, or moss stitch pattern, make the buttonhole over an odd number of stitches so that you can center it between two knit ribs.

- In a 2 x 2 rib pattern or double seed stitch pattern, make the buttonhole over an even number of stitches so that you can plant it symmetrically between knit stitches.

Simple vertical buttonhole

A vertical buttonhole (see Figure 3-7) is stretchier than a cast-off horizontal buttonhole. You work each side of the buttonhole with a separate ball of yarn. Test it with your buttons to know how many rows to work to achieve the right size hole. The instructions that follow are for working this buttonhole in 1 x 1 ribbing, where you can place the buttonhole in the purl trough to camouflage it.

FIGURE 3-7: Vertical buttonhole.

Photograph by Wiley, Composition Services Graphics

1. **Work Row 1 (RS).**

   1. Work in rib pattern to the spot for the buttonhole, ending with a knit stitch.

   2. Purl into the front and the back of the next (purl) stitch.

      See the bar increase instructions in Book 2, Chapter 3 if you don't remember how to do this. Increasing 1 stitch in the purl trough allows for symmetry — both sides of the buttonhole will be bordered by a purl stitch on the RS.

   3. Continue in the rib pattern to the end of the row.

2. **Work Row 2.**

   1. Work in the rib pattern to the increased stitch (look for a stray stitch between a knit and a purl) and knit the increased stitch.

   2. Drop the yarn and, with another ball of yarn and beginning with k1, work in the rib pattern to the end of the row.

3. **Work Row 3 by ribbing to the buttonhole; then pick up the yarn from the other side and work in the rib pattern to the end of the row.**

4. **Repeat Rows 2 and 3 as many times as needed for the right size buttonhole.**

5. **Close the buttonhole.**

- On a RS row, purl the 2 stitches at the top of the hole together.

- On a WS row, knit the 2 stitches at the top of the hole together.

6. **To finish, cut the separate strand and weave in the ends.**

Weaving the ends in along the edges of the buttonhole helps keep it from stretching.

To work a vertical buttonhole in a 2 x 2 rib (k2, p2, k2, p2), work the slit between 2 purl stitches.

Round (eyelet) buttonhole

The eyelet buttonhole (see Figure 3-8) may not appeal to you if you're a seamstress because it doesn't look like a sewn buttonhole — it's round, not slitlike. But this buttonhole has its charms: It's easy to remember, simple to execute, and adjusts to fit whatever button is appropriate for the yarn and needle size you're using.

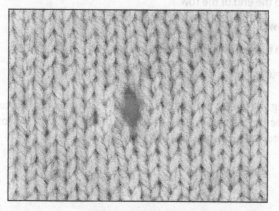

FIGURE 3-8:
Eyelet
buttonhole.

Photograph by Wiley, Composition Services Graphics

The instructions for working this buttonhole focus on stockinette fabric, but it also sits discreetly in the purl troughs of ribbing and is all but invisible in garter stitch, which is more than can be said for a lot of knitted slitlike buttonholes. You work this eyelet buttonhole over 1 stitch, and it takes 3 rows to complete. You may want to review how to make the different kinds of yarn overs in Book 2, Chapter 3 before you get started.

Always pair a decrease with the yarn over when you work an eyelet buttonhole.

To work the buttonhole in stockinette stitch, follow these steps:

1. **Work Row 1 (RS).**

   1. Knit to 2 stitches before the buttonhole stitch.

   2. Make a double yarn over by bringing the yarn through the needles to the front, over the RH needle to the back, and then to the front between the needles again.

   You can make a slightly smaller buttonhole by making a *single* yarn over rather than a double one. Just wrap the yarn once rather than twice.

   3. Knit the next 2 stitches together.

   4. Knit to the end of the row.

2. **Work Row 2.**

   1. Purl to the yarn over.

   2. Purl into the yarn over, letting the second wrap drop from the left needle.

   3. Purl to the end of the row.

3. **Work Row 3.**

   1. Knit to the stitch above the buttonhole.

   2. Knit into the hole (not the stitch above) and carry on.

If you're using the eyelet buttonhole in place of a horizontal buttonhole, work it in what would be the second bound-off stitch of a horizontal buttonhole. Use graph paper if needed to figure out where to place the eyelet.

Button Up!

Never underestimate the power of a button to make or break a sweater. The perfect button can enhance the theme of a sweater, such as a shimmery pearl button on a dressy sweater or a rustic bone button on an outdoorsy sweater. On the other hand, the contrast of a rugged button on a dressy sweater or a shell button on a bulky sweater may make an otherwise ho-hum garment really sing with originality. You can even design an entire sweater around a single spectacular button or sew on several buttons that share a theme but don't necessarily match. Be brave and experiment.

Plotting button placement

Knit up the front panel of your sweater (if you're planning a knit-in band) or the band that will carry the buttons before you work the piece with the buttonholes. This way, you can use safety pins or ties of contrasting yarn to mark where the buttons should go and plan where to make the corresponding buttonholes.

REMEMBER

For a woman's sweater, buttons generally go on the left front panel. For a man's sweater, they go on the right. For both, make sure to use enough buttons to prevent gaps.

Begin by positioning the top and bottom buttons on your band. Use your eyes to determine the best distance from the edge for these two buttons. The top button generally should start ½ inch to 1 inch from the top of the sweater. (For a delicate or medium-weight sweater, place the top button closer to the neck.) The bottom button on a standard cardigan should be ½ inch to 1 inch from the bottom edge. If you're working a jacket-type cardigan, you may want to place the bottom button higher up for freedom of movement.

After you place the top and bottom buttons, count the rows (or stitches for a picked-up band) between these buttons to determine where to place the others evenly between them. Don't rely on measuring with a ruler. For greater accuracy, chart your button placement on graph paper.

So happy together: Keeping your buttons buttoned

Cardigan instructions simply tell you to sew on your buttons opposite the buttonholes. But a couple of refinements will help your buttons stay snuggly in their holes and keep your bands lined up neatly.

>> **To place a button for a vertical buttonhole:** Center both the button and the buttonhole along the center lines of the front bands. Then plot your button/buttonhole pair so that the center of the button lines up with the top corner of the buttonhole. This placement will discourage the button from sneaking free.

>> **To place a button for a horizontal buttonhole:** Don't center both the buttons and buttonholes in their respective bands. When you button your sweater, the button won't stay centered in the hole; instead, the bands will pull apart until the button catches in the corner of the buttonhole. Avoid this sliding problem by positioning the button away from the center, toward the outer edge of the band. When you button up, your bands will remain aligned, one on top of the other.

Sewing on buttons

If you used a plied yarn for your sweater or project, you can unply a single strand and use it to sew on your buttons. You also can use embroidery thread.

REMEMBER

As you sew your buttons on, don't be afraid to go into the yarn strands of the sweater. If you try to secure a button by going around the strands and only in and out of the holes between stitches, your button will be unstable and will pull the stitch out of shape.

Most knitted fabric is dense enough to require a button with a *shank* — a small metal or plastic loop on the back of the button to sew through. If you want to use a button with holes in it instead, you can make a thread shank to allow room for the depth of the band fabric. The following steps tell you how:

1. Lay a toothpick or skinny double-pointed needle between the holes on the top of the button, and sew the button onto the sweater by stitching around the toothpick or needle, as in Figure 3-9.

FIGURE 3-9:
Create a thread shank by sewing over a toothpick or small needle.

Illustration by Wiley, Composition Services Graphics

2. Before knotting off, slide out the toothpick or needle, lift the button to take up the slack, and wind the thread several times around the "shank" on the underside of the button.

3. Bring the thread to the wrong side of the sweater, knot off, and weave in the end.

Voilà! A button that won't retract into the buttonhole.

Chapter **4**

Crocheting Your First Sweater

Although crocheting a sweater may seem like a daunting task, it's really quite easy. Many sweater designs are nothing more than squares sewn together. The simple shaping involved in these designs is as easy as increasing or decreasing a few stitches in the designated places. (Book 3, Chapter 3 gives you step-by-step directions for increasing and decreasing.) Of course, you'll want to take a few points into consideration before you dig in.

First off, you want to choose a design that you like and that suits your physique. And if you're new to the craft, you also need to consider the difficulty of the pattern. You want to choose your materials carefully, too, picking a yarn that's easy to work with so you don't become frustrated and give up before you finish.

This chapter shows you various sweater styles and how to construct them. You also see how sweaters are sized so you can adjust patterns to suit your needs. And at the end of the chapter, you find instructions for a simple shell top that you can crochet in no time flat.

Choosing Stitches and Yarn for Your Sweater

To guarantee your first sweater attempt isn't your last, choose your stitch pattern and yarn carefully. You can crochet beautiful sweaters with simple stitch patterns and readily available yarns. The sections that follow give you a heads-up on what to keep in mind.

Making the right pattern choice

First and foremost, make sure the pattern you're considering isn't too complicated for your skill level before you buy it or any of the materials. (Refer to Book 1, Chapter 4 if you need help reading patterns.) Here are some factors to consider:

» If you want a sweater design that has an open, lacy pattern, try a pattern that uses yarn (it's easier to work with than the cotton thread many lacy patterns call for) and a simple stitch repeat.

» If you want to crochet a sweater with more than one color, choose a pattern that has stripes or many different-colored motifs (see Book 4, Chapter 5 for more on motifs). Crocheting a pattern with color changes throughout is much more difficult than working a sweater in simple stripes or motifs. Another option is to use a multicolored or variegated yarn, both of which give you color variation without you having to worry about changing yarn colors constantly (see Book 1, Chapter 2 for info on substituting yarns).

» As a newbie, you want to avoid a pattern that calls for crocheting with two strands of yarn held together as one. Working with more than one strand of yarn can be confusing.

TIP

» For your first sweater, find a pattern that suggests a smooth yarn, such as wool or a wool blend, or a synthetic yarn, such as acrylic. These yarns are easier to work with than highly textured novelty yarns, such as *bouclé* or *eyelash* yarn. (Flip to Book 1, Chapter 2 for details on the various types of yarn.) The extra tufts on some novelty yarns make for a bumpy crochet experience, and if you happen to make a mistake and have to tear out some stitches, you may end up tearing out your hair as well.

» Choose a pattern that you like, or else be prepared to lose interest within the first ten minutes.

REMEMBER

If you're brave enough to go ahead and buy a pattern with new stitches, be sure to work a practice swatch to get a feel for them before beginning your sweater.

Finding the right yarn

Choosing the right yarn to work with means more than just picking your favorite color. You also need to select a yarn that complements the pattern yet won't tie you up in knots while you're crocheting with it. Of course, the pattern usually recommends a yarn so you have a ballpark idea of the yarn weight you need, such as sport weight or worsted weight, and the yarn material, such as acrylic or wool blend. (Head to Book 1, Chapter 2 for the full details on yarn weights and materials.)

Keep in mind the following factors when you go yarn shopping:

» **Feel:** For a softer sweater, choose a lighter-weight yarn or a pattern with looser stitches. Although some of the bulky weight yarns are relatively light, crocheting with the heavier weights of yarn quite often produces a stiff sweater that feels a bit like a cardboard box — definitely not an attractive (or comfortable!) option.

» **Fiber content:** Generally, natural fibers make for a more attractive and comfortable garment; however, they can be expensive and may require hand washing or dry cleaning. For your first sweater, blends (yarns that contain natural fibers along with synthetic fibers) and acrylic yarns may be more practical and easier to work with. Don't forget to check the label to see whether the blend is machine washable.

WARNING

Mixing materials can lead to disastrous results when you wash your sweater, so if a pattern calls for two or more yarn types or colors, be sure to compare the care instructions on the yarn labels. Always choose yarns with the same laundering requirements.

» **Twist:** Use yarns with a nice twist to the strand; yarns without much twist tend to split while you're crocheting.

» **Quantity:** When buying yarn for a project, be sure to purchase enough for the entire project. The materials list at the beginning of the pattern specifies the amount you need to complete the design. If you run out, you may not be able to find the color you need in the same *dye lot* (yarn dyed in the same batch), which means you may end up with an unplanned two-tone sweater.

REMEMBER

» **Quality:** Don't skimp on materials. You get what you pay for, and after all your hard work, you want a sweater that retains its beauty for years to come.

Crocheting Your First Sweater

Selecting a Super Sweater Style

You work most sweater designs in separate pieces — the back, the front (or fronts for a cardigan), the sleeves, and any desired borders — and sew or crochet them together after you complete them. (See Book 7, Chapter 2 for how to join pieces of crochet.) How you make these pieces and put them together determines the sweater's style. The simpler styles have little or no shaping to the pieces, but more complicated designs may have shaping or decreasing around the armholes and at the neck. The next sections show you several basic sweater designs you may want to consider.

REMEMBER

For your first sweater, choose a pattern with simple shaping. Most sweater patterns include a *schematic* — a diagram of the sweater construction. The schematic includes the important measurements, such as the width of the back and front(s), the *armhole depth* (the size of the opening that you put your arms through), the sleeve length, and the finished back length.

Baring your arms: Sleeveless sweaters

The simplest sleeveless sweater styles have two panels that you join at the center back and center front, producing a V-neck with a small overhang at the shoulders (see Figure 4-1a). You can make a shell, one of the other sleeveless styles, by merely skipping stitches at the side seams to make armholes and skipping across the center to make the neck opening (see Figure 4-1b).

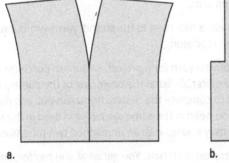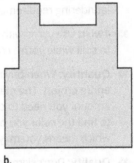

FIGURE 4-1:
Sleeveless
sweater styles:
(a) two-panel
V-neck and
(b) simple shell.

a.　　　　　　　　　　b.

With only minor shaping at the armholes and around the neck, you can make a simple tank top like the one in Figure 4-2a. The classic sleeveless vest cardigan (shown in Figure 4-2b) usually requires a bit more shaping at the armholes and neck, but you can still make it with relative ease.

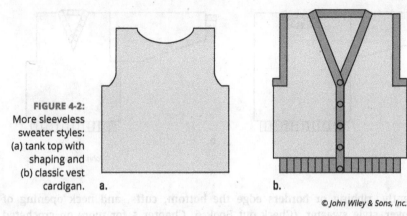

FIGURE 4-2:
More sleeveless
sweater styles:
(a) tank top with
shaping and
(b) classic vest
cardigan.

a.

b.

Going the classic route: Pullovers

You can make a pullover with almost any combination of sleeve and neck styles. Figure 4-3 shows you one of the simplest combinations. It has drop shoulders, wide cuffs, and a boat neck without borders or ribbing to complicate the design. A long sweater with no ribbing at the bottom is a *tunic* style, and a short sweater is sometimes called a *crop top*.

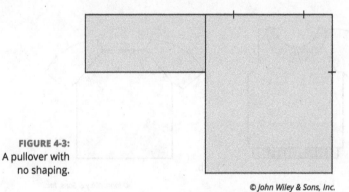

FIGURE 4-3:
A pullover with
no shaping.

Sweaters with tapered sleeves and some shaping at the neck are more common. Both sweaters in Figure 4-4 have tapered sleeves. (Tapered sleeves are easier than they look. You either start at the cuff edge and increase on each side until the sleeves reach the desired circumference or you start at the top edge and decrease until you get to the cuff.) The crew-neck sweater in Figure 4-4a has no armhole shaping and subsequently has dropped shoulders; the V-neck sweater in Figure 4-4b has inset sleeves for a more tailored look.

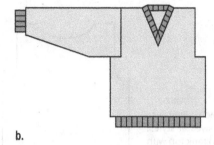

FIGURE 4-4:
Pullover styles:
(a) drop-shoulder
crewneck and
(b) inset sleeves
with a V-neck. **a.** **b.**

Frequently, ribbing or borders edge the bottom, cuffs, and neck opening of a pullover-style sweater. (Check out Book 6, Chapter 5 for more on crocheted ribbing and borders.)

The cap-sleeve pullover style is fitted to the shape of the body and produces less bulk under the arms. The upper sleeve edge is shaped in a curve to fit into the shaped armholes. The cap-sleeve sweater in Figure 4-5a sports a scoop neck and fold-down collar. You usually work the raglan-sleeve style shown in Figure 4-5b in one piece, starting at the neck and increasing at the "seam" point between the sleeves and the body of the sweater as you work down. This style has the advantage of having few, if any, seams to sew.

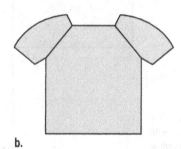

FIGURE 4-5:
More pullover
styles: (a) cap
sleeves with a
scoop neck and
(b) raglan styling. **a.** **b.**

Buttoning up: Cardigans

Cardigans can have tapered sleeves or straight sleeves, inset sleeves or dropped shoulders, scooped necks, V-necks or boat necks, just like pullovers. The only difference is that cardigans have two fronts, so you sew the front to the back a little differently. Figure 4-6 shows a V-neck cardigan and a hooded cardigan, both with tapered sleeves.

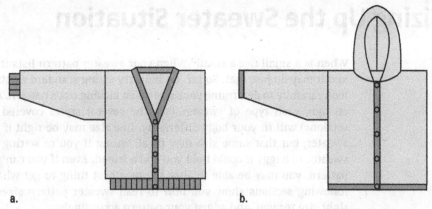

FIGURE 4-6:
Cardigan styles:
(a) V-neck and
(b) hooded.

a.

b.

© John Wiley & Sons, Inc.

Getting visually interesting: Motifs and vertical rows

Motifs and vertical rows are two fairly common design methods that can create a sweater with a lot of visual interest without you having to learn a bunch of complex stitch patterns:

» *Motifs* are small crocheted pieces worked in rounds that you sew or crochet together (see Figure 4-7a). You can use square, hexagonal, round, or triangular motifs of almost any size, providing that all the parts add up to the sweater measurements. Flip to Book 4, Chapter 5 for more on motifs.

» You can also crochet a one-piece sweater in vertical rows (see Figure 4-7b) by starting at one cuff edge, working to the shoulder, and then increasing for the length of the body of the sweater in the front and the back. Even though it seems a bit more complex, this technique is great for making a flattering sweater.

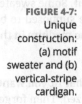

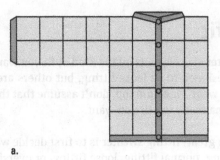

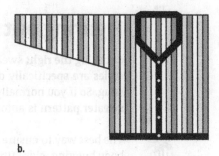

FIGURE 4-7:
Unique
construction:
(a) motif
sweater and (b)
vertical-stripe
cardigan.

a.

b.

© John Wiley & Sons, Inc.

Sizing Up the Sweater Situation

When is a small not a small? When your sweater pattern lists it as a medium — and it may do just that. So far, no industry sizing standard exists, so you need to look carefully to determine your size when picking out a pattern. As if that weren't enough, each type of sweater (see the several styles covered in the previous sections) will fit your body differently. One size may be right if you want a snug sweater, but that same size may be all wrong if you're setting out to crochet a sweater so baggy it could hold you and a friend. Even if you can't find the perfect pattern, you may be able to alter the next best thing to get what you want. The following sections show you how to read sweater pattern sizes, determine the right size for you, and adjust your pattern accordingly.

Understanding sweater pattern sizes

Most sweater patterns list the size ranges (and one pattern may include several sizes) at the beginning of the instructions. You may find the back length and sleeve length listed as well. In fact, you may even find a schematic diagram showing the measurements of all the different pieces.

Sweater patterns also include the instructions for making all the listed sizes. Typically patterns list the directions for the smallest size first, followed by changes for the larger sizes in parentheses. For example:

Sc in each of next 50 (54, 58) sts.

In this example, you work 50 single crochet stitches if you're making a small sweater, 54 single crochet stitches for a medium one, and 58 single crochet stitches for a large one.

TIP

To make a particular sweater pattern easier to follow, highlight all the numbers for your desired size before you begin.

Figuring out fit

Choosing the right sweater size depends on the kind of fit you want. Some sweater styles are specifically designed to be loose fitting, but others are supposed to be snug. So if you normally wear a medium top, don't assume that the medium in the sweater pattern is automatically the fit you want.

REMEMBER

The best way to ensure a great-fitting sweater is to first decide what fit you want: body hugging, close fitting, normal fitting, loose fitting, or oversized. Then forget what the pattern labels as small or large, measure your own bust line, and add to or subtract from the resulting measurement to get your desired fit. Table 4-1 tells you how many inches to add to (or subtract from) your own bust measurement to come up with a finished bust measurement that achieves the fit you desire. (The *finished bust measurement* is the total number of inches around the bust of the finished sweater — which isn't necessarily the same as your own bust measurement.) You then take this adjusted bust measurement and find the pattern size that matches it.

TABLE 4-1

Determining Sweater Fit

Fit You Want	Number of Inches to Subtract from or Add to Your Bust Measurement
Body hugging	– 1–2
Close	+ 1–2
Normal	+ 2–4
Loose	+ 4–6
Oversized	+ 6–8

For example, if you have a 36-inch bust and want to make a normal-fitting sweater, add 2 to 4 inches to your bust measurement for a total finished bust measurement of 38 to 40 inches. Now look at the pattern for the finished bust measurement closest to this range. If you don't find an exact measurement, choose the next largest size for a comfortable fit. Usually patterns offer sizes in 4-inch increments. However, that's not always the case. You may have a pattern that offers the bust sizes of 36 inches, 41 inches, and 46 inches. In this case, the 41-inch size is your best choice for a comfortable fit.

REMEMBER

Working to the designated gauge is especially important when making sweaters. The gauge determines how many stitches you use for a given finished bust size. If your gauge is off, then your finished garment will be as well. The sweater that's supposed to have a 38-inch finished bust measurement may very well end up being a 34 if your gauge is too tight, or a 42 if it's too loose. (Check out Book 1, Chapter 3 for gauge basics.)

Customizing your pattern

If you find a sweater that you want to make, but it doesn't have directions for your size, you may be able to alter it on your own. These sections show you how to get the size you need.

Crocheting Your First Sweater

Adjusting the finished bust measurement

For sweaters that you work in horizontal rows, adjusting the bust size is fairly simple; you just add inches to (or subtract them from) the front and back pieces evenly. Suppose that the pattern for a cardigan offers finished bust measurements of 36, 40, and 44 inches, but you need a 48-inch finished bust. To get the extra 4 inches you need, adjust the directions for the largest size by adding 2 inches to the back width and 1 inch to each of the two front pieces (or 2 inches to the front width if you're working the front as one piece). You work the armholes and the length in the same manner as in the size-44 pattern.

Now check the gauge (refer to Book 1, Chapter 3) for the pattern stitch and calculate approximately how many extra stitches you need to add to the back and the front to get your extra 4 inches. For example, if the pattern has just 1 stitch, such as single crochet, and the gauge is 9 stitches = 2 inches, you need to add approximately 9 stitches to the back width and approximately 5 stitches to each front piece of the cardigan.

But if you have a stitch pattern that repeats across the body of the sweater, you need to increase your stitch count in multiples of the stitch repeat. For example, if the pattern for the body of the sweater is * (double crochet, chain 1, double crochet) in next stitch, skip next 2 stitches *, then the multiple (or repeated part of the pattern) is 3 stitches. So any adjusting you do must be in a multiple of 3 stitches. For the back, you can easily add 9 stitches, which is a multiple of 3 stitches. But for the front, 5 stitches isn't divisible by 3 stitches, so you need to add the next multiple of 3, which is 6 stitches.

TIP

Sometimes you can make a good guesstimate from the existing multisized pattern. For example, if the differences between small and medium and between medium and large are both 4 stitches, then you can usually assume that the difference between a large and an extra-large is also 4 stitches. The benefit of this approach is that the pattern designer has (theoretically) already figured out the multiple sizes in relation to the repeats.

TIP

For patterns with large repeats, adjusting the size and maintaining the original pattern isn't always possible. Sometimes changing to a larger crochet hook and working the largest size offered creates a sweater that's a size larger. Crochet a gauge swatch (see Book 1, Chapter 3) with the next largest hook size and calculate how big the sweater would be if you used that hook size. If the result isn't large enough, try the *next* largest hook. Make sure the looser gauge produces a comfortable fabric that isn't too sloppy looking or so holey that you can see through it.

Lengthening the sweater and sleeves

If you want to adjust the sweater or sleeve length, you can usually just increase or reduce the number of rows you work:

>> Adjust the length of the sweater by adding or subtracting rows at the bottom edge (so you don't mess up the shaping around the arm holes).

>> Alter the sleeve length either above or below the shaping, depending on how it's made. Just make sure you've added all the stitches to ensure a comfortable fit around the upper arm and shoulder.

Shell Shock Project

The sleeveless design of this pretty shell gives you experience making garments without having to worry about the sleeves! The super soft, lightweight yarn used to make this top is cool enough for hot summer months and comes in a wide variety of colors.

Materials and vital statistics

>> **Size:** Directions are given for size Small (4–6). Changes for Medium (8–10), Large (12–14), and X-Large (16–18) are in parentheses.

>> **Yarn:** LB Collection Cotton Bamboo lightweight yarn (52% rayon from bamboo), (3.5 oz [100 g], 245 yds [224 m] each skein): 3 (for Small) (or 3 [for Medium], 4 [for Large], and 5 [for X-Large]) skeins of #139 Hibiscus.

>> **Hook:** Crochet hook sizes G-6 US (4 mm) and H-8 US (5 mm) or size needed to obtain gauge

>> **Yarn needle**

>> **Measurements:** Finished bust: 32 (36, 39, 43) in. Back length: 24 (25, 26.5, 27.5) in. Use sweater schematic in Figure 4-8 to determine which size to make.

>> **Gauge:** With larger hook, in body pattern, 2 repeats = 3.25 in.; 4 rows = 2.5 in. With smaller hook, 18 sts and 9 rows dc = 4 in.

>> **Stitches used:** Chain stitch (ch), slip stitch (sl st), single crochet (sc), double crochet (dc), **Dc2tog:** * (Yo, insert hook in next st, yo, draw yarn through st, yo, draw yarn through 2 loops on hook) twice, yo, draw yarn through 3 loops on hook*. **Shell:** * (3 dc, ch 2, 3 dc) in same st *. **Picot:** * Ch 3, insert hook through front loop and next loop below top loop of last st made, yo, draw yarn through all loops on hook (sl st) *.

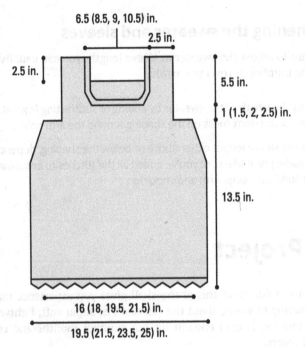

6.5 (8.5, 9, 10.5) in.

2.5 in.

2.5 in.

5.5 in.

1 (1.5, 2, 2.5) in.

13.5 in.

FIGURE 4-8:
Schematic for
the Shell Shock
project.

16 (18, 19.5, 21.5) in.

19.5 (21.5, 23.5, 25) in.

© John Wiley & Sons, Inc.

Directions

The row-by-row instructions for this top appear as you'd see them in any crochet publication. Figure 4-9 shows a reduced sample of the stitch pattern for the body, which is a repeat of Rows 2 through 7. If the instructions here seem like Greek to you, head on over to Book 1, Chapter 4 for pointers on reading crochet patterns.

Back

Starting at bottom edge, with larger hook, ch 88 (96, 104, 112) + 3 (first dc).

Row 1 (RS): Dc in 4th ch from hook, dc in each ch across (89 [97, 105, 113] dc), *turn.*

Row 2: Ch 4 (counts as dc, ch 1, here and throughout), skip next dc, * dc in next dc, ch 1, skip nxt dc; rep from * across, ending with dc in top of tch (44 [48, 52, 56] ch-1 spaces), *turn.*

Row 3: Ch 3 (counts as dc, here and throughout), skip next 2 ch-1 spaces, * shell in next dc, skip next 2 ch-1 spaces, dc in next dc; rep from * across, ending with last dc in 3rd ch of beginning ch-4 (11 [12, 13, 14] shells), *turn.*

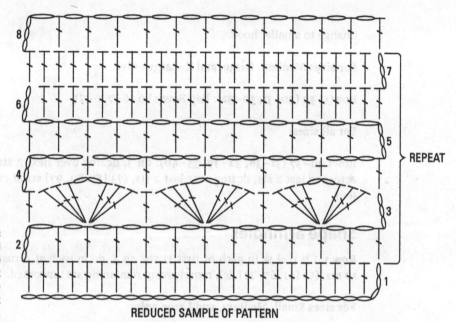

FIGURE 4-9:
A reduced
sample of the
stitch-repeat
pattern for the
Shell Shock
project.

REDUCED SAMPLE OF PATTERN

© John Wiley & Sons, Inc.

Row 4: Ch 6 (counts as dc, ch 3, here and throughout), * sc in next ch-2 space, ch 3, skip next 3 dc **, dc in next dc, ch 3, skip next 3 dc; rep from * across, ending last rep at **, dc in top of tch (22 [24, 26, 28] ch-3 spaces), *turn.*

Row 5: Ch 4, * dc in next ch-3 space, ch 1, dc in next sc, ch 1, dc in next ch-3 space, ch 1, dc in next dc; rep from * across, ending with dc in 3rd ch of beginning ch-6 (44 [48, 52, 56] ch-1 spaces), *turn.*

Row 6: Ch 3, * dc in next ch-1 space, dc in next dc; rep from * across, ending with last dc in 3rd ch of beginning ch-4, (89 [97, 105, 113] dc), *turn.*

Row 7: Ch 3, dc in each dc across, (89 [97, 105, 113] dc), *turn.*

Rows 8–25: Rep Rows 2–7 (3 times).

Rows 26–29: Rep Rows 2–5.

WARNING

The body pattern of this sweater has a lot of chain loops and spaces. Because most crocheters tend to crochet chains a little tighter than other stitches, the body pattern uses a larger hook than the solid double crochet section on the top of the sweater. Be sure to check your gauge for both stitch patterns to ensure that the final measurements will be correct.

Change to smaller hook.

For sizes Medium, Large, and X-Large only:

Row(s) 30 (30–31, 30–32): Rep Row(s) 6 (6–7, 6–7).

For all sizes:

Rows 30–37 (31–38, 32–39, 33–40): Ch 3, dc2tog over next 2 sts, dc in each st across to last 2 sts, dc2tog over last 2 sts, (73 [81, 89, 97] sts at end of last row), *turn*.

Shape armholes

Row 1: Ch 1, sl st in each of first 11 sts, ch 3, dc in each st across to within last 10 sts, (53 [61, 69, 77] dc), *turn*, leaving remaining sts unworked.

For sizes Small, Medium, and Large only:

Rows 2–9 (10, 12): Ch 3, dc in each st across, *turn*.

For size X-Large only:

Rows 2–5: Ch 3, dc2tog over next 2 sts, dc in each st across to last 2 sts, dc2tog over last 2 sts, (69 sts at end of last row), *turn*.

Rows 6–12: Ch 3, dc in each st across, *turn*.

FIRST STRAP

Row 1: Ch 3, dc in each of next 10 sts, (11 dc), *turn*, leaving remaining sts unworked.

Rows 2–5: Ch 3, dc in each st across, *turn*. Fasten off.

SECOND STRAP

Row 1: With first strap on the right, skip next 31 (39, 47, 55) sts, join yarn with a sl st in next st, ch 3, dc in each remaining st across, (11 dc), *turn*.

Rows 2–5: Ch 3, dc in each st across, *turn*. Fasten off.

Front

Work same as back through Row 1 of shape armholes.

Row(s) 2 (2–3, 2–4, 2–5): Ch 3, dc in each st across, *turn*.

FIRST STRAP

Row 1: Ch 3, dc in each of next 12 sts, dc2tog over next 2 sts, (14 sts), *turn*, leaving remaining sts unworked.

Row 2: Ch 3, dc2tog over next 2 sts, dc in each st across, (13 sts), *turn*.

Row 3: Ch 3, dc in each st across to last 2 sts, dc2tog over next 2 sts, (12 sts), *turn*.

Row 4: Rep Row 2 (11 sts).

Rows 5–13: Ch 3, dc in each st across, *turn*. **Fasten off.**

SECOND STRAP

Row 1: With first strap on the right, skip next 23 (31, 39, 47) sts to the left of first strap, join yarn in next st, ch 3, dc2tog over next 2 sts, dc in each st across, (14 sts), *turn*.

Row 2: Ch 3, dc in each st across to last 2 sts, dc2tog over next 2 sts, (13 sts), *turn*.

Row 3: Ch 3, dc2tog over next 2 sts, dc in each st across, (12 sts), *turn*.

Row 4: Rep Row 2 (11 sts).

Rows 5–13: Ch 3, dc in each st across, *turn*. **Fasten off.**

Assembly

With the right sides of the front and back facing each other, take a yarn needle and yarn and follow these steps:

1. **Using the whipstitch, sew front to back across the shoulders.**

    Check out Book 7, Chapter 2 for all things sewing related.

2. **Beginning at the lower edge of the right side of the sweater, match stitches across the side edges and sew side seam with whipstitch.**

3. **Repeat on other side edge.**

Refer to the schematic in Figure 4-8 to check your finished pieces for accuracy in sizing.

Finishing

Follow these directions to finish the bottom, neck, and armhole edgings.

BOTTOM EDGING

Rnd 1: With RS facing, using smaller hook, join yarn with a sl st in first foundation ch on bottom edge of front, ch 3 (first dc), dc in each ch across to last ch, skip last ch, dc in each ch across bottom edge of back, skip last ch, join with a sl st in top of beginning ch-3 (176 [192, 208, 224] dc).

Rnd 2: Ch 4, skip next st, * dc in next st, ch 1, skip next st; rep from * around, join with a sl st in 3rd ch of beginning ch-4 (88 [96, 104, 112] ch-1 spaces).

Rnd 3: Ch 1, sc in first st, skip next 2 ch-1 spaces, (4 dc, picot, 3 dc) in next dc, skip next 2 ch-1 spaces **, sc in next dc; rep from * around, ending last rep at **, join with a sl st in first sc (22 [24, 26, 28] shells). Fasten off.

NECK EDGING

Rnd 1: With RS facing, using smaller hook, join yarn with a sl st on neck edge in left shoulder seam, ch 4, (dc in next row-end st, ch 1) across to front neck edge, (dc in next st, ch 1, skip next st) across front neck edge, working across neck shaping, (dc in next row-end st, ch 1) across to back neck edge, (dc in next st, ch 1, skip next st) across back neck edge, working across back neck shaping, (dc in next row-end st, ch 1) across to beginning, join with a sl st in 3rd ch of beginning ch-4. Fasten off.

ARMHOLE EDGING

Rnd 1: With RS facing, using smaller hook, join yarn in one armhole opening at shoulder seam, ch 1, sc evenly around armhole opening, join with a sl st in first sc. Fasten off.

Rep armhole edging around other armhole opening.

Weave in ends. Block sweater.

IN THIS CHAPTER

» Tacking on edgings, borders, and collars

» Creating buttonholes in a crocheted garment

» Adding ties and drawstrings

Chapter **5**

Crocheting Sweater Edges and Buttonholes

You've conquered crochet and completed the body of a great new sweater or cardigan. But something's missing. How are you going to keep those wide-open sleeves from dragging without a cuff? Or how is that cardigan going to keep you warm if you can't fasten it shut? This chapter shows you how to make your new garments functional with important finishing touches such as borders, cuffs, collars, and buttonholes. And the best part is that creating these finishing touches is easy.

TIP

If you want to practice your buttonholes or collars before trying them in another pattern, grab a few of the practice swatches that you made when practicing new stitches and add a buttonhole or collar to them.

Adding Trims: Edgings, Borders, and Collars

If you're thinking that you can make only the most basic of sweaters — two squares hung on your shoulders — forget it. The following sections show you how to add simple edgings, ribbed borders, and elegant collars that bring your projects to life without a lot of work.

Outlining your designs with edging

Crocheting a basic edging of one or two rows or rounds on the outer edges of a design can smooth out the rough spots and add a finished, professional look to your crocheted items. You can even add crocheted edgings to other materials. Here are a few options:

>> Crochet a round of single crochet stitches around the bottom edge, neck edge, and cuffs of a sweater, especially one that you worked in a heavier-weight yarn. (Flip to Book 3, Chapter 1 for a refresher on single crochet.)

>> When making a patchwork afghan or sweater, edge each panel or motif with a row of stitches. (Typically the slip stitch or single crochet is used to create a smoother edge for joining.)

>> Crochet decorative strips of some of the fancier stitches (such as shells, clusters, and chain loops) with cotton thread and sew these edgings on pillowcases, sheets, handkerchiefs, and towels — or down the seam of your jeans! (Book 4, Chapter 3 describes a variety of fancy crochet stitches you can use. Book 5, Chapter 2 includes a pillowcase edging project.)

REMEMBER

Although knowing how to do a simple edging on your own is helpful, any pattern that includes an edging to finish off the design tells you in detail how to complete it.

Bordering your masterpieces with ribbing

Borders can be quite elaborate and may consist of a number of rows or rounds that are a design unto themselves. If intricate borders tickle your fancy, check out a few of the many publications available to find dozens of complex border designs. In the next sections, however, you learn how to make two of the most common borders used on garments: single crochet ribbing and post stitch ribbing.

Single crochet ribbing

Single crochet ribbing is a long strip of very short vertical single crochet rows. Because these rib rows lay perpendicular to the rows in the body of the finished sweater, you normally make the ribbing first and then work the body of the sweater off the row-end stitches along the long edge of the rib.

REMEMBER

Typically, you want the ribbing to cinch in a little around the bottom of the sweater and at the cuffs but still be flexible enough to stretch. You accomplish this by applying two techniques at the same time: (1) making the rib with a hook that's one size smaller than the one you use for the rest of the sweater, and (2) working in *only* the back loops of each single crochet stitch across the row.

You can make a wider border by increasing the stitches in each row (or you can create a narrower border by simply working fewer stitches). A typical bottom rib is 1 to 3 inches wide, or about 4 to 10 stitches.

To make ribbing that's approximately 2 inches wide using worsted-weight yarn and a size H-8 US (5 mm) hook, follow these steps:

1. **Chain 9 (ch 9).**

2. **Single crochet (sc) in the second chain from the hook and then single crochet in each chain across; _turn._**

   You now have 8 single crochet stitches.

3. **Chain 1 and then single crochet in the back loop of each single crochet across the row (like in Figure 5-1); _turn._**

4. **Repeat Step 3 until the rib reaches your desired length.**

REMEMBER

Typically, you make the rib an inch or two shorter than the width or diameter of the part of the sweater that you're crocheting. For example, if you have a sweater cuff that's 10 inches in diameter, you make the rib 8 or 9 inches in diameter. The amount of "cinching in" that you want to achieve and the elasticity of the yarn you're working with are determining factors in deciding the length of the rib strip.

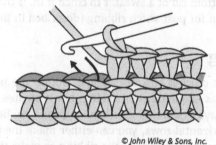

FIGURE 5-1:
Working single crochet ribbing.

© John Wiley & Sons, Inc.

Figure 5-2a illustrates how a standard single crochet ribbing should appear, and Figure 5-2b shows the stitch diagram.

You can add single crochet ribbing after you've crocheted the body of a sweater, but doing so takes more time (plus the appearance may not be as neat as if you worked the ribbing first). If the pattern you're working asks you to do this, it'll provide instructions.

FIGURE 5-2:
A swatch of single
crochet ribbing
with its stitch
diagram.

a.

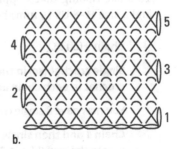

b.

TIP

Single crochet ribbing works better with some yarns than with others. For example, if the yarn you're using is soft and has little elasticity, it may not be suitable for single crochet ribbing. Yarns with some type of wool in them are the most suitable for ribbing projects.

TIP

If your ribbing looks flat, try working with a smaller hook to tighten it up. As a last resort, you can tighten up your flat ribbing by weaving elastic thread in several places around the bottom rib of a sweater to cinch it in. If that doesn't do the trick, you may want to opt for post stitch ribbing (described in the next section).

Post stitch ribbing

Post stitch ribbing (double crochet stitches worked around the posts of previous stitches) isn't as elastic as single crochet ribbing, but it creates a more rounded style of ribbing that always maintains its ribbed appearance. Because you work post stitch ribbing in horizontal rows, you can either make the ribbing first and then work the body across the top edge of the ribbing or make the body first and then work the ribbing off the bottom edge of the garment (which is normally how you want to do it).

To fashion a typical post stitch ribbing across a sweater's bottom edge:

1. **Work 1 row of double crochet (dc) across the bottom edge and *turn*.**

2. **Chain 2 (ch 2).**

This counts as your first post stitch.

3. **Work 1 front post double crochet (FPdc) around the post of the next double crochet, as shown in Figure 5-3a.**

   See Book 4, Chapter 3 for detailed information on working post stitches.

4. **Work 1 back post double crochet (BPdc) around the post of the next double crochet. (Refer to Figure 5-3b.)**

5. **Repeat Steps 3 and 4 until you reach the last stitch.**

6. **Work 1 half double crochet (hdc) in the last stitch; _turn._**

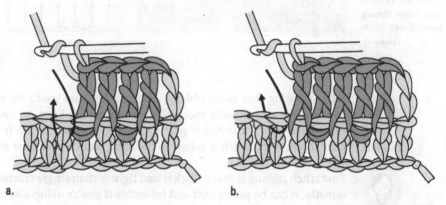

FIGURE 5-3:
Working post stitch ribbing. **a.**   **b.**

© John Wiley & Sons, Inc.

Here's how to work the next row:

1. **Chain 2 (ch 2) for your first post stitch.**

2. **If the next post stitch from the previous row is raised to the front, work 1 front post double crochet (FPdc) around its post. If the next post stitch is raised to the back, work 1 back post double crochet (BPdc) around its post.**

   In Figure 5-4a, the stitches that appear to be raised to the front are front post stitches.

3. **Repeat Step 2 across the row until you reach the last stitch.**

4. **Work 1 half double crochet (hdc) in the last stitch and then _turn._**

5. **Repeat Steps 1 through 4 until the rib measures the desired depth.**

Figure 5-4a shows a post stitch ribbing swatch, and Figure 5-4b depicts the stitch diagram.

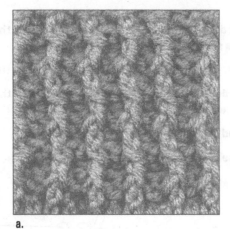

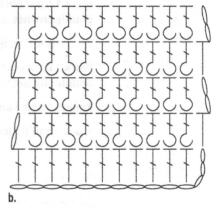

FIGURE 5-4:
Double crochet post stitch ribbing swatch with stitch diagram.

a.

b.

REMEMBER

When creating post stitch ribbing, always make sure your post stitches are raised to the same side in each successive row or round. Keep an eye on the ribs and remember this: If the stitch you're working is raised to the front, work a front post stitch; if the stitch is raised to the back, work a back post stitch.

TIP

Post stitch ribbing is much thicker and tighter than single crochet ribbing. Consequently, it can be pretty stiff and inflexible if you're using a heavier yarn. Using a larger crochet hook gets you a softer, more flexible feel.

Gracing your neck with a common collar

Collars are a broad subject, with variations too numerous to explain in detail. However, if you can work basic crochet stitches (like the ones described in Book 3, Chapters 1 and 2), you can fashion almost any style collar you can think of. Among the myriad collar options are soft, draping shawl collars, turtlenecks, and the traditional flared collar. (If you need to create another type of collar as part of a pattern, the pattern instructions tells you how.)

A common collar is the traditional flared collar, which features pointed ends like a standard shirt collar. This collar often appears on cardigans, crew neck pullovers, and polo-style sweaters with front openings and plackets. To work a flared collar, follow these steps:

1. **With the right side of the sweater facing you, join the yarn with a slip stitch (sl st) in the top right-hand corner of the right front neck edge. Chain 1 (ch 1).**

2. **Single crochet (sc) evenly from the right front neck edge around to the top left-hand corner stitch of the left front neck edge; *turn*.**

3. **Chain 1 and then work 2 single crochet stitches (sc) in the first single crochet stitch. Single crochet in each stitch across, ending with 2 single crochets in the last stitch; *turn*.**

   Work the extra stitch at both edges of the collar to add the flare to it.

4. **Repeat Step 3 until the collar reaches 3 inches deep, or your desired depth.**

   To figure out how deep your collar should be, try measuring the collar on one of your favorite shirts or sweaters.

TIP

5. **Fasten off at the end of the last row.**

Holding Things Together: Buttonholes, Ties, and Drawstrings

When you button your shirt in the morning, do you ever stop to think about which side the buttons are on and which side the holes are on? Or about how much space is between them? How about the ties on that cute new coverup? Are they flat or round? Do they have tassels or beads at the end, or are they just finished with a knot? The following sections show you all you need to know to keep your new clothes on — with buttons, ties, and drawstrings, that is.

Making room for buttons: Buttonholes

The design of the garment you're crocheting determines whether you work buttonholes horizontally or vertically, although both appear as vertical slits when finished.

>> If the garment has front *plackets* (those narrow bands that run up the inside edges of the front or back of a shirt or sweater opening), you create the buttonhole horizontally, right into the placket.

>> If the design doesn't have front plackets, you work buttonholes vertically into the garment itself.

On a woman's shirt, the buttonholes are on the right side of the shirt when you're wearing it; on a man's shirt, the buttonholes are on the left.

REMEMBER

Of course, there's no reason to have buttonholes if you don't have buttons. But in the meantime, take a look at the next few sections to see just how you can whip up some buttonholes. You also discover how to make button loops, which can be a pretty alternative to buttonholes.

Working buttonholes in front plackets

Making buttonholes in front plackets is easy. All you do is skip enough stitches in the designated row of the placket to accommodate the button size wherever you want a buttonhole. The buttonhole is usually created in a row close to the center of the placket, with a row or two following to add strength.

Here's how to fashion a standard buttonhole using this method:

1. Place markers across the front edge of the placket to mark the beginning and end of each desired buttonhole position.

2. Crochet across the row in the stitch designated by the pattern to the first marker, chain 2 (ch 2), skip the next 2 stitches, and then continue crocheting across to the next marker. (Refer to Figure 5-5a.)

If you have a larger button, chain the required number of stitches for that button size. Then skip the same number of stitches as you made chain stitches.

3. Repeat Step 2 for each marker until you reach the end of the row; *turn.*

4. Crochet evenly across the previous row, working an equal number of stitches into the chain space as it has chain stitches.

In this example, you work 2 stitches into the space because you made 2 chain stitches in the previous row. Refer to Figure 5-5b to see the completed buttonhole.

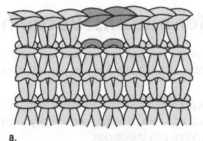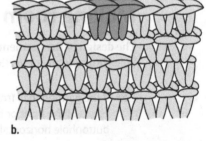

FIGURE 5-5:
Working a buttonhole horizontally.
a.
b.

© John Wiley & Sons, Inc.

REMEMBER

The number of stitches you skip, and therefore chain, depends on the size of the buttons you're using. Have your buttons on hand before crocheting any buttonholes — that way, you can better fit the hole to the button.

Working buttonholes in the garment body

If your sweater design doesn't have front plackets, you work a buttonhole right into the body of the sweater by first working across the row to the point where the buttonhole will appear and then turning your work, leaving several stitches unworked. Next, you fasten off and rejoin the yarn in the stitch on the other side of the buttonhole, skipping a stitch to create the buttonhole. You then work in the few stitches that you left unworked in previous rows to create the other side of the buttonhole. What all of this means is that you need to plan ahead and determine your buttonhole positions before you work the body of your sweater.

Here's how to crochet a vertical buttonhole (like the one illustrated in Figure 5-6b) on a single crochet sweater:

1. **When you're ready to begin the designated row for the bottom of the buttonhole, chain 1 (ch 1) to start the new row. Single crochet (sc) in each of the first 3 stitches and then turn, leaving the remaining stitches of the row unworked.**

2. **Chain 1 and then single crochet in each stitch across the first half of the buttonhole;** *turn.*

3. **Repeat Step 2.**

   Figure 5-6a shows what your buttonhole should look like after you complete this step.

4. **Fasten off the yarn and, with the right side facing you, skip 1 single crochet and rejoin the yarn on the other side to begin making the second side of the buttonhole.**

REMEMBER

   Rejoin the yarn so you work in the same direction as the other side; otherwise, you end up with a different stitch pattern. For example, if you work the first row of the buttonhole row with the right side of the project facing you, make sure that when you rejoin your yarn to work the second side, the right side of your work is once again facing you.

5. **Chain 1 and single crochet in each stitch across the remainder of the front;** *turn.*

6. **Work 3 more rows of single crochet across, ending with a wrong side row at the top of the buttonhole.**

7. **Chain 1, skip the space for the buttonhole, and single crochet in each of the next 3 single crochets on the first side of the buttonhole. (Refer to Figure 5-6b.)**

Repeat Steps 1 through 7 for each buttonhole.

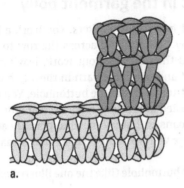
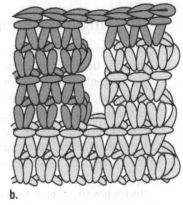

FIGURE 5-6:
Working a
buttonhole
vertically. **a.**

b.

Working button loops

Button loops are nice alternatives to buttonholes. You can use them in a lightweight garment where you don't need a tight closure to the front or as a simple
one-button closure at the top of a neckline. You work these loops into the final
rows of an edging of a garment, and the number of rows depends on the weight
of your yarn:

>> If you're using a lightweight yarn, work the loop in the last two rows to give it
more strength.

>> If you're using a heavier yarn, a loop worked in the last row is sufficient.

Here's how to make a button loop on the last two rows of an edging:

1. **On the next-to-last row of the edging, mark positions across the front
edge where you want the beginning of your loops to be positioned.**

2. **Crochet in the specified pattern stitch across the row until you reach a
marked position.**

3. **Make a chain that's just long enough to form a loop that the button can
slip through.**

4. **Without skipping any stitches, continue crocheting until you reach the
marker for the next loop.**

5. **Repeat Steps 2 through 4 across the row; *turn*.**

6. **For the last row, crochet evenly across, working the same number of stitches as there are chains in the chain space of each loop.**

   Check out Figure 5-7 to see a sample single crochet button loop.

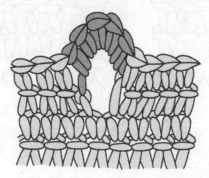

FIGURE 5-7: A completed button loop worked in the last two rows of edging.

© John Wiley & Sons, Inc.

TIP

When you're working the button loop stitches, you can also work each stitch into the chain stitch itself. However, most patterns tell you where to place your stitches for the button loop.

To make a button loop on the last row of an edging, proceed as follows:

1. **Before you begin the last row, mark positions where you want to place your loops across the front edge, marking both the beginning and ending of each loop.**

2. **Crochet in the specified pattern stitch across the row until you reach the second marker for the first loop (as shown in Figure 5-8a);** *turn.*

3. **Make a chain that's large enough to slip the button through.**

4. **Join the chain with a slip stitch (sl st) at the edge of the first marker of the first loop;** *turn.*

   Refer to Figure 5-8b for a visual of this step; note that the work shown hasn't been turned yet.

5. **To complete the button loop, work the same number of stitches as there are chain stitches into the chain space.**

   Figure 5-9 shows a completed button loop. To create additional button loops, repeat Steps 2 through 5 for each loop.

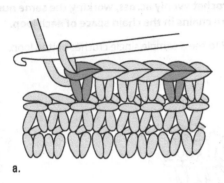

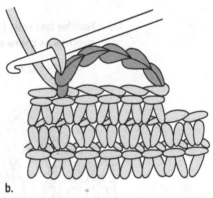

FIGURE 5-8:
Working a button
loop in the last
row of edging.

a.

b.

© John Wiley & Sons, Inc.

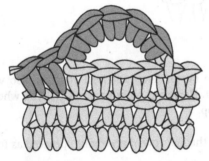

FIGURE 5-9:
A completed
button loop
on the edge
of a work.

© John Wiley & Sons, Inc.

Keeping your clothes on (or just spicing them up): Ties and drawstrings

Ties and drawstrings make fun and easy closures for the front (or back) of a garment. They can be as simple as a single tie attached to each side of a light sweater's front or as elaborate as a threaded drawstring crisscrossing the back of a summer halter top.

You usually attach ties to the top-front portion of a garment, close to the neck opening, or at the beginning of the front neck shaping, centered over the chest. However, you can also place ties in a row down the entire front of a sweater. You attach ties to garments with the excess lengths of yarn left from the beginning of the tie to "tie" them to the correct position on the garment.

Drawstrings, which you weave through a round with *eyelets* (a round created with a pattern of spaces) or post stitches (see Book 4, Chapter 3) crocheted into the body of a sweater or sleeve, often adorn the neckline, waistline, bottom edges, and cuff edges of some sweaters. You can also place drawstrings in the center-back area of a garment, weaving them back and forth between the open edges of, say, a halter top to draw the sides together.

TIP

The following list gives you a few options for crocheting a tie or drawstring:

» **Make a simple chain.** Chain the required length for the tie or the drawstring. (You may use one or more strands of yarn.)

» **Make a round cord.** Chain 5 (or the required number for the thickness of the cord) and slip stitch in the first chain to join. Single crochet in each chain around. Then, working in a spiral, continue to single crochet in each single crochet around until the cord reaches your desired length.

» **Single crochet or slip stitch a cord.** Chain the required length, turn, and slip stitch or single crochet in the back bump loop of each chain across.

To spice up your ties and drawstrings, add embellishments such as tassels or just tie each end in a simple knot.

7

Finishing Touches

Contents at a Glance

IN THIS CHAPTER

» Tidying up loose ends

» Blocking your work

» Shaping 3D projects

» Fulling (also known as felting)
to make study fabric

Chapter **1**

Blocking and Felting

H ooray! You're almost done with a knitting or crocheting project. In this
chapter, you discover how to neatly secure loose ends and block the pieces
of your work so the dimensions and shape reflect your pattern. This
chapter also explains how fulling (more often referred to as felting) can turn your
knitted or crocheted fabric into a denser, stronger fabric.

Tying Up Loose Ends

The first step in the finishing process is taking care of all the loose ends hanging
about. If you've managed to make all the yarn changes at the side edges, that's
where you'll find most of the ends. Otherwise, you'll have loose ends scattered here
and there that require different techniques for successfully making them disappear.

Although various techniques exist for weaving in ends (and weave you must;
there's no getting around it because knots will show on the right side of the work
and may unravel over time), keep in mind that your goal is a nice, smooth fabric
without glitches or an unattractive ridge in the middle of your work. You can hide
your loose ends by doing any of the following:

» Weaving them vertically up the side edges

» Weaving them in sideways on the wrong side of the fabric

» Weaving them in along a bound-off edge

Use whichever method safely tucks in your ends *and* results in a smooth, unblemished right side. Every situation (thickness of yarn, location of join) is different. Try the techniques in this section, and if you discover something that works better in a given circumstance, use it.

TIP

Here are some general tips for tidying up loose ends:

>> Weaving in the entire length of a 6-inch yarn end is unnecessary; you need to weave the end over only a few stitches.

>> With wool yarn, running a yarn end in over 3 or 4 stitches is enough to secure it. The fuzzy nature of the fibers helps the woven ends "stick" to the rest of the fabric.

>> With slick yarns, such as rayon and polished cotton, you need to weave the ends in over 5 or 6 stitches to prevent them from working their way out. Then cut away the excess, leaving about ¼ inch free.

>> If an end is too short to comfortably thread through a needle, run your needle through the appropriate nearby loops as if it were threaded. With the eye of the needle at the short yarn end, finagle the yarn end through the eye of the tapestry needle and pull the needle through the loops. The end will be woven in and secured.

Book 3, Chapter 1 has additional tips for tidying loose ends in crocheted pieces.

Weaving ends up the sides

If you joined yarns at the side edges by temporarily tying the two ends together in a bow, follow these steps to weave in the ends:

1. **Untie the bow.**

   Don't worry. Your knitting or crocheting won't unravel.

2. **Thread one end through the tapestry needle and weave it *down* the side loops at the edge of your work.**

3. **Thread the other end through the tapestry needle and weave it *up* the side loops at the edge of your work (see Figure 1-1).**

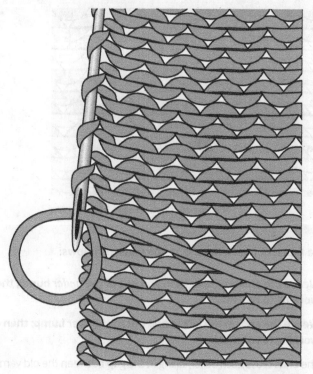

FIGURE 1-1:
Weave the yarn
end through the
side loops.

Illustration by Wiley, Composition Services Graphics

If you joined the ends by working the two strands together for the edge stitch (instead of tying your two ends together), use a tapestry needle to pick out one of the ends and then weave it up the side as outlined in the preceding steps. Weave the other end in the opposite direction. If the two strands are thin and won't add much bulk to the edge stitch, don't bother to pick out one of the ends. Just weave each end into the sides in opposite directions.

Weaving the ends horizontally

If you switched yarns in the middle of a row and have loose ends dangling there, you need to weave the ends in horizontally. Untie the knot or pick out one of the stitches if you worked a stitch with a double strand of yarn.

If you have a knitted piece, take a careful look at the purl bumps on the back side of your fabric. You'll notice that the tops of the purl stitches look like "over" bumps, and the running threads between the stitches look like "under" bumps (see Figure 1-2).

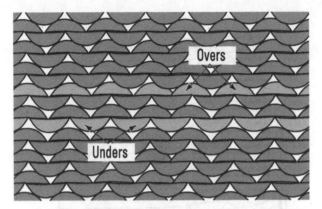

FIGURE 1-2:
Identify the over and under parts of the stitches on the purl side.

Illustration by Wiley, Composition Services Graphics

Using a tapestry needle, weave in the ends as follows:

1. **Weave the end on the right in and out of the *under* bump; then continue working to the left.**

2. **Weave the end on the left in and out of the *over* bump; then continue working to the right.**

   The ends cross each other, filling in the gap between the old yarn and the new, as shown in Figure 1-3.

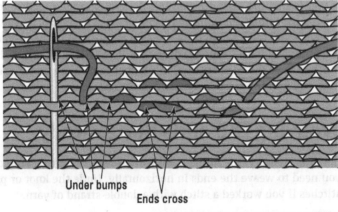

FIGURE 1-3:
Thread the strand through the under bumps on the purl side.

Under bumps

Ends cross

Illustration by Wiley, Composition Services Graphics

Work fairly loosely so as not to pull the fabric in any way. Check the right side of the fabric to make sure that it looks smooth.

TIP

If your yarn is particularly slippery, weave in the end by following the path of the neighboring stitches around the under and over bumps, as shown in Figure 1-4. This method creates a little extra bulk, but it completely secures the strand.

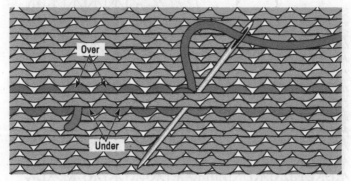

FIGURE 1-4:
Follow the path of the stitch.

Illustration by Wiley, Composition Services Graphics

After you work your ends into the fabric, snip them about ½ inch from the surface and gently stretch and release the fabric to pull the tails into the fabric.

Weaving ends into a bound-off edge

When you're weaving in an end at a bound-off edge that forms a curve, you can weave in the end in a way that creates an uninterrupted line of bound-off stitches. You can use this technique, for example, where you've joined a second ball of yarn at the start of neckline shaping or on the final bound-off stitch of a neckband worked on a circular needle. Here's how:

1. Thread a tapestry needle with the yarn end.

2. Find the chain of interconnected Vs that form the bound-off edge (shown in Figure 1-5).

3. Insert the needle under the legs of the first of the interconnected Vs, and then take it back through the initial stitch, mimicking the path of a bound-off stitch (see Figure 1-5).

Remember to start at the V next to the loose end.

4. Finish weaving in the end by running the needle under the series of V legs along one side of the bound-off edge.

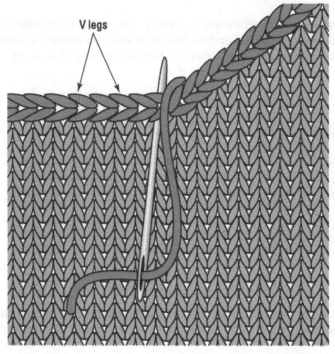

V legs

Illustration by Wiley, Composition Services Graphics

FIGURE 1-5:
Weave in an end
along a bound-off
edge.

TWEAKING VS

As you're weaving in ends, keep an eye out for loose or misshapen stitches on the right (front) side of your fabric. While you're holding the tapestry needle, you can tweak them back into line by using the tip of your needle to adjust the legs of the stitch, as shown in the following figure.

Remember that a row of stitches is connected. If you have a loose or sloppy stitch, you can pull on the legs of the neighboring Vs in either direction for as many stitches as you need to redistribute the extra yarn. If one side of the V is distorted or larger than the other, pull slightly on the other side or tweak the stitch in whatever way is necessary to even it out.

You don't need to get too fussy about the appearance of every single stitch. Blocking straightens any general and minor unevenness, but sometimes, especially in color work, the stitches around the color changes can use a little extra help.

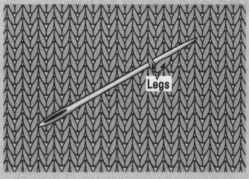

Illustration by Wiley, Composition Services Graphics

Blocking Your Way into Perfect Shape

To get most pieces — especially garments, such as sweaters, vests, and jackets — to match a pattern's finished measurements, you must block them. *Blocking* is a process used to shape knitted or crocheted work. It can be as simple as spraying your design with water or completely immersing it in a tub to get it good and wet. Or you may use some heat by applying steam from your steam iron. Some items, such as cotton doilies or three-dimensional designs, need a little extra shaping help from starch or another stiffening agent.

The final use of your design helps you determine which method of blocking to use. Another consideration is your yarn type. Different types of yarn respond differently to water, steam, and heat, and using the wrong method can have disastrous results. But don't be alarmed; the following sections help you avoid blocking-related pitfalls by explaining the various blocking methods and when you use each one. Of course, before you begin any project, you need to make sure you have the right tools on hand, so you find a list of these as well.

TIP

If your design has pieces that you join together, such as the sleeves and body of a sweater or the different motifs for an afghan, block each piece separately before joining. Doing so makes joining the pieces easier because each one is the correct size and shape. It also gives you a more accurate finished size.

REMEMBER

If the design that you're blocking is a garment and it doesn't fit correctly before blocking (it's too small or too large as is), don't try to stretch it (or squash it) to fit when blocking. Blocking only shapes the garment; it doesn't change its size. If you try to stretch (or squash) your garment during blocking, you may ruin it entirely. If your garment doesn't fit, chalk it up to experience and pass it along to someone who can use it. Don't despair if this happens; it's all part of the experience of becoming a better knitter or crocheter.

The essential tools

You probably already have most of the tools you need to correctly block your designs. First, make sure you have the finished design dimensions from the pattern so you know what shape you're shooting for.

Second, find a flat, padded surface that's large enough to accommodate your design when you stretch it to its finished measurements. (The surface must be padded so you can pin your piece down.) A bed, the floor, a large piece of sturdy cardboard covered in plastic wrap, an ironing board, or a mesh drying rack all work fine as a padded surface.

Here are some other tools you may need, depending on which blocking method you're using:

>> Large tub or sink

>> Several large, absorbent towels

>> Tape measure or ruler

>> Rustproof straight pins (always pin designs with this kind of pin to prevent nasty rust stains)

>> Spray bottle

>> Thin cotton towels (two or three should suffice) or a pressing cloth (an old sheet or T-shirt works well)

>> Steam iron

>> Spray starch, liquid starch, or fabric stiffener (available at most craft stores)

Wet blocking

To *wet block* an item, you submerge the whole thing in water. This method works for just about any yarn, but read the yarn label just to be sure it's not a dry-clean-only fiber. You can also gently wash your item at this time to rid it of the dirt and oils that the yarn is sure to have picked up from your hands. Use a mild soap made for delicate fabrics (*not* detergent) and rinse well in cool water before blocking. This method is useful for many items, including garments, afghans, and home decor.

WARNING If you're not sure whether your yarn is colorfast, be sure to test a swatch before dunking your whole design into a tubful of water. Bleeding colors, especially in a striped design, can ruin your work. If you use a solid color, the effect of bleeding isn't as bad, although you may encounter some fading if you continue to wash the piece over time.

To wet block your work, follow these seven simple steps:

1. **Fill a clean, large tub or sink with cool water and immerse your design completely, allowing it to become thoroughly wet.**

If you want to wash your design, now's the time. Add some soap to the water and swish your garment around. Rinse it well with cool, clean water, taking care not to twist or wring out the fabric.

2. **Drain the water from the tub or sink without removing your project.**

3. **Press down on your work in the tub to remove some excess water and then pick it up and gently squeeze it to remove more water, being careful not to let any part of it hang down and stretch.**

WARNING

Never wring your wet item. Doing so can cause friction between the fibers and alter the appearance of your design. More importantly, it can stretch the fibers beyond repair, and you could end up with a misshapen piece.

4. **Lay your design flat on top of a large towel and then roll the towel and design together like a jellyroll to absorb more of the water.**

You don't want to remove too much of the water — just enough so that the material isn't soaking wet.

5. **Place another large towel on your blocking surface and lay your work flat on it.**

REMEMBER

Your blocking surface needs to be a place where you can leave your design undisturbed for a day or two because it may take that long to dry completely.

6. **Following the schematic (garments) or measurements (afghans or other nonwearables) for the design, use a ruler or tape measure to gently shape and stretch the item to the correct size.**

If the design has three-dimensional elements to it, such as bobble stitches or popcorn stitches, gently puff them into shape. If the design is lacy, make sure to open up the loops so that the design is evident.

7. **Allow your design to dry thoroughly.**

If you need to dry your work in a hurry, place a large fan in front of the damp design to speed up the drying process. Don't place it so close that the fan can blow your masterpiece around, though.

WARNING

Don't ever use a blow-dryer to dry your design. The heat could shrink your piece or melt the fibers in a synthetic yarn.

Spray blocking

Spray blocking is similar to wet blocking, but instead of immersing the piece completely in water, you spray it with water to dampen the fabric. Use spray blocking when your piece needs only a little bit of help with shaping or when you don't want to take the time to wet block. Here's how to spray block:

1. **Prepare a blocking surface that's suitable for pinning down your design.**

   See the earlier section "The essential tools" for ideas on appropriate blocking surfaces.

2. **Lay out your design on the blocking surface, stretching it to the correct measurements; with rustproof pins, pin it in place along the edges every few inches to make sure it stays put.**

3. **Grab a clean spray bottle filled with lukewarm water and spray the design evenly to a uniform dampness.**

4. **Gently smooth the fabric with your hands to even it out, shaping any three-dimensional stitches as needed.**

5. **Allow the design to dry completely before removing it from the blocking surface.**

Heat blocking

You can *heat block* your design by either ironing it or steaming it. Faster than wet blocking and spray blocking, heat blocking works best on natural fibers, such as wool and cotton, but you must take extra care not to burn the fibers. The next sections fill you in on how to iron and steam your work.

WARNING

Avoid heat blocking synthetic fibers because they can melt, thereby ruining your design.

Ironing it out

The ironing method of heat blocking works well for flat items, such as doilies, that have no three-dimensional stitches. To block your design with the ironing method, follow these steps:

1. **Set your iron to the correct temperature as indicated on the yarn label.**

   If the label doesn't recommend a temperature, be cautious and set the iron on a medium-low setting (the steam function should be off as well). You can always make the iron warmer, but burns are irreversible.

2. **Lay out your design on a heat-resistant blocking surface and pin it to the proper dimensions.**

3. **Cover your design with a clean cotton towel or a pressing cloth. Then, using a spray bottle, spray it with water to slightly dampen the cloth.**

   If you prefer to dry press, cover the design with the cloth and omit the spraying step.

4. **Iron the item through the cloth by gently pressing and then lifting the iron and moving it to a new section.**

   Running the iron over the design while pressing down flattens your stitches and may harm the yarn fibers.

WARNING

5. **Allow your design to cool and then remove it from the blocking surface. If necessary, repeat the process on the other side.**

Steaming your fabric

Steaming works especially well for correcting curling edges. It's also quite useful when you have to shape just a small section, such as a cuff or collar that won't behave. All you need to steam press your work is a normal steam iron. To steam block your design, follow these steps:

1. **Set your iron to the correct temperature indicated on the yarn label.**

   If the label doesn't recommend a temperature, be cautious and set the iron on a medium-low setting.

2. **Lay out your design on a heat-resistant blocking surface and pin it to the proper dimensions.**

3. **Holding your steam iron about an inch above the fabric, steam separate sections of the design, being careful not to let the iron touch the fabric.**

4. **Give your design time to cool and dry before removing it from the blocking surface.**

Starch blocking

Doilies, collars, ornaments, edgings, and three-dimensional designs often require a little extra help when blocking to show off the stitches and, in some cases, to create the proper shape. When your design calls for a stiffer finish, it's time to call in the starch. *Note:* You use starch and stiffening agents almost exclusively with cotton thread.

For designs such as pillowcases or towel edgings, you want a lightly starched finish, or else your piece may become too scratchy to actually use. Doilies and filet crochet designs require a heavier finish, so use heavy spray starch or liquid starch to show off the stitch detail and maintain the proper shape. To permanently stiffen works such as ornamental snowflakes and other three-dimensional designs, use a commercial fabric stiffener, which you can find at most craft stores.

The following sections cover the how-tos of working with spray starch, liquid starch, and fabric stiffeners.

Achieving targeted stiffness with spray starch

Spray starch is your ticket for a light- to medium-crisp finish. To block a crocheted item with spray starch, follow these steps:

1. **Hand wash the crocheted design with a mild soap and cool water, rinsing several times to remove all the soap residue.**

   Make sure not to twist or wring out the design while rinsing it.

2. **With a clean towel (or several, if you need them), blot out any excess moisture until the design is just damp.**

3. **Prepare a blocking surface suitable for pinning down your design.**

   Not sure what constitutes a good blocking surface? See the recommendations in the earlier section "The essential tools."

4. **Spray one side of your design with starch, and place the starched side down on your blocking surface.**

5. **With rustproof pins, pin your design to the required dimensions, taking extra care to shape stitch patterns as shown in the photo that accompanies your pattern.**

   This could mean opening the spaces in lace patterns or straightening picot stitches.

   Work quickly so that you get the design pinned down before the starch dries.

REMEMBER

6. **Spray the other side of the design, making sure the fabric is lightly saturated.**

7. **Blot excess starch from the design with a clean, dry towel and allow it to dry completely.**

Immersing your piece in liquid starch or fabric stiffener

Blocking a crocheted design with liquid starch allows you a bit more range when determining the desired crispness. Follow the manufacturer's advice on the bottle of starch for the amount of starch you need and whether you need to dilute.

REMEMBER

If your final design has a permanent shape, such as snowflake ornaments, baskets, or other three-dimensional designs, use a commercial fabric stiffener rather than liquid starch. Liquid starch loses its hold over time, whereas a commercial stiffener is meant to last. A design blocked with a commercial fabric stiffener should hold up for years to come with the proper care.

To block with liquid starch or fabric stiffener, follow these steps:

1. **Using cool water, gently hand wash your design with a mild soap, rinsing several times to remove all the soap residue.**

   Avoid wringing out or twisting the fabric as you rinse it.

2. **In a clean tub or sink, prepare the solution as directed on the container.**

3. **Immerse your item in the solution and allow it to penetrate the fabric.**

   The fabric should be soaked through with the solution in a couple of minutes.

4. **Prepare a blocking surface suitable for pinning down your design.**

5. **Remove the item from the solution and, with a clean, dry towel, blot your item to remove any extra solution.**

6. **With rustproof pins, pin the design to the required dimensions on your blocking surface, taking extra care to shape stitch patterns as shown in the photos accompanying your pattern.**

7. **After pinning, blot the design again to remove any remaining excess solution.**

WARNING

If you're using commercial fabric stiffener, be extra careful to remove as much excess solution from the stitches and between the stitches as possible. When dry, the solution can leave a hard residue that obscures the design.

8. **Allow your masterpiece to dry completely before removing the pins.**

Shaping Three-Dimensional Designs

Not all knitting and crochet is designed to be flat. One of the beautiful aspects of this craft is that with it you can create three-dimensional designs, whether your creation is as simple as a hat or as complex as a decorative, three-dimensional Lilliputian village that you work in many pieces.

Many three-dimensional designs need to be coaxed and shaped after you finish the actual knitting or crocheting. Most patterns include detailed instructions on how to finish and shape your work. If yours doesn't, you can follow the wet-blocking instructions presented earlier in this chapter. But instead of pinning your design out flat, you mold it over the appropriate shape and pin down the edges so it can dry that way.

Here are some of the supplies you should have on hand to shape a three-dimensional design:

>> **A kitchen bowl:** Pick one an appropriate size (comparable to the finished design measurements) for wet blocking a hat or shaping a doily into a decorative bowl.

>> **Paper cups:** Shape cotton-thread Christmas ornaments, such as bells, with paper cups.

>> **Plastic wrap:** Probably the most useful tool, plastic wrap can stuff, prop up, and shape many three-dimensional designs.

>> **Preformed foam shapes:** Available in most craft stores, foam shapes, such as cones, can shape the bodies for objects such as crocheted Christmas tree toppers.

As you can see, you don't need any fancy supplies. Just look around your house, and you'll find that you already have many of the items you might need on hand.

Fulling (or Felting) to Make Sturdy Fabric

Many times, you hear knitters or crocheters say they're going to *felt* a bag. True, the end result will be a fabric that's feltlike, but because they're beginning with a fabric and not raw fleece, they're actually *fulling* a bag. These terms seem to be interchangeable in everyday vernacular, but the two are different. Here's how:

>> **Fulling:** Fulling is the process of adding heat, moisture, and tremendous agitation to a knitted, woven, or crocheted fabric made of wool to make it

shrink. The fabric becomes much stronger, fluffier, and warmer yet is still very pliable.

>> **Felting:** Felting is the process of adding heat, moisture, and agitation to raw fleece to create a fabric that's strong, warm, and typically a lot stiffer than a fulled fabric.

The major difference between the two is that felting uses raw fleece that has no initial structure to get the same result as fulling, which uses a knitted, woven, or crocheted fabric.

Fulling knitted or crocheted fabric makes it much denser. This technique is great for knitted and crocheted bags because your stuff is less likely to poke through the stitches and the stronger fabric holds up well.

You *felt* (or *full*) knitted or crocheted fabric by deliberately shrinking it in the washing machine, so don't put any good sweaters in the same load.

TIP

If you seam the sides of design with yarn *before* you full it (such as the pieces of a bag), the sides will be stronger than if you sew them together afterward. However, if you want a fulled strap for a bag, don't attach it before fulling the rest of the bag — put it in to shrink unattached. Straps can get caught on the center agitator of your washing machine and pull out of shape very easily.

Creating the right conditions to full knitted fabric

Fulling may be the intentional and controlled felting of a fabric, but it isn't an exact science. Too many variables can affect the result. Knowing these variables and maintaining their balance is the best way to ensure a good fulling experience.

Finding a fulling-friendly project

A project made of 100-percent wool can be fulled, but that doesn't mean it should be fulled. Fulling shrinks the stitches and meshes them together. So if your pattern wasn't written with this in mind, fulling may make the proportions of your project all wrong.

REMEMBER

Fulled fabric loses more length than width when it shrinks. To keep a fulled piece the same dimensions as its knit- or crochet-only counterpart, you need to stitch about one-third more rows . . . sometimes even more, depending on the yarn. So if you're supposed to make a piece 22 inches long, you should stitch about 28 to 29 inches instead. It should only shrink a little bit widthwise, but to be safe, add an extra 5 stitches to the width.

Most patterns for a fulled project use stitches that full pretty evenly. You can also full a project that has textured stitches, such as cables or ribbing, but to make sure the fabric doesn't get overfulled and become mush, you need to be vigilant. To make sure textured stitches full consistently, check your piece frequently and take it out of the washing machine at just the right moment — that point when the stitches are visible yet hazy and interlocked to create a solid fabric.

You can spice up any simple fulled project by adding colorwork to the pattern (such as stripes or mosaics). Sometimes even different colors in the same yarn brand and fiber don't full the same, so make sure you stitch and full the gauge swatch with the colors you plan to combine in your project. Fulling the gauge swatch also allows you to see whether the colors will bleed on one another.

Book 3, Chapter 5 has details about multicolor crochet; Book 4, Chapter 1 explains how to knit stripes; and Book 5, Chapter 4 includes several knitted mosaic patterns.

Choosing your fiber

Fulling works only with 100-percent wool that hasn't been chemically treated to be a super wash; it doesn't work on any synthetic. However, not all wool fiber fulls or felts well. Some animal fibers work better than others, and sometimes the dye used to color the wool makes the fiber do not want to cooperate.

Some common fiber choices for fulling include the following:

>> Sheep

>> Angora

>> Alpaca

>> Llama

>> Mohair

>> Yak

Most fulled projects use a bulky or super bulky yarn, but some double a worsted-weight yarn to achieve the bulky weight. Fulled projects also use a larger gauge (see the next section), which requires more yarn. If you're pulling yarn from your stash to complete a fulled project, make sure you have enough yarn.

To make sure your wool will give you the results you want, full the entire gauge swatch. Fulling the gauge swatch shows you how much the fabric fluffs up (also known as *bloom*), how pliable it will be, and how much it will shrink. Knowing that 4 sts per inch and 6 rows before fulling will become 3 sts per inch and 4 rows after fulling is important if you plan on fulling something that needs to fit, such as a hat or gloves.

Getting the right fabric gauge

When you plan to full a knitted or crocheted fabric, you need to stitch it in a loose gauge. Usually, that means stitching about 2 mm larger in size than you normally would for the yarn you're using. (*Note:* If you're using a pattern for a fulled project, the pattern gives you the exact size of needle or hook you need, so adjusting to an even larger needle or hook isn't necessary.) You want the stitches to be big enough so that the scales of the wool have room to expand and mesh with one another. If the fabric weave is too tight to begin with, the wool doesn't have space to move; the resulting fulled fabric will have textured stitch definition, and the end product can tear and break because it no longer has the stretch of knit.

When the fulling process is complete, not only is the project significantly smaller, but the stitches look hazier, like firm remnants of what they once were (see Figure 1-6) — or the stitches may not be visible at all. The visibility of the stitches depends on the amount of time you full the fabric.

FIGURE 1-6: Knitted fabric unfulled (a) and fulled (b).

a.   b.

Photograph by Wiley, Composition Services Graphics

TIP

Some knitters and crocheters love to full because it can hide mistakes. Because the fabric is going to be fulled, a little oopsie will never show up. So don't fret too much if you make a small error; the fulled project won't show the mistake!

Controlling water temperature, soap, agitation, and time

Whether you're using a washing machine or hand fulling, the fulling process relies heavily on four factors: water temperature, soap, agitation, and time. The more you can control these factors, the better your results.

>> **Water temperature:** For a more consistent finish, use water that's about as warm as a hot bath if you're new to fulling. As you become familiar with the process, try using hot water. Always rinse with cold water.

>> **Soap:** You can use laundry detergent to full, but a soap product works better. The pH balance in soap (like Ivory) helps the fibers open and adhere to one another. A teaspoon of liquid soap is enough to make the scales on the wool open up.

>> **Agitation:** Agitation makes the wool fibers mesh together.

>> **Time:** The amount of time needed to full something properly depends on the fiber used, the size of the piece, the temperature of the water, and the fulling method.

You know the fulling is complete when the project appears to be just about where you want it. Even if it's *almost* right, go ahead and take it out to air-dry. Later, you can full a little more if need be, but you can't reverse the fulling process.

The fulling experience: How to full

You can full a knitted fabric by hand or by machine. The two methods result in the same end product. Machine fulling is less work and is definitely faster than hand fulling, but hand fulling offers the most control.

To see which method of fulling you prefer, make two gauge swatches and try both methods. One way may work better for your project than another. It's best to find that out with the gauge swatches rather than the actual project.

Hand fulling

Hand fulling is a great way to jump into the fulling process because you can stop and check the fabric at every stage and as often as you like. You can also adjust the fulling amount per stitch pattern in any given project simply by agitating select stitches more or less.

To hand full a project, follow these steps:

1. **Fill a basin that's large enough to fit the project with warm to hot water.**

2. **Dissolve the soap in the water.**

   Add only enough soap to generate some suds on the fabric.

3. **Immerse the project in the water.**

4. **Start to knead the fabric.**

Use your hands to generate friction so that the scales of the wool open and fuse to each other. For more agitation, you can use a plunger on the fabric or even scrub the fabric on a washboard.

WARNING

Refrain from overstretching the fabric or pulling it too much, and do not rub the fabric together. If you rub the front of a bag to the back of the bag, for example, the two will adhere and the bag won't open.

5. **Remove the project from the water frequently to check on the process.**

If the stitches pull apart easily, the process isn't complete. Remember, you want the stitches to become a solid fabric but not total mush.

6. **When the fulling is complete, rinse out the soap in cold water. Squeeze out any excess water.**

7. **Roll the project in a towel to soak up any remaining moisture.**

8. **Lay the project out flat on a dry towel, away from sunlight, to air-dry.**

If you find that your project is taking too long to dry, change out the towel under it after a few hours. You can also place a fan to blow over it.

TIP

Machine fulling

You can full a project in a washing machine as long as the machine lets you open the door to check on the project.

To machine full a project, follow these steps:

1. **Set the washer on a hot water/cold rinse cycle, no spin, and minimum size load.**

Folds caused by the spin cycle are hard to remove.

2. **Dissolve soap in the water.**

Add only enough soap to generate some suds on the fabric.

3. **Place the project in a pillowcase or pillow cover and either zip it shut or close it with a heavy-duty elastic.**

This cover catches fibers that come off in the washing process so they don't clog your machine.

4. **Place the pillowcase in the washer and wash.**

Blocking and Felting

5. **Check the fulling process every 1 to 5 minutes.**

   The length of time required to full your project depends on your machine, soap, and local water conditions. Check frequently. As you do more fulling, you'll learn the amount of time your machine takes to do the work. For now, be vigilant. Don't get distracted and stray from the washing machine, or you could come back to a ruined project.

   WARNING

   The fulling process is irreversible. You can always full a little more, but you can't unfull! Remove the project before it's too late. If the project starts to full unevenly, you can always finish the fulling process by hand.

   TIP

   If the stitches pull apart easily, then the process isn't complete. If you find that the fibers of your project aren't meshing together well, add a couple of tennis balls, old jeans, or shoes to the basin of the washing machine. These items act as additional agitators and help the fibers interlock.

6. **When the fulling is complete, rinse out the soap in cold water. Do not use the spin cycle.**

7. **Roll the project in a towel to soak up any remaining moisture.**

8. **Lay the project out flat on a dry towel, away from sunlight, to air-dry.**

TAKING A STAB AT NEEDLE FELTING

Needle felting is the art of using special needles to attach wool yarn or fleece to a flat piece of wool fabric, creating a drawing or sculpture. Adding needle felting to a finished project is a form of appliqué felting. You can also use needle felting for sculptural felting or three-dimensional felting.

Needle felting does not require soap and water. Instead, sharp barbs on a needle actually grab at the scales on the wool and make them mesh with the wool fabric. To get started, you need the following tools:

- A thick piece of foam or a felting brush that allows the felting needles to go through the fiber and beyond without damaging the needles or surface below

- A needle-felting tool with either a single barbed needle or many needles

- Wool yarn or roving in a variety of colors

- A fulled or felted project to use as the fabric

Note: New to the market are needle-felting machines. Similar to a sewing machine, these machines use barbed needles to work wool into fabric.

With these supplies, needle felting is as easy as "painting" with the fiber. First think about your design. You can create an easy pattern like stripes or polka dots, or you can create a flower. Better yet, be creative and freeform random shapes.

When you have an idea of what you want to do, place the foam or felting brush under the fabric you want to needle felt. Then tear off bits of wool yarn or fleece. Lay the fiber on the fabric and begin to punch the needles through the fiber and the fabric repeatedly. Be sure to move the needles around so that the fiber attaches itself to the fabric.

As the fiber begins to attach itself, you can add more fiber in the same color or new colors or go in a totally different direction. With the fabric as your canvas and the fiber as your paint, the options are endless.

Not everybody can create freeform shapes, so here's a little tip: Use a cookie cutter as a guide for your needle felting. Place the cookie cutter on the fabric and fill it with fiber. Then punch the needle through both fiber and fabric, filling in the entire space of the cookie cutter. To get dimension, repeat the process with many layers of fiber, and the shape will really pop. Now you have some great shapes with little work!

Chapter 2

Joining Pieces

After you block your sweater or project pieces, it's time to put them together. You can choose between traditional sewing methods and techniques that mimic and work with knitted or crocheted stitches.

The techniques in the following sections help you join your pieces in ways becoming to the knitted or crocheted fabric. These techniques work with the structure of the stitches, creating seams that are smooth and flexible.

Sewing Pieces Together

Two sewing methods explained in this chapter — mattress stitch and backstitch — work with both knitted and crocheted pieces.

REMEMBER To sew sweater pieces together, you can use these stitches (and check out the section about assembling a sweater for additional help). When you've finished seaming your sweater pieces together, no matter which method you use, steam all the seams and press down on them with your fingertips to encourage them to lie flat.

Mattress stitch

Mattress stitch makes a practically invisible and nicely flexible seam for joining pieces side to side. You can't use it successfully, however, on pieces that have a difference of more than 2 rows. It's worth keeping track of your rows when working backs and fronts to be able to join them at the sides with this wonderful technique.

To join pieces with the mattress stitch, lay out your pieces next to each other, right sides facing up, bottom edges toward you. You seam from the bottom edge up. If you've left a tail of yarn at the cast on edge, you can use it to get started.

TIP

To work mattress stitch, you need to be able to recognize the running threads between the first 2 edge stitches. If you gently pull these stitches apart, you'll see the series of little horizontal — running — threads connecting them (see Figure 2-1).

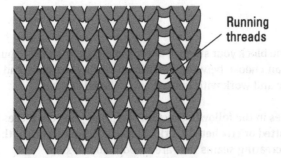

Running threads

FIGURE 2-1: Identify the running threads.

Illustration by Wiley, Composition Services Graphics

Thread the tail of yarn or a fresh piece on a tapestry needle. Working through the two threads on the cast on row, join the bottom edges of the pieces by using a figure 8, as shown in Figure 2-2. The direction you work the figure 8 depends on whether you begin on the right or left side. If you begin from the right piece, you work your figure 8 to the left; if you begin from the left piece, you work to the right.

To work the mattress stitch, follow these steps:

1. Locate the running thread between the first and second stitches on the bottom row of one piece (refer to Figure 2-1).

2. Bring your needle under the thread to pick it up; then pick up the running thread between the first and second stitches on the opposing piece, as in Figure 2-3.

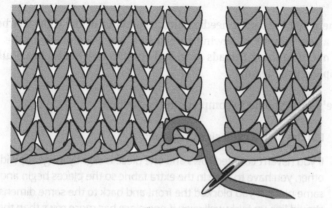

FIGURE 2-2:
Join the bottom
edges with a
figure 8 for
mattress stitch.

Illustration by Wiley, Composition Services Graphics

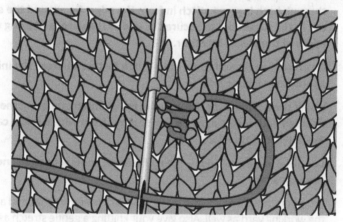

FIGURE 2-3:
Pick up the
running thread in
mattress stitch.

Illustration by Wiley, Composition Services Graphics

3. **Work back and forth from running thread to running thread to running thread, keeping the tension easy but firm.**

   Check the tension by pulling laterally on the seam from time to time. The amount of give should be the same as between 2 stitches.

When you've finished your seam, take a moment to admire it.

Sewing seams with backstitch

When you join pieces by using backstitch, you sew them together in the conventional manner: *right* sides together with your tapestry needle moving in and out along the seam line. Try to work the stitches consistently — either in the trough of running threads between the first 2 stitches when you're working vertically or along the same row of stitches when you're working with a horizontal edge.

TIP

To help you keep your needle going in and out of the right slot between stitches, run a few strands of sewing thread in a bright color along the seam line — in and out of running threads or in and out of a row of stitches. Pull it out after you complete your seam.

Here's what you do to complete the backstitch:

1. **Pin the pieces right sides together.**

   If you haven't counted rows and one piece is slightly longer or wider than the other, you have to ease in the extra fabric so the pieces begin and end in the same place. If you blocked the front and back to the same dimensions, they should line up fairly well even if one piece has more rows than the other.

2. **With a tapestry needle and yarn, bring the needle from the bottom up through both layers 1 stitch in from the edge. Go around the edge, come out in the same spot to secure the end of the yarn, and bring the bottom edges of the pieces together.**

3. **Go around again and come out 1 stitch farther up from the initial stitch, as shown in Figure 2-4a.**

4. **Insert the needle back through the initial stitch and bring the tip out through both layers again, a few stitches from where it last came out, as shown in Figure 2-4b.**

5. **Continue in this manner — going forward, coming back — and keep an even tension.**

   Bring your needle in and out in the spaces between stitches and avoid splitting the working yarn as well. Also give your knitting a gentle stretch as you work to keep it flexible.

Keep needle going in and out along running stitches (under bumps) between first two stitches

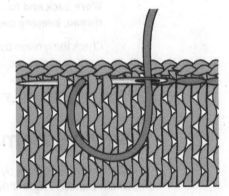

FIGURE 2-4:
Work a backstitch seam.

a. Beginning a backstitch seam.

b. Continuing the backstitch.

Illustration by Wiley, Composition Services Graphics

Knitting Pieces Together

If you choose the knitterly techniques discussed in this section, the one you use is determined by how the stitches are coming together: head to head, side to side, or head to side, all of which are shown in Figure 2-5.

Stitches side to side

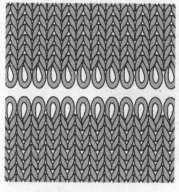

Stitches head to head

Stitches head to side

FIGURE 2-5: Assess how stitches are lined up for assembly.

Three-needle bind-off (head to head)

Use the three-needle bind-off when you're joining stitches head to head (refer to Figure 2-5). The technique is the quickest and easiest joining method and creates a stable — and visible — seam. With a three-needle bind-off, you get to do two things at once: bind off and join two pieces together — perfect for joining shoulder seams.

For the three-needle bind-off, you need three needles: one each to hold the shoulder stitches and one for working the actual bind-off. If you don't have three needles of the same size, use a smaller one for holding the stitches of one or both of the pieces to be bound off, and use a regular-size needle for binding off.

To work the three-needle bind-off, thread the open stitches of your pieces onto a needle — one for each piece. If you've left a long tail end (about four times the width of the stitches to be joined), you can use it to work the bind-off. Thread your first needle through the stitches on the first piece so the point comes out where the tail is. When you're threading the second needle through the second piece, make sure your needle tips will point in the same direction when your pieces are arranged with right sides together (see Figure 2-6). If you haven't left a tail end for this maneuver, you can start working with a fresh strand and weave in the end later.

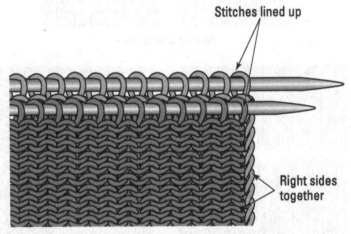

FIGURE 2-6:
Right sides together, needles pointing to the right, stitches aligned.

Stitches lined up

Right sides together

Illustration by Wiley, Composition Services Graphics

For this method, you knit and bind off the usual way, but you work stitches from two LH needles at the same time. Follow these steps:

1. Insert the third needle knitwise (as if you were knitting) into the first stitch on *both* needles, as Figure 2-7 shows.

2. Wrap the yarn around the RH needle as if to knit, and draw the loop through both stitches.

3. Knit the next pair of stitches together in the same way.

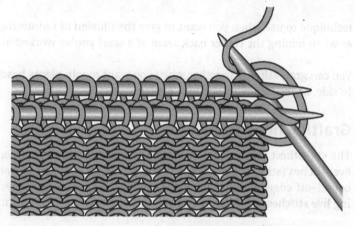

FIGURE 2-7:
Insert the RH needle into the first stitch on both needles.

Illustration by Wiley, Composition Services Graphics

4. **Using the tip of either LH needle, go into the first stitch knitted on the RH needle and lift it over the second stitch and off the needle, as shown in Figure 2-8.**

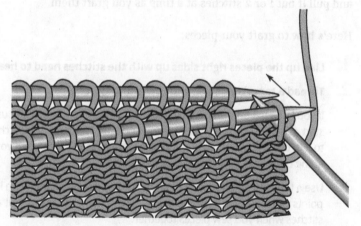

FIGURE 2-8:
Bind off the first stitch on the RH needle.

Illustration by Wiley, Composition Services Graphics

5. **Continue to knit 2 stitches together from the LH needles and bind off 1 stitch until you bind off the last stitch and pull the yarn tail through the last loop.**

Grafting stitches (the Kitchener stitch)

Grafting (also known as the *Kitchener stitch*) uses a tapestry needle to mock knit, creating a very stretchy and almost invisible join between pieces. It's a good technique to use when you want to give the illusion of uninterrupted fabric, such as when joining the center back seam of a scarf you've worked in two pieces.

You can graft stitches together when you want to join pieces head to head or head to side, as the following sections explain.

Grafting head to head

The smoothest join — and also the stretchiest — is made by grafting together *live* stitches (stitches that haven't been bound off yet). But you also can graft two bound-off edges if you want more stability. Just work the same steps for grafting live stitches, working in and out of the stitches just below the bound-off row.

If you plan to graft live stitches, don't bind off the final row. Instead, leave a yarn tail about four times the width of the piece, and with a tapestry needle, run a piece of scrap yarn through the live stitches to secure them while you block your pieces. Blocking sets the stitches, enabling you to pull out the scrap yarn without fear of the stitches unraveling. If you're working with a slippery yarn and the stitches want to pull out of their loops even after blocking, leave the scrap yarn in the loops and pull it out 1 or 2 stitches at a time as you graft them.

Here's how to graft your pieces:

1. **Line up the pieces right sides up with the stitches head to head.**

2. **Thread a tapestry needle with the working yarn.**

   If you left a tail on the side that you want to begin grafting from, use it. If not, start a fresh strand and weave in the end later. You graft the stitches from right to left, but if you're more comfortable working left to right, or if your yarn tail is at the other end, you can reverse direction.

   Use a tapestry needle with a blunt tip for any kind of seaming on knits. Sharp points can pierce the yarn too easily. Always aim to go in and out and around stitches when you sew pieces together.

3. **Starting in the bottom piece, insert the needle up through the first loop on the right and pull the yarn through.**

4. **Insert the needle up through the first right loop on the upper piece and pull the yarn through.**

   You can see Steps 3 and 4 in Figure 2-9.

5. **Insert the needle down into the first loop on the bottom piece (the same loop you began in) and come up through the loop next to it; pull the yarn through.**

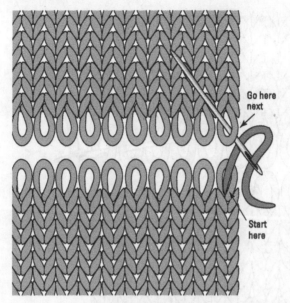

Go here
next

Start
here

FIGURE 2-9:
Insert the needle
up through the
edge stitches to
start grafting.

Illustration by Wiley, Composition Services Graphics

6. **Insert the needle down into the first loop on the upper piece (the same one you came up through in Step 4) and up through the stitch next to it; pull the yarn through.**

   You can see Steps 5 and 6 in Figure 2-10.

7. **Repeat Steps 5 and 6 until you come to the last stitch on both pieces.**

   Follow the rhythm down and up, down and up, as you move from one piece to the other. When you get going, you'll be able to see the mock stitches you're making, as in Figure 2-11.

8. **When you come to the last stitch, insert the needle down into the last stitch on the bottom piece and then down into the last stitch on the top piece; run the end along the side loops and snip.**

With the exception of the first grafting stitch (Steps 3 and 4) and the last one (Step 8), you go through 2 stitches on each piece — the stitch you've already come up through and the new stitch right next to it — before changing to the other piece. Work with even tension, trying to match the size of the stitches you're marrying. If, after you finish, you find any grafted stitches that look out of kilter, you can go back with the tip of your needle and tweak them, working out any unevenness.

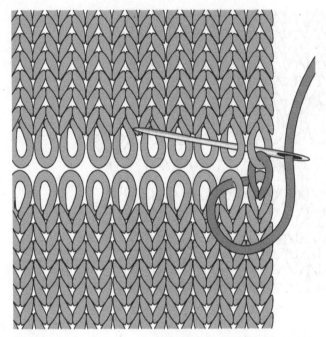

FIGURE 2-10:
Insert the needle into the first loop on the top piece and exit through the loop next to it.

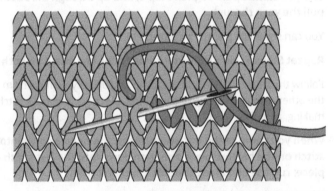

FIGURE 2-11:
Completed grafting stitches.

Grafting head to side

Grafting head to side makes a smooth and weightless seam. As in head-to-head grafting, you make a mock knit stitch, but instead of going in and out of stitches lined up head to head, you graft the heads of stitches on one piece to the *sides* of stitches on the other piece. (Actually, as in the mattress stitch explained earlier in this chapter, you pick up running threads when you're joining to the sides of the stitches.) Grafting head to side is a great method for joining a sleeve top to a sweater body on a dropped shoulder sweater, which has no shaped armhole or sleeve cap.

Before working this graft, make sure that you can recognize the running thread between the 2 side stitches. (See the following section for help identifying running threads.) Then line up your pieces, heads on the bottom and sides above, as shown in Figure 2-12.

REMEMBER

Keep in mind that 1 square inch of stockinette fabric has more vertical rows of stitches than stitches across. For every 1 inch of heads, you need to pick up 1 inch of sides (running threads). This task is actually quite easy. For example, if your gauge is 5 stitches and 7 rows to the inch, you should pick up five running threads out of every seven as follows: Pick up one running thread, then two running threads together, then one running thread, then two together, then one running thread. Then start over. If you look closely at Figure 2-12, you can see that two running threads have been picked up every few stitches to compensate for the difference in vertical and horizontal stitches per inch.

Follow these steps to graft heads of stitches to sides of stitches:

1. **With a tapestry needle and yarn, come up through the first head stitch on the right or left end of your work.**

   Figure 2-12 shows how to work from right to left, but you can work in either direction.

2. **Go around the running thread between the first 2 side stitches (see Figure 2-12).**

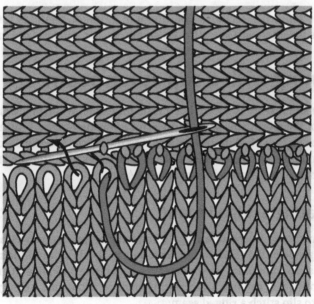

FIGURE 2-12: Graft heads of stitches to sides of stitches.

Illustration by Wiley, Composition Services Graphics

3. **Go back down into the same head stitch you came out of and up through the next head stitch — the stitch to the right if you're traveling in that direction or to the left if you're going that way.**

4. **Repeat Steps 2 and 3.**

The best version of this seam is made by grafting live stitches to the armhole edge, but you can use it with a bound-off edge as well. Just go into the stitches (heads) directly below the bound-off edge.

Crocheting Pieces Together

Sometimes a pattern asks you to crochet your seams, whether for functional or decorative purposes. A crocheted seam is strong and comes in handy when joining pieces that are going to be put through a lot of wear and tear, such as motifs in an afghan. It can also become a part of your design if you work it on the right side of the fabric.

REMEMBER

If the wrong sides of the pieces are facing each other when you join a seam, then the crocheted seam appears on the right side. If the right sides are facing, then the crocheted seam appears on the wrong side. Take a few seconds to make sure your pieces are facing in the correct direction based on where you want your seam to appear before joining them. Trust us, ripping out a seam is pretty frustrating.

In the following sections, you discover different methods for crocheting your pieces together with slip stitches, single crochet stitches, and more.

Joining with a slip stitch seam

A slip stitch seam is secure but a little inflexible. When you work it on the wrong side of the fabric, this seam is great for items that take a beating, like purses and tote bags. If worked on the right side of the fabric, the slip stitch seam looks like an embroidered chain stitch. You can join pieces with the slip stitch to create two different looks: a ridged seam or a flat seam.

Creating a ridged seam

If you choose to create a ridge along your seam, you can either hide it (on the wrong side of the fabric) or make it part of the design (on the right side). Ridged seams are sometimes used to create a decorative look, like in an afghan made up of motifs; you can use a contrasting color to add another design element. Here's how to slip stitch a ridged seam:

1. **Position the two pieces together with right sides facing (for a wrong side seam) or wrong sides together (for a right side seam).**

   Make sure the stitches across each edge match.

2. **Working through the double thickness of both pieces and using the same size crochet hook that you used in the design, insert your hook through the back 2 loops of the first 2 stitches, leaving a yarn tail about 6 inches long.**

   Figure 2-13 shows the correct positioning of the hook in the back loops.

3. **Yarn over the hook (yo).**

4. **Pull the yarn through and repeat Steps 2 and 3 in each stitch across; fasten off and weave in the ends.**

   Take a look at the completed ridged seam in Figure 2-14. Book 3, Chapter 1 and Book 7, Chapter 1 explain how to weave in ends.

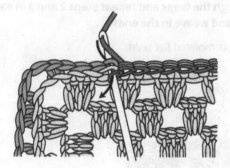

FIGURE 2-13:
Slip stitching pieces together.

© John Wiley & Sons, Inc.

FIGURE 2-14:
Two crocheted pieces joined with a ridged slip stitch seam.

© John Wiley & Sons, Inc.

Creating a flat seam

You can slip stitch two pieces together to create a flat seam, which crocheters often use when they want the seam to be invisible (think of a side seam joining the front and back of a sweater). To slip stitch a seam in this fashion:

REMEMBER

1. **Lay the 2 pieces to be joined side by side on a flat surface, with right sides facing up (for a right side seam) or wrong sides facing up (for a wrong side seam).**

   Check that the stitches across each edge match before moving on.

2. **Working in the top loops of the stitches only and using the same size crochet hook you used in the design, insert your hook through the loops of the first 2 stitches, leaving a yarn tail several inches long.**

   Figure 2-15 shows the correct positioning of the hook in the loops.

3. **Yarn over the hook (yo).**

4. **Pull the yarn through the loops and repeat Steps 2 and 3 in each stitch across. Fasten off and weave in the ends.**

   Figure 2-16 shows a completed flat seam.

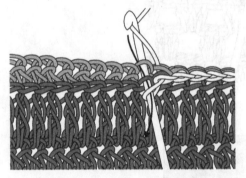

FIGURE 2-15:
Creating a flat seam by slip stitching.

© John Wiley & Sons, Inc.

Joining with single crochet

When you join two pieces with single crochet stitches, you create a sturdy seam that's more flexible than one created with slip stitches. A seam made with single crochet creates a raised ridge that looks like a decorative chain. If you work it in a matching or contrasting color, it can become an integral part of your design.

FIGURE 2-16:
Two pieces joined
with a flat slip
stitch seam.

© John Wiley & Sons, Inc.

REMEMBER

Using single crochet stitches to join the seam in a garment has both positive and negative sides. When used for a strictly functional purpose (to join pieces together), the single crochet seam can cause uncomfortable lumpiness if it's on the inside of the finished piece. However, used on the right, or outside of the work, it can add wonderful texture and another design element to your creation.

Follow these steps to work a seam using single crochet stitches:

1. **Position the pieces with the right sides (or wrong sides) together and match the stitches across each side edge.**

2. **Working through the double thickness of both pieces and using the same size crochet hook that you used when creating the design, insert your hook through the top 2 loops of the first 2 corresponding stitches.**

   Figure 2-17 shows the correct positioning of the hook in the top loops.

3. **Yarn over the hook (yo).**

4. **Pull the yarn through both stitches, as shown in Figure 2-17.**

5. **Yarn over and pull the yarn through the 2 loops on your hook.**

6. **Insert the hook through the top 2 loops of the next 2 corresponding stitches and then repeat Steps 3 through 5 in each stitch across.**

7. **Finish by fastening off and weaving in the ends with the yarn needle.**

   Figure 2-18 depicts a completed single crochet seam.

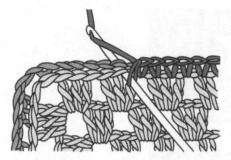

FIGURE 2-17:
Creating a seam with single crochet.

© John Wiley & Sons, Inc.

FIGURE 2-18:
A decorative single crochet seam on the right side of the work.

© John Wiley & Sons, Inc.

Joining with a row of stitches

Joining two pieces with another row of stitches creates a different look from the other seams presented earlier in this chapter. Instead of working through the double thickness of two crocheted pieces, you work back and forth between them, usually on the right side of the piece. The row between the two pieces can be as narrow as a single stitch, or it can be wide and lacy. You can use this joining method to connect motifs when making a shawl, to add interest to the side seams of a garment, or to join panels when crocheting an afghan.

To crochet a joining row that's a chain-2 space wide:

1. **Lay the pieces side by side on a flat surface, matching stitches across the adjacent edges that you're going to join.**

2. Insert your hook under the top 2 loops in the designated stitch on the first piece, chain 1 (ch 1), single crochet (sc) in the same stitch, and then chain 2 stitches for the joining row.

3. Insert your hook under the top 2 loops of the designated corresponding stitch on the second piece, yarn over (yo), and pull the yarn through the stitch. (See Figure 2-19.)

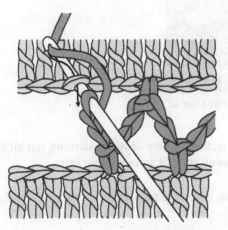

FIGURE 2-19: Crocheting a joining row.

© John Wiley & Sons, Inc.

4. Yarn over, draw the yarn through the 2 loops on your hook, and single crochet the stitch complete.

5. Chain 2, insert your hook under the top 2 loops of the designated stitch on the first piece, yarn over, and pull the yarn through the stitch.

6. Yarn over and draw the yarn through the 2 loops on your hook.

7. Chain 2; then repeat Steps 3 through 6 across the row to the ending point designated in the pattern.

8. Fasten off and weave in the ends with the yarn needle.

Check out Figure 2-20 to see a completed seam made with a row of stitches.

Joining motifs on the last row or round

Some pieces, like the motifs covered in Book 4, Chapter 5, are joined together while working the last row or round. Joining pieces as you go saves you from the daunting task of having to sew or crochet lots (and lots!) of pieces together at the end of a project.

FIGURE 2-20:
A seam made by joining with a row of stitches.

REMEMBER

Because motifs use an endless variety of stitch patterns, not all of them are joined in the same spot, but some general guidelines do exist:

>> Motifs that have side edges, like squares or triangles, are usually joined along one or more sides.

>> Motifs with points (think flowers and stars) are joined at one or more points.

Note: The pattern you're working should let you know exactly where to place your joining stitches. If not, just refer to the guidelines here.

The following steps walk you through the process of joining motifs using granny squares as an example:

1. **Work the first granny square completely and fasten off.**

2. **Work the next square until you reach the point where you want to join the 2 pieces together.**

   This point is usually a corner stitch or chain space.

3. **Work the corner stitch or chain for the square you're currently on, as described in Book 4, Chapter 5.**

4. **Holding the 2 pieces with wrong sides together, insert your hook from the back of the current square into the same corner stitch or space of the square you completed in Step 1.**

5. **Yarn over and draw your hook through the corner stitch, or space, and the stitch on your hook, as shown in Figure 2-21.**

   You now have a slip stitch seam at the corner.

FIGURE 2-21:
Joining pieces on
the last round.

6. **Continue working the stitches across the side of the square, joining stitches or spaces as directed.**

7. **Finish the square you're working on to the end of the round and fasten off; weave in any loose ends using a yarn needle.**

   Continue working any remaining motifs the same way. To see what two pieces joined together on the last round look like, see Figure 2-22.

FIGURE 2-22:
A seam created
by joining two
pieces on the last
round.

REMEMBER

If you're working a row of squares, such as for a scarf, you have to join squares on only one side. If you're working a blanket or a shawl, however, you need to join the pieces together on more than one side. Blanket and shawl designs often consist of several rows containing a number of motifs that must be joined, which is why you join them on more than one side.

Joining Pieces

CROCHETING SEAMLESSLY

If you think seams are pretty unappealing looking in sweaters, or if you just hate making them, you'll be delighted to know that you can create several interesting and attractive sweater styles with few, if any, seams. Here are some ideas:

- Search out a pattern for a raglan-style sweater. You can work this style of sweater without a single seam from the neck down, all in one piece.

- Work a cardigan in one piece across the fronts and the back to the armholes; then work the fronts and backs off of the body. The only sewing you have to do is the shoulder seams.

- Work the sleeves of a sweater in rounds and directly off of the armholes, thus eliminating the underarm and shoulder seams.

- Trim cuffs and bottom edges in post double crochet ribbing right off of the edges of the sweater (see Book 6, Chapter 5 for more on ribbing).

Assembling a Sweater

As you assemble sweaters, you usually follow a fairly predictable order of assembly that goes something like this:

1. **Tack down any pockets and work pocket trims or embroidery details on sweater pieces before seaming them together.**

2. **Sew the shoulder seams.**

   Sew both shoulders for a cardigan or a pullover with a neckband picked up and worked on a circular needle. Sew only one shoulder if you want to work the neckband on straight needles, and then seam the second shoulder and neckband together.

3. **Work the neckband and front bands on cardigans.**

4. **Sew the tops of sleeves to the sweater front and back.**

5. **Sew the side seams.**

6. **Sew the sleeve seams.**

7. **Sew on buttons on cardigans.**

If you've worked your sweater in a medium or lightweight plied yarn, you can use the same yarn for seaming the parts. If the yarn is heavy or a single ply that shreds, use a finer yarn *in the same fiber* in a similar color.

Although this section focuses on knitted sweaters, you can use many of the steps and techniques for crocheted sweaters, too.

TIP

Joining back to front at the shoulder

The first pieces to join after blocking are the front and back at the shoulder (stitches head to head). You have three choices for this seam:

>> Use the three-needle bind-off, which makes it possible to bind off the edges of two pieces and seam them together at the same time.

>> Graft the shoulder stitches together.

>> Use the backstitch to seam the pieces together.

Because most knitters would rather knit than sew, the first option is a good one to learn as you develop your finishing repertoire. For instructions on how to work any of these joins, see the relevant sections earlier in this chapter.

After you join your front and back pieces at the shoulder, work the neckband of the collar before adding the sleeves or seaming the sides so that you have less bulk to contend with. Book 6, Chapter 3 covers neckline details.

TIP

Attaching a sleeve to a sweater body

How you attach the sleeves to your sweater body depends on the design of your sleeve cap and armhole. If you're making a dropped-shoulder sweater or one with an angled armhole and straight cap, you can use the head-to-side grafting technique explained in the earlier section "Grafting head to side." If you're making a sweater with a set-in sleeve, you need to use the backstitch for seaming; see the earlier section "Sewing seams with backstitch" for instructions.

To attach a set-in sleeve to a sweater body, follow these steps:

1. **Mark the center of the sleeve cap at the top edge and align it with the shoulder seam on the sweater body, as shown in Figure 2-23.**

2. **With the right sides together, pin the center top of the sleeve cap to the shoulder seam.**

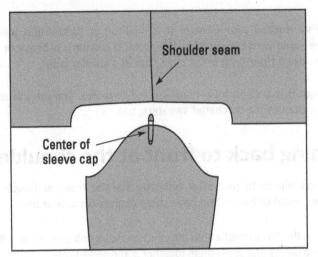

Shoulder seam

Center of
sleeve cap

FIGURE 2-23:
Align the set-in
sleeve and
armhole.

3. **Working on only one side at a time, line up the bound-off stitches at the beginning of the armhole, shaping both the sleeve and sweater body, and pin the pieces together there.**

4. **Pin the sleeve cap edge to the armhole every inch or so between the bound-off stitches and the shoulder, as in Figure 2-24.**

5. **Use the backstitch to sew the pieces together along the edge from the bound-off stitches to the shoulder.**

   When you come to the vertical section of the armhole in the sweater body, keep your stitches in the trough between the first 2 stitches.

6. **When you reach the shoulder, pin the other half of the armhole and sleeve and sew from the shoulder to the bound-off stitches.**

7. **Steam your seam well, pressing down on it with your fingertips as the moisture penetrates.**

Making side and sleeve seams

After you complete the shoulder seams and neckband and attach the sleeves to your sweater body, the rest is all downhill. If you counted rows and have the same number (almost) on the front and back pieces, you can use the mattress stitch to seam your pieces together — and you won't believe how good they look.

If your front(s) and back have a different number of rows (off by more than 2), use the backstitch technique to seam them together.

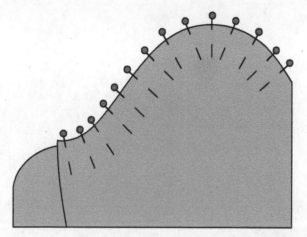

FIGURE 2-24:
Pin the sleeve cap
to the armhole.

Illustration by Wiley, Composition Services Graphics

TIP

Sometimes you may be off by a couple of stitches as you seam two sides together. If you seam the sleeves from the cuff to the armhole, hide these extra stitches in the armpit area. You can do the same if you seam the front and back together starting at the hem and working toward the armhole.

IN THIS CHAPTER

» **What to do when the work is done**

» **Maintaining the look of your crocheted pieces**

» **How to properly store your pieces of art**

Chapter 3

Caring for Your Work

Now that you've completed your design, the final step is making it look its best and making sure that it stays looking its best. Because of all the time you've invested, it would be a shame to have your project fall apart on the first wash, shrink to a baby-doll size, stretch so far out of proportion it's unrecognizable, or discolor by being improperly stored.

It's not difficult to preserve the beauty of the original finished piece, but you do need to take a few extra steps. Follow the appropriate tips given in this chapter to ensure that your work will stick around for a long time.

Keeping Care Instructions Handy

Don't throw out those yarn labels! Every yarn label has care instructions on it. Keep them organized in a binder, or keep a notebook of your projects with the yarn label attached. Write a note underneath the label with the name or description of the crocheted item so you'll have a handy reference when you need to launder that item. Figure 3-1 provides a complete list of care symbols and information about each one.

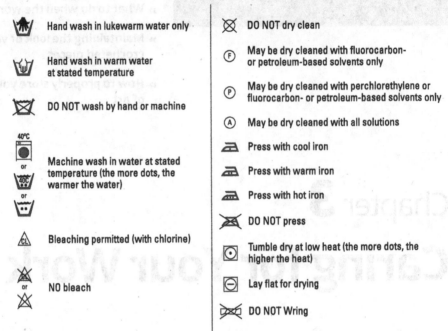

FIGURE 3-1:
Care instructions.

© *John Wiley & Sons, Inc.*

If you'd rather keep the care instructions with your creation, you can sew a care label onto the item itself. These are available at craft stores and some yarn shops. Use a permanent ink pen to write care instructions on the label before you attach the label to the item. (You don't want to ruin all of your hard work by getting permanent ink on it.) Attaching a care label works best for items such as garments and afghans. You can also include your name and the date you made the item, too.

The best way to attach the label is to sew it on with a sewing needle and matching sewing thread. Don't iron the label on because the heat can ruin your work.

It's especially important to include care information if you're giving the piece to someone as a gift. Even though you may know how to care for it, the recipient probably doesn't have a clue. If it's not practical to attach a label directly to the item, then a decorative card with the instructions works just as well. You don't have to go into great detail, just a simple phrase would do. Here are some ideas to help you word the instructions:

>> "I'm delicate. Please hand wash me and lay me flat to dry."

>> "I can be washed and dried."

>> "Take me to the cleaners — I need it."

Cleaning Knitted and Crocheted Items

Hand washing your items is the safest bet, but you can try washing and drying some items, too. The following sections give you tips for each method.

If the yarn label says "Dry clean only," then by all means, take the item to the cleaners. A word of advice, though: Bring the label (or a copy of the label) to the cleaners with you. That way they'll know what material they're working with and can use the appropriate chemicals.

Handwashing

Unless the yarn specifically states "dry clean only," handwashing is your best option. Here's how:

1. **Grab a bottle of mild detergent and make sure your sink or bathtub is clean.**

   The best soap to use is a mild laundry detergent formulated for delicate items or baby clothes, such as Woolite or Ivory Soap. For small items, the kitchen sink is the perfect size. For larger items such as afghans, the bathtub or washtub works better.

2. **Fill the sink or tub with enough cool to warm water so the item can be submerged.**

3. **Swish the item around gently.**

   By keeping the agitation to a minimum, you preserve the integrity of the stitches.

4. **After washing, rinse thoroughly and squeeze out excess moisture.**

   Rinse the item under cool water until it runs clear.

   Never wring a knitted or crocheted item because the twisting motion can stretch the stitches and ultimately ruin the item's shape.

   WARNING

5. **Wrap the item in towels to absorb the extra moisture and lay flat to dry, blocking as necessary. Book 7, Chapter 1 explains how to block items.**

   Never hang a crocheted piece to dry (it will stretch out of shape beyond recognition), and please, keep items out of the sun, which can cause fading.

   WARNING

Machine washing and drying

In some cases, it's perfectly fine to throw your masterpieces in the washing machine. This holds true for items made from synthetic yarns, such as acrylic, which won't sustain so much damage from the washing machine. Use the delicate cycle and, if size permits, throw the item into a mesh laundry bag. Be sure to check the yarn label for the correct water temperature settings.

TIP

It's always a safe bet to wash these items alone the first time around, just to make sure the colors won't bleed into the rest of your laundry. If you're not sure what the correct water temperature should be, opt for the safe route and use the cool water setting.

Sometimes tossing your afghan, scarf, or other piece of handiwork in the dryer is just fine. Again, check the yarn label to make sure it's okay. Most synthetic yarns will take a low heat setting unless it's got some stuff attached like sequins or mirrors. Add some smooth-textured items like pillowcases to the dryer to help absorb moisture.

WARNING

Don't machine dry wool — it will shrink! Find a spot large enough to accommodate the piece and lay it out flat, shape it if necessary, and allow to dry, preferably in a place that is out of direct sunlight and won't be disturbed by playful pets.

Iron only if you must

If you feel that you need to add some heat to an item to get all the wrinkles out, set the iron on the lowest heat setting suggested for the yarn. Place a slightly damp cloth, such as a clean cotton dish towel, on top of your piece before ironing.

WARNING

Never allow the iron to come into direct contact with the yarn. Excessive heat can ruin the integrity of the yarn fibers, and even cotton thread can flatten out too much and ruin the original look of the design.

Storing Your Work

By all means, use and enjoy your knitted and crocheted pieces. That's why you made them. But when you're not using an item, whether it's a sweater or tablecloth or anything in between, never, ever, ever store it on a hanger. Hanging stretches out the stitches, and the damage can't be reversed.

>> **For garments, find a spot to lay them flat with as few folds as possible.** If this means you have to rearrange your closet or drawers, go ahead and do it.

>> **For items such as tablecloths, doilies, runners, and even afghans, roll them up and store them that way to minimize creases and folds.**

You've put in a lot of time, so take the time to care for your pieces properly.

Home decor items are meant to be shown off, so go ahead and use them. If it's a table runner, then lay it out on the table. Afghans can be draped over the back of your favorite chair or sofa, but be sure to keep them out of direct sunlight or extreme temperatures.

If items are to be stored for any length of time, such as holiday designs or winter sweaters, invest in some acid-free tissue paper. Place the paper between the folds and around the outside of the piece. This ensures that the piece stays clean and dust free, and helps preserve the yarn fibers until you bring it out again.

WARNING

Always put your items away clean. Time in storage allows stains to set, and you may not be able to get them out a year later.

To avoid pulling out pieces that the moths have dined on (especially wool items), place these items in a plastic storage bin with a couple of cedar blocks and store the bin in a cool, dry place.

Removing Those Pesky Pills

It's inevitable — where there's yarn there are pills, those unsightly little balls that pop up on fabric after laundering or from normal wear and tear. Removing the pills can revitalize your pieces and make them look like new again.

You can get rid of pills two ways:

>> **By using a sweater stone:** This is the recommended preference because it is gentler on the fabric and you have more control over it.

>> **By using a sweater shaver:** These devices are typically battery operated or electric, and if you don't use them properly, you can put holes in your item.

To use a sweater stone properly:

1. **Lay the item on a flat surface.**

2. **Hold the stone in the palm of your hand and gently brush the fabric in smooth short strokes.**

The stone will crumble a bit, but don't worry, this is normal and won't damage your piece. Gently shake the item or use a lint roller to remove these tiny pieces.

WARNING

Never, ever try to remove pilling with scissors! Remember that knits and crochet are a series of interlocking loops; if you inadvertently cut even one of the strands of yarn, your whole piece can unravel.

Index

L

labels
- article number on, 34
- brand name on, 34
- care instructions on, 34
- color name and number on, 34
- company name and logo on, 34
- dye lot number on, 34–35
- gauge on, 35
- manufacturer's address on, 35
- overview, 33
- ply on, 35
- recommended needle or hook size on, 35
- weight on, 36
- yardage on, 36
- yarn content on, 36

lace edgings, 384
lace insertions, 383
lace knitting. *see also* stitch patterns
- arrowhead lace, 380
- blocking, 386
- Butterfly Runner project, 407–409
- charts, 374–376
- designing your own patterns, 377
- error, finding, 384–385
- eyelet patterns, 378–379
- faggot lace, 381–382
- incorporating into other pieces, 382–383
- lace edgings, 384
- lace insertions, 383
- Lace Leaf Shawl project, 406–407
- miniature leaf pattern, 380–381
- mistakes, avoiding and handling, 384–386
- no-stitch symbol, 375–376

open lace patterns, 379–381
- overview, 373
- pattern overview, 376–377
- practice projects, 404–409
- ridged ribbon eyelet pattern, 378–379
- ripping out lace, 385
- Scarf with Faggot Lace project, 404–406
- yarn-over increase and decrease symbols, 374–375

Lace Leaf Shawl project
- directions, 407
- materials, 406
- overview, 406
- vital statistics, 406

lace weight, 32
lacets, 401–403
lacy hexagon motif, 364–366
Lacy Shawl project
- directions, 428–429
- materials, 427
- overview, 426
- thickness, 429
- variations, 429
- vital statistics, 427

lamb's wool, 27
layered flower motif, 368–370
left-hand (LH), 57
left-handed knitters, 86
left-handers, yarn, how to hold, 156
left-slanting double decrease, 127
level of experience section, in crochet patterns, 63
LH (left-hand), 57
lifelines, 386
light tones, 256
light worsted weight, 32
linen stitch, 490–493
linen yarn, 28
linked stitches

first row of, 324–327
- overview, 324
- second row of, 327–328

linked triple crochets (Ltr), 324–327
liquid starch, 590
little boxes mosaic, 487–488
little mosaic, 486–487
llama, 594
long stitches, 328–329
long-tail cast-on, 80–82
Longways Multiyarn Stole project
- directions, 419
- materials, 418–419
- overview, 418
- variations, 420
- vital statistics, 418–419
- yarns, choosing, 420

looking at work, 140
loop, 67
loop stitch, 315–317
loop(s) (lp(s)), 57
Luxurious Washcloth with Border project
- directions, 183–185
- materials, 183
- overview, 182
- vital statistics, 183

M

m1 (or m) (make 1 stitch), 57
machine fulling, 597–598
machine washing, 628
magnetic board and strips, 22
magnetic line magnifier, 22
main color (MC), 57, 65, 256–257
make 1 increase
- defined, 117
- doubling increase with, 121
- twisting to the left, 119
- twisting to the right, 118

About the Authors

Pam Allen has been designing sweaters for more than 20 years, and her patterns have appeared in such publications as *Family Circle* and *Woman's Day*. In addition to *Knitting For Dummies*, she's the author of *Scarf Style* and co-author of *Wrap Style*, *Lace Style*, *Bag Style*, and *Color Style* (all published by Interweave Press). She lives in Portland, Maine.

Tracy L. Barr is a professional writer and editor. She learned to knit when she was 10 and in the three-plus decades since has continued to be an avid knitter.

Marly Bird is a crochet and knitwear designer, YouTube instructor, YarnThing Podcast host, national teacher, and author. She is a multi-crafty gal who both knits and crochets; the yarn is the star, not how you work with it. Like many folks, Marly learned how to crochet from her beloved grandmother, thus starting her down on this amazing yarn-covered path. Marly has a wildly successful podcast, blog, YouTube channel, and website. At www.marlybird.com you can find her list of published works, links to her podcast, her teaching schedule, and her super informational and fun blog. On Marly's YouTube channel, www.youtube.com/marlybird, you can find videos teaching you the basics of crochet, learn how to knit with Marly and her mom, specific stitches, as well as video tutorials for her myriad of different craft along projects! Marly is married to her amazing husband John, and they have three wonderful kids.

Susan Brittain's fascination with crochet began very early, when she was 4 or 5 years old. She would watch her grandmother, who had lost her sight in midlife, spend hours crocheting beautiful afghans for friends and family, counting the stitches with her fingers. By the age of 8, Susan was crocheting her own projects, starting with simple patterns such as scarves, and then moving on to afghans, toys, and sweaters. Although her creative streak has led her to learn many different crafts, crochet has been a steady thread throughout. Susan finally had the opportunity to combine work with pleasure, and she held the position of assistant editor for *Crochet Fantasy* magazine for a little more than two years, contributing as a designer as well. She is also the coauthor of *Crocheting For Dummies* (Wiley) and continues to design new projects for various yarn companies, as well as friends and family.

Karen Manthey discovered her passion for crochet during the 1970s while she was working as a graphic artist. In 1984, her training in art and understanding of crochet led her to a job illustrating the magazine *Crochet Fantasy*. She soon moved on to become editor of the magazine, all the while continuing to do the illustrations and frequently designing projects for publication. After 20 years of working in an office, Karen went on to work freelance doing technical editing and crochet diagrams for books, magazines, yarn companies, and designers. Now semi-retired, Karen continues to do crochet diagrams for hire, but makes time to pursue a life-long love of painting.

Shannon Okey is the author of more than a dozen books on knitting, has appeared on many crafty television shows, served as a knitting magazine columnist and editor, and is also the founder of cooperativepress.com. Vogue Knitting named her one of the New Guard of Knitting in its anniversary issue. You can find her online at www.knitgrrl.com and on most social media as knitgrrl.

Kristi Porter is an author, designer, technical editor, and teacher. She has written three other books: *Knitting for Dogs, Knitting in the Sun, and More Knitting in the Sun*. Her work has been featured in many books and on knitty.com. Kristi doesn't remember learning to knit as a child, but she captured the basics and an enthusiasm for the craft from her mother, her aunt, and her grandmother. She began her first projects as a designer and a knitter, realizing only later that not everyone designed their own patterns. Though her first attempts were boxy and oversized (thank goodness it was the '80s!), once she grasped the importance of gauge, she was on her way to creating wearable designs. She began approaching the craft in a serious way in the late '90s and learned how to read and write patterns in order to share her designs with others. As a knitting instructor, Kristi teaches students at all levels and ages. Getting feedback about what knitters want to knit, what they enjoy, and what they find difficult has given her a strong sense of what knitters need to know.

Publisher's Acknowledgments

Executive Editor: Lindsay Lefevere

Compiler: Rebecca Huehls

Development Editor: Rebecca Senninger

Proofreader: Debbye Butler

Production Editor: Mohammed Zafar Ali

Cover Image: © Dezene Huber/Getty Images